ECONOMIC DEVELOPMENT: A GLOBAL PERSPECTIVE

PARVIZ ASHEGHIAN

CALIFORNIA STATE UNIVERSITY SAN BERNARDINO

2003
GLOBE ACADEMIC PRESS

Economic Development: A Global Perspective, by Parviz Asheghian

Cover Design: Jonathan Gullery

Printer: Books, Just Books

Library of Congress Control Number: 2003094010

ISBN 0-9742079-0-X

COPYRIGHT ©2003 by Globe Academic Press
                                3734 Ridge Line Drive
                                San Bernardino, CA 92407

All rights reserved. No part of this book may be reproduced or used in any form or any means—graphic, electronic, electrostatic, magnetic, mechanical, tape, photocopying, recording — without the written permission of the publisher.

The author and the publisher have been careful in preparation of this book in order to provide accurate and authoritative information on the subject matter. However, they do not make any expressed or implied warranty of any type and presume no responsibility for any omissions or errors. No liability is assumed to any person or entity with respect to accidental or consequential damages in relation with or evolving out of information incorporated in this book.

Printed in the United States of America

TABLE OF CONTENTS

PREFACE .... *xvii*
ABOUT THE AUTHOR .... *xxi*

PART I : BASIC CONCEPTS AND PRINCIPLES 1

CHAPTER 1: THE GLOBAL ECONOMY AND DEVELOPING NATIONS 3

ECONOMIC DEVELOPMENT IN THE GLOBAL CONTEXT 4
GLOBAL INSIGHTS CASE 1.1: DEVELOPING NATIONS IN THE GLOBAL ECONOMY 5
GLOBAL INSIGHTS CASE 1.2: GLOBAL CONSUMPTION INEQUALITIES 6
WHY STUDY ECONOMIC DEVELOPMENT? 7
THE LIMITATIONS OF TRADITIONAL ECONOMICS 7
SUMMARY 8
QUESTIONS 8
NOTES 9
SUGGESTED READINGS 9

CHAPTER 2: THE DEFINITION AND MEASUREMENT OF ECONOMIC DEVELOPMENT 11

GROWTH AND DEVELOPMENT 11
GLOBAL INSIGHTS CASE 2.1: THE GLOBAL GROWTH EXPERIENCE 12
CLASSIFICATION OF NATIONS 14
MEASURING ECONOMIC DEVELOPMENT 15
GNP Measure 16
    Problems With Using GNP to Make Comparisons Over Time 16
    Problems With Using GNP To Make Comparisons Between Nations ... 17
GLOBAL INSIGHTS CASE 2.2: GILBERT AND KRAVIS EFFECT 19
THE PHYSICAL QUALITY OF LIFE INDEX (PQLI) 19
WEIGHTED INDICES FOR GNP GROWTH 20
BASIC NEEDS YARDSTICK 21
GLOBAL INSIGHTS CASE 2.3: ALTERNATIVE MEASURES OF GROWTH IN
    SOME DEVELOPING NATIONS 22

TABLE OF CONTENTS

THE HUMAN DEVELOPMENT INDEX (HDI) 24
GLOBAL INSIGHTS CASE 2.4: HUMAN DEVELOPMENT INITIATIVES IN
    SOME DEVELOPING NATIONS 25
Gender Related Development Index (GDI) 25
SUMMARY 27
QUESTIONS 28
NOTES 29
SUGGESTED READINGS 29

CHAPTER 3: ECONOMIC DEVELOPMENT IN A HISTORICAL CONTEXT AND A PROFILE OF DEVELOPING NATIONS 31

ECONOMIC GROWTH IN THE NON-WESTERN WORLD 32
    The Japanese Development Strategies 32
    Newly Industrialized Countries Development Strategies 33
GLOBAL INSIGHTS CASE 3.1: ECONOMIC DEVELOPMENT STRATEGIES OF EAST
    AND SOUTHEAST ASIA 34
GLOBAL INSIGHTS CASE 3.2: TURMOIL IN ASIAN ECONOMIES 35
    The Soviet Development Strategies 36
GLOBAL INSIGHTS CASE 3.3: THE FEL'DMAN INVESTMENT STRATEGY 38
    Recent Economic Growth in Developing Nations 39
PROFILE OF DEVELOPING NATIONS 39
    Low Standards of Living 40
    GNP Per Capita and its Growth Rate 40
    Distribution of National Income 40
GLOBAL INSIGHTS CASE 3.4: THE INCOME DISTRIBUTION IN BRAZIL 41
    Poor Health 41
    Political Framework 42
    External Dependence 42
GLOBAL INSIGHTS CASE 3.5: ELIMINATION AND ERADICATION OF
DISEASES: THE EXAMPLE OF POLIOMYELITIS AND A CASE FOR
    VACCINATION 43
GLOBAL INSIGHTS CASE 3.6: A GLOBAL LOOK AT THE AIDS (ACQUIRED
    IMMUNODEFICIENCY SYNDROME) EPIDEMIC 44
    Rapid Population Growth and Dependency Burdens 45
    High and Growing Rates of Unemployment and Underemployment 45
    High Dependence on Agricultural Sector 46
    Dependence on Primary Exports 46
    Low Levels of Labor Productivity 46
        Inadequacy of Physical and Human Capital 46
        Poor Health 47
    Presence of Imperfect Markets and Incomplete Information 47
    An Extended Family 48
SUMMARY 49
QUESTIONS 50
NOTES 50
SUGGESTED READINGS 51

TABLE OF CONTENTS

CHAPTER 4: ALTERNATIVE THEORIES OF ECONOMIC DEVELOPMENT 53

THE CLASSICAL THEORY OF ECONOMIC STAGNATION 54
THE MARXIST THEORY 55
   The Marxian Theoretical Framework 55
      Economic Interpretation of History 56
      Theory of Value and Wages 56
      Theory of Surplus Value and Capital Accumulation 57
      The Class Struggle 57
      Theory of Socialist and communist Revolution 58
   An Appraisal of Marxist Theory 59
GLOBAL INSIGHTS CASE 4.1: MCDONALD'S IN RUSSIA 60
DEPENDENCY THEORY 62
GLOBAL INSIGHTS CASE 4.2: INVESTMENT CLIMATE IN POLAND 63
   Criticisms of Dependency Theory 64
ROSTOW'S STAGES OF ECONOMIC GROWTH 64
HAGEN'S STAGES OF ECONOMIC INDUSTRIALIZATION 66
THE VICIOUS CIRCLE OF POVERTY 67
   Criticisms of Vicious Circle of Poverty 68
THE BIG-PUSH THESIS 69
   Criticisms of the Big-Push Thesis 70
THE BALANCED VERSUS UNBALANCED GROWTH 70
   Balanced Growth 70
   Criticisms of Balanced Growth 71
   Unbalanced Growth 71
   Criticisms of Unbalanced Growth 72
THE LEWIS THEORY OF DEVELOPMENT 72
THE HARROD-DOMAR GROWTH MODEL 75
GLOBAL INSIGHTS CASE 4.3: JAPANESE CAPITAL FLOW
   CONTROLS 77
GLOBAL INSIGHTS CASE 4.4: THE ASIAN GROWTH MODEL IN
   PERSPECTIVE 78
   The Application of the Harrod-Domar Model to the
   Stages-of-Economic Growth 79
SUMMARY 80
QUESTIONS 81
NOTES 82
SUGGESTED READINGS 83

PART II : THE ELEMENTS OF GROWTH 85

CHAPTER 5: POVERTY AND INCOME DISTRIBUTION 87

ABSOLUTE POVERTY 87
GLOBAL INSIGHTS CASE 5.1: POLICIES TO REDUCE POVERTY IN INDIA 88

TABLE OF CONTENTS

- THE PROBLEM OF DEFINING INCOME 89
- GLOBAL INSIGHTS CASE 5.2: THE DOZEN NATIONS INCLUDING MOST OF THE POOR IN THE WORLD 91
- FACTORS CONTRIBUTING TO INCOME INEQUALITY 92
  - Universal Causes of Inequality In Nations 92
  - Additional Causes of Inequality In Developing Nations 92
- ALTERNATIVE MEASURES OF INCOME INEQUALITY 93
  - Functional Distribution of Income 93
  - The Size Distribution of Income 94
    - The Income Shares Method 94
    - The Lorenz Curve and the Gini Coefficient 96
- THE HUMAN POVERTY INDEX 102
- IDENTIFYING THE POVERTY GROUPS 102
  - Rural Poverty 102
  - Women and Poverty 103
  - Ethnic Minorities 104
- GROWTH AND INEQUALITY: THE INVERTED-U HYPOTHESIS 104
- DOES INEQUALITY INDUCE GROWTH? 105
- POLICIES TO ALLEVIATE POVERTY AND INCOME INEQUALITY 107
- SUMMARY 109
- QUESTIONS 110
- NOTES 112
- SUGGESTED READINGS 112

CHAPTER 6: POPULATION GROWTH AND ECONOMIC DEVELOPMENT 115

- MALTHUSIAN THEORY OF POPULATION 115
- DEMOGRAPHY 117
  - Demographic Transition 118
  - Demographic Transition in Developing Nations as Compared to Advanced Nations ... 120
- CHANGES IN AGE DISTRIBUTION 121
- THE MICROECONOMICS OF FERTILITY 122
  - The Higher Fertility In Rural Areas than Urban Areas In Developing Nations 123
  - The Inverse Relationship Between the Level of Income and Fertility 123
  - A Microeconomic Model of Fertility 123
- NONECONOMIC VARIABLES AFFECTING FERTILITY 124
- GLOBAL INSIGHTS CASE 6.1: INTERNATIONAL CONFERENCE ON POPULATION AND DEVELOPMENT (ICPD) 125
- THE FALLACIES OF POPULATION DENSITY 126
- BENEFICIAL IMPACTS OF POPULATION GROWTH 127
- ECONOMIC DEVELOPMENT OR FERTILITY DECLINE? 128
- GLOBAL INSIGHTS CASE 6.2: POPULATION CONTROL STRATEGIES IN SOME DEVELOPING NATIONS 129
- POLICIES FOR DIMINISHING FERTILITY 129
  - Socioeconomic Development 130
  - Birth Control Programs 130

TABLE OF CONTENTS vii

POPULATION PROJECTIONS	131
SUMMARY	132
QUESTIONS	134
NOTES	135
SUGGESTED READINGS	135

CHAPTER 7: UNEMPLOYMENT, MIGRATION, URBANIZATION AND ECONOMIC DEVELOPMENT 137

UNEMPLOYMENT PROBLEMS IN DEVELOPING NATIONS	137
Types of Unemployment and Underemployment in Developing Nations	138
RURAL-URBAN MIGRATION	138
The Harris-Todaro Model	139
DISGUISED UNEMPLOYMENT	140
GLOBAL INSIGHTS CASE 7.1: EDUCATION AND UNEMPLOYMENT IN SOME DEVELOPING NATIONS	141
POLICIES TO REDUCE UNEMPLOYMENT	141
Policies to Discourage Rural-Urban Migration	142
Technology Adaptation Polices	142
Policies to Decrease Factor-Price Distortion	143
Educational Policy	144
INTERNATIONAL MIGRATION	145
Causes of International Labor Migration	145
Effects of International Labor Migration	146
The Output Effect	146
Income Distribution Effect	149
Other Effects	150
GLOBAL INSIGHTS CASE 7.2: THE PUSH AND PULL OF U.S. IMMIGRATION POLICY	151
SUMMARY	152
QUESTIONS	154
NOTES	154
SUGGESTED READINGS	154

CHAPTER 8: RURAL DEVELOPMENT AND AGRICULTURAL TRANSFORMATION1 157

INTEGRATED RURAL DEVELOPMENT APPROACH	157
THE HISTORY OF AGRICULTURAL GROWTH	158
GLOBAL INSIGHTS CASE 8.1:THE AGRARIAN STRUCTURE IN LATIN AMERICA	159
AGRICULTURAL PRODUCTIVITY IN ADVANCED NATIONS	160
THE STAGES OF AGRICULTURAL DEVELOPMENT	161
Subsistence Agriculture	161
GLOBAL INSIGHTS CASE 8.2: THE DETERIORATING RURAL CONDITIONS IN ASIA	162
Diversified (Mixed) Agriculture	163

TABLE OF CONTENTS

    Modern Agriculture 164
  STRATEGIES OF AGRICULTURAL AND RURAL DEVELOPMENT 164
  GLOBAL INSIGHTS CASE 8.3: THE IMPORTANCE OF AGRICULTURAL
    RESEARCH IN CHINA 165
    Research and Technological Improvements 165
    Supportive Social Services 166
    Pricing and Exchange Rate Policies 168
    Rural Industrialization 168
    Improving the Status of Women 169
    Land Reform 169
  GLOBAL INSIGHTS CASE 8.4: AGRICULTURAL REFORM IN CHINA 170
  SUMMARY 171
  QUESTIONS 173
  NOTES 174
  SUGGESTED READINGS 174

CHAPTER 9: TECHNOLOGICAL PROGRESS 177

  DEFINITION OF TECHNOLOGY AND RELATED TERMINOLOGIES 178
  TECHNOLOGY AND CULTURE 179
    Technology and Economic Systems 179
    Technology and Value Systems 180
    Technology and Religious Systems 180
    Technology and Political Systems 181
    Technology and Social Organization Systems 181
    Technology and Educational Systems 181
  FACTOR INTENSITY AND TECHNOLOGICAL PROGRESS 182
    Neutral Technological Progress 183
    Capital Saving (Labor Using) Technological Progress 185
    Labor Saving (Capital Using) Technological Progress 186
  INGREDIENT OF TECHNOLOGICAL PROGRESS 186
    Elasticity of Substitution 186
    Scale of Production 188
    New Products and Demonstration Effect 189
    Social Relations of Production 190
    Speed of Change 190
  GLOBAL INSIGHT CASE 9.1: THE ASIAN "MIRACLE" 191
    Technology Imitation 191
  SUMMARY 192
  QUESTIONS 193
  NOTES 194
  SUGGESTED READINGS 194

PART III: DOMESTIC RESOURCE POLICIES AND DEVELOPMENT STRATEGIES 197

CHAPTER 10: HUMAN RESOURCE DEVELOPMENT AND CAPITAL FORMATION 199

HUMAN RESOURCE DEVELOPMENT 199
GLOBAL INSIGHTS CASE 10.1: THE RELATIONSHIP BETWEEN POVERTY, EDUCATION AND EARNINGS 201
    Major Educational Policy Options 202
        External Educational Policies 202
        Internal Educational Policies 202
GLOBAL INSIGHTS CASE 10.2: EDUCATION AND GENDER DISCRIMINATION IN PAKISTAN 203
GLOBAL INSIGHTS CASE 10.3: HOW EDUCATING FOREIGN STUDENTS PROMOTES MARKETS AND DEMOCRACY 204
CAPITAL FORMATION 205
SUMMARY 206
QUESTIONS 208
NOTES 208
SUGGESTED READINGS 208

CHAPTER 11: MONETARY AND FISCAL POLICIES 211

IMPEDIMENTS TO MONETARY POLICIES IN DEVELOPING NATIONS 211
    Inadequacy of Financial Institutions in Developing Nations 212
    Insensitivity of Investment Decisions to Interest Rate Fluctuations in Developing Nations 213
REFORMING DEVELOPING NATIONS' FINANCIAL SYSTEMS 213
GLOBAL INSIGHTS CASE 11.1: THE ASIAN GROWTH MODEL IN PERSPECTIVE 214
OBSTACLES TO FISCAL POLICY IN DEVELOPING NATIONS 215
    Taxation 215
GLOBAL INSIGHTS CASE 11.2: PERFORMANCE OF THE INTERNATIONAL FINANCIAL INSTITUTIONS IN THE 1990s 216
        The Taxation Potential 217
        Sources of Taxation 217
    Government Expenditures 219
        Nondurable Goods and Services 220
        Interest Payments 222
        Subsidies 223
        Intergovernmental Transfers 224
REVAMPING DEVELOPING NATIONS' FISCAL SYSTEMS 225
    State-Owned Firms (SOFs) 225
        Enhancing SOFs' Effectiveness 226
SUMMARY 228
QUESTIONS 230
NOTES 230

TABLE OF CONTENTS

SUGGESTED READINGS 231

CHAPTER 12: DEVELOPMENT PLANNING: THEORY AND PRACTICE
THE DEFINITION OF DEVELOPMENT PLANNING 233

THE DEFINITION OF DEVELOPMENT PLANNING 233
THE ARGUMENTS FOR AND AGAINST DEVELOPMENT PLANNING 234
   Opponents' Arguments 234
   Proponents' Arguments 234
GLOBAL INSIGHTS CASE 12.1: PLANNING IN THE FORMER SOVIET UNION 235
THE PLANNING PROCESS 237
   Choosing Social Objectives 237
   Setting Various Targets 238
   Organizing a Framework for Implementation Coordination and Monitoring
      of a Development Plan 238
      Aggregate Growth Models 238
GLOBAL INSIGHTS CASE 12.2: DEVELOPMENT PLANNING IN INDIA 239
      Input-Output Tables 240
      Project Appraisal and Cost-Benefit Analysis 243
   Defining the Duration of the Plan 246
THE FAILURE OF PLANNING IN DEVELOPING NATIONS 246
   Limitations of Theory in Practice 248
   Inadequacy of the Planning Process 249
   Markets Over Planning 249
GLOBAL INSIGHTS CASE 12.3: THE STAGES OF ECONOMIC DEVELOPMENT
   AND PLANNING IN CHINA 250
SUMMARY 252
QUESTIONS 253
NOTES 254
SUGGESTED READINGS 254

PART IV: INTERNATIONAL ECONOMICS OF DEVELOPING
NATIONS 257

CHAPTER 13: TRADE THEORY, TRADE POLICIES, AND DEVELOPMENT
EXPERIENCE 259

HISTORICAL DEVELOPMENT OF MODERN TRADE THEORIES 259
   Theory of Mercantilism 260
   Theory of Absolute Advantage 260
   Theory of Comparative Advantage 262
HECKSCHER-OHLIN THEORY 263
GLOBAL INSIGHTS CASE 13.1: RELATIVE RESOURCE ENDOWMENTS AND TRADE
   PATTERNS OF LEADING DEVELOPED NATIONS 264
LEONTIEF PARADOX 265
TRADE THEORY AND ECONOMIC DEVELOPMENT 266

TABLE OF CONTENTS

    Theory of Immiserizing Growth 266
    Graphical Illustration of Immiserizing Growth 267
    Prebisch Theory 269
EXPORT INSTABILITY 270
    Factors Giving Rise to Export Instability 270
        Price Variability 270
        High Degree of Commodity Concentration 271
    Empirical Studies of Export Instability in Developing Countries 272
    Policies to Stabilize Export Prices or Revenues 273
        Domestic Marketing Boards 273
        International Commodity Agreements 273
        International Buffer Stock Agreements 273
        International Export Quota Agreements 274
    Multilateral Agreements 276
TRADE LIBERALIZATION IN DEVELOPING NATIONS 278
DEMANDS FOR A NEW INTERNATIONAL ECONOMIC ORDER 279
GLOBAL INSIGHTS CASE 13.2: U.S. POLICY ON TRADE WITH DEVELOPING
    COUNTRIES 282
SUMMARY 283
QUESTIONS 284
PROBLEMS 284
NOTES 285
SUGGESTED READINGS 286

CHAPTER14: THE INTERNATIONAL DEBT CRISIS **287**

MAGNITUDE OF THE DEBT CRISIS 287
ORIGIN OF DEVELOPING COUNTRIES' DEBT CRISIS 289
    Tight Monetary Policies of Advanced Countries 289
    The Second Oil Shock 290
    Poor Public Sector Investment in Developing Countries 290
    The World Wide Recession 291
    Capital Flight from Developing Countries 292
    Appreciation of the Dollar 294
    Excess Loanable Funds in Advanced Countries 294
THE MEXICAN DEBT CRISIS 294
GLOBAL INSIGHTS CASE 14.1: DEBTS OF TRANSITIONAL ECONOMIES 295
DEBT CRISIS IN OTHER DEVELOPING COUNTRIES 297
SOVEREIGN DEFAULT 297
THE INTERNATIONAL MONETARY FUND AND THE DEBT CRISIS 299
THE UNITED STATES AND THE DEBT CRISIS 300
SOLUTIONS TO THE DEBT CRISIS 300
    Debt-Equity Swap 300
    The Baker Plan 301
GLOBAL INSIGHTS CASE 14.2: TRADE LIBERALIZATION AND THE DEBT CRISIS 302
GLOBAL INSIGHTS CASE 14.3:TIED-AID AGREEMENTS 303
    The Brady Plan 303

THE CHALLENGE AHEAD	304
SUMMARY	306
QUESTIONS	306
PROBLEMS	307
NOTES	307
SUGGESTED READINGS	308

PART V: FOREIGN DIRECT INVESTMENT, MULTINATIONAL CORPORATIONS, AND FOREIGN DIRECT INVESTMENT 309

CHAPTER 15: FOREIGN DIRECT INVESTMENT AND MULTINATIONAL CORPORATIONS 311

DEFINITION OF MULTINATIONAL CORPORATION	312
THE WORLD'S MAJOR MULTINATIONAL CORPORATIONS	313
FOREIGN DIRECT INVESTMENT AND PORTFOLIO INVESTMENT	313
CHANNELS OF ENTRY INTO INTERNATIONAL BUSINESS	316
Exporting	317
Licensing	317
GLOBAL INSIGHTS CASE 15.1: PIZZA HUT GOES TO BRAZIL	318
Franchising	319
MNC-Owned Foreign Enterprise	319
GLOBAL INSIGHTS CASE 15.2: DISNEYLAND OVERSEAS	320
Joint Venture	321
GLOBAL INSIGHTS CASE 15.3: U.S. COMPANIES APPETITE FOR JOINT VENTURES	322
Wholly Owned Subsidiary	323
Management Contract	324
Turnkey Operation	324
SUMMARY	324
QUESTIONS	326
PROBLEMS	326
NOTES	327
SUGGESTED READINGS	327

CHAPTER 16: TECHNOLOGY TRANSFER BY MULTINATIONAL CORPORATIONS TO DEVELOPING NATIONS 329

CHOICE OF TECHNOLOGY	329
The Cost of Capital and Labor	329
The Availability of Technological Alternatives	330
The Size and the Growth of the Market	330
The Obsolescence of the Existing Technology	330
GLOBAL INSIGHTS CASE 16.1: GILLETTE'S BLUNDER	331
TECHNOLOGY TRANSFER AND APPROPRIATE TECHNOLOGY	332

TABLE OF CONTENTS xiii

    Appropriate Technology 332
GLOBAL INSIGHT CASE 16.2: THE GLOBAL DIFFUSION OF TECHNOLOGY 333
CONFLICTS SURROUNDING TECHNOLOGY TRANSFER BY MNCs: 333
    Home Countries' Reactions to Technology Transfer 334
    Host Countries' Reactions to Technology Transfer: 334
    Reconciling Host and Home Countries' Reactions. 335
MODES OF TECHNOLOGY TRANSFER 336
TECHNOLOGY TRANSFER STRATEGIES 336
    The Sophistication of the Technology 336
    The Environments of the Home and Host Countries 336
    The Characteristics of the MNC 337
    The Characteristics of Domestic Firms 337
PRICING OF TECHNOLOGY TRANSFER 337
    Transfer Pricing 337
TECHNOLOGICAL FORECASTING 338
GLOBAL INSIGHTS CASE 16.3: MATSUSHITA'S FORECAST OF THE GROWTH OF
    ELECTRONICS AND RELATED TECHNOLOGIES 339
SUMMARY 340
QUESTIONS 341
PROBLEMS 341
NOTES 341
SUGGESTED READINGS 342

CHAPTER 17: CONFLICTS BETWEEN HOME AND HOST COUNTRIES 343

MAJOR CRITICISMS OF MNCS 343
SOURCES OF CONFLICTS 344
    MNCs' Objectives 344
    Home Countries' Objectives 345
        Economic Goals 345
        Noneconomic Goals 345
GLOBAL INSIGHTS CASE 17.1: THE EXXON VALDEZ DISASTER 346
    Host Countries' Objectives 347
        Economic Goals 347
            The Economic Growth Goal 347
            The Distributive and Allocative Goal 347
            The Balance of Payments Goal 348
        Noneconomic Goals 348
GLOBAL INSIGHTS CASE 17.2: HISTORICAL EVIDENCE AGAINST
    MULTINATIONAL CORPORATIONS 349
        Colonialism 350
        The Income Distribution Effect of MNCs 351
        Transborder Data Flow 351
HOST COUNTRIES' REACTION TO MNCS 352
    Joint Venture Arrangements 352
    Controlling Entries and Takeovers 353
    Excluding Foreigners from Specific Activities 354

TABLE OF CONTENTS

    Controlling the Local Content and Local Employment 355
    Export Requirements 355
    Controlling the Local Capital Market 355
    Debt Equity Requirements 356
    Taking the Foreign Investment Package Apart 356
    Requiring Disinvestment 356
    Controlling Remittances, Rates, and Fees 357
    Other Policies 357
    WHO IS RIGHT? 357
  GLOBAL INSIGHTS CASE 17.3: U.S. TOBACCO EXPORTS:
    A HEALTH-TRADE CONTROVERSY 358
  SUMMARY 359
  QUESTIONS 360
  PROBLEMS 361
  NOTES 362
  SUGGESTED READINGS 363

CHAPTER 18: FOREIGN AID 365

  THE HISTORY OF FOREIGN AID 365
  THE MAJOR TYPES OF FOREIGN AID 368
    Public Aid 368
    Private Aid 368
  MEASUREMENT PROBLEMS IN CALCULATING DEVELOPMENT ASSISTANCE .. 369
  GLOBAL INSIGHTS CASE 18.1: PATTERNS OF U.S. AID TODAY 370
  THE FOREIGN AID INCENTIVES OF DONOR NATIONS 371
Political Incentives 371
  GLOBAL INSIGHTS CASE 18.2: FOREIGN AID AND U.S. PUBLIC OPINION 372
    Economic Incentives 372
  THE FOREIGN AID INCENTIVES OF THE RECEIVING NATIONS 373
  GLOBAL INSIGHTS CASE 18.3:GUGING PUBLIC SUPPORT FOR U.S.
    GOVERNMENT AID 374
  CONTROVERSIES SURROUNDING FOREIGN AID 374
  LOOKING INTO THE FUTURE 375
  SUMMARY 375
  QUESTIONS 377
  NOTES 378
  SUGGESTED READINGS 378

PART VI : CRITICAL ISSUES FOR THE NEW MILLENNIUM 379

CHAPTER 19: TRANSITION ECONOMICS 381

  POLITICAL EVENTS GIVING RISE TO ECONOMIES IN TRANSITION 381
    Eastern European Countries Economic Reforms 381
    Unification of Germany 382
    Demise of the Soviet Union 384

TABLE OF CONTENTS xv

GLOBAL INSIGHTS CASE 19.1: BILATERAL INVESTMENT TREATIES 385
TRANSITION AND ECONOMICS 387
PRINCIPLES OF ECONOMIC TRANSITION 388
   Macroeconomic Reforms 388
      Price Liberalization 388
   Launching Appropriate Fiscal and Monetary Policies 389
GLOBAL INSIGHTS CASE 19.2: THE 1948 WEST GERMAN
   EARHARD REFORMS 390
   Opening the Economy to International Market Forces 391
      Currency Convertibility 391
STRUCTURAL REFORMS 393
   Establishing Private Property and Property Rights 393
GLOBAL INSIGHTS CASE 19.3: IMPORTS OF FOREIGN TECHNOLOGY
   ON JAPAN'S ECONOMIC TRANSITION 394
      The Order of Privatization 394
      Creation of a Private Housing Market 394
      Privatization Experience 394
GLOBAL INSIGHTS CASE 19.4: PROPERTY RIGHTS AND PRIVATE PROPERTY
   IN THE FORMER SOVIET UNION, EASTERN EUROPEAN NATIONS
   AND LATIN AMERICAN COUNTRIES 395
   Advancing domestic Competition 396
   Experience with Economic Reform and the Need for a New Theory 396
GLOBAL INSIGHTS CASE 19.5: THE ECONOMIC HARDSHIP IN SUB-SAHARAN
   AFRICA 389
SUMMARY 400
QUESTIONS 401
NOTES 402
SUGGESTED READINGS 403

CHAPTER 20: GLOBALIZATION, LOCALIZATION, AND THE ENVIRONMENT . 405

GLOBALIZATION 405
   Globalization and Dependency 406
LOCALIZATION 407
GLOBALIZATION, LOCALIZATION, AND ECONOMIC DEVELOPMENT 407
THE ENVIRONMENT 408
   Acid Rain 408
   Causes of Acid Rain 408
GLOBAL INSIGHTS CASE 20.1: U.S. ACID RAIN PROGRAM 409
   The Effects of Acid Rain 409
   How to Reduce Acid Rain 409
      Cleaning Up Smokestacks and Exhaust Pipes 409
      Using Alternative Energy Sources 410
      Restoring A Damaged Environment 410
OZONE DEPLETION 410
   The Ozone Agreements 411
CLIMATE CHANGE 411
GLOBAL INSIGHTS CASE 20.2: GOOD AND BAD OZONE 412

TABLE OF CONTENTS

    Greenhouse Gases 412
  GLOBAL INSIGHTS CASE 20.3: THE IMPACT OF OZONE ON HUMAN HEALTH
  AND ENVIRONMENT 413
  GLOBAL INSIGHTS CASE 20.4: THE ANTARCTIC OZONE HOLE 414
    Global Warming 414
    Factors Giving Rise to Greenhouse Gases 414
  GLOBAL INSIGHTS CASE 20.5: CHANGING CLIMATE 415
    The Impact of Climate Changes on the Environment 415
    Rio Convention 416
    Tokyo Convention 416
  BIODIVERSITY 417
    Definition of Biodiversity 417
    Levels of Biodiversity 417
    The Significance of Protecting Diversity 417
  DEFORESTATION 418
  GLOBAL INSIGHTS CASE 20.6: BIODIVERISTY AND BASIN'S HUMAN
  POPULATION 419
    Causes of Deforestation 419
    The Rate of Deforestation 420
    The Impact of Deforestation on Climate 420
    Deforestation and Biodiversity 420
    The Impact of Deforestation on the Ecosystem 420
  GLOBAL INSIGHTS CASE 20.7: TROPICAL DEFORESTATION AND HABITAT
  DEGRADATION IN THE BRAZILIAN AMAZON BASIN 421
    Looking Into The Future of Deforestation 422
  GLOBAL INSIGHTS CASE 20.8: THE LEVEL OF INCOME AND DEFORESTATION IN T
  TROPICAL COUNTRIES 423
  GLOBAL INSIGHTS CASE 20.9: SELECTIVE LOGGING IN INDONESIA 423
  GLOBAL INSIGHTS CASE 20.10: REGIONAL VARIATIONS IN THE RATE OF
  DEFORESTATION 424
  GLOBAL INSIGHTS CASE 20.11: NASA MISSIONS TO STUDY DEFORESTATION .. 424
  DESERTIFICATION 425
    Causes of Desertification 425
    The Impact of Desertification on the Environment. 425
  GLOBAL INSIGHTS CASE 20.12: THE UNITED NATIONS CONFERENCE ON
  DESERTIFICATION (UNCOD) 426
    Global Monitoring of Desertification 427
    GLOBAL INSIGHTS CASE 20.13: HISTORY OF DESERTIFICATION 427
    Local Treatments of Desertification 428
  RELATIONSHIP BETWEEN ECONOMIC DEVELOPMENT AND ECONOMIC
  DEVELOPMENT 428
  SUMMARY 429
  QUESTIONS 432
  NOTES 433
  SUGGESTED READINGS 434

GLOSSARY 437
INDEX 463

PREFACE

The world economy has changed drastically during the last three decades. The international monetary system has been completely restructured. The immense growth in computer and telecommunication industries has contributed significantly to the flow of information across national boundaries and has given rise to the transborder data flow (TDF) problem. The volume of world trade and investment has been expanding significantly. Newly industrialized countries, such as Taiwan and South Korea, have captured a significant share of the world market for manufactured goods. Eastern European countries have switched to a market-oriented economic system, joining the rank of developing nations in their struggle to achieve economic development. The collapse of the Soviet Union and the unification of Germany have changed the political and economic climate of the world. The European Union (EU) members are still struggling to achieve complete economic integration which was supposed to be implemented by 1992. The United States has entered into some significant free trade agreements including the North American Free Trade Agreement (NAFTA). The U.S.-Mexico-Canada free-trade agreement is the first of its kind. Never before have advanced nations formed such a huge free-trade area with a developing nation. Because the union of a developing nation with two advanced nations is unprecedented, it produces uncertainty. This uncertainty is imbued with the voice of opposition from all three countries. Many developing countries, especially those in Latin America, have been grappling with the debt crisis that hit the world in the early 1980s. Unable to service their debt on time, they have been experiencing staggering unemployment, rampant inflation, and a lower standard of living. The debt crisis also threatened several U.S. banks with bankruptcy, emphasizing the need for a solution to the situation. Multinational corporations have expanded their operations around the globe, emerging as an important force in shaping the economies of the developing nations.

The above changes have contributed to the significance of foreign trade and investment in the process of economic development in the developing nations. This has resulted in an expanded demand for a textbook that addresses the recent developments in the world economy and discusses their impacts on developing nations. Unfortunately, most existing textbooks do not deal adequately with these issues. Instead, they discuss various development problems without paying sufficient attention to the recent events in the world economy and their impacts on the developing countries. They also lack an adequate discussion of the controversial role that is played by multinational corporations in the process of economic development. Additionally, most textbooks confront students with elaborate models and assumptions that are difficult for most undergraduates to comprehend without sufficient real-world examples. This textbook attempts to remedy these problems.

The idea of writing this textbook came from my experience in teaching economic development to undergraduate students over the last two decades. My belief is that economic development should be studied in the context of a global framework. I also believe that the best way to motivate students and to teach a theory is to show how it is used in practice. This textbook reflects these tenets by viewing economic issues from a global perspective and discussing theories along with ample examples, followed by case studies, and thought-provoking questions.

DISTINCTIVE TEXT FEATURES

The following features distinguish this textbook from others in the field:

Coverage of Contemporary Issues

Given the recent events in the world economy, it is easy for a textbook to become out of date. Unfortunately, most of the existing textbooks are concerned mainly with traditional issues and theoretical models, and have been either silent or inadequate in their coverage of the events that are taking place in these turbulent times. This textbook provides the most complete coverage of contemporary issues in comparison to competing books. Topics discussed include:

- Globalization, localization and the environment (Chapter 20)
- Transition economics (Chapter 19)
- Newly industrialized countries (Chapter 3)
- The demise of the Soviet Union (Chapter 17)
- Eastern European countries economic reforms (Chapter 19)
- Immigration (Chapter 7)
- Foreign direct investment and multinational corporations (Chapter 15)
- Technology transfer by multinational corporations to developing countries (Chapter 16)
- Conflicts surrounding multinational corporations (Chapter 17)
- The transborder data flow problem (Chapter 17)

Application of Theories

Theories are discussed along with numerous real-life examples and global insights cases to illustrate their relevance and application to real-world situations. For example, the discussion of economic growth in the non-western world is presented with the example of the Japanese development strategies (Chapter 3), and discussion of poverty and income distribution is presented with the example of policies that are employed to reduce poverty in India (Chapter 5). Further, the discussion of rural development and agricultural transformation is presented with case studies of the agrarian structures in Latin America, Asia, and China (Chapter 8). The discussion of technological progress is presented with a global insights case that elaborates on the Asian economic miracle (Chapter 9). Human resources development and capital formation is presented with a discussion of education and gender discrimination in Pakistan (Chapter 10). Monetary and fiscal policies are studied with a presentation of the Asian growth model and performance of international financial institutions in the 1990s. (Chapter 11). The subject of development planning is presented with a review of development planning in the former Soviet Union and China. The presentation of the Prebisch theory includes a demonstration of its usefulness in studying the import substitution policies that are practiced by Latin American countries such as Colombia, Peru, and Chile. Finally, our discussion of mercantilism is illustrated with the example of "high-tech mercantilism" that is practiced in France today (Chapter 13).

Global Insights Cases

The boxed Global Insights display contemporary and real world examples of concepts or theories that have been explained, immediately following presentation. As a result, students do not have to search for an example or ponder whether the theory has any real-world relevance.

Depth of Coverage

The presentation of often-ignored topics, including foreign direct investment and multinational corporations, immigration, technology transfer, newly industrialized countries, globalization, localization, and the environment, and transition economics make this textbook more comprehensive than most.

As a result of the increasing importance and attention given to foreign direct investment and multinational corporations, a complete and separate section is devoted to this topic.

A comprehensive treatment of debt crisis is presented in a separate chapter, elaborating on the elements that gave rise to this issue and discussing different solutions presented in resolving this problem. Finally, throughout the textbook, close attention is paid to the recent political and economic events affecting developing nations, placing such contemporary issues among the topics that receive more coverage in this textbook than most.

ORGANIZATION OF THE TEXT

The text consists of six parts subdivided into 20 chapters. Part one focuses on the basic concepts and principles. Topics include the global economy and the developing nations, the definition and measurement of economic development, economic development in a historical perspective, and alternative theories of economic development.

Part two deals with the elements of growth. Topics include poverty and income distribution, population growth and economic development, unemployment, migration and urbanization and economic development, rural development and agricultural transformation, and technological progress.

Part three elaborates on domestic resource policies and development strategies. Topics include resource development and capital formation, monetary and fiscal policies, and development planning.

Part four covers the international economics of developing nations. It includes trade theory, trade policies and development experience, and the international debt crisis.

Part five draws attention to foreign direct investment, multinational corporations, and foreign aid. Topics discussed are foreign direct investment and multinational corporations, technology transfer by multinational corporations to developing nations, conflict surrounding multinational corporations, and foreign aid.

Par six concentrates on the critical issues for the new millennium. Topics include transition economics, and globalization, localization and the environment.

Each chapter begins with the main learning objectives of the chapter and includes case studies that illustrate the applications of concepts and theories covered throughout the chapter. Each chapter concludes with a detailed summary, a number of thought provoking questions, and a list of suggested readings.

PEDAGOGY

Each chapter begins with a set of main learning objectives and concludes with a detailed summary, review questions, and a list of suggested readings. Additionally, some chapters include thought-provoking problems, that helps students to sharpen their analytical reasoning. Each chapter also includes a number of global insight cases that apply theories to real-world situations.

The text concludes with a complete glossary for easy access to the terminology used in economic development.

SUPPLEMENTARY MATERIALS

To aid instructors we have developed a support package that includes the following materials.

Instructor's Manual. For each chapter this manual includes lecture notes and answers to the problems that are included at the end of some of the chapters.

Test Bank. The test bank has been classroom tested. Each chapter contains 30 multiple-choice questions, 30 true/false questions, and 30 completion questions, with answers provided.

ACKNOWLEDGMENTS

A comprehensive textbook on international economics could not be written without the help of individuals who offer their valuable time and talents. My students at California State University, San Bernardino, have been instrumental in providing feedback and contributing to some of the cases presented in this book. I am grateful to all of them. I would like to thank Professor Michael LeMay (California State University, San Bernardino), who wrote a case on the subject of immigration.

I am indebted to the anonymous reviewers from the following universities who read the manuscript at different stages and provided me with constructive criticism and useful suggestions:

- State University of New York, Albany
- Southern Methodist University
- Washington State University, Pullman
- University of Nebraska, Lincoln

My deepest thanks go to my family who had to sacrifice on so many occasions so that I could work on this project. My wife, Dorothy Thurman, a lecturer at California State University San Bernardino, wrote three case studies and read most pages of the manuscript and provided me with valuable comments. My son, Daniel Thurman Asheghian, a student at UCLA, read every single page of the manuscript to ensure readability and provided me with valuable comments. I thank my daughter, Laila Thurman Asheghian, for her understanding, support, and tolerance throughout the whole project.

ABOUT THE AUTHOR

Parviz Asheghian (Ph.D., Georgia State University) is a professor of economics at California State University. He is the author of the following textbooks:

International Economics. 3rd. ed., Mason, Ohio, Thomson Learning, 2003.

The External Environment of Global Business, Leyh Publishing LLC, Austin, Texas, 2002 [with Bahman Ebrahimi].

The Internal Environment of Global Business, Leyh Publishing LLC, Austin, Texas, 2002 [with Bahman Ebrahimi].

The Multinational Corporations: Economics and Environments. Commack, N.Y.: Nova Science Publishing Co, 1998.

International Business: Economics, Environments, and Strategies. New York: Harper Collins, 1990 [with Bahman Ebrahimi].

Dr. Asheghian's major research interests are in the areas of international economics/finance, multinational corporations, and economic development. He has published more than two dozen articles in academic journals such as *Journal of Economic Development, Development Policy Review, The Asian Pacific Journal of Business Economics and Business, Journal of International Business Studies, Quarterly Journal of Business and Economics, Quarterly Review of Economics,* and *Managing International Development.*

Professor Asheghian has served on the editorial boards of several scholarly journals including *International Trade and Finance Journal, Journal of Third World Development,* and *Journal of Business and Economic Perspectives.*

PART I

BASIC CONCEPTS AND PRINCIPLES

CHAPTER 1

THE GLOBAL ECONOMY AND DEVELOPING NATIONS

Today, we have entered a new millennium, marked by a growing global competition that is characterized by a one-world market. In this market, significant economic and technological considerations are forcing the movements of traditional industries to developing countries and creating newly industrialized countries (NICs). This in turn, is triggering a reallocation of resources in the industrial nations from the traditional capital-intensive industries to the new knowledge and service industries.

Although globalization is not a new phenomenon, what is different today is the speed and the extent of growth in global markets. Two major factors have contributed to this growth. First, advances in communication technology and transportation methods have greatly expanded international trade and investment. As a result, the percentage of gross national product (GNP) absorbed by foreign trade for major developed (advanced) countries has roughly doubled since 1960. Second, long-term increases in the GNP per capita coupled with higher life expectancies and education levels have increased the role of some developing countries in global markets. For example, Brazil, Hong Kong, Singapore, and South Korea now rank among the top 20 exporters of manufactured goods, whereas in 1965 no developing country was even included in the top 30. The increasing importance of developing countries in global markets has decreased the capacity of developed countries to dominate these markets.[1] Nevertheless, the major beneficiaries of globalization have been the advanced nations. Today, more than three quarters of the world's 5.3 billion inhabitants live in poverty, but they account for only one quarter of the world's production and income. Occupying the vast regions of Africa, Asia, and Latin America, they have been referred to collectively as third-world countries, underdeveloped countries, developing countries, or less developed countries (LDCs). The majority of people living in these nations suffer from poor health, they are unable to read and write, they are unemployed, and their chance for a prosperous life is dismal or indeterminate. An investigation of these global inequalities in living standards is illuminating.

If we examine an average family in the United States or Canada, we find a family of four earning about $30,000 to $40,000 a year. They live comfortably in an apartment or suburban house equipped with modern appliances with separate bedrooms for each of the two children, a living room, a kitchen, and a garage for their car. Their house is filled with numerous consumer goods and electrical equipment, many of which were manufactured outside North America in countries such as Taiwan, South Korea, and Singapore. They can always have three meals a day which may include bananas from Central America, beef from Costa Rica, coffee from Brazil, and canned fish from Japan. Both parents have completed high school and their children are expected to finish high school and perhaps go to college. They work in a reasonably safe environment furnished with modern equipment and machinery that is conducive to physical and mental work. They have access to state-of-the-art medical care and are expected to live to an average age of 74 years. But, though the family seems to have a reasonably good life, they may suffer from the stress associated with the competitive pressure to excel financially. Their water may be polluted, and air dirty. The pressure of day-to-day living, and lack of time to enjoy simple pleasures of life may cause them to experience stress, frustration, and emptiness. Nevertheless, such a life style is envied by millions of less fortunate people in the world who would be happy with even a portion of the material opulence of an average family in North America.

If we examine a typical family in rural areas of Asia, Africa, or Latin America, we would find that the household is composed a dozen people who live in crowded quarters. This "extended" family includes not only the parents and their half dozen or more children, but also their grandparents, and some close relatives such as uncles or aunts. They all live in one room that is poorly constructed and may lack any electricity, plumbing, or other amenities that many people in advanced countries take for granted. All of the family members, except the younger children, must work on the land. All the adults in the family are all illiterate. Unable to read and write, they set a poor example for their children to follow. As a result, none of the children are expected to finish elementary school. The family members could hope only for one meal a day. The meal rarely changes and it is seldom adequate to appease the continuous hunger experienced by the children. The work is back-breaking physical labor in the hot sun, contributing to much sickness and poor health that stems from lack of sanitation and poor living conditions. Yet, trained doctors and nurses are far away in urban areas, treating their wealthier patients. In such an environment, the aspirations for a better life are constantly being crushed and the only assuagement from the daily exertion lies in the spiritual life.

Leaving the rural areas, suppose we were to visit a typical city in a developing nation, say New Delhi, India. We would be shocked by clear differences in living standards from one part of this city to another. In one extreme we find upper-income people, composed of professionals, business people, and civil servants who live comfortably in large houses that are composed of a half dozen rooms. Although they may have fewer electrical appliances than a typical family in North America, they attain the same level of comfort by employing maids and menial workers. On the other extreme, we find a large number of unemployed, underemployed and marginally employed people who basically live in the streets, where they bathe, cook, eat, defecate and sleep. Between these two extremes we find a family whose main breadwinner has a steady job and works either in an assembly line of a large company or is hired as a clerk by a government agency, living in a small house or an apartment.

Although there is a sharp contrast between the life styles and social institutions of the developing nations, the majority of developing countries suffer from the same degree of income inequality and poverty as in India. It is sufficient to say that even the poorest people who live in North America have a better standard of living than most inhabitants of developing nations.

ECONOMIC DEVELOPMENT IN THE GLOBAL CONTEXT

The objective of this book is to provide a better understanding of the major problems and prospects for economic development by concentrating specifically on the predicament of the three-quarter of the world's inhabitants who have low standards of living and continue to suffer from poverty.

It should be emphasized at the outset that economic development cannot be studied in a vacuum, without considering the role of the advanced nations in directly or indirectly facilitating or impeding the development process. As we explained earlier, advances in communication technology and transportation methods have greatly expanded international trade and investment. They have also intensified the interdependence among nations. Today, no nation is immune to events that occur in other nations. For example, the recent currency crisis in Asia has in one way or another, directly or indirectly, affected the

GLOBAL INSIGHTS CASE 1.1

DEVELOPING NATIONS IN THE GLOBAL ECONOMY

During the 1960s and the 1970s the rate of growth of the gross domestic product (GDP) in developing nations remained relatively strong. However, beginning with 1980, the growth rate of GDP in these nations declined from an average of 5.4 percent a year during the 1973-80 period to 3.9 percent during the 1980-87 period. Two important exceptions are India and China which because of their major growth fostering policy strategies during the 1980s, continued to experience a relatively strong growth. The decrease in the growth rate of GDP in developing nations can be partially attributed to unpredictable changes in the world economy. Such changes had an adverse direct effect on the developing nations. It also revealed that many of the macroeconomic policies that were adopted by the developing nations during the 1970s were not sustainable during the 1980s. The developing nations that were most significantly affected by the changes, starting in the 1980s, had the following four problems in common:

1. Unresponsive policies.
2. Significant macroeconomic imbalances, such as large fiscal deficits and high inflation.
3. Inflexible and distorted markets.
4. High level of external debts.

Global factors affected these nations in two major areas of trade and finance. From the international trade standpoint, between 1980 and 1986 the primary commodity prices declined significantly. During the same period, the crude oil prices declined even more significantly than those of other primary commodities. As a result, most of the developing countries, including all oil exporters experienced difficulties in adjusting to such a sharp decline in prices of their primary exports. However, given their ability, developing nations reacted differently to these changes. East Asian nations responded by enhancing the volume of their primary commodity exports, and thus preserving the level of their revenue from these commodities. In Latin America and South Asia, however, the growth of the export volume proved to be inadequate to overcome the declining prices and hence their purchasing power fell. In Sub-Saharan Africa, commodity export volumes stagnated, leading to a sharp decline in the purchasing power in this region. Finally, the growth in the value of manufactured exports from developing nations also declined sharply, reaching the average level of 9 percent after 1980, as compared to the average level of 25 percent during the 1970s. During the same period, the rate of growth in the volume of exports fell from 13 to 9 percent.

Besides international trade, another factor that affected the economic performance of the developing nations was the cost and availability of international finance. The early 1980s is marked as the beginning of the debt crisis. The adoption of anti-inflationary macroeconomic policies in advanced nations led to a sharp increase in nominal interest rates. The developing nations with large amount of foreign debt were deeply affected. The higher interest rates combined with the lower export prices for non-oil commodities led to escalating real costs for servicing all forms of new and existing debts. The depletion of resources, resulting from the debt crisis, made many nations adopt austerity measures. Although the unequivocal breakdown of the financial system that many had feared has not occurred, the debt burden in developing nations continues to present a major obstacle to economic growth in debt stricken countries and threatens the global economy.

Source: The World Bank, *world Development Report 1988* (New York: Oxford University Press, 1988), pp. 23-39.

> ## GLOBAL INSIGHTS CASE 1.2
>
> ## GLOBAL CONSUMPTION INEQUALITIES
>
> Over the past quarter of a century, consumption per capita in advanced nations has steadily increased at about 2.3 percent. During the same period, consumption per capita grew at an impressive rate of 6.1 percent in East Asia and at 2 percent in South Asia. Yet, these developing nations are still far from catching up to the level of consumption in advanced nations. Moreover, consumption growth in other developing nations has been either slow or stagnant.
>
> Today, 20 percent of the globe's inhabitants have been left out of the consumption explosion. Out of the 4.4 billion people in developing nations:
>
> - About 60 percent lack basic sanitation.
> - More than 30 percent have no access to clean water.
> - 20 percent have no access to modern health services.
> - About 20 percent of children do not attend school to grade five.
> - About 20 percent of children cannot get enough dietary energy and protein.
>
> Source: The World Bank, *Human Development Report 1998* (New York: Oxford University Press, 1998), pp. 1-13.

economic conditions of European and North American nations. As another example, the crash of the U.S. stock market on Monday, October 19, 1987, wiping out $500 billion in wealth in a few hours, affected other countries in the world. Within hours of the collapse of the U.S. stock market, the European and Asian markets were falling fast, experiencing an unprecedented decline in their stock prices and losing billions of dollars.[2]

One of the consequences of the globalization of the world's economy has been a remarkable increase in consumption. However, such growth has been badly distributed within and between nations, contributing to income inequality at the national and international level. In advanced countries, consumption per capita has accelerated at about 2.3% over the past quarter of a century. Yet, the average African today consumes 20% less than he/she did a quarter century ago. What is alarming is that the globe's dominant consumers live in advanced countries, but environmental decay resulting from the world's consumption falls more heavily on developing nations. For example, the fifth of the globe's highest-income countries generate 53% of carbon dioxide emission, the poorest 3%. Among the developing nations, Brazil, India, Indonesia, and Mexico account for the highest emission. Yet, with large populations, their per capita emissions are still very small as compared to advanced nations. For example, per capita emissions of Mexico (3.9 metric tons a year) are less than 1/5 of the United States' per capita emissions (20.5 metric tons a year). The global warming from carbon dioxide is devastating for many developing nations. For instance, with a rise in sea levels, Bangladesh's sea area could shrink by 17%.

In satisfying advanced nations' appetite for a variety of food, some developing nations have expanded the exports of cash crops at the expense of feeding their own people. Today, about a billion people in 40 developing nations risk losing access to their primary source of protein, as excessive fishing motivated by the growing export demand for animal feed and oils depletes their fish stocks.

CH.1/THE GLOBAL ECONOMY & DEVELOPING NATIONS

In this textbook we study economic development within a global economic framework, examining the whys and hows of ever increasing economic interdependence among nations. We consider the organizations and rules of conduct of the global economy. How are these rules devised? Who profits most from them? Who administers them?

WHY STUDY ECONOMIC DEVELOPMENT?

The purpose of studying economic development is to gain a better understanding of different problems faced by developing nations and discuss possible options available in resolving these problems. The following is a list of major questions that can be raised by every development economist in the study of economic development:

- What are the common characteristics of developing nations?
- What is meant by economic growth and economic development?
- What are alternative theories of economic development?
- Has economic growth been effective in improving the living conditions of developing nations?
- How can poverty be reduced in the rural areas of developing nations?
- Is the shortage of resources a main barrier to the process of economic development?
- What is the impact of population on economic development and income inequality?
- Why do developing countries experience such a high rate of underemployment?
- What elements influence labor skills in developing nations?
- How should we allocate capital between alternative uses?
- What elements augment the effective entrepreneurial activity in developing nations?
- How can a nation enhance its capital formations rate?
- What fiscal and monetary policies should a nation employ to realize economic development with price stability?
- What economic policies should a developing nation employ to alleviate foreign exchange shortages and high debt ratios?
- Should a developing nation employ tariffs to protect domestic industry?
- Should a developing nation depend on pricing systems or state planning in allocation of resources?
- How can the global community help developing nations?

THE LIMITATIONS OF TRADITIONAL ECONOMICS

When studying economic development, strict adherence to *traditional economics*, that is, classical and neoclassical economics, is problematic. Traditional economics is concerned with the notion of "perfect markets" as it applies to advanced nations. It deals mainly with the efficient, least-cost allocation of scarce resources. It investigates the optimal growth of these resources over time to produce a growing level of goods and services. However, unlike advanced countries, developing countries' markets are highly imperfect, and consumers and producers have scant information. These nations often lack a conducive climate for entrepreneurship, large number of entrepreneurs, a highly educated and mobile labor force, local ownership of industry, heavy dependence on direct taxes for revenue, large number of exportable goods, a well-developed capital market, high savings rate, local ownership of industry, an average income significantly above subsistence, commercial farmers with considerable land holdings, and a well-developed and utilized banking system.

Thus, the problems of economic development are often unique. In addition to being concerned with the efficient allocation of resources and their sustained growth over time, we must also deal with economic, political, and social frameworks in order to raise the standard of living of poverty-stricken, illiterate, and malnourished people who live in developing nations.

Given the diversity of developing nations, it must be realized that there are no universal principles or laws of economic development that are applicable to any or all developing nations. Economic development must be multifaceted in nature, that is to fuse germane concepts and doctrines from traditional economic theories with contemporary models and broader multi disciplinary approaches that are based on the historical and contemporary experience of the third world nations.

To be sure, the main focus of this is textbook is on the essence of economic development and its usefulness in comprehending issues of economic and social growth in developing nations. However, we continue to be aware of the fact that values, attitudes and institutions, both domestic and global, have significant effects on the process of economic development.

SUMMARY

1. Two major factors have contributed to the growth of globalization. First, advances in communication technology and transportation methods have greatly expanded international trade and investment. Second, long-term increases in the GNP per capita coupled with higher life expectancies and education levels have increased the role of some developing countries in global markets.
2. Today, more than three quarters of the world's 5.3 billion inhabitants live in poverty, but they account for only one quarter of the world's production and income. Occupying the vast regions of Africa, Asia, and Latin America, they have been referred to collectively as third-world countries, underdeveloped countries, developing countries, or less developed countries (LDCs).
3. The majority of people living in these nations suffer from poor health, they are unable to read and write, they are unemployed, and their chance for a prosperous life is dismal or indeterminate.
4. Economic development cannot be studied in a vacuum, without considering the role of advanced nations in directly or indirectly facilitating or impeding the development process.
5. The purpose of studying economic development is to gain a better understanding of different problems faced by developing nations and discuss possible options available in resolving these problems. Seventeen options are listed in the textbook.
6. When studying economic development, strict adherence to *traditional economics*, that is, classical and neoclassical economics, is problematic.
7. Unlike advanced countries, developing countries' markets are highly imperfect, and consumers and producers have scant information.
8. Given the diversity of developing nations, there are no universal principles or laws of economic development that are applicable to any or all developing nations.

QUESTIONS

1. Why are neoclassical theories inadequate in examining the economies of the third world nations.?
2. What factors have contributed to the globalization of the world economy in recent years?
3. What do you expect to learn from studying economic development?
4. Why do you think that economic development should be studied in a global context?
5. Elaborate on the ways in which developing nations may differ in terms of economic, social and political frameworks.

CH.1/THE GLOBAL ECONOMY & DEVELOPING NATIONS

NOTES

1. "Entering A New Age of Boundless Competition," *Fortune*, March 14, 1988, pp. 40-48.
2. "The Plunge in Stock Market has Experts Guessing About Market's Course," *The Wall Street Journal*, 26 October 1987, p.1; "Anguish Abroad: Foreign Ardor Cools Toward U.S. Stocks After Market's Drive," *The Wall Street Journal*, 26 October 1987, p.1; "How Bad? The Economy Will Have to Struggle to Avoid a Recession," *Business Week*, 2 November 1987, pp. 42-43; "How the Bull Crashed Into Reality," *Business Week*, 2 November 1987, pp. 48-50.

SUGGESTED READINGS

Berg, Robert J., and Jennifer Seymour Whitaker, eds. *Strategies for African Development*. Berkeley: University of California Press, 1968.
Cole, John P. *Development and Underdevelopment: A Profile of the Third World*. London: Routledge, 1987.
Goulet, Denis. *The Crucial Choice: A new Concept in the Theory of Development*. New York: Atheneum, 1971, chap. 2.
Harrison, Paul. *Inside the Third World*. New York: Penguin, 1982.
Hicks, Norman L, and Paul P. Streeten. "Indicators of Development: The search for a basic needs Yardstick." *World Development* 7 (June 1979).
Furtado, Celso. *Economic Development in Latin America*. London: Cambridge University Press, 1970.
Goldschmidt, Walter. "Toward an Anthropological Approach to Economic Development." *Human Organization* 41 (1982):80-82.
Heeger, Gerald A. *The Politics of Underemployment*. New York: St. Martin's Press, 1974.
Hoven, Allan."Anthropologists and Development." *Annual Review of Anthropology* 11 (1982): 349-375.
Ingham, Barbara. "The Meaning of Development: Interactions between 'new' and 'old' ideas." *World Development* 21 (November 1993): 1803-1821.
Myrdal Gunnar. *Asian Drama*. New York: Pantheon, 1968.
Raffaele, J.A. *The Economic Development of Nations*. New York: Random House, 1971.
Ruttan, Vernon W. "Cultural Endowments and Economic Development: What can we learn from Anthropology?" *Economic Development and Cultural Change* 36, Supplement (April 1988): 247-272.
Seers, Dudley. "The Meaning of Development." *International Development Review* 11 (December 1969): 1-16.
Sheahan, John. *Patterns of Development in Latin America*. Princeton, N.J.: Princeton University Press, 1978.
Smith, Stephen C. *Case Studies in Economic Development*, 2nd ed. Reading Mass.: Addison-Wesley, 1997, chapt. 1.
United Nations Development Program, *Human Resource Development Report 1994*. New York: Oxford University Press, 1994. Chaps. 1 and 2.
Wirada, Howard J. "Toward a Nontechnical Theory of Development: Alternative Conceptions for the Third World." *Journal of Developing Areas* 17 (July 1983).

CHAPTER 2

THE DEFINITION AND MEASUREMENT OF ECONOMIC DEVELOPMENT

As our discussion of the limitations of traditional economics theory in Chapter 1 indicated, economic development is a multidimensional subject that investigates economic problems within the political and social framework of the developing country in question. In fact, disappointment with the outcomes of development attempts during the past three decades prior to the 1980s led to refocusing the approach to address the issues of development. As a result, the growth of GNP is no longer considered the main objective or yardstick of economic development.

The purpose of this chapter is to define the meaning of economic development and to elaborate on the measures used to assess development.

In achieving these objectives, we first distinguish between economic growth and economic development and then turn our attention to the classifications of rich and poor countries. Finally, we elaborate on different measures that are used to assess economic development.

GROWTH AND DEVELOPMENT

Economic growth refers to the rate of increase in a nation's full employment real output or income over time. In other words, economic growth is the rise in full-employment output in constant prices. Economic growth can be measured as a rise in total full-employment real gross national product (GNP), or gross domestic product (GDP) over time. The "total" measure is employed to depict the expansion of a country's economic output or potential. The "per capita" measure is utilized to indicate a nation's material standard of living.

It is hard to provide an accurate meaning of "economic development." We may start by the following list that shows what is not considered "economic development":

- Economic development is not identical to total development of a nation. Rather it is a part of general development. Total (national) development includes, at a minimum, social and political development as well as economic development. Total development may encompass other types of development such as administrative or legal development. However, the major question raised in the subject of our study is how political and social development facilitate economic development and are, in turn, defined by it.
- Economic development is not equivalent to "economic independence." Given their colonial history,

GLOBAL INSIGHTS CASE 2.1

THE GLOBAL GROWTH EXPERIENCE

World income per capita grew at an annual rate of 1.3 percent, increasing a total of 28 percent over the 1990-2000 period. Performance in the East Asia and Pacific region (East and Southeast Asia plus Australia, New Zealand, and the Pacific island nations) far exceeded this benchmark: average income per capita in these countries more than tripled, from $396 in 1980 to $1,252 in 2000, with growth of more than 6.2 percent a year. In contrast, incomes per capita in Latin America rose only from $3,548 in 1980 to $3,856 in 2000, which translates to an annual average growth rate of less than 0.5 percent. Average annual income per capita in the countries of Sub-Saharan Africa actually fell by 14 percent during the period, from $658 in 1980 to $564 in 2000, or by 0.8 percent a year. (Unless otherwise noted, all income levels in this chapter are reported in constant 1995 dollars.)

Measures of countries' adherence to the pro-growth principles introduced above, and described in more detail below, suggest possible reasons for this huge variation. One is the presence or absence of macroeconomic stability: inflation varied substantially among the three regions, in a pattern that mirrors their growth outcomes. Annual inflation in Latin America as a whole remained relatively high during the 1980s and 1990s, averaging about 25 percent. In contrast, inflation in the fast-growing East Asia and Pacific region averaged only about 12 percent during these two decades but fell sharply in many countries over the period. Inflation in slow-growing Sub-Saharan Africa also averaged only about 12 percent. However, unlike East Asia and the Pacific, inflation in Sub-Saharan Africa rose over the period, from 10 percent in the 1980s to 16 percent in the 1990s.

Source: U.S. Government Printing Office, *Economic Report of the President* (Washington D C.: U.S. Government Printing Office, 2003), 216.

many developing nations have been unhappy with their dependence on export markets and foreign capital. They have viewed such a dependence as "foreign domination" or "exploitation". Such views have led many of these countries to pursue "inward looking" policies by restricting the inflow of foreign capital or reverting to import-substitution, that is, replacing their imports by domestic production. However, as we discuss in other chapters, the pursuit of such policies may prove to be detrimental to the very core of economic development.

- Economic development is not synonymous with industrialization. Because advanced countries are industrialized, the policy makers of some developing nations have viewed industrialization as the main path to riches. Given such a misconception, they may consider dependence on primary products undesirable, thus engaging in hasty industrialization. However, such a strategy might go against the comparative advantage of the developing nations. The appropriate question is whether industrial development or agricultural development is the proper policy for expediting a nations's economic development. In answering this question the following points should be kept in mind:

    1. Concentration of a large proportion of production in the agricultural sector by itself is not the

CH. 2/THE DEFINITION & MEASUREMENT OF ECONOMIC DEVELOPMENT

cause of poverty. Rather, it is the low productivity in agriculture that breeds poverty.
2. Advancement in the industrial sector is highly correlated with growth in the agricultural sector. In the absence of adequate primary production in providing inputs for the industrial growth, the industrialization polices will suffer significantly.
3. Economic development encompasses much more than mere establishment of industries. It comprises an upward movement of the whole society. It involves achieving a number of modernization objectives such as economic and social equalization, productivity growth, better institutions, improved attitudes, and a system of policy measures that are rationally designed and coordinated so that undesirable conditions that breed a state of underdevelopment are dismantled.

These considerations convey that economic development encompasses much more than economic growth. In a nutshell, economic development is growth plus change. More precisely, **economic development** can be defined as the *process* whereby a nation's *real per capita income* (its GNP) rises over a *long period* of time, provided that the number below an "*absolute poverty* line" does not rise, and that income distribution does not become more unequal. Given this definition, the following concepts need clarification:

- We accentuate that economic development is a process, implying that it involves causal relationships. This demands that the implementation of developmental activities is to be achieved in a logical, interconnected, and causal manner that is appropriate to the conditions existing in the developing country.
- Given that a primary objective of a developing country is the alleviation of mass poverty, then it should concentrate on raising the level of its *per capita* real income rather than just enhancing its GNP. If the emphasis were only on elevating GNP, then it would be probable for GNP to increase without an increase in per capita income. This might occur, because the rate of growth of population may exceed the rate of growth of GNP, or be equal to it. If this were the case, the result would be falling, or constant per capita income, which is not considered to be economic development.
- We place emphasis on a *long period* of time to avoid considering as economic development short run increases that may occur during an upswing of the business cycle. What is important in economic development is *sustained* rise in the level of GNP.
- We stressed that the number below a "*absolute poverty* line" does not rise, and that income distribution does not become more unequal. Otherwise, given a growing population, it would be possible for the number of those living below a poverty line to rise along with an increase in the average income of the population as a whole. Assuming the existence of a dual economy, that is, an economy composed of a modern sector and a traditional sector, it is also possible for the entire growth of income to accrue to the modern sector, and income per head might still rise although there had been no change in the traditional economy.*

To sum up, although it is customary to consider a rise in per capita real income as the best available measure of economic development, we should refrain from designating this as an increase in economic welfare, or social welfare, without taking into account other variables such as valuation, composition, and

---

*As we will explain later in Chapter 5, absolute poverty is below the income that secures the bare essentials of food, clothing, and shelter. Two poverty lines have been identified by economists: the lower (extreme) poverty line, and upper poverty line. The lower poverty line, considered as the absolute minimum by international standards, is based on a standard set in India and amounts to $275 per capita income. The upper poverty line amounts to $370 per capita. This figure is derived from studies for a number of nations with low average income -Bangladesh, the Arab Republic of Egypt, India, Indonesia, Kenya, Morocco, and Tanzania. Both of the figures are in constant 1985 prices.

the distribution of the augmented output. To be sure, development economists no longer envision GNP as the measure of economic development, but focus more directly on the quality of the development progression, portrayed by better living conditions, better nutrition, better health, and better employment opportunities for the poor segment of the population.

CLASSIFICATION OF NATIONS

When the systematic study of economic development began in the late 1940s and early 1950s, it was conventional to divide nations into the two categories of rich and poor. The rich nations included Australia, Canada, Japan, New Zealand, Western European countries, and the United States. The poor nations encompassed Africa, Asia, and Latin America.

It is risky to attempt to generalize too much about these categories. The distinction between poor and rich countries, oversimplified before, has become more obscured in the 1990s. Today, the classification schemes used to define developing countries differ, depending on the agency providing the scheme. The United Nations (UN) distinguishes between three major classes of third-world countries: the least-developed, or poorest nations; the non-oil-exporting developing nations; and the petroleum-rich OPEC (Organization for Petroleum Exporting Countries) nations.* The Organization for Economic Cooperation and Development (OECD) classifies developing nations into low-income countries, middle-income countries, newly industrialized countries (NICs), and members of OPEC. Finally, the World Bank divides all countries (both developing and advanced) into four categories: low-income, lower-middle-income, upper-middle-income, and high-income economies.

The members of **The United Nations Conference on Trade and Development (UNCTAD)**, are usually referred to as **third world nations**, a designation developed in the early post-World War II decades. By refraining from affiliating themselves with either the United States or the former Soviet Union, these 127 Asian, African, and Latin American members of the UNCTAD formed a third political unit in the United Nations. Today, the "third world" designation does not imply nonalignment, as it did originally. Rather, it is used to distinguish UNCTAD nations from the first world, and the second world. The term **first world** refers to the capitalist nations, where capital and land are owned by people. The term **second world** alludes to the socialist or the centrally directed nations, where the government owns the means of production.**

Today, the designation *second world* is hardly used. This has been especially the case since 1989-91, when the former Soviet Union, Eastern European nations, China, Mongolia, and Vietnam have been moving toward a market oriented economic system. Following the collapse of the Soviet Union and the economic reform of the Eastern Europe, these nations are now included among developing nations.

In spite of the diversity of classification schemes used to define developing countries, an examination of the characteristics of these nations is useful in demonstrating that they are very different from advanced countries. Table 2.1 provides data on selected indicators of development for both advanced and developing countries.

In the table, nations are divided into four categories reported by the World Bank. Low-income economies are defined as those with a gross national product (GNP) per capita of $755 or less in 1999. Lower-middle-income economies include those countries with a GNP per capita of $756 to $2,995 in 1999. Upper-middle-

---

*The least-developed nations are sometimes referred to as fourth-world nations to identify them as the "poorest of the poor." See H. C. Low and J. W. Howe, "Focus on the Fourth World." In *World Development, Agenda for Action 1975* Prager (New York: for the Overseas Development Council, 1974), 35-54.

**In contrast to Western usage of the term communism, the second world designated itself as socialist. As we explain later in Chapter 5, in Marxian theory, communism is a stage that is followed by socialism in which goods are distributed in accordance to individuals' needs, money is absent, and the state is non-existent.

income economies are those with a GNP per capita of $2,996 to $9,265 in 1999. Finally, high-income economies refer to countries with a GNP per capita income of $9,226 or more in 1999. [1] An examination of this data shows that, in general, as the level of GNP per capita rises, the life expectancy at birth rises; the adult illiteracy rate declines; the rate of population growth declines; the percentage of gross domestic product (GDP) allocated to the agriculture sector declines; and the percentage of GDP to the industrial sector rises. The relationship between income and some of these basic indicators is observed in most developing countries. Nevertheless, a high level of income alone is not sufficient to classify a country as an advanced nation. For example, in Table 2.1, high-income countries include Kuwait, which is considered a developing

Table 2.1
SELECTED INDICATORS OF DEVELOPMENT

Income Group	1999 GNP per Capita (U.S. $)	Population (Millions) 1999	Life Expectancy at Birth (years) 1996 Males Females	Adult Literacy Rate % of People 15 and above 1998 Males Females	Average Annual Population Growth Percentage Rate (1997-1999)	1999 Value Added as Percentage of GDP Agriculture Industry
Low Income	410	2,417	59 61	30 49	2.0	27 30
Lower Middle Income	1,200	2,094	67 72	10 23	1.1	
Upper Middle Income	4,900	573	67 74	9 11	1.4	15 40
High Income	25,730	891	75 81	32 49	0.6	7 32
						2 30

Source: The World Bank, *World Development Report 2000/2001* (New York: Oxford University Press, 1999), 275, 277, 279, 297.

country.* In general, however, developing countries have low levels of per capita income, and they share the following set of common problems in varying degrees:

- Vast disparities in distribution of income.
- Large and fast growing population.
- Low and sluggish levels of agricultural productivity.
- High and growing levels of unemployment and underemployment.
- Archaic, and inappropriate educational and health systems.
- Large and growing imbalances between urban and rural levels of living and economic opportunities.
- Considerable and growing dependence on foreign, often inappropriate, technologies, institutions, and value systems.
- Intense balance of payments (BOP) and international debt problems.

MEASURING ECONOMIC DEVELOPMENT

As we mentioned earlier, conventionally GNP has been used as a yardstick of economic development.

---

*Other developing countries that are included in the list of high-income countries are Israel, Hong Kong, Singapore, and the United Arab Emirates.

16 PART I/BASIC CONCEPTS AND PRINCIPLES

In this section, first, we elaborate on this method of comparison and then discuss better measures that have been developed to assess economic development.

GNP Measure

Although economists no longer consider GNP as the sole measure of economic development, it is still used either to compare a nation's GNP over time or compare the GNP of one developing nation to another developing nation or to a developed (advanced) nation. But, as we explain shortly, even such simple comparisons are not without problems.

Problems With Using GNP to Make Comparisons Over Time. When using national income data to make comparisons over time, we run into problems. For example, suppose that we learn that Costa Rica's GNP now is 60% higher than it was in 1990. This of course does not mean that Costa Rica is now producing 60% more goods and services than it did in 1990. As a student of economics we know that inflation impacts nominal income, making meaningful comparison problematic. To get around this problem, we need to use a weighted price index to make adjustment for price increases. However, because we are dealing with a developing country, we need to keep in mind that in general, the data produced by these nations are not accurate. More specifically, the goods included and the weights assigned to them might be out of date. For example, the weighting of commodity prices has not changed in Africa and Eastern Europe since 1972, in spite of substantial structural changes. But economic development shifts supply and demand for goods and services, causing their prices to change over time. A nation that has experienced development over time may find a good, say steel, that had a low demand at early stages of development, and hence received small weights in the nation's price index, has a high demand in late stages of development and must have been assigned large weights. This makes a significant difference in calculating real GNP, depending on the type of price index employed. There are three types of price indices: Laspeyres, Paashe, and Fisher. To illustrate how the use of these different price indices produces different results, let us use India as a hypothetical example. Assume that this country produces only two goods, transistor radios and leather gloves, and their hypothetical quantities (Qs) and prices (Ps) in Rupees (Rs) for 1990 and 2000 are as given in Table 2.2.

Table 2.2
PRICES AND QUANTITIES OF TRANSISTOR RADIOS AND LEATHER GLOVES PRODUCED IN INDIA: A HYPOTHETICAL EXAMPLE

Commodity	1990 P_0	Q_0	2000 P_n	Q_n
Transistor Radio	R800	45,000,000	R200	225,000,000
Leather glove	R200	400,000,000	R400	800,000,000

As the table 2.2 indicates, the output of leather gloves doubled as prices doubled, while the output of transistor radio raised fivefold and prices declined sharply, as the industries enjoyed economies of scale and experienced technological improvement.

To calculate **Laspeyres price index**, applying base-year or 1990 quantities to weight prices, we use the following formula:

CH. 2/THE DEFINITION & MEASUREMENT OF ECONOMIC DEVELOPMENT 17

$$P = \frac{\sum P_n Q_0}{\sum P_0 Q_0} \quad (2\text{-}1)$$

Where P is the price of the good produced, Q is the quantity of the good produced, 0 the base year (1990), and n the current year (1999). Plugging the data in equation 2-1, we get:

$$P = \frac{(R200 \times 45,000,000) + (R400 \times 400,000,000)}{(R800 \times 45,000,000) + (R200 \times 400,000,000)} = 1.46$$

To calculate a **Paashe price index**, applying terminal-year or 2000 quantities to weight prices, we use the following formula:

$$P = \frac{\sum P_n Q_n}{\sum P_0 Q_n} \quad (2\text{-}2)$$

Plugging the data into equation 2-2, we get:

$$P = \frac{(R200 \times 225,000,000) + (R400 \times 800,000,000)}{(R800 \times 225,000,000) + (R200 \times 800,000,000)} = 1.07$$

To calculate a **Fisher ideal index**, we take the geometric average of the other two indices, and we get:

$$P = \frac{1.46 + 1.07}{2} = 1.26$$

In our hypothetical example of Costa Rica, the Laspeyres price index (1.46) is greater than the Paasche index (1.07). To the degree that industries with faster growth, such as the electronic industry, display relatively less sharp increases or even decreases in price, Laspeyres index, which employs base period weights, will provide higher values than Paasche-type indexes, which adopt weights from a current period. Thus, the Laspeyres index is biased upward and Paasche index biased downward. By taking the geometric average of the two, the Fisher ideal index removes this bias. However, due to its complexity, this index is not used that often.

Problems With Using GNP To Make Comparison Between Nations. To compare the GNP of developing nations, one has to put the respective GNPs into the same currency. Conventionally the U.S. is used as the measuring yardstick. For example, to compare the GNP of India to that of Kuwait, we need to convert India's GNP in rupees and Kuwait's GNP in dinar into dollars at their respective exchange rates. This approach is followed in publications of the International Monetary Fund, the United Nations, and the World Bank. Aside from the fact that the GNP recorded by different countries is often based on different concepts and data collection, when comparing two countries, the following problems persist:

1. The country's exchange rates to the dollar may not reflect its real purchasing power. This happens because the currencies of many developing countries are kept fixed at some artificial level by their monetary authorities. This artificial level may not have any relationship to the interplay of demand and supply in the foreign exchange market.

2. Even if exchange rates are determined by free forces of demand and supply in the foreign exchange market, they do not reflect the purchasing power of a currency. This is due to the fact that market exchange rates are based on internationally traded goods. For example, consider a free market rate for Argentina, 0.9995 peso per one U.S. dollar. This rate only reflects the purchasing power of peso in the United States, or the dollar in Argentina over goods and services that are traded internationally. In other words, the relative purchasing power over goods and services that are not traded internationally is not portrayed by the foreign exchange rate. Given that nontraded goods and services are relatively cheaper in developing countries than developed countries, a dollar converted into a developing country's currency commands more in that country than it will in the United States. For example, in 1993, the annual salaries of elementary school teachers in the United States were about 10 times greater than the salaries of elementary school teachers in India. Thus, in general, the GNP of developing countries are understated because many of their nontraded goods are composed of cheap labor-intensive goods and services that do not have any impact on their exchange rates.
3. A larger proportion of goods and services in developing countries are produced for self-consumption relative to developed countries. Because these are not traded in the market place, they do not enter into GNP calculations. As a result, the GNPs are understated for developing countries.

To alleviate these problems, The International Commission Project (ICP) of the United Nations Statistical Office and the University of Pennsylvania, devised a new measurement system that is based on determination of the purchasing power of income. This new approach, referred to as ICP, changes a nation's GDP from domestic currency into international dollars ($1) by calculating P (the price level of GDP) as the ratio of the purchasing power parity (PPP) exchange rate to actual (or market) exchange rate, where both exchange rates are defined as the value of the U.S. dollars in terms of domestic currency.

Given the PPP exchange rate, goods and services included in domestic product cost the same in both nations that are being compared. For example, in 1992, a Big Mac cost 3.30 pesos in Argentina, and $2.19 in the United States, resulting in a PPP of peso 1.51 = $1[*], compared to the actual exchange rate of peso 0.99 = $1.[**] Thus, P was 152.5 percent and the peso was overvalued.[2]

The ICP economists employ a series of simultaneous equations to determine the PPP for 81 countries and world average prices for 400 to 700 goods and services. These figures are the best available for adjusting for purchasing power. However, the CPI calculations demand extra time to collect figures that are many years behind the most up-to-date figures that are disclosed in the world bank's *World Development Report*.

The whole exercise leads us to the conclusion that one needs to be very cautious when trying to compare national products or income of different nations. It should be kept in mind that GDP numbers are only rough estimates of reality. This of course does not imply that GDP comparisons should not be made but that they should be made with caution.

The ICP findings imply that the developing nations are not as poor as portrayed by the conventional data. Given the political implications of these findings, some developing nations have disapproved continuation of the project. As a result, it has been more difficult to obtain funding for the project. The PPP phenomenon should not, however, diminish our concern with poverty, rather, it should make our perception of income differential between developing and developed countries more real.

---

[*] 3.30/2.19 = 1.51

[**] (1.51/0.99) X 100 = 152.5

GLOBAL INSIGHTS CASE 2.2

GILBERT AND KRAVIS EFFECT

As we discussed in this chapter, when a country uses exchange rate to measure its real GNP for comparison purposes, its value might be understated. This event was once referred to as the Gilbert and Kravis effect since Milton Gilbert and Irvin Kravis first studied this phenomenon. Their research indicated per capita GNP in the United States and eight Western European nations during the 1950s, when labor was relatively cheaper in Western Europe than in the United States. Their research indicated that converting the GNP into dollars at prevailing exchange rates understated the 1955 output of the western European nations by 18% to 70%.

More recent research of developing nations on the use of exchange rates for comparative purposes, indicate that per capita GNP is understated by 200% for nations with real per capita GNP of $600, and it is understated by 300% for countries with real per capita income of $200.

Source: See Simon Kuznets, *Economic Growth of Nations: Total Output and Production Structure* (Cambridge, Mass., 1971).

THE PHYSICAL QUALITY OF LIFE INDEX (PQLI)

Given the shortcoming associated with using income as a measure of economic development, attempts have been made to replace the GNP per capita with a more reliable yardstick. One alternative measure of economic development is the **physical quality of life index (PQLI)**. This composite index combines indicators of infant mortality, life expectancy, and basic literacy to measure the performance of a nation in terms of the most basic needs of the populace. Table 2.3 shows the yardsticks by which these indicators are measured.

Table 2.3
COMPONENTS OF PQLI AND THEIR MEASUREMENT METHODS

Indicators	Yardsticks
Infant Mortality	The number of deaths of infants under one year of age per 1,000 live births
Life Expectancy	Measured at age one, so that it does not overlap with infant mortality
Literacy	Expressed in terms of percentage

PQLI is primarily designed to measure results rather than inputs such as income. The first two indicators included in PQLI indicate the impact of nutrition, income, public health, and the general environment. For instance, infant mortality echoes mother's health, availability of clean water, and the condition of the home environment. Literacy is an indicator of well-being and it is considered an essential element of economic development.

Critics argue that PQLI suffers from the following shortcomings:

1. There is a close relationship between the three components of this index and per capita income.
2. The PQLI indicators cannot distinguish levels of development beyond middle-income nations. All three components of PQLI are highly correlated to per capita income *until* nutrition, health, and education approach certain high levels, then the value of these indicators level off.
3. As a composite index, the PQLI requires scaling and weighting. This is problematic, because scaling the raw data to 0-1 range is fairly subjective and there is no definite theoretical basis for assigning equal weights to the core indicators.

In summary, the PQLI is subject to controversies. Its meaning is very narrow, causing some critics to label it as "quantity" of life index rather quality of life index. Additionally, in determining PQLI levels, purchasing power in circulation is not taken into account. Nevertheless, the PQLI data has added another angle to the intercountry comparison.

WEIGHTED INDICES FOR GNP GROWTH

One of the shortcomings of the GNP growth rate as an indicator of development, as we noticed earlier, is that it is heavily weighted by the income shares of the rich. As a result, a given growth rate for the rich has by far more effect on total growth than the same growth rate for the poor. For example, take the case of India where, according to 1994 data, the lowest income class (10% of population) earns about 4% of total income; the highest income class (10% of population) earns about 25%.[3] If we assume that GNP of India is $100 billion, then the highest income class receives $25 billion and the lowest income class receives only $4 billion dollars. A GNP growth rate of 10 percent in income for the highest income class results in 2.5 percent total growth, but, the 10% growth for the lowest income class leads to only 0.4 percent in total growth. However, the 10% growth for the lowest income class is more effective in reducing poverty than the same growth for the highest income class.

As the above example illustrates, if we use GNP per capita as a measure of social welfare, the same growth for the rich as the poor has much more effect on total growth; and a given dollar rise in GNP increases the income of the poor by a higher percentage than the rich. To alleviate these problems we may start by setting the following social welfare function:

$$S = \sum W_i G_i \qquad i = 1 \ldots n \qquad (2\text{-}3)$$

Where, S is an index of the growth of the total social welfare and W_i is the weight assigned to ith group, and G_i is the rate of growth of the ith income group. This function enables us to measure development, not just in terms of growth of GNP, but in terms of the pattern of income distribution. In this manner, we can set the weights in each income class according to the level of distributional emphasis desired. To illustrate, suppose the economy is composed of three income classes, as illustrated in Table 2.4. Given three income classes,

Table 2.4
INCOME CLASSES AND THEIR SHARES IN TOTAL INCOME

Income Class	Upper 40%	Middle 40%	Lowest 20%	Total
Share in Total Income	75%	20%	5%	100%

the equation (1) becomes:

$$S = W_1G_1 + W_2G_2 + W_3G_3$$

Where subscripts 1, 2, and 3, denote upper, middle, and lower income groups, respectively. If we use GNP as the measure of social welfare, then its growth basically reflects the income growth of the upper income class which accounts for three quarters of the population.

One alternative to this measure of GNP growth is to use an **equal-weights index**, whereby equal weight is given to a one percent increase in income of any member of the society. Thus, weights in equation (1) are set in proportion to the number of people in each income class, and would be equal to 4% for the upper income class ($W_1 = 0.40$), and 4% for the middle- income class ($W_2 = 0.40$), and 20% for the lowest income class. This approach causes a one-percent increase in income in the lowest income class to have the same weight in the overall performance as a one-percent rise in income of the other two incomes, in spite of the fact that the absolute increment is by far smaller for the lowest income class than the other two classes.

Another alternative is to use a **poverty-weighted index**, whereby a higher weight is given to a one-percent increase in income of the lowest income class than for the upper income. In this manner more emphasis is placed on the welfare of the lower-income classes. In our example, we may decide to assign 0.6 for the lowest-income class ($W_1 = 0.6$), 0.4 for the middle-income class ($W_2 = 0.4$), and 0.2 for the upper-income class ($W_3 = 0.2$).

It should be realized that the use of such indexes in assessing performance of developing nations is severely limited due to the lack of reliable data. However, their use underlines the significance of enhancing the rate of growth of the poor instead of concentrating on the overall picture of income distribution. In practice, economists usually use GNP per capita, due to its convenience and easy interpretation. It is much easier to evaluate poverty by employing both GNP per capita and income distribution than to determine poverty-weighted index or equal-weights index.

BASIC NEEDS YARDSTICK

In the late 1960s many economists realized that economic growth was not very effective in alleviating poverty in the developing nations. It became clear that mass poverty could exist along with a high degree of equality, and a decrease in absolute poverty was consistent with an increase in inequality. The growing disappointment with GNP per head and its growth led the developing economists in the late 1970s to realize that strategies that rely on increasing productivity in developing nations are inadequate in the absence of programs that directly concentrate on satisfying the basic needs of the poorest half of the populace through a variety of measures other than merely redistribution of incremental GNP.

The basic needs approach considers the conventional approach, that is, the income approach to be incomplete for the following reasons:

GLOBAL INSIGHTS CASE 2.3

ALTERNATIVE MEASURES OF GROWTH IN SOME DEVELOPING NATIONS

The table indicates the differences in welfare growth on the basis of three different weighting systems: (1) GNP weights for each income class; (2) equal weights for each income class; and (3) poverty weights of 0.6 for the lowest-income class, 0.3 for the middle income class, and 0.2 for the upper-income class.

		Income Growth			Annual Increase in Welfare		
Country	Period	Upper 20%	Middle 40%	Lowest 40%	(A) GNP Weights	(B) Equal Weights	(C) Poverty Weights
Korea	1964-70	10.6	7.8	9.3	9.3	9.0	9.0
Panama	1960-69	8.8	9.2	3.2	8.2	6.7	5.6
Brazil	1960-70	8.4	4.8	5.2	6.9	5.7	5.4
Mexico	1963-69	8.0	7.0	6.6	7.6	7.0	6.9
Taiwan	1953-61	4.5	9.1	12.1	6.8	9.4	10.4
Venezuela	1962-70	7.9	4.1	3.7	6.4	4.7	4.2
Columbia	1964-70	5.6	7.3	7.0	6.2	6.8	7.0
El Salvador	1961-69	4.1	10.5	5.3	6.2	7.1	6.7
Philippines	1961-71	4.9	6.4	5.0	5.4	5.5	5.4
Peru	1961-71	4.7	7.5	3.2	5.4	5.2	4.6
Sri Lanka	1963-70	3.1	6.2	8.3	5.0	6.4	7.2
Yugoslavia	1963-68	4.9	5.0	4.3	4.8	4.7	4.6
India	1954-64	5.1	3.9	3.9	4.5	4.1	4.6

If we compare GNP with the other two indices, we note the following differences:

1. In Colombia, El Salvador, Sri Lanka, and Taiwan, the weighted indexes are higher than growth. The data indicates that the distribution improved for these nations. More precisely, the lower-income class experienced a higher growth than the higher income class.
2. In Panama, Brazil, Mexico, and Venezuela, where relative income distribution worsen over time, the weighted indices portray worse performance than the GNP growth.
3. In Korea, the Philippines, Yugoslavia, Peru, and India, where income distribution remained fairly constant, the use of weighted indices does not change the GNP growth greatly.

Source: Hollis Chenery, Montek S. Ahuwalia, C.L.G., Bell, John H. Duloy, and Richard Jolly, eds., *Redistribution With Growth* (London: Oxford University Press, 1974), p.42.

CH. 2/THE DEFINITION & MEASUREMENT OF ECONOMIC DEVELOPMENT

1. Consumers in developing nations are not generally effective in maximizing health and nutrition. For example, the additional income earned by a subsistence farmer may be spent on food of low nutritional value, or on articles other than food.
2. The way in which additional income is obtained may not be conducive to good health. For instance, a mother may raise her income at the cost of nursing her baby, which is nutritionally preferable to alternatives.
3. Given the male-dominated cultures of most developing nations, in comparison to men, a lower proportion of women and children's needs are not satisfied. In other words, there is a maldistribution of income within the household, as well as outside the household.
4. A large percentage of individuals who are aged, disabled, sick, or orphaned, are not able to work. As a result their needs can be satisfied only through transfer payments or public services.
5. Some basic needs can be met only through subsidized goods and services, or through transfer payments. Examples include health, water, sanitation, and education.
6. Many developing nations either import or produce highly sophisticated, capital-intensive goods that satisfy the needs of rich elites. A basic feature of the basic needs approach is that it concentrates on the production of appropriate products, produced by appropriate technology. Such a strategy should generate more jobs, and a more even income distribution, which in turn gives rise to demand for these products.

The basic-needs approach focuses not only on *how much* is being produced, but also *what* is being produced, in *what ways*, for *whom*, and *with what impact*. To be sure, in this approach, the rapid growth of income is still considered a significant element in alleviating poverty. However, such growth should be supplemented with some indicators of the makeup and the recipients of the GNP.

Table 2.5 provides the list of basic needs and their measurement methods. Infant mortality is considered to be a desirable indicator of clean water facilities and sanitation, because of the vulnerability of infants to water-born illnesses. Additionally, data on infant mortality are usually more easily obtainable than data on water accessibility. Although literacy is a fair measure of advances in education, the proportion of the appropriate age group enrolled in primary school is included to measure country impact. Because the existing measures of housing, such as people per room, do not satisfactorily reflect the quality of housing, no measure is identified for housing.

Table 2.5
COMPONENTS OF BASIC NEEDS AND THEIR YARDSTICKS

Basic Needs	Yardsticks
Education	Literacy rates, primary school enrollment as percent of population aged 5-14
Food	Calorie supply per head, or calorie supply as percent of requirements; protein
Health	Life expectancy at birth
Housing	None
Sanitation	Infant mortality (per thousand births)
Water Supply	Infant mortality (per thousand births), percent of population with access to portable water

In spite of much research on designing a composite index that represents the basic needs, a rational weighting system that allows combining the core indicators has not yet been developed. An alternative is to cut the number of indicators from six to one or two that are highly correlated with basic needs. It is argued that some measure of health, such as life expectancy at birth, is a good sole indicator of basic needs. In other words, we can consider life expectancy as a type of weighted "composite" index of progress in satisfying basic needs.

THE HUMAN DEVELOPMENT INDEX (HDI)

In 1990, with the support of the United Nations, another measure of economic development, called the Human Development Index, came into existence. This index was designed to incorporate quality of life components with national products, adjusted for purchasing power. In elaborating on the HDI, the United Nations made the following statement:

> Human development is a process of enlarging people's choices. The most critical ones are to lead a long and healthy life, to be educated and enjoy a decent standard of living. Additional choices include political freedom, guaranteed human rights and self-respect — what Adam Smith called the ability to mix with others without being "ashamed to appear in publick."[4]

HDI is a composite index which includes three indicators. Table 2.6 provides the components of HDI and their measurement methods. On a scale of 0 to 1, where 0 is the worst and 1 is the best, in 1995, Canada, with score of 0.960, held the highest rank, followed by France (0.946). Norway and the United States, each with a score of 0.943, tied for third place. The worst HDI belonged to Sierra Leone which with a score of 0.507 ranked 174th among all the nations listed.[5]

In justifying the need to measure human development, the United Nations has argued that developing nations have made tremendous progress during the last three decades, as evidenced by an increase in life expectancy, adult literacy rates, and per capita calorie supply. However, the income gaps have been widening over time.

Some economists maintain that development is basically an economic problem, demanding stimulation of economic growth. For example, in his research, R. Reichel concludes that per capita income, adjusted for purchasing power, explains a large percentage of other components of HDI. As a result, he argues, we do not need to assess human development separately from per capita income. But most development economists and international organizations disagree with Reichel's opinion, asserting that income measures neglect many significant facets of the development mechanism, leaving much of human development undetermined.

Table 2.6
COMPONENTS OF HDI AND THEIR YARDSTICKS

Components of HDI	Yardsticks
Longevity	Life expectancy at birth (in years), calculated by conjecturing that infants born in a given year will experience the current death rate at each age cohort throughout their lifetime.
Education	2/3(adult literacy rate in percentage) + 1/3 (the mean years of schooling for adults over 25 years of age)
Standard of living	Per capita GNP in purchasing power (PPP) dollars

GLOBAL INSIGHTS CASE 2.4

HUMAN DEVELOPMENT INITIATIVES IN SOME DEVELOPING NATIONS

One of the impacts of preparing the national human development reports has been the efforts undertaken by some developing nations to promote human development. The following is a summary of the major strategies employed by these nations to improve their human development record:

1. **The Philippines—considering human development as a national priority.** Following the launch of 1997 Human Development Report, the president of the Philippines, Fidel Ramos, instructed all local government agencies to set aside at least twenty percent of their total revenue to human development priorities.
2. **Benin—monitoring human development for planning.** Benin's 1997 National Human Development Report portrays this country's commitment to human development by declaring a new "observatory of social change". The observatory combines quantitative and qualitative data, permits the report to concentrate on multidimensional facets of human poverty. The report provides a significant contribution to the National Development Plan for 1998-2002, making the elimination of poverty the country's first priority.
3. **Egypt—addressing socio-economic disparities.** Since this nation published its first report, all of its governors have been meeting on a regular basis to assess disparities among and within districts. Such meetings have resulted in the emergence of a number of new strategies in combating disparities. They changed their developmental preferences, giving more weight to the allocation of resources in underdeveloped areas. They used the national report's findings to monitor and assess development decreasing human development disparities. The report was used by the two houses of parliament in policy analysis.
4. **Brazil—allocating budget for human development needs.** Brazil's 1996 National Human Development Report encouraged several actions. For example, the state of Minas Gerais introduced the "Robin Hood Law" to ensure the allocation of more tax revenue to municipalities that have a low ranking on the Human Development Index. It was also decided that allocations to municipalities should be based on implementation of programs that successfully address the shortcomings detected. Economic power, geographic area, and population size should no longer be the only parameters for assessing resource allocations to municipalities. In other words, the budgets should also depend on the basis of human development.

Source: United Nations Development Programme, *Human Development Report*, 1998 (New York, Oxford University Press, 1998)., p18.

Gender Related Development Index (GDI)

In continuing the search for a better index of economic development, the United Nations realized that HDI does not echo the negative impact of gender inequality in social progress. Given this recognition, in 1995, it came up with yet another index, the **Gender Development Index (GDI)**, to reflect gender equality in developing nations. The following statement made by the United Nations clarifies the need for developing such an index:

The recognition of equal rights for women along with men, and the determination to combat discrimination on the basis of gender, are achievements equal in importance to the abolition of slavery, the elimination of colonialism and the establishment of equal rights for racial and ethnic minorities.[6]

GDI is HDI adjusted for gender inequality. It focuses on the same variables as HDI, but it considers inequality in accomplishment between men and women, perpetrating retribution for such inequality. The GDI is assessed on the basis of women's shares of earned income relative to men, and a weighted average of female literacy and schooling relative to those of males. It also considers the life expectancy of women relative to men, taking into account the biological advantage that females have in living longer than males. However, GDI does not account for variables that are effortlessly appraised such as female admittance to professional careers, female participation in community life and decision making processes, resource consumption within the family unit, personal security, and dignity.

Today, given the existence of gender inequality in every nation, developed or developing, the GDI continues to be smaller than HDI. On a scale of 0 to 1, where 0 is the worst and 1 is the best, in 1997, Canada, with score of 0.928, held the highest rank, followed by Norway (0.927), the United States (0.926), Japan (0.977), and Belgium (0.918). The worst HDI belonged to Sierra Leone which ranked 143rd among all the nations listed.[7]

In closing this chapter we may emphasize that there are benefits and costs associated with economic development and growth. Growth causes starvation, famine, infant mortality, and death to decline; it increases our leisure time; may cultivate music, art, and philosophy; and furnishes the resources for people to be good Samaritans. But economic growth and development have their costs as well.

The following is alist of some of the costs associated with economic growth:

- It is usually accompanied by increasing specialization and automation which may lead to more monotonous tasks, loss of craftsmanship, increasing individualism, and more discipline.
- Society's economic struggle may lead to materialism and acquisitions at the expense of nonmaterial and spiritual needs, generating dissatisfaction with one's present state.
- With its emphasis on scientific approach to technological change and innovation it may threaten religious and social authority.
- It may cause institutions and individuals, including artists, to conform to its needs.
- With its reliance on mobility, and self-reliance, it may disrupt the extended family system, in fact the current social framework.
- It may lead to an environment that is characterized by bureaucratization, and communication difficulties, requiring force to keep individuals "in line."

Thus, even if a society is dedicated to economic growth and development, its achievement cannot be attained at all costs. The society has to take into account other goals that may clash with economic growth maximization. For instance, a nation may prevent foreigners from obtaining high managerial positions in order to leave the control of its industrial sector in the hands of its own citizens. Such an action may decrease the nation's growth in the short run. Thus, it must be implemented by considering the tradeoff between the objective of fast economic growth and noneconomic goals such as maintaining culture and traditional values, championing political freedom, and achieving a peaceful and stable society. But, given the growing literacy rates, the formerly silent masses are now organizing and pressuring the political elites in developing nations to ensure a better life for all of their citizens. As a result, some developing nations want development despite some costs.

27   CH. 2/THE DEFINITION & MEASUREMENT OF ECONOMIC DEVELOPMENT

SUMMARY

1. **Economic growth** refers to the rate of rise in a nation's full employment real output or income over time. In other words, it is the rise in full-employment output in constant prices. Economic growth can be measured as a rise in total full-employment real gross national product (GNP), or gross domestic product (GDP) over time.
2. Economic development is not identical to total development of a nation. It is not equivalent to "economic independence," and it is not synonymous with industrialization.
3. **Economic development** can be defined as the *process* whereby a nation's *real per capita income* (its GNP) rises over a *long period* of time, provided that the number below an "*absolute poverty* line" does not rise, and that income distribution does not become more unequal.
4. Today, the classification schemes used to define developing countries differ, depending on the agency providing the scheme.
5. The United Nations (UN) distinguishes between three major classes of third-world countries: the least-developed, or poorest nations; the non-oil-exporting developing nations; and the petroleum-rich OPEC (Organization for Petroleum Exporting Countries) nations.
6. The Organization for Economic Cooperation and Development (OECD) classifies developing nations into low-income countries, middle-income countries, newly industrialized countries (NICs), and members of OPEC.
7. The World Bank divides all countries (both developing and advanced) into four categories: low-income, lower-middle-income, upper-middle-income, and high-income economies.
8. The members of **The United Nations Conference on Trade and Development (UNCTAD)**, are usually referred to as **third world nations**, a designation developed in the early post-World War II decades. The term **first world** refers to the capitalist nations, where capital and land are owned by people. The term **second world** alludes to the socialist or the centrally directed nations, where the government owns the means of production.
9. There are three types of price indices: Laspeyres, Paashe, and Fisher.
10. To calculate **Laspeyres price index** we use the following formula:

$$P = \frac{\sum P_n Q_0}{\sum P_0 Q_0}$$

Where P is the price of the good produced, Q is the quantity of the good produced, 0 the base year, and n the current year.
11. To calculate **Paashe price index** we use the following formula:

$$P = \frac{\sum P_n Q_n}{\sum P_0 Q_n}$$

12. To calculate the **Fisher ideal index**, we take the geometric average of the other two indices.
13. The country's exchange rate to the dollar may not reflect its real purchasing power.
14. In general, the GNP of developing countries is understated because many of their nontrade goods are composed of cheap labor-intensive goods and services that do not have any impact on their exchange rates.
15. The **physical quality of life index (PQLI)** is a composite index of economic development that combines indicators of infant mortality, life expectancy, and basic literacy, measuring the performance of a nation

PART I/BASIC CONCEPTS AND PRINCIPALS

in terms of the most basic needs of the populace.

16. **Equal weights index** is a measure of economic development whereby equal weight is given to a one percent increase in income of any member of the society.
17. **Poverty-weighted index** is a measure of economic development whereby a higher weight is given to a one-percent increase in income of the lowest income class than for the upper income.
18. **The basic-needs approach** focuses not only on *how much* is being produced, but also *what* is being produced, in *what ways, for whom*, and *with what impact*.
19. **The basic-needs yardstick** is a composite index of economic development that combines the indicators of food, education, health, water supply, and housing.
20. **Human Development Index (HDI)** is a composite index which includes three indicators of longevity, education, and standard of living.
21. **Gender Development Index (GDI)** is HDI, adjusted for gender inequality.

QUESTIONS

1. Distinguish between economic growth and economic development. Can we achieve economic growth without economic development? Is economic growth a prerequisite for economic development?
2. What is not considered economic development? Discuss.
3. How are nations classified by different international agencies?
4. Go to your library and find a developing nation that has enjoyed a good development record, and a nation that has exemplified a bad development record. Compare these two nations, elaborating on their major strategies.
5. What are different criteria used to measure economic development?
6. Choose a developing nation and elaborate on major costs and benefits associated with its economic growth.
7. Compare equal-weights index and poverty-weighted index, and explain why in practice economists usually use GNP per capita to assess poverty.
8. In comparing the GNPs of two nations, what major problems do we encounter, and how can we alleviate such problems?
9. What problems do we face if we use GNP to make comparisons over time? What methods can we use to alleviate such problems?
10. Suppose Argentina produces only two goods: personal computers and shirts. The following table shows their hypothetical quantities (Q_0, and Q_n) and prices (P_0, and P_n) in pesos (p) for 1990 and 1999. Calculate Laspeyres price index, Passche price index, and Fisher ideal index.

Commodity	1990 Q_0	1990 P_0	1999 Q_n	1999 P_n
Personal Computer	40,000,000	p800	200,000,000	p200
Shirts	400,000,000	P200	800,000,000	p400

11. Go to your library and obtain the most recent issue of the Human Development Report. Use this report to compare HDI, GDI, and GDP per capita for the United States. Elaborate on your findings. Why does the basic needs approach consider the income approach incomplete? Explain.

CH. 2/THE DEFINITION & MEASUREMENT OF ECONOMIC DEVELOPMENT

12. Why does the basic needs approach consider the income approach incomplete.

NOTES

1. The World Bank, *World Development Report, 2000/20101* (New York: Oxford University Press, 1999), p.335.
2. "Big MacCurrencies," *Economicst*, 18 Aprile 1992, p. 81.
3. The World Bank, *World Development Report, 2000/20101* (New York: Oxford University Press, 1999), p.198.
4. United Nations Development Programme, *Human Development Report*, 1990 (New York, Oxford University Press, 1990), p. 10.
5. United Nations Development Programme, *Human Development Report*, 1998 (New York, Oxford University Press, 1998), pp. 128-130.
6. United Nations Development Programme, *Human Development Report*, 1995 (New York, Oxford University Press, 1995), p. 1.
7. United Nations Development Programme, *Human Development Report*, 1998 (New York, Oxford University Press, 1998), pp. 128-130.

SUGGESTED READINGS

Arthur, Lewis W. *The Theory of Economic Growth*, Homewood, Ill.: Richard D. Irwin, 1955.

Aturupane, Harsha, Paul Glewwe, and Paul Isenman. "Poverty, Human Development, and Growth: An Emerging Consensus." *American Economic Review* 84 (May 1994): 232-37.

Behrman, Jere, and Mark Rosenzweing. "Labour Force: Caveat Emptor: Cross Country data on Education and the Labour Force." *Journal of Development Economics* 44 (June 1994):147-171.

Chamie, Joseph. "Population Databases in Development Analysis." *Journal of Development Economics* 44 (June 1994): 131-46.

Chenery, Hollis, and T.N. Srinvasan, eds., *Handbooks of Development Economic*. Vols. 1 and 2, Amsterdam: North-Holland, 1988 and 1989.

Chenery, Hollis, Montek S. Ahluwalia, C.L.G. Bell, John J. Duloy, and Richard Jolly, eds. *Redistribution with Growth*. London: Oxford Univeristy Press, 1976.

Gormely, Patrick J. "The Human Development Index in 1994: Impact of Income on Country Rank." *Journal of Economics and Social Measurement* 21 (January 1955): 1-15.

Heston Alan. "National Accounts: A Brief Review of Some Problems in Using National Accounts Data in Level of output Comparisons and Growth Studies." *Journal of Development Economics* 44 (June 1994): 29-52.

Hicks, Norman L. and Paul Streeten, "Indicators of Development: The Search for a Basic Needs Yardstick." *World Development* (June 1979): 572-75.

Hicks, Norman L. "Growth Versus Basic Needs: Is there a Trade-off? *World Development* 7 (November/December 1979): 985-94.

Kravis, Irving. "Comparative Studies of National Income and Prices." *Journal of Economic Literature* 22 (March 1984): 1-57.

Kuznets, Simon. *Economic Growth of Nations: Total Output and Production Structure*. Cambridge, Mass.: Harvard University Press, 1971.

_____. *Population, capital and Growth*. London: Norton, 1974.

Maddison, Angus. "A Comparison of the Levels of GDP per Capita in Developed and Developing Countries, 1700-1980." *Journal of Economic History* 43 (March 1983): 27-41.

Morawetz, David. *Twenty-five Years of Economic Development, 1950-1975*. Baltimore: Johns Hopkins University Press for the World Bank, 1977.

Ruggles, Richard. "Issues Relating to the United Nations System of National Accounts and Developing Countries." *Journal of Development Studies* 44 (June 1994): 77-85.

Seers, Dudley. "The Meaning of Development." *International Economic Review* 11 (December 1969): 3-4.

Sen, Amartya. *Inequality Reexamined*. Cambridge, Mass.: Harvard University Press, 1972.

Sewell, John W. and Stuart K. Tucker, *Growth, Exports and Jobs in a Changing World Economy: Agenda, 1988*. New

Brunswick, N.J.: Transaction Books, 1988.

Simonis, Udo E. "Least Developed Countries-Newly Defined." *Intereconomics* 26 (September/October 1991): 3-27.

Srinivasan, T.N. "Data Base for Development Analysis: An Overview." *Journal of Development Economics* 44 (June 1994): 3-27.

_____. "Human Development: A New Paradigm or Reinvention of the Wheel."*American Economic Review* 48 (May 1994): 238-43.

Stern, Nichols. "Public Policy and the Economic Development." *European Economic Review* 35 (1991): 243-50.

Summer, Robert, and Alan Heston, "The Penn World Table (Mark 5): An Expanded Set of International Comparisons, 1950-1988." Quarterly *Journal of Economics* 106 (May 1991):330-31.

Streeten, Paul. "Human Development: Means and Ends." *American Economic Review* 84 (May 1994): 232-237.

Trabold-Nubler. "The Human Development Index-A New Development Indicator?" *Intereconomics* 26 (September-October 1991): 236-43.

Usher, Dan. *The Mechanism and the Meaning of National Income Statistics* (Oxford: Clarendon Press, 1968).

Williamson, John, ed. *Estimating Exchange Rates*. Washington D.C.:Institute for International Economics, 1994.

Wolf-Phillips. "Why Third World?: Origin, Definition and Usage." *Third World Quarterly* 9 (October 1987): 1311-27.

CHAPTER 3

ECONOMIC DEVELOPMENT IN A HISTORICAL CONTEXT AND A PROFILE OF DEVELOPING NATIONS

The rapid, sustained economic growth started in the West. As a forerunner, Great Britain began experiencing industrialization and sustained economic growth by the second half of the eighteenth century. This path was followed by the United States and France in the first half of the nineteenth century; Belgium, Germany, and the Netherlands by the middle of that century and in Scandinavia, Canada, and Italy by the last part of the nineteenth century. Among the non-Western countries, Japan, and perhaps Russia, began their sustained economic growth and development in the last half of the nineteenth century.

History shows that the emergence of capitalism was the main element that fueled industrialization and sustained economic growth in the West. Capitalism flourished in the late medieval period. More specifically, following the eleventh century, the increasing long-distance trade between capitalist hubs contributed to the demise of the medieval economy. As the European trade activity increased during the next few centuries, some organizations, such as joint stock companies and deposit banking, accelerated the growth of capitalism. Before the twentieth century, only capitalist economies were successful in large capital accumulation and in creating and applying a vast scientific and technical know-how to production. The factors that contributed to such a success include:

- The emergence of powerful nation states in Western Europe between the sixteenth and nineteenth centuries generated the necessary conditions for fast growth under capitalism. The nation-states nurtured a market, free from trade barriers and laws and regulations that led to a more secure environment that was conducive to business activities. Eventually, the monarchy relinquished power to the **bourgeoisie**, that is, the capitalist and middle classes. This led to the creation of a representative government that was more sympathetic to the capitalists interests.
- The collapse of the power of the medieval Roman Catholic Church, along with the Protestant Reformation of the sixteenth and seventeenth centuries, induced a new economic condition. The Protestant ethic bred frugality, hard work, austerity, and efficiency, attributes instrumental to the growth of capitalism.
- The diminishing power of the church coincided with the Enlightenment, that is, an age of extensive intellectual endeavor in seventeenth- and eighteenth-century Europe which led to scientific innovations in agriculture, industry, trade, and transportation. Such innovations enhanced the efficiency of large-scale production, expanded markets, and increased profits resulting from capital

accumulation.
- Economic and intellectual transformations fueled the political revolution in England, France, and Holland in the seventeenth and eighteenth centuries. As a result, the power of the church and landed aristocracy was significantly diminished, enabling the bourgeoisie to take over much of the authority.
- The Protestant philosophy of spiritual individualism reinforced the philosophical rationalism and humanism of the Enlightenment, accentuating freedom from tyrannical power. In the economic area, this liberalism advanced a self-adjusting market, free from the state monopoly or political intervention. These ideas were conducive to the bourgeoisie struggle in dismantling the old pattern.
- The growth of capitalism was further amplified by the flow of species (gold and silver) from the Americas to Europe during the sixteenth and seventeenth centuries. The flow of species, inflated prices and profits and enhanced capital accumulation. Inflation led to the redistribution of income from wage earners and landlords, whose real income declined, to manufacturers, merchants, and commercial farmers who were more apt to invest in modern and productive ventures.

The growth of capitalism in the West was not without great human costs, and was imbued with brutality, physical violence, and exploitation of workers. The accelerated industrial growth in England and Belgium was accompanied by declining wages and rising poverty. In both nations, a half century had to elapse until the absolute income of the poor approached the pre-industrial revolution levels. But in spite of these costs, capitalism led to the improvement of the standards of living for a large percentage of the population in the West since the early nineteenth century.

ECONOMIC GROWTH IN THE NON-WESTERN WORLD

Capitalism did not lead to economic modernization in most non-Western nations. The factors that contributed to the slow development of non-Western nations include:

1. The existence of barriers to capitalism in these traditional societies.
2. The impacts of colonialism and other forms of Western political domination on the sluggish development of these non-Western nations.

Regardless of these factors, it is evident that these nations did not have the highly motivated domestic capitalists and the vigorous political and bureaucratic supervision that are basic to fast economic modernization.

The Japanese Development Strategies

Japan is one of the few non-Western nations that avoided Western colonialism. Japan's strategy of modernization under the Meiji emperor, 1868-1912, emphasized "**guided capitalism**." This strategy depended on state initiative for larger investments in infrastructure. Government established about half of the investment in non agricultural ventures and helped private industries through a number of schemes such as low taxes on businesses, subsidies, tax rebates, loans, and a low-wage labor policy. One of the remarkable Japanese development strategies has been the policy of importing others people's technology and adapting it to their national environment. Another notable Japanese strategy, from 1868 to World War II, was the policy of adherence to multilateral, nondiscriminatory foreign trade outside their empire.

Although a contemporary developing nation can learn from Japanese experience in economic development, it should be kept in mind that this country's success was accompanied by income inequality, labor union repression, zaibatsu concentration, imperialism, and militarism. This series of incidents connected with military destruction does not portray an appropriate pattern of economic development that should be followed by today's developing nations. Such a development pattern is unlikely to expedite economic development and promote democracy in developing nations as it did in Japan.

Newly Industrialized Countries Development Strategies

In recent years, a number of developing nations have been very active in the global market. By promoting their manufacturing sectors, they have reached the status of **Newly industrialized countries (NICs)**. These countries include Argentina, Brazil, Greece, Hong Kong, South Korea, Mexico, Portugal, Singapore, Spain, and Taiwan. These countries are at a relatively advanced stage of economic development. Each of these countries has a substantial and active industrial sector that is integrated into its international trade, finance, and investment systems.

Among the NICs, the four East Asian countries of South Korea, Hong Kong, Taiwan, and Singapore have achieved impressive economic performance and have been used as models for economic development by other developing countries. Table 3.1 provides selective data on the economic development performance

Table 3.1
SELECTIVE INDICATORS OF DEVELOPMENT OF
NEWLY INDUSTRIALIZED PACIFIC RIM COUNTRIES

	Hong Kong	Singapore	South Korea	Taiwan
Population (1999)	7M	4M	47M	22M
Labor force (1999)	3M	2M	22M	9.7M
Real growth rate of GDP	1.8%	5.5%	10%	5.5%
Unemployment rate	6%	3.2%	6.35%	2.9%
GDP per capita (1999)	$23,100	$27,800	$13,300	$16,100
inflation rate (1999)	-4%	0.4%	0.8%	0.4%
Exports (1999)	$169.98B	$114B	$144B	$121.6B
Imports (1999)	$174.4B	$111B	$116B	$101.7B
Average annual growth rate of exports (1990-1997)	14.4%	10.8%	12.0%	8.33%

Source: The World Bank, *World Development Report 2000/2001* (Washington DC: Oxford University Press, 2001); U.S. Department of Commerce, *Foreign Economic Trends and Their Implications for the United States* (Washington DC: International Trade Administration, 1989); *United Nations, Human Development Report 2001* (New York: Oxford University Press, 2001); and *FISonline*.

M = millions.
B = billions.

GLOBAL INSIGHTS CASE 3.1

ECONOMIC DEVELOPMENT STRATEGIES OF EAST AND SOUTHEAST ASIA

During the 1960-1993 period, eight of the world's ten fastest-growing nations were in East and Southeast Asia. Japan's GDP per capita, adjusted for differences in relative prices, was only 30 percent of the United States' GDP per capita during 1960-1982. By 1994, it grew to the level of 82 percent of the United States' GDP per capita. The four Asian "tigers" (Hong Kong, Singapore, South Korea, and Taiwan) experienced growth in GDP per capita averaging over 6 percent a year during the period in which U.S. GDP per capita grew less than 2 percent a year. Malaysia and Indonesia's growth averaged about 4 percent a year. China, the world's most populous nation with more than a billion people, experienced astonishing growth in GDP per capita, averaging 8.1 percent since 1978.

Although these nations' economic development strategies have differed in various ways, they all followed a sound economic development strategy that included the following features:

1. **Investment in Human Capital.** All of these nations invested in nearly universal primary and secondary education, and developed their scientific and engineering skills.
2. **Investment in Physical Capital.** Given the relatively high rate of domestic saving rates in most of these nations, they were able to use domestic sources of financing to invest heavily in physical capital.
3. **The Complementary Role of the Government.** In most of these nations, the government adopted the strategy of complementing markets and making them work more efficiently, rather than trying to replace them.
4. **Outward Orientation.** Realizing the contribution of exports to their economies, the East and Southeast Asian economies adopted free trade policies. Accordingly, firms were compelled to compete in export markets and adhere to international standards and increase their efficiencies.

Source: U.S. Government Printing Office, *Economic Report of the President* (Washington DC: U.S. Government Printing Office, 1997), 238-242.

of these nations. With a collective population of 80 million and a labor force of over 36 million, these countries possess substantial and formidable economic power. The unemployment rates in these nations are substantially below those of most advanced nations, ranging from 6.35 percent in South Korea to 2.9 percent in Taiwan. South Korea, the most dynamic of these countries, has even surpassed Japan in terms of rapid growth in a short time period. As a group, these nations have performed so well during the past three decades that they have sometimes been referred to facetiously as the **"Four Dragons"** or the **"Gang of Four."**

Given the shortages of natural resources and capital, these countries have tried to achieve development by pursuing a free-trade philosophy, creating a favorable investment climate and using a low-wage labor force that adheres to the Confucian ethic of emphasizing education and hard work. As a result, in recent years, their living standards have risen sharply, unemployment has stayed low, and their economies have continued to experience fast growth.

GLOBAL INSIGHTS CASE 3.2

TURMOIL IN ASIAN ECONOMIES

The outbreak of the financial crisis in Asia was one of the most notable and troubling developments in the global economy during 1997. Events began midyear as a currency crisis and intensified over the rest of the year, spilling over to the real sectors of the affected economies as well as the rest of the world.

By May 1997 Thailand was in the throes of the fourth speculative attack on its currency, the baht, since August 1996. By then the buildup of financial difficulties and balance of payments pressures had reached such a point that efforts to defend the baht could not be sustained. Pressures soon spilled over to other emerging Asian economies (especially Indonesia, Malaysia, and South Korea), most of which also had some balance of payments weaknesses, as well as to Eastern Europe. These countries difficulties shook financial market confidence elsewhere in Asia and in emerging markets around the world, even those with sounder policies and economic fundamentals, with a contagious effect.

Since June, four of the countries in the region (Indonesia, the Philippines, South Korea, and Thailand) have requested and received assistance from the International Monetary Fund (IMF). In each instance the adjustment programs developed by the domestic authorities and the IMF have included a heavy emphasis on financial and structural adjustment measures (for example, to reform bank lending practices and further liberalize the economy), as well as the more traditional macroeconomic adjustments necessary to restore financial market stability. For each of the affected economies, the question of when their financial and balance of payments situation will stabilize depends, first and foremost, on whether and how aggressively they implement their policy commitments, and second, on the easing of the contagion effect from those economies that continue to experience difficulties. In the medium term the return of these economies' strong growth performance will depend significantly upon the degree to which the structural and financial sector reforms are implemented.

Source: U.S. Government Printing Office, *Economic Report of the President* (Washington D.C: Government Printing Office, 1998, 50, Box 2-2. Reprinted.

Although their GNPs remain lower than those of North America, Europe, and Japan, their overall economic growth is remarkable, ranging from about 1.8 percent a year in Hong Kong to 10 percent a year in South Korea. Their continuous growth has resulted in the development of strong domestic markets. Besides their striking growth performance, the most prominent feature of the Gang of Four is their adherence to free international trade. The NICs' relative share in the global market is still not large when compared to Japan's in most products. They continue, however, to experience a very strong export growth, ranging from 8.33 percent in Taiwan to 14.4 percent in Hong Kong. Additionally, they are emerging as a formidable industrial force that advanced countries will have to compete with in the global market. Japan is already losing ground to these nations in some industries, such as steel and textiles. In the international market for automobiles, Japan now has to reckon with South Korea, which has successfully eradicated Japan's position as the principal Asian automobile exporter.

Although the Gang of Four nations have been able to achieve remarkable economic success, their accomplishments have not come without problems. The philosophy of emphasizing industrialization at all costs has left these nations with major pollution problems. Labor unrest has become more common. South Korea, for example, recently faced pressure from workers to increase wages and bonuses, improve working conditions, and free labor unions which have been suppressed by the government.

As a part of China, Singapore and Hong Kong represent city-states, and as such some economists question their use as a model for more populated nation-states. But, South Korea and Taiwan escape this criticism and serve as a good model for other developing nations. To be sure, the development path of these countries is similar to that of Japan. Like Japan, these two nations have followed a policy of systematic intervention to advance economic development by providing tax incentives and subsidies, building infrastructure, investing heavily in primary education, and other human capital. Both of these nations borrowed a considerable amount of technology from abroad, and followed a dual-industrial policy of import substitution and promotion of labor-intensive technology in export sector. Beginning in the 1960s, these two nations focused on promotion of capital-and technology intensive exports.

In recent years, a new group of NICs (Indonesia, Malaysia, and Thailand) has begun to displace the Gang of Four as the "engine of growth" in the region. However, this trend seemed to change in 1991 when the growth of the Gang of Four surpassed that of the new group of NICs.

In concluding this section, we must emphasize that it is unwise to emulate the Japanese, Taiwanese, or Korean strategy of economic development without modification. The Meiji Japanese and pre-1980 Koreans and Taiwanese were not democratic. These nations repressed labor organizations, and spent heavily on the military. Nevertheless, developing nations can learn from the experience of these Asian nations by adapting some of the following major components of success that proved to be helpful to their economic development processes:

- Japanese and Taiwanese emphasis on advancing the skills of small- and medium-scale industries.
- Promotion of high standards of performance in primary and secondary education.
- Government planning aimed at improving private-sector productivity.
- Considerable technological borrowing and modification.
- Exchange-rate policies that were nondiscriminatory against the exports.

The Soviet Development Strategies

The Communist revolution in 1917 led to the emergence of an alternative approach to capitalism as the path to economic modernization. This approach, referred to as the Stalinist Development Model is associated with Soviet leader Joseph Stalin from 1924 to 1953. The cornerstone of this model is development planning. Starting with the first 5-year plan in 1928, the Soviet planners incorporated the following main strategies into their planning process:

1. Replacing consumers' preferences with planners' preferences, as dictated by the Communist party.
2. State control of land and capital.
3. Collectivization of agriculture.
4. State monopoly trading with other countries.
5. The virtual elimination of private trade.
6. Monitoring of plan fulfillment by the state banks.
7. Maintaining a low ratio of trade to GNP.
8. Diversion of saving from agriculture to industry.

The pursuit of such strategies in a few decades allowed the former Soviet Union to become a major industrial power. As a result, the share of industry in net national product (NNP) rose from 28 percent in 1928 to 45 percent in 1945. During the same period, agriculture's share in NNP declined from 49 percent to 29 percent and the labor share declined form 71 percent to 51 percent. Additionally, an average life expectancy of about 40 years, an illiteracy rate of 60 percent, and extensive poverty prior to the revolution was replaced with a life expectancy of 70 years, general literacy, and economic strength.

CH. 3/ECONOMIC DEVELOPMENT IN A HISTORICAL CONTEXT

Many observers believed that Soviet-style central planning had paid off, transforming the economy from the economic sluggishness of the pre-revolution to a fast growing economy during the four decades after 1928. In the late 1950s, Nikita Khrushchev claimed that the Soviet economic output would overtake and surpass that of the United States. He told the United States, "We will bury you." Such statements set the stage for a bitter cold war between the two superpowers. The United States and the Soviet Union fought a political battle that most observers believed would end in a final nuclear war. However, economic and political problems within the Soviet Union created an inefficient, bureaucratic system. This led to shortages of agricultural and industrial products, forcing the nation to continue to expand its imports from Western Europe and, ironically, from the United States, the country Khrushchev was supposed to bury.

The political and economic problems in the former Soviet Union set the stage for the emergence of one of our century's pivotal leaders, Mikhail S. Gorbachev, who came to power in 1985. His reforms, referred to as "perestroika" (restructuring) and "glasnost" (openness), transformed the political and economic structure of the Soviet Union and helped to end the Cold War. However, he became the victim of the very reforms that he initiated. Gorbachev's reforms opened Soviet society to the world and ended the Communist party's seven-decade monopoly on power. He allowed the fall of the Communist regimes in Eastern Europe, introduced multiple-party and multiple-candidate elections, and strengthened the elected legislature. He stopped religious oppression, freed political prisoners, and gave Soviet citizens the freedom to travel and emigrate. In talks with the United States, Gorbachev agreed to drastic reductions in nuclear and conventional arms, thereby strengthening the world's prospect for peace. However, despite his accomplishments in reshaping his country's political and economic systems, he made some mistakes. Many observers believed Gorbachev moved too slowly on economic reforms. As a result, shortages of food, fuel, housing, and consumer goods worsened. In planning and implementing his reforms, Gorbachev did not consult sufficiently with the republics, nor did he give them enough autonomy. Finally, he chose his aides unwisely, ending up with colleagues who eventually turned against him. These mistakes not only cost Gorbachev his presidency, but they paved the way for the demise of the Soviet Union and the birth of the new Commonwealth of Independent States (CIS).

Western leaders welcomed the formation of the CIS; U.S. President George Bush referred to the demise of the Soviet Union as "a defining moment in history." He said that U.S. security would be enhanced by offering aid to the region, and added that "If this democratic revolution is defeated, it would plunge us into a world more dangerous in some respects than the dark years of the Cold War."[1]

From the outset of independence, it was clear that it would be extremely difficult for the CIS to be transformed to market-oriented systems without economic aid from the West. Realizing this, Western leaders have been quick to pour economic aid into the region, contingent upon market-oriented economic reforms. On April 2, 1992, President Bush and Allied leaders pledged to funnel a combined $24 billion of additional aid to Russia.[2] The aid was given to help Yeltsin implement market-oriented economic reforms. The U.S. and European officials made it clear that "any backpedaling on economic reforms could jeopardize billions of dollars in planned Western aid."[3] In July 1992, the leaders of the G-7 nations (Great Britain, Canada, France, Germany, Italy, Japan, and the United States) promised to provide debt relief to Russia. They also pledged to extend export credit to Russia, lift their trade barriers, and provide the Russians with more technical assistance.[4]

Following Bill Clinton's presidential victory over George Bush, Russia continued to receive billions of dollars in grants, credits, and special funds to sustain its demolished economy. However, the outflow of funds was just as massive as the inflow. An estimated $10 to $15 billion flew out of Russia in 1992—an amount totaling about 15 percent of Russia's gross domestic product (GDP) for the year. Capital flight is a manifestation of the malfunctioning economy and is expected to reverse itself once the Russian economy stabilizes.[5]

GLOBAL INSIGHTS CASE 3.3

THE FEL'DMAN INVESTMENT STRATEGY

C. G. Fel'dman is the architect of a growth model that was developed for the Soviet planning commission in 1928, laying the foundations for the investment strategy in that country. According to his model, long-run economic growth is a function of the percentage of the GNP allocated to investment in capital goods industry. The model implies not only foregoing the percentage of the GNP spent on current consumption to boost current investment, but also diminishing the percentage of investment in consumer goods to increase the percentage of the GNP spent on capital goods. In other words, the higher the sacrifice of the short-run growth of consumer goods capacity, the higher long-run growth rates for capital goods and consumption will be. In a nutshell, the model implies that the rapid growth of investment in machinery and equipment leads to the production of more machinery and equipment, providing for a higher consumption in the long-run.

Soviet investment and growth pattern was based on the Fel'dman model. Following the dictates of this model, between 1928 and 1937, the share of heavy manufacturing in total manufacturing increased from 31 percent to 63 percent. In the meantime, the share of light manufacturing declined from 68 percent to 26 percent. During this period, the percentage of investment to GNP doubled from 13 percent to 26 percent, while the share of consumption in GNP, measured in 1937 prices, decreased from 80 percent to 53 percent.

The implementation of the Fel'dman investment strategy in the former Soviet Union led to impressive economic growth and industrialization. However, it also created a consumption level that was lower than almost all of the Western European countries, setting the stage for the eventual collapse of this superpower.

The Fel'dman model was not only used in the former Soviet Union, but it was also adopted by India and China in their economic planning. India's second 5-year plan (1995/56-1960/61), headed by Mahalanobis, an Indian statistician, tried to combine the Fel'dman investment strategy with democratic socialism to alleviate capital shortages. Like the Fel'dman model, the Mahalanobis model emphasized raising the share of investment in steel and capital goods. Unfortunately, the Mahalanobis strategy failed to meet the stated targets, and as a result, the plan was abandoned in the late 1960s.

Although China used the Fel'dman model, emphasizing capital goods investment as the core of planning during the 1950s, in 1960, it abandoned the model. Such an action was taken, in part, because the Soviet aid agency, angered by the Chinese missionary movement against Soviet Premier Nikita Khrushchev's criticism of Stalinism, withdrew financial and technical assistance to China. But, Chinese policy makers realized that a major problem of the Fel'dman model was that it placed too much emphasis on capital accumulation at the expense of consumption. They also noted that the model diverted too much investment in heavy industry and too little in light industry and agriculture, resulting in disproportionate development of the economic system. China's present economic readjustment objectives are to provide a balance between various economic variables that are significantly out of proportion, and to ease undue emphasis on heavy industry such that the process of production, distribution, and consumption can be accelerated to improve economic outcomes. To meet these objectives, a high priority is given to the production of consumer goods.

Sources: Paul R. Gregory and Robert C. Stuart, *Soviet Economic Structure and Performance* (New York: Harper & row, 1981); Paul R. Gregory and Robert C. Stuart, *Soviet and Post-soviet Economic Structure and Performance* (New York: Haper Collins, 1994); India, Planning Commission, *Fourth Five-Year Plan*, 1969-74 (Dehli, 1969); 119-27;Maddison, *Class Structure and Economic Growth: India and Pakistan Since the Moghuls* (New York: Norton, 1971); Angus Carl Riskin, *China's Political Economy: The Quest for Development Since 1949* (Oxford University Press, 1987); and Lance Taylor, *Macro Models for Developing Countries* (New York: McGraw-Hill, 1979).

With the focus on international trade at their September 1994 summit in Washington, both presidents of the United States and Russia signed a Partnership for Economic Cooperation that serves as a framework for reducing barriers to expanded economic cooperation. A number of U.S. agencies, including the Overseas Private Investment Corporation, the Export-Import Bank, the Trade and Development Agency, and the Department of Commerce, have programs that are aimed at facilitating trade and investment in Russia. Since 1992, the U.S. Agency for International Development (USAID) has offered about $2 billion in assistance to helping Russia develop democratic and market institutions.[6] However, despite aid from the Western world and Russia's progress on reform, it is anticipated that this country will face a decade- long process of economic reform that promises to be marked by many upheavals such as rising inflation, growing unemployment, and falling output.[7]

The Soviet-style unbalanced approach to economic development, placing undue emphasis on investment in heavy industry at the expense of light industry and agriculture, provides the following important lessons for today's developing nations:

- The allocation of a large proportion of total investment to capital goods industry is likely to enhance economic growth if it is accompanied by sufficient demand for capital goods.
- The pressure on current consumption resulting from the unbalanced investment approach may last as long as a generation.
- The implementation of the Soviet economic development strategy requires substantial control over total investment. However, planners in capitalist and mixed economies usually have limited control over total investment.

Recent Economic Growth in Developing Nations

Data on the economic performance of developing nations before World War II are generally poor, making a precise assessment of economic growth in these nations very difficult. However, the available data in the case of India, the developing nation with the best estimates, indicates that from the beginning of the twentieth century until its independence in 1947, this country's growth was not more than 0.2 percent per year, compared to an annual 1.9 percent growth from 1950 to 1992. Such estimates suggest that the economic growth in developing nations was much faster after World War II than before.

Unfortunately, such rapid growth does not reveal a wide diversity of experience among the 4.2 billion who live in developing nations. Sub-Saharan Africa, Latin America, and the Middle East have endured negative growth and a drastic debt crisis since 1980. East Asia, with newly industrialized countries and China have grown at annual rates in excess of 6 percent since 1980. Nevertheless, because of its earlier development, Latin America still portrays the highest GNP per capita among all the developing regions. On the other hand, South and Southeast Asia, because of their pervasive slow growth in the beginning of the post World War II period, indicate the lowest GNP per capita among developing regions.

Given the diverse experience of developing nations with regard to economic growth, it appears that the overall postwar growth of developing nations as a whole has been neither faster nor slower than the growth of developed nations, suggesting that the real per capita income of developing nations does not show any signs of approaching the level of per capita income in developed countries.

PROFILE OF DEVELOPING NATIONS

It is often too risky to attempt to generalize too much about developing nations. Although most of these countries are economically poor, they have diverse cultures, economic conditions, and social and political structures that make each country unique. Nevertheless, these nations share certain economic characteristics that allow us to place them in a broadly similar structure. The purpose of this section is to ascertain these similarities and elaborate on their importance. We may begin by classifying these common characteristics into the following general classes:

1. Low standards of living, exemplified by low income, high inequality, bad health, and insufficient education.
2. A political framework that is marked by dominance, dependence, and vulnerability in international relations.
3. Rapid population growth and dependency burdens.
4. High and growing rates of unemployment and underemployment.
5. High dependence on agricultural sector.
6. Dependence on Primary Exports.
7. Low levels of labor productivity.
8. Presence of imperfect markets and incomplete information.
9. An extended family.
10. Inadequate technology, capital, and saving.

Low Standards of Living

One of the major characteristics of developing nations is the existence of low standards of living for the great majority of their people. This is the case not only in comparison to their corollary in advanced nations, but also with respect to small upper classes within their nations. These low standards of living are portrayed in terms of low income, slow growth, poor health and inadequate education. In this section we examine each of these variables by looking at some recent statistics.

GNP Per Capita and its Growth Rate. In 1997, the total GNP of the world was about $30 trillion, of which about $24 trillion originated in developed nations and $6 trillion was generated in developing nations. If we take account of the distribution of world population, this means that about 80 percent of the world's GNP is generated in the developed nations, comprising only 20 percent of the world's population. In other words, the Third World with almost 80 percent of the world population, lives on less than 20 percent of the world's income.

In addition to experiencing a much lower level of GNP per capita, many developing nations have endured slower GNP growth than the advanced nations. Among all developing nations, for instance, growth decelerated significantly during the 1980s and real GDP in fact decreased by 0.2% in 1990 and again in 1991. As a result, the income gap between rich and poor nations grew at the fastest rate in more than three decades.

Distribution of National Income. Although all the countries portray some degree of *income inequality*, the gap between rich and poor is generally wider in developing nations as compared to advanced nations. For example, if we compare the share of national income received by the poorest 40 percent of a nation's population with that of the wealthiest 20 percent as an arbitrary measure of the degree of income inequality we can distinguish between the following three groups of nations on the basis of income inequality:

1. **High level of income inequality**, including countries such as Brazil, Colombia, Ecuador, Guatemala, Jamaica, Kenya, Mexico, Moldova, Sierra Leone, and South Africa.
2. **Moderate level of income inequality**, including countries such as Chile, Costa Rica, Malaysia, Libya, India, and Tanzania.
3. **Low level of income inequality**, including countries such as Canada, Indonesia, Japan, Sweden, South Korea, and Taiwan.

CH. 3/ECONOMIC DEVELOPMENT IN A HISTORICAL CONTEXT

GLOBAL INSIGHTS CASE 3.4

THE INCOME DISTRIBUTION IN BRAZIL

Brazil is one of the fastest growing developing nations in the world. Over the past three decades this country has experienced periods of high economic growth that reached the level of over 6 per cent for some years. Yet, during this prosperity a majority of Brazilian people have not benefitted much from its remarkable economic growth. While a majority of city workers live in poverty, a small percentage of the population enjoys enormous profit made possible by low industrial wages. This inequality can be detected from data on income distribution. According to the latest available data published by the World Bank, in 1995, the poorest 20 percent of the Brazilian population received only 2.5 percent of the national income, while the highest 10 percent received 47.9 percent of the income and the highest 20 percent received 64.2 percent of the income.

Despite its fast economic growth, a large percentage of the population in Brazil suffer from severe poverty. According to World Bank data, in 1995, 23.6 percent of population, almost 40 million Brazilian lived on less than a dollar a day. 43.5 percent of the population, over 70 million Brazilian, lived on less than two dollars a day. Two thirds of the poorest people in Brazil inhabited agrarian areas where 44 percent of the arable land belonged to the richest one percent of the landlords, and more than fifty percent of farmers worked on less than three percent of the land.

The existence of such enormous poverty and income inequality in Brazil has contributed to a new social and political movement, called the "landless movement", known as MST in Portuguese. During the 1995-1997 period about 600 stretches of arable land which were not under cultivation were seized by MST and 200,000 families settled. In many cases, these families were able to obtain legal title to the land from the government.

Sources: World Bank, *World Development Report, 1998/1999* (New York: Oxford University Press, 1999); World Bank, 1988 *World Development Indicators* (Washington, D.C.: World Bank, 1998); World Bank, *The World Bank Atlas, 1988* (Washington, D.C.: World Bank, 1998); United Nation's Development Program, *Human Development Report, 1998* (New York: Oxford University Press, 1998).

It is interesting to note that there is no clear relationship between levels of per capita GNP and the degree of income inequality. For example, India, with the same low per capita income as Kenya, portrays a much lower income inequality between the top 20 percent and bottom 40 percent. As another example, Belgium, with almost the same high per capita GNP As Kuwait, has a much higher portion of its income distributed to the bottom 40 percent of its populace. These examples underline the significant point that economic development cannot be assessed only in terms of the level and growth of GNP per capita. As we mentioned in Chapter 1, we also need to look at the distribution of income to the inhabitants of the country to determine the beneficiaries of the economic development process.

Poor Health. As a by-product of low income, poor health is another major problem that many people in developing nations have to deal with. Not only do they have to struggle on low incomes to satisfy their needs, but they also constantly have to fight against malnutrition, disease, and ailing health. Although there have been some important improvements since the 1960s, in 1996 the life expectancy at birth in the low-income countries was 58 years for male and 60 years for females, compared to 66 years for males and 71 years for females in middle-income nations, and 74 years for males and 81 years for females in high-income nations. In 1996, **infant mortality rates** —the number of children old who die before their first birthday out of every 1000 live births —averaged 113 in low-income nations as compared with 43 in middle-income nations and only 7 in high-income nations.[8]

In the mid-1970s over one billion people, almost half of the population of the developing nations (excluding China), were surviving on diets inadequate in fundamental calories. The vast majority of these people lived in the poorest nations, and within these nations, in the lowest income classes. During the 1980s and 1990s the condition worsened in both Asia and Africa where more than sixty percent of the people barely met minimum calorie requirements needed to preserve adequate health. It is interesting to note that this calorie deficit is estimated to amount to less than two percent of the world's cereal production. This challenges the generally held opinion that malnutrition is the eventual consequence of an imbalance between world food supplies and world population. But in fact, the more plausible explanation is the existence of a huge imbalance in world income distribution.

As one of the most important measures of sanitation, water plays an important role in the maintenance of good health. Water born illnesses like cholera, typhoid fever, and a range of serious or fatal diseases account for more than 35 percent of the deaths of children in Africa, Latin America, and Asia. The majority of these sicknesses and subsequent deaths could be eliminated with sanitary water reserves.

Finally, another major problem in developing nations is the severe scarcity of medical care. According to the most recent available data, in 1993, the number of physicians per 100,000 people averaged only 14 in the least developed countries, compared to 287 in the advanced countries. In the same year, the number of nurses per 100,000 people averaged 26 in the least developed countries, compared to 780 in advanced nations. Given that most of the medical facilities in developing nations are located in cities which include only 25 percent of the inhabitants, the inadequacy of the health care system in developing nations becomes very clear.

Political Framework

One of the major factors that affects the process of economic development is the political framework in a developing nation. Today there are only 36 developing nations that enjoy political democracies, imbued with wide competition between organized political parties and elections that are held regularly and are fairly implemented.[9] Unlike Western democracies, political structures in developing nations are controlled by a relatively small **political elite**. This group encompasses two major factions. The first faction is composed of people who play a significant role in government affairs and includes traditional princes and chiefs, political leaders, senior servants and administrators, public corporation executives, and high-ranking military officers. The second faction includes land owners, major business people, urban industrialists, bankers and foreign manufacturers.

For the political elite, economic development and modernization usually present a paradox. Economic modernization leads to stability by empowering the governing groups to maintain law and order, select leaders, and promote political community. But the resulting industrialization, urbanization, and educational expansion lead formerly passive ethnic, religious, regional, or economics clusters into politics. Given the limited capacity of developing nations in absorbing the influx of new political participants, the stage is set for instability.

Thus, a successful economic development demands either that the support of elite groups be secured or that the influence of the elites be offset by more assertive democratic forces.

External Dependence

Today, no nation can live in isolation and all the countries in the world are dependent on each other to some extent. The extent to which a country is dependent on foreign trade, political and social forces, is correlated

GLOBAL INSIGHTS CASE 3.5

ELIMINATION AND ERADICATION OF DISEASES: THE EXAMPLE OF POLIOMYELITIS AND A CASE FOR VACCINATION

Poliomyelitis, commonly referred to as polio, has been one of the world's greatest scourges. Prior to polio vaccine development in the 1950's, about a half million people a year were paralyzed or died from this disease. In 1988, the World Health Assembly resolved to eradicate poliomyelitis globally by the year 2000 (1). Although this goals was not met, substantial progress has been made towards this achieving this goal. Once eradicated, the U.S. alone estimates a $230 million a year saving in health care costs associated with the vaccination of the 4 million Americans born every year.

Public health officials define elimination and eradication of disease in the following manner:

- *Elimination* of a communicable disease involves controlling the disease within a specific country, continent, or region, with the goal of eventual eradication within that geographical area.
- *Eradication* is reducing the incidence (number of new cases per year) of a communicable disease worldwide to zero, with no additional necessary control measures.

Vaccination has been one of the most significant health care measures to prevent and control infectious diseases. Smallpox was the first vaccine-preventable disease to be eradicated (in 1977, and certified by the World Health Organization in 1980). Much suffering has been avoided, and children are no longer vaccinated for smallpox.

Many criteria must exist for a disease to be targeted for eradication, including, but not limited to, epidemiological factors such as the disease having a human host only (no host in nature), and an easy diagnosis with obvious clinical manifestations. Necessary criteria also include factors involving political will, such as a substantial global morbidity and mortality associated with the disease, and the cost effectiveness of a eradication campaign.

The progress towards the eradication of polio has been great. The region of the Americas eliminated poliomyelitis in 1991. The Pacific Rim, Europe, and central Asia appear to be polio-free. (The countries in this region, including the U.S., must continue to vaccinate its children because infected travelers can easily spread polio.) The remaining reservoirs where it is endemic are confined to India and contiguous countries, and to sub-Saharan Africa. Ongoing armed conflict in countries like Somalia, and parts of southern Sudan, as well as the poor infrastructure (health-care facilities, schools, roads, power plants) of many developing countries provide the greatest obstacles. The use of health care delivery strategies have included major events called National Immunization Days, and partnerships between local and international non-governmental organizations. Not only can vaccinations be given house-to-house, but can be given boat-to-boat, as was the case in the Mekong River area of Cambodia, Laos, and Vietnam, in an attempt to reach previously undervaccinated children residing on the extensive waterways. Creativity at the local level is often the final key to a successful program.

Sources: *World Health Assembly. Global eradication of poliomyelitis by the year 2000.* Geneva, Switzerland: World Health Organization, 1988; WHA resolution no. WHA 41.28; Swanson, Janice, and, Mary Nies *Community Health Nursing: Promoting the Health of Aggregates*, 2nd. Ed., W.B. Saunders and Company, p.658-659, 1997; Centers for Disease Control. *Recommendations of the International Task Force for Disease Eradication. Morbidity and Mortality Weekly Report* 42:1-38, 1993.4.Centers for Disease Control. *Progress Toward the Global Interruption of Wild Poliovirus Type 2 Transmission*, 1999. MMWR 48(33):736-738, 1999; Centers for Disease Control: *Final Stages of Poliomyelitis Eradication - Western Pacific Region.* 1997-1998. MMWR 48(2):29-31, 1999.
This case was written by Dorothy L. Thurman, instructor of community health and maternal-child health, California State University, San Bernardino.

GLOBAL INSIGHTS CASE 3.6

A GLOBAL LOOK AT THE AIDS (ACQUIRED IMMUNODEFICIENCY SYNDROME) EPIDEMIC*

Although reports regarding increased longevity and health of the U.S. HIV (human immunodeficiency virus) infected population has given us some of the most optimistic news we've heard since the identification of the virus in the early 1980's, it does not tell the story of the epidemic worldwide.

The epidemic is huge and has shown no signs of stabilization. The disparities in disease rates between rich and poor countries are great and increasing. More than 90 percent of the HIV infected people live in developing countries, where few precautions are being taken to prevent the spread of the infection. Many of the infected persons don't know their HIV status.

Two thirds of the total number of people worldwide who are infected with HIV live in sub-Saharan Africa, one of the poorest regions in the world. In Botswana, one of the worst hit areas, the number of adults infected has doubled in the last 5 years alone, with approximately 30 percent of that aggregate infected. Contrast those statistics with the ones in Western Europe and North America that show a 30 percent decline in the number of new cases between 1995 and 1997. Of course, within the United States, the infection rates, which showed a 6 percent decline in 1996, are still increasing among the poorest groups, particularly African-American and Hispanic men and women. Access to costly antiviral drugs, and access to health care generally, is more limited in these groups.

Asian surveillance systems have been less well developed, but the available evidence reflects increasing rates of HIV infection in China, India, Cambodia and Vietnam. Thailand has been able to reduce the rate of new infections by using massive condom campaigns and other educational campaigns.

Eastern Europe and countries that comprise the former Soviet Union are expected to have rising rates as the numbers of newly infected shift from predominantly IV drug users to those having unsafe sexual practices.

Latin America and the Caribbean have fairly low rates of infection, but again, the growth in the numbers of poor, and women, who are newly infected individuals shift from the previous aggregate of homosexual men and IV drug users. Rates are expected to increase as the virus makes its way into a different population.

Source: The *1998-99 World Resources: A Guide to the Global Environment.*
*This case was written by Dorothy L. Thurman, instructor of community health and maternal and child health nursing, California State University, San Bernardino

to its size, resource endowment, and political history. For most developing nations, this dependency is substantial and in some nations affects almost every aspect of life. Such a dependency stems from the need of these nations to engage in foreign trade, to transfer technology and know-how, to seek foreign aid, and to secure foreign sources of capital. A by-product of this process is the transfer of government systems, educational systems, value systems, consumption patterns, and attitudes towards life, work and self, from the advanced nations to these developing nations. As we discuss in later chapters, this transfer turns out to be a double-edged sword for most developing nations, especially for those who demonstrate the greatest potential for self-reliance. A developing nation's ability to control its own economic and social agenda is significantly impacted by the extent of its dependence on advanced countries.

CH. 3/ECONOMIC DEVELOPMENT IN A HISTORICAL CONTEXT

Rapid Population Growth and Dependency Burdens

In 1997, the world's population reached the level of 5.829 billion people, out of which more than three quarters (85 percent) lived in developing nations and less than one quarter in advanced nations. The **population density,** the number of people per unit area of land (e.g., per square kilometer) in developing nations was 54 per cultivated square kilometer, compared to 22 per cultivated square kilometer in advanced nations.

The problem in developing nations is not population density per se, but low productivity coupled with fast population growth. The rapid population growth in developing nations is related to the higher birth rates than death rates in these nations as compared to the advanced countries. Although better public health and preventive medicine have cut the death rates in developing nations by more than half since 1945, the death rates in these nations are still high as compared with those in developed nations. In 1998, while the population growth in advanced nations was only 0.3 percent per year, the developing nations' birth rates stayed at high levels, leading to a volatile annual growth rate of 1.9 percent.

A major problem associated with high birth rates in developing nations is the composition of their age distribution. In these nations, children under 15 constitute about 40 percent of total population as compared with 20 percent of the total population in advanced nations. By contrast, the percentage of people older than 65 is much higher in advanced nations as compared to developing nations. Children and older people are usually considered as an economic **dependency burden**, in the sense that they are nonproductive members of the society and must be supported by others. The overall dependency burden–people between ages 15 and 64–represents about 45% of the populations of the developing nations but only about 33% of the populations of advanced nations. Additionally, in developing nations about 90% of the dependents are children, while only 66% are children in advanced nations. Given the relatively higher rate of unemployment in developing nations, the working individuals in these nations have to support twice as many people as compared to their counterparts in advanced nations.

High and Growing Rates of Unemployment and Underemployment

One of the major factors that contributes to low standards of living in developing nations is that their labor is not used efficiently as compared to the advanced nations. Inefficient utilization of labor portrays itself in the following two shapes:

1. **Open Unemployment**, that is, people who are willing and able to work but cannot find jobs. The average unemployment rate in developing nations is about 10 to 15 percent. What is worse is that unemployment among young people, aged 15 to 24, most of whom have considerable education, is about two times as high as the overall average.
2. **Underemployment**, that is, a condition in which workers are overqualified for their jobs or work less than they prefer. This includes people who work on an hourly, weekly, or seasonally basis.

If we add the "**discouraged workers**"—those who have given up looking for work—to the openly underemployed and underemployed in the developing nations, we would find that about 35 percent of the labor force in developing nations is unutilized.

Given the high birth rates in the developing nations, their labor is expected to continue growing at high rates. This implies that jobs should be generated at equivalent rates in order to keep up with the growth of labor. We discuss this topic in detail in Chapter 6.

High Dependence on Agricultural Sector

The economies of most developing nations are dominated by the agricultural sector. Today, about 62 percent of the labor force of developing nations is engaged in agriculture as compared to 7 percent in advanced nations. Additionally, the agriculture sector in developing nations accounts for 19 percent of GDP as compared to only 3 percent in advanced nations.

The fact that most of developing nations are predominantly agricultural societies stems from their low productivity in the agricultural sector which is caused by the following two factors:

1. The high population density in these nations.
2. The utilization of traditional methods of agricultural production, characterized by primitive technologies, poor organization, and limited capital.

The factor that fuels technological backwardness in the agricultural sectors of developing nations is the existence of noncommercial peasant farming. Peasant farmers are composed of a household whose primary concern is survival. Most of the land in these nations is worked by land tenure provisions whereby a peasant rents the land as opposed to purchasing it. Such a provision removes much of the economic incentives to enhance productivity or expand the output. Even where the land is plentiful, the traditional method of farming demands that family's land holding not to exceed 12 to 20 acres, in which 10 to 15 people work on each acre to make their ends meet.

Given that one of the major problems in developing nations is the lack of productivity in the agricultural sector, improvement in agricultural efficiency continues to be among the major objectives of economic development.

Dependence on Primary Exports

One of the attributes of many developing nations is that their production and exports are mainly composed of primary products, including agriculture, raw materials, fuel, and forestry. In other words, the contribution of the manufacturing sector to the total exports in developing nations is much smaller in comparison to developed nations. For example, as Table 3.2 indicates, in 1998, the exports of the manufacturing products of low-income countries accounted for 52 percent of the total exports, as opposed to 82 percent for developed nations.

Low Levels of Labor Productivity

Labor productivity, that is, output per worker in developing nations, is very low when compared with those in advanced nations. Such a low productivity stems from two major factors: Inadequacy of physical and human capital, and poor health .

Inadequacy of Physical and Human Capital. The law of diminishing returns (variable proportions) states that in a given state of technology, if we add a variable factor of production, say labor, to other fixed factors of production (e.g capital, land, materials), the amount of output associated with each additional unit of labor (marginal product of labor) declines beyond a certain point. Given the lack or severe shortages of "complimentary" factors of production such as physical and human capital, it is no wonder that labor productivity is low in developing nations.

Table 3.2
THE SHARE OF THE MANUFACTURING IN TOTAL EXPORTS OF DEVELOPING AND DEVELOPED NATIONS

Economies	Total Exports Millions of dollars	Manufacturing % of total exports
Low income	165,177	52
Lower middle income	499,085	66
Upper middle income	625,765	74
High income	3,963,915	82

Source: World Bank, *World Development Report, 2000/2001* (New York: Oxford University Press, 2001), 313.

To raise the productivity in these nations, one needs to elevate the level of technology by triggering domestic savings and foreign capital in order to generate new investment in physical and human capital. This requires a revamping of the existing institutions to maximize the potential of such investment. Institutional improvement might take the following divergent forms:

1. Reforming the tax system, land tenure, credit, and banking structure.
2. Administrative reform, including the generation or bolstering of an independent, trustworthy, and effective administration.
3. Reforming educational and training programs to make them more conducive to the requirement of the developing nations.
4. Nurturing an environment that is conducive to innovation, experiments, the desire to do a good job, the relationship between workers and managers, and self-improvement.

In summary, the creation of economic opportunities for self-improvement in developing nations will not lead to a successful economic development unless it is accompanied by the appropriate institutional and structural reforms.

Poor Health. There is a close relationship between physical/mental health and the level of labor productivity. Studies show that inadequate nutrition in childhood can lead to mental and physical problems in adulthood. Even when a person reaches adulthood, inadequate food, poor dietary habits, and bad personal hygiene can lead to further deterioration of health, adversely affecting the individual's attitude and ability to work. This in turn causes workers' productivity to decline. Thus, laborers' low productivity in developing nations can be attributed mainly to lethargy and the weakness, both physical and psychological, to tolerate the day-to-day pressures of work.

In summary, low standards of living and low productivity are self-augmenting elements in developing nations that fuel underdevelopment.

Presence of Imperfect Markets and Incomplete Information.

The decades of the 1980s and 1990s can be marked as a period during which many developing nations embarked on policies of promoting free markets and strengthening competitive forces in order to facilitate their development process. Such policies were partially in response to the World Banks advocacy of "market-friendly" economic policies as a prerequisite for loans.

The success of such policies depends on the existence of cultural, institutional, and legal environments that are either absent or extremely weak in developing nations. Unfortunately, however, most developing nations suffer from the following shortcomings:

1. The nonexistence of a strong legal system that affirms property rights and implements contracts.
2. A lack of stable and reliable currency.
3. The nonexistence of an infrastructure that provides for low communication and transportation costs, facilitating interregional trade.
4. The inadequacy of market information regarding prices, quantities, and qualities of goods and services, as well as the creditworthiness of borrowers.
5. The absence of an advanced banking system and credit appropriation that chooses projects on the basis of relative economic worthiness and executes rules of repayments.
6. The nonexistence of economies of scale in major industries, such as extractive industries.
7. The existence of scant markets for many goods due to inadequate demand and few sellers.
8. The prevalence of extensive externalities, in consumption and production.*
9. The predominance of common property resources such as grazing lands and waterholes.

The above listing implies that markets in developing nations are highly imperfect. It also exemplifies that information is inadequate and costly to acquire, leading to the misallocation of resources, goods and finances. Does the existence of imperfect markets and incomplete information justify a more actively involved government? This is a question that we will be discussing in later chapters.

An Extended Family

In most developing nations the **extended family** is composed of two or more nuclear families of parent(s) and children. Some scholars consider the extended family a hindrance to economic development. They argue, if one of the family member's income rises, allowing his/her savings to increase, other members may put demand on that saving. This leads to the diversion of the funds from potential capital formation, hampering the process of economic development. Other scholars, however, elaborate on the positive aspects of the extended family. They argue, for example, if one of the family members plans to extend formal education, or start a new business venture, other members may pool risks to support him/her financially, thus contributing to the process of economic development.

To be sure, in most developing nations, family entrepreneurship can bring together large amounts of resources, make collective decisions, put faithful people into management positions, and fund apprentice training and initial investment. But, it may also hinder the firms's expansion by diverting resources to current consumption.

In concluding this chapter, we must emphasize that the road to economic development is not smooth and is imbued with uncertainty. A successful journey requires managerial know-how, technical expertise, and immense financial resources that are lacking in most developing countries. As a result, advanced countries have a crucial role in assisting developing countries to achieve their economic development goals. However, as newly industrialized countries (NICs) have demonstrated, the major effort should come from developing countries themselves. In other words, malnutrition and poor health in developing nations are possibly even more an issue of poverty than of food production, even though the two variables are indirectly linked.

---

*costs or benefits that accrue to individuals not doing the producing or consuming.

CH. 3/ECONOMIC DEVELOPMENT IN A HISTORICAL CONTEXT

SUMMARY

1. The rapid, sustained economic growth started in the West. As a forerunner, Great Britain began experiencing industrialization and sustained economic growth by the second half of the eighteenth century. This path was followed by the United States and France in the first half of the nineteenth century; Belgium, Germany, and the Netherlands by the middle of that century and in Scandinavia, Canada, and Italy by the last part of the nineteenth century.
2. Among the non-Western countries, Japan, and perhaps Russia, began their sustained economic growth and development in the last half of the nineteenth century.
3. History shows that the emergence of capitalism was the main element that fueled industrialization and sustained economic growth in the West. Capitalism flourished in the late medieval period.
4. Before the twentieth century, only capitalist economies were successful in large capital accumulation and in creating and applying a vast scientific and technical know-how to production. As are listed in the book, a number of factors contributed to such a success.
5. The growth of capitalism in the West was not without great human costs, and was imbued with brutality, physical violence, and exploitation of workers.
6. The factors that contributed to the slow development of non-Western nations include: (a) the existence of barriers to capitalism in these traditional societies; and (b) the impacts of colonialism and other forms of Western political domination on the sluggish development of these non-Western nations.
7. Japan is one of the few non-Western nations that avoided Western colonialism. Japan's strategy of modernization under the Meiji emperor, 1868-1912, emphasized **"guided capitalism."** This strategy depended on state initiative for larger investments in infrastructure.
8. The **Newly industrialized countries (NICs)** include Argentina, Brazil, Greece, Hong Kong, South Korea, Mexico, Portugal, Singapore, Spain, and Taiwan. These countries are at a relatively advanced stage of economic development. Each of these countries has a substantial and active industrial sector that is integrated into its international trade, finance, and investment systems.
9. Among the NICs, the four East Asian countries of South Korea, Hong Kong, Taiwan, and Singapore have achieved impressive economic performance and have been used as models for economic development by other developing countries. As a group, these nations have performed so well during the past three decades that they have sometimes been referred to facetiously as the "**Four Dragons**" or the "**Gang of Four.**"
10. The Communist revolution in 1917 led to the emergence of an alternative approach to capitalism as the path to economic modernization. This approach, referred to as the Stalinist Development Model, is associated with Soviet leader Joseph Stalin from1924 to 1953. The cornerstone of this model is development planning.
11. The Soviet-style unbalanced approach to economic development, placing undue emphasis on investment in heavy industry at the expense of light industry and agriculture, provides important lessons for today's developing nations.
12. Data on the economic performance of developing nations before World War II are generally poor, making a precise assessment of economic growth in these nations very difficult.
13. Given the diverse experience of developing nations with regard to economic growth, it appears that the overall postwar growth of developing nations as a whole, has been neither faster nor slower than the growth of developed nations, suggesting that the real income per capita of developing nations does not show any signs of approaching the level of per capita income in developed countries.
14. We may classify common characteristics of developing nations into the following general classes:

1. Low standards of living, exemplified by low income, high inequality, bad health, and insufficient education.
2. A political framework that is marked by dominance, dependence, and vulnerability in international relations.
3. Rapid population growth and dependency burdens.
4. High and growing rates of unemployment and underemployment.
5. High dependence on agricultural sector.
6. Dependence on Primary Exports.
7. Low levels of labor productivity.
8. Presence of imperfect markets and incomplete information.
9. An extended family.
10. Inadequate technology, capital, and savings.

QUESTIONS

1. What factors contributed to the success of capitalists economies before the twentieth century? Explain.
2. What factors contributed to the slow development of non-Western nations? Explain.
3. What is meant by "guided capitalism?" Explain.
4. What nations are classified as NICs? What do these nations have in common? What is the major development strategy of the "Four Dragons?"
5. What can developing nations learn from the experience of the NICs? Explain.
6. What are the main strategies that were included in the Soviet's development planning, starting with the first 5-year plan in 1928?
7. What major reforms were implemented by Mikhail S. Gorbachev in the former Soviet Union? What major mistakes were committed by him that cost him his presidency?
8. What can developing nations learn from the Soviet-style unbalanced approach to economic development?
9. List the common characteristics of developing nations.
10. What are the major factors that give rise to the low level of productivity in the agricultural sectors of developing nations? What institutional improvements can be undertaken to alleviate these problems?
11. What factors contribute to the presence of imperfect market and incomplete information in developing nations?

NOTES

1. "Bush, allies Pledge $24 billion to Russia," *The Wall Street Journal*, 2 April 1992, A2.
2. Ibid.
3. "Russian Cabinet Offers to Quit to Save Reforms, *The Wall Street Journal*, 14 April 29, A 14.
4. "G-7 Nations Offer Yelstin Relief on Debt," *The Wall Street Journal*, 9 July 1992, A2.
5. "Russia Should Turn to Latin America for Advice as Capital Flight worsens," *The Wall Street Journal*, 15 November 1993, A 9.
6. "U.S. Printing Office, *Economic Report of the President* (Washington, D.C.: United States Government Printing Office, 1997), 258.
7. "Russia Faces Years of Crisis, CIA Contends," *The Wall Street Journal*, 9 June 1992, p. A14.; "U.S., Allies to Ease More Curbs on High-Tech Sales to East Europe," *The Wall Street Journal,* 20 February 1990, A20.
8. The World Bank, *World Development Report 1998/99* (New York, Oxford University Press, 1999)., p.193.
9. *Africa Demos: A Bulletin of the African Governance Program, the Carter Center 3* (March 1995):35.

CH. 3/ECONOMIC DEVELOPMENT IN A HISTORICAL CONTEXT

SUGGESTED READINGS

Adelman, Irma and Cynthia Taft Morris. "Growth and Impoverishment in the Middle of the Nineteenth Century." *World Development* 6 (March 1978): 245-73.

Amsden, Alice H. "Why Isn't the Whole World Experimenting with the East Asian Model to Develop: Review of the *East Asian Miracle,*" *World Development* 22 (April 1994): 635-44.

Baumol, William, Sue Anne Batey Blackman, and Edward N. Wolff. *Productivity and American Leadership: The Long View* Cambridge, Mass.: MIT Press, 1989.

Brautigam, Deborah. "What Can Africa Learn form Taiwan? Political Economy, Industrial Policy, and Adjustment." *Journal of Modern African Studies* 32 (March 1994): 111-38.

Chenery, Hollis, Sherman Robinson, and Moshe Syrquin. *Industrialization and Growth: a Comparative Study*. New York: Oxford University, 1968.

Dillard, Dudley. *Economic Development of the North Atlantic Community: Historical Introduction to Modern Economics.* Englewood Cliffs, N.J.: Prentice Hall, 1967.

Dobb, Maurice. *Capitalism Enterprise and Social Progress*. London: Routledge, 1926.

Franko, Lawrence G. *The Threat of Japanese Multinationals–How the West Can Respond*. Chichester, U.K.: Wiley, 1983.

Gregory, Paul R. and Robert C. Stuart. *Soviet and Post-Soviet Economic Structure and Performance*. New York, 1994.

Hicks, Norman, and Paul Streeten, "Indicators of Development: The Search for a Basic Needs Yardstick." *World Development* 7 (June 1979): 572-73.

Huntington, Samuel P. *Political Order in Changing Societies*. New Haven: Yale University Press, 1968.

Ito, Takatoshi. *The Japanese Economy*. Cambridge, Mass.: MIT Press, 1992.

Kennedy, Paul. *The Rise and Fall of the Great Power: Economic Change and Military Conflict from 1500 to 2000*. New York: Random House, 1987.

Krugman, Paul. "The Myth of Asia's Miracle." *Foreign Affairs* 71 (November/December 1994): 62-78.

Kuznets's, Simon. *Economic Growth of Nations and Modern Economic Growth: Rate, Structure and Spread*. New Haven: Yale University Press, 1966.

_____. *Modern Economic Growth: Rate, Structure, and Spread*. New Haven: Yale University Press, 1966.

Lall, Sanjana. "*The East Asian Miracle:* Does the Bell Toll for Industrial Strategy?" *World Development* 22 (April 1994): 645-54.

Maddison, Angus. *Class Structure and Economic Growth: India and Pakistan Since the Moghuls*. New York: Norton 1971.

Morawwtz, David. *Twenty-five Years of Economic Development, 1950 to 1975*. Baltimore: Johns Hopkins University Press for the World Bank.

Morris-Suzuki. *The Technological Transformation of Japan: From the Seventeenth to the Twenty-First Century*. New York: Cambridge University Press, 1974.

Nafziger Wayne E. *Inequality in Africa: Political Elites, Proletariat, Peasants, and Poor*. Cambridge: Cambridge University Press, 1968.

_____. *Learning form the Japanese: Japan's Prewar Development and the Third World*. Armonk, N.Y.: M.E. Sharpe, 1955.

North, Douglas C. and Robert Paul Thomas. "An Economic Theory of the Growth of the Western World." *Economic History Review* 23 (April 1970): 1-17.

Ohkawa, Kazushi, and Gustav Ranis, eds. *Japan and the Developing Countries*. Oxford: Blackwell, 1985.

Ohno, Koichi and Hideki Imalka. "The Experience of Dual-Industrial Growth: Korea and Taiwan." *Developing Countries* 25 (December 1987): 310-23.

Olson, Mancur. *The Rise and Decline of Nations: Economic Growth, Stagflation, and Social Rigidities*. New Haven: Yale University Press, 1982.

Riskin, Carl. *China's Political Economy: The Quest for Development Since 1949*. Oxford: Oxford University Press, 1987.

Robertson, H.M. *Aspects of the Rise of Economic Individualism: Criticism of Max Weber and His School*. New York: Kelly and Millman, 1959.

Romer, Paul M. "The Origins of Endogenous Growth." *Journal of Economic Perspectives* 5 (Winter 1994): 3-22.

Samuelson, Kurt. *Religion and Economic Action: A Critique of Max Weber.* New York: Harper & Row, 1957.
Squire, Lyn. *Employment Policy in Developing Countries: A Survey of Issues and Evidence.* New York: Oxford University Press, 1981.
Tawny, R.H. *Religion and the Rise of Capitalism.* New York: Harcourt, Brace, and Co., 1926.
Taylor, Lance. *Models for Developing Countries.* New York: McGraw-Hill, 1979.
Weber Max. *The Protestant Ethic and the Spirit of Capitalism.* New York: Charles Scribner's Sons, 1930.
Wilber, Charles K., ed. *The Political Economy of Development and Underdevelopment.* New York: Random House, 1979.
World Bank. *The East Asian Miracle: Economic Growth and Public Policy.* New York: Oxford University Press, 1993.
Yanagihara, Toru. "Anything New in the Miracle Report? Yes and No." *World Development* 22 (April 1994): 663-70.
Yoshihara, Kunio. *Japanese Economic Development.* Oxford: Oxford University Press, 1994.

CHAPTER 4

ALTERNATIVE THEORIES OF ECONOMIC DEVELOPMENT

The world of economic development is extremely complicated. It includes many nations with different cultural, economic, and social backgrounds. Such complexity is further amplified by the fact that all nations are economically related to each other in one way or another. For example, the increase in oil prices by the Organization of Petroleum Exporting Countries (OPEC) in 1973, from $2.59 to $11.65 per barrel, was felt by almost everyone in the world. In the United States this resulted in an increase in oil prices and fueled inflation for years to come. As a consequence, the entire economic picture of the United States took on a new dimension. Foreign trade, investment, consumption, and government spending were all affected.

In the area of foreign trade, for example, the demand for fuel-efficient Japanese cars increased. In the meantime, demand for the U.S. manufactured automobile, the "gas guzzler," declined. This contributed to the gloomy picture of the U.S. automobile industry in the 1970s, as evidenced by the bankruptcy crisis of one of the major automobile manufacturers, Chrysler Corporation, which the U.S. government finally "bailed out." In the area of investment, the U.S. automobile manufacturers were forced to retool their industry in order to respond to the ever-increasing demand for small cars. In the area of consumption, many consumers changed their driving habits and rebudgeted their income to account for the higher fuel cost. Other industrialized nations in the world experienced similar problems in facing what was then the deepest recession since the depression of the 1930s. Oil-producing nations, however, became richer overnight and found themselves confronted with the whole range of opportunities that were setting the stage for new prosperity and the host of economic problems that could accompany it.

The decline in oil prices, starting in the early 1980s, once again changed the economic picture of the world. Some of the oil-producing nations faced one of the most serious economic crises that they have ever experienced. For example, Mexico found itself on the brink of bankruptcy, unable to pay its huge debt; Iran and Iraq, in need of additional funds to finance the Iran-Iraq war (1980-1988) were badly hurt by their shrinking oil revenues. In desperation, both countries kept cutting their oil prices in order to capture a larger portion of the market, worsening their economic conditions in the long run.

In developed nations, lower oil prices in the early 1980s allowed some nations like the United States to enjoy one of the lowest inflation rates they had ever experienced. Yet, the United States kept struggling to resolve its balance of trade deficit (an excess of imports over exports), especially with regard to Japan, which continues to capture a large percentage of the U.S. market, mainly because of its high quality products.

The global economic picture changed once again when the threat of a war in the Persian Gulf led to a surge in oil prices, adversely affecting the world economy and contributing to the U.S. recession in the early 1990s. The military defeat of Iraq, which ended the gulf crisis, led to the collapse of oil prices, thus contributing to U.S. economic recovery which gradually started to emerge from recession in March 1991.

As the previous examples indicate, an increase or decrease in the price of one commodity, such as oil, creates such an enormous chain of events that it makes the analysis of all the causal relationships virtually impossible. In this situation, one finds a mass of data that is unmanageable and meaningless without a theoretical framework. To be able to use these data and to discover an orderly relationship between different economic variables, it is necessary to develop a theory. A **theory** is an abstraction of reality and is based on certain simplifying assumptions. In our example of the rise and then decline of oil prices, rather than trying to examine all the variables involved, we may concentrate on a few of them. For instance, we may ask what happens to the quantity demanded of oil as the result of an increase or decrease in the price of oil, assuming that all other things that affect the demand for oil stay constant. Such an assumption would allow us to simplify and to abstract from the myriad data related to the impact of a change in the price of oil. In fact, every theory, whether in the biological, physical, or social sciences, uses the same approach, simplifying and making assumptions, and actually distorting reality. Such a methodology allows the development of a theory that, if it holds up under empirical testing, would provide us with the understanding of diverse empirical data. It will allow us to predict the future course of events with a reasonable degree of certainty.

In summary, we use theories to arrive at conclusions about the real world. A theory is an abstraction from reality and is based on certain simplifying assumptions. The test of the usefulness of a theory is its power to predict. We continue to use a given theory until certain events show it to be false. In this case a new theory could replace the old one.

Having realized the importance of theory we devote this chapter to a discussion of economic development theories. An understanding of these theories is significant because it enables us to comprehend scientific rationales about how and why development does or does not occur. Such a comprehension not only enables us to understand the world of economic development better, but it also provide us with a better basis for policy prescription and implementation in developing nations. However, it is important to keep in mind that these theories are abstractions from reality, and as such they provides us with a framework that may be useful in the analysis of economic development. To be useful, such a framework should be employed along with the additional information that is gathered in the real world with regard to a given problem.

THE CLASSICAL THEORY OF ECONOMIC STAGNATION

The classical economists of the late eighteenth and early nineteenth centuries assumed that technological progress was taking place at a steady rate. As long as sufficient capital was forthcoming to permit the exploitation of resources, technological change was assured. The rate of capital accumulation, in turn, depended on profits. As the population grew, however, according to the classical economists, technological progress would be incapable of overcoming the process of diminishing returns in agriculture.[*] As a result, food prices would rise. Because the cost of food is the major component of wage costs, the classical economists assumed that this would lead to higher wages in the industrial sector. The higher wages in industry would, in turn, lead to lower profits. The lower profits would lead to a decline in investment and retard technological progress. Thus, the continuous growth of population would lead to economic stagnation. At this so-called

---

[*]Assuming that technology stays constant, the addition of a variable factor of production (for example, labor) to some fixed factors of production (for example, land) may initially lead to increasing amounts of extra output per unit of the variable factor added. However, a point will be reached beyond which each additional unit of the variable factor will yield diminishing amounts of extra output. This is the point of the diminishing returns.

CH. 4/ALTERNATIVE THEORIES OF ECONOMIC DEVELOPMENT

stationary state there would exist low income for the masses and population growth would be checked by poverty.

The classical economists, however, did not generally appreciate the role that could be played by the entrepreneur in the process of technological change. The appreciation of the role of the entrepreneur was recognized by many writers who followed the classical economists. For example, Schumpeter referred to the entrepreneur as the innovator who operates in a capitalist environment of monopolistic competition. He distinguished between profits and the entrepreneur. With a banking system in place, Schumpeter explained, the entrepreneur could use people's savings to finance the introduction of technological change. The motivating force behind the entrepreneur's quest for technological innovation was still profit. These innovations allowed the entrepreneur to introduce a new idea or a new product that allowed him or her to enjoy monopolistic profit for some time.

Today the significance of the individual entrepreneur as an innovator and contributor to the process of economic development is emphasized by many economists. The work of Everett Hagen, which characterizes the individual entrepreneur as the prime mover of development for today's developing countries, will be discussed in this section.

THE MARXIST THEORY

Karl Marx is one of those influential intellectuals of the nineteenth century whose radical philosophies surfaced as reactions to capitalism. As the theorist of doom for capitalism and chief saint in the Communist hierarchy he is praised by masses of his supporters and criticized by his innumerable opponents. Because of the continuing importance of his ideas in shaping policies in the former Soviet Union, China, and other Communist nations, some knowledge of Marxist thought is essential for an understanding of economic development within a global context.

Marx was a "philosophical economist" who was profoundly influenced by the distinguished nineteenth century German philosopher, George Hegel. The cornerstone of Hegelian philosophy is the **Hegelian dialectic**, a method of logic or reasoning which maintains that any concept called a *thesis*, can have meaning only when it is compared to its opposite concept, called an *anthesis*; the interplay of the two then generates a new concept of comprehension referred to as *synthesis*. For example, the concept of "high" (thesis) induces the opposite concept of "low" (antithesis), and the two interact to shape the new concept of "height" (synthesis).

In Hegelian philosophy, the dialectic process, by its interplay of opposite forces, presents an approach of comprehending history. In this context, the evolution of cultures is market by the triumph of the higher form of culture over the lower form; in the history of religion, simplistic and primitive kinds of worship give way to more sophisticated forms and methods.

To understand the impact of Hegelian philosophy on Marx's ideas, we begin to review briefly Marx's principal theories that are presented in his tremendous work, *Das Kapital*, the first volume of which was published in 1867.

These theories form the Marxian theoretical framework, and were developed by Marx during his many years of fellowship with his intellectual associate Friedrich Engles.

The Marxian Theoretical Framework

The Marxian theoretical framework is composed of five fundamental doctrines: economic interpretation of history, theory of value and wages, surplus value and capital accumulation, the class struggle, and theory of socialistic and communistic revolution.

Economic Interpretation of History. In order to predict the future course of events, Marx believed that one must understand the causal forces that were at work. In following such a philosophy, he searched for the basic determinants of historical events, and he discovered them in economic environments in which societies flourish. In other words, Marx maintained that all great social, political, ethical, and intellectual activities of history are ascertained by the manners in which societies organize their social institutions to perform the basic economic activities of production, exchange, distribution, and consumption of commodities. Although economic incentives may not consistently be the only reason for human behavior, every critical historical development is essentially the outcome of changes in the method by which one or more of these economic activities are executed. This in effect is the *economic interpretation of history.*

Building upon the Hegelian dialectic process, Marx developed the concept of ***dialectic materialism***, that is, a logical method of historical analysis which suggests that every economic system develops to a stage of maximum efficiency and then breeds internal opposing forces that eventually leads to its own demise. At this stage, the foundations of an opposing system have already been shaped and it eventually replaces the old system. This metamorphoses continues pulling the society from one historical stage to another as each old system yields to the new one.

Theory of Value and Wages. According to Karl Marx, the value of each commodity is determined by the amount of labor embodied in its production. In his own words:

We see that which determines the magnitude of the value of any article is the amount of labour socially necessary, or labour-time socially necessary for its production.[1]

Based on Marx's definition of value, if it takes two times as much labor time to produce jackets as pants, the price of jackets should be two times greater than the price of pants. In his own words:

Commodities, therefore, in which equal quantities of labour are embodied, or which can be produced in the same time, have the same value. The value of one commodity is to the value of any other, as the labour-time necessary for the production of the one is to that necessary for the production of the other.[2]

Unlike the classical economists that preceded him, Marx did not confine his definition of labor-time only to direct labor spent on production of goods. He also included the labor-time needed to build the equipment and machineries which are in turn used to produce commodities. In other words, he considered capital as *accumulated labor* or *congealed labor*. Thus, according to Karl Marx, all commodities are made up of the common denominator of labor-time and will exchange for one another in proportion of labor-time embodied in their production. As Marx put it, "As values, all commodities are only definite masses of congealed labour-time."[3]

Having developed his theory of value, Marx adopted the classical *subsistence theory of wages* to advance his own theory of wages. In his view, in an advanced capitalist society the land-owning class has lost its prominence, leaving only the following two classes:

1. The capitalist class (entrepreneur) which controls and owns the means of production and distribution.
2. The working class (proletariat) which is subservient to the capitalist class and does not control anything.

In its quest for profit maximization, the capitalist class ends up paying the lowest possible wages, that is, subsistence wages, to the working class. At the subsistence wage, the working class is only able to meet its basic physical and biological necessities, having not much left for social needs.

CH. 4/ALTERNATIVE THEORIES OF ECONOMIC DEVELOPMENT

Theory of Surplus Value and Capital Accumulation. According to Karl Marx, in production of a commodity, the capitalist hires a worker and sets the length of the working day. Although the value of a commodity that is produced is defined by the amount of time embodied in its production, the capitalist pays only a constant subsistence wage to the worker. Because the worker does not stop producing when the value of the commodity that is created is equal to the subsistence wage, the value of the commodity that is produced is greater than the subsistence wage that the worker receives. This difference, referred to as the surplus value, is the driving force of capitalist system. In order to enhance the surplus value, the capitalist may revert to the following schemes:

- Increasing the length of the working day.
- Intensifying or speeding up the workers', output by offering "piece rates" or other impetuses.
- Allowing some workers to be released, while others continue to work harder and/or longer hours.

According to Karl Marx, the surplus value, which is the difference between the value that is created by the worker and the subsistence wage, is actually stolen from the worker. The capitalist uses part of this surplus for personal consumption, leaving the other part for acquisition of more labor and machinery. The continuous inflow of surplus over and above the expenditures, generates a sequence of capital accumulation. In this process capital is not created by the capitalist, but it is acquired by him/her through the exploitation of labor. In this manner the capitalist is a robber who steals the products of the worker's drudgery.

It is interesting to note that Marx had no personal grudge toward the capitalist, even though he referred to them as robbers. Rather, Marx viewed the competitive capitalist system itself as the source of problem. In this system, the capitalist was merely a participant in the exciting competition. As such, the capitalist either had to exploit and accumulate or be exploited and accumulated.

The Class Struggle. To elaborate on the consequences of capitalist production, Marx used the dialectic analysis and looked at the past to predict the future. He said that all history is imbued with the struggle between classes. In ancient Rome, there were struggles between plebeians and patricians and between masters and slaves. In the Middle Ages, there were conflicts between lords and serfs, and between guildmasters and journeymen. In the new society that has bloomed from the ruin of feudalism, class antagonism has diminished to the struggle between the following two classes:

1. The oppressed proletariat, or working class, who own nothing but their labor power. Because they are dependent on wages for survival, they have to sell their labor power.
2. The oppressing capitalist or bourgeois class who own the means of production and derive their income by exploiting workers.

What is the role of the state in this process? Marx's answer is that "The state is nothing but the organized collective power of the possessing class." In other words, "the state is an agency of oppression." The power of state "grows stronger in proportion as the class antagonisms with the state grows sharper." In a nutshell, the state is an instrument of repression.

According to Marx, if it were not for certain "contradictions" that automatically and continually emerge within the capitalist system, the class struggle might persist. The major factors that fuel these contradictions include:

1. **Increasing Unemployment.** The capitalists' desire to augment their surplus value and to accumulate capital leads to the use of more capital intensive technology and the displacement of workers. This process advances to growing misery as a "reserve army of unemployed" emerges.

2. **Declining Rate of Profits.** In the process of capital accumulation, the capitalist allocates an increasing portion of the capital to labor-saving machinery that yields no surplus. A decreasing proportion of it is allocated to labor and human capital which is the main source of surplus. As a result, the capitalist surplus value that is extracted from labor continues to decline. In Marx's own words:

> Moreover, the development of capitalist production makes it constantly necessary to keep increasing the amount of the capital laid out in a given industrial undertaking, and competition makes the imminent laws of capitalist production to be felt by each individual capitalist, as external coercive laws. It compels him to keep constantly extending his capital, in order to preserve it, but extend it he cannot, except by means of progressive accumulation.[4]

3. **Business Cycles.** With a declining rate of profit and a growing unemployment, and the wages kept at the subsistence level, instability and uncertainty emerge in the system. The competitive pressure leads the capitalists to continue accumulating more capital and displacing labor. As a result, depressions resume "each time more intensively."

4. **Concentration and Monopolization of Capital.** As the process of capital expansion continues, Marx explained, it gives rise to an increasing concentration of capital by fewer and fewer capitalists. In the meantime, such a concentration, by itself, calls for more capital accumulation. The process of concentration, he maintained, appears in two different shapes, which are interrelated. The first is the dissemination of large-scale production, and the second is the enlargement of enterprise via takeover and expansion. Marx explained that the organizational structure that is more appropriate to capital expansion is a joint-stock company—what today we call a corporation. At this stage the small capitalist either weakens or is taken over by a few larger ones, or as Marx put it, "one capitalist always kills many."[5]

5. **Finance Capitalism and Imperialism.** Marx implied that a final stage would follow the concentration and monopolization of capital. However, it was left to V. I. Lenin, the founder of Russian communist ideology in the early twentieth century, to elaborate on this stage. Lenin argued that concentration and monopolization of capital would lead to an economic system that is controlled by "finance capital." This is the stage in which large banks in cooperation with huge monopolies control and manipulate the masses. The expansion of these giants would necessitate their penetration into foreign markets. This is achieved by crossing national boundaries and forming multinational corporations (MNCs), which would then control the market and resources of other nations. When this happens, the economy has reached the highest and final stage of capitalism, which is called "capitalistic imperialism."

Theory of Socialist and communist Revolution. Marx believed that capitalism will eventually die and the class struggle is resolved when the bourgeoisie is ousted by the proletariat. At this stage, capitalism will be replaced by socialism, which Marx considered a *transitionary stage* preceding communism. **Socialism** will have two major features:

1. **"Dictatorship of Proletariat."** This is a stage in which the bourgeoisie has been stripped from power and is controlled by the proletarians. Capitalists' properties are under the control of the workers who also run the state. As Marx put it, this is a stage in which "expropriators have been expropriated."
2. **Payment according to work accomplished.** The wages received by workers depends on their contribution to the production process. In Marx's own words, each worker receives "for an equal quantity of labor an equal quantity of products," and "he who does not work shall not eat."

CH. 4/ALTERNATIVE THEORIES OF ECONOMIC DEVELOPMENT

Thus, socialism is a transitory stage between capitalism and communism. It is a stage in which means of production are owned by the state, and the state in turn is controlled by the proletarians, and the output is allocated according to the following motto:

"from each according to his ability to each according to his labor"

In Marxist ideology, **Communism,** that is, the final and perfect goal of historical development, is characterized by the following features:

1. A classless society in which all people live by earning and no one lives by owning.
2. The wage system is entirely eliminated and all people live according to the following motto:

    "From each according to his ability to each according to his needs."

3. The state has been dismantled and transferred to the museum of antiques "along with the bronze ax and the spinning wheel."

An Appraisal of Marxist Theory

The economic thoughts of Marx have been criticized on many grounds. Some of the major criticisms of Marx include:

1. "Holding real wages constant, he was simply incorrect in believing that on his assumption it was possible for the rate of profit to fall as a result of technical change. If capitalists act rationally (as according to Marx they do) ....The only technical changes which will be adopted will be those associated with a rising or constant rate of profit."[6]
2. In his interpretation of history, Marx put undue emphasis on economics and failed to give sufficient weight to many non-economic forces and institutions in history. This resulted in a one-sided, oversimplified interpretation of history.
3. By ascribing all values to labor, Marx neglected the entrepreneurial functions. It is the entrepreneur who takes the risks, organizes the production and advances money to workers. To be sure, in socialist and communist societies these tasks are undertaken by the government or committee of government-authorized worker-managers, but they are tasks that must be implemented.
4. Marx theorized that the workers will revolt in the industrialized West, but the revolution occurred in Russia which was one of the least developed capitalist nations in Europe. Marxists present the following reasons why Western workers have not yet overthrown capitalism:

    a. Given the threat of dissident workers in the industrialized West, the capitalists have devised a strategy of "divide and rule" that is based on exploitation of workers overseas.
    b. Churches, the news media, and educational establishments have given rise to false consciousness supporting ruling class ideologies.
    c. The capitalist state has strong legal, political, military and organizational tools to defeat potential rebellion.

GLOBAL INSIGHTS CASE 4.1

MCDONALD'S IN RUSSIA

When the world's biggest McDonald's first opened in Moscow in January 1990, it was hard to believe that a symbol of American Capitalism would ever be profitable in a former communist nation. As it turned out since McDonald's opened its doors it has been serving 35,000-45,000 customers a day. Customers were willing to wait in a three-hour line to get their favorite food from McDonald's. Some Russians even got into the business of buying sandwiches for resale at a slight profit. It was evident that McDonald's had problems in meeting such a high demand.

Historically, Russians have always been very curious about life in America and McDonald's gave them a taste of American culture. It seems ironic that McDonald's demand continued to stay strong despite the fact that inflation kept rising, with Russian salaries averaging about 10,000 rubles ($16.95) a month, failing to keep up with inflation. McDonald's experienced no significant change in its sales revenue.

Given the growing demand for its product, McDonald's decided to expand its domain of operation in Russia by opening additional restaurants at the rate of one per month. At this rate, McDonald's is expected to have 100 restaurants in Russia by the year 2000.

By the mid-1990s, the demand for McDonald's product in Russia started to weaken. The long lines began to disappear as the number of customers dwindled to a more manageable size than the 35,000-45,000 daily that once waited for 3 hours for a big Mac. It seems that inflation had finally taken its toll. Several customers found that they were no longer able to afford to "eat out". Many citizens were locked into state jobs and while inflation increased, their salaries stayed the same forcing them to cut back on their discretionary spending.

In response to this weakening demand, McDonald's marketing department had to come up with some innovative ideas for advertising in order to stimulate demand and accept the fact that probable future inflation related incidents can hardly guarantee the same sales growth rate when operating in an unstable economy like Russia.

Currently, McDonald's offers a streamlined menu. It does not include breakfast, Happy Meals, chicken or many other items that are offered in America. However the menu does cater to the Russian market. The menu includes Russian favorites such as pirogi, mushroom soup, sugary tea, Kvas (a Russian drink that is made from fermented bread), blini (thin pancakes), and of course McDonald's in Russia would not be complete without serving Russia's favorite drink: vodka. Two new products that McDonald's is planning to add to its menu are chicken sandwiches, and a fish sandwich that is made of Alaskan pollack fillet.

Given McDonald's effort in adapting its products to the Russian environment, it is expected that its sales will increase in the future. McDonald's ability to run a profitable operation in a country that does not offer much political and economic stability is indicative of its ability to adapt to the environment of the country in which it operates. Having proved to be profitable in Moscow, McDonald's future plans include expansion into the rest of Russia and other former Soviet Republics.

Sources: Gribanov, Valeri., "Fast Food St. Petersburg Style," *Kommersant-Food* 11 April 1997, p.2;"Five McDonald's Outlets To Be Built In Nizhny Novgood," *Finansovye Izvestia* September, 1996, p 2; Plotnikova, Tatyana. "McDonald's Picks Out An Advertiser In Russia," *Kommersant* 4 March 1997, p.10; RICA News Agency. "American Investments Into Russian Economy," *Rica Biznes Yezhenedelnik* 24 January 1994; Vardanyan, Raznik. "The Impact of Economic Reform On International Migration," *Sotsis*, 20 October 1995, p58-67.

CH. 4/ALTERNATIVE THEORIES OF ECONOMIC DEVELOPMENT

5. Marx did not foresee that the interest of workers and capitalists might overlap. The workers in the West may have helped capitalism because they benefitted more in the long run by earning a comparatively constant portion of a fast growing output than by aspiring to obtain a big portion of what might have been more slowly growing output under an alternative system.
6. With regard to large corporations specifically, an economic historian writes "Marx failed to recognize, however, that the large corporations, while facilitating the concentration of control, have at the same time been instrumental in diffusing property among many capitalists."[7] In fact, evidence shows that countries such as Taiwan and South Korea have experienced a healthy economic growth and a more equitable income distribution while they have been highly dependent on the United States and other capitalist countries for their trade and investment.[*]

In spite of the above criticisms, Marx injected certain notions into the theory of economic development that have contributed to our understanding of the development mechanism. His major contributions to the subject of economic development include the following:

1. Almost every writer on the subject of economic development, since Marx, has subscribed to the notion that technological progress is the source of economic growth, and that innovation is the major task of the entrepreneur. By the same token, investment decisions and capital accumulations are the center of most growth theories. In all theories, decisions are correlated with the rate of return on capital.
2. Another main contribution of Marx to the economic development literature is the idea that economic growth under capitalism is destabilizing. More specifically, Marx demonstrated that stable growth demands preservation of an appropriate balance between investment and consumption, and hence between savings and investment. He also pointed to the relationship between the savings-investment and the distribution of income. This notion has become an integral part of trade theory ever since.
3. Marx elaborated on the fragility of the bridge to steady economic growth, which could be marked either by too high or too low ratio of wages to output, and hence could impede investment and lead to depression. This character of the boom has remained a recognized feature of any complete analysis of cycles and trends. Marx also made unemployment and employment a major part of the system.

Thus, Marx contributed to the literature in the area of economic development by elaborating on the major building blocks that shape a theory of growth, even if Marx's own structure disintegrated because some of its columns were defective.

The Marxist theory provides us with some clues to the economic history of the third world nations. It proposes that one should look at the power structure between social classes to discover potential impediments to economic growth. It tells us that we need to look at the roots of colonial policies in the economic environments of the home countries, rather than the economic condition of colonies by themselves. It also suggests that underdevelopment in the former colonies might be partially related to these policies.

The Marxist theory has attracted the attention of many political groups as a rationale for opposing MNCs. Consequently, some countries, such as Cuba, have gone so far as to break their economic ties with the capitalist economies of the West. Evidence shows, however, that as the result of their actions these same countries have suffered from stagnation by reducing or severing their economic relations with the West.

In today's world, pragmatism has undermined the philosophical ideologies of the Marxist sympathizers. This is evident by the collapse of the Soviet Union and the Eastern European countries. It is also apparent by a significant shift in the People's Republic of China's economic policies following the demise of Mao

---

[*]Both Taiwan and South Korea have experienced a real per capita income growth of over 6 percent per year during the 1960s and 1970s.

Tse-tung in 1976. Since then the Chinese have reversed their policies with regard to foreign direct investment (FDI), openly inviting Western entrepreneurs to invest in their country.

We close this section by stating that although we must be wary of the pitfalls in the Marxist system, for all its errors, the Marxist theory of economic development has much to contribute to an understanding of development or lack of it.

DEPENDENCY THEORY

Dependency theory was developed by an influential group of writers sympathetic to Karl Marx. This theory attributes the sluggishness of economic growth and development in developing nations to their dependent relationships with advanced countries. The dependency literature is based primarily on Latin American experience and has been recognized as a method of study only since the mid-1960s.

A major contributor to dependency theory, Andre Gunder Frank, challenges the idea that developing countries resemble the now-advanced countries in their earlier stages. He criticizes the scholars who view the modernization of developing countries as simply the adoption of advanced countries' economic and political structures. He considers underdevelopment the outcome of modern capitalism permeating the antiquated economic systems of the third world. He perceives the upsetting of African communities by slave trade and resulting colonialism, the deindustrialization of India under British colonialism, and the total eradication of Incan and Aztec civilizations by Spanish conquistadors as cases of origination of underdevelopment.

According to Frank, Latin American countries and other developing nations have been assimilated into the global economy since the initial phases of their colonial periods. Such assimilation has transformed these nations into essentially capitalist economies. The integration of these presumably capitalist economies into the global economy is inevitably accomplished through an endless metropolis-satellite chain, in which surplus created by each satellite (developing nation) is absorbed by the metropolis (advanced) nations.

Frank writes:

> It is this satellite status that generates underdevelopment, then a weaker or lesser degree of metropolis-satellite relations may generate structural underemployment and/or allow for more possibility of local development.[8]

Given this scenario, according to Frank's analysis, the only options available are to break with the metropolis-satellite network entirely, through socialist revolution, or to stay "underdeveloped" within this network.

Frank's ideas are echoed by Paul Baran, considered the father of dependency theory by some scholars, who writes:

> What is decisive is that economic development in underdeveloped countries is profoundly inimical to the dominant interests in advanced countries.[9]

To evade such development, advanced countries form coalitions with precapitalist native elites who will be unfavorably influenced by the metamorphosis brought about by capitalist development. The aim of these coalitions is to suppress the metamorphic process. Such an alliance allows advanced countries easy conditions, the prospect of economic growth in dependent nations would be unduly restricted. The surplus created by developing countries would be expropriated to a large extent by foreign capital and otherwise wasted on luxury consumption by traditional elites. Additionally, because capital goods would have to be purchased abroad, resources that could be set aside for investment significantly decline. This mechanism would essentially lead to economic stagnation, and the only solution would be political (that is, a socialist

GLOBAL INSIGHTS CASE 4.2

INVESTMENT CLIMATE IN POLAND

Following the drastic reforms launched in January 1990, Poland gradually turned into the fastest-growing economy in Europe. To survive, Polish authorities restructured their organization. New accounting rules emerged that helped improve management quality, and Polish workers began to realize that foreign direct investment (FDI) could bring with it the new technology that they needed to strengthen their economic development process.

Today, Polish workers no longer consider foreign capital as a tool of imperialism or an instrument of capitalism to exploit their resources. They now believe that foreign direct investment plays an important role in the modernization of the Polish economy and can rationalize the economic activity in accordance with the market mechanism. Today, Poland's major objectives are to become an industrial free trade system, to harmonize legislation, and to develop economic cooperation that supports its goal of becoming a member of the European Union (EU).

Two actions that are indicative of Poland's openness to FDI are the Foreign Investment Act of 1991, and its accession to the OECD. The Foreign Investment Act of 1991 provides the basis for opening the Polish economy to FDI. Poland's accession to the OECD in mid 1996 has accelerated procedural changes that should help enhance foreign investment. This includes equal treatment of foreign and domestic investors, thus making it more efficient to purchase land, and easing restrictions on capital flows.

Although Poland has welcomed FDI in many business sectors, the road to FDI in Poland has not been a smooth one. Currently, foreign investors face potential discrimination in public procurement contracts. Poland's public procurement law allows for a 20 percent price advantage for domestic firms, and there is a 50 percent domestic material and labor content minimum for all bids. In some cases, the Polish authorities have reverted to protectionism to preserve its national sovereignty. This has resulted in the control of some business sectors by the government. These sectors include telecommunications, mining, steel, defense, transportation, energy, and banking. One of the countries that has been a major beneficiary of Poland's privatization efforts is the United States. In 1995, the U.S. was the top foreign investor in Poland, accounting for 25 percent of the total foreign investment. The top 20 U.S. investors include: Polish American Enterprise Fund, International Paper Corp, Philip Morris, Proctor and Gamble, Curtis, Epstein, D.Chase Enterprises, Schooner Capital, Ford Motor, Goodyear Tires, Mars, McDonald's, Ameritech, RJ Reynolds, Airtouch, Liquid Carbonic, Citibank, General Motors, and Gerber.

Currently, trade regulations and standards of doing business in Poland have become a concern for the U.S. Tariff rates are subject to frequent change as Poland moves toward becoming a market economy. Customs duties apply to all products imported into Poland ranging from 0 to 90 percent with the average between 8 and 12 percent. In 1992, Poland signed the European Community Association Agreement with the EU which lowered or eliminated tariffs on many EU produced goods imported into Poland, while tariffs on U.S. products remained the same. This has put the United States in a disadvantageous position relative to the EU, in trading with Poland.

Sources: "Poland Emerges As The Test Case For EU Expansion," *The Wall Street Journal* 30 Oct. 1996, B9A; Graham Field, "A Guide to Poland," *Euromoney* (September 1996): 248; Gene Koretz, "Paths Toward A Free Market," *Business Week*, (January 1997): 27; "Polish Program of Privatization Shows Progress," *Wall Street Journal*, 8 July 1996; "Poland Allows Foreign Buyers For Some Banks," *Wall Street Journal*, 1 July 1996, B7F; "Booming Economy In Poland Brings Jobs, Wealth, and Apathy," *Wall Street Journal* 25 November 1996, A1; "For Polish Firms, Mass Privatization Moves Glacially," *Wall Street Journal*, 6 January 1997, A7C; *National Trade Data Bank*.

revolution). This is because, according to Frank, within the framework of capitalism there would be no alternative to underdevelopment.[10]

Criticism of Dependency Theory

The dependency theory has been subject to many criticisms, on both theoretical and empirical grounds. Most economic historians concede that economic dependency under foreign control and domination proved to be very costly for colonies. Under colonial power, production was guided toward foreign rather than indigenous requirements. Economic practices restrained regional industrial endeavors, leading to unbalanced national and regional economic development. This condition led to the rise of an elite that was oriented to foreign interests. Nevertheless, these sufferings were partially counterbalanced by the growth of roads, schools, railroads, and administrative services under colonial rule.

It is unjust to compare the experiences of countries under colonialism to what might have occurred in the absence of foreign rule. For example, Afghanistan, Ethiopia, and Thailand, which were not colonized although they were influenced by advanced countries, are severely underdeveloped. Additionally, the theory does not present a verifiable and independent explanation of the mechanism causing underdevelopment. Rather, dependence is defined in a circular fashion by saying the developing countries are underdeveloped because they are dependent. It is argued that the attributes usually ascribed to underdevelopment in dependent nations are not limited to these nations. Such attributes are also found in "nondependent" economies. Consequently, they are characteristics of capitalist development in general and not of dependent capitalism exclusively.

Today, most advanced nations are also dependent on foreign economies. Belgium and Canada are more dependent on foreign investment than India or Pakistan. However, according to dependency theory, they are not regarded as dependent nations. Thus, instead of dividing the world into dependent and independent nations, it seems more rational to consider a spectrum of dependence from the weakest developing country to the strongest capitalist nation.

In spite of the aforementioned criticism, dependency theory should not be totally dismissed. Developing countries have been subject to exploitation on a number of occasions. For example, economic growth in Indonesia was not very beneficial to the indigenous people during the Dutch colonial period. As another example, economic growth in Mexico under foreign domination during the Porfirio Diaz rule (1876-1911) led to a decrease in living standards for the rural masses and fueled the revolution which began in 1910. Finally, there are several examples of nations that could have developed faster with less dependence on foreign countries. Bangladesh, Guatemala, Honduras, Pakistan, Zaire, and the Philippines were likely hindered by unreasonable economic dependence on advanced nations. The solution to these problems, however, is not necessarily detachment from the capitalist economic system, but the pursuit of more sensible policies when interacting with capitalist nations. Economic aid, trade, capital flows, and technology transfers from advanced countries must be conducted in a manner that directs investment to priority industries. Promoting domestic firms, deterring foreign monopoly power, evading significant technological dependence on foreigners, and avoiding excessive foreign investment should all be part of sensible policies. Also, as we study in Chapter 14, there are other policies that a country can employ when dealing with multinational corporations, allowing that country to enjoy the benefits of foreign investment without yielding to total control and ownership.

ROSTOW'S STAGES OF ECONOMIC GROWTH

W. W. Rostow, a prominent economist, presented his analysis as an alternative to Marx's theory of economic history. In his famous book, *The Stages of Economic Growth,* published in 1961, he describes his theory as "non-communist manifesto." Rostow positions his five stages of growth against Marx's five stages of feudalism, bourgeoisie, capitalism, socialism, and communism. In analyzing the process of economic development, he studies the history of economic growth in industrialized nations. His study shows that, based on the experience of the advanced nations, growth can be divided into the five following stages:[11]

1. **The Traditional Stage.** A predominantly agricultural society that is based on "pre-Newtonian science and technology." The level of productivity is limited by the unavailability of modern science and technology.
2. **The Preconditions for Takeoff.** A transitional stage that is marked by the following characteristics:
    a. A significant change in the agricultural sector in order to feed the growing urban population.
    b. An increase in transportation investment to facilitate the emergence of larger markets and enhance production and specialization.
    c. An increase in imports, including capital, funded conceivably by exportation of some natural resources.
3. **The Takeoff.** During this stage, resistance to growth is subdued and factors contributing to economic growth expand. This stage requires that the following conditions be met:
    a. The rate of productive investment rises, say from 5 percent or less to 10 percent of national income (or net national product).
    b. One or more substantial manufacturing sectors develop.
    c. The existence or rapid inception of social, political, and institutional structure that utilizes stimulus to growth in the modern sector and capitalizes on the potential external economy impacts of the takeoff, allowing growth to become a continuous process.
4. **The Drive to Maturity.** During this stage, an era of about 60 years after the inception of takeoff, modern technology expands to include the whole range of economic activities. This is a period of regular and sustained economic growth that is characterized by the following characteristics:
    a. Industry comes to use more complex technologies.
    b. An urbanized labor force that is highly skilled, less individualistic, more bureaucratic, and exemplifies a growing dependence on the state for the provision of economic safety.
    c. The application of these complex technologies to a wide range of resources allows the production of anything that the society desires, given the market conditions and any constraints on resources.
5. **The Age of Mass Consumption.** The leading sectors of the economy shift toward durable consumer goods and services. During this stage, the percentage of the population in urban areas increases, and the percentage of the population employed in offices and in skilled factory jobs soars. As a result, the composition of the working class changes, and the real income per capita increases, enabling the population to attain a higher standard of living, as marked by automobiles, suburbanization, countless durable consumer goods and gadgets. The United States reached this stage in the 1920s and Western Europe in the 1950s.

The theories of both Marx and Rostow attempt to analyze the evolution of whole societies, primarily from an economic angle. Both theories recognize that economic changes have social and cultural ramifications.

Rostow's stage theory has been subject to the following criticisms:

1. The stages are arbitrarily established and hence it is not possible to clearly distinguish one stage from another.

2. It is not necessary for a nation to go through all these stages of development. For example, history shows that England, Germany, and Sweden did not go through the takeoff stage. Rather, these countries experienced a steady growth that extended over a long period of time.
3. Because the stages are not defined precisely, they are difficult to test empirically.
4. Unlike Marx's dialectic materialism, Rostow's method does not indicate how the features and process of one stage move a society to the next stage.
5. Rostow assumes that the development of developing nations follows the same pattern as developed nations. The fact is that developing nations are not traditional economies as developed nations were, as Rostow implies. Today's developing nations are influenced by and controlled by the developed nations. Additionally, each developing nation has its own highly individual history.

In general, "stage making" approaches are misleading because they rely on a linear interpretation of history and connote that all economies have to pass through the same series of stage. In spite of these criticisms, Rostow's theory has gained some popularity because it seems to provide some simple answers to the questions that are raised regarding economic development. Rostow's theory emphasizes the significance of savings, investment, and technology in the process of economic development. It also teaches us that economic development is a time-consuming process that demands certain changes occur before a country can depart from the traditional stage and realize some degree of economic growth.

HAGEN'S STAGES OF ECONOMIC INDUSTRIALIZATION

Everett Hagen's stages of economic industrialization are similar to Rostow's stages in the sense of being based on historical observations. However, unlike Rostow's stages, which are based on data from the advanced countries of the West, Hagen's stages are formed from his observations of Japan and the developing countries in Latin America.[12]

Hagen's stages of economic industrialization describe how an industrialized system is likely to be developed by domestic entrepreneurs who are equipped with the knowledge of technologies that are employed in other nations. He divides the process of industrialization into the following six stages:

1. **The Emergence of the Self-Contained Factory Processes**. This is a stage during which some of the entrepreneurs who are engaged in small manufacturing shops feel secure enough in their ventures to contemplate a change. This change is achieved by the adoption of simple machinery and techniques that are used abroad in the production of familiar goods, such as footwear, matches, rice, soaps, sugar, textiles, and wheat flour. These are goods that have already been produced indigenously by traditional methods and are well known to the home country residents. The new method of production introduced in this stage is a "straight line, self-contained" process that does not require a large number of suppliers and components from other sectors. In this stage, workers are organized into teams, foremanship is developed, and there is an increase in the delegation of authority.
2. **The Development of Initial Interrelationships**. Further advances in technology that occur during this stage lead to the use of more capital-intensive methods of production. Growth in the volume of production allows for the specialization of production in some products, such as paper specially produced for packing, bottles made to contain beer, and coal mined for steam engines. "Forward" linkages also occur; that is, some plants that are producing a given product extend their operations to include further processing of that product. For example, sugar refineries engage in the production of alcohol and sugar syrup as well. The expansion of industrial activities leads to the local production of simple tools and machinery that were formerly imported.

3. **The Expansion of Light Engineering.** In this stage, light engineering begins to expand at a faster rate than industry in general. Consequently, products that do not require too exact specifications are produced domestically. Examples of such products include refrigerators, bicycles, and commercial air-conditioning systems.
4. **The Improving Control of Quality and Industrial Tolerances.** In this phase, the country is capable of employing more complicated technologies than the technologies that were used in the previous stages. This allows advancements in metallurgy and chemicals. There is improved quality control and the size tolerances in the metal-working industries become more exact. This stage can be marked by an increase in management's ability to manage more complex industrial establishments.
5. **The Elaboration of the Industrial Complex.** In this stage further advances in technical capability ultimately lead to heavy metal working processes, and an advanced electronics industry may develop.
6. **The Stage of Industrial Complexity.** In this stage, there is a continuous increase in specialization. The supply interrelationships increase to the extent that no productive establishment can operate independently. Thus, these establishments become part of a productive complex that can produce any product within some area of specialization.

The stages of economic industrialization show that economic development is a timely process that involves a progressive evolution of the industrial structure. One implication is that a technology that is used in an advanced country may not be appropriate for a developing country that is in a given stage of economic development. This raises the issue of "appropriate technology" that we will discuss later in Chapter 8. Another implication of Hagen's stages is that the foreign firms play a significant role in supplying technology to developing countries. According to Hagen, those firms do not play a role in the process of economic development until a developing country has reached stage four of its economic industrialization.

THE VICIOUS CIRCLE OF POVERTY

The vicious circle of poverty is a well known theory which is based on the notion that a lack of capital is the major impediment to growth and economic development. In other words, this theory relates economic stagnation to very low levels of per capita output. The theory was developed during the early 1950s, when many developing nations were suffering from low per capita income. However, following that period, many third world nations reached higher per capita GNPs and experienced improvements in other socioeconomic indicators. As a result, there is nothing in this model to show why growth and development occur.

The model is depicted in Figure 4.1, indicating that there are in fact two circles, one portraying the supply conditions and the other the demand forces.

On the supply side, the low income generates a limited capacity to save, and this in turn, leads to meager investment, generating insufficient capital. Lack of capital indicates that productivity is low, leading to low income and hence closing the circle. On the demand side, low income leads to limited purchasing power, and hence inadequate impetus to investment. As a result, a limited capital will be used in production, leading to low productivity and generating low income. This completes the circle.

Figure 4.1

THE VICIOUS CIRCLES OF POVERTY

The model indicates that there are in fact two circles, one portraying the supply conditions and the other the demand forces.

On the supply side, the low income generates a limited capacity to save, and this in turn, leads to meager investment, generating insufficient capital. Lack of capital indicates that productivity is low, leading to low income and hence closing the circle. On the demand side, low income leads to limited purchasing power, and hence inadequate impetus to investment. As a result, a limited capital will be used in production, leading to low productivity and generating low income. This completes the circle.

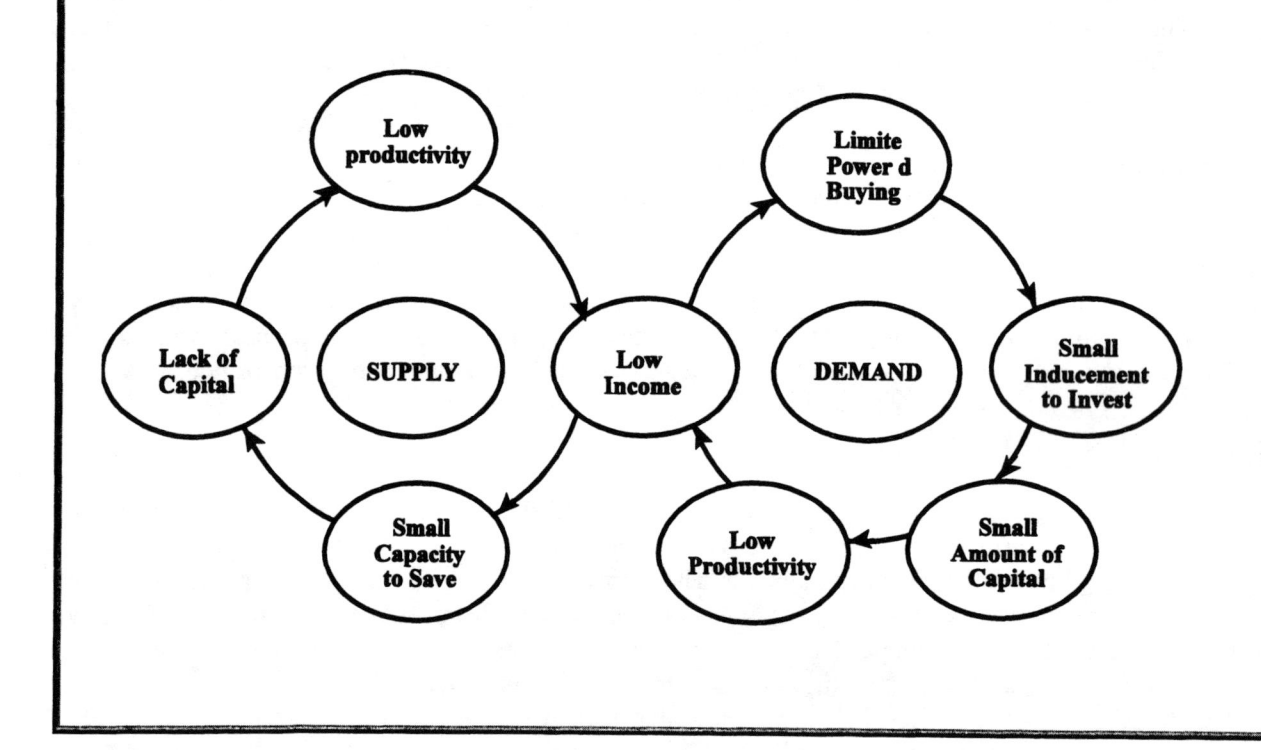

Criticisms of Vicious Circle of Poverty

The model is subject to the following two criticisms:

1. The model misconstrues levels of savings with rates of savings. It assumes that the source of the problem on the demand side is the low level of absolute savings in developing nations. What really matters is the rate of savings. Absolute levels of per capita savings in developing nations will be limited for many years even after savings rates start to increase. Nevertheless, the increase in savings rates, assuming that all other things stay constant, will lead to economic growth. The low rates of savings should not be ascribed to poverty, that is, a low level of income. Rather, it stems from social,

CH. 4/ALTERNATIVE THEORIES OF ECONOMIC DEVELOPMENT

political and other institutional factors. In many poor developing nations, the poorest people manage to a set aside a certain amount of their income for religious purposes, or for the acquisition of opium, cocoa leaves, alcoholic beverages, or other substances. Thus, it is evident that the poor have some capacity to save. What seems to be the source of the problem is the lack of incentives to save. If the social structure does not provide the poor with a reasonable chance for economic progress, then savings may not be directed to productive investment. For instance, a peasant may not be induced to save if the land belongs to the landlord and the farmer knows that with improved technology the rent increases or the landlord's share of the harvest rises. Even if the farmer owned the land, the higher output might lead to lower prices, and with an inelastic demand for agricultural products, his/her total revenue would decrease. In this situation, spending money for personal pleasure is a rational behavior. Thus, what seems to be needed is a social structure that is conducive to mobilization of these potential savings.

Although the poor people comprise the bulk of the population in developing nations, the 5 percent of the upper income class families who are relatively wealthy, receive about 15 to 35 percent of the national income, that is, an amount per head 8 to 20 times larger than that of the poorest 10 percent of the people. Thus, rich people in developing nations have great savings potential.[13] However, part of their income might be sent to rich countries in search of a higher return or a safer investment environment in those nations. The other parts may be spent on conspicuous consumption such as large buildings, elegant sport stadiums, or luxurious religious institutions. If this wealthy class could diminish its consumption, the national saving rates could rise, contributing to the rate of growth of income.

2. The model does not make any provision for savings in terms of foreign direct investment, foreign aid, and public or private lending. As the experience of some developing nations indicates, such savings could boost investment, generating economic growth.

In spite of these criticisms, it is evident that the majority of people who live in developing nations have difficulty in saving. Given the rapid population growth in these nations, a relatively high rate of savings is needed to merely hold per capita income at a steady level. This calls on government authorities to design policies that lure potential savings, both within their boundaries and from abroad, to productive investment.

THE BIG-PUSH THESIS

The origin of the big-push thesis can be traced back to an article by Paul Rosenstein-Rodan, published in 1943.[14] Rosenstein-Rodan considered industrialization as the major method for bringing about more equal distribution of income between various parts of the world, by enhancing incomes in depressed parts at a higher rate than in affluent parts. Rosenstein-Rodan defined industrialization as the increase in capital-labor ratio, both in agricultural and nonagricultural sectors. Thus, he assigned a major role to capital in the process of economic growth and development. In this process, he considered capital as the core of economic growth and development.

According to Paul Rosenstein-Rodan, the factors that contribute to economic growth do not rise smoothly, but they are subject to sizeable jumps or **indivisibilities.** These indivisibilities stem from flaws generated in the investment market by external economies. **External economies** refers to conditions that lead to decreases in a firm's long-run average costs. These conditions that are totally outside of the firm as a producing unit, depend on adjustment of the industry. They are related to the firm only to the extent that the firm is part of the industry. For example, the development of an industry in an area may lead to external economies that stem from the improvement in public transportation and marketing facilities. This leads to benefits for every individual firm in the industry. Another example of external economy is the creation of a public technical school in response to enhanced demand for a large number of people with technical expertise. This decreases a firm's on-the-job-training costs.

Rosenstein-Rodan argued that a big push was required because the twentieth century's firms were larger and more capital-using than those in the nineteenth century. Thus, larger amounts were ventured by entrepreneurs who had to trigger a significant amount of savings in a condition where formal capital markets might not even exist. Extensive markets for their output had to be created, to assure a satisfactory rate of return. Social overhead capital also had to be furnished on a larger scale.

On the demand side, the demand for industrial products is limited by the relatively small number of buyers whose incomes are in cash. To illustrate this point, suppose a new shoe factory were created in a sluggish economy, composed of numerous subsistence farm workers whose marginal productivity is zero, that is, they add nothing to the total output. In this condition, the demand for shoes would be limited to the small number of formerly unemployed workers now paid cash wages by the new factory. With such an insignificant demand the shoe factory could not survive. This is the case for any factory that produces other products. However, if a large number of factories, each making a different good, could be created at the same time, the total product demand generated would be sufficient enough to make all of them viable.

In summary, the big-push thesis states that massive activity is fundamental to defeat the sluggishness that is deep-seated in the stagnant economy of a developing nation. This situation resembles a wagon that is stuck in the mud and will not move with a gradually accelerating push; What is needed is a big push. Thus, according to the advocates of the big-push theory, the strategy of gradualism is destined to collapse.

Criticisms of the Big-Push Thesis

The big-push thesis has been subject to the following criticisms:

1. Most developing nations have sufficient high-and moderate income recipients to foster small but technically productive industrial firms.
2. The income of people demanding industrial goods in developing nations is not always stagnant. It can be expected to rise due to enhanced agricultural or mineral exports, tourism, or remittances by immigrants. As a result, demand for industrial output can rise gradually and induce new firms to begin operation without reliance on a big push.
3. The big-push thesis ignores the possibility that developing nations can also take advantage of foreign markets.
4. All social overhead capital is not necessarily highly indivisible. For example, electric power can be generated with small generators at first, followed by a massive hydroelectric project later.
5. The big-push thesis ignores the conditions that are conducive to investment. High up on the list are the existence of honest and stable governments, the absence of inflation, development of general and technical education, and improvements in agriculture.

THE BALANCED VERSUS UNBALANCED GROWTH

Between the 1940s and 1960s, a major debate that developed among economists was the theory of balanced growth versus the theory of unbalanced growth. The purpose of this section is to define these theories and discuss their shortcomings.

Balanced Growth

Balanced growth calls for simultaneous application of capital to a wide range of various industries. This

CH. 4/ALTERNATIVE THEORIES OF ECONOMIC DEVELOPMENT

theory was proposed by Rangar Nurkse who in his version of minimum effort theory advocated "a frontal attack...a wave of capital investment in a number of different industries," to achieve economic development.

Nurkse's basic argument is a mixture of the vicious circle of poverty and Rosenstein-Rodan's thesis. In fact, he cites Rodan's example of the shoe factory to support his view. According to Nurkse, low real income "is a reflection of low productivity, which in turn, is largely due to a lack of capital. The lack of capital is a result of small capacity to save, so the circle is complete." The inducement to invest, in turn, is limited by the size of the market. But the crucial determinant of the size of the market is productivity. Productivity "depends largely, though by no means entirely, on the degree to which capital is used in production... But, for any individual entrepreneur, the use of capital is inhibited, to start with, by the small size of the market." Another vicious circle.

How can we break this circle? According to Nurkse the only way out is "more or less synchronized application of capital to a wide range of different industries. Here is an escape from the deadlock; here the result is an over-all enlargement of market...Most industries catering for mass consumption are complementary in the sense that they provide a market for, and thus support, each other... the case for 'balanced growth' rests on the need for a 'balanced diet.'"

Criticisms of Balanced Growth. According to Hans Singer, a development economist, the balanced growth doctrine suffers from the following two major problems:

1. The doctrine is inadequate in handling the real problem of the developing nations, that is, the shortage of resources. "Think Big" is a good recommendation to the developing nations, but "Act Big" is bad advice if it induces them to do more than their existing resources allow.
2. The doctrine presumes that developing nations start from scratch. In fact, every developing nation begins from a condition that reflects early investment decisions and past development. Thus, at any given time there exists highly beneficial investment undertakings which are not balanced investment proposals by themselves. Rather, they embody unbalanced investment to complement current imbalance. When such an investment incurs, a new imbalance is likely to emerge which will necessitate yet another "balancing" investment, and so on.

Unbalanced Growth

This theory was developed by Albert O. Hirschman, who contends that *deliberate unbalancing* of the economy, according to a pre-formulated strategy, is the best approach for accomplishing economic growth.[15] He agrees with Nurkse's big-push thesis, but unlike Nurkse who calls for simultaneous expansion of all industrial sectors, Hirschman recommends undertaking a big push in strategically selected industries or sectors. To defend his position, he points out that today's advanced nations, did not get where they are through "balanced" growth. In these nations development has proceeded "with growth being communicated from the leading sectors of the economy to the followers, from one industry to another, from one firm to another."[16] Thus, he emphasizes that we should not take the "defeatist view that growth has to be balanced from the start or can not take place at all."

Hirschman points out that one of the shortcomings of traditional economic theory is the assumption that the profitability of different investment projects are independent. However, this does not to have to be the case. For example, suppose the interest rate stands at 8 percent and there are two investment projects, A and S, requiring equal amounts of capital. Project A involves investment in an auto manufacturing plant and yields a 10 percent rate of return. Project S is related to a steel manufacturing plant, yielding an 8 percent rate of return. If it was left to the market, only investment in auto manufacturing would be launched. When the auto manufacturing plant is in operation, demand for steel rises. As a result, the rate of return in steel manufacturing rises to, say 10 percent, and hence it will be undertaken.

Suppose, however, that the creation of a steel manufacturing plant would increase the rate of return in auto manufacturing from 10 percent to 14 percent. Society as a whole would be better off investing in the steel manufacturing plant first, and the auto manufacturing plant second, rather than making an independent decision on the market's rate of return. Thus, economic planners must consider the interdependence of different investment projects in order to maximize the overall social profitability. In other words, they should concentrate on investments that generate the greatest amount of new investments. To achieve this goal they should choose industries that portray the greatest linkages, encompassing **forward linkages** to enterprises that purchase output from the industry and **backward linkages** to firms that sell inputs to the industry. For example, according to Hirschman, the steel industry which has forward linkages to auto and construction industries, and backward linkages to iron and coal production, is a good example of an investment with great potential.

Criticisms of Unbalanced Growth. Unbalanced growth doctrine is subject to the following criticisms:

1. The failure to emphasize the significance of agricultural investment. According to Hirschman, agriculture does not induce linkage formation as directly as other industries. But, research indicates that agriculture has significant linkages to other sectors of the economy. Additionally, agricultural growth makes a crucial contribution to the nonagricultural sectors through growing food supplies, labor supply, capital transfer, larger markets, and additional foreign exchange.[17]
2. For nations launching development, unbalance is unavoidable. All investments in developing nations generate unbalanced growth due to rigidities and the sluggishness of responses of both demand and supply and because of mistakes. Thus, governments and economic development planners do not need the advice of theoreticians in following an unbalanced growth path.
3. The theory focuses on inducements to expansion and tends to ignore or minimize reaction generated by imbalances. Shortages generate vested interests; they lead to monopoly profits. Thus, people might lose money from bad investment or get frightened by the growth of competition.

In spite of these criticisms, Hirschman's thought of forward and backward linkages seems to be enticing and useful. It points out the formerly neglected effects of one investment on the investment at the beginning and the subsequent stages of production.

THE LEWIS THEORY OF DEVELOPMENT

In the mid-1950s, Sir W. Arthur Lewis, an economist, developed a well-known theory of economic development to explain how economic growth takes place in labor-abundant third world nations. The theory was later modified, and extended by John FDI and Gustav Ranis. Their efforts gave rise to the **Lewis two-sector model** which served as the general theory of development process in labor-abundant developing nations during the 1960s and early 1970s. Today, this theory still has many followers, especially among American scholars of economic development.

The Lewis model considers a developing economy that is composed of the following two-sectors:

1. **The Traditional Sector**, that is, an overpopulated agricultural sector that is marked by a zero marginal product of labor. Lewis describes this condition as **surplus labor** to signify the fact that the withdrawal of workers from the agricultural sector can be accomplished without any loss of output.
2. **The Modern Sector,** that is, a high-productivity urban industrial sector that absorbs the workers that

CH. 4/ALTERNATIVE THEORIES OF ECONOMIC DEVELOPMENT

are transferred from the traditional sector.

Given the above two sectors, the model is set up to explain the mechanism of labor transfer and the growth of output and employment in the modern sector. The model is based on the following assumptions:

1. Both the labor transfer and the modern sector employment are caused by output expansion in the modern sector.
2. The speed of the output expansion, in turn, depends on the rate of industrial investments and capital accumulation.
3. Industrial investments stem from the profits over wages, assuming that capitalists reinvest all of their profits.
4. The level of wages in the modern sector is constant and is determined by a premium over the fixed subsistence level of wages in the traditional sector. More specifically, Lewis assumed that the level of wages in the modern sector would have to be at least 30% higher than the level of wages in the traditional sector to entice workers to leave their homes.

We can illustrate the Lewis model by using Figure 4.2. W_T in the lower diagram portrays the average level of subsistence income in the traditional sector, and W_M represents the real wage in the modern sector. At this wage, the supply of labor in the traditional sector is assumed to be unlimited and hence perfectly elastic, as shown by the horizontal portion of S_L curve. At this point, Lewis assumes that at modern wage W_M above traditional average income W_T, the modern sector's entrepreneurs can employ as many workers as they want without worrying about increasing wages. Given a constant stock of capital K_0, shown in the upper part of the diagram, in the initial stage of modern sector growth, the demand curve for labor is determined by labor's diminishing marginal product and is illustrated by the negatively sloped MPP_{L0} curve in the lower diagram.

In pursuit of profit maximization, modern-sector entrepreneurs are assumed to employ workers up to the point where their marginal physical product of labor is equal to the real wage rate. This is shown by point P_0 in the lower diagram, where the labor demand and supply curves intersect. Total modern- sector output Q_0 would be given by point A_0 in the upper diagram and the area $OD_0P_0L_0$ in the lower diagram. The share of this total output received by the workers in the form of wages would be equal, therefore, to the area of the rectangle $OW_MP_0L_0$. The balance of the output, area $W_MD_0P_0$, would be the total profit that is collected by the entrepreneur. Lewis assumes that all of these profits are reinvested by the entrepreneur, causing the total capital stock in the modern sector to rise from K_0 to K_1. This larger capital stock causes the output in the modern sector to increase to Q_1, which in turn leads to an increase in the marginal physical product of labor to a new level, as shown by the outward shift of the labor demand from MPP_{L0} to MPP_{L1}. As a result, a new modern-sector equilibrium employment level will be established at point P_1 with L_1 workers are now hired. Total modern-sector output, Q_1 would be given by point A_1 in the upper diagram and the area $OD_1P_1L_1$ in the lower diagram. The share of this total output received by the workers in the form of wages would be equal, therefore, to the area of the rectangle $OW_MP_1L_1$. The balance of the output, area $W_MD_1P_1$ would be the total profit that is collected by the entrepreneur. Once again, these higher profits of $W_MD_1P_1$ are reinvested, increasing the total capital stock to K_2. This larger capital stock causes the output in the modern sector to increase to Q_2, which in turn leads to an increase in the marginal physical product of labor to a new level, as shown by the outward shift of the labor demand from MPP_{L1} to MPP_{L2}. As a result, a new modern-sector equilibrium employment level will be established at point P_2 with L_2 workers are now hired. Total modern-sector output, Q_2, would be given by point A_2 in the upper diagram and the area OD_2P2L_2 in the lower diagram. The share of this total output received by the workers in the form of wages would be equal, therefore, to the area of the rectangle $O\ W_MP_2L_2$. The balance of the output, area $W_MD_2P_2$ would be the total

Figure 4.2

THE LEWIS MODEL

In pursuit of profit maximization, modern-sector entrepreneurs are assumed to employ workers up to the point where their marginal physical product of labor is equal to the real wage rate. This is shown by point P_0 in the lower diagram, where the labor demand and supply curves intersect. Total modern-sector output Q_0 would be given by point A_0 in the upper diagram and the area $ODoP_0L_0$ in the lower diagram. The share of this total output received by the workers in the form of wages would be equal, therefore, to the area of the rectangle $OW_MP_0L_0$. The balance of the output, area $W_MD_0P_0$, would be the total profit that is collected by the entrepreneur.

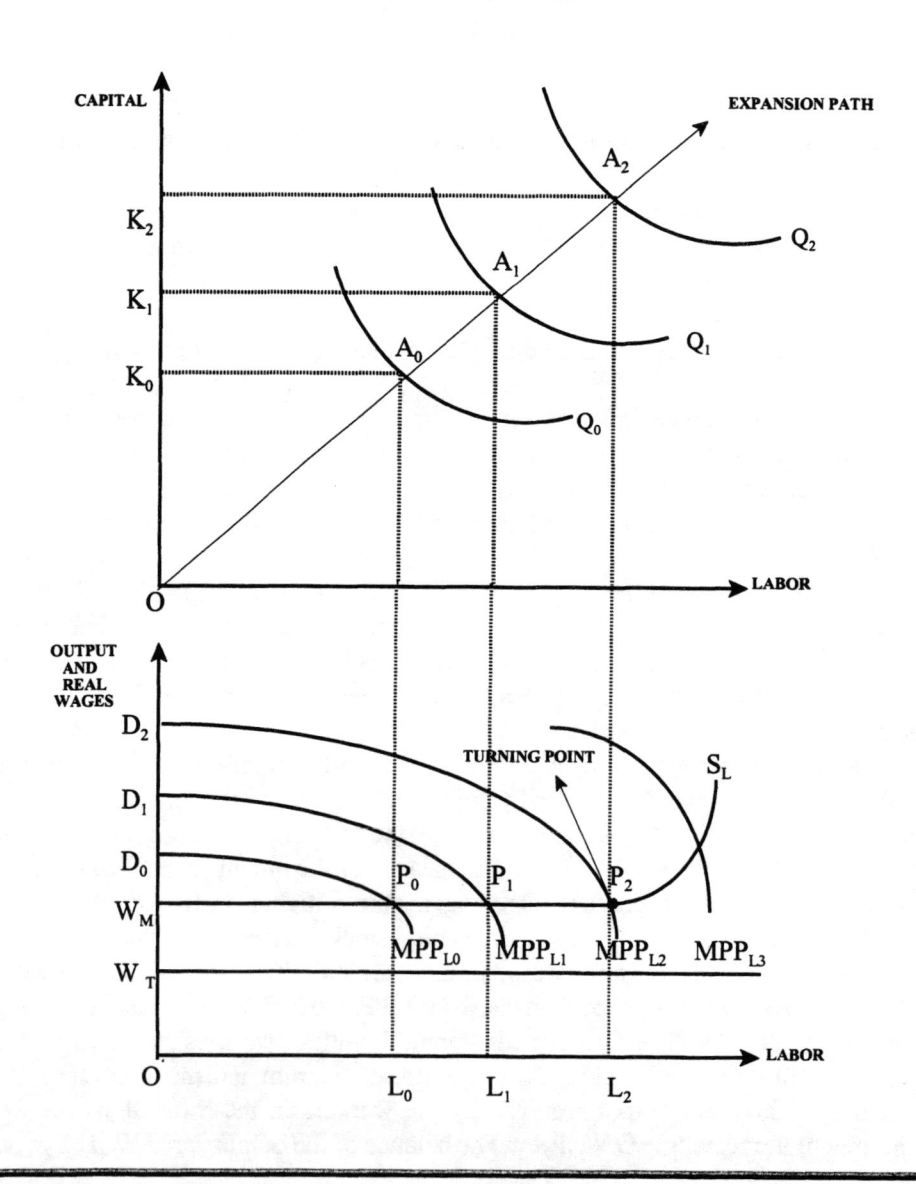

profit that is collected by the entrepreneur.

Up to the point L_2 additional workers can be lured into the industrial sector at a constant wage rate. However, beyond that point the real wage rate should be increased in order to attract more workers away from the traditional sector. This happens either because labor becomes more scarce in the traditional sector or costs of a food increase or both. After this "turning point," capital accumulation in the industrial sector must proceed at an even faster rate—or something else must happen to shift the marginal productivity curves upward and to the right. For success, we need capital accumulation, technological progress in the modern sector, preferably of a labor-using type, and improvement in the agricultural productivity, to prevent increases in the industrial real wage which should slow down the relative transfer of labor form the traditional sector to the modern sector.

From this model the authors recommend the following simple strategies for launching economic development:

1. The total agricultural surplus should be increased.
2. The economy should accumulate as much capital as possible.
3. There should be as much investment and labor-using innovation in the industrial sector as possible.

Although no one could quarrel with these strategies, the dilemma is to arrange its application in particular cases.

THE HARROD-DOMAR GROWTH MODEL

One of the significant factors that contribute to the maintenance and growth of an economic system is domestic savings which serves the following two main functions:

1. Providing funds for the replacement of worn out equipment and machinery.
2. Helping the economy to grow by providing funds for new investments representing net addition to **capital stock**.

The Harrod-Domar growth model shows the elements that give rise to economic growth. This model can be constructed in the following order:

1. Investment (I) is determined as the change in the capital stock (K), that is:

$$I = \Delta K \qquad (4.1)$$

2. Savings (S) is a fixed proportion (s) of national income or output (Y), that is:

$$S = sY$$

$$(4.2)$$

3. Capital-output ratio (K/Y) ratio is always equal to a constant (k), that is:

$$\frac{K}{Y} = k$$

or

$$\frac{\Delta K}{\Delta Y} = k$$

or, finally,

$$\Delta K = k \Delta Y \tag{4.3}$$

3. National savings (S) must be equal to total investment (I), that is:

$$S = I \tag{4.4}$$

But, from Equation 4.1, we know that S = sY, and from Equations 4.2 and 4.3, we know that I = Δk = k ΔY. Thus, we can rewrite Equation 4.4 as:

$$S = sY = \Delta k = k \Delta Y = I \tag{4.5}$$

or

$$sY = k \Delta Y \tag{4.6}$$

Dividing both sides of Equation 5.6 first by Y and then by k, we get:

$$\frac{\Delta Y}{Y} = \frac{s}{k} \tag{4.7}$$

Note that the left hand side of equation 4.7 ($\Delta Y/Y$), shows the rate of change or rate of growth of output (GNP). In other words it represents the percentage change in output. Equation 4.7, representing a simplified form of the familiar equation in the Harrod-Domar theory of economic growth, states that the rate of growth of output ($\Delta Y/Y$) is defined simultaneously by the national savings ratio (s), and the national capital-output ratio (k). In particular, according to the equation, in the absence of government, the growth rate of national output will be directly or positively related to the savings ratio and inversely or negatively correlated to the economy's capital output ratio.

The economic implication of Equation 4.7 is straightforward. For a nation to grow, it must save and invest a certain percentage of its GNP. The more a nation can save and invest, the faster it can grow. Given the levels of saving and investment, the rate of growth of a nation can be measured by the inverse of the capital-output ratio, that is 1/k. This is because 1/k is simply the output-capital or output-investment ratio, that is:

$$\frac{\Delta Y}{\Delta K} = \frac{\Delta Y}{I} = \frac{1}{k} \tag{4.8}$$

GLOBAL INSIGHTS CASE 4.3

JAPANESE CAPITAL FLOW CONTROLS

In 1949, after World War ll, Japan enacted a law that severely restricted foreign trading. This law was gradually liberalized over the years, allowing freer trade in goods and services. However, during the 1960s and 1970s, Japan continued to impose restrictions on capital outflows and inflows. These restrictions were primarily dismantled by the early 1980s, under the Foreign Exchange and Foreign Control Law.

With regard to capital outflows, Japanese residents were not allowed to buy foreign securities prior to 1970. In 1970, Japan's Ministry of Finance abolished the restriction and allowed the Asian Development Bank—an international development bank similar to the World Bank with its headquarters in Manila—to sell 6 billion yen in yen-denominated bonds to Japanese residents. These bonds, referred to as *Samurai bonds*, allowed nonresidents seeking sources of finance to enter the Japanese financial market. However, selective restriction of investment remained throughout the 1970s.

With regard to capital inflows, foreigners were not allowed to buy numerous types of Japanese assets. The causes for the restrictions varied. One common reason was that the Japanese government feared that the capital inflows into Japan would increase the demand for the yen, leading to its appreciation. Such fear was not without basis. During the late 1970s, the yen significantly appreciated in value. The Japanese government was afraid that further appreciation would weaken Japan's competitive position in the world markets. As a result, the government prohibited any significant capital inflows. In 1979, however, the yen depreciated against the U.S. dollar, prompting Japanese authorities to eliminate their restrictions of capital inflows. This allowed foreigners to buy a wide range of Japanese securities. In 1980, capital flows were liberalized further under the Foreign Exchange and Trade Control Law. This law abolished the constraint that foreigners acquire government permission before they investment in Japan.

The liberalization of investment flows in Japan significantly merged the Japanese financial system with the financial systems across its boundaries. This has resulted in the globalization of Japanese investment, as evidenced by the upsurge of Japan's investment in the United States and other nations. Today, the Japanese securities industry is both powerful and concentrated. The top four financial firms in that industry now rank among the world's chief and most profitable financial firms on the New York Stock Exchange and deal directly with the U.S. Treasury in treasury securities.

Sources: J. R. Lothian, " A History of Yen Exchange Rates," in W. T. Ziemba, W. Bailey, and Y. Hamao, eds., *Japanese Financial Market Research* (Amsterdam: Elsvier, 1991); J. Frankel, *The Yen/Dollar Agreement: Liberalizing Japanese Capital Markets* (Washington, D.C.: Institute for International Economics, 1984).; F. McCall Rosenbluth, *Financial Politics in Contemporary Japan* (Ithaca, N.Y.: Cornell University Press, 1989); H. Ueno, "Deregulation and Reorganization of Japan's Financial System," *Japanese Economics Studies* (Spring, 1988); Y Suziki, ed. *The Japanese Financial System*(Oxford: clarendon Press, 1987).

GLOBAL INSIGHTS CASE 4.4

THE ASIAN GROWTH MODEL IN PERSPECTIVE

The Asian crisis caught most analysts by surprise. Some had warned of economic policy flaws in Asia, but few expected them even to produce a sharp slowdown, and no one predicted the profound crisis that actually materialized. Until recently many observers thought that the East Asian countries possessed the strong economic fundamentals and structural characteristics necessary for sustained long-run growth.

If structural weaknesses in the Asian economic system lie at the origin of the crisis, as many observers contend, a natural question is why the crisis occurred when it did. One hypothesis is that countries pass through natural stages of economic development, and that the Asian financial system, based on such practices as relationship banking is better suited to countries in the early stages. After all, financial intermediation by banks (even in the context of relationship, banking) is a tremendous step to take for countries where firms are used to financing all investment out of family savings or retained earnings. Relationship banking may mimic the close ties of extended family lending and thus ease the transition to a more arm's-length financial system. Moreover, as long as growth is rapid, high leverage (that is, a high ratio of debt to equity) is sustainable. But when growth slows, the financial system needs to adapt, and firms need to reduce their high leverage.

Some slowdown in East Asia's growth was probably inevitable at some point, after the breakneck growth of the preceding decades, for the simple reason that economic convergence served as one of the driving forces of that growth. An economy that starts out behind the world leaders in income per capita can close part of the gap over time by growing more rapidly, provided of course such fundamentals as an outward orientation and investment in physical and human capital are in place. Convergence occurs for two reasons: the high rate of return on capital in labor-abundant economies, and the opportunity to emulate the most advanced technology and management practices of the leaders. But as the income gap closes, this impetus to growth diminishes. Economies encounter diminishing returns to capital, limits on labor supply growth from rural-to-urban migration, and infrastructure constraints. Also, as they draw closer to the technological frontier, they have less to learn from those who have gone before. Japan had achieved convergence by the 1980s, and Hong Kong and Singapore by the 1990s. Korea and the others still had some way to go—a very long way in some cases. Nevertheless, the basic principles remain that the smaller the remaining gap, the less the forces of convergence contribute to further growth.

One controversial view is that East Asia's growth from the beginning had more to do with the rapid accumulation of the factors of production—both labor, through increased labor force participation rates, and capital, due to very high investment rates—than with growth in the productivity of these factors. Some studies have found only modest underlying growth rates of multi-factor productivity (a measure of increased efficiency in the use of all factors, resulting in part from technological progress). This view is correct, it means that East Asia's high growth rates were not sustainable in the long run, given that the rate of employment growth must at some point decline, and given an expected reduction in the rate of investment. However, even this view implies at worst gradual slowdown of growth, not the sudden and severe crisis that occurred.

The answer to why the East Asian crisis struck when it did is thus probably a complex one. As discussed below, it appears that, around mid-1997, the factors working to produce an eventual slowdown in growth interacted in unfortunate ways with existing financial sector weaknesses, excessive corporate leverage, financial fragility resulting from poorly designed capital market liberalization, foreign indebtedness, a slowdown in export markets, worsening terms of trade, and the development of overcapacity in many sectors. The crisis was the result.

Source: U.S. Government Printing Office, *Economic Report of the President* (Washington D.C.: U.S. Government Printing Office, 19999), 2 32; Reprinted.

Thus, multiplying the rate of new investment, that is, s = I/Y by its productivity, that is, 1/k = ΔY/I, we get the rate at which national output or GNP (Y) will grow, that is:

$$\frac{\Delta Y}{I} \times \frac{I}{Y} = \frac{\Delta Y}{Y}$$

The Application of the Harrod-Domar Model to The Stages-of-Economic-Growth

Application of Equation 5.7 of the Harrod-Domar model to the stages-of-economic-growth theories, discussed at the beginning of this chapter, will tell us that to accelerate economic growth all we have to do is raise the percentage of national income that is saved. In other words, if we increase s in equation 5.7, we can increase the rate of growth of output (ΔY/Y). For example, if we assume that the national capital-output ratio (K/Y = k) is 2, and the aggregate saving ratio (S/Y = s) is 4%, according to Equation 5.7, we can write:

$$\frac{\Delta Y}{Y} = \frac{s}{k} = \frac{4\%}{2} = 2\%$$

Now if the national savings rate is increased, from 4% to, say, 12%, then GNP growth would rise from 2% to 6%, that is:

$$\frac{\Delta Y}{Y} = \frac{s}{k} = \frac{12\%}{6\%} = 6\%$$

Indeed, Rostow and others determined the takeoff stage exactly in this manner. Nations that were able to save 15% to 20% of their GNP could grow more rapidly than those that saved less. Thus, according to the model, economic growth and development can be accelerated simply by enhancing national savings and investment.

The main barrier to economic growth, according to the theory of stages of growth, was the relatively low level of new capital formation in most poor nations. But if a nation decided to grow at, say, a rate of 6% per year and if it could not induce savings and investment at a rate of 18% of its national income or output (assuming that k = 3) but could only generate a 14% savings, it could close this "savings gap" of 4% by means of foreign direct investment or foreign aid.

The "capital constraint" stages method to growth and development provided a rationale for qualifying huge flows of capital and technical assistance from the advanced nations to the developing nations. However, in practice such flows proved to be ineffective in accelerating economic development. This is not because more savings and investment is not a **necessary condition** for rapid rates of economic growth, but rather because it is not a **sufficient condition**. More specifically, the underlying assumptions of the Harrod-Domar model and Rostow's model are not appropriate for today's developing nations. These models implicitly assume the existence of the same arrangements and attitude in developing nations as in advanced nations. Yet, as we already know, the environment in developing nations is very different from that in developed nations. In many cases, developing nations lack the complimentary factors such as managerial competence, skilled workers, and the ability to plan and manage a wide range of development projects. Setting this problem aside, the more fundamental problem with these models is the failure to recognize that today's developing nations do not operate in a vacuum. Rather, they are part of a highly integrated and inextricable global system in which even the best and most astute development strategies can be counterbalanced by outside forces beyond the nation's control. One can no longer claim, as many economists did in the 1950s and 1960s, that development is simply a task of dismantling barriers and providing different missing ingredients such as foreign-exchange, managerial and technical expertise, and capital. In fact, it was the frequent disappointment with this strictly economic theory of development that gave rise to a radically different approach such as the dependency theory, discussed at the beginning of this chapter. This theory was advanced chiefly by Third World scholars in an attempt to blend economic and institutional elements into a social system model of international development and underdevelopment.

SUMMARY

1. We use theories to arrive at conclusions about the real world. A theory is an abstraction from reality and is based on certain simplifying assumptions. The test of the usefulness of a theory is its power to predict. We continue to use a given theory until certain events show it to be false. In this case a new theory may replace the old one.
2. According to the classical economists, continuous growth of the population would lead to economic stagnation. At this so-called stationary state there would exist low income for masses and the population growth would be checked by poverty.
3. The cornerstone of Hegelian philosophy is the **Hegelian *dialectic***, a method of logic or reasoning which maintains that any concept, called a *thesis*, can have meaning only when it is compared to its opposite concept called an *anthesis*; the interplay of the two then generates a new concept of comprehension referred to as *synthesis*. For example, the concept of "high" (thesis) induces the opposite concept of "low" (antithesis), and the two interact to shape the new concept of "height" (synthesis).
4. The Marxian theoretical framework is composed of five fundamental doctrines: economic interpretation of history, theory of value and wages, surplus value and capital accumulation, the class struggle, and theory of socialistic and communistic revolution.
5. According to Marx, if it were not for certain "contradictions" that automatically and continually emerge within the capitalist system, the class struggle might persist. The major factors that fuel these contradictions include: (a) increasing unemployment, (b) declining rate of profits, (c) business cycles, (d) concentration and monopolization of capital, and (e) finance capitalism and imperialism.
6. The economic thoughts of Marx have been criticized on many grounds.
7. The dependency theory was developed by an influential group of writers sympathetic to Karl Marx. This theory attributes the sluggishness of economic growth and development in developing nations to their dependent relationships with advanced countries.
8. The dependency theory has been subject to many criticisms, on both theoretical and empirical grounds.
9. According to Rostow, the process of economic growth can be divided into five stages: (a) the traditional stage, (b) the preconditions for takeoff, (c) the takeoff, (d) the drive to maturity, and (e) the age of mass consumption.
10. According to Hagen, the process of economic industrialization can be divided into six stages: (a) the emergence of self-contained factory processes, (b) the development of initial interrelationships, (c) the expansion of light engineering, (d) the improving control of quality and tolerances, (e) the elaboration of the industrial complex, and (f) the stage of industrial complexity.
11. The vicious circle of poverty is a well known theory which is based on the notion that a lack of capital is the major impediment to growth and economic development. In other words, this theory relates economic stagnation to very low levels of per capita output.
12. The vicious circle of poverty is subject to the following two major criticisms: (a) The model misconstrues levels of savings with rates of savings; and (b) the model does not make any provision for savings in terms of foreign direct investment, foreign aid, and public or private lending.

CH 4/ALTERNATIVE THEORIES OF ECONOMIC DEVELOPMENT

13. The origin of the big-push thesis can be traced back to an article by Paul Rosenstein-Rodan, published in 1943. Rosenstein-Rodan considered industrialization the major method for bringing about more equal distribution of income between various parts of the world, by enhancing incomes in depressed parts at a higher rate than in affluent parts.
14. Balanced growth calls for simultaneous application of capital to a wide range of various industries. This theory was proposed by Rangar Nurkse.
15. The theory of unbalanced growth was developed by Albert O. Hirschman who contends that *deliberate unbalancing* of the economy, according to a pre-formulated strategy, is the best approach for accomplishing economic growth.
16. In the mid-1950s, Sir W. Arthur Lewis, an economist, developed a well known theory of economic development to explain how economic growth takes place in labor-abundant third world nations. The theory was later modified, and extended by John FDI and Gustav Ranis.
17. The Lewis model recommends the following simple strategies for launching economic development: (a) the total agricultural surplus should be increased; (b) the economy should accumulate as much capital as possible; and (c) there should be as much investment and labor-using innovation in the industrial sector as possible.
18. The Harrod-Domar growth model shows the elements that give rise to economic growth.
19. Application of Equation 5.7 of the Harrod-Domar model to the stages-of-economic-growth theories tells us that to accelerate economic growth all we have to do is raise the percentage of national income that is saved.

QUESTIONS

1. Elaborate on the dependency theory by answering the following questions:
    f. What is a "metropolis-satellite chain"?
    b. What are the major criticisms of this theory?
    c. Should this theory be dismissed at face value?
2. Discuss the classical theory of economic stagnation by answering the following questions:
    a. What does classical theory state?
    b. What assumptions are underlying this theory?
    c. What is the major shortcoming of this theory?
3. Elaborate on Rostow's stages of economic growth by answering the following questions:
    a. What are these stages?
    b. What are the main criticisms of this theory?
    c. What can we learn from Rostow's theory?
4. Elaborate on Hagen's stages of economic industrialization:
    a. What are these stages?
    b. What are the main criticisms of this theory?
5. Compare Rostow's stages of economic growth with Hagen's stages of economic industrialization by answering the following questions:
    a. What do these theories have in common?
    b. How do these theories differ from each other?
6. Name the five fundamental doctrines of the Marxian economic framework, and answer the following questions:
    a. What is meant by "Hegelian dialectic" and "dialectic materialism"?
    b. What is the labor theory of value?

7. Compare the theories of socialism and communism by answering the following questions:
   a. What do these theories have in common?
   b. How do these differ from each?
8. Appraise Marxist theory by answering the following questions:
   a. What are the major criticisms of this theory?
   b. What are the major contributions of the Marxist theory to the theory of economic development?
9. Elaborate on the vicious circle of poverty by answering the following questions:
   a. What does this theory state?
   b. What are the major criticisms of this model?
   c. What can we learn from this theory?
10. Elaborate on the theory of balanced growth by answering the following questions:
    a. What does this theory state?
    b. What are the major criticisms of this theory?
11. Explain the Lewis model, by answering the following questions:
    a. What are the assumptions underlying this theory?
    b. What does the theory state?
    c. Use graphs to demonstrate this model.
    d. What are the main strategies recommended by this model for launching economic development?
12. Elaborate on the Harrod-Domar model by answering the following questions:
    a. What is the economic implication of this model for a nation?
    b. Using algebra, derive this model.
    c. What can we learn from this model?

NOTES

1. Karl Marx, *Capital: A Critique of Political Economy,* Vol. 1 (Moscow: Progress Publisher, 1978), p.47.
2. *Ibid.*
3. *Ibid.*
4. Karl Marx, *Capital*, 3 vols. (Moscow: Progress Publisher, 1975), vol. 1, p. 555.
5. *Ibid.*, p. 714.
6. M. C. Howard and J. E. King, eds., *The Political Economy of Karl Marx*, 2nd ed. (New York: Longman), p. 202.
7. H. William Spiegel, *The Growth of Economic Thought* (Englewood Cliffs, N.J.: Prentice-Hall, 1971), p.475.
8. Andre G. Frank, *Capitalism and Underdevelopment in Latin America: Historical Studies of Chile and Brazil* (New York: Monthly Review Press, 1967), p. 11.
9. Paul Baran, *La Economica Politica del Crecimiento, Mexico.* (Mexico: F.C.E., 1957), p. 28.
10. Andre G. Frank, *Capitalism and Underdevelopment in Latin America: Historical Studies of Chile and Brazil* (New York: Monthly Review Press, 1967).
11. W. W. Rostow, *The Stages of Economic Growth: A Non-Communist Manifesto* (Forge Village, Mass.: Murray, 1960), chap. 2.
12. Evertt E. Hagen, *The Economics of Development*, 3rd ed. (Homewood, Ill.: Irwin, 1980), chap. 6.
13. Shail Jain, *Size Distribution of Income* (Washington D.C.: world Bank, 1975).
14. Paul N. Rosentein-Rodan, "Problems of Industrialization of Eastern and Southern Europe," *Economic Journal*, 53 (June-September 1943), 202-211.
15. Albert Hirchman, *The Strategy of Economic Development* (New Haven,1958), p. 36.
16. *Ibid*, pp.62-63.
17. Bruce F. Johnson and John W. Mellor, "The Role of Agriculture in economic Development," *American Economic Review* 51(September 1961): 571-81.

SUGGESTED READINGS

Adelman, Irma. *Theories of Economic Growth and Development*. Stanford: Stanford University Press, 1961.
Arndt, H. W. "Market Failure and Underdevelopment." *World Development* 16 (February 1988).
Baran, Paul A. *The Political Economy of Growth*. New York: Monthly Review Press, 1957.
Barro and Xavier Sala-i-Martin. "Convergence." *Journal of Political Economy*. 100 (April 1992) 223-51.
Bettelheim, Charles. *Class Struggles in the USSR*. New York: Monthly Review Press, 1978.
Brewer, Anthony. *Marxist Theories of Imperialism: A Critical Survey*. New York: Routledge & Kegan Paul, 1980.
Coase, Ronald. "The Institutional Structure of Production." *American Economic Review* 82 (December 1992).
Domar, Evsey D. "The Problem of Capital Accumulation." *American Economic Review* 37 (March 1947): 34-55.
Dutt, Amitava K., Kwan S. Kim, and Ajit Singh. eds. *The States, Markets and Development*. London: Elgar, 1994.
Frank, Andre Gunder. *Capitalism and Underdevelopment in Latin America: Historical Studies of Chile and Brazil*. New York: Monthly Review Press, 1969.
———. *Latin America: Underdevelopment or Revolution?* New York: Monthly Review Press, 1969.
Furtado, Celso. *Economic Development of Latin America: A Survey from Colonial Times to the Cuban Revolution*. Cambridge: Cambridge University Press, 1977.
Hagen, Evrett E. *On the Theory of Social Change: How Economic Growth Begins*. Homewood, Ill.: Dorsey Press, 1962.
Harrod, Roy F. "An Essay in Dynamic Theory." *Economic Journal* 49 (March 1939): 14-33.
Higgins, Benjamin. *Economic Development: Problems, Principles, and Policies*. New York: Norton, 1968.
Hirschman, Albert O. *The Strategy of Economic Development*. New York: Yale University Press, 1958.
Howard, M. C. and J. E. King. eds. *The Political Economy of Karl Marx*. New York: Longman, 1985.
Khan Mohsin S., Peter J. Montiel, and Nadeem U. Haque. "Adjustment with Growth: Relating the Analytical Approaches of the IMF and the World Bank." *Journal of Development Economics* 23 (January 1990): 155-79.
———. *Macroeconomic Models for Adjustment in Developing Countries*. Washington, D.C.: International Monetary und, 1991.
Lal, Deepak. *The Poverty of Development Economics*. Cambridge, Mass.: Harvard University Press, 1985.
Lall, Sanjaya. "Is 'Dependence' a Useful Concept in Analyzing Underdevelopment?" *World Development* 3 (November-December 1975): 799-810.
Lewis, Arthur W. "Economic Development with Unlimited Supplies of Labor." *Manchester School* 22 (May 1954): 139-91.
Lim, David. *Explaining Economic Growth: A New Analytical Framework*. Cheltenham, U.K.: Edward Elgar, 1996.
Little, Ian. *Economic Development: Theories, Policies, and International Relations*. New York: Basic Books, 1982.
Marcus and Fleming. "External Economies and the Doctrine of Balanced Growth." *Economic Journal* 65 (June 1955):241-56.
Nurkse, Rangar. *Problems of Captial Formation in Underdeveloped Countries*. New York: Oxford University Press, 1953.
Ranis, Gustav and John C. H. FDI. "A Theory of Economic Development." *American Economic Review* 51 (September 1961): 533-65.
Rosenstein-Rodan, Paul. "Problems of Industrialization of Eastern and Southeastern Europe." *Economic Journal* 53 (June-September 1943): 202-11.
———. "Notes on the Theory of the Big Push." In Howard S. Ellis, ed., *Economic Development for Latin America*. London: Macmillian, 1951.
Rostow, Walter W. *The Stages of Economic Growth: A Non-Communist Manifesto*. Cambridge: Cambridge University Press, 1961.
———. *The Economics of Takeoff into Sustained Growth*. London: Macmillan, 1963.
Sen, Amartya. "Development: Which Way Now?" *Economic Journal* 93 (December 1983): 745-762.
Singer, Hans. "The Concepts of Balanced Growth and Economic Development Theory and Facts." University of Texas Conference on Economic Development, April 1958.
Streeten, Paul. "Markets and States: Against Minimalism." *World Development* 21 (August 1993): 1281-1298.
———. "Dualism Revisited: New Approaches to the Problems of Dual Society in Developing Countries." *Journal of Development Studies* 7 (January 1970): 60-71.

PART II

THE ELEMENTS OF GROWTH

CHAPTER 5

POVERTY AND INCOME DISTRIBUTION

The 1970s can be marked as the period in which both the advanced nations and the developing nations began to question the wisdom of the persistent quest for economic growth as the main objective of society. In advanced nations, such a concern exemplified itself in terms of environmental quality. The environmentalists warned us of the by-products of industrial growth such as air and water pollution, environmental decay, and destruction of other species. In the developing nations, the attention was shifted from pursuing economic growth to growth versus income distribution. The main issue became not only how to make GNP grow faster, but also who would cause the growth, the small percentage of the population that is rich, or the masses of poor people. If such growth were to be generated by the rich, then they would most likely be the beneficiaries of the growth, and the masses of poor people continue to suffer from poverty. On the other hand, if the GNP growth were induced by the poor, they would be the main benefactors of such growth and the society's income would be more evenly distributed.

In spite of the attention given to the question of income inequality in developing nations since the early 1970s, the attempt to investigate this issue has been hampered by the inadequacy of data that are even weaker than national income statistics. Most of the data published on income distribution by the officials of the developing nations or international agencies are not compatible and reliable over time. Nonetheless, careful research has helped scholars to answer some of the questions that are raised on poverty and income inequality, and suggest policies to alleviate them.

In this chapter, we first explain the concept of absolute poverty; second, we elaborate on the problems of defining income; third, we discuss factors contributing to income inequality; fourth, we explain the human poverty index; fifth, we identify the poverty group; sixth, we elaborate on the inverted-U hypothesis; finally, we present policies to alleviate poverty and income inequality.

ABSOLUTE POVERTY

Absolute poverty is below the income level that secures the bare essentials of food, clothing, and shelter. This income level, referred to as the absolute poverty line, is a global measure of poverty. In other words, it is an international poverty line that does not recognize any national boundary. The absolute poverty line is independent of the level of per capita income and it does not take into account the various price levels in different nations. As an international line of poverty it considers anyone who lives on less than a dollar a day in **purchasing parity power (PPP)** dollars as poor. PPP can be defined as the number of units of a nation's currency needed to buy the identical quantity of goods and services in the domestic market as $1 would purchase in the United States. Given this definition, poverty can and does exist in advanced nations like the United States as in developing nations like India. However, in general, the magnitude of poverty, measured

GLOBAL INSIGHTS CASE 5.1

POLICIES TO REDUCE POVERTY IN INDIA

Today, over 50% of the globe's poor live in India. Poverty afflicts about 35% of India's rural population and 20% of its urban dwellers. Encompassing one of the highest poverty rates in the world, and the greatest number of people living on less than $1 a day, India symbolizes the problem of absolute poverty. This is partially due to the fact that India is geographically the largest nation in South Asia and the seventh largest in the world.

Having realized the extent and severity of poverty in India, policy makers were pressured to take action to improve the standard of living of the masses of poor in this country. As a result, the constitution of 1949, and 5-year plans which started in 1951, emphasized abolishing poverty and improving income distribution. This resulted in implementation of various programs beginning in the 1950s. These programs included land reform, community development, credit and services for the rural poor, education and food subsidies, village cooperatives, sanitation, health, drinking water, communication, transportation, electricity for the poor, employment, and nutrition.

Unfortunately, these programs were not successful in resolving the poverty and income distribution problems in India. According to the available data, income share of the poor dropped from the 1950s through the late 1970s, while at the same time no significant change was made on absolute poverty. The failure of these programs could be attributed to the machinery of government in India which was controlled by the landlords and business classes. These classes, dominating government services and legislatures, did not find it in their best interest to implement programs effectively that improved the standard of living of the poor at their own expense. Laws were often passed with loopholes and exemptions that permitted land transfers to relatives, leading to concentration of lands in the hands of few families. Additionally, large landlords, money lenders, and traders dominated village cooperatives and utilized most of the social and capital programs established by community development programs.

The fastest poverty alleviation apparently took place after liberalization reforms stimulated growth, starting in the mid-1980s, but peaking in the New Industrial Policy in 1991 when a new government initiated a new set of economic reforms. These reforms included the following schemes:

1. Currency devaluation to increase exports and decrease imports.
2. A reduction of quantitative import restrictions, production subsidies, and import duties on capital goods.
3. A revision of the personal income tax system.
4. A speedup of the privatization mechanism with further incentive to foreign investors.
5. A reduction of production subsidies.

Following seven years of reforms and relatively satisfactory economic growth, in 1998, India's new nationalist government declared a change in policy that emphasized economic nationalism. More specifically the government was going to reexamine the policy of lowering import tariffs and welcoming investors with open arms. It remains to be seen how India can balance growth with equity, free markets with poverty reduction, employment with growth, and food production with distribution in the face of a rapidly growing population and ethnic unrest between Hindu and Muslim fundamentalists.

Source: Pranab K. Barhan, "India," in Hollis Chenery, et.al, eds., *Redistribution with Growth* (London: Oxford University Press, 1974), pp. 255-62; David Morawetz, *Twenty-five Years of Economic Development, 1950-1975* (Baltimore: John Hopkins Press, 1977), pp. 39-41; R.P. Pathak, K.R. Ganapathy, and Y.U.K. Sarma, "Shifts in Patterns of Asset Holding of Rural Households, 1961-62 to 1971-72," *Economic Political Weekly* 12 (March 19, 1977): 507-1; and Inderijit Singh, *The Great Ascent: The Rural Poor in South Asia* (Baltimore: John Hopkins University, 1990).

CH. 5/POVERTY AND INCOME DISTRIBUTION

by the **headcount index**, that is, ratio of number of poor people to population, is much lower in advanced nations as compared to the developing nations.

Two lines have been identified by economists: the lower (extreme) poverty line, and the upper poverty line. The **lower (extreme) poverty line**, considered as the absolute minimum by international standards, is based on standards set in India and amounts to $275 per capita income. The **upper poverty line** amounts to $370 per capita. This figure is derived from studies of a number of nations with low average income–Bangladesh, the Arab Republic of Egypt, India, Indonesia, Kenya, Morocco, and Tanzania. Both of the figures are in constant 1985 PPP.

Although the headcount index is a useful measure of poverty, it has its limitations. This index ignores the degree by which the poor fall below the poverty line. For example, if the poverty line is set at $300, it makes a significant difference whether most of the absolute poor receive $340 or $310 per year. This happens because in calculating the proportion of population that lies below the poverty line, both cases are given the same weight. However, the poverty level is clearly worse in the latter case. To alleviate this problem, a poverty gap can be calculated. A **poverty gap** measures the total amount of money needed to bring the income of every poor person up to the poverty line, thereby eradicating poverty.

Using the upper poverty line as the measure, in 1985 about 1.115 billion people were poor. That is approximately 30 percent of the total population of the globe. Of this total, about 630 million or 18 percent of the population of the developing nations were extremely poor, that is, they lived below the lower (extreme) poverty line of $275. In spite of such a massive amount of poverty, the total poverty gap, based on the $370 poverty line, was only 3 percent of consumption. The total poverty gap, based on the $275 poverty line, was, of course, even smaller, amounting to only 1 percent of the developing nations' consumption.

Today, about 50 percent of the developing nations' poor people and almost 50 percent of those in extreme poverty live in South Asia. Sub-Saharan Africa houses about one third as many poor. The Middle and North African nations have the next highest poor. They are followed by Latin America, the Caribbean, and East Asia.

It should be emphasized that there is not a necessary correlation between the levels of per capita income and the distribution of that income. In other words, higher per capita income does not ensure the absence of a significant number of poor people in a developing nation. Given that the percentage share of income accrued to the poor people varies significantly across various nations, it is conceivable for a high per capita nation, which has a large proportions of its inhabitants below an international poverty line, to portray a larger poverty gap than a nation with lower per capital income. For example, in 1996, Brazil had a per capita income of $4,720, a poverty rate of 23.6 percent, and a poverty gap of 10.7 percent, while Indonesia had a per capita income of $110, a poverty line of 11.8 percent and poverty gap of a 1.8 percent. Thus, poverty and income maldistribution do not stem just from the economic growth process. Rather, they hinge on the kind of economic growth and the political and economic environment in which the growing national incomes are distributed among the masses of population.

THE PROBLEM OF DEFINING INCOME

Even in an advanced country like the United States, where income data are relatively reliable, there have been considerable controversies, regarding both the degree of income inequality and trends in income inequality over time. Because the question of income inequality circles around the definition of income, it is necessary to understand what income is and how it is measured. The following is the list of the main factors that enter the calculations and measurement of income in a given nation:

1. **Noncash Income.** Almost all estimates of personal income distribution either do not take noncash (imputed) income into consideration, or limit its measurement to the value of food produced and

consumed at home. Noncash income includes items such as the value of personal services rendered within a community or household, the rental value of the owner-built home, and the value of clothing, fruit, vegetables, and similar items produced from raw material grown or collected by household members. Because the exclusion of these items underestimates an individual's true income, that is, noncash plus cash income, a systematic upward bias is implanted in income inequalities. This happens because the importance of noncash transactions varies inversely with income. In other words, poor people are more apt to engage in cash transactions than rich people. As a result, the true income of poor people is underestimated.

It is difficult to measure the value of goods and services that do not pass through the market mechanism. Given this difficulty, in the United States nonmarket income is restricted to the rental value of owner-occupied housing, and the value of the produce directly consumed by the farm household producing it. In developing nations, estimates exclude not only noncash income but also entire classes of workers. For instance, estimates for some nations are based not on surveys or census but on income tax returns which include less than half of the nation's population. Such estimates are bound to understate the extent of income inequality by not counting those too poor to pay income taxes.

2. **Pretax or Aftertax Income.** Some nations use pretax income while other nations use aftertax income as the basis of their income distribution estimates. This makes intercountry comparison of income distribution less accurate.
3. **Demographic Factors.** Most estimates of income distribution are based on family or household income. Although this is a more appropriate basis for assessing income distribution, it is subject to the following problems:
    - The families or households differ significantly by size. A given amount of income leads to a higher relative *per capita* spending income in a small family or household than in a large one. Consequently, small families with low income may sometimes be better off than large families with higher income, depending on their relative *per capita* spending income.
    - Income data are not adjusted for age differentials among income groups. To a large degree, income differentials at a given point in time stem from differences in age. Usually, young people who have recently entered the market and old people who left it, have lower income than people who are in midcareer.
4. **Geographic Factors.** The purchasing power of money differs within the region of a country. The costs of housing and domestically produced food are relatively lower in the rural sector than the urban sector. In addition, clothing and housing needs for preserving a given level of personal comfort depend on the temperature. Geographic factors, however, are not taken into account when measuring income to assess inequalities.
5. **Public Goods and Services.** The quality of life is significantly affected by the consumption of public services that are not paid for in the market. Public health facilities, schools, roads and streets, are examples of public services that make important contributions to welfare. These services are usually less accessible to rural dwellers than urban residents. Again, these items are not taken into account when measuring income to determine inequalities.

In summary, the definition of income used to assess inequality differs significantly from nation to nation. Even for the same nation, income inequality estimates for two various years may be based on different concepts of income. This makes the task of assessing income inequality over time difficult. This of course does not imply that income data are not valuable for comparative purposes. Rather, it means that a careful assessment of income inequality in any nation should be based on a definite comprehension of what the data in fact evaluate.

GLOBAL INSIGHTS CASE 5.2

THE DOZEN NATIONS INCLUDING MOST OF THE POOR IN THE WORLD

In 1993, a dozen nations accounted for about eighty percent of the globe's poor people. The following table lists these nations and provides estimates of their total number of poor people in 1997. These estimates are arrived at by multiplying the number of people in each country by the percentage below the poverty line in a given year. As the table indicates, if these percentages had stayed constant in these nations, the number of poor people in 1997 would be 996 million. It should be noted that some other developing nations which have much higher poverty rates, however, are excluded from the list due to smaller populations. In other words, the dozen nations listed in the following table have large populations that contribute significantly to the global poverty total.

POPULATION BELOW THE POVERTY LINE IN THE DOZEN NATIONS, ACCOUNTING FOR 80% OF THE GLOBE'S POOR IN 1997

Nation	1997 Population (millions)	Head Count Index Percent blow Poverty line	Year	Estimated Number of poor (millions)
India	970	52.5	1992	509
China	1,236	22.2	1995	274
Brazil	160	23.2	1995	38
Nigeria	107	31.1	1993	33
Ethiopia	59	46.0	1982	27
Indonesia	204	11.8	1995	24
Philippines	73	28.6	1991	21
Pakistan	138	11.6	1991	16
Kenya	29	50.2	1992	15
Mexico	96	14.9	1992	14
Peru	24	54.0	1991	13
Nepal	23	53.0	1995	12
Total				996

Source: World Bank, *1998 World Development Indicators* (Washington D.C.:World Bank, 1998), tab. 2.7; Population Reference Bureau, *1997 World Population Data Sheet* (Washington, D.C.: Population Reference Bureau, 1997).

FACTORS CONTRIBUTING TO INCOME INEQUALITY

Why is there such a difference between the income levels of different groups of people within a nation? In answering this question, first we elaborate on the universal factors of inequality, that is, factors that are responsible for income inequality in a given nation, regardless of whether it is a developing or advanced nation. Second, we list some additional factors that are responsible for further income inequality in developing nations.

Universal Causes of Inequality In Nations

There are many factors that give rise to differences in income among households in a given nation. The most significant factors are:

1. **Earning Ability and Opportunity Differentials.** People differ in terms of intelligence, skills, motivation, energy, talents, and education. Such differences lead to earning differentials. Additionally, many people may suffer from job barriers in the form of sex, age, or race. Although the legislation has made these barriers less invincible, they still account for some of the inequality that exists in a given society.
2. **Differences in Wealth.** Wealth is an important source of income. Examples include income from financial investment, income from interest, and income from real estate.
3. **Differences in Age.** Young people, who have recently entered the job market, and the old people who have left it have relatively much lower income than those in the middle of their careers. This is because young people have less experience than those in the middle of their career and old people generally live on retirement income or social security payments which are significantly lower than the earnings of those in midcareer.
4. **Differences in Opportunities.** An individual who is born in a favorable condition and accorded the opportunities to advance inborn abilities has a better chance of earning a higher income than a person who is not so lucky.
5. **Differences in Human-Capital Investment.** Investment in human capital, that is, education and training, usually leads to higher paying jobs. This explains why professionals and skilled workers make more money than unskilled workers.
6. **Differences in Security, Risk, and Uncertainty.** Occupations vary in terms of risk, security, and uncertainty. Such differences are reflected in the earning differentials of individuals. Some individuals prefer lower incomes in return for security in the less risky and more certain occupations. For example, given the risks associated with mining, miners earn more than road-construction workers. In the same manner, the financial executive of a corporation earns considerably more than an economics professor with the same level of education.
7. **Differences in Resource Mobility.** Many individuals are precluded by the lack of financial means or information from moving into higher-paying locations or occupations. This may result in low levels of income or even extensive poverty for years to come. This is true even in parts of the United States where some miners, farm workers, and factory workers are able to earn only a substandard level of living.

Additional Causes of Inequality In Developing Nations

Besides the universal factors of inequality that affect both developing and developed nations, other factors that give rise to the widening income inequality in developing nations are:

1. **Rapid Population Growth.** The rapid population growth in developing nations leads to a rise in the percentage of young people in the population. As a result, inequality increases even though the distribution of income remains fairly constant within any age group.
2. **Taxes and Government Expenditure Patterns.** Government policies regarding taxes, subsidies, foreign exchange allocation, credit, land policies and other similar policies may be used to reward supporters and penalize adversaries and the weak. Even if the government wanted to narrow income inequality, taxes and transfer payments are less effective in changing income distribution in developing countries relative to developed nations, due to the fact that such mechanisms themselves are less developed.
3. **Discrimination.** The existence of a social framework that excludes individuals on the basis of sex, religion, race, or cast, from land-holding, jobs, and other means to earn an income.
4. **Skill Shortages.** The scarcity of skilled workers and professionals, such as engineers, teachers, physicians, economists, accountants, and computer specialists in developing nations. Such scarcity leads to a relatively higher remuneration for these jobs as compared to other jobs, contributing to income inequality in these nations.
5. **Unequal Distribution of Land Ownership.** In many developing nations, based on historical and social reasons, land ownership and access to land are highly unequal.
6. **Market Imperfection.** The prevalence of imperfect information, imperfect factor mobility, and monopoly power based on political or economic power may make existing disparities hard to eradicate.

ALTERNATIVE MEASURES OF INCOME INEQUALITY

There are a number of different measures of income inequality. However, economists generally differentiate between two main measures: functional distribution of income, and size distribution of income. In this section we discuss these measures of income inequality and elaborate on their advantages and disadvantages.

Functional Distribution of Income

A rather crude measure of income inequality is **functional** or **factor share distribution of income**. As the name implies this measure of income inequality deals with the distribution of income to factors of production. More specifically, this measure compares the percentage of total income that the labor receives as a whole, with the percentages of total income distributed in the form of rent, interest, and profit to land, capital, and entrepreneur, respectively. Assuming other things stay the same, the higher the level of wages, the more equally total income will be distributed. This is due to the fact that wealth, which is the source of property income, has always been more unequally distributed than current income.

Theoretically, the concept of functional income distribution is based on the assumption of perfect competition which states that each factor of production is paid according to the value of its marginal product. It is assumed that the unit price of each factor of production is determined by the market forces of demand and supply. Given this assumption, each factor of production would be compensated according to its contribution to production. For example, the demand and supply of labor are presumed to determine the wage rate. If we multiply this wage rate by the total hours of work, we end up with the total wage payment, also referred to as the *total wage bill*. Unfortunately, however, the relevance of the functional theory is significantly reduced due to the fact that we do not live in the world of perfect competition. In the real world, factor prices are significantly affected by nonmarket forces such as labor unions, and monopoly power.

In practice, the greatest advantage of the functional distribution of income is that it is available on a yearly basis for many developing nations, thus allowing an assessment of changes for a given country over time. However, such an approach is subject to the following serious problems:

1. In a given nation, factor shares can oscillate sharply from year to year, especially if government intervention influences the wage rate. This makes use of the measure to make intercountry comparisons problematic.
2. The measure does not provide for adequate disaggregation of income types. For example, top executives who receive high salaries are lumped together along with production workers whose wages are much lower than the executive's salaries. As a result, great inequality can exist within the salary-and -wage class.
3. The measure is inadequate in comparing functional shares of developing and advanced nations. This is the case, because top executives in developing nations are less likely to receive salaries and more likely to acquire income that would be recorded as property income.

In summary, the usefulness of the functional distribution of income is limited as an analytical tool for measuring income inequality.

The Size Distribution of Income

The **size** or the **personal distribution of income** is the most commonly used measure of income inequality by economists and it is usually employed as a direct indicator of welfare. Theoretically, income distribution is largely determined by the ownership structure of the productive factors of production and the function that each factor performs in the production process, and as such, it is an important measure of welfare. For example, if the distribution of land and capital ownership is narrow, then anything that raises remuneration to these factors of production will serve to deteriorate the size of income distribution. On the other hand, a higher return to unskilled labor, that is, the most widely distributed resource, will lead to a more equal size distribution of income.

The size distribution of income focuses on individuals, households, and the total incomes they receive. The manner by which the income is earned is immaterial. What counts is how much was earned by a person regardless of the occupational source (e.g. manufacturing, agriculture, service, or commerce) of income or the location (rural or urban) in which the income was generated.

In practice, the size distribution of income suffers from some measurement problems. Inhabitants of developing nations usually experience wide variations in their income due to the market, nature's vagaries, and their own governments. There are also systematic variations in earnings by age. Given such income fluctuations, ideally, average income over several years, or even accumulated lifetime earnings should be employed in the analysis. However, such an approach is not commonly practical. As a result, most researchers end up considering income over a specific recent interval, a year or a month, as the basis of their analysis. Questions are also raised with regard to the precise definition of income and the manner by which the data are collected. Commonly, a sample survey of households is chosen. But even when extreme care is exercised, the resulting statistics may be questionable. When collecting the sample, the respondents may not know their income or may be fearful to acknowledge it, possibly due to the suspicion that their taxes will increase.

Having collected the data, the next step is to analyze them. The data can be analyzed in various ways. The two most common methods used by economists are the income shares method and the Lorenz curve method.

The Income Shares Method. In this method, the first step is to divide the population into successive quintiles (fifth) or deciles (tenth) in accordance to ascending income levels. The next step is to determine

CH. 5/POVERTY AND INCOME DISTRIBUTION

what percentage of the total national income is received by each income group. For instance, Table 5.1 illustrates a hypothetical but quite common income distribution in a developing nation. In this table the annual personal incomes of twenty individuals are presented in an ascending order. The individual income ranges from the lowest level of 0.75 units to the highest level of 15.50 units. The national income is equal to 100 and is obtained by adding up the individual incomes, as shown in column 2 of the table. In column 3, the population is sorted into quintiles composed of four individuals each. The first quintile portrays the bottom 20% of the population on the income scale. As a group, these individuals receive only 4.65%, that is, a total of 4.65 money units, of the total national income. The bottom 40% of the population, that is, quintile 1 plus quintile 2, receive only 13.70 % of the income. The top 20%, that is, the fifth quintile, receives 51% of the total income. A conventional yardstick of income inequality that can be obtained from column 3 is the ratio of the incomes received by the bottom 40% and the top 20% of the population. This ratio is usually presented as a yardstick of the extent of inequality between the two extremes of the very poor and the very rich in a nation. In our example, this inequality is equal to the ratio of 13.70/51, or roughly 0.22.

Table 5.1

A HYPOTHETICAL SIZE DISTRIBUTION OF INCOME IN A DEVELOPING NATION BY INCOME SHARES-QUINTILES AND DECILES

Personal Income		Percentage Share in Total Income	
Individuals	(Money Unit)	Quintiles	Deciles
1	0.75		
2	1.25		2.00
3	1.20		
4	1.45	4.65	2.65
5	1.85		
6	2.00		3.85
7	2.50		
8	2.70	9.05	5.20
9	2.75		
10	2.85		5.60
11	3.45		
12	3.90	12.95	7.35
13	4.75		
14	4.50		9.25
15	5.80		
16	7.30	22.35	13.10
17	1.50		
18	12.00		22.50
19	13.00		
20	15.50	51.00	28.50
Total (national income)	100.00	100.00	100.00

In column 4, the population is sorted into deciles of 2 individuals each to provide a more detailed division of the size distribution of income. The first decile represents the bottom 10% of the population on the income scale. As a group, these individuals receive only 2% of the total national income. The top 10% of the population, that is, the two richest individuals, receive 28.5% of the total income.

This provides a more detailed breakdown of the size distribution of income, finding out what the top 5% receives, one can divide the total population into 20 equal groups of individuals, and calculate the percentage of the total income received by the top group. In our example, it turns out that each group is composed of only one individual, and the top 5% of the population, that is, the twentieth individual, receives 15.5% of the total income. This amounts to a higher share than the 13.7% shares of the total income received by the lowest 40% of the population.

The Lorenz Curve and the Gini Coefficient. Another common way of analyzing personal income data is to construct a **Lorenz Curve**. This curve was devised in 1905 by Conrad Lorenz, an American statistician. The Lorenz curve is the most widely used diagram that shows the relationship between population groups and their respective income shares. Figure 5.1 depicts the Lorenz curve that is constructed on the basis of the data given in Table 5.1. In this figure, the horizontal and vertical axis are divided into 10 equal portions according to each of the 10 decile group. Both the table and the curve show what percentage of population, ranked from poorest to richest, received what percentage of the total national income in a given year.

The graph is drawn by indicating the percentage of income recipients (population) on the horizontal axis. Commonly families, rather than individuals, are presented in a Lorenz diagram. The point denoted 20 indicates the lowest 20 percent of the population; the point denoted 40, the lowest 40 percent and so one. The vertical axis shows the percentage of total money income. Both axes are of the same length and scale. Thus, a diagonal line, starting at zero and sloping upward from left to right at a 45 degree angle portrays the **line of perfect equality**.

Along the line of perfect equality, 20 percent of the population receives 20 percent of the national income. Similarly, 40 percent of the population receives 40 percent of the national income, and so on. The line of perfect equality provides a basis of comparison with the curve of actual distribution, the Lorenz curve, that is derived from the data given in the table. Point "a" indicates that the bottom 10% of the population receives only 2 percent of the national income, point "b" indicates that the bottom 20% receives 4.65 percent of the national income, and so on for each of the other cumulative decile groups. The area between the line of perfect equality and the Lorenz curve measures the degree of income inequality. Hence, the more the Lorenz curve is bowed away from the diagonal, the higher the inequality of income distribution. This point is illustrated in Figure 5.2, which portrays two representative distributions, one for relatively equal income distribution (Figure 5.2a) and the other for a more unequal income distribution (Figure 5.2b).

The Lorenz curve can be used to provide us with a shorthand summary yardstick of income inequality in a nation. This yardstick, the **Gini coefficient of inequality**, is named after Corrodo Gini, an early-twentieth-century Italian statistician. Referring back to Figure 5.1 again, the Gini coefficient may be defined as the numerical value of the area between the Lorenz curve and the line of perfect equality divided by the numerical value of the entire area beneath the line of perfect equality. In other words, it is the ratio of the inequality area to the whole triangular area under the line of perfect equality, That is:

$$\text{Gini coefficient of inequality} = \frac{\text{inequality area}}{\text{triangular area}}$$

Figure 5.1

THE LORENZ CURVE

The graph is drawn by indicating the percentage of income recipients (population) on the horizontal axis. The vertical axis shows the percentage of total money income. Both axes are of the same length and scale. Thus, a diagonal line, starting at zero and sloping upward from left to right at a 45 degree angle portrays the **line of perfect equality**.

Along the line of perfect equality, 20 percent of the population receives 20 percent of the national income. Similarly, 40 percent of the population receives 40 percent of the national income, and so on. The line of perfect equality provides a basis of comparison with the curve of actual distribution, the Lorenz curve, that is derived from the data given in the table.

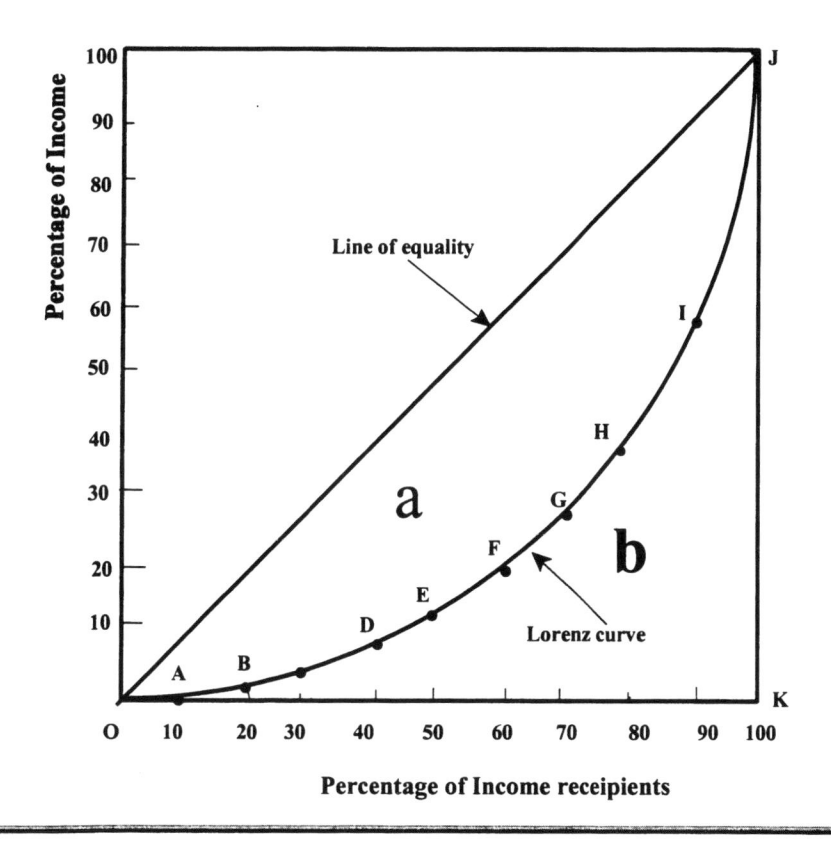

98 PART II/THE ELEMENTS OF GROWTH

Figure 5.2

INTERPRETING THE CURVATURE OF THE LORENZ CURVE

The more the Lorenz curve is bowed away from the diagonal, the higher the inequality of income distribution. This point is illustrated in the figure, which portrays two representative distributions, one for relatively equal income distribution (panel a) and the other for a more unequal income distribution (panel b.)

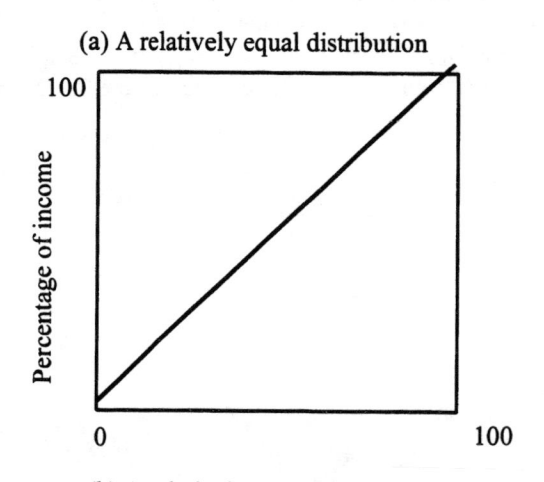

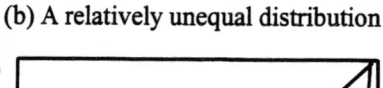

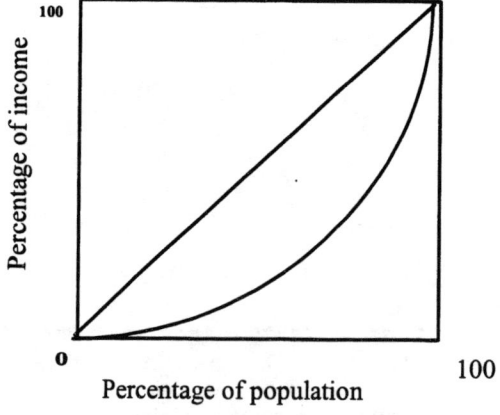

(a) A relatively equal distribution

(b) A relatively unequal distribution

Percentage of population

CH. 5/POVERTY AND INCOME DISTRIBUTION

The value of the Gini coefficient ranges from 0 to 1. As incomes become more equal, the inequality area gets smaller in comparison to the triangular area under the line of perfect equality. In other words, as income becomes more equal, the Gini coefficient approaches zero. At zero, no inequality exists, that is, all incomes are equal. As incomes become more unequal, the inequality area gets larger relative to the triangular area. Thus, the Gini coefficient approaches 1. However, given the existence of income inequality in the real-world society, the Gini coefficient is always less than 1.

Although the Gini coefficient is a widely used measure of income inequality it has the following disadvantages:

1. As a single coefficient, the Gini coefficient does not show the degree by which different income groups are accountable for the overall index of inequality. For example, the dotted Lorenz curve in Figure 5.3 has the same Gini coefficient as the solid Lorenz curve. However, according to the dotted curve, the poor people have less of the national income, while income is distributed more equally among the upper-and middle-income groups.

2. Another problem associated with the Gini coefficient is related to the measurement of area "a". This area is commonly measured by determining area "b" and subtracting it from (a + b). Area b can be calculated by using integral calculus. However, the first step, describing the Lorenz curve algebraically, is a cumbersome task. A common approach for approximating the area under the curve is to connect the various points (O, A, B, C, ... J in Figure 5.1) with the straight lines, and then calculate area b by adding the areas under the curve. The following example demonstrates this approach:

Suppose a society is composed of four income classes with a combined money income of $20 billion. The distribution of income among families is given in Table 5.2. The Lorenz curve is portrayed in Figure 5.4 and the Gini coefficient is calculated by:

a. Calculating the total triangular area beneath the diagonal, that is, the area of AEF (Figure 5.4). Note that for a triangle, the area A in terms of the base b and height h is found by the following formula:

$$A = 1/2 bh$$

Thus, the area of AFG is : $1/2 \times 100 \times 100 = 5{,}000$

b. Calculate the sum of the areas under the Lorenz curve. This is equal to the small triangular area and the three remaining trapezoid areas under ABCDE. Note that the area of a trapezoid in terms of the base b and heights h_1 and h_2 is found by the following formula:

$$A = 1/2 b(h_1 + h_2)$$

Thus, the area under the Lorenz curve is:

$125 + 500 + 1{,}125 + 2{,}000 = 3{,}750$

100   PART II/THE ELEMENTS OF GROWTH

Figure 5.3

TWO LORENZ CURVES WITH THE SAME GINI COEFFICIENT BUT DIFFERENT CURVATURES

The dotted Lorenz curve in the figure has the same Gini coefficient as the solid Lorenz curve. However, according to the dotted curve, the poor people have less of the national income, while income is distributed more equally among the upper-and middle-income groups.

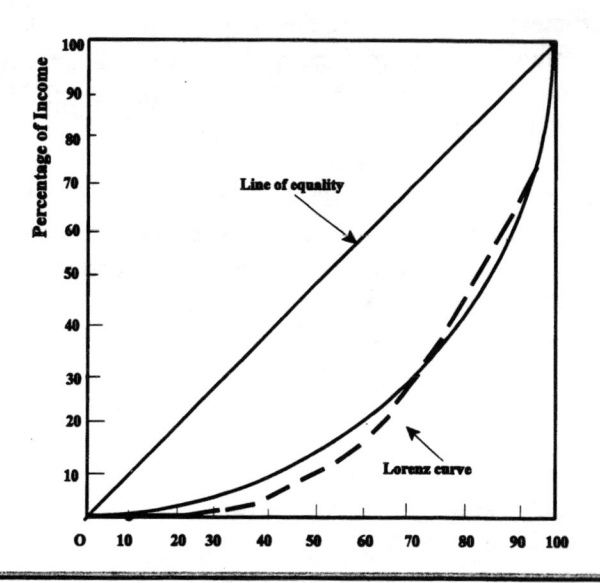

Table 5.2

THE DISTRIBUTION OF INCOME IN A HYPOTHETICAL SOCIETY COMPOSED OF FOUR INCOME CLASSES

1	2	3	4	5	6
Percent of families	Income received (in billions of dollars)	Percent of income received	Cumulative percent of families	Cumulative percent of income received	Point on Lorenz curve
0	0	0	0%	0	A
Lowest Fourth	2	10	25	10	B
Second Fourth	4	20	50	30	C
Third Fourth	6	30	75	60	D
Highest Fourth	8	40	100	100	E

Figure 5.4

THE LORENZ CURVE: A HYPOTHETICAL EXAMPLE

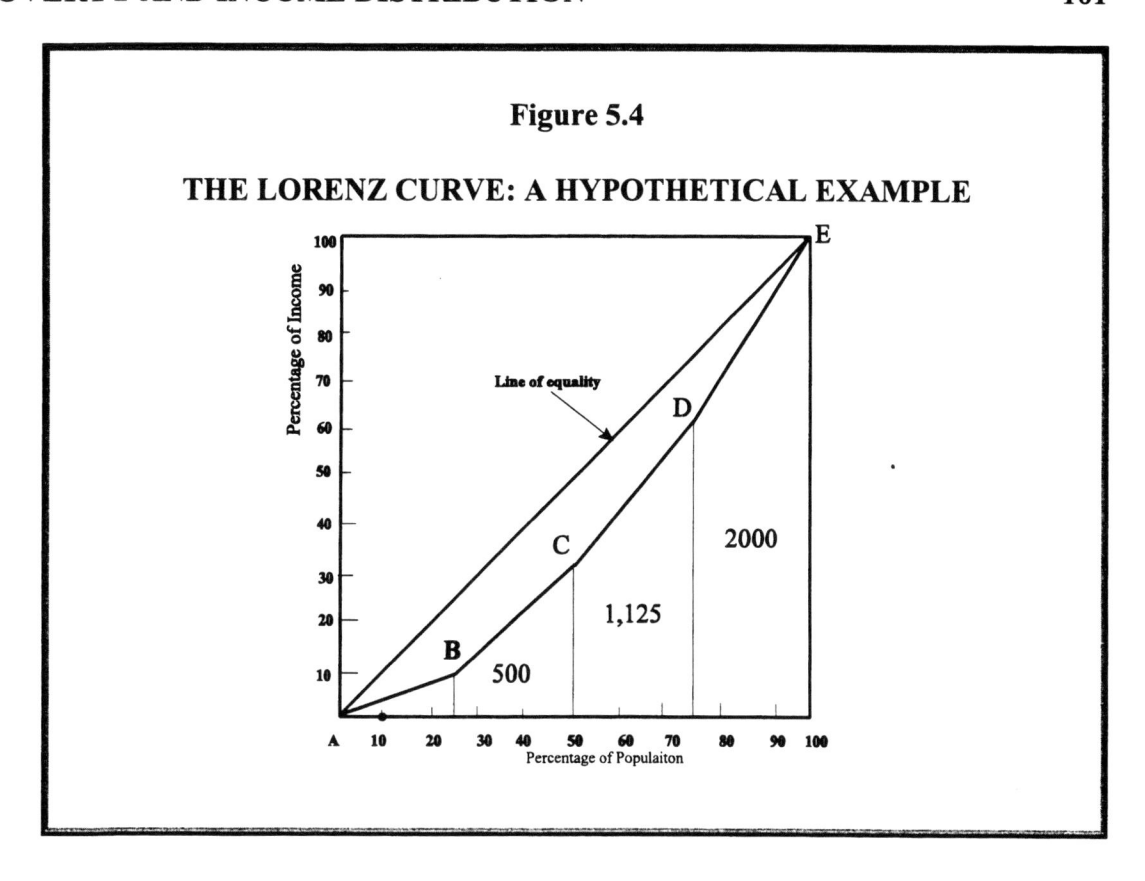

c. Subtracting the answer obtained in step (b) from the answer obtained in step (a), we get:

5,000 - 3,750 = 1,250

d. Expressing the result as a fraction of the total triangular area obtained in step (a) we get the Gini coefficient of inequality:

$$\frac{1,250}{5,000} = 0.25$$

Although the calculation of area b by the procedure outlined above is relatively simple, it leads to an upward bias in estimating area b, thus underestimating the degree of income concentration. The fewer the number of income classes into which the population is broken, the fewer the number of points that can be plotted, the higher the underestimate tends to be.

Thus, different methods of measuring the Gini coefficient can provide us with significantly different figures. This is problematic because not all researchers use the same methods. As a result, comparisons among nations may yield misleading results. This problem, coupled with the difficulty in defining and measuring income discussed earlier, makes it clear that inequality ranking of any specific nation should be considered with caution and must be supplemented by other evidence before any judgement is made about the pattern of income distribution in that country as compared to other nations.

THE HUMAN POVERTY INDEX

In 1997, a new measure of poverty was introduced by the United Nations Development Program (UNDP). The development of this index stemmed from the UNDP's dismay with the dollar-a-day World Bank measures. The UNDP attempted to supplant a measure of "human" poverty for the World Bank's "income" poverty. Thus it devised the **Human Poverty Index (HPI)**, similar in ways to the Human Development Index (HDI), discussed in Chapter 2. The construction of this index is based on the assumption that human poverty should be measured in terms of the following three major deprivations:

1. **Survival.** This variable reflects the vulnerability to death at relatively early age. It is measured by the percentage of people who are expected to die before reaching the age of 40.
2. **Knowledge.** This variable is measured by the percentage of adults that are illiterate.
3. **Overall Economic Provision.** This variable is measured by the percentage of people with access to health services and safe water plus the percentage of children younger than five years of age who are malnourished.

The incorporation of the above three variables into a single composite index, HPI, is based on a complex formula developed by the World Bank. Using this formula, in 1997, the World Bank ranked 78 nations from the lowest to the highest HPI and learned that these rankings could vary significantly from both UNDP's own HDI ranking and the World Bank's income poverty rankings.

Given that the value of HPI shows the percentage of population negatively impacted by the three major deprivations indices, the lower the HPI for a nation, the better off that nation is in terms of human development. Table 5.3 portrays the five lowest-ranked (high HPI) and the highest ranked (low HPI). It also shows the HPI deviations from the HDI and income ranking of these same nations.

IDENTIFYING THE POVERTY GROUPS

Our discussion of poverty in previous sections indicates that higher levels of per capita income do not warrant lower levels of poverty. Thus, a comprehension of the nature of the size distribution of income is a prerequisite to a meaningful analysis of the poverty issue in developing nations. But before we can devise strategies to eradicate poverty at its core, we need to identify these poverty groups and understand their economic features. We may distinguish between three poverty groups: rural, women, and ethnic minorities.

Rural Poverty

The existing data from a wide cross section of developing nations indicate the following:

1. A majority of poor people live in rural areas.
2. The primary occupations of poor people are agriculture and related activities.
3. Women and children, as opposed to adult males, make up the bulk of poor people.
4. A large percentage of poor people are composed of minority groups and ethnic groups.

Today, in Africa and Asia, about 80% to 90% of the poor live in rural areas. This percentage decreases to 50% for Latin America.

Given the relatively larger proportion of poor people in rural sectors as opposed to urban sectors, it is

CH. 5/POVERTY AND INCOME DISTRIBUTION

ironic that the lion's share of the GNP of most developing nations over the past quarter of a century has been allocated toward the urban areas and, within those areas, toward the comparatively rich commercial and agricultural sectors. Such an urban bias in government expenditures is the source of many development problems that will be discussed in forthcoming chapters.

Women and Poverty

Today, women constitute more than 70 percent of the globe's poor people. The poorest portion of developing nations' people live in households headed by women. In these households there is usually no male wage earner. Women head about 40% of households in rural Kenya, and 20% in India. Other developing nations experience similar problems and the percentage of women heading a household continues to rise.

Women and children are more likely to be malnourished and poor than men. They are less likely to get medical attention or receive clean water, sanitation, or other necessities of life. Medical care evidence shows that, given equal treatment, women have lower death rates than men. This is evident from the available data in Europe and North America, where although males outnumber females at birth, females enjoy lower mortality rates, outnumbering males by 105 to 100. Gender bias is also reflected in the differential treatment of boys and girls in developing nations. For example, it is estimated that in India, girls are four times as likely to endure acute malnutrition and boys are forty times more likely to be taken to the hospital when sick. Such gender biases have resulted in a significant reduction in the survival rates of female infants, as evidenced by the recorded female-male sex ratios in nations such as China. According to the available data this ratio is so

Table 5.3

HUMAN POVERTY INDEX RANKINGS FOR THE TEN TOP-AND BOTTOM-RANKED DEVELOPING NATIONS, 1997

\multicolumn{5}{c	}{Top Ten Nations}	\multicolumn{5}{c}{Bottom Ten Nations}
Rank	Nation	HPI Index Value (%)	HPI Rank minus HDI Rank*	HPI Rank minus $1-a-day Poverty Rank*	Rank	Nation	HPI Index Value (%)	HPI Rank minus HDI Rank*	HPI Rank minus $1-a-day Poverty Rank*
1	Trinidad and Tobago	4.1	-4	-	1	Mali	54.7	0	-
2	Cuba	5.1	-18	-	2	Ethiopia	56.2	2	14
3	Chile	5.4	1	-13	3	Burkina Faso	58.3	1	-
4	Singapore	6.6	3	-	4	Sierra Leone	59.2	-1	-
5	Costa Rica	6.6	2	-15	5	Niger	66.0	2	3

Source: United Nations Development Program, *Human Development Report, 1997*, (New York: Oxford University Press, 1997), p. 21, table 1.1.

* A negative number denotes that the nation performs better on the HPI than on other measures (HDI or income poverty); a positive, the opposite.

much lower than the expected value that it is said that 200 million girls are "missing" in China.[1]

In many developing nations, gender ideologies commonly advocate the idea that males have the right to personal spending money, while females' money is for common ends. In the job market, such ideologies have been marked by the existence of large wage differentials between men and women. According to the International Labor Organization (ILO), females receive an average income half that of males in developing nations. This stems partly from **crowding**, that is, the inclination to discriminate against females in high-paying occupations, compelling them to accept low-paying and menial jobs.

The male-dominated cultures of many developing nations have led to legislation that often prevents females from property ownership, signing financial contracts without their husband's signature, applying for a passport without their husband's consent, and applying for institutionally provided resources such as training and credit. In these nations, generally, income-generating programs and government employment are reserved exclusively for men, worsening the existing income disparities between males and females.

Research has indicated that development activities can in fact enhance females' workloads, while simultaneously, decreasing the percentage of household resources that are controlled by them. Such findings underline the fact that women and their dependents constitute the most economically deprived class in developing nations. Thus, economic planners who are serious about improving living standards for the poorest individuals must bring women into the economic mainstream. This means that they should adopt strategies that aim at increasing women's participation rates in formal-sector employment, training and educational programs, and agricultural extension programs. It also means ensuring that women are not discriminated against in obtaining governmental resources set aside for formal education, training, employment, services, and social security programs.

Ethnic Minorities

Today, about 40 percent of the globe's nation-states include more than five major ethnic populations, some of which suffer from considerable economic, political, and social discrimination. Such conditions have resulted in domestic conflicts and even civil wars, stemming from the ethnic group's perception that they are losing the battle in the race for the exploitation of scant resources and diminishing employment opportunities. The situation is even worse for the indigenous people who constitute more than 300 million in 70 nations. Most of these people live in utmost poverty and suffer from discrimination in access to education, health care, and employment opportunities. For instance, in Guatemala about 87% of the indigenous are poor, compared to 45% for the nonindigenous population. A similar situation exists in Bolivia, Mexico, and Peru. The poverty predicaments of ethnic minorities, whether we consider Muslims in India, Kurds in Iraq, Tibetans in China, Tamils in Sri Lanka, or Karens in Myanmar, is as severe as that of indigenous peoples who occupy the Third World nations. The gravity of this situation was underlined by the United Nations which labeled 1993 as the year of indigenous peoples.

GROWTH AND INEQUALITY: THE INVERTED-U HYPOTHESIS

As we already know, the mere dependence on economic growth to reduce the degree of absolute poverty in developing nations is probably inadequate. Given the significance of this issue to development theory and policy, an understanding of how income distribution changes over the course of development calls for further examination. The question to ask is whether the pursuit of economic growth improves, deteriorates, or has no impact on the distribution of income and the degree of poverty in developing nations. In his pioneering work, Simon Kuznets proposed the **inverted-U hypothesis** to explain the secular behavior of income inequality. According to Kuznets, there is a wide oscillation in the income inequality gap characterizing the secular income framework: expanding in the initial stages of economic growth, when the transition from the traditional sector to the modern sector is fast; stabilizing for a while; and then narrowing in the final stages. This is, in fact, where the theory got its name. This can be detected from Figure 5.5 which shows the relationship between a longitudinal (time-series) plot of changes in income distribution (measured by the Gini coefficient), and GNP per capita which traces a U-shaved curve.

The U-shaped pattern of income inequality can be related to the nature of structural change. According to Lewis, early growth maybe concentrated in the modern industrial sector, which is characterized by limited employment, high wages, and high productivity. The income inequality between the two sectors may expand quickly initially, before starting to narrow down. The income gap in the growing modern sector may be much larger than the stagnant traditional sector.

Although research on Western nations seems to support the inverted-U hypothesis, studies on developing nations are too mixed and inconclusive to affirm the inverted U-hypotheses.[*][2]

DOES INEQUALITY INDUCE GROWTH?

Until the late 1980s, it was widely believed that a high degree of income inequality was a necessary condition for triggering rapid growth. The main economic argument in support of this proposition was that individuals in the upper income brackets save and invest a significant percentage of their income, whereas individuals in the lower income brackets spend their entire income on consumption goods. Given that the rate of growth of GNP is positively correlated to the percentage of national income saved, then clearly an economy marked by high income inequality would save more and grow more rapidly than one with less income inequality. It was further assumed that eventually national and per capita income would be large enough to allow significant redistribution of income from the rich to the poor through tax and subsidy policies. However, before such time is approached any policy that aims at sizeable income distribution would lead to lower growth rates and postpone the time when a larger income size allows a bigger share for the entire population's classes.

Kuznets did not buy into the proposed relationship between income inequality and rates of economic growth concerning the now developed nations. Additionally, he was not at all persuaded that large income inequalities in today's developing nations would have a positive impact on their rate of economic growth. He wrote:

> Because they may have proved favorable in the past, it is dangerous to argue that completely free markets, lack of penalties implicit in progressive taxation, and the like are indispensable for growth of the now underdeveloped countries. Under present conditions the results may be quite opposite- withdrawal of accumulated assets to relatively "safe" channels, either by flight abroad or into real estate; and the inability of governments to serve as basic agents in the kind of capital formation that is indispensable to economic growth. It is dangerous to argue that, because in the past foreign investment provided capital resources to spark satisfactory economic growth in some of the smaller European countries or Europe's descendants across the seas, similar effects can be expected today if only underdeveloped countries can be convinced of the need of a "favorable climate".[3]

---

[*]Part of the difficulty stems from the absence of time-series data for most of the developing nations, causing researchers to employ cross sectional data, that is, to examine many different nations at one point in time instead of one nation over a long period of time. Deducing results from cross-sectional data for a time-series event is highly questionable. Additionally, some critics have argued that research in support of the inverted-U hypothesis can sometimes be reserved by deleting one or two nations from the data pool.

Figure 5.5

KUZNET'S INVERTED-U CURVE

The figure shows the relationship between a longitudinal (time-series) plot of changes in income distribution (measured by the Gini coefficient), and GNP per capita which traces a U-shaved curve.

[Graph: Gini coefficient (y-axis, 0.25, 0.50, 0.75) vs Gorss national product per capita (x-axis), showing an inverted-U curve]

Most economists share Kuznet's view and reject the proposition that a high degree of income inequality has a favorable impact on economic growth. They, in fact, argue that greater equality in developing nations may be a prerequisite for self-preserving economic growth. The following four general reasons can be presented in support of their arguments:

1. It is not necessarily true that the rich generate more productive domestic savings and investment than the poor. In fact, the rich are known to exhaust much of their incomes on imported luxury goods, jewelry, gold, expensive homes, foreign travel, or to pursue safe havens abroad for savings in the shape of capital flight. Such savings and investments do not contribute to the country's productive investment. Rather, they portray massive depletions of these resources which are generated from the toil and sweat of the workers. Thus, a growth policy based on wide and growing income inequality may in fact be nothing more than strategies devised to serve the vested interests and preserve the status quo of the economic and political elites of the developing nations, often to the detriment of the masses of poor people in these countries.[4]
2. Enhancing the income levels of the poor will induce an overall rise in the demand for indigenously produced necessity goods such as clothing and food, while the rich are inclined to disburse more of their additional income on luxury goods. Increasing demand for domestic products contributes to domestic production, domestic employment, and domestic investment, generating the conditions for fast economic growth and a wider participation in that growth.[5]
3. A decrease in mass poverty, achieved through a more equitable income distribution, can trigger

robust economic growth by serving as a potent material and psychological stimulus to widespread public collaboration in the development mechanism. On the contrary, large income inequality can serve as a potent material and psychological disincentive to economic progress. It may even set the stage for an eventual disapproval of progress by the baffled and fiery people, in particular those who are highly educated.[6]

4. The low levels of income and standard of living of the poor, which are displayed in poor education, health, and nutrition, can lower their economic efficiency, and thus slow down economic growth. Thus, policies that aim at enhancing incomes and living standards of poor people do not only lead to their economic well-being, but also cause the productivity and income of the entire economy to grow at a faster rate.[7]

POLICIES TO ALLEVIATE POVERTY AND INCOME INEQUALITY

As our preceding discussion indicates, most economists argue that greater equality in developing nations may be a prerequisite for self-preserving economic growth. Given this position, to reduce poverty and income inequality, the developing nations' authorities have many options and alternative policies to choose from. The following provides a list of four major policies that can be adopted by a developing nation's government.

1. **Altering Relative Factor Prices.** This policy is based on the presumption of **factor-price-distortions** in developing nations. It is argued that due to inappropriate government polices and institutional constraints, the price of labor (the wage rate) is higher and the price of capital is lower than what is warranted by the free market forces of demand and supply in a developing nation. The higher price of labor reflects the power of trade unions in raising minimum wages to artificially higher levels than those resulting from the interaction of supply and demand, even in the face of widespread unemployment. The lower price of capital reflects the government's desire to encourage investment through various policies, such as tax allowances, investment incentives, subsidized interest rates, overvalued exchange rates, and low tariff on capital goods imports such as tractors and automated equipment. It is argued that the removal of factor price distortions which allow wage rates to decline and the price of capital to rise to their market determined values will lead employers to substitute labor for capital in their production processes. Such an action entices producers to increase their utilization of the abundant factor of production, that is, labor, and lower their employment of the scarce factor of production, that is, capital. This enhances the overall level of employment and eventually increases the incomes of the poor, who basically own their labor services. It also causes more efficient utilization of the relatively scarce factor of production, that is capital, and lowers the artificially high incomes of owners of capital. Thus, given a rise in the income of the poor, accompanied by a simultaneous decline of the incomes of the owners of capital, poverty will be alleviated and income will become more equal.

    In summary, dismantling of factor-price distortion kills many birds with one stone, so to speak. It fuses growth, and the induced efficiency, with higher employment, less inequality and less poverty.

2. **Redistributing Wealth.** The major cause of unequal distribution of personal income in developing nations is the concentration of the wealth. Today, less than 20% of the population of developing nations control more than 90% of wealth composed of physical capital, land, stocks, bonds, and human capital in the form of better education. Given such a high concentration of wealth, it is no wonder that less than 20 percent of the population in developing nations receive more than a 50% share of the national income. Thus, correcting factor price distortion is not sufficient to alleviate income inequality. It is also necessary to attack the problem at the source, that is, to focus attention on alleviating the control of wealth, unequal access to education, unequal distribution of power, and

income generating opportunities that exemplify many developing nations. In achieving these objectives, the following policies can be adopted:

    a. **Land Reform.** The objective of this policy is to alter tenant farmers into small farm owners who have motives to increase output and advance their income levels. However, as we will explain in Chapter 7, as an income redistribution tool, such a policy may not be very effective if the existence of institutional and price distortions in the economic framework inhibit small farm owners to have access to badly needed resources such as seeds, fertilizers, credit, marketing channels, and agronomy education.

    b. **Asset Redistribution.** This policy can be implemented in two different ways. The first strategy calls on government to redistribute the existing assets from the rich to the poor. The second strategy, known as "**redistribution from growth,**" requires the government to transfer a certain percentage of annual savings and investments to low-income classes in order to provide for a gradual redistribution of assets as they agglomerate over time. Given the gradual nature of such a transfer, it may prove to be politically more acceptable than the first strategy.

    c. **Education.** Given the unequal distribution of human capital in the form of education, the government can promote wider access to educational opportunities as a main strategy for alleviating poverty. However, the success of such a strategy requires adoption and implementation of complementary policies such as the provision of more productive employment prospects. The relationship between education, employment and development will be further discussed in Chapter 8.

3. **Imposing Progressive Income and Wealth Taxes.** Direct and progressive taxation on both income and wealth not only provides the developing nation with a major source of funds needed to implement development plans, but also provides for more equitable income/wealth distribution. **Progressive income taxes** concentrate on personal and corporate income, requiring the rich to pay a progressively higher proportion of their total income than the poor. Taxation on wealth usually includes personal and corporate property taxes and may also involve progressive inheritance taxes. The burden of this tax is devised to fall on the upper-income classes. In practice in many countries, both developed and developing, progressive taxes end up to be **regressive taxes** in the sense that the lower-and middle-income classes pay a relatively larger percentage of their incomes in taxes than the upper-income classes. This happens because the poor are usually taxed at the source of their incomes or expenditures by withholding taxes from general poll taxes, wages, or **indirect taxes** imposed on retail purchases of goods and services. On the contrary, the rich generate the largest percentage of their incomes from return on their assets which usually are not reported for tax purposes. They often know how to manipulate the system to avert paying taxes without worrying about government retribution.

4. **Direct Transfer Payments and Public Expenditures.** This policy calls on government to pay money directly to the poor and/or engage in a number of social programs that are financed by taxes. Examples include school lunches, preschool nutritional supplementary schemes, subsidized food programs for the rural and urban poor, public health projects in rural and poverty stricken urban areas, and the provision of clean water and electricity to distant rural areas.

CH. 5/POVERTY AND INCOME DISTRIBUTION

SUMMARY

1. Absolute poverty is below the income level that secures the bare essentials of food, clothing, and shelter. This income level, referred to as the absolute poverty line, is a global measure of poverty. As an international line of poverty it considers anyone who lives on less than a dollar a day in **purchasing parity power (PPP)** dollars as poor.
2. PPP can be defined as the number of units of a nation's currency needed to buy the identical quantity of goods and services in the domestic market as $1 would purchase in the United States.
3. A **poverty gap** measures the total amount of money needed to bring the income of every poor person up to the poverty line, thereby eradicating poverty.
4. In general, the magnitude of poverty, measured by the **headcount index**, that is, ratio of number of poor people to population, is much lower in advanced nations as compared to the developing nations.
5. Two poverty lines have been identified by economists: the lower (extreme) poverty line, and the upper poverty line. The **lower (extreme) poverty line**, considered as the absolute minimum by international standards, is based on standards set in India and amounts to $275 per capita income. The **upper poverty line** amounts to $370 per capita.
6. The main factors that enter the calculations and measurement of income in a given nation are noncash income, pretax or aftertax income, demographic factors, geographic factors, and public goods and services.
7. Factors that contribute to income inequality can be divided into two groups. The first group is composed of the universal factors of inequality, that is, factors that are responsible for income inequality in a given nation, regardless of whether it is a developing or an advanced nation. The second group includes some additional factors that are responsible for further income inequality in developing nations.
8. The universal causes of income inequality in nations include the following:
    a. Earning ability and opportunity differentials.
    b. Differences in wealth, differences in age.
    c. Differences in opportunities.
    d. Differences in human-capital investment.
    e. Differences in security, risk, and uncertainty.
    f. Differences in resource mobility.
9. Additional causes of inequality in developing nations include the following:
    a. Rapid population growth.
    b. Taxes and government expenditure patterns.
    c. Discrimination.
    d. Skill shortages.
    e. Unequal distribution of land ownership.
    f. Market imperfection.
10. Economists generally differentiate between two main measures of income inequality: functional distribution of income, and size distribution of income.
11. Functional or factor share distribution of income is a measure of income inequality that deals with the distribution of income to factors of production.
12. The size or the personal distribution of income is the most commonly used measure of income inequality by economists and it is usually employed as a direct indicator of welfare. It focuses on individuals, households, and the total incomes they receive. The two most common methods used by economists to calculate the size distribution of income are the income shares method and the Lorenz curve method.
13. The income shares method is composed of two steps. The first step is to divide the population into successive quintiles (fifths) or deciles (tenths) in accordance to ascending income levels. The second step

is to determine what percentage of the total national income is received by each income group.
14. The Lorenz curve is the most widely used diagram that shows the relationship between population groups and their respective income shares.
15. Gini coefficient may be defined as the numerical value of the area between the Lorenz curve and the line of perfect equality divided by the numerical value of the entire area beneath the line of the perfect equality. In other words, it is the ratio of the inequality area to the whole triangular area under the line of perfect equality, That is:

$$\text{Gini coefficient of inequality} = \frac{\text{inequality area}}{\text{triangular area}}$$

16. The Human Poverty Index (HPI) is similar to the Human Development Index (HDI), The construction of this index is based on the assumption that human poverty should be measured in terms of the following three major deprivations:
    a. Survival.
    b. Knowledge.
    c. Overall Economic Provision.
17. We may distinguish between three poverty groups: rural, women, and ethnic minorities.
18. According to the inverted-U hypothesis, there is a wide oscillation in the income inequality gap characterizing the secular income framework: expanding in the initial stages of economic growth, when the transition from the traditional sector to the modern sector is fast; stabilizing for a while; and then narrowing in the final stages.
19. The following provides a list of four major policies that can be adopted by a developing nation's government in order to alleviate income inequality:
    a. Altering factor prices.
    b. Redistributing wealth, including land reform, asset redistribution, and education.
    c. Imposing progressive income and wealth taxes. Encompassing progressive income taxes, regressive taxes, and indirect taxes.
    d. Direct transfer payments and public expenditures.

QUESTIONS

1. Elaborate on the concept of absolute poverty by answering the following questions:
    a. What is meant by absolute poverty?
    b. What is meant by the headcount index? Does this index differ between developing and developed nations? Explain.
    c. What is meant by poverty gap?
    d. What are the two poverty lines identified by economists? What are the major differences between the two poverty lines?
2. Elaborate on advantages of utilizing income-gap approach, headcount approach, and Gini coefficient to portray poverty instead of using only the headcount index.
3. What are the main factors that enter the calculation and measurement of income in a given country?
4. Devise a plan for collecting data on poverty and income distribution for a low-income nation of your choice. Show data and measures you would emphasize, and discuss how this information can be utilized to effect government policy.
5. According to the textbook, what are the two main groups of factors that contribute to income inequality in a given nation? What is the major difference between these two groups?
6. What are the universal causes of income inequality? Explain.

CH. 5/POVERTY AND INCOME DISTRIBUTION 111

7. According to your textbook, besides the universal causes of inequality, what other factors contribute to further income inequality in developing nations?
8. Economists usually differentiate between two main measures of income inequality. What are these two measures? How do they differ from each other?
9. Elaborate on the Lorenz curve by answering the following questions:
   a. What does this curve measure?
   b. What is meant by the Gini coefficient and how is it measured and interpreted?
   c. What are disadvantages of the Gini coefficient?
10. What is meant by HPI? How is it differentiated from HDI? What are the major assumptions underlining the construction of this index?
11. Elaborate on the inverted-U hypothesis by answering the following questions:
    a. Who proposed this theory?
    b. What does this theory explain?
    c. According to Lewis, how can the U-shaped be explained?
    d. Do the existing empirical studies support the U-hypothesis?
    e. Does the increasing portion of the inverted U-shaped curve connote that the poor's condition deteriorates with economic growth? Explain.
12. Elaborate on the major policies that can be adopted by a developing nation's government to alleviate poverty, by answering the following questions:
    a. Name these policies.
    b. What policies do you think would be more effective in alleviating poverty and income inequality in developing nations? Explain.
    c. Why do women in developing nations have higher poverty rates than men?
    d. What polices can a developing nation adopt to alleviate women's poverty rates?
13. Suppose that a society consists of only four families with a combined money income of $200,000. The distribution of income among families is given in the following table:

1	2	3	4	5
Percent of Families	**Income Received**	**Percent of Income Received**	**Cumulative Percent of Families**	**Cumulative Percent of Income Received**
0		0	0%	
Lowest Fourth		5	25	
Second Fourth		10	50	
Third Fourth		30	75	
Highest Fourth		55	100	

Given the above table:

a. Fill in columns 2 and 5.

b. Construct a Lorenz curve and calculate the Gini coefficient of income inequality, using the technique explained in the textbook.
c. What is the usefulness of the Gini coefficient for a developing nation?

NOTES

1. Amartya Sen, "Missing Women," *British Medical Journal* 304 (1992): 587-588.
2. Irma Adelman and Cynthia Taft Morris, *Economic Growth and Social Equality in Developing Countries* (Stanford, Calif.: Stanford University Press, 1973).
3. Simon Kuzenet, "Economic Growth and Income Inequality," *American Economic Review*, 45 (March 1955), p.26.
4. Donald R. Lessard and John Willimson, *Capital Flight: The Problem and Policy Responses* (Washington, D.C.: Institute for International Economics, 1987); Gustav Ranis, "Investment Criteria, Productivity and Economic Development: An Empirical Comment," *Quarterly Journal of Economics* (May 1962); K. L. Gupta, "Personal Saving in Developing Countries: Further Evidence," *Economic Record* (June 1970); and Andrew Mason, "Savings, Economic Growth and Demographic Change," *Population and Development Review* 14 (March 1988): 113-144.
5. Norman L. Hicks, "Growth vs. Basic Needs: Is There a Trade-Off?" *World Development* (1997): 985-994; and Adriana Marshall, "Income Distribution, the Domestic Market and Growth in Argentina," *Labour and Society* 13 (January 1998): 79-103.
6. Alberto Alesina and Roberto Perotti, "The Political Economy of Growth: A Critical Survey of the Recent Literature," *World Bank Economic Development Review* 8 (September 1994): 351-371; and Alberto Alesina and Dani Rodrik, "Distributive Policies and Economic Growth," *Quarterly Journal of Economics* 109 (May 1994): 465-490.
7. Partha Dasgupta and Dbragi Ray, "Inequality As Determinant of Malnutrition and Unemployment Policy," *Economic Journal* 97 (March 1987): 177-188.

SUGGESTED READINGS

Adelman, Irma, and Sherman Robinson. "Income Distribution and Development." in Hollis B. Chenery and T.N. Srinivasan, eds. *Handbook of Development Economics*. Vol. 2. Amsterdam: Elsevier-North Hollan, 1989; pp. 950-1008.

_____. "A Poverty-Focused Approach to Development Policy." in John P. Lewis and Valeriana Kaleb. eds. *Development Strategies Reconsidered*. Washington, D.C.: Overseas Development Council, 1986, pp. 49-65.

Ahluwalia, Monteck S. Nicholas G. Carter, and Hollis B. Chenery. "Growth and Poverty in Developing Countries. *Journal of Development Economics* 6 (September 1979): 299-341.

Alesina, Alberto and Dani Rodrik. "Distributive Politics and Economic Growth." *Quarterly Journal of Economic* 109 (May 1994): 465-90.

Atkins, Anthony B. *The Economic of Inequality*. New York: Oxford University Press, 1975.

Barhan, Pranab, "Efficiency, Equity and Poverty Alleviation: Policy Issues in Less Developed Countries." *Economic Journal* 106 (September 1996): 1344-1356.

Bruce, Judith and Daisy Dwyer. eds. *A Home Divided: Women and Income in the Third World*. Stanford, Calif.: Stanford University Press, 1988.

Bhagwati, Jagdish N. "Poverty and Public Policy." *World Development* 16 (May 1980: 539-555.

Bigsten, Ann. "Poverty, Inequality and Development." in Norman Gemmell. ed. *Survey in Development Economic*. Oxford: Blackwell, 1987., ch. 4.

_____. *Income Distribution and Development Theory, Evidence and Policy*. London: Heinemann, 1983.

Buvinic, Margaret A. Lycette, and William P. McGreevey. eds. *Women and Poverty in the Third World*. Baltimore: Johns Hopkins University Press, 1983.

Cardoso, Eliana and Ann Helwege. "Below the Line: Poverty in Latin America." *World Development* 20 (January 1992): 19-37.

Chenery, Hollis, *Structural Change and Development Policy*. London: Oxford University Press, 1980.

Chenery, Hollis, John Duloy, and Richare Jolly. eds. *Redistribution with Growth: An Approach to Policy*. Washington, D.C.: World Bank, 1974.

Dasgupta, Partha. *An Inquiry into Well-Being and Destitution*. New York: Oxford University Press, 1993.

De Kant, Emanuel. "Of Markets, Might and Mullaks: A Case for Equality, Pluralism, and Tolerance in Development." *World Development* 13 (1985): 549-556.

Fields, Gary. "Data for Measuring Poverty and Inequality Changes in Developing Countries." *Journal of Development Economics* 44 (1994): 87-102.

_____. *Povery, Inequality and Development*. Cambridge: Cambridge University Press, 1980.

_____. "Employment, Income Distribution and Economic Growth in Seven Small Economies." *Economic Journal* 94 (1984): 74-83.

Haddad, Lawrence. *Gender and Poverty in Ghana: A Descriptive Analysis*. Washington, D.C.: World Bank, 1991.

Papanek, Gustav, and Lodrich Kyn. "The Effect on Income Distribution of Development, the Growth Rate and Economic Strategy." *Journal of Development Economics* 23 (1986): 55-65.

Persson, Torsten and Guido Tabellini. "Is Inequality Harmful for Growth." *American Economic Review* 84 (June 1994): 600-21.

Ravallion, Martin, Gaurav Datt, and Dominique van de walle. "Quantifying Absolute Poverty in the Developing World." *Review of Income and Wealth 37 (December 1991): 345-61.*

Ravallion, Martin and Shaohua Chen. "What Can New Survey Data Tell Us About Recent Changes in Distribution?" *World Development Review* 11 (May 1977): 357-382.

Robinson, Joan. *An Essay on Marxian Economics*. London: Macmillan, 1949.

Sen, Amartya. "The Economic of Life and Death." *Scientific American* 268 (May 1993): 40-47.

Srinivasan, T. N. "Destitution: A Discourse." *Journal of Economic Literature* 32 (December 1994): 1842-655.

Sugden, Robert. "Welfare, Resources, and Capabilities: A Review of Inequality Reexamined by Amartya Sen." *Journal of Economic Literature* 31 (December 1993): 1947-62.

Sundrum, R. M. *Income Distribution in Less Developed Counties*. London: Routledge, 1992.

Ul-Haq, Mahbub. *The Assault on World Poverty*. Baltimore: Johns Hopkins University Press, 1975.

CHAPTER 6

POPULATION GROWTH AND ECONOMIC DEVELOPMENT

One of the major factors that has severely limited the economic development potential of the Third World nations is rapid population growth. In fact, in academic circles, few development issues induce as much cynicism as does the high rate of population growth in developing nations. Such cynicism is rooted in the classical theory of economic stagnation. As you recall from Chapter 4, according to this theory, in the long run, development of an economy will lead to a so called "stationary state" in which low income for the masses and the population growth will be checked by poverty. Such a pessimistic attitude toward economic development led to labeling economics as the "dismal science"a long time ago.

To date, the classical pessimistic view on economic growth has proved to be baseless for the advanced nations. The history of these nations attests to their success in achieving economic progress. Such progress is exemplified by a high rate of increase in real income, that is, population and per capita real income have both risen. Unfortunately, however, in many poor developing nations, per capita income has continued to stay at a very low level. Such conditions have given rise to increasing concern about the possibility that economic improvement will be checked by undue population pressure. It has become customary to characterize the development issue as "increasing the fertility of the soil and reducing the fertility of human beings."

Some of the major problems that are highly associated with the subject of population in developing nations are employment, migration, and urbanization. We will examine these issues in the next chapter. In this chapter we examine other problems relating population growth to economic development. First, we explain Malthusian theory of population; second, we elaborate on demography; third we discuss the microeconomics of fertility; fourth we talk about the noneconomic variables affecting fertility; fifth, we present the fallacies of population density; sixth, we evaluate the beneficial impacts of population growth; seventh, we examine the question of economic development versus fertility decline; and finally, we address policies for diminishing fertility.

MALTHUSIAN THEORY OF POPULATION

The systematic study of population dates back to the late eighteenth century, when Thomas R. Malthus, an English economist, published his book *The Essay on Principles of Population* in 1798. Although Malthus had many precursors, his ability to systematically combine many strands of thought made his work stand out and gain much greater recognition. He presented his pessimistic view on the growth of population by stating that population tends to grow faster than food supply. That is, population unchecked would increase according to a geometric progression (1,2,4,8,16,32,...), while food supply would increase according to an arithmetic progression (1,2,3,4,5,6, ...). Malthus illustrated the two progressions as shown in Table 6.1.

Table 6.1

THE MALTHUSIAN POPULATION GROWTH

Year	1	25	50	75	100	125	150	175	200	225
Population	1	2	4	8	16	32	64	128	256	512
Food Supply	1	2	3	4	5	6	7	8	9	10

According to Table 6.1, population, when unchecked, would have increased 512 times after 225 years. However, the food supply would have increased only 10 times after the same amount of time. Malthus's theory is based on the law of diminishing returns. According to this law, with a given state of technology, a growing population and a fixed amount of land would eventually lead to diminishing returns for agricultural workers. That is, each additional worker would add smaller amounts to output. This simply means that at a certain point in time the world would run out of food supply, and hence humanity would be doomed to misery and poverty unless the rate of population growth is somehow checked. This may be achieved, according to Malthus, either by **positive checks**, such as famine, disease, and war, or, by **preventive checks**, such as late marriage and the restraining of sexual desires.

Theoretically speaking, the Malthusian and neo-Malthusian theories as applied to the now developing nations can be rejected for the following reasons:

1. Inability of these theories to predict the miracle of technological progress that has drastically changed food production in the world. In fact, rapid technological progress, resulting from technological, and social inventions and innovations, has led to increasing rather than decreasing returns to scale.
2. Such theories are based on the assumption of a positive correlation between population growth and levels of per capital income. Such an assumption, however, is not supported by the empirical evidence. Given the improvement in medical science and publicly funded health programs, death rates have fallen abruptly and have become less dependent on the level of per capita income. Additionally, birth rates do not tend to indicate a definite correlation with per capital income levels. Thus, it is not the level of aggregate income that accounts so much for population growth but the manner by which the income is distributed. More specifically, it is the level of household income, not the level of per capita income, that appears to count most.
3. These theories concentrate on an invalid variable, that is, per capita income, as the major determinant of the rate of population growth. A more valid method is to focus on the microeconomic of family-size decision-making process where the individual level of living, as opposed to the aggregate level of living serves as the major determinant of a family's choice with regard to the number of children desired.

Given the above theoretical shortcomings associated with the Malthusian proposition, most economists refute his idea that rapid population growth will inevitably be limited by food production. They point out that in practice, aside from drought regions, population has not yet approached the capacity of the land to support it. In fact, in many developing nations the food problem would be easily alleviated if it were allocated in accordance to the need and not on the basis of income.

It should be noted that the population problem is greater than the food problem in that it puts pressure on human resources, savings and foreign exchange. The population explosion that has been encountered by most of the developing nations during the last three decades is in sharp contrast with the history of the current advanced nations when they were in their early stages of the economic development process. During the nineteenth-century preindustrial stage, the Western European nations experienced a rate of population growth that was generally less than fifty percent of the rate that exists in today's developing nations. Thus, one should not compare the population growth of these nations with the population growth of the developing countries that are experiencing different population growth patterns which demand immediate attention and call for serious efforts to curb population before it gets out of control.

Today, Malthus's name has become symbolic of the alarming growth of population in certain underdeveloped areas of the world, such as in Africa, Asia, and South America, where there is not enough food for the growing population. Another aspect of population growth that has attracted increasing attention in recent years is its adverse effect on the environment. This is clearly stated in the following excerpts of a United Nations report:

> Today the footprints of humanity are impossible to miss. Human activity has affected every part of the planet, no matter how remote, and every ecosystem, from the simplest to the most complex. ...Our numbers have doubled since 1960 to 6.1 billion, with growth mostly in poorer countries. Consumption expenditures have more than doubled since 1970, with increases mostly in richer countries. During this time, we have created wealth on an unimaginable scale, yet half the world still exists on less than $2 a day. We have learned how to extract resources for our use, but not how to deal with the resulting waste: emissions of carbon dioxide, for example, grew 12 times between 1900 and 2000. In the process we are changing the world's climate.[1]

DEMOGRAPHY

Demography is the formal study of population and the elements that affect its rate of change. Since the study of demography is based on certain universally accepted terminologies, we start our exploration of this subject by first elaborating on the following three major concepts employed in this area of study:

1. **The fertility rate** is the number of children born alive per 1,000 women within the childbearing age group (usually between ages 15 and 49 years) during a given year. **The age-specific fertility rate** is the number of babies born alive per 1,000 women within a given age-group of population during a year. **The crude birth rate** designates the number of births per 1,000 of population. The fertility rates are more accurate than crude birth rates in assessing the inclination of a population to have children. The crude birth rate, however, is a better measure in portraying changes in the age-specific birth rate, changes in age the structure, and changes in the death rate. The **net reproduction rate** refers to the number of daughters a newborn female will deliver throughout her life, given constant age-related and fertility and mortality rates. In other words, this rate portrays the degree to which a group of newborn females will reproduce themselves. If this rate is equal to one, it implies that fertility is at replacement level. This means at this rate a female will deliver, on average, only sufficient daughters to replace herself.
2. **Mortality (death) rate** can be defined as the number of deaths per 1,000 population in a given year. The **age-specific death rate** is the number of deaths per 1,000 for a given age group during a year. The **infant mortality (death) rate** refers to the number of deaths per 1,000 births during the first year of life. **Life expectancy** refers to the average number of remaining years that people of a specific age group can expect to live, given that the age-specific death rate stays constant. **Life expectancy at birth** refers to the average number of years a newborn infant is expected to live,

assuming that the existing pattern of mortality at the time of birth were to stay the same throughout the child's life. The **crude death rate** is the number of deaths per 1,000 of the population in a year. It portrays changes in the birth rate, the changes in age structure, and changes in the age-specific death rate. **Maternal mortality rate** measures the number of deaths of women from pregnancy-related causes per 100,000 live births in a year.

3. The **rate of natural increase of population** can be defined as the difference between the crude death rate and crude birth rate. The **total population increase** of a population is the natural increase plus net migration during a given period of time. A **stationary population** can be defined as a population in which age-and sex-specific mortality rates have stayed at a replacement stage, that is, one. In other words, birth rates and death rates have remained constant and equal, the age structure has stayed constant, and the rate of population growth has remained at zero. If a population has an age distribution that is characterized by a disproportionate number of females, then it will continue to grow even after fertility has declined to the replacement level. If fertility stays at the replacement level, then the birth rate will keep surpassing the death rate until the age structure stabilizes and a stationary population is attained.

Demographic Transition

Demographic transition is a process by which a population pattern eventually shifts from a stage characterized by high birth rates and high death rates to a stage in which both birth and death rates are low and almost equal. This process is composed of four distinct stages, as depicted in Figure 6.1 The demographic transition describes why all contemporary advanced nations have gone through three stages of demographic transition and when developing nations are expected to enter the fourth stage. The four stages of demographic transition are as follows:

1. **Stage I: High Fertility and Mortality.** Before their economic modernization which occurred in early 19th century, advanced nations were in this stage through most of their history. During this stage, most of these nations had stable or very slow growing population, stemming from a mixture of high death rates and high birth rates. This led to a population growth rate of about 5 per thousand, or 0.5% a year. High death rates resulted from the absence of modern sanitation, medicine, transportation, communication, agriculture, industry, and trade. For such populations to thrive, fertility rates must at least match mortality rates. No wonder the existing ideology, religion, values, and social structure at that time supported high birth rates. During that period, large families were regarded as a blessing from God. By bearing a child, a woman acquired acceptance not only in her husband's family but also in the neighborhood. However, with the passage of time institutions and values advocating high fertility altered gradually as mortality rates diminished.

2. **Stage II: Decreasing Mortality.** This stage started in the first quarter of the 19th century in Europe, when modernization along with improved public health methods, high income, and healthier diet led to gradual reduction of mortality rates which raised life expectancy from under 40 years to over 60 years. Improvement in transportation, communication, and trade made people less susceptible to food inadequacies. However, a decrease in mortality was not immediately followed by a decline in fertility. Consequently, the growing gap between high fertility and declining mortality led to rapid rate of growth of that population as compared to the rate of growth in earlier centuries. Thus, stage II can be labeled as the start of the demographic transition, that is, transition from stable or slow-growing population initially to rapidly growing levels and then to diminishing rates.

Figure 6.1

THE DEMOGRAPHIC TRANSITION

Demographic transition is a process by which a population pattern eventually shifts from a stage characterized by high birth rates and high death rates to a stage in which both birth and death rates are low and almost equal. This process is composed of four distinct stages, as depicted in the figure. The demographic transition describes why all contemporary advanced nations have gone through three stages of demographic transition and when developing nations are expected to enter the fourth stage.

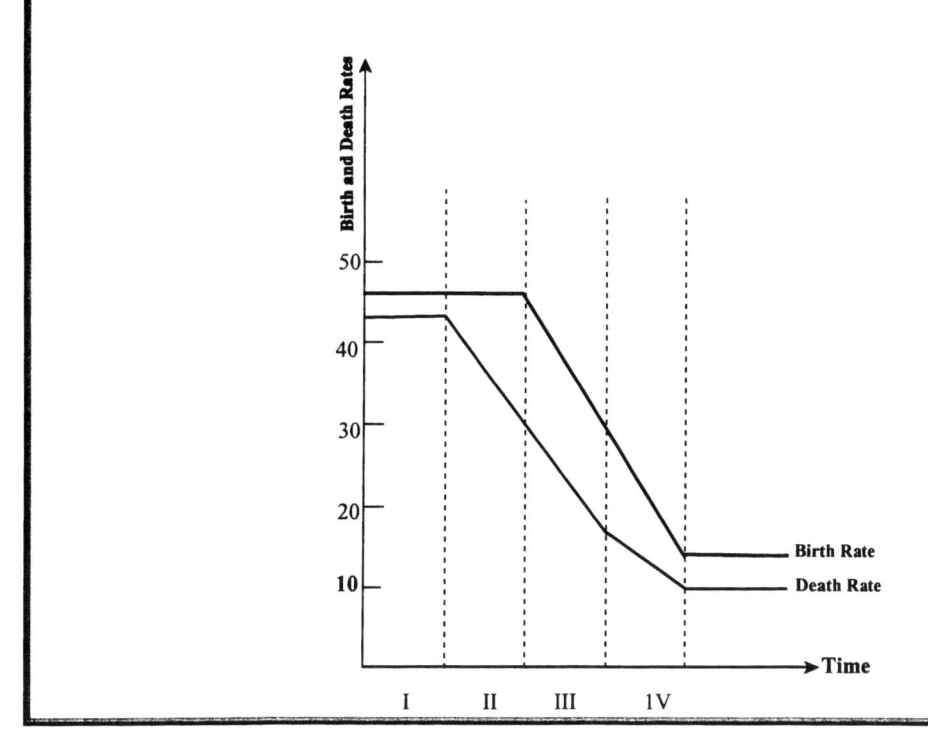

3. **Stage III: Declining Fertility**. Stage III began in the late 19th century when the effects of modernization and development triggered a decrease in fertility. During this stage, declining birth rates amassed with lower death rates, eventually led to an overall rates of population growth which hardly surpassed the 1% level even at their peak.
4. **Stage IV: Stationary Population**. At this stage, birth and death rates are low and almost equal. In other words, the rate of growth of population is equal to zero. The World Bank predicts that most developing nations will not approach a precise replacement rate until 2020 to 2040. At this rate, an average childbearing woman delivers only one daughter which can be conceived as her replacement in the population. However, as we mentioned earlier if a population has an age distribution that is characterized by a disproportionate number of females, then it will continue to grow even after fertility has declined to the replacement level. Given the structure of age distribution in developing nations, it is expected that most of these nations will not experience

Figure 6.2

THE DEMOGRAPHIC TRANSITION IN THIRD WORLD NATIONS

The following figure portrays the population histories of developing nations, which contrast with those of Western Europe and fall into two patterns.

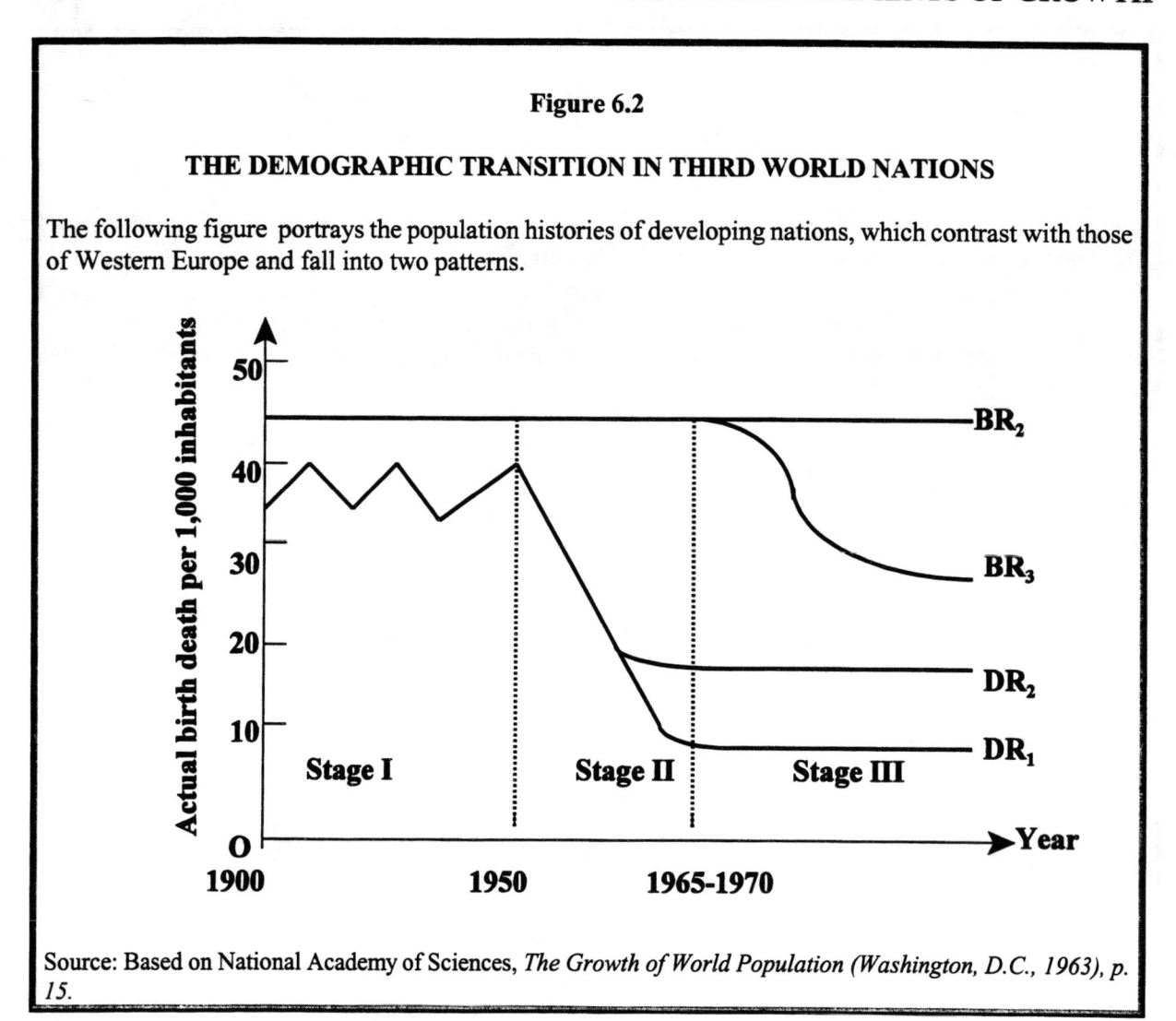

Source: Based on National Academy of Sciences, *The Growth of World Population (Washington, D.C., 1963)*, p. 15.

a stationary population until 2075 to 2175, that is, approximately 5 decades to 1.5 centuries after reaching exact replacement level.

Demographic Transition in Developing Nations as Compared to Advanced Nations. Figure 6.2 portrays the population histories of developing nations, which contrast with those of Western Europe and fall into two patterns. Today, birthrates in many poor developing nations are greater than they were in Western Europe before industrialization, when they were in stage I of their demographic transition. This is due to the fact the majority of women in developing nations marry at earlier ages as compared to women in advanced nations. This not only leads to an increase in the number of families for a given population size in these nations, but it also extends the child bearing periods. Stage II of demographic transition occurred in most of the developing nations beginning in the 1940s and particularly in the 1950s and 1960s. The importation of advanced medical and public health technologies led to a much greater decline in developing nations's death rates as compared to the death rates experienced by Western Europe in the 19th century. Considering the historically high birthrates of developing nations, amounting to about 40 per 1000, this means that stage II of the developing nations demographic transition can be marked by population growth rates exceeding the level of 2% to 2.5% per year.

In terms of stage III, developing nations may be classified into the following two groups.

1. This first group is composed of developing nations in which advanced methods of death control along with sharp and rapid increases in the standard of living have led to low death rates of 10 per thousand, and rapidly declining birth rates that range between 20 and 30 per thousand. These nations, including China, Chile, Costa Rica, Cuba, South Korea, Sri Lanka, and Taiwan, have arrived at stage III of their demographic transition and have enjoyed diminishing overall population growth rates. During the 1980s and 1990s, a number of developing nations, encompassing Colombia, Indonesia, the Dominican Republic, Thailand, Malaysia, Mexico, Kenya, South Africa, and Brazil, seemed to be arriving at stage III. In Figure 6.2, BR_1, and DR_1 portray the birth rate and the death rate respectively of this first group of developing nations.
2. The second group include the majority of developing nations. In these nations, following a beginning phase of rapid decrease, death rates have not declined further. This is mainly due to the existence of extensive absolute poverty and low standards of living. Additionally, the preservation of high birth rates, stemming from the low standards of living, have caused the overall population growth rate to stay relatively high. These nations, encompassing many of those in the Middle East and sub-Saharan Africa, are still in stage II of their demographic transition. In Figure 6.2, BR_2 and DR_2 portray the birth rate and the death rate respectively of this second group. In Figure 6.2 BR_1, and DR_1, portray the birth rate and the death rate respectively of this first group of developing nations.

CHANGES IN AGE DISTRIBUTION

Some of the consequences of rapid population growth that have the most significant impact on economic development in developing nations are those related to shifts in age composition. When death rates decrease, they decrease most abruptly among infants, composed of children less than one year old. Although some infants' deaths stem from genetic shortcomings, a large number of deaths are caused by gastrointestinal illnesses and respiratory disorders like bronchitis, pneumonia, or diarrhea. Changes in age structure of population can be summarized in the **dependency burden**. This is an index which measures the proportion of the total population aged 0 to 14, and 65 years and older, which are considered unproductive years and thus not included in the labor force. In many developing nations, individuals under the age 15 make up about fifty percent of population. This condition imposes a burden on the commonly small labor force and the government, which has to distribute the scant resources between alternative uses such as public health, education, and housing, for use by people who do not contribute to the production process.

Table 6.2 presents the percentage of population under age 15, the percentage of population aged 65 and over, and the dependency ratios for different groups of nations in 1999. As this table indicates, the dependency ratio for all developing nations (38.15%) is higher than the dependency ratio for high-income nations (33.1%), including mainly advanced nations. It is interesting to note that sub–Saharan Africa has the highest dependency ratio (47.7) and East Asia and the Pacific has the lowest dependency ratio (33.4%) among developing nations listed in the table. Dependency burdens within developing nations differ in accordance to income level. High fertility and large family size impose a heavy burden in the poor segment of the population in these nations, where each adult supports more dependents than is the case in advanced nations.

The above explanations illustrate the degree to which most developing nations continue to face high population growth rates in the future. As they plan for ideal population numbers in the future, they may as well admit that growth rates in the order of 65% to 125% are arriving in spite of policies they implement. However, this should not diminish their determination in alleviating the population problem, because with the passage of each year the population momentum leads to a larger multiple of the present total population size, before it can finally reach a stationary stage.

Given the preceding explanations, regarding rapid population growth in developing nations, the important questions to ask are the following:

1. When and under what circumstances can we expect developing nations to enjoy declining birth rates and slower population growth?
2. What are the major factors that give rise to high fertility rates in developing nations?
3. Can government policy control the factors that give rise to high fertility rates in developing nations?

Malthusian and neo-Malthusian theories of population have tried to answer some of these questions. However, as we explained earlier in this chapter, application of these theories to contemporary developing countries are largely rejected by economists. We may now turn our attention to a contemporary and highly influential neoclassical microeconomics model, the household theory of fertility.

Table 6.2
Dependency burdens of developing Nations and Advanced Nations, 1997

Nations	Population under age 15 (as % of total)	Population aged 65 and above (as % of total)	Dependency* Ratio (%)
All developing countries	33.1	5.0	**38.1**
Least developed countries	43.2	3.1	46.3
Arab States	38.1	3.7	41.8
East Asia and the Pacific	27.3	6.1	33.4
Latin America and Caribbean	32.3	5.2	37.5
South Asia	35.5	4.5	40.0
Sub Saharan Africa	44.7	3.0	47.7
High income	18.6	14.5	**33.1**
Middle income	27.8	6.5	**34.3**
Low income	37.2	4.4	**41.6**
World	30.2	6.9	**37.1**

Source: United Nation Development Programme, *Human Development Report 2001* (New York: Oxford University Press, 2001), p. 157.
* This column was calculated by the author

THE MICROECONOMICS OF FERTILITY

The demographic transition and the consequent change in the age distribution can be clarified in terms of conventional microeconomic analysis. Beginning with the 1960s, economists expanded the applications of the analysis of consumer behavior to understand the microeconomic determinants of family fertility. The microeconomic analysis of the household behavior starts by conjecturing that a couple's decision to bear children, or avoid bearing them is, based on the same decision-making process they utilize in other aspects of their lives. To be sure, this hypothesis does not connote that the couple is perfectly "rational" regardless of how it might be determined, nor does it conjecture that their only objectives are economic ones. Rather, it simply assumes that children are knowingly pursued or evaded and that decisions justifying conception or contraception are not essentially different from other choices.

Two major questions may be raised in terms of microeconomic analysis. First, why is the fertility rate higher in rural areas as compared to urban areas in the developing nations? Second, why as the level of income of a couple rises do they decide to have fewer children? The answers to these questions are given in the following two sections.

The Higher Fertility In Rural Areas than Urban Areas In Developing Nations

Conventional wisdom purports that each mouth comes supplied with two hands. In terms of simple cost and return analysis, children may be considered as assets on the farm from an early age. The marginal costs of bearing them and raising them are low. Additionally, they may soon contribute to their own expenses as well as that of the family. In fact, it is not unusual for children of six or seven years old to function as scarecrows, herders, carriers of wood and water, messengers, weeders, and babysitters.

In urban areas, the cost of raising children is higher than in rural areas, due to the higher costs of food, clothing, and school accessories. Additionally, children in urban areas of developing nations do not have much opportunity to engage in productive work. This is because the type of jobs that are obtained by children in urban areas consist of unproductive tasks, such as washing cars, shining shoes, peddling newspapers, and carrying baggage. In these types of jobs the marginal productivity of their labor maybe as close to zero as that more routinely associated with *rural* **disguised unemployment**, that is, a condition in which the available functions are distributed among workers in such a manner that all appear to be fully employed, but in fact much of their time is wasted in unproductive endeavors. The large number of abandoned children in some of the urban areas of developing nations also confirms their relative low value and high cost to their parents.

We conclude that the higher human fertility in rural areas as compared to urban areas is perfectly compatible with the higher economic cost of children in cities.

The Inverse Relationship Between the Level of Income and Fertility

In low income nations, where the national system does not provide for old age, children are valued as sources of support to their parents in old age. In fact, the culture in most developing nations expects children to take care of their parents. Children may be viewed as lottery tickets in human terms. The more children in the family, the more assured the parents can be of support. Also, the more children one has, the higher the possibility that at least one would be successful. As income rises, however, couples usually decide to have fewer children. This happens because, in microeconomic analysis, children can be viewed as a special kind of consumption good. As with any other consumption good, certain amounts of time must be spent with children in order for them to generate utility. The time spent with children not only yields utility to the parents, but it also improves the quality of children. In the mean time, the capability of children to generate more income in the future also increases. For these reasons, as modernization proceeds and the level of income rises, parents tend to desire higher quality children. As the quality of children improves, cost rises. Thus, the observed decrease in fertility is compatible with the rise in costs.

So far we have not elaborated on contraception costs and its impact on fertility. Today, this issue constitutes an important part of modern microeconomic analysis. The economic principles imply that if the costs of dependable contraception declined, the quantity demanded would rise, and, assuming that other things stay constant, fertility would diminish.

We thus conclude that microeconomic causes of fertility downturn encompass not only the changes in costs and benefits of having children, but also changes in costs of avoiding them. Today, in most cultures, the costs have risen, the benefits have declined, and the costs of avoidance have decreased.

A Microeconomic Model of Fertility

Having elaborated on the microeconomic variables that affect human fertility, we are now equipped with the knowledge to build a fertility model.

The theory of consumer behavior conjectures that a person with a given set of tastes and preferences for a bundle of commodities, portrayed by a utility function, attempts to maximize the utility (satisfaction) deduced from consuming these commodities subject to the income constraints and the relative prices of all other commodities. In applying this theory to fertility behavior, children are considered as consumption goods. In this context, fertility presents a rational economic reaction to family's (consumer's) demand for children relative to other commodities. Thus, the common income and substitution effects are assumed to be applicable in this type of analysis as well. This means that if we keep other factors constant, the desired number of children (N_d) can be expected to change directly with the following variables:

1. **The level of family income (Y)**. The higher the family's income level, the larger the demand for children.
2. **The net price of children (P_n)** that is, the difference between expected costs and benefits. Expected costs are mainly composed of the opportunity costs associated with mother's time. Expected benefits stem from the potential of the child to earn income and provide support for parents at old age. The higher the net price of children, the lower quantity demanded.
3. **The prices of all other commodities (Po)**. The higher the prices of all other commodities, relative to children, the greater the quantity of children demanded.
4. **Tastes for commodities, relative to children (To)**. The better the tastes for commodities relative to children, the fewer children demanded.

Mathematically, these relationships can be expressed in terms of the following equation:

$$N_d = f(Y, P_n, Po, To), O = 1..., n,$$

Where, $\delta N_d / \delta Y \rangle 0$, $\delta N_d / \delta P_n \langle 0$, $\delta N_d / \delta Po \rangle 0$, and $\delta N_d / \delta To \langle 0$.

NONECONOMIC VARIABLES AFFECTING FERTILITY

Microeconomic analysis enables us to comprehend the economic causes of fertility. However, noneconomic variables also play a significant role in fertility. This happens because besides economists, other individuals such as religious leaders, political theorists, and military leaders are involved in decisions that affect the size and growth of population.

Religious leaders who find themselves threatened are likely to consider population control against their teaching and hence undesirable. Ethnic groups within a nation may defy official policies on population reduction if they perceive them to be tactics employed by the government authorities to control their numbers.

Small nations concerned with being swallowed up by larger countries may also perceive that their

GLOBAL INSIGHTS CASE 6.1

INTERNATIONAL CONFERENCE ON POPULATION AND DEVELOPMENT (ICPD)

The International Conference on Population and Development (ICPD) is the largest intergovernmental conference on population and development that meets periodically to discuss major population and development issues and offers recommendations for action at the local, national, and international levels. Its participants are composed of government officials, specialized agencies and organizations, intergovernmental organization, non-governmental organizations and the media.

The conference was first convened in Cairo in 1974. This resulted in the creation of the Cairo Plan of Action which draws upon the World Population Plan of Action that was adopted by the participants in the conference. In the 1984 conference, additional recommendations were adopted by the members which includes a statement of principles, projections of future population growth, and a set of 20-year goals for population, infant mortality, life expectancy, maternal mortality, education, contraceptive use, and gender quality.

At its 1994 conference in Cairo, Egypt, with 11,000 registered participants from more than 180 states, the ICPD created a plan of action on population for the next 20 years. Accordingly, the following two goals were adopted:

1. To implement more effective local action to satisfy individual needs and aspirations, specifically those of women.
2. Adopt more effective national policies and programs in order to create a balance between population and the available resources.

The Conference also addressed major population and development issues and suggested the following recommendations to be implemented at the local, national and international levels:

1. Linkage between population, the environment, and economic growth, and the need to take population factors into account in planning for sustainable development.
2. Integrating population concerns into all development activities; stabilizing population growth rates to balance human demands with available resources; and addressing important demographic trends, such as urbanization, national and international migration, and aging.
3. Economic opportunities for women and the removal of barriers to their empowerment.
4. Acknowledging the needs of individuals, families, communities, and countries for: better health services, especially reproductive health care and family planning, education, housing, employment and other measures to alleviate poverty.
5. The rapid growth of world population, the diversity among and within regions in growth rates and distribution, the challenges posed by the high proportion of young people in many countries populations, and the growing numbers of elderly people in developing countries.

Continued

> *Global Insights 6.2, continued*
>
> 6. Reproductive rights, and provision of voluntary reproductive health programs and family planning, encompassing such issues as adolescent sexuality, abortion, and sexually transmitted diseases including HIV/AIDS.
> 7. Increase male responsibility towards family planning issues and female reproductive rights.
> 8. Enable informed choices by: ensuring access to and awareness of safe, affordable family planning methods; forging partnerships among governments, local communities, NGOs and the private sector; and by increasing domestic spending and international assistance for population activities.
> 9. Maintain awareness of internal shifts of population due to rural/urban inequity, and the resulting explosion of urban growth.
> 10. International migration, its causes and effects, and the protection of the rights of documented and undocumented migrants and refugees.
>
> Source: *The Population Institute*

national survival depends on their numbers, and hence resist population control. However, evidence shows that on purely military grounds, this presumption proves to be false. For example, the experience of Egypt in the Six-Day War of 1967 with Israel, and of the United States in Vietnam demonstrates that a larger nation does not necessarily have a military advantage over the smaller nation. Even in peaceful times, a nation with a relatively large size does not necessarily have a greater influence or more clout than a relatively smaller nation. Does Nigeria portray more clout in world issues than Canada? Pakistan more than Saudi Arabia? India more than Sweden? Nevertheless, the slogan that larger numbers mean greater influence seems to be popular among those who stand to benefit from it.

The population issue has not only attracted the attention of policy makers and social scientists in market economies, but it has also been subject to scrutiny in command economies. The traditional Marxist-Leninist approach maintains that the "population problem" could not exist in a socialist society. The population problem is viewed only as part of the greater problem of unemployment. Because capitalist nations suffer from unemployment while socialist nations do not, the population problem exists only in capitalist countries. Thus, strategies aimed at controlling birth rates should be considered as capitalist ploys to lower unemployment and thus delay the day of unavoidable revolution.

As communist nations, one might expect China and Cuba to subscribe to the Marxist view on the population problem. However, far from the traditional Marxist endorsement of unrestrained births, both the Chinese and Cuban governments have instituted elaborate programs that aimed at population control.

The movement toward population control in China began with the death of Mao Tse-tung in 1976. To control the population, the Chinese started a program that aimed at encouraging a one-child family norm. To achieve this goal they crafted a set of incentives to lure married couples to have only a single child. These incentives included a subsidy, better housing, preference in school admission and employment for the single child, greater pension, and higher grain rations.

Although the Cuban fertility rate from the 1950s onward was among the lowest in Latin America, the Cuban leader, Fidel Castro, has continued to consider high rates of population growth as a real impediment to the national development. In fact, his statements on many occasions starting in 1970 have centered on the age distribution aspect of population, such as providing education to disproportionately large numbers of children.

THE FALLACIES OF POPULATION DENSITY

Much of the literature on the impact of population growth, both classical and modern, falters by

CH. 6/POPULATION GROWTH AND ECONOMIC DEVELOPMENT

concentrating on population as a credible yardstick of overpopulation. Such a flaw would become obvious if we examine the real world in which we find some densely populated nations such as Hong Kong and Singapore prospering, while some of the most sparsely populated nations, such as those on the margin of Africa's Sahel Desert continue to suffer from poverty.

In reality, the following two related fallacies are committed:

1. In already densely populated areas, where land is the only factor of production that is combined with labor in the production process, population growth is overly destructive. In reality, however, only in specific tropical conditions, where capital is extremely scarce and where conventional labor-using agricultural techniques are employed, the threats from density are clear.
2. Population growth should be endured or even advocated in sparingly populated regions. According to this fallacious argument, some nations in Africa and Latin America would even benefit from rapid population growth since they occupy large barren lands. However, the idea that glutting empty lands connotes the desirability of rapid population growth, disregards basic ingredients of development. Indeed, regional migration within a nation has been overwhelmingly from rural to urban regions and between already existing cities. In other words, the migration tendencies have been away from rural regions. The filling of empty lands necessitates the reversal of such a movement. This can be achieved by building an economic infrastructure, such as housing, roads, and storage facilities, to make lands agriculturally productive. Unfortunately, in practice, such projects have not proven to be successful. Examples include resettlement of Bolivians from their previous homes in the Altiplano to new homes in lowland regions, and interisland "transmigration" in Indonesia. Thus, rapid population growth, far from helping resolve the problem and potential of empty lands, is likely to block those solutions.

BENEFICIAL IMPACTS OF POPULATION GROWTH

The literature on population growth is imbued with studies that enumerate its negative economic impact on the country in question. Most of these studies warn that population size, growth, or density have led or will lead to problems such as climate change, overgrazing, unemployment, inflation, and loss of individual freedom in both developing and advanced nations. Such skepticism has made some scholars wonder if the sheer number of people can be accountable for a wide range of individual and social problems. This has resulted in the development of a counter argument in favor of larger population. Accordingly, it is argued, the favorable impact of population growth could be related with any of the following factors:

1. **Accelerator Principal.** As you already know from your introductory microeocnomics course, the accelerator principal proposes that net investment in capital goods is the function of changes in the level of output, that is, GDP. Given this proposition, a favorable impact of population growth, it is argued, is that it leads to higher output and hence to an increase in net investment. Of course for the accelerator principal to work, the mere desire for more output must be turned into real demand for output. In other words, the larger number of people stemming from high population growth must somehow generate a faster rate of growth in output to make the mechanism operational. However, the problem in developing nations is inadequacy of effective demand for output and a slow reaction, at best, in terms of growth in output resulting from higher population growth.
2. **Counterpressure.** Population pressure generates counterpressure. In Albert Hirschman's words:

   > The activity undertaken by the community in resisting a decline in its standard of living causes an increase in its ability to control its environment and to organize itself for development.[2]

However, such an argument is not necessarily true. In fact, some believe that Hirschman has it backwards. This is because a nation's resistance to a decrease in the standard of living indicates the lack of its ability to go forward, rather than "breeding" ability. If the extent of poverty were indeed effective in inducing people to forge forward, then poor nations such as Haiti and Peru must be ranked along side of the fastest growing developing nations in the world. However, as we know, this happens not to be the case.

3. **Technological Progress**. A larger population encompasses more creative people, and hence is better equipped to make technological progress. However, this argument suffers from the following shortcomings:
   a. The rapid population may lead to a greater number of creative people. In the past, some geniuses were born to large families. However, such a proposition fails to recognize that high population growth also deteriorates the quality of life, for both parents and children. This, in turn, may lead to mental retardation of potential geniuses, stemming from malnutrition caused by lower income.
   b. A higher number of births would not only increase the number of creative and genius people, such as Newton and Einstein, but it would also give rise to destructive people, such as Hitler and Stalin in equal proportions.

4. **Economies of Scale**. A larger population allows economies of scale, that is, as the size of a firm's plant increases, its long run average declines. Such a proposition is subject to the following shortcomings:
   a. The argument assumes that a larger population somehow leads to a higher demand for goods, generating economies of scale. However, as we explained in part 3.a, the problem in developing nations is inadequacy of effective demand for output and a slow reaction, at best, in terms of growth in output resulting from higher population growth.
   b. The argument implies that the nation in question engages in no international trade, operates in a world in which trade barriers cause export expansion to become so costly as to prevent international trade. However, as the theory of international trade proposes, it is better for developing nations to advocate free international trade and, particularly, possibilities of export expansion.

ECONOMIC DEVELOPMENT OR FERTILITY DECLINE?

On some occasions economic development and fertility decline have been described as alternatives to each other. Thus, it is argued that as a matter of policy we should not focus on fertility. If we concentrate on developmental functions, the fertility problem will resolve itself. For example, such a proposition dominated the mood of the Population Conference in Budapest in 1974. However, economic development and fertility decline are not alternatives to each other. To date, none of the advocates of fertility decline has seriously proposed that we should give up promoting development, and instead concentrate on controlling fertility decline. In fact, economic development and fertility decline policies are interrelated and they should be orchestrated harmoniously. The synchronous and interdependent character of development and a decrease in fertility rate is outlined in the following statement that appeared in one of the World Bank's publications in 1981:

> Except in an initial phase when mortality falls before fertility decline follows, rapid population growth results from failed development—failed human development in particular. The response required is active promotion of those features of development associated with fertility decline—education, improved health, advancement of women, modern-sector development and family planning programs.[3]

To be sure, policies that aim at advancing social and economic development by promoting health, nutrition, education, women rights, and urban development will eventually decrease fertility rates. Additionally, ameliorating income inequality by advocating more job and educational opportunity for females, low-income classes, and underprivileged groups, will also lead to fertility decline. In a nutshell, lower fertility is an outgrowth of schemes commonly viewed socially advantageous in themselves. Thus, development and fertility decline are correlated, each affecting the other.

GLOBAL INSIGHTS CASE 6.2

POPULATION CONTROL STRATEGIES IN SOME DEVELOPING NATIONS

Almost fifty developing and newly industrialized countries employ family planning programs specifically designed to reduce the rates of population growth. The more personally coercive a program is, the more likely it has resulted in a backlash, which is counterproductive. A fully informed client is better able to make choices that he or she will feel responsible for in later years.

India's program dates back to the pre-1960's, and was probably the first modern program. They have experimented with cash incentives to both men and women for sterilization; and cash deposits by employers into savings accounts for women workers when they weren't pregnant, with the understanding that the woman who had too many children would lose all the money in their account.

Singapore has scarce public housing so the government policy of assigning housing to families regardless of the families' size is specifically designed as a disincentive for large families. Maternity leave is paid for a maximum of two pregnancies; birth fee reimbursements are prorated with additional children receiving less money than the first two children; and income tax relief applies only to the first three children.

China's policies have been the most strict and far-reaching, with the adoption in the early 1980's of the one child per family policy. Enforcement of the policy has resulted in neighborhood committees being consulted prior to a family's decision to conceive, with permission granted for pregnancy for most first pregnancies. Second pregnancies are allowed occasionally when a woman has remarried or when the first child has a birth defect. A family who doesn't follow the one child policy can expect to be fined heavily, and incur discrimination in housing, medical care, education, and job promotion.

Unexpected outcomes may result from population control policies. For instance, the Chinese have traditionally had a preference for male children, and of the generation now coming of age (births post-1980) there are tens of thousands fewer females than males. It is believed that female infanticide and the abortion of female fetuses is the cause of the disproportion. Currently, in some parts of China, men are finding it more difficult to find wives.

Source: This case was written by Dorothy L. Thurman, instructor of community health and maternal-child nursing, California State University, San Bernardino.

POLICIES FOR DIMINISHING FERTILITY

As our preceding discussion in the previous section indicates, development and fertility decline are interrelated. Given this fact, we may distinguished between two sets of policies that are aimed at reducing fertility rates: (1) socioeconomic development and (2) birth control programs. These policies are discussed in the next two sections, respectively.

Socioeconomic Development

This approach is based on the realization that long run development polices will eventually reduce the fertility rate in a developing nation. It is realized that the cause of the population problem is not numbers per se or parental irresponsibility. The problem is rooted in the widespread absolute poverty and low standards of living that give rise to the economic justification for large families and flourishing populations. Undoubtedly, there are noneconomic rationale as well. The following constitute different strategies that can be employed in the long run by a developing nation in order to advance its development and hence promote fertility decline:

a. Alleviation of poverty.
b. Improving income inequalities.
c. Improving educational opportunities, especially for females.
d. Improving job opportunities for both males and females.
e. Providing modern preventive medicine and public health programs, in particular, clean water and sanitation to urban and rural poor.
f. Advancing maternal and child health by providing more food, better diets, and enriched nutrition in order to decrease infant mortality.
g. Providing other social services to broad segments of populations, on an equitable basis.

Birth Control Programs

Although long run development, enumerated in the last section, is necessary for eventual population stabilization, there exist some additional specific strategies that developing nations' governments could use to lower birth rates in the short run. These strategies include:

1. Use the media and educational network, both formal (school system) and informal (adult education) to convince people to opt for smaller family sizes.
2. Devise family planning programs to furnish health and contraceptive services to promote the preferred behavior. Although such services exist for 47 developing nations at the present time, a few large nations such as Congo (Dem. Rep.), Ethiopia, and Nigeria lack such government sponsored services.
3. Deploy economic incentives and disincentives to control the fertility rate. These strategies include the following:
    - Abolish or cut maternity leaves and benefits.
    - Eliminate or decrease financial incentives, or charge financial fines for having children above a specific number.
    - Devise minimum-age child labor laws.
    - Establish old-age social security programs.
    - Increase the school fees and eliminate high public subsidies for secondary and higher education.
    - Subsidize smaller families through direct money payments.
        Today, some form of population oriented incentives or disincentives exist in over 30

developing nations. However, other developing nations have yet to devise such polices to eliminate the population explosion that seriously threatens the process of their economic development.

4. Channel population away from rapidly growing urban sectors by eradicating the existing imbalance in economic and social opportunities in urban versus rural sectors.

5. Advance the social and economic status of women to generate an environment that is conducive to deferred marriage and diminished marital fertility. An important component of any strategy aimed at curtailing fertility rates is broadened education of females followed by the generation of gainful employment for them. Such a strategy will lead to the following benefits:
    - Directs young women to postpone marriage by allowing them to become economically self-sufficient. This, in turn, puts them in a better position to exert control over the choice of husband and the timing of marriage.
    - Alleviates family coercion for early marriage by permitting women to contribute to the family's household income.
    - Reduces female dependence on other family members, in particular, males, for financial safety.
    - Allows women to take into account the additional cost of childcare when childbearing competes with income-earning endeavors.
    - Alleviates women's isolation, which is usually a barrier in providing family-planning services.

The significance of these strategies in improving the status and function of women was emphasized in two international conferences on population held in Bucharest in 1974, and in Mexico in 1984. Recently, at the 1994 Cairo International Conference on Population and Development, this issue attracted more attention. In this conference it was emphasized that the general "empowerment" of women, in particular, with respect to **reproductive choice**, is an important ingredient of population and development programs. This position was summarized in the Cairo Program Action as follow:

> The empowerment and autonomy of women and the improvement of their political, social, economic and health status...[are] essential for the achievement of sustainable development and... for the long-run success of population programs. Evidence shows that population and development programs are most effective when steps have simultaneously been taken to improve the status of women.[4]

6. Force people to have smaller families via the power of state legislation and penalties. However, in practice, such a strategy not only is often morally abominable and politically inappropriate, but it is also very difficult to implement. For example, the popular resentment of the government forced sterilization in India, led to the fall of Indian Prime Minister Indira Gandhi's government in 1977. Her subsequent return to power in 1980-84 was guided by a promise not to use coercive birth control strategies.

POPULATION PROJECTIONS

The population growth, and its projection to the year 2015, are shown in Table 6.3. According to this table, the human population of the Earth reached the level of 5,862.7 billion in 1999. As the table indicates, although the rate of growth of the population is expected to slow down in the future, the annual population figures keep on increasing every year. If this trend continues, the world population would reach 7.048 billion by the year 2015. As Table 6.3 shows, the most striking feature of the forecast is that most of the population growth would occur in developing countries. The available data show that populations of many of the developed nations of the world have stabilized and are now beginning to decline to more comfortable levels. However, it is expected that the population of the whole of Europe (a total of 31 separate countries) will decline by 123 million over the next 50 years, while Asia and Africa will experience massive population growth.[5]

Table 6.3
POPULATION GROWTH, 1960-1994, AND PROJECTED TO 2000

Countries	Total Population (millions) 1975	Total Population (millions) 1999	Total Population (millions) 2015	Annual Population Growth Rate (%) 1975-99	Annual Population Growth Rate (%) 1999-2015
Developing	2,898.3	4,606.8	5,759.1	1.9	1.4
High Income	746.1	876.2	928.4	0.7	0.4
Middle Income	1,843.1	2,632.6	3,018.6	1.5	0.9
Low Income	1,398.2	2,356.9	3,101.2	2.2	1.7
World	3,987.4	5,862.7	7,048.2	1.6	1.2

Source: *Human Development Report 2001* (New York: Oxford University Press, 2001)

Some conservative thinkers anticipate that population in the West will drop, resulting in economic problems for these countries. For the United States they predict that by the year 2025 the population will have leveled off and that it will then begin to gradually decline. They fear that such a decline will have serious economic consequences for the United States and other Western countries, such as Germany and Denmark, which are already losing population. They believe that the depopulation of the West means a gradual decline in demand and a shrinking market. This will cause the loss of world influence for the United States and democratic allies. Fortunately, most economists and demographers dismiss such predictions as "alarmist hyperbole."

Some economists even believe that the fertility rates in the West will soon turn upward. But even if the conservative thinkers are correct, and the population in the West levels off or declines, many experts argue that this does not necessarily mean the loss of economic power for these countries. These experts argue that the engine of economic growth is education, technology, and capital, not the sheer size of the population. Additionally, if necessary, a shortage of population can be alleviated by more liberal immigration policies.[6] In any event, one thing is clear: The rate of population growth for developing countries is expected to be much faster than for advanced countries.

SUMMARY

1. According to the Malthusian theory, unchecked population growth would increase at a geometric ratio, while food supply would increase at an arithmetic ratio. Thus, unchecked population growth would have

CH. 6/POPULATION GROWTH AND ECONOMIC DEVELOPMENT 133

increased 512 times after 225 years, but the food supply would have increased only 10 times during this same period. There are positive checks and preventive checks to population growth.

2. Demography is the formal study of population and the elements that affect its rate of change.
3. Fertility can be defined as the inclination of a population to have children. The age-specific fertility rate is the number of babies born to a certain group of population at a specific point in time. The total fertility rate refers to the total of the age-specific fertility rate for a specific group over time, that is, over the total childbearing years.
4. The crude birth rate designates the number of births per thousands of population.
5. The net reproduction rate refers to the number of daughters a newborn female will deliver throughout her life, given constant age-related and fertility and mortality rates.
6. Mortality can be defined as the rate of death of a specific population. The age-specific death rate is the number of deaths in a given of population during a specific period of time. The infant death rate refers to the number of deaths per thousand of births during the first year of life. Life expectancy refers to the average number of remaining years that people of a given age group can expect to live, given that the age-specific death rate stay constant. The crude death rate is the number of deaths per thousand of the population. It portrays changes in the birth rate, the changes in age structure, and changes in the age-specific death rate.
7. The rate of natural increase of population can be defined as the difference between the crude death rate and crude birth rate. The total population increase of a population is the natural increase plus net migration.
8. A stationary population can be defined as a population in which age and sex-specific mortality rates have stayed at replacement stage, that is, one.
9. Demographic transition is a process by which a population pattern eventually shifts from a stage characterized by high birth rates and high death rates to a stage in which both birth and death rates are low and almost equal. This process is composed of the following four distinct stages:
    Stage I: High Fertility and Mortality.
    Stage II: Decreasing Mortality.
    Stage III: Declining Fertility.
    Stage IV: Stationary Population.
10. Dependency burden is an index which measures the proportion of the total population aged 0 to 14, and 65 years and older, which are considered unproductive years and thus not included in the labor force.
11. The microeconomic analysis of the household behavior starts by conjecturing that a couple's decision to bear children, or avoid bearing them is based on the same decision-making process they utilize in other aspects of their lives.
12. The desired number of children (N_d) can be expected to change directly with the following variables:
    a. The level of family income (Y).
    b. The net price of children (P_n).
    c. The prices of all other commodities (Po).
    d. Tastes for commodities, relative to children (To)
    Mathematically, these relationships can be expressed in terms of the following equation:
    $N_d = f(Y, P_n, Po, To), O = 1..., n,$
    Where, $\delta N_d/ \delta Y \rangle 0$, $\delta N_d/ \delta P_n \langle 0$, $\delta N_d/ \delta Po \rangle 0$, and $\delta N_d/ \delta To \langle 0$.
13. Noneconomic variables also play a significant role in fertility. This happens because besides economists, other individuals such as religious leaders, political theorists, and military leaders are involved in decisions that affect the size and growth of population.
14. The two related fallacies of population are:
    a. In already densely populated areas, where land is the only factor of production that is combined

with labor in the production process, population growth is overly destructive.
    b. Population growth should be endured or even advocated in sparingly populated regions.
15. The favorable impact of population growth could be related with any of the following factors:
    a. Accelerator Principal.
    b. Counterpressure.
    c. Technological Progress.
    d. Economies of Scale.

16. We may distinguish between the following two sets of policies that are aimed at reducing fertility rates:
    a. Socioeconomic development.
    b. Birth control programs.
17. The following constitute different strategies that can be employed in the long run by a developing nation in order to advance its development and hence promote fertility decline:
    a. Alleviation of Poverty.
    b. Improving income inequalities.
    c. Improving educational opportunities, especially for females.
    d. Improving job opportunities for both males and females.
    e. Providing modern preventive medicine and public health programs, in particular clean water and sanitation to urban and rural poor.
    f. Advancing maternal and child health by providing more food, better diets, and enriched nutrition in order to decrease infant mortality.
    g. Providing other social services to broad segments of populations, on an equitable basis.
18. Some specific strategies that developing nations' governments could use to lower birth rates in the short run are:
    a Use the media and educational network, both formal (school system) and informal (adult education) to convince people to opt for smaller family sizes.
    b. Devise family planning programs to furnish health and contraceptive services to promote the preferred behavior.
    c. Deploy economic incentives and disincentives to control the fertility rate.
    d. Channel population away from rapidly growing urban sectors by eradicating the existing imbalance in economic and social opportunities in urban versus rural sectors.
    e. Advance the social and economic status of women to generate an environment that is conducive to deferred marriage and diminished marital fertility.
    f. Force people to have smaller families via the power of state legislation and penalties.

QUESTIONS

1. Discuss Malthusian population theory by answering the following questions:
   What does the theory state?
    a. What are the major assumptions underlying this theory?
    b. Is the Malthusian theory applicable to today's developing nations?
    c. Does the Malthusian theory explain Western population growth?
2. Explain demographic transition theory by answering the following questions:
    a. What does the theory state?
    b. At what stages of demographic transition are developing nations?
    c. Why are developing nations at different stages of demographic transition?

3. Over the past few decades population growth in developing nations has proceeded at unprecedented rates. Given this fact, answer the following questions:
   a. What are the major factors that give rise to high fertility rates in developing nations?
   b. Why are fertility rates declining in some developing nations and not in others?
   c. What are the main policy options available to developing nations' governments to control population growth?
4. Discuss the microeconomics of fertility by answering the following questions:
   a. What does the theory state?
   b. Do economic incentives or disincentives affect family size decisions? Explain your answer by providing some specific examples of such incentives and disincentives.
   c. What are the major variables that determine the number of children desired by a couple?
5. Discuss the arguments *against* and in *favor* of the idea that population growth is a crucial issue in developing countries.
6. Compare and contrast the demographic transition patterns of today's developing nations. Why are these patterns different?
7. Elaborate on the concept of dependency burden by answering the following questions:
   a. What is meant by dependency burden and how is it measured?
   b. Is there a relationship between the dependency burden and the age structure of a population?
   c. Is the dependency burden lower or higher in developing nations as compared to advanced nations? Explain.

NOTES

1. United Nations Population Funds (UNFPA) *The State of World Population 2001*, Chapter 1: Overview. http://www.unfpa.org/swp/2001/english/ch01.html.
2. Albert O. Hirschman, *The Strategy of Economic Development*, Yale University Press, New, Conn., 1958., Haven p. 177.
3. *World Development Report 1981*, Oxford University Press, 1981, p.114.
4. United Nations, *International Conference*, para. 4.1. See also Nancy Folbre, "Engendering Economics : New Perspective on Women, Work and Demographic Change," in Michael Bruno and Boris Pleskovic (eds.), *Proceedings of the World Bank Conference on Development Economics, 1995* (Washington, D.C.:World Bank, 1996).
5. UNFPA Report, "Population Projections 2001-2050." http://www.population.org.au/factfigs/popproj2001.htm.
6. "British Dearth: Some Thinkers Expect Population to Drop and Trouble to Result," *The Wall Street Journal*, 18 June 1987, p. 1.

SUGGESTED READINGS

Bongaarts, John. "Population Growth and Global Warming." *Population and Development Review* 18 (June 1992): 299-319.

_____. "The Supply-Demand Framework for the Determinants of Fertility: An Alternative Implementation." *Population Studies* 47 (November 1993): 437-56.

_____., W. Parker Mauldin and James Phillips. *The Demographic Impact of Family Planning Programs* Washington, D.C.: Population Council, 1990.

Cassen, Robert, H. "Population and Development: A Survey." *World Development* 4 (October 1976).

_____. *Population Policy: A New Consensus*. Washington, D.C.: Overseas Development Council, 1994.

Chamie, Joseph. "Demography: Population Databases in Development Analysis." *Journal of Development Economics* 44 (June 1994): 131-46.

Cochrane, Susan. " A Review of Some Microeconomic Models of Fertility." *Population Studies* 29 (1975).

Dasgupta, Partha. "The Population Problem: Theory and Evdence." *Journal of Economic Literature* 33 (December

1995): 1879-1902.

Daugherty, Helen, and Kenneth Kammeyer. *An Introduction to Population*. New York: Guilford, 1995.

Demeny, Paul. "The World Demographic Situation." in Jane Menken, ed. *World Population and U.S. Policy*. New York: Norton, 1986, pp. 27-66.

Easterlin, Richard, ed. *Population and Economic Change in Developing Countries*. Chicago: University of Chicago Press/National Bureau of Economic Research, 1980.

_____. Easterlin, Richard A. "An Economic Framework for Fertility Analysis." *Studies in Family Planning* (March 1975).

Germain, Sen A. and Lincoln Chen, eds. *Population Policies Reconsidered*. New York: International Women's Health Coalition, 1994.

Hartmann, Betsy. *Reproductive Rights and Wrongs: The Global Politics of Population Control and Contraceptive Choice*. New York: Harper & Row, 1987.

Johnson, Gale D. Effects of Institutions and Policies on Rural Population Growth with Application to China." *Population and Development Review* 20 (September 1994): 503-31.

King, Timothy and Allen Kelly. *The New Population Database: Two Views on Population Growth and Economic Development*, Population Trends and Public Policy Paper No.7. Washington, D.C.: Population Reference Bureau, 1985.

Lutz, Wolfgang. "The Future of World Population." *Population Bulletin* 49 (June 1994):1-47.

Merrick, Thomas W. "World Population in Transition." *Population Bulletin* 41 (April 1986): 1-51.

Mauldin, Parker W. and John A. Ross. *Family Planning Programs: Efforts and Results, 1982-89* Washington, D.C.: Population Council, 1991.

Nerlove, Marc. "Household and Economy: Toward a New Theory of Population, and Economic Growth." *Journal of Political Economy* 82 (June 1974).

Pritchett, Lant H. "Desired Fertility and the Impact of Population Policies." *Population and Development Review* 20 (March 1994): 1-55.

Ridker, Ronald, ed. *Population and Development: The Search for Selective Interventions*. Baltimore: Johns Hopkins University Press, 1980.

Schultz, Paul T. *Fertility Determinants: A Theory, Evidence, and Application of Policy Evaluation*. Santa Monica, Calif.: Rand Corp., 1974.

Teielbaum, Michael S. "Population and Development: Is a Consensus Possible?" *Foreign Affairs* (July 1974): 749-757.

The World Bank. *Averting the Old Age Crisis: Policies to Protect the Old and Promote Growth*. New York: Oxford University Press, 1994.

United Nations Population Fund. *Population, Resources and Environment: The Critical Challenges*. New York: United Nations, 1991.

World Resources Institute. *World Resources, 1994-95. New York: Oxford University Press, 1994, chap.2*.

CHAPTER 7

UNEMPLOYMENT, MIGRATION, URBANIZATION AND ECONOMIC DEVELOPMENT

Having discussed population and development in the previous chapter, we note that some of the major problems that are highly associated with the subject of population in developing nations are employment, migration, and urbanization. The dependency burden of the working age population stems from fertility rates, and the labor force growth is determined by the natural growth of population and migration, both regional and international. The purpose of this chapter is to examine these issues. First we explain unemployment problems in developing nations, second we discuss urbanization, third we elaborate on regional migration, and finally, we study international migration.

UNEMPLOYMENT PROBLEMS IN DEVELOPING NATIONS

Like other economic issues, the unemployment problem in developing nations is quite different than in advanced nations. The openly unemployed individuals in developing nations are usually young people 15 to 24 years old, educated males, and residents of cities. The unemployed individuals in a developing nation are less likely to be from the poorest 20% of the population as is the case in advanced nations.

High unemployment presents a major problem for developing nations, reflecting vast underutilization of human resources. It contributes to the potential source of social unrest and political discontent by often young, urban and educated males who makeup the bulk of unemployed people.

In advanced nations, economic development was followed by a sizeable internal and international migration from agrarian areas to urban areas. Such a migration was fueled by the increasing demand for labor in the urban areas, resulting from industrial expansion in cities. Given the pattern of development in the now developed nations, many economists assumed that rapid industrialization would resolve the unemployment in today's developing nations. However, for reasons to be explained below, this approach of rapid industrial growth has not created the same results in developing nations as it did in advanced nations.

Types of Unemployment and Underemployment in Developing Nations

To understand the nature of unemployment in developing nations, we begin by elaborating on the following terminologies that are used in describing different types of unemployment in developing nations:

1. **Open Unemployment** consists of individuals without work who are actively seeking and presently available for work among a given age range. They usually encompass those age groups relating to significant participation in economic activities. To be sure, this definition excludes individuals who work even one hour in paid employment, are self-employed, or engage in an unpaid apprenticeship.
2. **Underemployment.** A situation in which individuals work less than they would like to work.
3. **Visible Underemployment.** A condition in which workers are compelled to work short hours as an alternative to being out of a job.
4. **Invisible Unemployment.** A situation in which workers' capabilities are used inadequately.
5. **Disguised Unemployment.** A condition in which present work functions are divided among resources (typically labor) such that all seem fully employed, but in fact much of their time is spent in unproductive endeavors.
6. **Hidden Unemployment.** A situation in which individuals are engaged in nonemployment endeavors, such as education and household chores, as a "second choice." The two major reasons giving rise to this condition are:
   a. Job opportunities are not accessible at the level of education already attained.
   b. Job discrimination prevents women from obtaining a job that they desire.

Equipped with these terminologies, we devote the rest of this chapter to the discussion of rural-urban migration, disguised unemployment, policies to reduce unemployment, internal migration, and finally, international migration.

RURAL-URBAN MIGRATION

History shows that the economic development of Western Europe and the United States was accompanied by the migration of workers from rural to urban areas. With an urban sector concentrated on industrialization and a rural sector focusing on agricultural endeavors, overall economic development in these nations was marked by the steady reallocation of labor out of the agriculture sector and into the industrial sector via rural-urban migration, both on internal and international levels. This pattern of development served to breed the idea that industrialization and development were essentially identical. Such an idea set the foundation for a blueprint of development that exemplified itself in the original Lewis theory of labor transfer, discussed in Chapter 4. As a result, until the 1960s, rural-urban migration was considered favorable by economists. Internal migration was regarded as a natural process in which surplus workers were slowly released from the rural sector to furnish required labor for urban industrial growth. This mechanism was viewed as socially desirable because laborers were being channeled from the rural sector where their marginal social product was commonly zero to the industrial sector where their marginal product was not only positive but also rapidly increasing as a consequence of capital accumulation and technological progress.

However, during the 1960s and 1970s when developing nations experienced an extensive migration of their rural workers into urban areas in spite of increasing unemployment and underemployment in these areas, the validity of the Lewis two-sector model of development became questionable.

Today, based on the experiences of developing nations, it is clear that rates of rural-urban migration continue to outstrip rates of urban job creation and to exceed considerably the absorptive capacity of both

CH. 7/UNEMPLOYMENT, MIGRATION AND ECONOMIC DEVELOPMENT

industry and urban social services. As a result, economists no longer consider migration as a beneficial process needed to resolve problems of rising urban labor demand. Rather, they perceive such a process as the main element that fuels urban surplus labor and continues to worsen the existing acute urban unemployment problems stemming from structural and economic disparities between urban and rural sectors.

Migration worsens the existing structural disparities between urban and rural both on the supply side and the demand side. On the supply side, the flow of migration from the rural sector to the urban sector enhances the rate of growth of labor supply relative to the rate of growth of urban population. On the demand side, urban job generation is usually more difficult and costly to implement than rural job generation. This difficulty stems from the provision of massive complementary resources needed for most jobs in the industrial sector. Additionally, given the growing urban wages and fringe benefits along with the lack of appropriate, more labor-using technologies, an increasing percentage of the modern-sector output growth comes from increases in labor productivity. This in turn decreases the demand for additional workers. Collectively, this fast rising supply and lagging demand growth change a short-run problem of resource imbalances into a long-run condition of chronic and growing labor surplus in the industrial sector.

We should point out that migration is both a sign of and a contributor to developing nations' underdevelopment. Thus, the comprehension of the elements that give rise to rural-urban migration is a prerequisite to an understanding of the nature and character of the development process and to devising strategies to affect this process in a socially desirable manner. In answering these issues, we examine the Harris-Todaro model and discuss its major criticisms in the next section.

The Harris-Todaro Model

As you recall from Chapter 4, the Lewis model showed how developing nations' economic growth generated from the rise in the size of the modern industrial sector relative to the traditional agricultural sector. However, this model does not explain why rural migration continues in spite of high urban unemployment. John R. Harris and Michael P. Todaro try to close this gap by devising a model that is based on the assumption that a worker's decision to migrate from the rural sector to the urban sector is based on wages and probability of unemployment. More specifically, according to the model, migrants respond to urban-rural differences in expected as opposed to actual earnings. Assume an unskilled Indian farm worker can choose between working on a farm for an annual average income Rs. 4,000 or migrating to New Delhi, receiving an annual wage of Rs. 8,000. Most economists who assume the existence of full employment conclude that the worker would end up accepting the higher paying job in New Delhi. However, given the existence of high unemployment in developing nations, such an assumption is not valid. Suppose that the probability of the laborer finding a job in New Delhi during a one-year period is 30 percent. The laborer would not move to New Delhi because the **expected income** is Rs. 8,000 × 0.30 = 2,400. This amount is much less than Rs. 4,000 (4,000 × 1) that the worker could earn in the rural sector. However, if the probability of finding a job in New Delhi is 70 percent, expected urban earning would be Rs.8,000 × 0.70 = Rs. 5,600. In this situation it would be rational for the Indian farm worker to seek the job in New Delhi. And because most migrants are young people under the age of 25, it would be rational to presume that they have an even longer time span during which they could make their migration decision. As a result, if the present value of expected life time earnings in urban occupation is greater than on the farms, it would be rational to migrate.

Harris and Todaro argue that creating urban jobs by enhancing industrial output is not sufficient for resolving the urban unemployment problem. Instead, they suggest that government should decrease urban wages, remove other factor price distortions, create labor-using technologies, and advance rural employment.

The major shortcoming of the Harris-Todaro model is that it does not consider other factors that affect the decision to migrate. To be sure, the decision to migrate is not based simply on earning differentials between the urban sector and rural sector. Other factors also enter into the decision process. The migrant compares housing, transport, schools, shops, entertainment centers and other amenities before deciding to migrate. Transportation, housing, fuel, sewerage, and staple foods are commonly subsidized by the developing nations' government in urban areas, where their costs are by far higher than the rural areas. In fact, the concentration of social services in developing nations' urban sectors is one of the main variables that contribute to overurbanization, especially in Africa.

Even setting aside such amenities, according to a study by the International Labor Organization (ILO), the ratio of average urban income to rural income is more than two in Asia and Latin America and four to five in Africa, after making adjustment for the costs of living. Given a ratio of two, urban unemployment rate should be fifty percent to make urban and rural expected income equal to each other. However, urban unemployment in developing nations seldom surpasses ten to twenty percent, implying that migration does not close the urban and rural expected wage gap. The gap can be explained by adding the urban informal sector, to Harris-Todaro urban formal and rural sector. The urban informal sector includes street venders, shoe shiners, car washers, street entertainers, garbage collectors, repair persons, artisans, petty traders, hawkers, cottage industrialists, and other self-employed individuals who generate income and employment for themselves by engaging in activities that do not require much skill or start-up costs. These minor entrepreneurs negotiate agreements outside the legal framework, and pay their workers below minimum wages. Statistics show that a considerable percentage of developing nations' urban labor force is composed of the informal sector. For example, 45 percent of workers in Bogota, and 50 percent of workers in Lagos, Nigeria come from the informal sector's labor supply.

The supply of labor by the informal sector is influenced mainly by wages and population growth in the rural sector. The considerable absorption of rural emigrant workers into the informal sector provides an explanation for the tendency of migration to end long before rural expected income reaches the level of income in the urban formal sector. In fact, many immigrants are neither receiving the current formal sector wage nor are unemployed, but are engaged in informal occupations, which paves their way toward the urban economy.

DISGUISED UNEMPLOYMENT

Rising unemployment in developing nations is caused by a labor force that is growing faster than the rate of growth of employment opportunities. The developing nations' labor force reached the level of 1,325 million in year 2,000, which is 2.5 times larger than its level of 500 million in 1950. Today, developing nations have to deal with a much faster labor force growth than the advanced nations had at a similar stage in their economic growth process. The labor force in Japan, North America, and Western Europe grew at 0.8 percent a year in the nineteenth century as compared to 1.9 percent a year in developing nations, during the 1992-1996 period. The available statistics show that it took approximately 90 years for the labor force to double in advanced nations; it currently takes about 38 years in developing nations.

Slow employment growth in the industrial and service sectors of developing nations has contributed to high rates of urban unemployment, underemployment, and low rural productivity. Many economists maintain that disguised unemployment, that is, zero marginal revenue productivity of labor, is endemic among developing nations' agricultural labor. In other words, withdrawing a worker from the agricultural sector does not diminish output. However, the available evidence does not support such a contention.[*]

---

[*]The term *disguised unemployment* originated during the Great Depression and was used to refer to workers in developed nations who took inferior jobs as a consequence of being laid off. Between the 1930s and early 1950s, developing nations did not have much industrial unemployment, so economists surmised that the developing counterpart of mass unemployment in the West was disguised unemployment: people continued to work

GLOBAL INSIGHTS CASE 7.1

EDUCATION AND UNEMPLOYMENT IN SOME DEVELOPING NATIONS

Education and training are commonly considered as the main road to employment in developed nations. Given the existence of a positive correlation between the level of education and the rate of employment in developed nations, one might expect to detect the same relationship in developing nations. In reality, however, many highly educated people in developing nations suffer from unemployment. What is even worse is that for many developing nations, unemployment increases with level of education. For example, in India, in 1989, the unemployment rate for individuals with no education was 2%, as compared to 9% for those with secondary education and 12% for university graduates. One explanation for this unemployment picture is that the least educated people are not able to financially support themselves and need to find any kind of job in the urban informal sector. Although these people might be severely underemployed, working only a few hours a week, they are not counted as being unemployed. Secondary school and high school graduates are more likely able to financially support themselves and remain unemployed until a higher paying job becomes available. As a result, these people are more likely to be counted among the openly unemployed during the period that they are waiting for an appropriate job to come along. During the 1973-1983 period, Thailand's unemployment rates among high school graduates ranged from 20% to 35%. In Bangladesh, 40% of individuals with master's degrees are either underemployed or unemployed. In Africa, where the educational system continues to produce a larger supply of graduates than is warranted by demand for their services, the problem is especially becoming critical. For example, in 1986, the unemployment rates among Algerian secondary school graduates was about 29%.

The basic problem is the inadequacy of demand to absorb the supply. The solution to this problem requires implementation of appropriate strategies in both the short-run and the long-run. The short-run strategy could concentrate on offering the unemployed more vocationally-oriented training. This strategy may be complemented by providing the private sector with some incentives in order to hire the vocationally trained graduates. The long-run strategy should nurture and facilitate the educational and training systems that are conducive to the provision of relevant skills needed by society. This demands changes at all levels of learning, ranging from literacy training to university education.

Source: United Nations Development Program, *Human Development Report, 1993* (New York: Oxford University Press, 1993), p.38; Michael P. Todaro, *Economic Development*, 7th ed. New York: Addison-Wesley, 2,000), po. 264-265.

POLICIES TO REDUCE UNEMPLOYMENT

As you recall from your introductory macroeconomics course, the classical economists believed that in the long-run an economy would be in equilibrium at full employment. In other words, they assumed that wage

---

on the farm despite depressed conditions.

and price flexibility ensures full employment. In such an economic system, according to classical thought, there would be no such thing as involuntary unemployment. Such a view was prevalent in the West for about 100 years before the Great Depression.

The failure of the classical model in the West in the 1930s, set the foundation for the emergence of Keynesian economics. In his famous book, *The General Theory of Employment, Interest and Money* (1936), Keynes strongly criticized the classical theory and formulated a theory of his own. In Keynesian theory, a nation's employment rises with GNP. Unemployment arises because aggregate (total) demand is insufficient to absorb aggregate supply at full employment. To resolve this problem, the aggregate demand should be enhanced by any of the following means:

1. Reducing taxes or lowering interest rates to increase private consumption and investment, and hence increasing aggregate demand.
2. Increasing government spending, and thus enhancing aggregate demand.

According to Keynes, as long as there is unemployment and unutilized capital capacity in the economy, output responds automatically to rise in demand through higher employment. However, as we will discuss later in Chapter 9, Keynesian theory is not applicable to developing nations. This is mainly due to the slow response in output to demand increases, and inefficiency of fiscal policy, calling for the reformation of the financial system of the developing nation in question.

Having dismissed the effectiveness of Keynesian economics in resolving the problems of unemployment, developing nations are left with four general policies that can help to alleviate unemployment problems. These include policies to discourage rural-urban migration, technology adaptation, policies to reduce factor price distortion, and educational policy.

Policies to Discourage Rural-Urban Migration

These policies rely on greater rural economic development schemes in order to discourage the migration of workers from rural to urban areas, thus reducing the unemployment rate. Such policies include the following:

1. Promoting amenities such as housing, schools, food, entertainment, health services, hospitals, and roads in rural areas.
2. Eliminating the price ceiling on food and other agricultural goods.
3. Establishing new industries in rural areas.
4. Enhancing labor-using, technological progress in the agriculture sector.
5. Adjusting the foreign exchange price close to a market-clearing rate.

Although such expenditures might reach the point of diminishing returns too quickly, however, unemployment among even a small percentage of urban migrants may be preferable to extensive low labor efficiency in the rural sector. To be sure, in some cases the issue of urban migration might be political in nature rather than economical.

Technology Adaptation Polices

As we will explain later in Chapter 8, the technology that is developed in advanced nations is not appropriate for the developing nations. Given that developing nations are relatively more labor-abundant than advanced nations, in general, appropriate technologies in developing nations are relatively more labor-

CH. 7/UNEMPLOYMENT, MIGRATION AND ECONOMIC DEVELOPMENT 143

using compared to advanced nations. Such technologies help increase the employment of more unskilled labor in developing nations, and thus alleviates the unemployment problem. The use of more labor-using technologies in developing nations can be encouraged by the following policies:

1. **Utilizing Less Modern Equipment.** For example, using typewriters for typing as opposed to computers.
2. **Promoting Greater Income Equality.** Because commodities that are consumed by poor people are relatively more labor intensive than those consumed by rich people, greater income equality may lead to an increasing demand for labor intensive goods such as sandals and cotton shirts.
3. **Promoting the Use of Labor Intensive Technologies in the Production Process Substitution.** Promoting the production of more labor-intensive commodities within each industry. For example, producing sandals instead of fancy shoes.
4. **Promoting the Use of Labor Intensive Technologies Auxiliary Activities.** Using labor as opposed to heavy equipment (e.g. conveyer belts or fork lifts) in activities such as storage, packing, materials receiving, and handling which allow more factor substitution than materials processing.
5. **The Local Generation of Technologies.** Generating the needed technology domestically.
6. **Government Purchases of Labor-Using Goods.** Because a large percentage of a developing nation's national income is used by the government in the purchase of goods and services, the government can impact employment by choosing to buy more labor-using commodities.

Policies to Decrease Factor-Price Distortion

As we explained in chapter 5, due to inappropriate government polices and institutional constraints, the price of labor (the wage rate) is higher and the price of capital is lower than what is warranted by the free market forces of demand and supply in a developing nation. Developing nations can enhance employment by diminishing factor distortions. This causes wages to decline to a lower level, dictated by the free forces of market demand and supply, thereby increasing employment. The policies to decrease factor-price distortions include the following:

1. **Promoting Small-Scale Industry.** Small firms commonly require less capital and more labor per unit of output. As a result, the promotion of such firms leads to the employment of more labor, helping to reduce unemployment problems in the developing nations that employ such a policy. Governments can encourage the development of small-scale industry by schemes such as technical assistance, industrial extension service, and preferred official buying.
2. **Utilizing Capital Stock More Efficiently.** Because developing nations seem to have low capital utilization rates compared to advanced nations, this policy calls on increasing the use of capital stock by working two or three shifts rather than one.
3. **Diminishing Subsidies to Domestic Industry.** This policy calls on cutting credit and capital subsidies to the domestic firms in order to decrease capital-using technology and unemployment.
4. **Cutting Wages in the Organized Sector.** If demand for labor is relatively elastic, that is, greater than one, then as microeconomic theory tells us, a decline in wages (the price of labor), causes the wage bill to increase. However, such a policy is not effective if demand for labor is relatively inelastic, due to the following reasons:
    a. Product demand is relatively inelastic.
    b. Labor constitutes a relatively small percentage of the total cost.
    c. Other factors of production cannot be easily substituted for labor.
    d. The supplies of factors of production other than labor are inelastic.

     e. The goods administered price is not flexible.
5. **Decreasing Social Security Programs and Payroll Taxation.** Such a decrease will raise the demand for, and supply of, labor at any given wage rate, thus enhancing employment.
6. **Establishing Market-Clearing Exchange Rates.** Foreign trade policies in some developing nations have called on lowering the exchange rate (the price of foreign currency in terms of the domestic currency). This has caused the price of the capital-goods imports in terms of the domestic currency to decline, leading to a rise in their quantity demanded. If we allow the price of foreign exchange to adjust to a market-clearing rate, the price of the foreign-made capital goods in terms of domestic currency increases, causing their quantity demanded to decline. This, in turn, stimulates demand for the labor-intensive technologies, helping to increase employment.
7. **Reforming Labor Legislation.** Labor legislation in many developing nations is not conducive to industrial employment. For example, in some developing nations legislation makes it hard to discharge a worker, who usually requires a large severance pay when dismissal takes place. Such conditions call on the developing nations to revise worker legislation to improve termination polices and the severance payment standard.

Educational Policy

The educational system of many developing nations is not tuned to their requirements for the type of labor they need to achieve economic development. Often these nations lack public primary education and suffer from the shortages of managerial and technical expertise. Such conditions fuel unemployment and impede the economic development process. The following is a list of policies that these nations could adopt in order to achieve a proper balance between their educational output and their labor requirements:

1. **Allocating a Larger Percentage of the Educational Budget to Primary Education and Managerial and Technical Training.** One of the characteristics of unemployment in developing nations is the existence of a growing number of unemployed secondary school graduates and dropouts where secondary school has expanded rapidly in recent years. Additionally, many secondary school graduates have been trained in the humanities and social sciences, lacking technical, managerial skills and knowledge needed in the process of economic development. This calls on the developing nations' policy makers to change their educational-budget priorities, placing more emphasis on primary education, and technical and managerial expertise, when politically feasible.
2. **Reducing Subsidies for Higher Education.** Some developing nations have continued to subsidize higher education at the expense of primary education and technical expertise. As a result, they have created a large number of highly educated people some of whom cannot find proper employment. Reducing this type of subsidy not only decreases the unemployment of highly educated people, but it also contributes to income equality. This happens because the reduced subsidies are channeled toward primary education and technical training of the poor segment of the population.
3. **Minimizing Inequality and Discrimination in both Education and Employment.** In some developing nations, ethnic, regional, and sex discrimination keep highly qualified and productive people out of work. To rectify this problem, the developing nation should pursue polices that recognize job-related education and experience for advancement, stopping discriminatory practices.
4. **Enhance the Pay Scales' Flexibility.** In some developing nations the pay scales are not flexible enough to adjust to market prices, resulting from the interaction of demand and supply. Thus, if there is a surplus of a given profession, say engineers, their salaries do not decline to the market level. Thus, both graduates and prospective students do not receive the right signal from the market

CH. 7/UNEMPLOYMENT, MIGRATION AND ECONOMIC DEVELOPMENT

to shift to another field. As a result, the unemployment problem in the field of engineering keeps worsening.

5. **Set Realistic Job Qualifications.** Some developing nations have a tendency to overstate the job qualifications, requiring educational certification for employment. This has the effect of keeping some well experienced people who do not have the certification out of the job. It seems counterproductive, for example, to make a bachelor's degree in accounting a prerequisite for a bank teller position. Thus, employers should be encouraged to establish realistic job qualifications, increasing the employment of qualified, experienced people.

INTERNATIONAL MIGRATION

International migration, like births and deaths, is one of the factors that affect the size of population in a given nation. Although labor is generally less mobile than capital across national boundaries, it represents one of the most sensitive issues of our time. For some countries, having natives migrate to other nations could tarnish national dignity and lead to economic losses for those who are left behind. In receiving nations, immigration might raise nationalist fervor and fuel xenophobia and ethnic prejudice, mainly among those who fear that competition from immigrants could lead to loss of their jobs and economic well-being. For migrants themselves, the road to another nation with a different culture has its costs and is filled with uncertainty. The costs consist of transportation expenses and loss of income during the transitory stage of resettling and looking for a job in the new country. A migrant leaving friends and family behind has to endure the "cultural shock" of adjusting to a new culture and, often, a new language. Also, subject to new potential ailments and possible exploitation by others, a migrant may fail to find a better income in the new nation and return home frustrated. Nevertheless, on average, migrants should benefit from migration; if this were not the case, they would not decide to migrate.

The purpose of this section is to shed some light on the main issues surrounding labor migration. First, we describe the causes of international labor migration. Second, we provide a theoretical explanation of labor migration by examining its welfare effects in the context of demand and supply analysis.

Causes of International Labor Migration

The factors giving rise to international labor migration are both economic and noneconomic in nature, and often the two are interconnected. In some instances, noneconomic factors, such as political, religious, and physical freedom gained by refugees who escape oppressive governments constitute the major reason for migration. This was certainly the case for some of the migrations that occurred in the nineteenth century and earlier in Europe. In other cases, the expectation of higher real wages and income constitute the main cause of migrating to another country. In fact, most international labor migration, especially following World War II, has been inspired by the possibility of securing higher earnings abroad. Highly educated professionals from developing countries have increased their income substantially by migrating to countries such as Australia, Great Britain, Canada, Germany, and the United States.

The United States has been an especially attractive place for migration, admitting more than 57 million migrants from 1820 through 1990. Western Europe was the chief origin of migrants during this period; Britain, Germany, and Italy were among the major contributors. In recent years, however, the percentage of immigrants from developing countries has increased, whereas the percentage of European migrants has declined. This can be seen from Table 7.1 As this table indicates, in 1998, out of 660,500 immigrants, 90,800 (13.75 percent) were European, whereas 219,700, (33.26 percent) were Asian. In other words, the number of Asians that migrated to the United States was more than two times greater than the number of European immigrants. As Table 7.2 shows, in 1998, the top three popular states for immigration were

California, New York, and Florida.

To be sure, an intricate mesh of elements affects a person's decision to emigrate. For simplification of the analysis, however, in the next section we focus on economic causes and assume that an individual's decision to emigrate is only motivated by higher wages in the country of his or her destination.

Table 7.1

IMMIGRANTS ADMITTED TO THE UNITED STATES BY COUNTRY OF BIRTH: 1981-1998
(In thousands)

COUNTRY OF BIRTH	1981-90, total	1991-96, total	1997	1998
All Countries	7,338.1	6,146.2	798.4	660.5
Europe	705.6	875.6	119.9	90.8
Asia	2,817.4	1,941.9	265.8	219.7
North America	3,125.0	2,740.7	307.5	253.0
Central America	458.7	342.8	43.7	35.7
South America	455.9	344.0	52.9	45.4
Africa	192.3	213.1	47.8	40.7
Other countries	41.9	31.0	4.5	10.9

Source: U.S. Bureau of Census, Statistical Abstracts of the United States: 2001. (Washington, DC: Government Printing Office, 2001), http://www.census.gov/prod/2002pubs/01statab/pop.pdf, p. 11.

Effects of International Labor Migration

The effects of international labor migration can be investigated in terms of output effect and income distribution effect. Let us first study these effects in the context of demand and supply analysis. Next, we elaborate on other effects of international labor migration that are not apparent from the demand and supply analysis.

The Output Effect. In Figure 7.1, assume the world is composed of only two countries, the United States and Mexico; there are only two factors of production, capital and labor. O_U represents the origin of the United States, and O_M represents the origin of Mexico. The length of the horizontal axis ($O_U O_M$) represents the fixed supply of labor in the world. The initial allocation of this supply between the two countries is shown by the intersection of the entirely inelastic supply curve (S) with the horizontal axis at L_0. Accordingly, the United States has $O_U L_0$ units of labor, and Mexico has $O_M L_0$ units of labor. The demand schedule for each nation is represented by the value of the marginal product of labor (VMPL) in that nation. The United States demand for labor (D_U) is denoted by $VMPL_U$; Mexico's demand for labor (D_M) is denoted by $VMPL_M$.

CH. 7/UNEMPLOYMENT, MIGRATION AND ECONOMIC DEVELOPMENT

Table 7.2
IMMIGRANTS ADMITTED TO THE UNITED STATES BY LEADING COUNTRY OF BIRTH: 1998

State and other area	Total*	Mexico	China	India	Philippines	Dominican Republic	Vietnam	Cuba	Jamaica
Total	660,477	131,575	36,884	36,482	34,466	20,387	17,649	17,375	15,146
Alabama	1,608	178	117	165	85	2	51	29	15
Alaska	1,008	105	56	14	254	32	13	1	1
Arizona	6,211	3,209	253	230	220	7	96	7	7
Arkansas	914	305	46	59	42	2	38	3	-
California	170,126	62,113	12,582	7,177	16,202	72	6,519	289	186
Colorado	6,513	2,293	317	218	143	10	287	27	6
Connecticut	7,780	272	304	478	181	186	145	43	856
Delaware	1,063	135	79	141	26	11	23	8	28
District of Colombia	2,377	42	112	36	80	46	111	4	83
Florida	59,965	2,788	628	1,079	837	1,483	437	14,265	4,795
Georgia	10,445	1,630	435	882	163	44	592	110	211
Hawaii	5,465	75	482	16	3,140	2	101	-	3
Idaho	1,504	984	63	29	25	4	37	1	-
Illinois	33,163	10,127	1,357	3,446	1,350	67	306	98	131
Indiana	3,981	904	208	375	117	9	78	20	25
Iowa	1,655	366	78	129	56	4	218	1	1
Kansas	3,184	1,357	91	184	78	4	279	8	6
Kentucky	2,017	141	72	119	50	5	195	243	7
Louisiana	2,193	132	94	129	70	32	201	83	4
Maine	709	9	80	41	9	5	23	8	9
Maryland	15,561	364	697	1,108	625	137	251	44	545
Massachusetts	15,869	105	1,355	958	179	1,138	443	40	340
Michigan	13,943	1,055	557	1,484	330	72	206	124	93
Minnesota	6,981	536	270	455	156	10	328	14	34
Mississippi	701	56	69	94	64	1	31	27	4
Missouri	3,588	491	197	271	139	7	184	23	16
Montana	299	21	42	8	17	-	6	-	-
Nebraska	1,267	542	52	88	36	2	71	3	1
Nevada	6,106	2,881	231	145	712	14	95	195	9
New Hampshire	1,010	28	73	91	56	28	39	3	8
New Jersey	35,091	772	1,318	4,284	1,648	2,478	271	437	1,037
New Mexico	2,199	1,359	76	116	32	1	43	59	4
New York	96,559	1,616	8,850	4,017	1,490	10,719	646	322	5,874
North Carolina	6,415	880	318	618	151	33	310	78	40
North Dakota	472	12	9	41	9	2	16	18	-
Ohio	7,697	311	493	900	221	32	263	18	51
Oklahoma	2,273	812	96	204	60	2	131	3	5
Oregon	5,909	1,879	411	239	165	1	365	81	8
Pennsylvania	11,942	625	938	1,127	265	245	586	78	349
Rhode Island	1,976	27	73	62	38	284	15	1	6
South Carolina	2,125	259	96	182	96	2	63	4	11
South Dakota	356	36	13	8	19	-	6	13	1
Tennessee	2,806	300	148	291	60	9	118	43	19
Texas	44,428	22,956	1,159	2,663	851	97	1,576	218	108
Utah	3,600	1,035	120	101	72	5	133	17	6
Vermont	513	9	30	53	6	4	13	1	2
Virginia	15,686	541	523	910	921	31	689	60	117
Washington	16,920	4,129	843	599	1,159	5	940	47	27
West Virginia	375	10	23	65	20	-	2	5	4
Wisconsin	3,724	680	234	314	106	5	50	4	44
Wyoming	159	42	10	15	7	-	2	-	-
Guam	1,835	1	54	10	1,507	-	9	-	-
Northen Mariana Islands	103	-	10	1	76	-	-	-	-
Puerto Rico	3,251	39	36	1	1	2,647	1	147	-
Virgin Islands	979	-	5	12	6	349	-	-	9
Armed Services Posts	88	1	-	-	38	-	-	-	-
Other	6,030	-	1	-	-	-	-	-	-

- Represents zero.
* Includes other countries, not shown separately.
Source: U.S. Bureau of Census, Statistical Abstracts of the United States: 2001 (Washington, DC: Government Printing Office, 2001), http://www.census.gov/prod/2002pubs/01statab/pop.pdf 12.

As we know from microeconomics courses, VMPL is equal to the marginal physical product of labor (the amount of output associated with the last unit of labor hired) multiplied by the price of the product produced. In other words, VMPL measures the amount of money producers receive from the sale of the output produced by the last unit of labor hired. As the quantity of labor in a given nation increases, the marginal physical product of labor decreases and VMPL declines. Because under competitive conditions VMPL is equal to the wage rate, it follows that an increase in the quantity of labor leads to a decline in the wage rate. In other words, the VMPL curve in each country is the labor demand schedule, portraying a negative relationship between the wage rate (W) and the quantity of labor employed.

The premigration equilibrium wage rate in each country is found at the intersection of labor demand and supply curves for that country. In the United States, this equilibrium occurs at point A where S and DU intersect. At this point, the U.S. wage rate is $O_U W_U$, and the value of total output is measured by $O_U CAL_0$ (areas h + g + f). Out of this total, area g + f represents total labor income, that is, the wage rate ($O_U W_U$) multiplied by the quantity of labor ($O_U L_0$). The rest (area h) represents the share of national income collected by the owners of capital.** In Mexico, the equilibrium occurs at point B where S and D_M intersect.

Table 7.3

THE OUTPUT EFFECT OF MIGRATION

	Before Migration	After Migration	Gain (+)/Loss (-)
U.S. Output	Areas h + g + f	Areas h + g + f + d + e + j + i	Areas i + j + e + d
Mexican Output	Areas a + b + c + d + e	Areas a + b + c	- e - d
Net Gain In World Output			Areas i + j

At this point, the equilibrium wage rate in Mexico is $O_M W_M$, and the value of total output is measured by $O_M DBL_0$ (areas a + b + c + d + e). Out of this total, area a + d measures total labor income ($O_M L_0 \times O_M W_M$). The rest (areas b + c + e) denotes the share of income collected by the owners of capital. Now assume free international labor migration, meaning that labor can move freely between the two nations solely in response to wage differentials. Because wages are higher in the United States than in Mexico, there is an incentive for Mexican workers to migrate to the United States to compete for the higher wages. This process continues until the wage differential between the two nations is eliminated. Graphically, this is represented by the shift of the supply of labor from S to S`, where it intersects both D_U and D_M at equilibrium point E. At this postmigration equilibrium point, the wage rate in both countries is equal ($O_U W_E = O_M W_E$), and the quantity of labor employed in the United States and Mexico is $O_U L_1$ and OML_1, respectively. Thus, wage rates rise in Mexico and fall in the United States. However, the value of total output falls from $O_M DBL_0$ (areas a + b + c + d + e) to $O_M DEL_1$ (areas a + b + c) in Mexico, and rises from $O_U CAL_0$ (areas h + g + f) to $O_U CE_1$ (areas h + g + f + d + e + j + i) in the United States. These results are summarized in Table 7.3. As this table indicates, free immigration leads to a net gain in the value of world output shown by areas i + j.

**In our analysis, we are assuming capital and labor are the only two productive factors of production.

CH. 7/UNEMPLOYMENT, MIGRATION AND ECONOMIC DEVELOPMENT

Figure 7.1

OUTPUT AND INCOME DISTRIBUTION EFFECTS OF INTERNATIONAL LABOR MIGRATION

Given a supply of $O_U L_0$ units of labor, the United States has a wage rate of $O_U W_U$, and the value of its total output is measured by $O_U CAL_0$, or areas h + g + f. Given a supply of $O_M L_0$ units of labor, Mexico has a wage rate of $O_M W_M$, and the value of its total output is measured by $O_M DBL_0$, or areas a + b + c + d + e. The migration of $L_0 L_1$ labor from Mexico to the United States equalizes wage rates in both nations at $L_1 E$. This increases total output by areas d + e + j + i in the United States and reduces Mexico's total output by areas d + e. Thus, immigration leads to a net gain in the value of world output as shown by areas j + i.

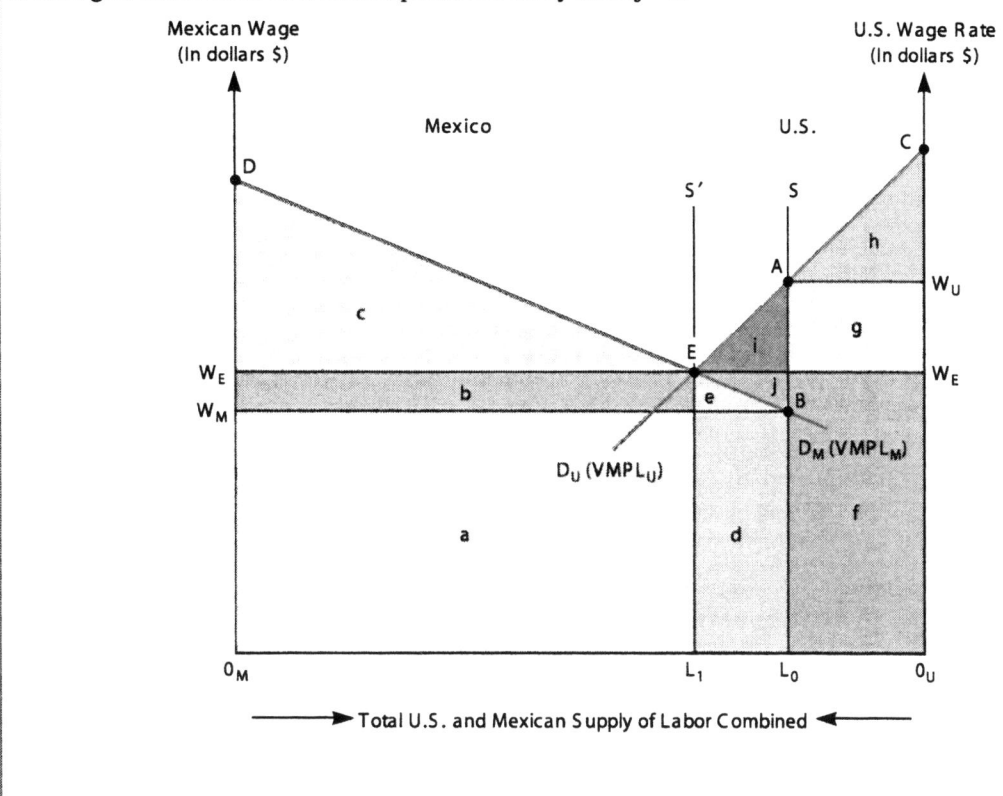

Income Distribution Effect. Migration also alters the income distribution in both nations. As Table 7.1 indicates, the United States' total gain in output is measured by area i + j + e + d. Out of this total, area d + e + j represents total labor income ($O_U W_E$ x $L_1 L_0$) paid to Mexican migrant workers, and the rest (area i) represents the extra earnings gained by U.S. owners of capital due to the availability of additional labor. However, immigration causes wage rates to go down in the United States from $O_U W_U$ to $O_U W_E$. As a result, the earnings of native U.S. workers decrease by area g, which is transferred to U.S. owners of capital. In the case of Mexico, as our analysis showed, labor emigration causes its output to fall by area d + e. This total represents a transfer from Mexico to the United States. The remaining workers in Mexico gain area b at the expense of the owners of capital due to higher wage rates following emigration.

expense of the owners of capital due to higher wage rates following emigration.

To summarize, under competitive conditions, labor migration causes overall world output to increase. It also causes a redistribution of income from capital to labor in the sending country (Mexico) and from labor to capital in the receiving country (the United States).

Other Effects. In the preceding analysis, we tacitly conjectured that workers are unskilled. However, in real-world settings, migrants are people with different skills and educational backgrounds. The effect of skilled workers' migration is likely to be significantly different from that of unskilled workers. Economically speaking, highly skilled workers are considered human capital, obtained by incurring great cost in education and training. Thus, the departure of these workers from developing countries to advanced countries results in a gain in the advanced countries' capital stock at the expense of developing countries. This limits the growth potential of a developing country, retarding its economic development process. Given the scarcity of capital in most developing countries, the emigration of highly skilled workers from these countries to advanced countries has continued to be a sensitive issue and has been referred to as **brain drain.**

Brain drain is often encouraged by national immigration laws (like those in the United States, Canada, Great Britain, Australia, and other advanced countries) that encourage immigration of skilled workers while discouraging the immigration of unskilled workers. This has resulted in the exodus of a large number of highly skilled workers, such as medical doctors, scientists, engineers, and nurses, from developing countries and Europe to the United States, especially since the 1950s. For example, during the 1980s, more than 200 well-known scientists left Britain to accept positions in the United States' top universities. As another example, following the collapse of the Soviet Union, a large number of scientists continued to emigrate to the United States.

To be sure, the brain drain inflicts clear costs on the sending nations. Closing borders to unskilled migrants causes more of the globe's work force to be trapped in less-efficient economies, contributing to the divergence of income between developing and advanced countries. A case can be made for a brain drain tax that remunerates sending nations for their human capital investment in emigrants.

In our demand and supply analysis of labor migration, we also implicitly assumed that the decision of Mexican workers to migrate to the United States was essentially permanent. In the real world, however, a large number of workers migrate to another country on a temporary basis. This has been the case especially for the European Union (EU). Members of the EU, such as France and Germany, permit migration of foreign workers, referred to as *guest workers,* on a temporary basis, depending on the members' domestic economic conditions. In a recessionary period, when foreign workers are no longer needed, these countries refuse to issue work permits. During a recovery period, however, they issue new work permits or renew the old ones. Such a practice tends to shield their economies and their labor forces from labor shortages during recovery periods and labor surpluses in recessionary periods. The pursuit of such a practice shifts the labor adjustment problem to the labor-emigrating nations, such as Turkey, Portugal, and Spain, which are relatively poorer and less prepared to handle the problem.

Given the low wages paid to guest workers, in 1991 the EU commission called for new regulations regarding pay levels and social conditions for guest workers.[1]

Another issue that is not apparent from our demand and supply analysis is the question of illegal immigration. This has been especially problematic for the United States. Today, millions of illegal immigrants work in the "underground economy" in the United States at below minimum wages. Many of these workers coming from Mexico to southwestern states (especially California), join the ranks of unskilled workers and provide a cheap supply of workers for the U.S. agricultural, restaurant, and garment industries. Although these workers receive few, if any, social benefits in the United States, they have been subject to resentment by low-skilled U.S. workers, mainly for depressing the wage level. This has made the subject of immigration, both legal and illegal, a "political hot potato" in the United States and has put pressure on policymakers to come up with a viable solution. One outcome of this pressure has been the passage of the

GLOBAL INSIGHTS CASE 7.2

THE PUSH AND PULL OF U.S. IMMIGRATION POLICY

The elements that give rise to international migration can be classified into "push" and "pull" forces. The extent of migration depends on the interaction of these two forces. Push forces are those factors that drive many persons to decide to emigrate, leaving their nation of origin. These factors may be major events causing widespread civil disorder and disruption of lives and a nation's economy---war with other countries, civil war, or large-scale ethnic persecutions. Examples of such situations can be seen in the refugee flows leaving Haiti, Bosnia, and Rwanda; the 800,000 Cuban refugees who have fled to the United States; and the tens of thousands of Russian Jews fleeing the former Soviet Union. Other push factors of significance may be natural disasters, including floods, earthquakes, and massive crop diseases, such as the infamous potato famine of the 1840s. Sometimes a nation's economy falters to the extent that droves of residents seek employment elsewhere, as in the case of the estimated millions of undocumented Mexicans coming to the United States.

Pull forces are those factors that attract large waves of immigration to a specific country. They are often linked in some way to push forces. In times of civil unrest and war, a nation that promises political and social stability draws people from the fighting countries. In times of religious and ethnic persecution, a country where freedom of religion is an important value again attracts the persecuted. And in times of economic disruption, a nation with a strong economy and the hope of jobs will, like a powerful magnet, draw millions of migrants.

Figure A traces the immigration patterns in the United States from 1820 to 1990. It clearly illustrates the ebb and flow of immigration and briefly highlights some of the major push and pull forces that have contributed to the process over the years.[1]

United States immigration policy responds to the ebb and flow of immigration by attempting to influence the push and pull forces. Two recent policy initiatives exemplify an attempt to control the immigration flow into the nation by influencing the push and pull forces perceived to be causing the influx.

The North American Free Trade Agreement (NAFTA) is first and foremost a matter of economic policymaking, not of immigration policy. But by having a positive impact on Mexico's economy by creating jobs there, it will reduce the push forces driving millions of Mexican nationals to the United States. More jobs will result in people remaining in Mexico rather than flowing across the over-2,000 miles of border between the two nations.

In 1986, the United States enacted the most sweeping immigration laws reform in 20 years-the Immigration Reform and Control Act (IRCA). This law exemplifies an attempt to influence pull forces. A major provision was the enactment of a new device to control immigration, employer sanctions. The most significant immigration problem of the 1970s and 1980s was perceived to be the annual flow of hundreds of thousands of illegal aliens into the United States, drawn by the economy. The IRCA was conceived as a way to "demagnetize" the draw of the U.S. economy by making every employer an agent of the Immigration and Naturalization Service (INS); the act made it illegal to hire an undocumented alien. While initially successful in causing a nearly 30-percent decline in the number of illegal aliens apprehended at the nation's borders, the impact of IRCA clearly has been largely temporary. The available data B shows that the number of illegal aliens apprehended at U.S. borders has gradually risen back to pre-IRCA levels. Perhaps the ineffectiveness of IRCA to control the flow of illegal aliens is in large measure due to the fact that push forces are as strong or stronger than the pull forces influencing international migration.[2]

Notes

1. Michael LeMay, *From Open Door to Dutch Door: An Analysis of U.S. Immigration Policy Since 1820.* New York: Praeger, 1987.
2. Michael LeMay, *Anatomy of a Policy: The Reform of Current U.S. Immigration Policy.* Westport, CT: Praeger, 1994.
Source: This case was written by Professor Michael LeMay of California State University, San Bernardino.

U.S. Immigration Reform and Control Act in 1986. According to this act illegal aliens who could prove they had lived in the United States since before January 1, 1982, would be granted amnesty and the chance to obtain legal status and, ultimately, citizenship. Also, employers would be subject to fines, ranging from $250 to $10,000, for every illegal alien they employed. May 4, 1988, was set as the registration deadline. This act resulted in granting legal status to 3 million illegal immigrants of all nationalities. However, the act does not seem to have either slowed down the flow of illegal immigrants to the United States or significantly deterred employers from hiring undocumented immigrants. According to a report by the U.S. Immigration and Naturalization Service (INS), the number of illegal immigrants entering California seems to be increasing overall. In fact, the apprehension of illegal immigrants along the California and Arizona borders has increased 30 percent over the last decade, from 970,000 in 1982 to 1,258,000 in 1992. Additionally, according to random audits of all businesses by the INS, one third of them are in violation of the act. Violations encompass both the employment of illegal immigrants and shoddy documentation of workers' citizenship status.[2]

Unfortunately, there are no definite empirical studies to assess the impact of illegal immigrants on the U.S. economy. However, according to a report by Los Angeles County, illegal immigrants cost the county government $308 million, primarily in education and public assistance expenses, in 1991-1992. But the same group paid about $904 million in local and federal government taxes. In other words, illegal immigration provided a net gain of $596 million ($904 million - $308 million).[3] Thus, judging from the available data, the popular belief that illegal immigrants are a financial burden is apparently inaccurate. Overall, legal and illegal immigrants taken as a whole are likely to induce a net gain in the receiving country.

In closing this section it should be emphasized that the policies to reduce unemployment discussed in this chapter may not always be politically viable. The changes introduced by these polices might lead to the loss of the political support of the government. Thus, before embarking on such polices, government authorities should make sure that the political environment in their nation is conducive to the changes that are introduced by the implementation of employment enhancing policies.

We conclude this chapter by stating that theories of international factor movements and MNCs, like those of trade theories, are abstractions from reality. As such, they help us to understand the "why" and "how" of factor movements and MNCs. One must be careful, however, not to read too much into theories. We should keep in mind that these theories provide only some comprehension of the general elements that explain FDI and MNCs. These theories should be employed along with additional data gathered in the real world when trying to answer the questions that are raised by FDI, MNCs, and immigration.

SUMMARY

1. The following terminologies are used in describing different types of unemployment in developing nations:
    a. **Open Unemployment** consists of individuals without work who are actively seeking and presently available for work among a given age range.
    b. **Underemployment. A situation in which individuals work less than they would like to work.**
    c. **Visible Underemployment**. A condition in which workers are compelled to work short hours as an alternative to being out of a job.
    d. **Invisible Unemployment**. A situation in which workers' capabilities are used inadequately.
    e. **Disguised Unemployment**. A condition in which present work functions are divided among resources (typically labor) such that all seem fully employed, but in fact much of their time is spent in unproductive endeavors.
    f. **Hidden Unemployment**. A situation in which individuals are engaged in nonemployment endeavors, such as education and household chores, as a "second choice."
2. During the 1960s and 1970s when developing nations experienced an extensive migration of their rural

CH. 7/UNEMPLOYMENT, MIGRATION AND ECONOMIC DEVELOPMENT 153

workers into urban areas in spite of increasing unemployment and underemployment in these areas, the validity of the Lewis two-sector model of development became questionable.

3. Today, economists no longer consider migration as a beneficial process needed to resolve problems of rising urban labor demand. Rather, they perceive such a process as the main element that fuels urban surplus labor and continues to worsen the existing acute urban unemployment problems stemming from structural and economic disparities between urban and rural sectors.

4. Migration worsens the existing structural disparities between urban and rural both on the supply side and the demand side.

5. According to the Harris-Todaro model, migrants respond to urban-rural differences in expected as opposed to actual earnings.

6. The major shortcoming of the Harris-Todaro model is that it does not consider other factors that affect the decision to migrate.

7. Policies to discourage Rural-Urban Migration include the following:
   a. Promoting amenities such as housing, schools, food, entertainment, health services, hospitals, and roads in rural areas.
   b. Eliminating the price ceiling on food and other agricultural goods.
   c. Establishing new industries in rural areas.
   d. Enhancing labor-using, technological progress in the agriculture sector.
   e. Adjusting the foreign exchange price close to a market-clearing rate.

8. The use of more labor-using technologies in developing nations can be encouraged by the following policies:
   a. Utilizing Less Modern Equipment.
   b. Promoting Greater Income Equality.
   c. Promoting the Use of Labor Intensive Technologies in the Production Process Substitution.
   d. Promoting the Use of Labor Intensive Technologies Auxiliary Activities.
   e. The Local Generation of Technologies.

9. The policies to decrease factor-price distortions include the following:
   a. Promoting Small-Scale Industry.
   b. Utilizing Capital Stock More Efficiently.
   c. Diminishing Subsidies to Domestic Industry.
   d. Cutting Wages in the Organized Sector.
   e. Decreasing Social Security Programs and Payroll Taxation.
   f. Establishing Market-Clearing Exchange Rates.
   g. Reforming Labor Legislation.

10. The following is a list of policies that these nations could adopt in order to achieve a proper balance between their educational output and their labor requirements:
    a. Allocating a Larger Percentage of the Educational Budget to Primary Education and Managerial and Technical Training.
    b. Reducing Subsidies for Higher Education.
    c. Minimizing Inequality and Discrimination in both Education and Employment.
    d. Enhancing the Pay Scales' Flexibility.
    e. Setting Realistic Job Qualifications.

11. The factors giving rise to international labor migration are both economic and noneconomic in nature, and often the two are interconnected.

12. The impact of international labor migration can be studied in terms of output effect, income distribution effect, and other effects. Other effects include brain drain, temporary migration, and illegal migration.

13. Theoretically, labor migration causes overall world output to increase. It also causes a redistribution

of income from labor to capital in the receiving country and from capital to labor in the sending country
14. Overall, immigrants are likely to induce net gain in the receiving country.

QUESTIONS

1. Discuss the problem of unemployment in developing nations by answering the following questions:
   a. What factors contribute to unemployment?
   b. What policies can a developing nation adopt in order to alleviate unemployment problems?
   c. What specific factors give rise to unemployment among educated people in a developing nation.
2. Explain international immigration by answering the following questions:
   a. What factors contribute to international immigration?
   b. What is the impact of international immigration on labor and capital in the sending country and the receiving country?
   c. What policies can a developing nation adopt in order to slow down international immigration?
3. Discuss the Harris-Todaro model by answering the following questions:
   a. What does the model explain?
   b. How does this model differ from the Lewis model?
   c. What is the major criticism of this model?
4. According to the Harris-Todaro model, creating urban jobs by enhancing industrial output is not sufficient for resolving the urban unemployment problem. Given this statement, answer the following questions:
   a. What do you think underlines this statement?
   b. What can governments do to resolve the urban unemployment problem?
5. A paradoxical implication of the Harris-Todaro model is that government strategies aimed at generating more urban employment may trigger more unemployment. Do you agree with this statement? Discuss.
6. The urban sector of a developing nation is composed of two distinct sectors. Distinguish between these sectors and elaborate on their positive and negative aspects.
7. How does migration affect the existing structural disparities between urban and rural sectors? Explain by elaborating both on the supply side and the demand side.

NOTES

1. "Temporary Workers in Europe," *The Wall Street Journal*, 21 June 1991, A 8.
2. "The Day-Laborer Bottom Line: Demand Fuels Phenomenon," *Inland Valley Daily Bulletin*, 8 August 1993, A1.
3. Ibid.

SUGGESTED READINGS

Bairoch, Paul. *Urban Unemployment in Developing Countries*. Geneva: International Labor Organization, 1973.
Becker, Charles M.., Andrew M. Hammer, and Andrew R. Morrison. *Beyond Urban Bias in Africa: Urbanization in an Era of Structural Adjustment*. Portsmouth, N. H.: Heinemann, 1994.
Bencivenga, Valerie R. and Bruce D. Smith. "Unemployment, Migration, and Growth." *Journal of Political economy*. 105 (September 1997): 582-608.
Berghall, Pii Elina, *Habitat II and the Urban Economy: A Review of Recent Development and Literature*. Helsinki: United Nations University, World Institute for Development Economics Research, 1995.
Berry, Albert. "The Labour Market and Human Capital in LDCs." in Norman Gemmell, ed. *Surveys in Development*

Review 3 (Winter 1974.

Edward, Edgar O. and Michael P. Todaro. "Education, Society, and Development: Some Main Themes and Suggested Strategies for International Assistance." *World Development* 2 (January 1974): 29-30.

Emmerij, Louis. "The Employment Problem and the International Economy." *International Labour Review* 133 (December 1994): 449-466.

Field, Gary S. "Public Policy and the Labor Market in Less Developed Countries." in David Newbery and Nicholas Stern, eds. *The Theory of Taxation for Developing Countries*. New York: Oxford University Press, 1987.

Gallup, John L. "Theories of Migration." Discussion Paper No. 569. *Harvard Institute for International Development* (January 1997).

Ghai, Dharam. *Economic Growth, Structural Change and Labour Absorption in Africa, 1960-85*. Geneva: United Nations Research Institute for Social Development, 1987.

Gugler, Josef and William G. Flangan. *Urbanization and Social Change in West Africa*. London: Cambridge University Press, 1978.

Harris, John R. and Michael P. Todaro. "Migration, Unemployment, and Development: A Two-Sector Analysis." *American Economic Review* 60 (March 1970): 126-142.

International Labor Office. *World Development Report, 1995*. Geneva, 1955, pp. 15-21.

International Labor Organization. *Employment in Africa: Some Critical Issues*. Geneva: International Labor Organization, 1974.

_____. *Employment, Growth and Basic Needs: A One-World Problem*. Geneva: International Labor Organization, 1976.

_____. *World Development Report 1996/97*. Geneva: International Labor Organization, 1996.

Jolly, Richare et al., eds. *Third World Employment: Problems and Strategy*. Harmondsworth, England: Penguin, 1973.

Kannappan, Subbiah. *Employment Problems and the Urban Labor Market in Developing Nations*. Ann Arbor: University of Michigan Press, 1983.

Kao, Charles, H.C., Kurt A. Anschel, and Carl K. Eicher. "Disguised in Unemployment in Agriculture: A Survey." in Carl K Eicher and Lawrence Witt, eds. *Agriculture in Economic Development*. New York: McGraw Hill, 1964. pp. 129-44.

Khundker, Nasreen. "The Fuzziness of the Informal Sector: Can We Afford to Throw Out the Baby with the Bath Water? " *World Development* 16 (October 1988): 1263-65.

Morawetz, David. "Employment Implications of Industrialization in Developing Countries." *Economic Journal* 84 (September 1974).

Peattie, Lisa. "An Idea in Good Currency and How it Grew: The Informal Sector." *World Development* 15 (July 1987): 851-60.

Shrestha, M. "Institutional Policies and Migration Behavior: A Selective Review." World Development 15 (1987).

Squire, Lyn. *Employment Policy in Developing Countries: A Survey of Issues and Evidence*. New York: Oxford University Press, 1981.

Stark, Oded. "Rural-to-Urban Migration in LDCs: A Relative Deprivation Approach." *Economic Development and Cultural Change* 32 (July 1987): 851-60.

_____. *The Migration of Labor*. Oxford: Blackwell, 1991.

_____, and David Levhari. "On Migration and Risk in LDCs." *Economic Development and Cultural Change* 31 (October 1982): 191-96.

Toaro, Michael P. *Internal Migration in Developing Countries: A Review of Theory, Evidence, Methodology and Research Priorities*. Geneva: International Labor Organization, 1976.

Tolley, George S. and Vinod Thomas. *The Economics of Urbanization and Urban Policies in Developing Countries*. Washington, D.C.: World Bank, 1987.

Turnam, David. *"Employment and Development: A New Review of Evidence*. Paris: Organization for Economic Cooperation and Development, 1993.

Unitd Nations. *Report on the World Social Situation, 1997*. New York: United Nations, 1997., chap. 7.

World Bank. *World Development Report, 1995: Workers in an Integrating World. New York: Oxford University Press, 1981*.

CHAPTER 8

RURAL DEVELOPMENT AND AGRICULTURAL TRANSFORMATION

One of the common characteristics of developing nations is the continuous migration of people from rural areas to urban areas in search of employment. Today, cities in Africa, Asia, and Latin America are flooded with rural poor migrants who continue to add to urban unemployment and social dilemmas. The problem is especially alarming because 63% of 4.9 billion inhabitants of developing nations, that is, 3.1 billion people live in rural areas. This figure is expected to rise to about 3.3 billion by the year 2010. Given the relatively higher rate of population growth in rural areas as compared to urban areas, arable land bases are pushed to their limits and cannot support the growing rural population. It is estimated that over 800 million or 70% of the world's poorest people who live in rural areas and engage primarily in agriculture do not have enough food to satisfy their most basic nutritional requirements.[1] Under this condition, the rural poor are eventually transformed to urban poor as they migrate to densely populated cities in their quest for a job.

The urban population as a percentage of total population of the developing nations grew from 27 percent in 1975 to 35% in 1992, and it is projected to rise to 47% in 2010.[2]

These statistics makes one thing clear, that is, if development has to take place, it must focus on rural development areas where rapid population growth, widespread poverty, income inequality, and rising unemployment are rooted. The purpose of this chapter is to provide us with a basic understanding of the issues that are raised in rural development. In pursuing this objective, first we discuss the integrated rural development approach. Second, we review the history of agricultural growth. Third, we compare agricultural productivity in advanced and developing nations. Fourth, we elaborate on the stages of agriculture development. Finally, we, present strategies of agriculture and rural development.

INTEGRATED RURAL DEVELOPMENT APPROACH

Traditionally, economic development has placed a major role on industrialization, viewing agriculture as a passive and supportive sector that provides low-priced food and manpower to the growing industrial sector. Such an attitude stems from the historical experience of Western nations. In these nations economic development was viewed as needing speedy structural transformation of the economy from one dominated by agricultural activities to one that is primarily focused on the industrial sector. The Lewis two-sector model that we studied in Chapter 4, is indicative of the traditional view. As you recall from Chapter 4, this model places heavy emphasis on rapid industrial growth with the agricultural sector providing surplus labor and cheap food for the expanding industrial sector. In other words, in Lewis's model the function of agriculture in economic development is viewed as passive and supportive.

Today, economists question the rationale of placing so much emphasis on rapid industrialization. It has become clear that unlike the earlier view that agriculture should be passive and supportive in the process of economic development, it must play an essential role in the overall strategy of economic progress. This demands an integrated rural development approach, which requires at least the following three basic complementary elements:

1. Enhancing domestic demand for agricultural products through employment-oriented urban development strategy.
2. Rapid output growth via institutional, technological, and price incentive variations aimed at raising the productivity of small-scale farmers.
3. A labor-intensive rural development strategy that is composed of nonagricultural and diversified activities that directly or indirectly support or are supported by the rural society.

During the last two decades there has been a significant transformation in development thinking in which agricultural rural development came to be viewed by many as the prerequisite of national development. In the absence of such an integrated rural development approach, industrial progress either would be stultified, or if attained, would lead to such a profound internal imbalance in the economy that would further the problems of widespread poverty, inequality, and unemployment.

THE HISTORY OF AGRICULTURAL GROWTH

History shows that during the last half a century agricultural growth has proceeded at an uneven rate across the globe. During the 1950-1970 period, per capita food production and per capita agriculture production grew, on average, less than 1% per year.[*] More specifically, the historical data show that the rate of growth of these two indicators of agricultural performance was much smaller in the 1960s as compared to 1950s. In fact, the 1960s can be marked as a decade during which the agricultural sector in many developing nations stagnated. As developing nations increasingly focused their attention on raising agricultural productivity during the decade of 1970s, agricultural growth began accelerating. Consequently, during the 1970-1980 period per capita food production grew at an annual rate of growth of 0.5 percent. This rising pattern of growth continued and even accelerated during the 1990s. Unfortunately, per capital growth in the agricultural sector did not improve in some developing regions of the world. More specifically, the agricultural sector experienced significant growth only in parts of Asia, notably in China. However, it showed spotty growth in Latin America and sizeable decrease in Africa. Such a disharmonious pattern of growth across different continents exemplifies the magnitude and extent of Third World poverty that can be marked by marginal improvement in Asia and Latin America, and steady deterioration in Africa. The condition in Sub-Saharan Africa is especially severe. The severity of food shortages in Africa is well documented by the United Nations Food and Agriculture Organization (FAO). According to FAO estimates of 750 million people residing in Africa, more than 270 million suffer from some type of malnutrition stemming from the inadequacy of food supplies on that continent.

A major cause of this poor performance of the agricultural sector in developing nations has been the failure of developing nations' governments to assign a high priority to the agriculture sector. This failure

---

[*]Per capita agriculture food production includes not only food but also agricultural products such as rubber and cotton that are used as raw materials in the production of other goods.

GLOBAL INSIGHTS CASE 8.1

THE AGRARIAN STRUCTURE IN LATIN AMERICA

The agrarian structure in Latin America can be classified into the following four distinct structures:

1. **Latifundios.** These are very large landholdings that are defined in Latin America as farms large enough to secure employment for more than twelve people. In Latin American nations with dense population such as Ecuador, Guatemala, and Peru, *Latifudios* comprise less than 10% of all farms, yet they occupy about 80% of the agricultural land.
2. **Minifundios.** These are the smallest farms, defined as farms so small they can provide employment only for a single family that is composed of two workers.
3. **Family-Farms.** These farms provide work for 2 to 4 people.
4. **Medium-Sized (Multi Family) Farms.** These are farms that employ 4 to 12 workers. In Brazil, Uruguay, and Venezuela, these farms account for about half of the agricultural output and employ roughly 50 percent of the agricultural workers.

Economic theory tells us that large firms, enjoying economies of scale, are more efficient, that is, have lower costs than small firms. Given this theory, one would expect that *latinfundios* to be more efficient than *minifudios*. However, evidence from a number of developing nations indicate that this is not the case. For example, *minifudios* in Argentina, Brazil, and Chile produce more than two times the value of output per hectare under cultivation than *latinfundios* and more than 10 times the value per hectare of total farmland. The main factor that give rise to the relative inefficiency of *latinfundios* in comparison to *minifudios* is the rich landowners usually consider their landholding as vehicles for gaining power and prestige as opposed to a potential source for agricultural output. As a result, much of the *latinfundios* is either left untouched or farmed less intensively than *minifudios*. Additionally, transaction costs, in particular the costs of supervising the workers are much higher than the relatively lower cost of using family labor on peasant farms. This means that improving the agricultural productivity in Latin America demands much more than economic policies that are aimed at the provision of better seeds, less distorted factor prices, improved marketing skills, and higher output prices. It also calls on revamping rural social and institutional frameworks to help Latin American peasants who account for 70% of rural population, to elevate themselves out of their existing condition of economic subsistence.

Sources: R. Albert Berry and William Cline, *Agrarian Structure and Productivity in Developing Countries* (Baltimore: John Hopkins Press, 1979), chap. 3 and app. B; G. A. Cornia, "Farm size, Land Yields and the Agricultural Production Function: An Analysis of Fifteen Developing Countries," *World Development* 13 (December 1985): 513-534; K. Otsuka, H. Chuma and Y. Hyami, "Land Reform and Labor Contracts in Agrarian Economies," *Journal of Economic Literature* 30 (September 1992): 1965-2018; Nancy L. Johnson and Vernon ruttan, "Why Are Farms So Small?" *World Development* 22 (May 1994): 691-705; Celso Futado, *Economic Development in Latin America* (Cambridge: Cambridge University Press, 1970); United Nations Development Program, *Human Development Report, 1996* (New York: Oxford University Press, 1996), 98.

coupled with their bias toward investment in the urban industrial sector is rooted, to a large extent, in undue emphasis placed upon rapid industrialization through import-substitution and exchange rate overvaluation. Such a development strategy that permeated development thinking and strategy during the postwar period.

One major outcome of this rural neglect and undue emphasis of urban growth has been the massive migration of rural poor into the highly populated cities of Third World nations. The results have been high and rising unemployment, urban decay, and the host of social and political problems that accompanies the rural poor as they join the hoard of urban poor in cities.

Given this disappointing experience and the understanding that the future of most developing nations hinges to a large extent on the condition in their agricultural sector, there has been a significant change in development thinking and implementation. This transformation, which started in the late 1970s and has continued into the 1990s, can be characterized by a development philosophy that dismisses exclusive emphasis on rapid industrialization and realizes the overwhelming significance of agriculture and rural development in achieving national development. A prerequisite for the implementation of such a strategy is a comprehension of the nature of the agricultural systems in diverse development regions of the world and the stages of agricultural development. These are the subjects of the subsequent sections.

AGRICULTURE PRODUCTIVITY IN ADVANCED AND DEVELOPING NATIONS

In comparing the agricultural productivity in advanced and developing nations, the following generalizations can be made:

1. The agricultural sector in developing nations can be characterized by such a low productivity that in many cases not only is it incapable of supporting the growing urban population even at a subsistence level, it can barely provide for the rural population.
2. The agriculture sector in advanced nations can be marked by such a high productivity that it allows a very small number of farmers to feed an entire nation.

History shows that advanced nations have continued to experience a steady growth in their agricultural productivity. Such a growth has been fueled by technological and biological improvements which accelerated after World War I and continued to gather momentum after Word War II. This is especially true in the case of the United States, which in 1988 had only 2% of its labor force engaging in agriculture as compared to 70% of its labor force in the early 19th century.

The experience of developing nations with regard to agricultural productivity is entirely different than advanced nations. In many developing nations, agricultural methods have changed relatively slowly over time. As a result, agricultural productivity has continued to stay at a very low level when compared to advanced nations. Much of this technological stagnation stems from the particular conditions of peasant agriculture, which can be marked by high risks and uncertain rewards. The problem has been intensified by the rapid growth of urban population which has placed intense pressure on the existing resources. Given the scarcity of arable lands, especially throughout South and Southeast Asia, rapid population growth has increased the number of people living on each acre of land. As the principle of diminishing returns tells us, given the relatively unchanged traditional method of agriculture (constant technology), the higher number of workers added to a piece of land has led to a decline in the marginal and average product of the workers. As a result, the living standards of rural peasants have continued to deteriorate in developing nations and the gap between rich and poor has continued to grow over time.

We may note that although the agrarian structures prevailing in Africa, Asia, and Latin America differ from each other, the present status of the small farmer is not very different among the three regions. Achieving subsistence continues to remain the major goal of agriculture of peasants living in the Third World. Although at one time the small African peasant had more room in which to cultivate than the typical peasant in Asia or Latin America, the fast growth of rural populations throughout sub-Saharan Africa has created a similar fragmentation of smallholder agriculture.

CH. 8/RURAL DEVELOPMENT & AGRICULTURAL TRANSFORMATION

Today, the available data shows that the gap between the two types of agriculture exercised in advanced nations and developing nations is vast and continues to grow. Measuring productivity in terms of output per capita, in 1960, advanced nations produced a total output amounting to $680 per capita, as compared to $52 per capita in developing nations. In other words, in that year agriculture productivity was over 13 times greater in advanced nations as compared to developing nations. By 1995, this productivity gap had grown to over 50 to one. To avoid massive starvation and increase the living standards of the average rural dweller, there is a dire need to enhance agricultural production and the productivity of both land and labor throughout Asia, Africa, and Latin America. This calls on major economic, institutional, and structural changes in the farming sectors to allow developing nations to become self-sufficient in their food production, rather than depending on advanced nations, especially North America, to provide them with handouts.

THE STAGES OF AGRICULTURAL DEVELOPMENT

The evolution of agricultural production can be divided into the following three distinct stages:

1. Subsistence agriculture
2. Diversified agriculture
3. Modern agriculture

Because an understanding of the evolution of the agricultural system of a developing nation is a prerequisite for the comprehension of the economics of agriculture and rural development, we devote this section to the explanation of the process by which a predominantly subsistence agriculture is eventually transformed to a large-scale commercial enterprise. Given this understanding, in the next section we examine the strategies that can be employed to enhance agricultural and rural development.

Subsistence Agriculture

This stage is characterized by the existence of subsistence farming, that is marked by the most primitive agricultural production method and low productivity. At this stage, although some agricultural products may be sold or traded in local markets, most output is produced for family consumption. Few staple food crops, such as wheat, barely, rice and corn are the major sources of food intake.

Today, the agriculture sectors of most developing nations are still at this subsistence stage. Subsistence agriculture is a very risky and uncertain activity. In most of these nations, farms are very small and cultivation is dependent on the uncertainty of rainfall. As a result, the output is low, and in bad years the farmer and his family may face starvation. Given the risky nature of agricultural production at this stage, peasants are usually reluctant to switch from an archaic technology and cultivation method that they have come to comprehend and trust to a modern one that is expected to yield higher output but may involve greater risks of crop failure. This risk aversion behavior of peasant farmers helps explain the domination of sharecropping in most regions of Latin America and Asia. **Sharecropping** is an arrangement by which a peasant farmer utilizes the landlord's farmland in return for a percentage of food output, such as 50% of the wheat or rice that is grown. The economic and social structure in which sharecropping takes place can be marked by extreme social inequality. This is due to the extreme control that is exercised by the landlord who acts as the peasants' prospective employer, the loan officer, and the ultimate customer for the crops. These conditions, referred to as **interlocking factor markets**, provide the rural landlord with extreme monopoly and monopsony power. Trying to regulate several of these interlocked markets simultaneously is problematic and usually leads to inefficiency. For example, assume that the government in a developing nation tries to put a ceiling on the interest rate that is charged by the landlord. In response, the landlord can simply lower

GLOBAL INSIGHTS CASE 8.2

THE DETERIORATING RURAL CONDITIONS IN ASIA

History shows that throughout much of the twentieth century, rural conditions in Asia deteriorated. Accordingly, many rural Asians are gradually being transformed by going through the following stages of transformation, changing from small proprietor to migrant slum dwellers on the perimeters of contemporary urban areas:

1. Small proprietors.
2. Tenant farmers and sharecropper.
3. Landless rural workers.
4. Jobless vagrants.
5. Migrant slum dwellers on the perimeters of contemporary urban areas.

As a result of such a transformation, not only have these rural Asians' standards of living deteriorated, but their sense of self esteem and pride that have been high in spite of low incomes, has continued to dissipate. According to Gunnar Myrdal, the elements that have given rise to such a predicament can be classified into the following three interrelated factors:

1. **The Imposition of European Rule.** Before European colonization, the traditional Asian agrarian framework was structured around the village. Peasant families and local chiefs each provided goods and services. In such a framework, labor and produce flowed from the peasant to the chief in return for protection, rights to utilize community land, and the provision of public services. However, the arrival of Europeans significantly changed this traditional agrarian framework, replacing it with the European land tenure system of private property ownership which were both encouraged and reinforced by law.
2. **The Introduction of Monetized Transactions and the Increasing power of the Moneylender.** The emergence of individual titles to land led to the rise of moneylenders to power. With the introduction of private property into the Asian rural society, land became an asset that could be used by peasants as security of loans. In the case of default, land could be seized and transferred to the usually corrupt moneylender.
3. **Rapid Population Growth in Asia.** The rapid population growth in Asia led to severe fragmentation of landholdings. As these holdings become even smaller, the percentage of population below the subsistence level decreases, breeding persistent poverty. Farmers are forced to borrow more from the moneylenders at skyrocketing interest rates that can be as high as 200%. Because most of the peasants can not pay such loans they end up selling their lands and become tenants with large debts. Given the relative scarcity of land and abundance of labor, rents are high and wages are extremely low. As a result, peasants are trapped in chronic poverty and the only way out is major rural restoration and reform.

Sources: Gunner Myrdal, *Asian Drama* (New York: Pantheon, 1968).

wages, decreasing the tenant's share of crop, or cutting the price that is paid by the landlord to the crop that the tenant plans to sell.

The uncertainty associated with the agricultural endeavors calls on government to initiate and support programs that are aimed at raising agricultural productivity in developing nations and to provide adequate insurance against the risk of crop failure. Unfortunately, however, in practice many of these programs have not been successful. An examination of farming in Asia and Latin America reveals that the failure of these programs stems from the following factors:

1. The appropriation of all the profits by either the moneylenders or the landlords.
2. The government never paid the "guaranteed" price.
3. The complementary inputs such as water, credit, pesticides, and fertilizers were never delivered.

Diversified (Mixed) Agriculture

This is a stage in which part of the agricultural output is used for self-consumption and the other part for sale to the commercial sector. Production extends to include other crops and no longer is dominated by the staple crops. New cash crops such as vegetables, tea and coffee are produced and simple animal husbandry is established. These new activities are triggered by productivity improvement that stems from technological progress, capital formation, or utilization of underemployed resources in subsistence farming. This is especially helpful to developing nations in which there is an abundant supply of rural labor that can be used more efficiently. The introduction of these new activities can prove to be helpful in the following ways:

1. During those times of the year when disguised unemployment is commonplace, the new endeavors can take up the slack in farm workloads. For example, if the land is devoted to the production of staple crops during only part of the year, new crops can be introduced in the slack season. This allows the farmer to use both the idle land and family labor.
2. During peak planting seasons, when labor is in short supply, simple labor-saving devices, such as mechanical seeders, animal-operated steel plows, and small tractors can be introduced to reduce labor requirements.
3. The utilization of better seeds, fertilizers, and simple irrigation to enhance the production of staple crops such as rice, wheat, and maize, releases part of the land for the cash crop cultivation and ensures a sufficient supply of the staple food.

Given the above helpful effects accompanying new activities, the farm operator can have a marketable surplus, which can be sold to raise the family's consumption standards or invest in farm improvement. Thus, diversified farming can minimize the effect of staple crop failure and provide a security of income previously unattainable. To be sure, the success of such endeavors to transform traditional agriculture hinges upon the following factors:

1. The social, commercial, and institutional conditions under which the farmer must operate. These conditions include:
    a. The availability of reasonable, and reliable credit, water, fertilizer, crop information, and marketing facilities to the farmer.
    b. The payment of a fair market price for the farmer's output.
    c. The assurance that the farmer will be the main beneficiary of any improvements.
2. The farmers' capabilities in enhancing his/her productivity.

The existing evidence from countries such as Colombia, Ghana, Kenya, India, Mexico, Nigeria, Pakistan, the Philippines, and Thailand indicates that under the right conditions, small farmers are sensitive to price stimuli and economic opportunities and will embark on drastic changes in the type of their output and the method used in their production process.[3]

Modern Agriculture

This is the final stage of agricultural development in which substantial productive capacity and high output per worker allows a very small number of farmers to feed entire nations. Today, the highly efficient agricultural sectors of advanced nations characterized by specialized farms are at this stage.

Specialized farms have emerged in reaction to development in other areas of the national economy. Its evolution has been stimulated by the following major factors:

1. General rises in living standards.
2. Biological and technical progress.
3. The expansion of national and international markets.

In specialized farming, the major production goal is no longer limited to the provision of food for the family members with some surplus. Rather, the major objective is profit maximization, measured by the maximum per hectare yield from both the natural resources and synthetic resources, such as fertilizer, irrigation, pesticides, and hybrid seeds.

Given the objective of profit maximization, unlike the subsistence and often mixed farming, in modern agriculture the emphasis in resource utilization is no longer on land, water, and labor. Rather, technological growth, capital formation, and scientific research and development are considered to be the major elements that give rise to the higher levels of output and productivity. Although specialized farms differ in terms of both function and size, ranging from intensively cultivated fruit and vegetable farms to the huge corn and wheat farms in North America, they all share the following common characteristics:

1. The utilization of capital-using (labor-saving) technologies such as huge tractors, the combine harvester, and airborne spraying techniques.
2. Specialization in production of only one type of crop.

To be sure, from a practical standpoint, specialized farming does not differ from a large industrial firm, in terms of both concept and operation. Indeed, some of the biggest specialized farms that are operating in both the advanced and especially the developing nations are owned and operated by huge agribusiness multinational corporations.

STRATEGIES OF AGRICULTURAL AND RURAL DEVELOPMENT

Equipped with a knowledge of agricultural and rural conditions in developing nations we devote this section to the study of strategies that can be employed in achieving the following two main objectives:

1. To enhance average rural incomes, output, and productivity.
2. To diminish the percentage of rural population in poverty by improving income distribution.

These two objectives are interrelated, and their achievement can be facilitated by the implementation of a number of strategies discussed in the remaining part of this chapter.

GLOBAL INSIGHTS CASE 8.3

THE IMPORTANCE OF AGRICULTURAL RESEARCH IN CHINA

China provides us with an example of a country that has not engaged in any significant basic agricultural research. As a result, this country has continued to suffer from a very slow growth in per capita food output, especially from the 1950s through the late 1980s. During the 1966-1970 period when the country was at the height of the Cultural Revolution, the educational system was shut down, disturbing the matriculation of agricultural students. At that time, China sent some leading agricultural scientists to rural areas in order to observe agricultural techniques that were utilized by workers and peasants. Deng Xiaoping, China's foremost political leader during the late 1970s, stated that dawdling research and low quality education especially in agriculture, comprise the "greatest crisis" in contemporary China. Such a statement accentuates the importance of fundamental agriculture research in economic development.

Sources: Christopher Howe, *China's Economy: A Basic Guide* (New York: Basic Books, 1978), pp. 26-27, 81; and Guy Hunter, ed., *Agricultural Development and the Rural Poor: Declaration of Policy and Guidelines for Action* (London: Overseas Development Institute, 1978), pp. 78-82.

Research and Technological Improvements

As our study of population in Chapter 6 indicated, technology plays a significant role in providing food for a growing population. This underlines the importance of research and technology, especially as created by an international network of agricultural centers, in improving agricultural productivity in developing nations. The following are the two major approaches to technological innovation that a nation can choose from:

1. **The Mechanical Approach.** This approach calls on the utilization of tractors, combines, and other types of machinery primarily as a substitute for labor. The introduction of mechanized agriculture can have a significant impact on labor productivity, as measured by output per worker. This is especially true when land is extensively cultivated and labor is scarce. However, as we already know, such an approach is inappropriate for developing nations where land parcels are small, capital is scarce and labor is abundant. As a result, the introduction of capital using agricultural technology only leads to more rural unemployment in these nations. Additionally, the introduction of heavy equipment is often ill-suited to the physical environment of developing nations. Even worse, the importation of such equipment may intensify the already critical problems of rural poverty and unemployment in these nations. This happens because the efficient utilization of heavy machinery requires large tracts of land, leading to expropriation of small holdings by landlords and moneylenders.

2. **The Biological Approach.** This approach calls on increasing yield through the utilization of improved plant varieties such as hybrid corn or the new varieties of rice developed at the International Rice Research Institute in the Philippines. Due to the significant effect on yields of some of these new varieties, the phenomenon is frequently referred to as the **green revolution**. These varieties increase yields only if combined with appropriate and timely supplies of water and augmented amounts of chemical fertilizers. To be sure, the biological approach is scale-neutral, that

is, it can be employed in both large and small farms. Additionally, since it does not require large capital inputs or mechanized machinery, it is appropriate for tropical and subtropical areas and provides developing nations with great potential for increasing agricultural production.

Supportive Social Services

Because the new hybrid seeds demand access to complementary inputs, such as water and chemical fertilizers, in the absence of any supportive social services, they may only be supplied to a small minority of large landowners. As a result, the masses of poor rural peasants would be left out in the cold, so to speak, unable to reap the benefits of the green revolution. Large landowners, with ample access to complementary inputs and support services would be able to gain a competitive edge over small peasants, and eventually push them out of the market. The inevitable outcome is further impoverishment of the masses, the widening of the gap between rich and poor, and the increased integration of agricultural land in the hands of a very few powerful landowners. Thus, for the green revolution to alleviate rural poverty and raise agricultural output, it must be accompanied by the following appropriate supportive services to enable the active participation of the small farmers in the evolving agricultural framework:

1. **Agricultural Extension Programs.** These programs are designed to familiarize farmers with the results of agricultural research. To be effective, such programs must be composed of personnel who engage in the following activities:
    a. Keep up with the knowledge of the sources of technical advice and training.
    b. Make contact with the farmers, informing them of simple technical information.
    c. Demonstrate the application of the new technical information.
    d. Distinguish farmers who are good credit risks.
    e. Arrange for seeds, fertilizers and other inputs from government depots.
    f. Report farm problems to planners and researchers.

    Unfortunately, in practice, most agricultural extension programs in developing nations have proven to be ineffective. They often lack adequate number of qualified personnel who are well paid and well equipped to render technical advice. In many cases, they cater to the large, powerful farmers at the expense of the small farmers who are poorly educated and lack any political clout.
    It should be emphasized that extension services that pattern after the U.S. are not appropriate for developing nations. The research on Latin America and other developing nations shows that the U.S. model introduces few innovations and does not make any significant contribution to rapid growth in these nations. To be more effective, extension personnel must be integrated with development organizations, such as irrigation authorities, agrarian reform agencies, cooperative organizations, loan banks, and seed and fertilizer distribution centers.
2. **Provision of Water and Other Inputs.** In most developing nations, water access and availability is often problematic for small farmers. In these nations, usually large, influential farmers get first chance at available water, using it inefficiently, because cost is not related to the amount used. Setting water access problems aside, the small farmers ordinarily do not have incentives or the financial resources to invest in water generating projects such as wells. This situation calls on government to play an active role in water management by (a) enforcing water rights and planning user fees in order to avoid inequality and inefficiency; and (b) monitoring the salinity or the sedimentation problems by competent technical personnel.
    Beside water access, the farmers need other inputs such as fertilizers, pesticide and seeds. Because these inputs are usually supplied through governmental institutions, it is important for the

government to guarantee input quality, quantity, and accessibility.

To be sure, the provision of water and other inputs is not a cure-all for developing nations' agricultural problems. In fact, many irrigation plans in developing nations have failed to enhance agricultural output to the level that they compensate for their high construction and operating costs. Such a failure calls on developing nations' governments to engage in feasibility studies on irrigation projects. To be effective, such studies should be aimed at estimating personnel, capital, inputs, maintenance costs over time, and the appropriate approach in raising the output.

3. **Transportation.** One of the major factors that weakens the competitive position of most developing nations in the global market for agricultural output and raw materials is the inadequacy of transportation, leading to a higher cost of production. This condition calls on the government of developing nations to increase investment in roads, railroads, port facilities, canals and other forms of transportation in order to decrease the cost of producing farm goods and transporting them to the international market.

4. **Marketing and Storage Facilities.** Given the competitive nature of the market for farm products at both national and international markets, poor marketing channels and inadequate storage facilities are two of the factors that often hinder sales outside the production center and hamper production gains from the benefits of the green revolution. This condition calls on government to take the following actions:
   a. Enhance and improve the existing infrastructure, such as roads and grain bins.
   b. Establish uniform grades and standards in order to trigger incentives to improve agricultural output quality.
   c. Disseminate national price information.
   d. Assist farmers in their decision making process with regard to the type of crop planted, the timing of sale, and the appropriate storage facilities to be built.

Today, many marketing facilities that are established in some developing nations suffer from inefficiency and are open to abuses by the officials involved. Some of these nations have chosen to set up marketing boards to purchase crops from farmers to sell on the global market. However, these boards have shown a tendency to gain monopsony power in order to ensure financial success and they usually accumulate funds to transfer from the agricultural sector to the industrial sector. Some developing nations have established marketing organizations to substitute open markets which are considered to be inefficient and open to exploitation by private intermediaries. Unfortunately, such organizations are more apt to annihilate the small competitive grain traders than the agents or distributors for the large, powerful agribusinesses. Given the disadvantages associated with monosony and monopoly of aforementioned arrangements, it is necessary for the developing nations' officials to undertake a cost/benefit analysis to determine if the utilization of their scarce resources to establish marketing boards or marketing institutions in place of the private intermediaries is socially beneficial.

5. **Enhancing Rural Services.** In general, urban areas in developing nations have far more medical services, schools, fire protection, health care services, clean water, and so on, than rural areas. This calls on devising policies that aim at lessening urban-rural imbalances in incomes and economic opportunities by providing the rural areas their fair share of such services. An important service that is important in closing the urban-rural imbalance is education. Enhancing the percentage of public educational expenditures in rural areas is very effective in redistributing income to the poor. More specifically, if rural schools put more emphasis on educational programs that better prepare students for rural employment, the rural areas would be able to keep and lure more skilled workers.

Pricing and Exchange Rate Policies

In pursuing the objectives of rapid industrialization and urban development, many developing nations have chosen to maintain low agricultural prices in order to provide cheap food for the growing urban modern sector. Farmers often have been paid prices that are either below global competitive prices or free-market domestic prices. As a result, the domestic price ratio between food and manufactured goods, that is, domestic terms of trade, has turned against farmers and in favor of manufacturers.

The lower prices of farm products as compared to manufactured goods, in turn, has left the farmers with no incentives to increase their output or to invest in new equipment that leads to a higher productivity. Consequently, local food supplies have continued to fall short of demand in many developing nations, especially in sub-Saharan Africa, leading them to substitution of imports for domestic production. This condition has put further pressure on the balance of payments of these nations, as evidenced by the worsening of foreign-exchange and international debt crisis of the 1980s, discussed in Chapter 14 of this textbook.

If developing nations' governments are serious about enhancing agricultural output through research, technology, extension services, and so on, they must also provide incentives for small- and medium-sized farmers by price and exchange rate policces that reflect the interplay of demand and supply in their internal and external markets. This calls on developing nations' governments to take the following actions:

1. To minimize their intervention in the forms of public agricultural marketing boards, which leads to monopsony power and generates producer prices that are usually far below global market prices.
2. To refrain from setting up exchange rates that discourage exports and encourage import substitutes, that is, replacing imports with domestic production. Such rates lower the price farmers receive for their crops, further deteriorating their welfare.

Rural Industrialization

Two major characteristics of most developing nations are:

1. A relatively slow growth in demand for food, characterized by an income elasticity of demand for food that is only about 50 percent. This means that a one percent increase in income level leads only to a one-half percent increase in demand for food. This condition contributes to the slow growth of demand for agricultural labor, further aggravating unemployment problems that might accompany technical advances and capital accumulation.
2. The rate of population growth in rural areas is usually faster than the overall rate of population growth. As a result, the supply of labor in the rural areas continues increasing at a relatively steady rate.

Given these characteristics, to enhance the relative incomes of farmers and to decrease unemployment and underemployment problems in rural areas, developing nations' governments should undertake public works projects and promote small and medium-scale manufacturing businesses and processing. Development of industries and retail firms that are complementary to agriculture, such as repair and maintenance shops, may especially prove to be useful. However, any effort to establish major industries in rural areas must proceed with caution. This is due to the fact that many industrial operations are not able to survive competition in the absence of the required materials and services that are often concentrated in the urban areas. Skilled labor, power, financial institutions, and communication networks are examples of services that are vital to firms' operations and are usually offered in urban areas. For example, given the high costs of transportation, China learned the hard way that the strategy of insisting on the local production of lathes and tractors by rural communes during the Chinese Revolution was economically unwise.

Improving the Status of Women

An important and usually neglected characteristic of Third world agrarian sectors is the important function of women in the agricultural sector. Women render a variety of services in this sector which is composed of the following functions:

1. Cultivate food for household consumption.
2. Participate in the production of cash crops.
3. Raise and market livestock.
4. Look after their children.
5. Collect firewood.
6. Perform household functions such as sewing, cleaning, and cooking.
7. Provide additional income through cottage industries.

Given the multiplicity of functions performed by women in the agricultural sectors of developing nations, women usually end up working longer hours than men. Current estimates show that in addition to their work within the household, women supply 60% to 80% of agricultural labor in Africa and Asia and about 40% in Latin America. However, much of their work is statistically "invisible," that is, women commonly are not compensated for the services that they render. Unfortunately, government extension programs in Third World nations which devote their resources to men tend to intensify existing disparities between women's and men's access to the available resources. Given that in most developing nations, a relatively higher proportion of women's income than men's is used for nutrition and basic necessities, such discriminatory practices that lead to the lower level of income for women end up deteriorating the overall well-being of the household members. Yet, government-funded programs in developing nations have continued to engage in discriminatory practices by excluding women's access to their resources for the following reasons:

1. The lack of collateral for loans by women.
2. The existence of laws prohibiting women from owning property or engaging in financial transactions without their husband's permission.

The existing evidence shows that the efforts to increase the status of women by either raising their productivity or providing them with direct access to credit and inputs have proven to be very successful. However, programs that work indirectly with women have usually failed to achieve all of their stated objectives. Research has shown that projects are more apt to induce women's cooperation if they directly control the resources. Such findings call on governments of developing nations to engage in policy designs that ensure that women are not discriminated against in reaping the benefits of development endeavors.

Land Reform

In many developing nations land ownership is extremely concentrated, that is, a small percentage of land owners own and control the bulk of the land. As a result, the masses of farmers are left with less than two hectares of land for each to own and operate. Given the unequal distribution of land in most developing nations, rural peasants are not left with much hope of economic improvement. Often the land tenure system in developing nations does not offer the farmer with much incentive for hard work, innovation, long-term investment, improved seed, and enhanced fertilization. In many cases, landlords increase rents and crop

GLOBAL INSIGHTS CASE 8.4

AGRICULTURAL REFORM IN CHINA

Beginning in 1978 to reform its agricultural sector, China took the following actions:

1. Decontrolled farm prices for farm commodities.
2. Essentially eliminated compulsory deliveries of commodities to the state.
3. Promoted rural markets.
4. Eased interregional farm trade restrictions.
5. Permitted direct sales of farm products to consumers residing in cities.
6. Instituted a household responsibility system, that is, switched farm management from a production team, the size of a village, to a household. This action enabled farmers to have more latitude in choosing both farm and nonfarm affairs.
7. Encouraged direct sales by the peasants to the market.

These actions were accompanied by a reversal of China's pre-1979 dependence on imported grains, exporting corn, other coarse grains, soybeans, and raw cottons. These noticeable gains were accomplished only by adding a few chemical fertilizers to the production process. As a result, China experienced a high growth in food per capita, averaging 4.6 percent a year during 1977-1984 period. In 1984, however, agricultural output slowed down significantly to the extent that the Minister of Agriculture declared that the "situation in agricultural production is grim". The factors that contributed to such an outcome include the following:

1. Most rural areas had already seized the onetime gains stemming from instituting household responsibility.
2. The distribution of rights to communal land in fragmented plots on the basis of household size rather than farm management ability, implemented since the 1970s, provided few highly-productive farmers with the opportunity to flourish. The reduction of massive government subsidies in the late 1980s, causing the procurement price that the state paid to farmers to decrease.
3. The reforms of 1984 allowed interprovincial trade, private ownership of capital, access to urban markets, hiring of wage labor, and subcontracting. These changes promoted private and collective nonstate rural enterprises. As a result, employment and sown hectares in crop decreased, causing farmers to experience diseconomies of small-scale production.
4. The politicization of government lending by the Agricultural Bank of China, under the control of local party officials, led to the availability of few loans at market interest rates for expanding households.
5. Given the experience of farmers with previous volatility and uncertainty, they feared a reversal in land tenure system. As a result, they became reluctant to invest in agriculture and engage in innovation.

Sources: Peter M. Lichtenstein, *China at the Brink: The Political Economy of Reform and Retrenchment in the Post-Mao Era* (New York: Praeger, 1991); E. Wayne Nafziger, *The Economic of Development* 3rd. ed. (Upper Saddle River, NJ: Prentice Hall, 1997, pp. 598-599; World Bank, *World Development Report, 1986* (New York: Oxford University Press, 1986), pp. 104-6; and Louis Putterman, *Community and Change in China: Collective and Reform Eras in Perspective* (New York: Oxford University Press, 1993).

shares when production increases. Thus, the farmer does not gain much from higher output. Additionally, the legal systems in many developing nations have failed to define property rights to agricultural land. Such a failure, in turn, has adversely affected land use and improvement.

Land reform is frequently advocated as a necessary first step toward agricultural development in many developing nations and has taken the following forms:

1. The confiscation of large lands for new settlement, such as in Kenya.
2. Transformation of land ownership to tenants who already work the land to establish family farms. Examples includes Japan, South Korea, and Taiwan.
3. Transfer of land from large estates to small farms, such as in Mexico.
4. Transfer of land from large estates to state farms, such as in Peru.
5. Transfer of land from large estates to rural cooperatives, such as in Cuba.

The significance of land reform as a major ingredient of economic development has been underlined by an FAO report which presents the following reasons to underline the urgency of such a reform in today's world:

1. Rapid population growth threatens to further aggravate existing inequalities.
2. Unemployment and income inequality in rural sectors have deteriorated.
3. The green revolution can be exploited mainly by powerful and large land owners. This may further enhance their wealth, power, and political clout, further strengthening their ability to resist potential reforms.

The evidence shows that in many developing nations land reforms have failed simply because governments have yielded to the political duress from dominating landowning classes, failing to execute the planned improvements. Nevertheless, it must be emphasized that even an egalitarian land reform program by itself does not insure the success of agricultural and rural development. To be successful, such a program must be accompanied by a host of supportive social services that we discussed throughout this chapter.

SUMMARY

1. An integrated rural development approach requires at least the following three basic complementary elements:
    a. Enhancing domestic demand for agricultural products through an employment-oriented urban development strategy.
    b. Rapid output growth via institutional, technological, and price incentive variations aimed at raising the productivity of small-scale farmers.
    c. A labor-intensive rural development strategy that is composed of nonagricultural and diversified activities that directly or indirectly support or are supported by the rural society.
2. A major cause of the poor performance of the agricultural sector in developing nations has been the failure of developing nations' governments to assign a high priority to the agricultural sector. This failure, coupled with their bias toward investment in the urban industrial sector, is rooted to a large extent in the undue emphasis placed upon rapid industrialization through import-substitution and exchange rate overvaluation. Such a development approach permeated development thinking and strategy during the postwar period.
3. In comparing the agricultural productivity in advanced and developing nations, the following generalizations can be made:

a. The agricultural sector in developing nations can be characterized by such a low productivity that in many cases not only is it incapable of supporting the growing urban population even at a subsistence level, it can barely provide for the rural population.
   b. The agriculture sector in advanced nations can be marked by such a high productivity that it allows a very small number of farmers to feed an entire nation.
4. Today, the available data show that the gap between the two types of agriculture exercised in advanced nations and developing nations is vast and continues to grow.
5. The evolution of agricultural production can be divided into the following three distinct stages:
   a. **Subsistence agriculture.** This stage is characterized by the existence of subsistence farming that is marked by the most primitive agricultural production method and low productivity.
   b. **Diversified agriculture.** This is a stage in which part of the agricultural output is used for self-consumption and the other part for sale to the commercial sector.
   c. **Modern agriculture.** This is the final stage of agricultural development in which substantial productive capacity and high output per worker allow a very small number of farmers to feed an entire nation. Today, the highly efficient agricultural sectors of advanced nations characterized by specialized farms are at this stage.
6. The following are the two major approaches to technological innovation that a nation can choose from:
   a. **The Mechanical Approach.** This approach calls on the utilization of tractor, combines, and other types of machinery primarily as a substitute for labor.
   b. **The Biological Approach.** This approach calls on increasing the yields through the utilization of improved plant varieties such as hybrid corn or the new varieties of rice developed at the International Rice Research Institute in the Phillippines. Due to the significant effect on yields of some of these new varieties, the phenomenon is frequently referred to as the **green revolution**. These varieties increase yields only if combined with appropriate and timely supplies of water and augmented by use of chemical fertilizers.
7. For the green revolution to alleviate rural poverty and raise agricultural output, it must be accompanied by the following appropriate supportive services to enable the active participation of the small farmers in the evolving agricultural framework:
   a. **Agricultural Extension Programs.** These programs are designed to familiarize farmers with the results of agricultural research.
   b. **Provision of Water and Other Inputs.** This calls on government to play an active role in water management by (a) enforcing water rights and planning user fees in order to avoid inequality and inefficiency; and (b) monitoring the salinity or the sedimentation problems by competent technical personnel.
   c. **Transportation.** This calls on the government of developing nations to increase investment in roads, railroads, port facilities, canals and other forms of transportation in order to decrease the cost of producing farm goods and transporting them to the international market.
   d. **Marketing and Storage Facilities.** This calls on government to take the following actions: (I) Enhance and improve the existing infrastructure, such as roads and grain bins; (II) Establish uniform grades and standards in order to trigger incentives to improve agricultural output quality; (III) Disseminate national price information; (IV) Assist farmers in their decision making process with regard to the type of crop planted, the timing of sale, and the appropriate storage facilities to be built.
   e. **Enhancing Rural Services**. This calls on devising policies that aim at lessening urban-rural imbalances in incomes and economic opportunities by providing the rural areas their fair share of such services. An important service that is important in closing the urban-rural imbalance is education. Enhancing the percentage of public educational expenditures in rural areas is very

effective in redistributing income to the poor.
8. An important and usually neglected characteristic of the Third World agrarian sector, is the important function of women in the agricultural sector. Women render a variety of services in this sector. Given the multiplicity of functions performed by women in the agricultural sector of developing nations, women usually end up working longer hours than men. Yet government-funded programs in developing nations have continued to engage in discriminatory practices by excluding women's access to their resources.
9. Research has shown that projects are more apt to induce women's cooperation if they directly control the resources. Such findings call on governments of developing nations to engage in policy designs that ensure that women are not discriminated against in reaping the benefits of development endeavors.
10. In many developing nations land ownership is extremely concentrated, that is, a small percentage of land owners own and control the bulk of the land. As a result, the masses of farmers are left with less than two hectares of land to own and operate.
11. Land reform is frequently advocated as a necessary first step toward agricultural development in many developing nations and has taken various forms in different nations.
12. The evidence shows that in many developing nations land reforms have failed simply because governments have yielded to the political duress from dominating landowning classes, failing to execute the planned improvements.

QUESTIONS

1. What is meant by an integrated rural approach? Explain, elaborating on the three basic complementary elements that are required for the implementation of such an approach.
2. Elaborate on the history of agricultural development during the last half a century by answering the following questions:
   a. What is the major characteristic of the rate of growth of the agriculture sector across the globe during this period?
   b. What is the major cause of the poor performance of the agricultural sector in developing nations during this period?
   c. What are the consequences of the poor performance of the agriculture in these nations?
   d. What significant change in development thinking and implementation started in the late 1970s?
3. Compare agricultural productivity in advanced and developing nations by answering the following:
   a. What generalization can be made regarding the comparative productivity of advanced and developing nations?
   b. Why is agricultural productivity in advanced nations so much higher than in developing nations?
4. Elaborate on the stages of agricultural development by answering the following questions:
   a. Name these stages and describe the major characteristics of each stage.
   b. What form (s) dominate (s) farming in the majority of developing nations?
   c. What variables block the transition of developing nations to modern ones? Explain.
5. Elaborate on strategies of agricultural and rural development by answering the following questions:
   a. What are the two main objectives of implementing such strategies?
   b. Name the major strategies, and briefly describe each strategy.
6. Discuss rural poverty in developing nations by answering the following questions:
   a. What elements contribute to the existence of the high level of poverty in developing nations?
   b. What strategies can be employed to raise the level of rural income and reduce rural poverty?
   c. What strategies can be adopted to avert rural development policies from raising rural poverty through agricultural terms of trade?

7. Discuss urban bias in developing nations by answering the following questions:
   a. What are the forms of bias in developing nations?
   b. What is the major consequence of such a bias for developing nations?
   c. Give examples of urban bias in a developing nation that you are familiar with and discuss their impact on the development process.

NOTES

1. United Nations Food and Agricultural Organization, "Rome Declaration on World Food Security," *Population and Development Review* 22 (December 1969): 807-809; Lester R. Brown, "Facing the Prospect of Food Scarcity," in Worldwatch Institute, *State of the World, 1997* (New York: Norton, 1997): pp. 23-41; and Nikos Alexandratos, "The World Food Outlook: A Review Essay," *Population and Development Review* 23 (December 1997): 877-888.
2. Idriss Jazairy, Mohiuddin Alamgir, and Theresa Panuccio. *The State of World Rural Poverty: An Inquiry into its Causes and Consensus.* Published for International Fund for Agricultural Development. (New York: New York University Press, 1992), p.1.
3. World Bank, *World Development Report, 1986* (New York: Oxford University Press, 1986), chaps. 4 and 5.

SUGGESTED READINGS

Binswanger, Hans P. and Klaus Deininger. "Explaining Agricultural and Agrarian Policies in Developing Countries." *Journal of Economic Literature* 35 (December 1997): 1958-2005.

Bouis, Howarth E. "The Effects of Income on Demand for Food in Poor Countries: Are Our Food Consumption Database Giving Us Reliable Estimates?" *Journal of Development Economics* 44 (June 1994): 199-226.

Eicher Carl K. and Doyle C. Baker. *Research on Agricultural Development in Sub-Saharan Africa: A Critical Survey.* East Lansing: Michigan State University International Development Paper no. 1, 1982, pp.20-23.

Evenson, Robert E., and Carl E. Pray. "Food Production and Consumption: Measuring Food Production (with Reference to South Asia." *Journal of Development Economics* 44 (June 1994): 173-97.

Fong, Monica and Heli Perrett. *Women and Credit Institutions for the Poor and Reducing Barriers to Access for Women.* World Bank Discussion No. 117. Washington, D.C.: World Bank, 1991.

Ghonemy, M. R., K. H. Parsons, R. P. Sinha, N. Uphoff, and P. Wignaraja. *Studies on Agrarian Reform and Rural Poverty.* Rome: Food and Agriculture Organization of the United Nations, 1984. Pp. 19-57.

Ghose, Ajit Kuman., ed. *Agrarian Reforms in Contemporary Developing Countries.* Prepared for the ILO. London: Croom Helm, 1983, pp. 3-28.

Hayami, Yujiro and Vernon W. Ruttan. *Agricultural Development: An International Perspective.* Baltimore: Johns Hopkins University Press, 1971.

Howe, Christopher. *China's Economy: A Basic Guide.* New York: Basic Books, 1978.

Jazairy, Idriss, Mohiuddin Alamgir, and Theresa Panuccio. *The State of World Rural Poverty: An Inquiry into its Causes and Consequences.* Published for the International Fund for Agricultural Development. New York: New York University Press, 1992.

Lete, Uma. *The Design of Rural Development: Lessons from Africa.* Baltimore: John Hopkins University Press, 1975.

Lipton, Michael. *Why Poor People Stay Poor: A Study of Urban Bias in World Development.* London: Maurice Temple Smith, 1977.

Mudlak, Yari, Donald Larson, and Al Crego. *"Agricultural Development: Issues, Evidence and Consequences."* (memorandum) World Bank International Economic Development. Washington, D. C. ,1996.

Myrdal, Gunnar. *Asian Drama.* New York: Pantheon, 1968, chaps. 22, 23 & 26.

Nafziger, Wane E. "India Versus China: Economic Development Performance." *Dalhousie Review* 65 (Fall 1985): 366-92.

Prybyla, Jan S. *The Political Economy of Communist China.* Scranton, Pa.: International Textbook, 1970.

Riskin, Paul. *China's Political Economy: The Quest for Development Since 1949.* Oxford: Oxford University Press, 1987.

Robson, Peter and Dennis A. Lury, eds. *The Economics of Africa.* London: Allen & Unwin, 1969.

Sanders, John H., Sunder Ramaswamy, and Barry I. Shapiro. *The Economics of Agricultural Technology in Semi-Arid*

Sub-Saharan Africa. Baltimore: Johns Hopkins University Press, 1996.

Singh, Inderifit. *The Great Ascent: The Rural Poor in South Asia.* Baltimore: Johns Hopkins University Press, 1990.

Stavenhagen, Rodoflo. *Agrarian Problems and Peasant Movements in Latin America.* New York: Doubleday, 1970.

Tomich, Thomas P., Peter Kibly, and Bruce F. Johnson. *Transforming Agrarian Economies: Opportunities Seized, Opportunities Missed.* Ithaca, N.Y.: Cornell University Press.

Weitz, Raanan. *From Peasant to Farmer: A Revolutionary Strategy for Development.* New York: Columbia University Press, 1971.

Wittwer, Sylvan, Yu Youtai, Sun Han, and Wang Lianzheng. *Feeding a Billion: Frontiers of Chinese Agriculture.* East Lansing: Michigan State University Press, 1987.

World Bank. *Adjustment in Africa: Reforms, Results, and the Road Ahead.* Oxford: Oxford University Press, 1994.

CHAPTER 9

TECHNOLOGICAL PROGRESS

Since the mid-nineteenth century the United States, Canada, Japan, and most Western European nations have experienced a rapid economic growth, marked by an average annual per capital income growth of 1 percent per year. Such a fast rate has led to more than quadrupling of these nations' real per capita GNP during the past half of the century. Technology is one of the most important factors that has contributed to economic well-being in the advanced countries, and it has helped these nations to maintain their present standard of living. Technological improvement has enabled us to reduce our working hours, to increase production efficiency, to improve our working conditions, and to enhance the flow of the goods and services that we produce. In manufacturing, for example, about four decades ago an ammonia plant was capable of producing 150 tons of ammonia a day; in 1970, it could produce 1,500 tons a day; and in the early 1980s it could produce 3,000 tons of ammonia in a single day.[1] In agriculture, for example, technological innovations over the last generation have significantly increased the productivity of labor and land in the U.S. agricultural sector. In the production of corn, for instance, from 1910 to 1914, each acre of land required 35.2 hours of labor to produce 26 bushels of corn. From 1972 to 1982, however, each acre of land required only 3.4 hours of labor to produce 105.3 bushels of corn. Such improvements have drastically changed the structure of the U.S. agricultural sector over time. The U.S. agriculture sector has been transformed from a relatively labor-intensive system to a relatively capital-intensive one. As a result, in the late 1980s there were about 2.2 million farms in the United States, as compared with roughly 5.5 million farms 60 years ago, which is a 60 percent decrease. The number of workers in the agriculture sector has declined substantially. Today, only 2.6% percent of the U.S. labor force engages in agricultural activities, including farming, fishing, and forestry.[2]

Presently, there is not a day that goes by without news of some type of technological progress that will affect our lives. The invention of computer chips, for example, has had an enormous impact on production, education, and health care, to name just a few areas. The introduction of robots in many factories has reduced the need for labor. The use of VCRs and microcomputers has become commonplace in our homes, businesses, and schools. The advancements in medical technology have contributed to longevity in our society.

Unfortunately there is a negative side to our technological progress. The introduction of nuclear weapons has completely changed the balance of power in the world and has made the destruction of the human race a real possibility. Factories using modern technologies have polluted our air and water, contributing to the causes of cancer, birth defects, and other health-related problems. Despite this, we have come to rely on more technology to resolve the problems that are created by the technology in the first place. For instance, in the area of military technology, the Reagan administration announced research on "Star Wars" technology to combat the possibility of nuclear attack. To fight pollution, we use high-tech antipollution devices. It seems that our passion for technological advancement is a never-ending process.

In the past, most technologies have been developed by the advanced industrial nations, spreading to other countries only after different time lags. For example, the Industrial Revolution that started in England in the eighteenth century later spread to North America and Western Europe in the nineteenth century, and finally to Japan and Russia in the early twentieth century. However, this process has not yet been completed and many developing countries in Africa, Asia, and South America are still using the pre-Industrial Revolution technologies. As a result, the developing countries have become technologically dependent on the advanced nations for their economic growth and development. To obtain the needed technology, many developing countries have turned to the international market as a channel for modern technology transfer.

Today, technology is considered as one of the most significant factors that contribute to the process of economic development in developing countries. To emphasize the importance of this factor in the course of development, economists have referred to technology as the "prime mover" and the "vital growth component."[3]

Throughout history, technologies have been developed and advanced in modern nations at such a fast pace that a technological gap has been created between the advanced nations and the developing countries. To bridge this gap, many developing countries have turned to the international market as a channel for the transfer of modern technology. This view is clearly stated by the Organization for Economic Cooperation and Development:

> The efficient exploitation of advanced technologies calls for both technological resources beyond national boundaries and access to markets that are international in scope.[4]

The concern of the developing countries with the subject of technology has led economists to investigate more rigorously the process of technology transfer. This has resulted in the creditability of technology as a vital element of economic development.

The purpose of this chapter is to provide us with a broad understanding of the issues that are related to the concept of technology and technological progress. First, we define the concept of technology and discuss its different classifications. Second, we discuss the relationship between technology and culture. Third, we elaborate on factor intensity and technological progress. Finally, we examine the ingredients of technological progress.

DEFINITION OF TECHNOLOGY AND RELATED TERMINOLOGIES

Technology can be defined as the method or technique for converting inputs to outputs in accomplishing a specific task.

In the above definition, the terms "method" or "technique" are used to mean not only the knowledge, but also the skills and the means for accomplishing a task. **Technological progress** means an increase in **technical efficiency**, which can be defined in either of the following two ways:

1. Producing more output with the same inputs.
2. Producing the same quantity of output with fewer inputs.

Changes in technical efficiency stem from invention and innovation. **Invention** is the discovery of a technique. **Innovation** means the practical application of an invention to production for a market. The difference is indicative of the distinction sometimes made between "pure" and "applied" science. Invention is achieved by the inventor, while innovation is performed by the entrepreneur who applies the innovation to production for market.

Economic analysis makes a distinction between autonomous and induced technological change. **Autonomous technological progress** results from scientific curiosity. The inventor makes discoveries for the sheer pleasure of it. **Induced technological progress** results from the desire for profit, in the private sector. It may also be caused by aspiration for social progress in the public sector.

TECHNOLOGY AND CULTURE

Because a technological innovation requires advances in scientific knowledge and demands exploitation of human and nonhuman resources, it interacts with the culture within which it is introduced. Such an interaction leads to changes in the many variables that affect and are affected by the introduction of a new technology. These variables are the economic systems, the value systems, the religious systems, the political systems, the social organization systems, and the educational systems (see Figure 9.1).[5]

Technology and Economic Systems

The impact of a new technology on an economic system stems from the increase in efficiency that is caused by the introduction of that technology. Efficiency in this context can be defined in three different ways: (1) an increase in output with the same amount of input, (2) the production of the same output with a smaller amount of input, and (3) an improvement in the quality of products produced.

Given the above definitions, the increase in efficiency of an economic system leads to changes in factor proportions; that is, it leads to changes in the relative amount of resources that are used in producing a unit of a given commodity or service. Additionally, improvement in efficiency causes the system either to produce more goods and services with the same amount of resources or to produce better products that command higher prices in the national or the international market. In other words, the increase in efficiency introduced by a new technology causes the GNP of a country to increase, changing the economic picture of that country. In fact, transfer of new technology is one of the major factors that has contributed to the development process in the developing countries, and this is why some developing countries count on the multinational corporations (MNCs) to facilitate this technology transfer to them.

Several studies have attempted to measure the impact of a nation's rate of technological change on its rate of economic growth. For example, a study by Robert Solow, an economist, concluded that about 40 percent of the total increase in national income per person employed in the United States from 1929 to 1957 can be attributed to technological change.[6] As a more recent example, a study by Edward Denison, also an economist, reported that about 55 percent of the total increase in national income per person employed in the United States from 1929 to 1982 is attributed to technological improvements.[7] Although such studies are useful in highlighting the importance of technology for a nation's economic growth, their conclusions are very inexact. This is because it is extremely difficult to take into account the myriad factors that affect an economic system. Nevertheless, it is certain that technology has a significant impact on a nation's economy.

In addition to raising economic efficiency and contributing to economic development, technology plays a significant role in the international trade of a nation. According to the technological gap theory and the product life cycle theory discussed in international economic courses, technology is considered to be the most important element in explaining the pattern of international trade.[*]

---

[*] See for example, Asheghian, Parviz. *International Economics*. St. Paul, MN: West Publishing Co., 1995, pp. 81-84.

Figure 9.1

TECHNOLOGY AND THE REST OF THE CULTURE

Because a technological innovation requires advances in scientific knowledge and demands exploitation of human and nonhuman resources, it interacts with the culture within which it is introduced. Such an interaction leads to changes in the many variables that affect and are affected by the introduction of a new technology. These variables are the economic systems, the value systems, the religious systems, the political systems, the social organization systems, and the educational systems.

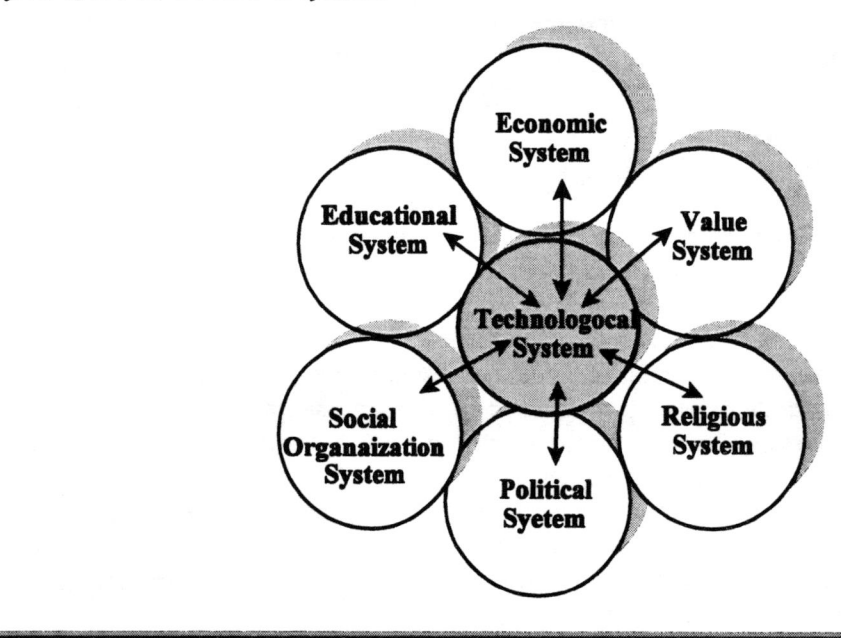

Technology and Value Systems

The cultural values, that is, the attitudes and beliefs of a society regarding what is right and wrong, play a significant role in determining the technologies that are developed and used in that society. For example, the development and the wide use of smoke detector alarms in the United States in recent years could be viewed as a response to an increasing regard for safety among many Americans. Other examples of technologies that reflect cultural values in the United States include technological improvements in pollution control devices, diet foods, exercise equipment, contraceptive devices, and fast foods.

Technology and Religious Systems

Because a society's value system is affected by its religious beliefs, religion has a significant impact on a society's view of change and technological improvement. For example, conservative Amish and Mennonite sects in the United States oppose the introduction of any new technology into their societies on the grounds that it will lead to the sociological ills that accompany all modern societies. Thus, they continue to ride in their horse and buggies, arguing that the use of the automobile is just a first step in a series of steps leading toward modernization and its resultant social problems, such as teenage pregnancy, drunk driving, and drug addiction.

As another example, Mahatma Gandhi, who was opposed to India's dependence on England, used the Hindu concept of "Nirvana" or "wantlessness" to oppose technological industrialization. He advised his followers to beware of infatuation with machinery, arguing that by working with machines people will become like machines, losing all sense of art and craftsmanship.[8]

Technology and Political Systems

The political system (that is, the governing institutions of a country) is affected by technology. The political system also affects the nature of the technology and its development and future direction.

Technology can be advanced because of certain goals that have been set by the political system. For example, U.S. plans regarding the "Star Wars" weapons system have set in motion research and development that is pushing forward the frontiers of technology concerned with laser beams and electronics. As another example, the U.S. space program has resulted in numerous advances in satellite technology, which have greatly improved communications.

Advancements in technology can disturb the tranquility of a political system and create resistance toward change. For example, labor union leaders have resisted technology on the grounds that it would create "technological unemployment," that is, they feel technology would replace humans with machines. Advances in technology have also resulted in toxic waste, environmental pollution, and urban decay, giving rise to the emergence of environmentalist groups whose activities have resulted in the enactment of laws that are aimed at the protection of the environment. Ironically, the environmental problems caused by technology have resulted in the development of still more technology that is used to clean up the environment.

Technology and Social Organization Systems

Social organization, that is, the order or the norm by which individuals or groups in a society relate to each other, is affected by technology, and the social organization also affects technology.

Japanese technological advancement in recent years provides a good example of the impact of social organization on technology. Many observers believe that one of the main reasons for Japanese technological progress is related to their social organization, that is, their feudalistic social order that recognizes a definite hierarchy and specifies individual responsibilities.

Technology can affect the social order by encouraging the migration of laborers to the technologically advanced areas. This is especially true in developing countries, when industrialization brought about by technology causes the movement of workers from the agricultural sector to the industrial sector where wages are higher. Such a migration goes against the social order in the agricultural sector, which is based on the extended family that works together on the same farm.

Technology and Educational Systems

Educational systems, both formal and informal, affect technology and are also affected by technology.

In the formal educational setting, universities and the research and development (R&D) departments of corporations provide the primary source for the development of technologies through their continuous scientific endeavors, conducted by groups of scientists. In the informal educational setting, different technologies are developed by individuals every day. Some of these technologies have had an enormous impact on our lives. Examples of this include the Wright brothers' invention of the airplane and Alexander

Graham Bell's invention of the telephone.

Technology has a significant impact on educational systems by providing them with new methods of research and development and instruction. For example, today microcomputers are used to teach preschool children to learn mathematics, to draw pictures, and to learn the alphabet. The invention of the video cassette recorder (VCR) has contributed significantly to education by simplifying the recording and playing of educational programs.

In summary, technology is significantly affected by the different aspects of a culture. Because MNCs are sought by many developing countries as the primary source of technology transfer, the success of their operation in such developing countries depends on their ability to introduce and implement modern technologies. The introduction and implementation of modern technology, in turn, require an understanding of the elements that shape a culture and demand a comprehension of their interaction with technology. This is an especially sensitive issue in developing countries, where MNCs have to tackle the question of which technology is the appropriate one in different cultural environments.

FACTOR INTENSITY AND TECHNOLOGICAL PROGRESS

Because the inputs of production can be combined in different proportions to produce the same type of output, we have different technological alternatives in the production of a given product. For example, a table can be built in many different ways. A primitive technology would use labor with hand tools to get the job done. A highly advanced technology would use a computer to design the table, to organize an assembly line, and to employ the skills of trained laborers using power tools to accomplish the task. Between these two extremes, one could picture a wide variety of combinations of laborers and machines, each representing a specific level of technology. At one extreme, when a primitive technology is used, the technology is referred to as "labor-intensive" or "capital-saving." The other extreme represents "capital-intensive" or "labor-saving" technology. As we move from the labor-intensive extreme to the capital-intensive extreme, we create different production alternatives by simply increasing the capital intensity of our production technology.

As we mentioned earlier, technological progress can be defined in two ways: (1) producing more output with the same inputs; or (2) producing the same quantity of output with fewer inputs.
Given the first definition, graphically, technological progress can be portrayed by the shift of an isoquant. Recall from your introductory microeconomics course, an **isoquant** is a curve that shows various combinations of two factor inputs, such as capital (K) and labor (L) that yield the same level of total output, say 100 units. Figure 9.2a illustrates technological progress by a parallel shift of the isoquant toward the origin, implying that the given amount of output (100 units) can now be produced with fewer inputs. As the figure indicates, less labor and less capital are required after the change to produce the same level of output (100) units.

Given the second definition, technological progress can be portrayed by the **production possibilities frontier (PPF),** or production possibilities curve, also known as the transformation curve. This curve shows all possible combinations of two products that a country can produce with available technology and full employment of all resources. In figure 9.2b, it is assumed that resources stay constant, and the economy produces only two products, video cassette recorders (VCRs) and Wheat (W). Furthermore, assume that the production of VCRs requires a relatively capital-using technology, whereas, production of wheat requires a labor-using technology. Given these assumptions, technological progress can be portrayed by the rightward and parallel shift of the PPF, indicating that the same quantity of output can now be produced with fewer inputs.

CH. 9/TECHNOLOGICAL PROGRESS 183

Figure 9.2

EFFECTS OF TECHNOLOGICAL PROGRESS ON THE ISOQUANTS AND THE PRODUCTION POSSIBILITIES FRONTIER

Panel a illustrates technological progress by a parallel shift of the isoquant toward the origin, implying that the given amount of output can now be produced with fewer inputs. In panel b, technological progress is portrayed by the rightward and parallel shift of the PPF, indicating that the same quantity of output can now be produced with fewer inputs.

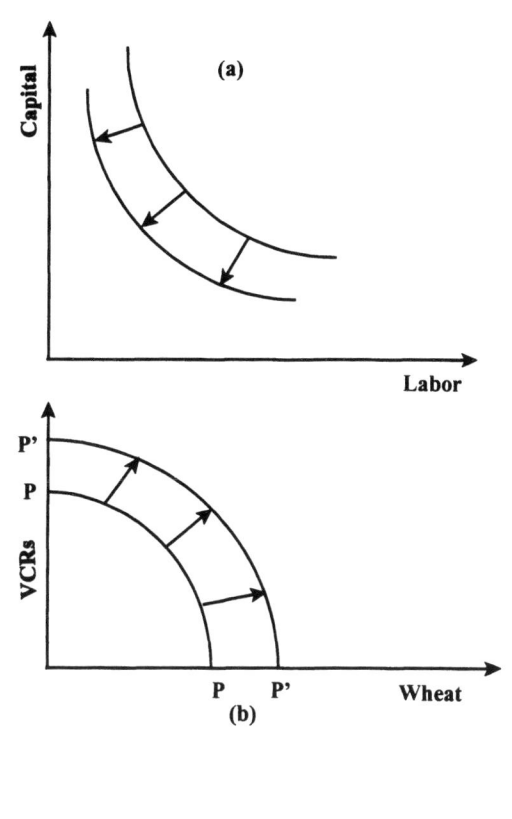

Having understood the concepts of technological progress and factor intensity, it is now the time to elaborate on the classification of technological progress on the basis of factor intensity. There are three basic classifications of technological progress: neutral, capital-using, and labor-using.

Neutral Technological Progress

Using the first definition of technological progress, neutral technological progress occurs when the same

184   **PART II/THE ELEMENTS OF GROWTH**

level of output can be obtained with less inputs, combined at the same proportion. The inward shifting of the isoquant of Figure 9.3a portrays this case. As the figure shows, the capital/labor ratios associated with points A and B are equal, because these points lie on the same ray from the origin.

Using the second definition of technological progress, neutral technological progress takes place when higher output levels are obtained with the same quantity and combinations of factor inputs, assuming that factor prices stay constant. Neutral technological progress implies that optimal capital/labor output stays constant. The outward shifting of PPF of Figure 9.3b provides a diagramatic presentation of neutral technological progress. Simple innovations such as those that stem from the division of labor can lead to higher total output levels and greater consumption for all persons.

Figure 9.3

NEUTRAL TECHNOLOGICAL PROGRESS

Neutral technological progress occurs when the same level of output can be obtained with less inputs, combined at the same proportion. The inward shifting of the isoquant of portrays technological progress. As the figure shows, the capital/labor ratios associated with points A and B are equal, because these points lie on the same ray from the origin.

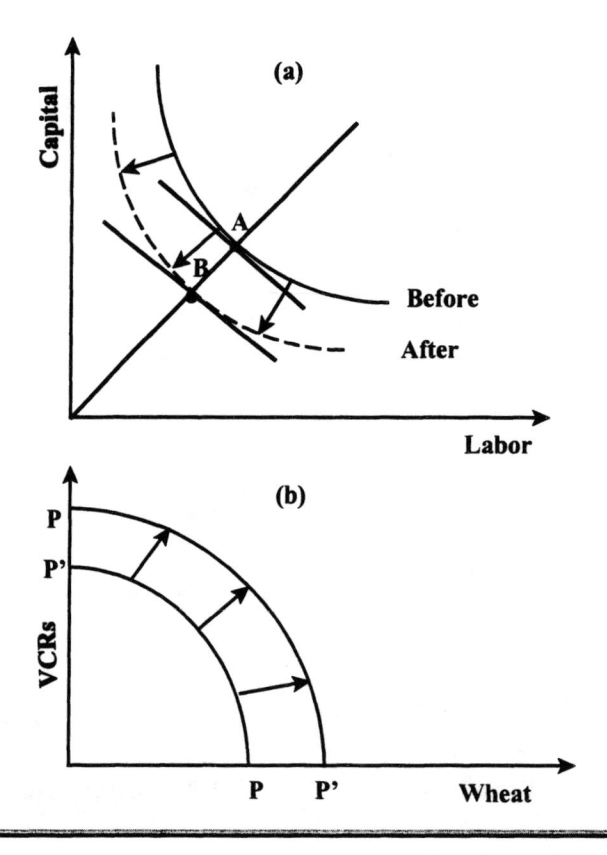

CH. 9/TECHNOLOGICAL PROGRESS

Capital Saving (Labor Using) Technological Progress

Using the first definition of technological progress, capital saving (labor using) technological progress occurs when the nature of the technological progress leads to a lower capital/labor ratio, assuming that factor prices stay constant. In Figure 9.4a, this is portrayed by the shift of the isoquant inward, which causes the equilibrium to move from point A to point B. Given the same factor prices, as shown by the slopes of the two

---

Figure 9.4

CAPITAL SAVING (LABOR USING) TECHNOLOGICAL PROGRESS

Capital saving (labor using) technological progress occurs when the nature of the technological progress leads to a lower capital/labor ratio, assuming that factor prices stay constant. In panel a, this is portrayed by the shift of the isoquant inward, which causes the equilibrium to move from point A to point B. Given the same factor prices, as shown by the slopes of the two parallel lines at tangency points A and B, the capital/labor ratio becomes lower after technological progress. In panel b, this is portrayed by the outward shift of the PPF that is more pronounced toward the VCR axis. The slight outward shift of the PPF along the wheat axis is due to the fact that in normal conditions both products call for the use of both factors as productive inputs although in different proportions.

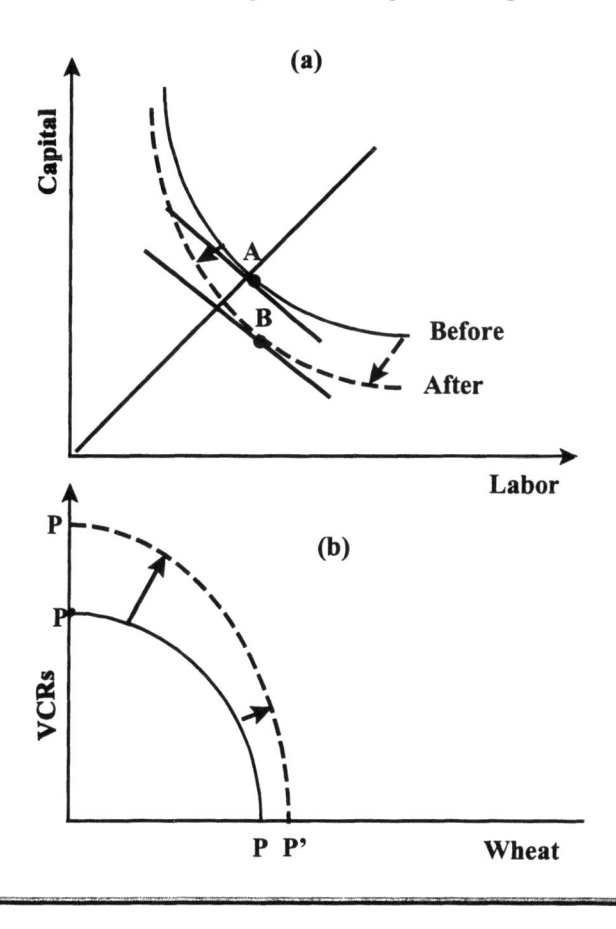

parallel lines at tangency points A and B, the capital/labor ratio becomes lower after technological progress.

Using the second definition of technological progress and our hypothetical example of VCR and wheat production, capital saving technological progress is portrayed in Figure 9.4b by the outward shift of the PPF that is more pronounced toward the VCR axis. The slight outward shift of the PPF along the wheat axis is due to the fact that in normal conditions both products call for the use of both factors as productive inputs although in different proportions.

Labor Saving (Capital Using) Technological Progress

Using the first definition of technological progress, labor using (capital saving) technological progress occurs when the nature of the technological progress leads to a higher capital/labor ratio, assuming that factor prices stay constant. In figure 9.5a, this is portrayed by the shift of the isoquant inward, which causes the equilibrium point to move from point A to point B. Given the same factor prices, as shown by the slopes of the two parallel lines at tangency points A and B, the capital/labor becomes higher after technological progress.

Using the second definition of technological progress and our hypothetical example of VCRs and wheat production, labor saving technological progress is portrayed in Figure 9.5b by the outward shift of the PPF that is more pronounced toward the wheat axis. The slight outward shift of the PPF along the VCR is due to the fact that in normal conditions both products call for the use of both factors as productive inputs although in different proportions.

INGREDIENT OF TECHNOLOGICAL PROGRESS

Having realized the significance of technological progress as the key element in enhancing productivity and output, we devote this section to a discussion of the ingredient of technological progress, which is composed of elasticity of substitution, scale of production, new products and demonstration effect, social relation of production, and speed of change.

Elasticity of Substitution

When the prices of factors of production, say, capital (K) and labor (L) change, we would expect the proportions in which they were combined to alter as well. In other words, we would expect the K/L ratio to change. The responsiveness of a firm to a change in the relative prices of inputs can be measured by the **elasticity of substitution**. This measure determines the relative responsiveness of the K/L ratio to a change in relative factor prices (r/w), where i is the interest rate and w is the wage rate. Mathematically, the elasticity of substitution is measured by the following formula:

$$\sigma = -[\frac{\Delta(K/L)}{K/L} \div \frac{\Delta(r/w)}{r/w}]$$

σ (*sigma*), the Greek letter used to denote elasticity of substitution measures the percentage change in capital labor ratio over the percentage in the relative price of capital (r) to the price of labor (w). When σ = -1, a 1 percent change in price of capital relative to the price of labor leads to a 1 percent change in the K/L ratio in the opposite direction. Although our formula deals with combinations of capital and labor, the principal is applicable to any factors of production or combinations of them.

Figure 9.5

LABOR SAVING (CAPITAL USING) TECHNOLOGICAL PROGRESS

In panel (a) labor saving technological progress is portrayed by the shift of the isoquant inward, which causes the equilibrium point to move from point A to point B. Given the same factor prices, as shown by the slopes of the two parallel lines at tangency points A and B, the capital/labor becomes higher after technological progress. In panel (b), labor saving technological progress is portrayed by the outward shift of the PPF that is more pronounced toward the wheat axis.

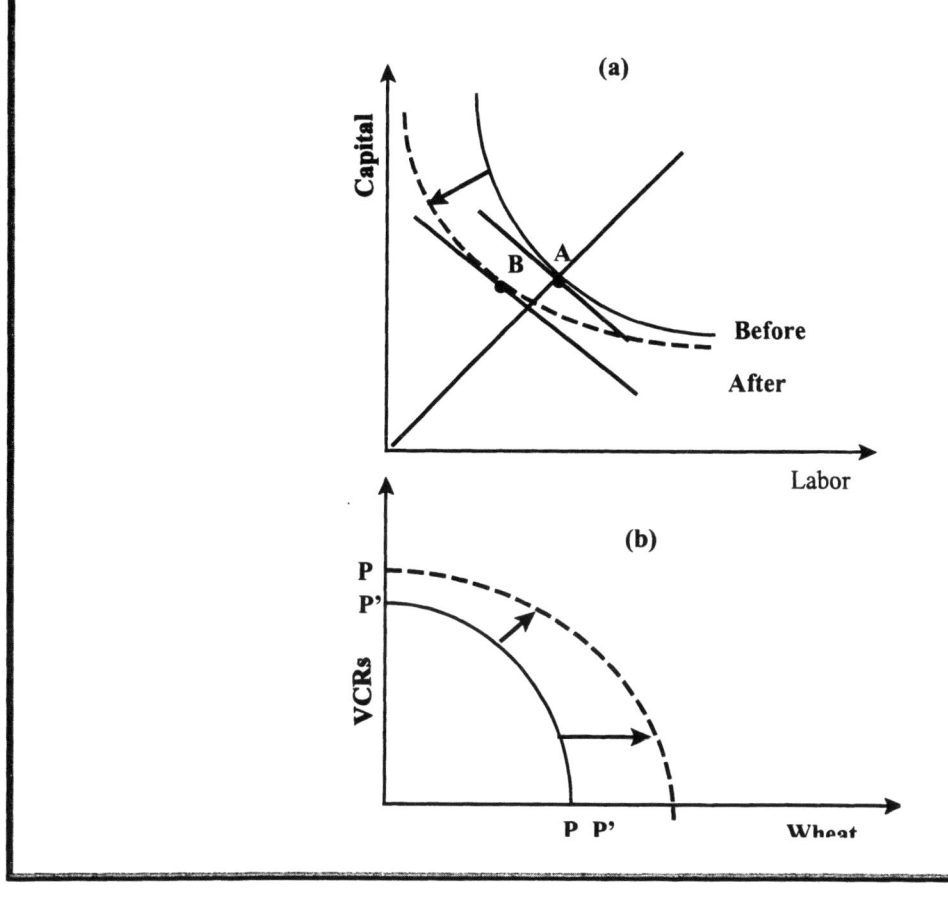

Various studies have tried to estimate the elasticity of substitution of capital for labor. Notably a few have reported that it is numerically close to -1; but it changes from industry to industry and from short-run to long-run. Empirically, the firm can and does respond to changing relative input prices. Thus, the notion that elasticity of substitution is equal to zero does not hold up in the real world.

The most significant implications of elasticity of substitution analysis stem from its affects on labor employment. When technological improvements causes displacement of labor, no change in wages may be sufficient to offset the resulting unemployment. In fact, some evidence proposes that technological change may be followed by increasing insensitivity to relative factor prices. In other words, technological improvement may be accompanied by successively lower elasticity of substitution. This scenario may be portrayed in terms of **technological dualism**, defined as an economy which is composed of the following two sectors, each with its own type of technology:

1. **Traditional Sector.** In this sector, technology is characterized by factor proportion flexibility, that is, high elasticity of substitution. In this sector, which is predominantly agricultural, workers and their implements could be combined in broadly flexible proportion.
2. **Modern Sector.** In this sector, technology is characterized by a very low elasticity of substitution that is close to zero. In this sector, one skilled worker is combined with one machine, as an inseparable team. For example, modern petrochemical, chemical, and metallurgical process are very inflexible in their requirement of inputs of all kinds.

Unfortunately, K/L ratio in many developing nations have not been very responsive to r/w ratio. This problem stems from the following two causes:

1. The inefficiency of managers in developing nations to respond to factor prices by changing the factor proportion to the appropriate level.
2. The existence of labor unions and politicians who apt to satisfy their constituencies by pushing to raise the wage rate. The insensitivity of wages to employment is even stronger when the short-run demand for final product is inelastic, which is the case of many agricultural products and primary goods.

The discussion of the elasticity of factor substitution connotes specific directions for imported technology and for local research and development. If our objective is the generation of more productive employment for labor, then the technology must concentrate on job creation. Imported technology, impacted by the factor prices and factor proportion in the nation where it was created, is usually incompatible with full employment in developing nations. The only technology that is conducive to rapid economic development is labor-intensive as well as productive. Such a technology allows broad types of factor combinations and is compatible with the adaptability and flexibility called for in the process of economic development.

Scale of Production

Technological improvement during the last two centuries has been marked by the following two features:

1. Enhanced volumes of production, that is, an increase in the scale of output.
2. Economies of mass production or economies of scale, that is, a decrease in a firm's long-run average costs as the size of its plant increases.

To be sure, efficiency of production is partly a function of its scale, which in turn is limited by the size of the market. The larger the scale, the cheaper the cost of the product when there exist economies external or internal to the firm.[*] In economic development, moreover, one expects to meet opportunities for internal

---

[*]External economies refer to conditions that result in decreases in a firm's long-run average costs as a consequence of elements totally outside of the firm as a producing unit. For example, external economies may stem from improvements in market facilities and public transportation as an industry develops in a given region. Internal economies, on the other hands, refer to conditions that result in decreases in a firm's long-run average costs or scale

economies of scale blocked by the existence of monopolies where entry is limited by lack of knowledge, capital, skills, etc.

The growth process can be led by a widening of the market, which in turn may result from increased efficiency in transport or communications. Cheapening transport fuses markets, bringing additional buyers and sellers into contact with one another, increasing elasticities of demand and supply. Or markets can grow through an increase in efficiency and income in any commodity, which increases effective demand for other products and spreads in cumulative fashion. Even where the growth process is led by efficiency in production, however, the requirements of distribution are inescapable.

New Products and Demonstration Effect

So far, our discussion of technological change has focused on *existing* products, emphasizing improvements in methods and processes instead of better products. However, technological improvement also leads to the production of new products as well as modern procedures to build them. Innovation can enhance demand, change its makeup, and decrease costs. The new products are prominent among labor-intensive goods, mass-produced goods and mass-marketed goods. In general, the new products have higher quality than the old ones.

Economically, a consumer's decision to purchase a new product is not formed in a vacuum. An important factor that affects such a decision is the "**demonstration effect**," as described by Nurkse who writes:

> when people come into contact with superior goods or superior patterns of consumption, with new articles or new ways of meeting old wants, they are apt to feel after a while a certain restlessness and dissatisfaction. Their knowledge is extended, their imagination stimulated; new desires are aroused, the propensity to consume is shifted upward.[9]

Domestically, the demonstration effect shows how increases in consumption drain most of the increase in income, while savings may stay constant or decrease. The introduction of new goods gives rise to new desires. The demonstration effect in consumption may thus entice the individual to work harder to satisfy the desire to obtain the new good. Domestically, the demonstration effect has a stabilizing effect on expenditure and output. Thus, it can be argued that economic growth hinges on consumers as much as or more than on entrepreneurs.

Internationally, the demonstration effect breeds a sense of instability and disequilibrium. The introduction of a new product through international trade may change the demand patterns in a country. As history shows, before trade, a developing nation consumes domestic foodstuff and other goods and services without final products imported from an advanced nation. However, the introduction of trade, particularly in highly advertised and well marketed goods, alters tastes, and demands by all income groups change toward imported products and away from domestic goods. Internationally, the strength of the demonstration effect not only hinges on the desirability of the new products but also on information and transportation costs. Today, given technological improvements in communication and transportation, the transfer of information about new products and modern methods of production occurs at a very fast rate. Additionally, transport costs have decreased over time, enhancing the exposure of people in remote areas to new products. Either they travel less costly to market centers, or the products are shipped to them at lower costs, or both. These changes have led to demonstration effects, portrayed in the adoption of Northern standards in food, music, dress, amusement, durable goods, as well as artistic literacy. The impact of the demonstration effect on standards of food consumption is well documented. Examples include the use of the European breakfast

---

of operations as a consequence of size adjustment within the firm as a producing unit. For example, internal economies may stem from greater specialization and more efficient utilization of the firm's resources as its scale of operations rises.

instead of fish and soybean soup in Thailand, the adoption of wheat in place of rice in Japan, and promotion of powdered milk as a substitute for breast milk in south Africa. As these examples demonstrate, the demonstration effect works against comparative advantage and may reduce dietary level. No wonder that a literature critical of the "cultural dependence" by developing nations on advanced nations has evolved.

Although changes in tastes and standards can be superseded, they are irrevocable. Thus, the task of development policy is to stimulate these dynamic economic impetuses to work in socially efficient manners.

Social Relations of Production

As technological improvement proceeds, the institutional framework for production and distribution goes through the following changes:

1. Increases in the numbers and proportions of skilled workers brought about by technological improvement imply that the ownership of capital, in particular human capital, is extended. This leads to a significant shift in the relations between capital and labor.
2. State-sponsored activities assume a greater role at the expense of private activities.
3. More inclusive provision of social benefits, including unemployment insurance, alleviate the greater threat of unemployment.
4. More emphasis is placed on managerial performance as the number of people with managerial tasks increases.
5. Agriculture mergers may raise the number of landless peasants, while agriculture relinquishes its plantation ownership and aptitude.

The above changes interact with technological improvement. The introduction of capital-using equipment and machinery, and the increasing flow of wage goods alters the relative factor prices. Such changes breed an environment that is conducive to the introduction of modern managerial and technical training.

Speed of Change

Today, given the speed and the lower cost of information transmission, the rate of technological improvement continues to accelerate like never before. Although the transferred technology may not be appropriate for developing nations, as we will explain later, it is increasingly easier to transmit it at the global level.

Because technological progress stems from innovation, the question to ask at this time is what are the determinants of innovation. In answering this question, we must realize that for new knowledge to be put into practice, the following conditions must be satisfied:

1. The potential innovators must be cognizant of potential for innovations.
2. The potential innovators must be confident that the product after innovation would be better than the original product.
3. The potential innovators must be willing to assume the risks associated with the innovation.
4. The potential innovator must be willing to undertake the cost of innovations either through borrowing or past savings.
5. The required materials must be accessible at the appropriate time and the appropriate place.

Problems may stem from any of the above conditions. To begin with, for the potential innovators to be cognizant of the possibilities of change they should have connections with media or change agents. A variety

GLOBAL INSIGHT CASE 9.1

THE ASIAN "MIRACLE"

Per capita gross national product (GNP) in East Asia grew, on average, by over 5 percent per year between 1965 and 1990. During the same period, per capita GNP in the industrialized countries that make up the Organization for Economic Cooperation and Development (OECD) grew by less than 2.5 percent per year. What explains this relatively rapid growth in East Asia? A recent World Bank book argues that a major part of the explanation is that the average OECD member was much more technologically advanced than the average East Asian country in 1965. By adopting and adapting techniques from the industrial countries, the East Asian countries were able to increase both productivity levels and per capita GNP at a rapid pace.

This is undoubtedly true. But other countries that were poor in 1965 did not grow as fast as the successful East Asian nations. Why did East Asia experience faster growth? One key factor is almost certainly the macroeconomic nvironment: inflation and budget deficits were kept relatively low, and national currencies were kept from becoming overvalued. Macroeconomic policies encouraged, or at least did not discourage, high saving and investment rates as well as strong export growth. Governments also emphasized education. The focus was primarily on the quality of basic education, rather than on higher education. As a result of these policies, East Asian countries accumulated substantial physical and human capital, which spurred relatively rapid growth in GNP per capita.

The impact of other, more interventionist policies on growth in several East Asian countries remains a source of controversy. Some government interventions in the market may have improved economic performance, particularly when they were not excessively distortionary, were administered competently, were aimed at particular market imperfections, and were adapted to meet changing circumstances.

The Asian countries are expected to account for increasing shares of world income and trade. By 2000 it is likely that Asia will have surpassed North America and Europe as the world's largest economic zone. As its share of world income rises, so will its share of world trade - the Asian share of U.S. trade is projected to rise to 40 percent by the end of the decade.

Source: U.S. Government Printing Office, *Economic Report of the President*, (Washington, D.C: U.S. Government Printing Office, February 1994), 232.

of channels exist and their efficiency hinges upon their requirements for literacy or further education, on the degree to which extension agents are available to people, and the size of innovation effort required. Given that the environment in developing nations is not conducive to any of the above conditions, it is no wonder that they severely lag behind the advanced nations in terms of technological progress.

Technology Imitation

Today in virtually all developing nations, handicraft production coexists alongside modern factories attesting to the intrasectoral dualism in these nations. One may ask why does imitation not enhance the technology of all firms to the level of the most modern technology? Where it is feasible, it must cost less than undertaking invention and innovation. The following answers might be given to this question:

a. Legal restrictions existing in the developing nations.
b. The existence of discrepancies between managerial incentives and cost minimization objectives.
c. Noneconomic variables, such as political considerations.
d. The lack of competition. In a competitive environment, when a leading firm attempts to lower prices, enhances its market share, and improves output and production efficiency, the industry as whole is left with no choice but to follow suit. In other words, it either has to engage in imitation and innovation, or it has to perish. However, when the economic environment is not conducive to competition and the market entry is restricted by factors such as weight of product, inadequate transportation, initial capital requirements, or a class structure that discriminates against potential entrants, imitation dwindles.

As the above list suggests, the barrier to imitation may be rooted in the social structure or in capital formation in the developing nation rather than in technological innovation.

Japan provides the classic example of a nation that followed a development policy that was initially aided by imitation of foreign technology. Before World War II, the nation was ridiculed for its copying, even duplicating, of equipment and machinery whose utilization was not completely comprehended. Over time, however, Japanese imitation began to proceed with an eye on adaptation. They became masters in borrowing technology from advanced nations and adapting it to their national requirements. Such an approach eventually enabled them to gain an independent capacity to innovate in fields such as electronics, photography, and automobiles.

SUMMARY

1. Technology can be defined as the method or technique for converting inputs to outputs in accomplishing a specific task.
2. **Technological progress** means an increase in **technical efficiency**, which can be defined in either of the following two ways:
   a. Producing more output with the same inputs.
   b. Producing the same quantity of output with fewer inputs.
3. Changes in technical efficiency stem from invention and innovation. **Invention** is the discovery of a technique. **Innovation** means the practical application of an invention to production for a market.
4. **Autonomous technological progress** results from scientific curiosity. The inventor makes discoveries for the sheer pleasure of it. **Induced technological progress** results from the desire for profit in the private sector.
5. The interaction of technology and culture produces variables that affect and are affected by the introduction of a new technology. These variables include (a) the economic systems, (b) the value systems, (c) the religious systems, (d) the political systems, (e) the social organization systems, and (f) educational systems.
6. Technological progress can be defined in two ways: (1) producing more output with the same amount of inputs; or (2) producing the same quantity of output with fewer inputs. Given the first definition, graphically, technological progress can be portrayed by the shift of an isoquant. Given the second definition, technological progress can be portrayed by the **production possibilities frontier (PPF),** or curve, also known as the transformation curve.
7. There are three basic classifications of technological progress: neutral, capital-using, and labor-using.
8. Using the first definition of technological progress, technological progress can be portrayed by the inward shifting of the isoquant. Using the second definition of technological progress, technological progress can be portrayed by the outward shifting of the PPF.
9. The ingredient of technological progress is composed of elasticity of substitution, scale of production,

new products and demonstration effect, social relations of production, and speed of change.
10. The elasticity of substitution determines the relative responsiveness of the K/L ratio to a change in relative factor prices (i/w), where i is the interest rate and w is the wage rate. Mathematically, the elasticity of substitution is measured by the following formula:

$$\sigma = -[\frac{\Delta(K/L)}{K/L} \div \frac{\Delta(r/w)}{r/w}]$$

11. Technological improvement during the last two centuries has been marked by the following two features:
    a. Enhanced volumes of production, that is, an increase in the scale of output.
    b. Economies of mass production or economies of scale, that is, a decrease in a firm's long-run average costs as the size of its plant increases.
12. Economically, a consumer's decision to purchase a new product is not formed in a vacuum. An important factor that affects such a decision is the "**demonstration effect.**"
13. As technological improvement progresses, the institutional framework for production and distribution goes through the following changes:
    a. Increases in the numbers and proportions of skilled workers brought about by technological improvement imply that the ownership of capital, in particular human capital, is extended. This leads to a significant shift in the relations between capital and labor.
    b. State-sponsored activities assume a greater role at the expense of private activities.
    c. More inclusive provision of social benefits, including unemployment insurance, alleviate the greater threat of unemployment.
    d. More emphasis is placed on managerial performance as the number of people with managerial tasks increases.
    e. Agriculture mergers may increase the number of landless peasants, while agriculture relinquishes its plantation ownership and aptitude.
14. Because technological progress stems from innovation, the question to ask is what are determinants of innovation? In answering this question, we must realize that for new knowledge to be put into practice, the following conditions must be satisfied:
    a. The potential innovators must be cognizant of potential for innovations.
    b. The potential innovators must be confident that the product after innovation would be better than the original product.
    c. The potential innovators must be willing to assume the risks associated with the innovation.
    d. The potential innovators must be willing to undertake the cost of innovations either through borrowing or past savings.
    e. The required materials must be accessible at the appropriate time and appropriate place.
15. Why does imitation not enhance the technology of all firms to the level of the most modern technology? The following answers might be given to this question:
    a. Legal restrictions existing in the developing nations.
    b. The existence of discrepancies between managerial incentives and cost minimization objectives.
    c. Noneconomic variables, such as political considerations.
    d. The lack of competition.

QUESTIONS

1. Define the concept of technology and answer the following questions:
    a. What is meant by technical efficiency?
    b. What are the major elements that give rise to technological progress?
    c. What are the links between technological progress and capital accumulation? Discuss.
2. What are the major cultural variables that affect and are affected by technology? What are the

implications of such relationships for economic development? Discuss.
3. Elaborate on the concept of technological progress by answering the following questions:
    a. What are different types of technological progress? Explain.
    b. What type of technological progress is more appropriate for a developing nation? Discuss.
4. Do you think that technological progress results in a decrease in demand for factors of production? Explain.
5. How is the concept of the elasticity of factor substitution related to the fixity or flexibility of factor substitution? What generalization can be made about the elasticity of factor substitution in developing nations as compared to advanced nations? Discuss.
6. Does technological progress necessarily imply a higher level of output? Explain.

NOTES

1. Bela Gold, "Changing Perspectives on Size, Scale, and Returns: An Interpretive Survey," *Journal of Economic Literature* 19 (March 1981): 5-33.
2. "Country Profile: United States,"http://www.fisonline.com/top_b1.htm.
3. Charles P. Kindleberger, *Economic Development* (New York: McGraw-Hill, 1958); James B. Quinn, "Scientific and Technical Strategy of the National and Major Enterprise Level," *The Role of Science and Technology in Economic Development* (Paris: UNESCO, 1970), chap. 4.
4. Organization for Economic Cooperation and Development, *Gaps in Technology, General Report* (Paris: Organization for Economic Cooperation and Development, 1968), p. 41.
5. Thomas Neil Gladwin, "Technology and Material Culture," in Vern Terpstra and Kenneth David, eds., *The Cultural Environment of International Business* (Cincinnati, OH: South-Western, 1978), chap. 6.
6. Edwin Mansfield, *The Economics of Technological Change*, pp. 4-5.
7. Edward Denison, *Trends in American Economic Growth: 1929-1982* (Washington, D.C.: Brookings Institution, 1985), p. 30.
8. D. P. Mukergi, "Mahatma Gandhi's Views on Machines and Technology," *International Science Bulletin*, vol. 6, no. 3 (1954), p. 441.
9. R. Nurkse, *Problems of Capital Formation in Underdeveloped Countries*, Oxford University Press, New York, 1967, pp. 58-59 (first published in 1953).

SUGGESTED READINGS

Arrow, Kenneth, "The Economic Implications of Learning by Doing," *Review of Economic Studies* 29 (June 1962): 154-94.
Delasanta, David W., and Robert P. Morgan. "The Choice of Sugar Cane Processing Technique for Pakistan." *World Development* (September 1980): 725-739.
Dosi, Giovani, Christopher Freeman, Richard Nelson, Gerald Silberberg, and Luc Soete, eds. Technological Change and Economic Theory. London: Pinter, 1988.
Eckaus, Richard. *Appropriate Technologies for Developing Countries*. Washington, D.C.: National Academy of Sciences, 1978.
Franman, Martin. *Technology and Economic Development*. Boulder, Colo: Westview, 1986.
Griliches, Zvi. "Hybrid Corn: An Exploration in the Economics of Technological Change." *Econometrica*, vol. 25, no. 4, October 1957, pp. 501-52.
_____. "Productivity, R & D, and the Data Constraint." *American Economic Review* 44 (March 1994): 1-23.
Kennedy, C. and A. P. Thirlwall, "Technological Progress: A Survey." *Economic Journal* (March 1972).
Landes, David S. *The Unbound Prometheus: Technological Change and Industrialization in Western Europe from 1750 to the Present*. London: Cambridge University Press, 1969.
Leibenstein, Harvey. *X-Efficiency Theory and Economic Development*. New York: Oxford University Press, 1978.
Mansfield, Edwin. *The Economics of Technological Change*. New York: W. W. Norton & Company, Inc., 1968.
Rogers, E.M., and F. F. Shoemaker. *Communication of Innovations*. Second ed. New York: Free Press, 1971.

Schumacher, E. F. *Small is Beautiful: Economics as if People Mattered.* New York: Harper & Row, 1973.
Schumpeter, J. A. *The Theory of Economic Development.* New York: Oxford University Press, 1961.
Sen, A. K. *Choice of Techniques: An Aspect of the Theory of Planned Economic Development.* Third ed. New York: A. M. Kelley, Publisher, 1968.
_____. ed. *Growth of Economics.* Harmondsworth, England: Penguin, 1970.
Stewart, Frances. *Technology and Underdevelopment.* Second ed. Macmillian, London, 1978.
Thirlwall, A. P. *Growth and Development with Special Reference to Developing Countries.* New York: Wiley, 1977.

PART III

DOMESTIC RESOURCE POLICIES AND DEVELOPMENT STRATEGIES

CHAPTER 10

HUMAN RESOURCE DEVELOPMENT AND CAPITAL FORMATION

Having realized the significance of technology in the process of economic development in Chapter 9, we realize that two of the main factors that contribute to economic development and technological progress are investment in human capital, and capital formation. The purpose of this chapter is to examine these issues and elaborate on their significance to the process of economic development. In achieving this objective, first we explain human resource development, and then we discuss capital formation.

HUMAN RESOURCE DEVELOPMENT

Human resource development includes expenditures on training, education, research, and health. Education raises individuals' productivity by allowing them to fulfill and apply their abilities and talents, thereby accelerating the process of economic development. Germany and Japan, two countries that were devastated by World War II, provide us with examples of nations that experienced rapid economic growth after the war. Although much of the physical capital in these nations was depleted as a result of the war, their rapid economic growth was due to education, skills, training, health, and the fact that the motivation and discipline of their labor force remained relatively intact. To underline the significance of education, Simon Kuznets argues that the major asset of a nation is not its physical capital but its human capital. As he put it, human capital is :

> the body of knowledge amassed from tested findings and discoveries of empirical science, and the capacity and training of its population to use this knowledge effectively.[1]

Kuznets' view is shared by most economists. For example, the late professor Frederick Harbison of Princeton University writes:

> Human resources...constitute the ultimate basis for the wealth of nations. Capital and natural resources are passive factors of production; human beings are the active agents who accumulate capital, exploit natural resources, build social, economic and political organizations, and carry forward national development. Clearly, a country which is unable to develop the skills and knowledge of its people and to utilize them effectively in the national economy will be unable to develop anything else.[2]

Not only does education raises productivity, improve health and nutrition, and reduce family size, it also gives rise to higher income equality in developing nations. Poor nutrition and health reduce labor productivity.

Having realized the significance of education to economic development, there is disagreement among economists who analyze the relative rates of return on investment to primary education and secondary education in developing nations. Setting aside such a disagreement, one thing is clear, that is, education affects income distribution and calls on government to devise the right strategies in order to alleviate income inequality. This happens because the students who go to schools receive high rates of return to the amount invested in their education by their parents or relatives. Yet, poor families who might like to borrow for more education commonly are not able to do so. A simple solution is for government to decrease the direct cost of education by making public school, especially basic primary education, accessible and free. Promoting primary education decreases income inequality and positively affects equality of opportunity. As primary schooling extends, children in agrarian regions, the poorest urban children, and girls will all have more opportunity of attending school. In general, public expenditures on primary education redistribute income toward the poor, who have larger families and almost no access to private school. Public spending on secondary and higher education, on the other hand, redistribute income to the rich, because poor children do not have much opportunity to benefit from such education. The problem becomes even more clear in light of the fact that public expenditures per student for higher education in developing nations are about ten times higher than for primary education. This of course does not mean that secondary and higher education should be ignored. A developing nation may want to charge its richer citizens for the full cost of secondary and higher education, and continue to support the secondary and higher education of poor people to the extent that is warranted by its educational requirement.

Although primary education in developing nations remains an important element of development, one of the problems of some developing nations is the existence of high numbers of educated unemployed individuals in the fields of humanities and social sciences, while at the same time there are serious shortages of technical and managerial expertise in these nations. In order to resolve such shortages a developing nation may employ the following two strategies:

1. **Utilizing More on-the-Job Training.** On-the-job training serves to balance demand for, and supply of, training. Additionally, training at short-term vocational or technical schools help individuals improve their skills without appreciably disrupting the production process.
2. **Using Input-Output Relationships.** To determine future demand for various types of high-level personnel, a developing nation may use the fixed input-output planning method. In this approach, past information is used to devise a relationship between
specialized human inputs and outputs. First, the future level and composition of output is estimated. Second, given the assumed input-output relationship, the demand for persons to fill the expected jobs is determined. Given the duration of training needed for highly skilled jobs, the production of highly trained individuals to fill them is nearly fixed in the short run. Nevertheless, plans could be designed for, say, 5 years, 10 years, and 20 years hence, with educational programs to satisfy the requirements of skilled workers. These programs would comprise training teachers by the time required. However, the fixed input-output method does not recognize the possibility of substituting one skill for another or adapting output to the skills array. More specifically, the plan does not make any provision for the following possibilities:

   a. If the supply of teachers is too costly or inappropriate, then planners could hire teachers from other nations or send students abroad.

GLOBAL INSIGHTS CASE 10.1

THE RELATIONSHIP BETWEEN POVERTY, EDUCATION AND EARNINGS

Our core democratic values affirm that each individual should have the opportunity to reach his or her full potential, regardless of race or the income or educational attainment of his or her parents. Yet numerous studies confirm that our Nation today is far from reaching this ideal. That shortfall imposes great costs both on individual Americans and on the country as a whole.

A recent study by a group of economists chaired by a Nobel laureate and commissioned by the Children's Defense Fund examined the effects of childhood poverty on an individual's future living standards. The study concluded that childhood poverty itself, as distinct from such factors as family structure, race, and parental education, has a significant adverse effect on both the educational attainment and the future wages of the Nation's poor children. The study found that children who experience poverty between the ages of 6 and 15 years are two to three times more likely than those who are never poor to become high school dropouts. Using years of schooling as a predictor of future hourly wages, the study concluded that just one year of poverty for the 14.6 million children and their families in poverty in 1992 costs the economy somewhere between $36 billion and $177 billion in reduced future productivity and employment.

Significantly, one of the studies that the group examined concluded that each $1 reduction in monthly assistance through the aid to families with dependent children, program may reduce future output by between $0.92 and $1.51 (in present value terms) solely by reducing the educational attainment and future productivity of the children who are AFDC's beneficiaries.

Source: U.S. Government Printing Office, *Economic Report of the President* (Washington D.C.: U.S. Government Printing Office, 19995), 31, Box 1-3. Reprinted.

- **b.** One type of skill may be substituted for another. For example, a physician assistant could be substituted for a medical doctor. As another example, technicians may be substituted for engineers.
- **c.** It is not necessarily true that the battery of skills created should adapt to the desired output composition. Maybe the relationship can be reserved, in particular in an economy receptive to international trade and specialization. For example, if a nation has an abundance of rug weavers and a scarcity of metal engineers, it may be less costly, especially in the short run, to export rugs and import metal. Other alternatives would be to employ foreign metal engineers or offer economic incentives to goad foreign firms to engage in the domestic production of metal.

Another problem of the educational system in most developing nations is that boys are sent to school far more often than girls. In 66 out of 108 nations, female enrollment in primary and secondary education is lower than that of males by at least 10 percentage points. Yet, a number of studies indicate that educating girls has a high payoff in improving nutrition, reducing fertility and child mortality, and increasing labor force productivity.

Major Educational Policy Options

Because the educational system in a nation reflects its economic and social organization, any policy devised to improve education must simultaneously consider both internal and external forces that affect the educational system.

External Educational Policies. These policies concentrate on reforming the economic and social cues and impulses *outside* the educational structure that determine the aggregate private demand for education and consequently the political reaction in terms of supplying public schools. Such policies include the following strategies:

1. **Remedying Major Economic Imbalances, Incentives, and Distortions.** These policies call on:
   a. Elimination of income and wage differentials between the modern sector and the traditional sector.
   b. Eliminating social and political constraints on upward mobility.

   These policies have the multiple positive impact of enhancing job opportunities, decelerating the rate of rural-urban migration, and easing development related reformation of educational systems.

2. **Reforming Job Rationing by Educational Certification.** In many developing nations entry to office jobs is contingent upon official certification. This is especially true in the public sector, where the salaries of college and secondary graduates are artificially inflated and bear little relation to efficiency. In such cases, educational requirements serve simply to ration access to these inflated salaries. To break this pattern, policies are needed that will stimulate or make public and private employers set realistic job requirements. The key to this approach would be the elimination of school certificates for many jobs, in particular in the public sector which seems to set the example for the private sector. For example, requiring a high school diploma for a file clerk in a developing nation seems to be unnecessary, when the job could be done with a capable person who does not hold such a certification.

3. **Controlling the Brain Drain.** As we mentioned in Chapter 7, from a developing nation's standpoint the problem of brain drain is apparent, that is, development at home is preferable to sending workers abroad and living on their remittances. Some economists argue that it seems both morally and economically defensible to either temporarily confine the exodus of indigenous professionals abroad in the national interest, or better, to tax foreign earnings of professional migrants and reinvest those proceeds in development programs of the nation. Such a tax on foreign earnings would function as a financial disincentive to international immigration. Its implementation, however, would demand the cooperation and assistance of the government of the nations who receive these professional migrants in developing nations. Given such arguments, as we mentioned in Chapter 7, some nations have restricted immigration, and some other nations have suggested doing so.

Internal Educational Policies. These policies concentrate on reforming the *internal* efficiency and equity of educational systems by making appropriate changes in course content, systems of public versus private financing, procedures of selection and promotion, and approaches for professional certification by the level of education. Such policies include the following strategies:

1. **Educational Budgets.** To facilitate the generation of rural and urban employment opportunities, the public educational budgets should grow at a slower rate than in the past, where politically plausible. Additionally, a larger percentage share of educational budgets must be set aside for the development of elementary education as compared to secondary and higher education. This is

because elementary education advances self-education and rural work-related learning experiences in later life.

GLOBAL INSIGHTS CASE 10.2

EDUCATION AND GENDER DISCRIMINATION IN PAKISTAN

Pakistan provides us with the prime example of a developing nation in which females suffer from a relatively higher educational deprivation than males. Like many other developing nations, such as Bangladesh, Jordan, Nepal, South Korea and Syria, in Pakistan boys are most favored by their parents. Gender discrimination impacts the poorest Pakistani females the most and does not appear to affect the daughters of urban elite to a noticeable degree. As a result, poor females do not have the political power to resolve their problems. According to a 1981 census, only 16% of women are literate as compared to 26% of population. The available data show that only 1.7% of the GNP is set aside for education. What is even worse is that this small amount is very inequitable, providing 30 times more money per pupil for higher education in comparison to primary education. Additionally, the allocation of primary educational expenditures are very unequal, distributing the lion's percentage of funds to schools that more often train the few pupils who will eventually pursue higher education.

Like many other developing nations, poverty in Pakistan is concentrated in rural areas, which encompasses over two-thirds of Pakistan's population which suffers from high illiteracy rates, especially for girls. Today, only 7.3% of rural females in Pakistan are literate as compared to 55.3% males.

Given that returns are usually highest in the earliest years of schooling, and given that girls receive less education than boys it seems rational to put more emphasis on enhancing years of schooling for girls. Unfortunately, however, more than two thirds of primary school dropouts in this country are girls. This has contributed to the scarcity of female teachers in many areas of the country where it is considered inappropriate for male teachers to teach female students.

In additional to the scarcity of female teachers in Pakistan, the nation suffers from the shortages of female agricultural extension workers. Although women are often involved in agricultural activities almost all extension agents are male, who due to traditional values usually refuse to train women. This condition calls on training female agents. But, even if the government is willing to resolve this issue, literate females capable of assuming the role are hard to come by.

Given the existing conditions for females in Pakistan, it is no wonder that a women's rights movement has been thriving in Pakistan. Such a climate has given rise to an active debate on whether Islamic fundamentalists' view on women represents a "biased" interpretation of Islamic holy book, the Koran.

Source: Stephen C., Smith, *Economic Case Studies in Economic Development* (New York: Longman, 1994):80-85.

> # GLOBAL INSIGHTS CASE 10.3
>
> ## HOW EDUCATING FOREIGN STUDENTS PROMOTES MARKETS AND DEMOCRACY
>
> The United States has a clear comparative advantage in higher education. Many foreign students, especially from developing countries, come to America to study for college and graduate degrees. Their spending on tuition counts as U.S. exports of educational services and rivals U.S. exports of corn or wheat, our two largest agricultural exports. When these students return home, they take with them an appreciation of the benefits of an open society and an open economic system. The U.S. system of higher education has done much to spread our values throughout the world, including our belief in democracy and the market system.
>
> This phenomenon is particularly evident with respect to Latin America. Many Latin Americans have come to the United States to study for graduate degrees in economics or public policy, and many have entered government service on returning home. The last two presidents of Mexico and the finance ministers of Argentina, Brazil, Chile, and Mexico, for example, all received doctorates in economics from U.S. universities. Partly because of their leadership, Latin America has embraced market-oriented economic policies.
>
> Source: U.S. Government Printing Office, *Economic Report of the President* (Washington D.C.: U.S. Government Printing Office, 1997), 260, Box 7-2. Reprinted.

2. **Quotas.** Under the current systems, implicit quotas by income levels usually define which student goes through the educational system. To break this pattern, to ensure that the percentage of low-income students at secondary and higher educational levels reflects their proportion in the overall population, some form of quota may be needed. The nature of the quota system should clearly depend on the nation's economic and political environment.

3. **Subsidies.** In order to eliminate distortions in aggregate private demand for education, subsidies for the higher levels of education must be decreased. Strategies should be devised that cause the beneficiaries of education, but not the student's family or society as a whole, to assume a larger percentage of educational costs as the student advances through the educational system. This can be achieved directly by means of loan repayments, or by providing service to rural areas. In the meantime, low-income classes must be accorded with adequate subsidies to allow them to endure the considerable private costs of education.

4. **Elementary School Curriculum in Relation to Rural Needs.** To enhance the efficiency of farm workers, elementary school curriculum and informal educational programs for adults and school dropouts must be directed more toward the occupational needs of the rural population, including nonfarm artisan and entrepreneurial activities, small-farm agriculture, and public and commercial services. Such a strategy, however, will not be effective in winning popular support unless it is accompanied by rural economic opportunities to allow individuals in these occupations to utilize

their vocational knowledge and training. In the absence of such incentives, such formal and informal educational schemes will be viewed with skepticism by the public.

CAPITAL FORMATION

Most developing nations suffer from the shortage of capital. This view was echoed by U.N. economists in the late 1950s, who considered capital shortages to be the major element that hinders the process of economic development in the Third World. By capital they meant machinery, equipment, tools, plants, inventory stock, and so on, but not human capital. Given this condition, where can a developing nation acquire its needed capital? To answer this question, consider an open economy, that is, an economy that engages in international trade, has no government sector. Given this assumption, we proceed with a presentation of a simple Keynesian model. Recall from introductory economics courses that in such model, national income (NI) is equal to consumption expenditure (C) plus desired or planned saving (S):*

$$NI = C + S. \tag{10-1}$$

Aggregate expenditure (AE) is equal to C plus desired or planned investment (I), plus exports (X), minus imports (M):

$$AE = C + I + (X - M) \tag{10-2}$$

Because at equilibrium NI = AE, we can set equations 10-1 and 10-2 equal to each other to get the following equation:

$$C + S = C + I + (X - M) \tag{10-3}$$

It follows from this that

$$I = S + (M - X) \tag{10-4}$$

According to equation 10-3, a nation's investment opportunities are defined by its potential for domestic saving (S) plus any net capital inflows from abroad, M ⟩ X. Of course, the only way for imports to be greater than exports is for the country to borrow abroad. In other words, M ⟩ X is a capital inflow, which must be generated as the savings of foreigners. That capital, which eventually comes from the savings of foreigners, may be generated in the following ways:

1. Long-term international loans, as from the World Bank.
2. Medium- or short-term loans from the International Monetary Fund (IMF).
3. Medium- or short-term loans from commercial banks.
4. Official development assistance (foreign aid) from foreign nations.
5. Foreign private investment.

The shorter-term borrowing, which came to involve the debt crisis in the 1980s, will be discussed in Chapter 13, and foreign direct investment and foreign aid in Part V. In this chapter we concentrate on the

---

*Although saving takes place in both the business and household sectors, for simplicity we assume that all savings are personal.

domestic savings.

Domestic savings can come from the following two sources:

1. Private and voluntary, which can be loaned to government or businesses by financial institutions.
2. Government savings, that is, the excess of taxes over government expenditures.

The components of government savings— taxation and government expenditures— will be studied in detail in Chapter 10. The private and voluntary savings will be discussed in the rest of this chapter.

Household savings, including the savings of small family businesses accounts for about 60% of domestic savings. Even in the poorest developing nations, some household savings can be important for development in spite of the low income levels. As our discussion of the Vicious Circle of Poverty in Chapter 4 indicated, low rates of savings should not be ascribed to poverty, that is, a low level of income. Rather, they stem from social, political and other institutional factors. In many poor developing nations, the poorest people manage to set aside a certain amount of their income for religious purposes, or for the acquisition of opium, cocoa leaves, alcoholic beverages, or other substances. Thus, it is evident that the poor have some capacity to save. What seems to be the source of the problem is the lack of incentives to save. If the social structure does not provide the poor with a reasonable chance for economic progress, then savings may not be directed to productive investment. For instance, a peasant may not be induced to save if the land belongs to the landlord and the farmer knows that with improved technology the rent increases or the landlord's share of the harvest rises. Even if the farmer owned the land, the higher output may lead to lower prices, and with an inelastic demand for agricultural products, his/her total revenue would decrease. In this situation, spending money for personal pleasure is a rational behavior.

Another factor that discourages saving in developing nations is the relatively high level of inflation in these nations as compared to developed nations. A normal response to inflation is to avoid its impacts by purchasing and hoarding tangible goods, by buying land or buildings, or by any other type of purchase that acts as a hedge against increasing prices. Similarly, government taxation policies may discourage savings. This happens because the interest on an account is easy to detect and tax. Additionally, the accounts themselves could be subject to a wealth tax. As a result, households might avoid saving in bank accounts as excessively risky.

Thus, what seems to be needed is a social structure that is conducive to the mobilization of these potential savings. Governments have the ability to attack inflation, to restore incentives to save, and to undertake pro-saving campaigns. A major way in which a government can help to stimulate saving is by assisting banks to find a solution to the high cost of managing small accounts. Incentives to save can stem from new institutions such as credit cooperatives, conceivably building on traditional systems such as the *enusu* credit societies of Ghana, the *hui* in China, and many others, in which monies are collected by a small group of people and lent to one of them at a time, in turn. Governments can also blend insurance and savings plans and create pension funds and post-office savings accounts to include small depositors. In many nations, banks have an urban bias.[3] To overcome this problem, governments can promote branch banking outside main metropolitan areas. Although the response to such a promotion is not likely to be overwhelming, it is a step in the right direction.

SUMMARY

1. Human resource development includes expenditures on training, education, research, and health.
2. Having realized the significance of education to economic development, there is disagreement among economists who analyze the relative rates of return to investment in primary education and secondary

education in developing nations. Setting aside such a disagreement, one thing is clear, that is, education affects income distribution and calls on government to devise the right strategies in order to alleviate income inequality.

3. One of the problems of some developing nations is the existence of high numbers of educated unemployed individuals in the fields of humanities and social sciences, while at the same time there are serious shortages of technical and managerial expertise in these nations.

4. In order to resolve shortages of technical and managerial expertise, a developing nation may employ the following two strategies:
   a. Utilizing More on-the-job Training.
   b. Using Input-Output Relationships.

5. Because the educational system in a nation reflects its economic and social organization, any policy devised to improve education must simultaneously consider both internal and external forces that affect the educational system.

6. External educational policies concentrate on reforming the economic and social cues and impulses *outside* the educational structure that determine the aggregate private demand for education and consequently the political reaction in terms of supplying public schools. Such policies include the following strategies:
   a. Remedying major economic imbalances, incentives, and distortions.
   b. Reforming job rationing by educational certification.
   c. Controlling the brain drain.

7. Internal Educational Policies. These policies concentrate on reforming the *internal* efficiency and equity of educational systems by making appropriate changes in course content, systems of public versus private financing, procedures of selection and promotion, and approaches for professional certification by the level of education. Such policies include the following strategies:
   a. Educational budgets.
   b. Quotas.
   c. Subsidies.
   d. Elementary school curriculum in relation to rural needs.

8. Most developing nations suffer from the shortage of capital. This view was echoed by U.N. economists in the late 1950s, who considered capital shortages to be the major element that hinders the process of economic development in the Third World.

9. The capital that eventually comes from the savings of foreigners may be generated in the following ways:
   a. Long-term international loans, as from the World Bank..
   b. Medium -or short-term loans from the International Monetary Fund (IMF).
   c. Medium- or short-term loans from commercial banks.
   d. Official development assistance (foreign aid) from foreign nations.
   e. Foreign private investment.

10. Domestic savings can come from the following two sources:
    a. Private and voluntary, which can be loaned to government or businesses by financial institutions.
    b. Government saving, that is, the excess of taxes over government expenditures.

11. What seems to be needed in developing nations is a social structure that is conducive to the mobilization of potential savings. Governments have the ability to attack inflation, to restore incentives to save, and to undertake pro-saving campaigns.

QUESTIONS

1. Elaborate on human resource development by answering the following questions:
   a. What expenditure items are included in human resource development?
   b. Between primary education and secondary education which one leads to a relatively higher rate of return? Discuss.
   c. What is the main economic variable that is affected by education.
2. Elaborate on unemployment problems in developing nations, by answering the following questions:
   a. What are the problems associated with the supply of skills needed in developing nations?
   b. What two strategies can a developing nation devise in order to resolve the supply problem?
3. What are the differences between formal and informal educational policies? Explain.
4. What are the main ingredients of formal educational policies? Explain.
5. What are the main ingredients of informal educational policies? Explain.
6. What are different ways by which a developing nation can generate foreign capital?
7. What are different sources of domestic savings?
8. Suppose that in a developing nation, NI= $100 billion, C = $ 70 billion, and I = $10 billion. Given this data answer the following questions:
   a. What is the level of domestic savings?
   b. What is the amount of aggregate expenditures at the equilibrium?
   c. What is the amount of net exports at the equilibrium?

NOTES

1. Simon S. Kuznets, "Toward a Theory of Economic Growth," in Robert Lekachman, ed., *National Policies for Economic Welfare at Home and Abroad* (Garden City N.Y.: Doubleday, 1955), p.39.
2. Frederick H. Harbison, *Human Resources as the Wealth of Nations* (New York: Oxford University Press, 1973), p.3.
3. World Bank, *World Development Report 1989* (New York: Oxford University Press, 1989), p.116.

SUGGESTED READINGS

Becker, Gary S. *Human Capital.* New York: Columbia University Press, 1975.
Behrman, Jere R. and Mark R. Rosenzweig. "Labor Force: Caveat Emptor: Cross-Country Data and Education and the Labor Force." *Journal of Development Economics* 44 (June 1994): 147-71.
Borjas, George J. "The Economics of Immigration." *Journal of Economic Literature* 32 (December 1994): 1667-1717.
Dasgupta, Partha. *An Inquiry into Well-Being and Destitution.* Oxford: Clarendon Press, 1993.
Goldsmith, Raymond. *Financial Structure and Development.* Bew Gaveb, Conn.: Yale University Press, 1969.
Hagen, Everett E. *On the Theory of Social Change: How Economic Growth Begins.* Homewoood, Ill.: Dorsey Press, 1962.
Hinchliffe, Keith. "Education, Individual Earnings, and Earnings Distribution." *Journal of Development Studies* 11 (January 1975): 152-56.
Knight, Hohn B. Richard H. Sabot, and D.C. Hovey. "Is the Rate of Return on Primary Schooling Really 26 Per Cent?" *Journal of African Economics* 1 (August 1992): 192-205.
McClellan, David C. *The Achieving Society.* Princeton: D. Van Nostrand, 1961.
Myrdal, Gunnar. *Asian Drama: An Inquiry into the Poverty of Nations.* Vol. 2. Middlesex, Eng: Penguin Book, 1968.
Nafziger, Wayne E. *Inequality in Africa: Political Elites, Proletariat, Peasants, and Poor.* Cambridge: Cambridge University Press, 1988.
Nair, Kusum. "Asian Drama-A Critique." *Economic Development and Cultural Change* 17 (July 1969): 435-56.
Nurkse, Rangar. *Problems of Capital Formation in Underdeveloped Countries.* New York: Oxford University Press,

1967 (first published in 1953).

Pascharopoulos, George, and Maureen Woodhall, *Education for Development: An Analysis of Investment Choices.* New York: Oxford University Press, 1985.

———. "Returns to Education: A Further International Update and Implications." *Journal of Human Resources* 22 (Fall 1985): 583-604.

———. "Return to Investment in Education: A Global Update." *World Development* 22 (September 1994): 1325-43.

Mikesell, Raymond, and James E. Zinser. "The Nature of the Savings Function in Developing Countries." *Journal of Economic Literature* (March 1973).Schultz, Theodore W. *The Economic Value of Education.* New York: Columbia University Press, 1963.

———. "Investment in Human Capital." *American Economic Review* 1 (March 1961): 1-17.

Shaw, Edward S. *Financial Deepening in Economic Development.* New York: Oxford University Press, 1973.

CHAPTER 11

MONETARY AND FISCAL POLICIES

As we already know from the introductory macroeconomics courses, two major policy tools that are employed in advanced nations to combat unemployment and inflation are monetary policies and fiscal polices. **Monetary policy** which is based on *monetarist theory* of economic activities is intentional implementation of the Federal Reserve's authority to stimulate expansions or contractions in the money supply in order to attain price stability, to help mitigate the swings of business cycles, and to bring countries' output and employment to the preferred level. Essentially, monetary policy operates on two major economic variables, aggregate supply of money in circulation and the level of interest rates. It is assumed that money supply, that is, currency plus commercial bank demand deposits, is positively correlated to the level of economic activity. Given this relation, an increase in money supply enables people to purchase more goods and services, leading to an expansion in economic activities. Thus, monetarists argue that by controlling the growth of money supply, the government of an advanced nation can control its economic activities and check inflation.

Fiscal policy which is based on *Keynesian economics* is deliberate taxation and spending decisions by the government to attain efficiency and growth. Efficiency is obtained by stabilizing the economy at full employment, hence mitigating the swings of business cycles. Growth is achieved by extending tax incentives to work, save and invest. Contemporaneous fiscal policy places considerable emphasis on achieving growth.

In practice, advanced nations do not usually achieve their macroeconomic objectives due to inadequate monetary and fiscal policies, incompatible objectives, or political constraints. Developing nations face even more constraints than advanced nations in employing such polies to attain their desired macroeconomic objectives. In this chapter, first we elaborate on the impediments to monetary policy in developing nations. Second, we discuss the obstacles to fiscal policy in developing nations, and finally, we explain policies that could be employed to revamp developing nations' fiscal systems.

IMPEDIMENTS TO MONETARY POLICIES IN DEVELOPING NATIONS

The impediments to monetary policies in developing nations could be classified into two major categories: Inadequacy of financial institutions in developing nations, and insensitivity of investment decisions to interest rate fluctuations in developing nations.

212   PART III/DOMESTIC RESOURCE POLICIES & DEVELOPMENT STRATEGIES

Inadequacy of Financial Institutions in Developing Nations

The ability of advanced nations to implement their monetary polices, by changing their money supplies or manipulating their interest rates, stems from the nature of their financial systems which have the following major characteristics:

1. Efficiently functioning money markets that are very organized, and economically independent.
2. Free flow of financial resources into and out of nationally regulated financial intermediaries, such as savings banks and commercial banks.
3. Interest rates that are determined by both market forces of supply and demand and administrative controls, resulting in consistency and relative uniformity of rates in various economic sectors and regions of the nations.

Given the above characteristics, financial intermediaries in advanced nations are able to channel savings into productive investment, contributing to long-term economic growth. In developing nations, however, financial institutions are poorly organized, externally dependent, and fragmented. More specifically, they have the following characteristics:

1. Many of the chief commercial banks in developing nations are subsidiaries of huge private banks in advanced nations. As a result, they are externally oriented, that is, they are concerned with profits in terms of their own currencies as opposed to domestic currencies of the nations in which they operate. As a result, they are not sensitive to their host government's monetary policies.
2. As open economies, many developing nations' currencies are pegged to the dollar or a basket of advanced countries' currencies. Given such fixed exchange rates and their high dependence on international transactions, they have to restrict the banking system's domestic expansion of money supply to some multiple of foreign exchange held by their central bank. As a result, the monetary authorities in developing nations are not always able to control the money supply due to the volatility of the foreign exchange rates.
3. The prevalence of **currency substitution**, that is, the use of foreign currency (e.g., U.S. dollars) as a medium of exchange instead of or along with the domestic currency (e.g., Mexican pesos in Mexico), in many developing nations makes the measurement and control of money supply very difficult.
4. Commercial banks in developing nations usually confine their loans to large and medium firms, such as modern manufacturing and mining. Small firms, such as artisans and farmers, usually acquire the needed funds from relatives or borrow at unreasonable interest rates from landlords and local money lenders. As a result, the banking systems in developing nations are less effective in manipulating interest rates as compared to the banking systems in advanced nations.
5. Because security markets are generally not well established in the developing nations, the central bank's activities in these markets are very limited. As a result, the power of the central bank to use the open market operation (i.e. buying and selling of securities) in order to control the money supply is very limited in these nations.
6. The percentage of the total money supply held in terms of demand deposits (checking accounts) is usually much lower in developing nations than in advanced nations. Because checks are not widely accepted in these nations, most transactions are performed in cash. As a result, commercial banks in developing nations control a smaller percentage of the money supply than in advanced nations.

Insensitivity of Investment Decisions to Interest Rate Fluctuations in Developing Nations

The second major impediment to monetary policy in the developing nations is the assumption of direct links between interest rate, investment, and output. More specifically, it is assumed that the lower interest rates lead to higher investments and expanded output. Although such an assumption is plausible for advanced nations, it is questionable in developing nations. This is because investment decisions are not usually very sensitive to interest rate fluctuations due to the following two factors:

1. Most loans are made outside the banking systems through money lenders, landlords and relatives.
2. Given the supply limitations (low elasticities of supply) in developing nations, a rise in investment demand may trigger inflation instead of boosting the real output. These limitations stem from poor management, bureaucratic particularities, the shortage of fundamental intermediate goods, a general lack of industrial-sector interdependence, and licensing restrictions. Whatever the causes, supply limitations imply that any rise in the demand for goods and services triggered by the growth of money supply will not be adjusted by rises in supply. Rather, the excess demand for investment goods will simply raise prices and fuel inflation. In some Latin American countries, such as Brazil and Argentina, such "structural" inflation has appeared as a chronic problem which has been worsened by the workers' demand to index wage rises to price increases.

In spite of the aforementioned impediments to monetary polices in developing nations, their financial systems continue to serve as an essential part of their overall economic system. For instance, in the presence of serious macroeconomic instability in Latin America, marked by high inflation, large budget deficits, and great trade deficits, monetary policies have served as significant tools in achieving overall stabilization.

In developing nations, financial systems satisfy different financial needs such as credit allocation, risk controls, insurance protection, mobilization of savings, and foreign exchange transactions. Nevertheless, until laws are passed to facilitate small entrepreneurs access to credit, or more government-assisted schemes are created to serve the needs of the noncorporate sector, the financial systems of most developing nations continue to be insensitive to the principles of cooperative national development.

REFORMING DEVELOPING NATIONS' FINANCIAL SYSTEMS

During the 1980s many developing nations were facing the so called "credit crunch." Such a phenomenon stemmed from the following factors:

1. The existence of high and extensive inflation.
2. The limitation of loans to a few big borrowers.
3. Growing budget deficit and negative interest rates.
4. Numerous lending restrictions imposed on financial institutions.
5. The imposition of mandatory ceilings on loanable funds at rates well below market-clearing levels. These ceilings often were imposed by developing nations' governments in order to finance their budget deficits by means of low interest bonds to private commercial banks. As the standard demand and supply analysis tells us, these restriction led to the shortages of loanable funds. To deal with such shortages, the banks had to resort to **rationing** the accessible credit. This phenomenon is referred to as **financial repression** since investment is restricted by the shortage of savings that results from artificial interest rates well below the market-clearing levels.

Given the above conditions, and assuming the absence of any corruption in the appropriation of the

GLOBAL INSIGHTS CASE 11.1

THE ASIAN GROWTH MODEL IN PERSPECTIVE

The Asian crisis caught most analysts by surprise. Some had warned of economic policy flaws in Asia, but few expected them even to produce a sharp slowdown, and no one predicted the profound crisis that actually materialized. Until recently many observers thought that the East Asian countries possessed the strong economic fundamentals and structural characteristics necessary for sustained long- run growth.

If structural weaknesses in the Asian economic system lie at the origin of the crisis, as many observers contend, a natural question is why the crisis occurred when it did. One hypothesis is that countries pass through natural stages of economic development, and that the Asian financial system, based on such practices as relationship banking is better suited to countries in the early stages. After all, financial intermediation by banks (even in the context of relationship banking) is a tremendous step to take for countries where, firms are used to financing all investment out of family savings or retained earnings. Relationship banking may mimic the close ties of extended family lending and thus ease the transition to a more arm's-length financial system. Moreover, as long as growth is rapid, high leverage (that is, a high ratio of debt to equity) is sustainable. But when growth slows, the financial system needs to adapt, and firms need to reduce their high leverage. Some slowdown in East Asia's growth was probably inevitable at some point, after the breakneck growth of the preceding decades, for the simple reason that economic convergence served as one of the driving forces of that growth. An economy that starts out behind the world leaders in income per capita can close part of the gap over time by growing more rapidly, provided of course such fundamentals as an outward orientation and investment in physical and human capital are in place. Convergence occurs for two reasons: the high rate of return on capital in labor-abundant economies, and the opportunity to emulate the most advanced technology and management practices of the leaders. But as the income gap closes, this impetus to growth diminishes. Economies encounter diminishing returns to capital, limits on labor supply growth from rural-to-urban migration, and infrastructure constraints. Also, as they draw closer to the technological frontier, they have less to learn from those who have gone before. Japan had achieved convergence by the 1980s, and Hong Kong and Singapore by the 1990s. Korea and the others still had some way to go–a very long way in some cases. Nevertheless, the basic principles remains that the smaller the remaining gap, the less the forces of convergence contribute to further growth.

One controversial view is that East Asia's growth from the beginning had more to do with the rapid accumulation of the factors of production-both labor, through increased labor force participation rates, and capital, due to very high investment rates-than with growth in the productivity of these factors. Some studies have found only modest underlying growth rates of multi-factor productivity (a measure of increased efficiency in the use of all factors, resulting in part from technological progress). If this view is correct, it means that East Asia's high growth rates were not sustainable in the long run, given that the rate of employment growth must at some point decline, and given an expected reduction in the rate of investment. However, even this view implies at worst gradual slowdown of growth, not the sudden and severe crisis that occurred.

The answer to why the East Asian crisis struck when it did is thus probably a complex one. As discussed below, it appears that, around mid-1997, the factors working to produce an eventual slowdown in growth interacted in unfortunate ways with existing financial sector weaknesses, excessive corporate leverage, financial fragility resulting fróm poorly designed capital market liberalization, foreign indebtedness, a slowdown in export markets, worsening terms of trade, and the development of overcapacity in many sectors. The crisis was the result.

Source: U.S. Government Printing Office, *Economic Report of the President*, (Washington, D.C.: U.S. Government Printing office, February 1999), Box 6-3, p.232.

available loanable funds, most commercial banks opt to disburse the accessible funds to a few large borrowers in order to minimize the administrative overhead as a percentage of the total costs of lending. Additionally, to cover the additional administrative costs and the added risks of smaller loans, they end up charging higher interest rates to small investors, as compared to the large borrowers. Thus, the net impact of government interference in the market for loanable funds is that fewer loans will be provided to small investors. As a result, small farmers and entrepreneurs are led to search for finance in the unorganized money market, where they end up paying above the market-clearing interest rates. To deal with this problem, one solution is to liberalize the financial system by letting the nominal interest rates increase to the market-clearing levels. These higher interest rates, in turn, dislodge the explicit interest subsidy given to large borrowers, and trigger more domestic savings and investment. As a result, some borrowers would be able to switch from unorganized to organized markets for loanable funds. To be sure, however, financial liberalization of the organized money system by itself does not necessarily cure the problems of the financial systems of developing nations. This is due to the fact that financial markets in developing nations are significantly different from those in advanced nations. As we explained before, market failures are likely to be more pervasive in developing nations as compared to advanced nations. Thus, financial liberalization in developing nations must be accompanied by a host of direct measures to ensure that small farmers and investors can access the needed credit. Additionally, it requires a careful supervision of the financial system to avert domination by the local elites. This calls on the governments of the developing nations to play crucial roles that include the following strategies:

1. Regulating financial systems.
2. Establishing new organizations to fill the gaps in the types of credit awarded by the private institutions, for example, to provide micro loans to small farmers and traders.
3. Enhancing consumer protection.
4. Assuring bank solvency.
5. Promoting fair competition.
6. Improving the allocation of financial resources.
7. Fostering macroeconomic stability.

In closing this section, it should be emphasized that like other aspects of economic development, the central problem of financial policy does not stem from the issue of government interventions versus free markets. Instead, the question is how should government and free markets work in harmony in order to satisfy the crucial needs of the masses of poor in developing nations.

OBSTACLES TO FISCAL POLICY IN DEVELOPING NATIONS

Having elaborated on the limitations of monetary policy in the developing nations, we now devote this section to an explanation of fiscal policy and discuss its limitations in developing nations. As we already know, the two major tools that are used in the implementation of fiscal policy are taxation and government expenditures. We continue our discussion of fiscal policy by providing a detailed explanation of these tools, and elaborate on their limitations in the developing nations.

Taxation

Taxes can be divided into two general groups: direct taxes and indirect taxes. **Direct taxes** are taxes that are composed of primary property, wealth, income, and inheritance taxes. Indirect taxes include items such as import, export, sales, purchase, and turnover, and value-added taxes.

GLOBAL INSIGHTS CASE 11.2

PERFORMANCE OF THE INTERNATIONAL FINANCIAL INSTITUTIONS IN THE 1990s

The turmoil in the international financial system in the second half of the 1990s indicated a shift in the nature of financial crises. The increase in the size of capital flows during the 1990s, documented earlier in this chapter, led to larger, more sudden crises when those flows reversed. These crises also appeared harder to contain, and the result often was large-scale IMF lending. The nature of these new crises focused attention on the role of the IFIs and raised key questions for policymakers. First and foremost, were the resources of the IFIs adequate to deal with these crises? Second, was the provision of assistance itself encouraging further crises? And finally, were countries becoming overly dependent on crisis financing provided by the IFIs?

From the mid-1980s through the mid-1990s, the IMF's resources available for crisis lending (also called its available liquidity) were adequate. However, over the 6-year period beginning in 1995, the average size of IMF stand-by arrangements (traditional lending programs), relative to the recipient country's IMF quota, more than tripled compared with the 6 years beginning in 1989. This is not surprising given the increase in gross capital flows over the 1990s. The new type of crisis was met with a larger official sector response. As a result, it became clear that, in the second half of the 1990s, IMF resources were shrinking relative to private financial flows. This was especially apparent during the Asian financial crisis, when IMF available liquidity fell to $56 billion in December 1997 from $83 billion the year before. By December 1998, available liquidity had dwindled to $54 billion.

Over the mid- to late 1990s, as crises developed and the size of IMF assistance programs increased, policymakers began to revisit the concern that the provision of official assistance was contributing to the development of new crises. The logic in support of such a proposition emphasizes the expectations of private investors. If investors come to expect that countries will automatically receive assistance in the event of a financial crisis, they are likely to exercise less prudence when making loans. Countries that are pursuing unsound policies may still get loans from private investors, since the investors believe that any future problems are likely to be resolved by the provision of funds by the IFIs. This is an example of moral hazard: an increase in risky behavior (in this case on the part of the borrowing countries and their lenders) when insurance or a guarantee is provided (in this case by the IMF). Thus the concern is that IFIs support can encourage risky activity on the part of private lenders and borrowing countries, which often ends badly in further rounds of crises.

The resolution of the crises of the late 1990s was also complicated by a shift in the composition of capital flows away from syndicated bank loans toward bond issuance. Such a shift protected the banking and payments systems of the industrial countries from the worst consequences of international financial crises. However, it also complicated the task of crisis resolution, because restructuring a country's debt now required dealing with a large number of bondholders spread around the world, rather than a small group of bank creditors. When a country's creditors are few in number, it may prove possible to coordinate an orderly restructuring that does little to interrupt economic activity (although this proved surprisingly difficult with bank loans to Latin American governments in the 1980s). But when the lenders are a large, diffuse group of bondholders, an orderly restructuring may be next to impossible. In fact, the switch from bank finance in the 1980s to bond finance in the 1990s in part may have reflected efforts by creditors to safeguard their positions by making such a restructuring more difficult for borrowers. In addition, the shift from bank to bond finance is part of a larger trend, seen not just internationally but in domestic capital markets as well, away from financial intermediaries to direct finance.

Source: U.S. Government Printing Office, *Economic Report of the President*, (Washington DC: U.S. Government Printing office, February 2002), pp. 284-285. Reprinted.

Today, direct taxes constitute roughly 30% of the total tax revenue for developing nations and make up about 16% of their GNPs. Indirect taxes are the major source of revenue in developing nations. In recent years, a number of developing nations have initiated the **value-added tax**. Devised by French economists, the value-added tax is a tax imposed on the value that is added at each stage of production of a given good. It is calculated as the difference between the sales of the firm and its purchases from other firms. The advantages of value-added tax are uniformity and simplicity, and the generation of buoyant revenues. These advantages stem from the fact that the tax paid by the producer at each stage of production is proportional to the value added to the product at that stage. Traditionally, taxes in developing nations are imposed to satisfy the following objectives:

1. **To Finance Public Expenditures.** Regardless of the prevailing political or economic ideology, a developing nation's survival and its social progress hinge upon the ability of its government to raise the needed revenue to finance its various nonrevenue- generating social programs such as transportation, health, education, sanitation, communications and similar services to maintain and promote its economic and social infrastructure. Moreover, most developing nations' governments are directly connected with the economic endeavors of their nations through possession and control of public firms and state trading institutions. Direct taxation provides a source of financing these types of operations that in many cases produce losses.
2. **To induce investment.** In many developing nations tax concessions and other incentives have been employed to induce private firms. Such concessions and incentives are often given to foreign private investors in order to encourage them to move their operations to the developing nation. Although such incentives are effective in encouraging the inflow of foreign funds to the developing nations, as we discuss in Chapter 16, the benefits of such strategies for the developing nations remain controversial.

The Taxation Potential. The ability of a nation to generate taxes usually depends on the following factors:

1. Administrative efficiency, integrity and honesty of the officials collecting taxes.
2. The level of per capita income.
3. The political, social and institutional framework, and the relative power of various groups. Unfortunately, in many developing nations, political ties to the ruling class, nepotism, and bribery, as opposed to rules and regulations, dominate the system, leading to gross injustices in tax collection practices.
4. The extent of income inequality.
5. The industrial composition of the economy and the significance of various types of economic endeavors. For example, the importance of the modern industrial sector, the significance of foreign trade, the degree of foreign participation in private firms, and the extent to which the agricultural sector is commercialized as compared to self-subsistence orientation.

Sources of Taxation. Having elaborated on the tax potential of a country, we now examine the following four major sources of direct and indirect taxes:

1. **Personal Income Taxes.** In general, personal income taxes generate less revenue in developing nations as compared to advanced nations. The income tax framework in advanced nations is **progressive,** that is, there is a positive relationship between the level of income and the percentage of taxes paid by an individual. In other words, people at the higher level of income are supposed to

pay a larger proportion of their income in taxes. In practice, however, the average level of taxation does not differ by much between middle- and upper-income groups. This happens because of the existence of tax loopholes that allow wealthy individuals avoid paying their fair share of taxes. A similar situation persists in the developing nations. Furthermore, a mixture of lower rates on smaller income, administrative deficiency in collecting taxes, bribery, nepotism, and various exemptions leaves only less than 3% of the developing nations' population to pay taxes, as compared to the level of 70% of the advanced nations' population who pay taxes. Given the existence of severe income inequalities in the developing nations', progressive taxes could provide the government with an appropriate tool for narrowing the income disparities. Unfortunately, however, most developing nations have not been effective enough in collecting taxes owed by the very wealthy individuals.

2. **Property Taxes**. In most developing nations, the ownership of property is heavily concentrated, further fueling income inequalities in these nations. Given this condition, property taxes could prove to be an efficient means both for inducing public revenues and alleviating severe income inequalities in developing nations. However, in most developing nations, where the large landowning and dominant classes control the political and economic scene, the share of property taxes as well as overall direct taxation has stayed about the same for the past quarter of a century. Clearly, the successful implementation of development plans requires the political will to derive revenue from the most appropriate bases in order to fund development activities.

3. **Corporate Income Taxes**. In general, corporate income taxes do not constitute a significant source of revenue for the developing nations. Taxes on corporate profits, of both foreign-owned and domestic firms, amount to only 3% of GDP in the developing nations as compared to 6% of GDP for the advanced nations. The major reasons that taxes account for such a small percentage of total revenue in developing nations are:

   a. **Tax Incentives and Concessions Offered**. In order to encourage industrialization, many developing nations offer a variety of tax incentives and concessions to manufacturing and commercial firms. Usually, the newly established firms are provided with tax holidays which last as long as 15 years. During such a period the firms enjoy specific tax write-offs, depreciation allowances and other measures to reduce their tax liability. Consequently, the ability of government to generate the potential tax revenue is significantly reduced.

   b. **Limited Corporate Activities**. Given that most developing nations are agricultural-based economies, they are far behind in terms of the number and the level of corporate activities operating on their soil as compared to advanced nations. As a result, their ability to generate corporate taxes is significantly lower than advanced nations.

   c. **The Use of Transfer Pricing by Multinational Corporations (MNCs)**. As we will explain in Chapter 11 transfer pricing refers to the pricing of goods and services between a parent company (a multinational corporation) and its subsidiaries or between subsidiaries themselves. Because tax rates are different between nations, a parent company exporting goods and services to a subsidiary in a high-tax nation (as compared with the taxes charged in the home country) could set a high transfer price. This has the effect of decreasing the profits of the foreign subsidiary, and leads to lower taxes in the host country. In the same manner, if the subsidiary is located in a low-tax nation, an MNC could minimize taxes by charging a low transfer price. However, if import tariffs are present, the MNC will consider both taxes and tariffs in formulating the transfer pricing policy. This is because a high transfer price means a high value for the goods and services sold. Similarly, a low transfer price means a low value for the goods and services sold. Because import tariffs are imposed on the declared value of imports, this leads to a higher or lower tariff cost as the case may be. Thus, an MNC should measure the tax benefit of a higher or lower transfer price against the resulting higher or lower tariff cost. A high transfer price will be charged if the savings on the host country's taxes are greater than the additional tariff costs. A low transfer price will be used if the savings on tariffs are greater than the additional taxes. Thus, to the extent that the transfer pricing is practiced by an MNC in a developing nation, the ability of that nation to collect its fair share of taxes is diminished.

4. **Indirect Taxes on Goods.** These taxes, paid indirectly by individuals and corporations through the purchase of goods, are composed of import, export, and excise duties. They constitute the most important source of public revenue in developing nations. A major advantage of these taxes is the ease by which they can be collected. This is especially true in the case of foreign-traded goods, which pass through national boundaries. The ease of collecting such taxes provides an explanation as to why nations with a significant volume of foreign trade usually collect a larger percentage of public revenues in the form of export and import duties than nations with insufficient foreign trade. In addition to serving as a major source of public revenue, indirect taxes can also prove to be an efficient substitute for corporate income taxes in developing nations. To the degree that importers are unable to pass on to the final consumers the total cost of the tax, an import duty can function as an alternate tax on the profits of the importers, and only partly a tax on the domestic consumer. In the same manner, an export duty can serve as an effective tool for taxing the profits of firms, including subsidiaries of MNCs that engage in transfer pricing practices. Nevertheless, export duties devised to create revenue should not be increased to such a high level that it deters domestic producers from expanding their output of the commodities exported.

In deciding what commodities to tax, the following general principals should be kept in mind:

a. To be able to control tax evasion, the goods must be produced or imported by a relatively small number of licensed firms.
b. The goods should have a low price elasticity of demand so that the rise in consumer prices resulting from higher taxes does not stifle the total demand.
c. The goods should have a high income elasticity of demand so that a rise in income leads to a higher tax revenue.
d. Taxes should be imposed on goods such as automobiles, household appliances, and imported exotic foods, that are primarily used by the upper income classes. However, items of mass consumption such as simple clothing and basic goods, should be exempted from taxes.

In closing this section it should be emphasized that the ability of a developing nation to collect taxes, either for public expenditures or as a tool to improve income distribution, hinges not only on the existence of proper tax laws but, more importantly, on the effectiveness and decency of the tax officials who must administer these laws.

Government Expenditures

As we explained earlier, the second major tool that is used in the implementation of fiscal policy is government expenditures. Government expenditures can be divided into the following two main categories:

1. **Capital Spending.** This item is composed of expenditures on the purchases of machinery and equipment.
2. **Recurrent Spending.** For most nations this item includes the following:
    a. Expenditures on nondurable goods, and services, consisting of those for maintenance, public sector employees, and all expenditures on military equipment.

220 PART III/DOMESTIC RESOURCE POLICIES & DEVELOPMENT STRATEGIES

    b. Interest payments of the government debts.
    c. Subsidies and other transfers to individuals.
    d. Transfers to substantial governments.

The impact of government capital spending on growth was long perceived as clearly positive. Critics later demonstrated that not all such investments have augmented growth, much less development. Nevertheless, the pervasive view is that any trade-offs between government recurrent spending and capital spending should be solved in support of investment, since recurrent spending is considered to be unproductive. In fact, recurrent costs of development have been marked as "government consumption," connoting that expenditures for such objectives have no impact on boosting the productive capacity of a developing nation. A number of economists have attempted to correct this misunderstanding. They explain that although most governments concentrate their attention on new investments, they usually lack adequate provision for recurrent operations and maintenance outlays of early investments. This leads to needless underutilization of public-sector capital, and in some instances to its fast deterioration.[1] In spite of such a view, in practice, it is true that in many developing nations there may be avenues for increasing public savings by controlling the growth of several kinds of recurrent spending. In this section we will examine the main items of recurrent spending, to find out how wide these avenues are.

Nondurable Goods and Services. In developing nations, *nondurable goods and services* make up on average about 60% of total recurrent spending. The major items included in this spending include:

1. Salaries and benefits for civil servants and military personnel.
2. Expenditures on maintenance and repair.
3. Other military spending.

In most developing nations, salaries and benefits make up about 50% percent of total expenditures for goods and services. The classic portrayal of a public sector institution in a developing nation is an organization marked by corruption, inefficiency, inflated payrolls, and lackadaisical behavior. However, since international comparisons of civil service performance are almost nonexistent, some economists believe that such views are not defendable. Rather, they are based essentially on anecdotal evidence. As a result, it is argued that no firm judgement can be made on the degree of overstaffing of public institutions, or bureaucratic extravagances in developing nations as compared to advanced nations. Setting such an argument aside, it is safe to say that civil systems in developing nations are in general more bureaucratic, less efficient and they are more open to bribery and misuse as compared to the civil systems of advanced nations. Additionally, it seems that the public sector in developing nations is no more or less sensitive to the socioeconomic variations that guide development of any other sector in these nations. For example, during the 1950s, one could repeatedly hear the famous word of *mordida* (bite) that was commonly demanded by civil servants at that time for doing their jobs. It was widely believed then that such behavior stemmed from both low civil salaries and cultural habits.

High public expenditures on nondurable goods and services are frequently mentioned as the main element that contributes to the low level of public savings in developing nations. But even this case, anecdotal evidence constitutes much of the basis for such a view.

If there are misuses in the government acquisition in some cases, they stem from the inadequacy of funds. More specifically, the government has been too thrifty in allocating funds, especially with regard to the provision of maintenance outlays for preserving public sector capital-stock and for many essential operating expenditures. As a result, painfully acquired public-sector capital stock has been deteriorating fast, needing eventually not routine maintenance but costly new public expenditures. This approach is worsened by the policies of aid donors who wholeheartedly support capital projects, and as a general policy, are unwilling to provide funds for routine costs of these projects.

An item of nondurable goods and services that has stirred significant controversy among economic development scholars in recent years is military expenditures. Beginning with the early 1970s, despite a world recession, declining growth in export revenues, and mounting foreign debts, military outlays in the developing nations began skyrocketing. In 1995, total military outlay of developing nations reached the level of $1.54 billion, making up 19.3% of world's military outlays. In recent years, not only have military expenditure of developing nations risen, but there has also been a change in their compositions, away from paying armies and toward the acquisition of advanced military equipment. Such conditions have fueled debates regrading the impact of military expenditures on economic development.

The proponents of military expenditures argue that such outlays have a positive effect on economic growth, resulting from enhanced aggregate demand triggered by military expenditures, the building of fundamental infrastructure, job creation, and training possibilities. They also maintain that the opportunity costs of military expenditures are relatively lower for the following two reasons:

1. The resources set aside for military consumption could instead be directed to private consumption or social investment, including such items as medical care, education, sanitation, and housing, which hardly contribute to economic growth.
2. The resources used for military objectives are usually obtainable only through foreign military aid and loans, and as such they are earmarked by the donor for military purposes. Otherwise they might not be available for public use.

The major empirical work presented in support of this idea is research undertaken by Emile Benoit, who finds a positive relationship between military spending and economic growth for 44 developing nations during the period of 1950-1965. The study concludes that nations with large defense expenditures have the most rapid growth rates, while those with the lowest defense budget seem to have the lowest growth rates.[2]

The opponents of military expenditures refute the idea that such outlays lead to large benefits for developing nations. In defending their positions, they present the following arguments:

1. Given that much of the military demand is directed toward imports, it is unlikely that it will have a significant impact on domestic demand.
2. The advantages of employment and training stemming from military expenditures are highly exaggerated, since the trend is toward procurement of weapons rather than paying armies.
3. If military expenditures are financed by a decrease in private or public investment, overall employment is likely to deteriorate.
4. It is not necessarily true that the training of military personnel makes valuable contributions to the labor force since skills learned in military are not readily applicable to the civilian sector.
5. The building of essential infrastructure for the military is less defensible, on the basis of the long-run economic growth and employment creation, than the generation of an infrastructure to satisfy public- and private-sector requirements.
6. It is not true that the opportunity costs of diverting funds that could otherwise be spent on items such as medical care, education, sanitation, and housing are low since such outlays do not make much contribution to future economic growth. The argument neglects the impact of investment in human capital, which forms a basis for the long-run economic growth.
7. Given the decrease in foreign aid in recent years, it is not necessarily true that resources used for military objectives are usually obtainable only through foreign military aid and loans. Most developing nations must now rely on domestic resources to satisfy their military requirements. Since the rise in military expenditures is mostly directed toward imports from abroad, substantial foreign exchange of the developing countries is depleted. If the source of foreign exchange earnings is

exportation, then they compete with investment that could be used to enhance the nation's foreign exchange earning potential in the future. On the other hand, if the source of foreign exchange earnings is external loans, then the debt burden is increased and may require the nation to implement monetary and fiscal polices that are aimed at the curtailment of private consumption and investment, and hence, lowering economic growth.

There are a number of empirical studies that support the view that military spending has a negative effect on economic growth. For example, a study of 54 nations by David Lim examined the relationship between military spending and economic growth over a more recent time period than the Benoit's study (1965-1973) and came up with an opposite conclusion. More specifically, Lim's study reports that there is no negative relationship between military spending and the rate of economic growth in developing nations. It has been argued that Benoit's conclusion regarding the positive relationship between military spending and economic growth is invalid since high military spending was correlated with high foreign aid during the period under study. Given the decrease in foreign aid beginning with the 1970s, it is argued, the correlation between military expenditure and rate of economic growth has been inverted.

Today, it is evident that high military expenditures are depleting developing nations of scarce resources that are badly needed to support their long-run economic endeavors. However, it is not apparent what impact the end of "the Cold War" will have on the military expenditures of developing nations. Before the end of the Cold War, the United States and the former Soviet Union supplied more than 80% of the developing nations' import demands. With the cessation of the Cold War, it is expected that tensions between nations previously supported by the former Soviet Union and the United States will diminish. The demise of the Soviet Union has basically ended its intervention in developing nations. The present policies of the United States are likely to lead to a considerable rise in the military engagement of the United States in developing nations' major economic and strategic interests. To stay on favorable terms, developing nations that aspire to preserve continued development assistance are likely to follow military spending molds compatible with the United States economic and military concerns. Such strategies imply serious constraints for developing nations' disarmament. However, the speed of disarmament in developing nations will eventually hinge on the determination of all nations to employ peaceful means of conflict resolution.

It is widely believed that advanced nations can significantly facilitate the peace process by encouraging the transformation of wasteful military outlays into productive economic and social expenditures. Such a transformation could be achieved by policies that include the following components:

1. The imposition of conditionality on development aid to assure that development funds are not channeled into military purposes.
2. Stricter arms export policies in supplier nations.
3. Enhanced economic assistance to developing nations to advance economic prosperity, resulting in internal political stability.
4. The reallocation of scarce resources in developing nations away from military expenditures and toward human investment.

Interest Payments. A major budgetary expenditure for many developing nations is interest payments on government debt, measured by the **debt-service ratio,** that is, payments of interest on total debt plus amortization as a percentage of total exports. Interest payments stem from past government budgetary deficits that are funded by internal and/or external borrowing. Interest payments on external debts have grown rapidly in several developing nations beginning with the early 1970s. As we explain later in detail in Chapter 14, this is due to a number of factors including tight monetary policies of advanced nations, the second oil shock, poor public investment in developing nations, the worldwide recession and capital flight from developing nations.

CH. 11/MONETARY AND FISCAL POLICIES

The debt-service ratio is an indicator of indebted countries' burden. As Table 11.1 indicates, there are noticeable differences among regions with regard to the debt burden. More specifically, the Western Hemisphere's burden is much larger than Asia's, and has not declined nearly as fast as Asia's. Asia's debt burden is expected to decrease to 4.4 percent in 2003. It is also expected that the Western Hemisphere's debt burden will fall to 12.8 percent in 2003.

Although the total amount of debt in Africa is smallest among the regions, as Table 11.1 shows, Africa's debt-service ratio is the second largest among the regions. In other words, like Western Hemisphere developing nations, African nations have also been suffering from a severe debt problem. However, unlike Western Hemisphere developing nations, which have been dependent on bank financing, the bulk of African nations' debt is owed to official agencies and governments.

Since interest payments on government debt stem from past decisions, this item of expenditures is hard to decrease. Even if a nation prevents further budget deficit and imposes a moratorium on external borrowing for several years, expenditures of this sort can not be readily condensed in the short-term. As we will discuss in detail in Chapter 14, the debt crisis has caused policymakers in developing countries to shift economic discussion away from income distribution and poverty, which are the crucial problems that exist in many of these countries. If the debt crisis was under control, there would be enormous pressure on policymakers in both developing and advanced countries to address these problems. This is a challenge that policymakers will have to deal with in the future.

Table 11.1

DEBT-SERVICE RATIOS OF DEVELOPING COUNTRIES (AS A PERCENTAGE OF EXPORTS OF GOODS AND SERVICES)

	1994	1995	1996	1997	1998	1999	2000	2001	2002*	2003*
Developing Countries										
Africa	**8.9**	**8.9**	**8.3**	**7.7**	**8.8**	**8.6**	**7.4**	**7.4**	**7.3**	**6.8**
Sub-Sahara	10.0	9.7	9.2	8.6	8.8	8.3	6.9	7.0	9.5	6.7
Developing Asia	804	7.9	7.9	7.6	7.7	7.6	6.4	6.8	10.2	6.7
Excluding China &	6.4	6.2	6.0	5.1	6.0	5.8	5.0	4.6	4.4	4.4
India	6.1	6.3	6.3	6.7	7.5	6.5	6.1	5.7	5.7	5.5
Middle East & Turkey	6.1	4.9	4.0	4.0	4.8	4.2	3.6	4.0	4.5	5.0
Western Hemisphere	16.2	16.9	16.0	15.4	17.2	17.8	16.0	16.1	14.2	12.8

*Estimated data.
Source: International Monetary Fund, *World Economic Outlook* (Washington, DC: IMF, May/ April 2002) 217, table A42.

Subsidies. A number of subsidies account for a major portion of recurrent expenditures in developing nations. This proportion ranges roughly from 2 percent in the poorest developing nations such as Democratic Republic of Congo and Kenya to about 60 percent in middle-income developing nations such as Argentina.

Recurrent budget subsidies take a variety of forms, including direct money transfers, subsidized food programs for the urban and rural poor, and direct government subsidies to keep the price of essential foodstuffs down. The common approach is the distribution of price-controlled foods through state-owned institutions and the recuperation of losses in food distribution by means of budgetary transfers to these institutions. Another form of subsidy, widespread in oil-rich developing nations, is that of domestic consumption of oil products. For example, in Bolivia, Colombia, Indonesia, Pakistan, and several other oil-rich nations, subsidies are granted for the consumption of petroleum products, in particular, kerosene which is used for cooking and heating in many of these nations. In all four cases mentioned, the principal justification offered for such subsidies was that of assisting low-income classes.

In basically all nations that grant budgetary subsidies, the stated objective has commonly been that of income redistribution. For foods, especially grains, the argument seems appealing, even if the final impact is not always what was planned. The effect of many other subsidies in serving the objective of income redistribution, however, is less clear. The most striking example is consumption oil subsidies granted in Bolivia, Colombia, Indonesia, and Pakistan. As we mentioned earlier, the main justification for granting such subsidies was to assist low-income groups. In practice, however, such subsidies failed to achieve the stated purpose. For example, in Bolivia through 1980, and in Colombia through 1974, the subsidy was extended to consumption of gasoline, although in both nations car ownership was by and large limited to the upper 5 percent of the income distribution. As another example, in Indonesia, gasoline has been only slightly subsidized, but budget subsidies kept prices of kerosene and diesel fuel at less than 50 percent of the cost of production and distribution. Although it seems logical that subsidizing kerosene favor the poor, in practice, this turns out not to be the case. The poorest 40 percent of families use only 20 percent of the kerosene sold. This means that for every $1 subsidy given to the poor, the relatively rich families received a $4 benefit. Given the substitutability of kerosene for diesel fuel, consumers would change to the former if the latter were unsubsidized Thus, the subsidized program ends up subsidizing consumption of fuel as well.

Unfortunately, during the last two decades, overall, subsidization policies have not been effective in meeting their stated objective, that is, raising the real personal income levels of the very poor above their actual market-determined monetary incomes. In the 1980s and 1990s, with the developing nations' debt crisis and the mechanism of World Bank and IMF initiated structural adjustment programs, the first casualties of prescribed public expenditure reductions were the rural and urban poor, in particular, women.

Intergovernmental Transfers. Subnational governments include provinces, departments, counties, and municipalities. Transfers from central to subnational governments are usually considered as recurrent expenditures, in spite of the fact that they may utilize the proceeds for capital formation. Nonetheless, in some nations, like Indonesia, some transfers are classified as capital expenditure and others as consumption. Such differing standards of classification make international comparison of nations problematic.

The proportion of the total expenditures that is transferred from the central government to subnational government differs among developing nations, depending on the degree of control that is exercised by the central government over the total spending, and may take one of the following forms:

1. In most unitary states, like Argentina and Chile, basically all government activities are managed at all levels by the capital city, and subnational units of government have few tasks to perform with their small local income.
2. In most federal states, the transfer of funds from the central government to subnational units is essential because the center has monopolized the most productive source of tax revenue. In most cases this monopoly is based on the following technical reasons:
    a. National governments levy income taxes since subnational governments do not have the resources and skills needed to manage such a complex tax.
    b. The main source of tax income for most nations, that is, import duties, must necessarily remain as a government resource.
3. Transfers to subnational units, including revenue sharing, make up a substantial percentage of recurrent expenditures in some developing nations such as India, Indonesia, and Korea. In some other developing nations, such as Bolivia, Malaysia, and Zaire, this percentage is very small.
4. In a few nations, the small percentage of such transfers stems from the fact that subnational units can tap into very rich sources of income. For example, in Bolivia, where oil-generating provinces acquire large royalties. As another example, in Malaysia, the eastern Malaysian governments of Sabah and Sarawak receive notable tax income from the exports of tropical timber gathered there.

CH. 11/MONETARY AND FISCAL POLICIES

Apparently, then, there are only a few simple approaches to decreasing most kinds of recurrent expenditures in order to generate higher public savings. Also, given the limited levels of income and the inadequacy of tax structures in developing nations, there are only few easy ways in which tax revenues can be augmented in order to attain the same goal. Finance ministers are accountable for both. Finance ministers who have met with some success in controlling the rising current expenditures and assuring healthy revenue growth seem to be as disdained as they are exceptional. In fact, in some nations an efficient finance minister may have facilitated income growth more than all the development planning machinery, over some periods. The distributional and stabilization effects of fiscal policy can expand the ability of a finance minister's central role in the development process.

REVAMPING DEVELOPING NATIONS' FISCAL SYSTEMS

One of the major problems faced by most developing nations is the scarcity of managerial and technical expertise in both the private and public sectors. Many scholars of economic development believe that administrative and managerial expertise is the scarcest public resource in developing nations. As a result, such scarcity has constituted a major roadblock in achieving the objectives of economic development. Unfortunately, the problem is not only rooted in inadequacy of training and experience, but it also stems from the political instability that dominates many developing nations. When authority is continually changing hands, concern over political loyalty is likely to be more important than effectiveness and public welfare. Additionally, the higher the number of public officials impacted by a change in authority, the harder it will be to preserve consistency in the composition and fulfillment of the state policies.

One could not expect the public administration in a developing nation to operate effectively if the following conditions exist:

1. The legal system is flimsy, and the rule of law is in question.
2. The existence of public disturbance, stemming from acute conditions of class, tribal, and religious conflict within the society.
3. There is not much agreement on basic problems.
4. The government has civil service objectives other than performance. Such objectives may include nationalizing civil service, conforming to ideological correctness, breaking up traditional elites, preferring an ethnic proportion, and excluding or including minorities.
5. The bureaucracy is highly understaffed at the top and highly overstaffed at the bottom.
6. There are acute shortages of individuals with managerial talents who are able to make independent decisions.
7. There are acute shortages of technical skills needed to operate nationalized industries that are staffed by the government.
8. Political concern affects the ability to employ capable managers with specific expertise.

One of the factors that has contributed to the problems of public administration in developing nations is the extensive use of state-owned firms (SOFs), as discussed in the next section.

State-Owned Firms (SOFs)

State-owned firms (SOFs) are public enterprises that are owned and managed by government.
The factors that have given rise to the creation of these firms include the following:

1. The prevalence of monopoly in developing nations calling on government control to ensure that

prices are not set above the marginal costs of producing the product.
2. Many products, such as education and health services have high social values that are not reflected in their market prices. Since such products must be made available to the public at prices below their costs or even free, the private sector has no incentive to produce them. As a result, government should step in to ensure a minimum welfare.
3. The scarcity of capital and inadequacy of private savings, especially at the early stages of development, lead to the serious lack of capital formation in most developing nations. Given the importance of capital formation in the process of economic development, government's investment in infrastructure is significant at this stage in order to set a foundation for projected investment.
4. The existence of uncertainty about the size of the local markets, the unreliability of sources of supply, and shortages of managerial and technical expertise in developing nations discourage the private sector to engage in promising economic endeavors. This may call on government to engage in economic activities for the following reasons:
    a. To enhance export revenues by establishing export industries, especially those industries that might otherwise be incapable of competition.
    b. To promote employment and training of the labor force by engaging in public production.
    c. To improve income distribution by establishing firms in certain sectors, especially in the economically backward regions which lack private motives for generating such economic endeavors.
    d. To gain national control over strategic sectors of the economy like defense and multinational corporations (MNCs) whose interest might not match those of the developing nation, and the chief sectors for planning objectives.
    e. To promote certain ideology.
    f. To support recent independence or to take the place of a recently bankrupted major private industry

During the past half century, developing nations have experienced a rapid increase in the number of public firms. Traditionally, these firms have dominated the following industries in developing nations:

1. Transportation, including railroads, airplanes, and buses.
2. Utilities, including gas, water, and electricity.
3. Communications, including telephone, telegraph, and postal services.

Today, besides dominating the traditional industries, SOFs have expanded their presence in such major sectors as construction, agriculture, large-scale manufacturing, finance, services, and natural gas. As a result, they account for, on average, more than 10% of GDP in developing nations. They also consume a significant amount of resources, and in many developing nations, inflict large fiscal burden on government. For example, a study of 27 developing nations showed that the net payments to nonfinancial SOFs averaged more than 3% of GDP.

Enhancing SOFs' Effectiveness. Despite their potential to contribute to the process of economic development, many SOFs in developing nations have failed to show a profit. As a result, they have continued their operation at a deficit, draining the scarce financial resources in these nations. The low performance of SOFs in terms of profitability and efficiency can be contributed to the following factors:

1. Because SOFs are public institutions, they may not pursue the objective of profit maximization in the same manner that private institutions would. This happens because, unlike private institutions that are aimed at satisfying commercial goals, SOFs are expected to pursue both commercial and social

goals. As a result, they may end up providing goods at prices below costs in order to subsidize the public, or employ additional workers to satisfy national employment goals. Such actions invariably diminish their profits.
2. The decision making process in most of developing nations is extremely centralized. Such overcentralization does not allow much flexibility for managers in performing their day-to-day operations.
3. The organizational bureaucracy is such that many decision makers are not responsible for their performance. Additionally, not much incentive is provided to enhance the productivity of managers.
4. In spite of labor abundance and employment directives, the use of capital-intensive technology has frequently led to the needless capital-deepening in many developing nations.

In alleviating the above problems, a developing nation can choose one of the following alternatives:

1. **Decentralization.** This calls for reorganization of the SOFs to allow for more flexibility, and provide better incentives for managers in order to enhance efficiency. It also calls for providing capital at its market price to prevent wasteful use of capital-intensive technology. An example of a nation that has adopted this strategy is the Chinese government which during the 1980s gave greater independence to and enhanced competition among its various SOFs.
2. **Privatization.** This calls for transferring the ownership and control of SOFs from the government to the private sector. This approach is rooted in the neoclassical theory that privatization leads to a higher productivity. More specifically, the proponents of this strategy present the following arguments in support of their position:

    a Privatization improves efficiency, enhances output, and decreases costs.
    b. Privatization checks the expansion of government expenditures, and increases cash to decrease government debts, at both domestic and international levels.
    c. Privatization advances individual initiative, and at the same time rewards entrepreneurship.
    d. Privatization widens the ownership base, enhances participation in the economy, and breeds a sense of belonging in individuals who feel that they have a direct interest in the economy.

The existing empirical studies to date show that privatization has been relatively successful in promoting efficiency and higher output, especially in high- and middle income nations.[3] In the case of poorer nations, however, the success of privatization in improving the SOFs' performance remains an open question. Although some positive results have been obtained in these nations, the impact of privatization on income distribution seems to be enhancing the gap between poor and rich. This stems from the fact that privatized assets are controlled by small classes of domestic and foreign elites. For instance, in many cases the sale of SOFs in Latin America were implemented in the absence of competitive bidding, frequently at predetermined negotiated prices.

Thus, privatization gives rise to many difficult questions, including the following issues:

a. The feasibility of implementing privatization.
b. Appropriateness of financing to the privatization project.
c. The legal and property rights framework.
d. The position of elites and rivaling interest groups, such as bureaucrats as opposed to indigenous and international interest groups, and government administrators.
e. The impact of privatization on the existing dualistic economic, social, and political framework.

As the above list indicates, the neoclassical's proposition that privatization leads to higher profits, larger output, and lower costs, is not necessarily true. The central question to ask is if such privatization better satisfies the long-run development objectives of a country by advancing a sustainable economic progress that is characterized by equitable income distribution.

Today, in spite of the aforementioned shortcomings associated with privatization, the popularity of this strategy continues to increase on the global level. During 1980-1992, more than 15,000 firms were privatized around the globe. More than 11,000 of these firms were located in East Germany. During the same period, in developing countries, more than $100 million of privatization transactions took place. It is interesting to note that almost all of these transactions occurred in Latin America, especially Mexico. Among low-income developing nations, however, the privatization process has been viewed with much more caution, where most of transfers occur in the from of low-value, small enterprises.

SUMMARY

1. **Monetary policy** which is based on *monetarist theory* of economic activities is intentional implementation of the Federal Reserve's authority to stimulate expansions or contractions in the money supply in order to attain price stability, to help mitigate the swings of business cycles, and to bring countries' output and employment to the preferred level.
2. Essentially, monetary policy operates on two major economic variables, aggregate supply of money in circulation and the level of interest rates.
3. Monetarists argue that by controlling the growth of money supply, the government of an advanced nation can control its economic activities and check inflation.
4. **Fiscal policy** which is based on *Keynesian economics* is deliberate taxation and spending decisions by the government to attain efficiency and growth. Efficiency is obtained by stabilizing the economy at full employment, hence mitigating the swings of business cycles. Growth is achieved by extending tax incentives to work, save and invest. Contemporaneous fiscal policy places considerable emphasis on achieving growth.
5. The impediments to monetary policies in developing nations could be classified into two major categories: inadequacy of financial institutions in developing nations, and insensitivity of investment decisions to interest rate fluctuations in developing nations.
6. The ability of advanced nations to implement their monetary polices by changing their money supplies, or manipulating their interest rates, stems from the nature of their financial systems which have the following major characteristics: (1) efficiently functioning money markets that are very organized, and economically independent; (2) free flow of financial resources into and out of nationally regulated financial intermediaries, such as savings banks and commercial bank; and (3) interest rates that are determined by both market forces of supply and demand and administrative controls, resulting in consistency and relative uniformity of rates in various economic sectors and regions of the nations.
7. In developing nations, financial institutions are poorly organized, externally dependent, and fragmented. More specifically, they have the following characteristics: (1) many of the chief commercial banks in developing nations are subsidiaries of huge private banks in advanced nations; (2) as open economies, many developing nations' currencies are pegged to the dollar or a basket of advanced countries' currencies; (3) the prevalence of currency substitution; (4) commercial banks in developing nations usually confine their loans to large and medium firms, such as modern manufacturing and mining; (5) because security markets are generally not well established in developing nations, the central banks' activities in these markets are very limited; and (6) the percentage of the total money supply held in terms of demand deposits (checking accounts) is usually much lower in developing nations than in advanced nations.

8. The second major impediment to monetary policy in developing nations is the assumption of direct links between interest rate, investment, and output. More specifically, it is assumed that lower interest rates lead to higher investments and expanded output. Although such an assumption is plausible for advanced nations, it is questionable in developing nations. This is because investment decisions are not usually very sensitive to interest rate fluctuations due to the following two factors: (1) most loans are made outside the banking systems through money lenders, landlords and relatives; and (2) given the supply limitations (low elasticities of supply) in developing nations, a rise in investment demand may trigger inflation instead of boosting the real output.
9. During the 1980s many developing nations were facing the so called "credit crunch." Such a phenomenon stemmed from the following factors: (1) the existence of high and extensive inflation; (2) the limitation of loans to a few big borrowers; (3) growing budget deficit and negative interest rates; (4) numerous lending restrictions imposed on financial institutions; and (5) the imposition of mandatory ceilings on loanable funds at rates well below market-clearing levels.
10. Financial liberalization in developing nations must be accompanied by a host of direct measures to ensure that small farmers and investors can access the needed credit. Additionally, it requires a careful supervision of the financial system to avert domination by the local elites. This calls on the governments of the developing nation to play crucial roles that include the following strategies: (1) regulating financial systems; (2) establishing new organizations to fill the gaps in the types of credit awarded by the private institutions; (3) Enhancing consumer protection; (4) assuring bank solvency; (5) promoting fair competition; (6) improving the allocation of financial resources; and (7) fostering macroeconomic stability.
11. The two major tools that are used in the implementation of fiscal policy are taxation and government expenditures.
12. Direct taxes are taxes that are composed of primary property, wealth, income, and inheritance taxes. Indirect taxes include items such as import, export, sales, purchase, turnover, and value-added taxes.
13. Devised by French economists, the value-added tax is a tax imposed on the value that is added at each stage of production of a given good. It is calculated as the difference between the sales of the firm and its purchases from other firms.
14. Traditionally, taxes in developing nations are imposed to satisfy the following objectives: (1) to finance public expenditures; and (2) to induce investment.
15. The four major sources of direct and indirect taxes: (1) personal income taxes; (2) property taxes; (3) corporate income taxes; and indirect taxes on goods.
16. The second major tool that is used in the implementation of fiscal policy is government expenditures. Government expenditures can be divided into the following two main categories: (1) capital spending; and (2) recurrent spending.
17. A major budgetary expenditure for many developing nations is interest payments on government debt, measured by the debt-service ratio, that is, payments of interest on total debt plus amortization as a percentage of total exports. Interest payments stem from past government budgetary deficits that are funded by internal and/or external borrowing.
18. A number of subsidies account for a major portion of recurrent expenditures in developing nations. This proportion ranges roughly from 2 percent in the poorest developing nations such as Democratic Republic of Congo and Kenya to about 60 percent in middle-income developing nations such as Argentina.
19. Subnational governments include provinces, departments, counties, and municipalities. Transfers from central to subnational governments are usually considered as recurrent expenditures, in spite of the fact that they may utilize the proceeds for capital formation.
20. One of the major problems that is faced by most developing nations is the scarcity of managerial and technical expertise in both private and public sectors.
21. State-owned firms (SOFs) are public enterprises that are owned and managed by government.

PART III/DOMESTIC RESOURCE POLICIES & DEVELOPMENT STRATEGIES

22. Despite their potential to contribute to the process of economic development many SOFs in developing nations have failed to show a profit.
23. In alleviating the problems associated with SOFs, a developing nation can choose one of the following alternatives: (1) decentralization; and (2) privatization.

QUESTIONS

1. Differentiate between fiscal policies and monetary policies and elaborate on the appropriate tools that are used in implementation of these policies.
2. What are the two major impediments to monetary policies in developing nations? Discuss.
3. What factors gave rise to the so called "credit crunch" in developing nations during the 1980s? Explain.
4. Elaborate on strategies that the government of a developing nation could adopt in order to avert the domination of its financial system by local elites.
5. One of the major tools that can be employed in implementation of fiscal policy is taxation. Elaborate on this tool by answering the following questions:
    a. What are the two general groups of taxes?
    b. Traditionally, what two major objectives have been satisfied by taxation in developing nations?
    c. What factors determine the ability of a nation to generate taxes?
    d. As a general rule, what factors determine the ability of a nation to collect taxes?
6. One of the major tools that can be employed in implementation of fiscal policy is government expenditures. Elaborate on this tool by answering the following questions:
    a. What are the two main categories of government expenditures?
    b. What are the main arguments for and against military expenditures as a tool of fiscal policy?
7. What are the elements that contribute to the ineffectiveness of public administration in developing nations?
8. Elaborate on SOFs by answering the following questions:
    a. What is meant by SOFs?
    b. What factors have given rise to the creation of SOFs?
    c. What sectors are dominated by SOFs in developing nations?
9. What are the main factors that have contributed to the low performance of SOFs in terms of profitability and efficiency? What are the two main alternatives that a developing nation could chose in order to alleviate the low performance of SOFs?
10. According to the neoclassical economists, privatization leads to higher profits, larger output, and lower costs. Is this proposition necessarily true? Discuss.

NOTES

1. Pete Heller, "The Under-Finance of Recurrent Development Costs," *Finance and Development* 16, No. 1(March 1979): 38-41.
2. Emile Benoit, "Growth a Defense in Developing Countries," *Economic Development and Cultural Change* 25 (January 1978).
3. Snita Kekeri, Hohn Nellis, nd Mary Shirley, "Privatization: Lessons from Market Economies," *World Research Observer* 9 (July 1994): 249-253; See also World Bank, *World Development Report*, 1997 (New York: Oxford University Press, 1977), Chap. 4.

SUGGESTED READINGS

Cardoso, Elina. "Hyperinflation in Latin America." *Challenge* 32 (January/February 989): 11-19.

Chelliah, Raja J., Hessel J. Baas, and Margaret R. Kelly. "Tax Rations and Tax Effort in Developing Countries, 1969-71." *International Monetary Fund Staff Papers* 22 (March 1975): 187-205.

De Olivria, Roberto. "Economic Development and Inflation With Special Reference to Latin America." in Organization for Economic Cooperation and Development, *Development Plans and Programmes*. Paris: OECD Development Center, 1964.

Dronbusch, Rudiger. *Stabilization, Debt, and Reform: Policy Analysis for Developing Countries*. Englewood, Cliffs, N.J.: Prentice Hall, 1993.

Eshag, Eprime. *Fiscal and Monetary Policies and Problems in Developing Countries*. Cambridge University Press, 1983.

Perry, David B. "International Tax Comparisons." *Canadian Tax Journal* 28 (January-February 1980): 89-93.

Lewis, Jr., Stephen R. *Taxation for Development: Principles and Applications*. New York: Oxford University Press, 1984.

Saches, Jeffery D. and Felipe, Larrain B. *Microeconomics in the Global Economy*. Englewood Cliffs, NJ: Prentice Hall, 1993.

Tait, Alan A., Wilfred L. M. Gratz, and Barry J. Eichengreen. "International Tax Comparisons of Taxation for Selected Developing Countries, 1972-1976." *International Monetary Fund Staff Papers* 26 (March 1979): 123-56.

Tanzi, Vito. "Quantitative Characteristics of the Tax Systems of Developing Countries." in David Newbery and Nicholas Stern, eds. *The Theory of Taxation for Developing Countries*. l: Oxford University pres, 1987.

Wai Tun U. "Interest Rates in the Organized Money Markets of Underdeveloped Countries." *International Monetary Fund Staff Papers* 5 (Agust 1956): 249-78.

CHAPTER 12

DEVELOPMENT PLANNING: THEORY AND PRACTICE

One of the controversial issues in economic development is the extent of government involvement in the process of economic development. Following World War II, there was considerable support for government intervention in the process of economic development by the means of development planning. Few people in the Third World questioned the wisdom of economic planning, and considered it as the surest and the most direct road to economic advancement. Planning had become the accepted strategy by the government authorities, and every five years or so the newest development plan was brandished with great publicity. However, starting with the 1970s many economists began to question the validity of such a strategy in ensuring economic development. Such a skepticism stems from the poor planning records of many developing nations marked by their failure in meeting the stated objectives.

In this chapter, first we elaborate on the definition of development planning. Second, we present the arguments for and against development planning. Third, we describe the planning process. Finally, we discuss the failure of planning in developing nations.

THE DEFINITION OF DEVELOPMENT PLANNING

Development planning may be defined as the intentional government action to orchestrate the economic decision process over the long run and to direct, affect, or even control a nation's major economic variables in order to achieve a contemplated set of economic goals. Development planning is implemented by the means of an economic plan. An **economic plan** is composed of a set of quantitative economic objectives to be attained during a given period of time. Economic plans can be divided into the following two categories:

1. **Comprehensive Plans.** These plans aim at covering all aspects of the national economy.
2. **Partial Plans.** These plans only deal with a part of the national economy, such as agriculture, industry, the foreign sector, and so forth.

A **planning process** can be described as an activity that is implemented by the government and composed of the following steps:

1. Choosing social objectives.
2. Setting various targets.

234 PART III/DOMESTIC RESOURCE POLICIES & DEVELOPMENT STRATEGIES

3. Organizing a framework for implementation, coordination and monitoring of a development plan.
4. Defining the duration of the plan.

THE ARGUMENTS FOR AND AGAINST DEVELOPMENT PLANNING

As we explained earlier, beginning with the 1970s, many economists began to question the wisdom of economic planning as a tool in achieving economic development. Such questions have given rise to heated debates among economists. The proponents of the detailed planning are considered as left of center or maybe even radical by the opponents. On the other hand, the opponents are branded as reactionary or conservative by the proponents. Neither side seems to accepts the other side's point of view, and the controversy continue to exist. In this section, first we review the proponents' views and then elaborate on the opponents' ideas.

Opponents' Arguments

The opponents arguments are based on the concept of market efficiency. They argue that the market efficiently allocates scarce resources among alternative uses, leading to the following outcomes:

1. Firms produce those goods that maximize their profits.
2. Consumers obtain commodities for which they are willing to pay.
3. The market determines available capital and labor.
4. The market distributes income between resources and thus, individuals.
5. Resources are hired out to maximized income.

Under these conditions, the market triggers growth and efficiency automatically, without government interventions. The only job left for the government to do is to enforce contracts and maintain the legal system. If the government interferes with the market process and begins allocating scarce resources, bribery, black markets, corruption, and nepotism are more likely to occur, leading to inefficient allocation of resources.

Proponents' Arguments

The plea for development planning by its proponents is based on the following two major arguments: market failures and undesirable market outcomes.

1. **Market Failures.** This first argument of proponents of development planning is that the market system does not work optimally. This contention is based on the following reasons:
    a. **The Existence of Externalities.** As we already know from standard microeconomic theory, the objective of profit maximization leads a perfectly competitive firm to the produce the output level at which price (P), or marginal private benefit (MPB) is equal to marginal private cost (MPC). However, MPC, reflecting the cost incurred by the firm as the result of its own decisions, may not be equal to marginal social cost (MSC), which portrays the costs incurred by the society as the results of the firm's production activities. In the same manner, MPB, reflecting the benefits accrued to the firms, may be different from marginal social benefits (MSB), that is, the costs sustained by the society as the result of the firms operation. Thus, a perfectly competitive market may not lead to the equality between MSC and MSB. As a result, the social welfare is not maximized and scarce resources are misallocated. This situation leads to market failure.

GLOBAL INSIGHTS CASE 12.1

PLANNING IN THE FORMER SOVIET UNION

The distinguishing characteristic of the economic system of the former Soviet Union was the fact that it operated on the basis of comprehensive planning. A basic principal of economic planning was to give priority to the development of certain key industries, such as chemical, gas, and electric power, which were considered to be essential to the overall rate of growth of industrial and agricultural production.

Economic planning consisted of a system of plans including the following:

1. **The National Plan.** A single plan for the economic development of the nation as a whole.
2. **Sectoral Plans.** A subset of plans for various sectors of the economy.
3. **Territorial Plans.** A subset of plans for various geographical areas.

The economic plans also differed in terms of their functional characteristics. There were physical output plans, which dealt with production, distribution, and investment objectives, and financial plans, which were derivative of these plans. Additionally, plans differed in terms of time limits. There were medium-term plans which covered a period of five to seven years, and specified goals or targets that had to be met during the period. There were also annual plans which comprised production plans to be implemented by the Soviet enterprises and other organizations during the year. The annual plan could be conceived as an operational plan which could be subdivided into quarterly or monthly plans. To provide harmony between different plans in order to maintain a proper relationship between production and consumption and between national requirements and resources, the planning agencies had to ensure that all of these plans were interconnected and interrelated.

The organization of economic planning in the former Soviet Union could be divided into the following stages:

1. Drafting of the plan in accordance with the goals of the Communist party and the Soviet government.
2. Endorsement of the plan by appropriate government organizations.
3. Control over the approval and execution of the plan.

It should be noted that Soviet planning, perhaps more comprehensive than any other nation ever achieved, was not as rigid as one might think. In the early 1960s, the rate of growth of the Soviet economy began to deteriorate. This phenomenon caused the Soviet leaders great concerns and made them reevaluate the strict adherence to planning in managing their economic system. In particular, leadership felt a need to reform the administrative structure for planning and managing their economy. As a result, in 1965 premier Kosygin launched a new system of planning, management, and incentives to be used by the Soviet Union. This system was designed to impact all the sectors of the economy, including industry, agriculture, transportation, and communications. To encourage enterprises' achievements, it was decided to retain more of their profits in a specially created fund to be used for bonuses, cultural expenditures, and investments. In a nutshell, the Soviet Union tried to devise a system which provided its economy with some of the results of the market price system without actually adopting that system.

Until the late 1980s many developing nations used Soviet planning as a pattern for their own planning. Beginning with the late 1980s, Mikhail Gorbachev's economic reforms, referred to as "perestroika" (restructuring), and "glasnost" (openness), transformed the political and economic structure of the Soviet Union, casting doubt on

Continued

> *Global Insights Case 12.1 Continued*
>
> the virtue of adherence to strict planning in achieving the economic goals. This event, along with decades of failure of economic planning in the developing nations, contributed to the developing nations increased used of the market mechanism as the a road to economic prosperity.
>
> *Sources:* Martin C. Schnitzer and James W. Nordyke, *Comparative Economic Systems*, 2nd ed. (Pelham Manor, N.Y.: South-Western Publishing Co., 1977, Ch. 16, pp.376-396; Paul R. Gregory and Robert C. Stuart, *Soviet and Post-Soviet Economic Structure and Performance* (New York: Harper Collins, 1994).

The deviation of MPC/MPB from MSC/MSB, and the resultant market failure stem from the existence of externalities. There are two kinds of externalities: external economy, and external diseconomy. An **external economy** is said to exist when marginal social cost is less than marginal social benefit. On the other hand, an **external diseconomy** persists if marginal social cost is greater than marginal social benefit. For example, production of some goods, such as chemical, rubber, and steel, pollute the environment and may lead to cancer. In this case, MPC only includes payments to the factors of production. However, MSC not only includes the payments to the factors of production, but also the cost of treating the cancer to the society. Thus, MSC〉MPC and market failure occurs. In the same manner, production of some goods, such as park facilities, education, labor training, and sanitation services, enhances the community satisfaction and thus contributes to *social benefits,* causing MSB〉MPB and leading to market failure.

In summary, these externalities may not always be fully accounted for in the prices of goods and services. To the degree that they are not, demand and supply curves fail to portray all the costs and benefits of production. Consequently, either too little, or too much is produced, leading to misallocation of resources.

b. **Lack of Information**. Market dependence assumes that people are well informed and want to maximize gains. But, there may be ignorance and lack of information.

c. **Monopoly Distortions**. Although studies on the degree of monopoly power in developing nations are rare, there are indications that such power is more prevalent in developing nations than advanced nations. In these nations, antitrust laws are usually nonexistent, small market sizes prevent competition, labor unions are commonly weak, and concentration of land ownership may lead to monopoly power in the agriculture sector as well as industrial sector. A monopolist produces less output and charges higher prices than does a perfectly competitive firm. Thus, profit maximization in a free market does not lead to the efficient allocation of the scarce resources if perfect competition does not prevail.

d. **Government Intervention**. Interference with interest rates, exchange rates and foreign trade by government authorities may alter competitive price system. In particular, if foreign trade is limited by the means of quota barriers, the monopoly power may be enhanced even further. As a result, prices do not reflect the social opportunity costs. In other words MSB diverts from MSC, leading to market failure.

e. **Low Savings Rate**. Free markets may lead to a low savings rate that is not socially desirable. However, government can usually save in excess of firms and households by imposing turnover taxes, establishing low procurement prices for state monopolies, and producing surplus from its own production.

2. **Unacceptable Market Outcomes**. Planning may be necessary, because the market mechanism could produce outcomes that policy makers may find unacceptable. This position is of course normative, calling for a value judgement. The following two situation illustrate the point:
   a. **Maldistribution of Income**. The government may consider the present income distribution socially unacceptable. If the problem can not be rectified through taxes and subsidies, then the market results will be considered unacceptable, and the government intervention through planning is called for.
   b. **Interests of Future Generations**. Government may decide to weight the interests of future generations more heavily than the market does. This may be the case if the rate of time discount is high, encouraging people to prefer income now to income later. This will cause a decline in investment and deteriorate the ultimate rate of growth.

THE PLANNING PROCESS

As we explained before, a planning process can be described as an activity that is implemented by the government and composed of the following steps:

1. Choosing social objectives.
2. Setting various targets.
3. Organizing a framework for implementation, coordination and monitoring of a development plan.
4. Defining the duration of the plan.

The purpose of this section is to provide detailed explanations on each of these steps.

Choosing Social Objectives

The first step in an economic planning process is to set the desirable economic goals that the government officials hope to achieve. These goals may or not may reflect the people's priorities. Planning goals vary, depending on the objective that a nation wishes to achieve during the planning period. A plan may include the following objectives:

a. Fast economic growth.
b. High basic needs attainment.
c. Reduction in poverty and improvement in income distribution.
d. Greater educational attainment.
e. Higher employment level.
f. Price stability.
g. Lower international economic dependence.
h. Greater regional balance.
i. Adequate environmental quality.

It should be noted that some of the objectives, such as price stability are independent, while other objectives such as high basic-needs attainment, reduced poverty and inequality are complementary. When there are conflicts between objectives, government authorities need to decide what relative weight should be assigned to each objective. To accomplish this task, a planner may take the following steps:

a. **Interpret economic data to ascertain objectives**. Examples of objectives include resolving the balance of payments problem, reducing rural poverty, and controlling inflation.
b. **Explicitly state the objectives**. Planners usually express objectives as **target variables**, that is specific quantitative goals that they wish to achieve. Examples include achieving annual GDP growth rate of 8 percent, reducing poverty by 2 percentage points of population, and reducing the balance of payments deficit to $100 million. Objectives are implemented through **instrumental variables**, which include policy devices such as monetary, fiscal, subsidy, tariff, quota, labor training, exchange rate, technology transfer, foreign investment, foreign aid, education, wage, price control, capital rationing, business incentives, and interest rate policies.
c. **Formulate the cost of one objective in terms of another objective**.

Setting Various Targets

In this second stage of economic planning the planners express their objectives as **target variables** -for example, 5 percent growth in annual GNP, 2 percent reduction in poverty, 6 percent growth in the manufacturing sector, and 8 percent growth in the agricultural sector. In order to achieve the stated goals, the planners should specify their **instrumental variables**. These variables are composed of economic instruments that are used to achieve the stated targets. They include monetary, fiscal, tax, tariff, quota, technology, labor training, health, social welfare, education, health, price control, capital rationing, foreign aid, foreign investment, population control, business incentive, and transfer policies.

Organizing a Framework for Implementation Coordination and Monitoring of a Development Plan

Traditionally, three major planning techniques have been used in organizing a framework for implementation of a development plan: (1) aggregate growth models, (2) input-output tables, and (3) project appraisals and cost-benefit analysis.

Aggregate Growth Models. Conventionally, an aggregate growth model constitutes the most elementary macroeconomic planning approach that has been employed in almost all developing nations. These models provide an accessible method for forecasting. As a macroeconomic approach, the aggregate growth model focuses on the major economic variables that affect the level and growth of national output. Examples include: capital stock, exports, imports, foreign aid, savings, investment, and so on.

Essentially all aggregate growth models are based on some version of the Harrod-Domar model discussed in Chapter 4. As we explained in that chapter, the Harrod-Domar model considers limited savings as the major obstacle to economic growth in developing nations. Given the targeted GNP growth rate and a national capital-output ratio, the Harrod-Domar model can be employed to determine the amount of domestic savings needed to trigger such a growth. For economic planning purposes, the following modified Harrod-Domar can be used:

$$k(g + d) = (S\pi - S_w)(\pi/Q) + S_w \qquad (12.1)$$

Where, k is capital stock, g is the targeted rate of growth, d is the fraction of capital stock depreciated in each period, π is profit income, Q is total output, and S_p and S_w are the savings propensities from π and W, respectively.

GLOBAL INSIGHTS CASE 12.2

DEVELOPMENT PLANNING IN INDIA

After years of struggle against British rule India gained its independence in 1947. Jawaharlal Nehru, India's first prime minister following its independence, was influenced by both English democratic socialism and Soviet industrial planning. Under his leadership, India was the first market-oriented developing nation to have its own planning commission in 1950. India's 5-year plans, during the 1950-1980 period, are marked by too much control over the private sector and insufficient commitment to programs in the public sector. During this period, the Indian planners often selected public sector investment without complete information and cost-benefit analysis for alternative project locations. Having chosen a project, the government often failed to adequately implement the project. The project implementation suffered from lack of detailed technical preparation, work scheduling, and bureaucracy. Poorly stated criteria for assigning input licenses and production quotas induced charges of bribery. Chief public sector products were frequently priced lower than scarcity prices, enhancing waste and depleting savings. Additionally, the political environment in public enterprises led to overstaffing of unskilled labor in many projects. Such planning practices led to profit rates for public firms that were lower than for domestic private firms.

Given the inadequacy of the planning during 1950-1980 in India, the planners became increasingly aware of the inappropriateness of controlling private output and prices, and the cost of licensing and quota policies. Beginning in 1980, the Indian government started to enhance efficiency and savings by improving public sector plans, easing import restrictions, loosening control on private business, relaxing production and material licensing, and improving consumption and savings. More specifically, the following three major policies were included in the seven five-year plan (1985-1990):

1. Increased emphasis on an export-oriented growth program to generate foreign exchange.
2. Expansion of antipoverty efforts and human resource development.
3. Increased efforts in slowing down the rate of population growth.

The aforementioned policies were only slightly successful in enhancing India's economic growth. However, the growth rate started to increase more rapidly after 1991. In that year a new government launched a set of economic reforms, including the following schemes:

1. Currency devaluation to enhance exports and diminish imports.
2. A speed up of the privatization process with further encouragement to foreign investors.
3. A revision of the personal tax system, including cutbacks in income and wealth taxes.
4. A progressive liberalization of interest rates to encourage savings and investment.
5. A reduction of production subsidies, import duties on capital goods, and quantitative import restrictions.
6. The deregulation of industry.

As the Indian government marches toward more dependence on the market mechanism and a more open economy the question that is raised is if any improvement in the economic growth might come at the expense of higher unemployment, greater income inequality, worsening of income distribution and environmental decay. Although no one knows the future, one thing is clear, that is, the major challenge facing the Indian government is how to balance economic growth with efficiency, equity, and rapid population growth. This is a question that only time will tell.

Continued

240 PART III/DOMESTIC RESOURCE POLICIES & DEVELOPMENT STRATEGIES

> **Global Insights Case 12.2, Continued**
>
> Source: Jagdish N. Bhagwati and Padma Desai, *India: Planning for Industrialization-Industrialization and Trade Policies Since 1951* (London: Oxford University Press, 1970), and Jagdish Bagwati, *India in Transition: Freeing the Economy* (Oxford: Clarendon Press, 1993), University Press.

The formula can be used to determine the adequacy of current saving out of profit and wage income. For example, if a 5 percent growth desired, that is $g = 0.05$, and if $d = 0.04$, $k = 4.0$. and $\pi/Q = 1/2$, equation 12.1 reduces to the following:

$$4.0(0.05 + 0.04) = (S_\pi - S_w)(1/2) + S_w$$
$$0.36 = \tfrac{1}{2}(S_\pi - S_w)$$
$$0.72 = (S_\pi - S_w)$$

According to the above equation, if savings out of profit income amounts to 30%, that is, $S_\pi = 0.03$, then wage earners must save at a 42% rate to attain the targeted rate of growth. If such a savings rate cannot be secured out of labor income, the authorities could follow an array of policies to increase domestic savings or pursue foreign aid.

Given the simplicity and the relatively low data-collection cost of the aggregate growth model, one might be tempted to overlook the very limitations of this approach, especially when it is implemented in a very mechanical manner. This point is elegantly explained by Noble Laureate W. Arthur Lewis who writes:

> The principal danger of a macroeconomic exercise lies in its propensity to dazzle. The more figures there are in a plan, produced by an army of professionals who have labored mightily to make them consistent, the more persuasive the plan becomes. Attention shifts from policy to arithmetic. Consistency can be mistaken for truth. Revision is resisted. Yet the plan is not necessarily right merely because its figures are mutually consistent.[1]

It should also be noted, that mistakes can arise in the calculations, because variables such as savings rates can be very unstable, and average capital-output ratios are very difficult to estimate. For example, when Nigeria's First National Plan (1962-1968) was published, Lewis writes:

> Argument broke out as to whether the planner had "chosen" the right rate of growth whether they had used the right capital-output ratios, and whether they had determined correctly the amount of capital which private entrepreneurs would be required to invest.[2]

To be sure, the aggregate growth models provide us with only a rough blueprint of the general directions that an economy might follow. However, they seldom comprise the operational development plan. The operational development plan calls for a more integrated economic model such as the familiar input-output model.

Input-Output Tables. The most useful approach to development planning is to employ some variant of the **interindustry** or **input-output table**. This approach is composed of a set of simultaneous equations that express the specific production processes or technologies of each industry, taking into consideration the interrelationship of all the major industrial sectors of the economy. All industries are considered both as

CH. 12/DEVELOPMENT PLANNING: THEORY AND PRACTICE

employers of inputs and producers of output.

To begin with, a model in the form of a table is created in which each of the economy's industries are listed twice: Once across the top as the purchaser of inputs and once down the left side as the seller of outputs. The squares within the body of the table are referred to as "cells," indicating the buying-selling relationships among industries depicted in the model in monetary terms. Table 12.1 portrays a very simplified version of an input-output table for an economy that consists of only four industries. In reality, an input-output table consists of hundreds of industries. In studying this table and elaborating on its application, we should note the following:

1. **Reading the Columns**. Each column indicates the value of the input bought by each industry at the top, from the industries itemized along the left side of the table. For example, during the given period, the auto industry bought $900 million worth of goods from the steel industry, $600 million

Table 12.1

Input-Output Table for an Economy with four Industries
(millions of dollars; hypothetical data for a given period)

Output (sellers) / Input (buyers)	Steel Industry	Auto Industry	Rubber Industry	Glass Industry	Inter-industry Sales Total	Direct Consumption *	Total Output
Steel Industry	$600 (0.25)	$900 (0.30)	$300 (0.18)	$150 (0.17)	$1950	$450	**$2,400**
Auto Industry	$300 (0.13)	$600 (0.20)	$150 (.09)	$300 (0.33)	$1350	$1,650	**$3,000**
Rubber Industry	$150 (0.06)	$750 (0.25)	$450 (0.27)		$1,350	$300	**$1,650**
Glass Industry		$600 (0.20)		$150 (0.17)	$750	$150	**$900**
Other Resources	$1,350 (0.56)	$150 (0.05)	$750 (0.46)	$300 (0.33)	$2,550		**$2,550**
Total Input	**$2,400**	**$3,000**	**$1,650**	**$900**	**$7,950**	**$2,550**	**$10,500**

* Includes all other sales consisting of direct sales to households, government, foreign sources, and sales for capital formation (investment goods)

worth of autos for its own use, $750 million worth of goods from the rubber industry, and $600 worth of goods from the glass industry. In addition, it purchased $150 million from "other resources." Thus, the total value of all inputs purchased by the auto industry adds up to $3000 million ($3 billion). Other columns for each industry are interpreted in the same manner. The dollar amount in each cell indicates how an industry's total input was allocated among different sellers itemized at the left of the table.

2. **Reading the Rows**. Each row indicates the value of the output sold by each industry at the left to the industries itemized along the top of the table. For example, during the given period, the glass industry sold $150 million worth of goods to the steel industry, $300 million worth of goods to the auto industry, nothing to the rubber industry, and $150 million to worth of goods to itself. In addition, direct consumption of glass by other sources amounted to $300 million. Thus, the total

value of all outputs sold by the glass industry adds up to $900 million. Other rows for each industry are interpreted in the same manner. The dollar amount in each cell indicates how an industry's total output was allocated among different buyers itemized along the top of the table.

3. **Input Coefficients**. An input coefficient shows the value of each input needed to produce an additional dollar's worth of output. In Table 12.1, the value of each coefficient for each cell, indicated in parentheses, is calculated according to the following formula:

$$\text{Input coefficient} = \frac{\text{industry's specific input}}{\text{industry's total input}}$$

For example, reading down from the top of the table, the auto industry's specific input from steel industry was $900 million, whereas the auto industry's total input was $3,000 million ($3 billion). Thus, the auto industry's input coefficient, IC, for steel is:

$$_{STEEL}IC_{rubber} = \frac{\$900}{\$3,000} = 0.03$$

In the same manner, reading down again from the top of the table, the rubber industry's specific input from auto industry was $150 million, whereas the rubber industry's total input was $1,650 million ($1.650 billion). Thus, the rubber industry's input coefficient for autos is:

$$_{RUBBER}IC_{autos} = \frac{\$150}{\$1,650} = 0.09$$

Other input coefficients are calculated in the same manner. Note that the sum of all input coefficients in each column should be equal to 1.

4. **Application of the Table**. The analysis based on the input-output tables has a number of applications in planning. Information collected for the construction of the table provides the sectoral data that may be useful in other aspects of planning. More specifically, the table can be used to predict the effects of changes in demand on industry supplies. For example, the economic planner might be interested in knowing the impact of a 10 percent increase in demand for auto industry on the sale of steel, autos, rubber, glass, and other resources. A 10 percent increase in demand for autos would raise their direct consumption by $165 million, from $1,650 to $1815. This additional $165 million is obtained by multiplying each impacted industry by its input coefficient:

Steel	0.30 X $165 million = $	49.5 0 million
Auto	0.20 X $165 million =	33.0 0 million
Rubber	0.25 X $165 million =	41.25 million
Glass	0.20 X $165 million =	33.00 million
Other resources	0.05 X $165 million =	8.25 million
Total value of additional inputs	= $165.00 million	

Thus, the total value of additional inputs to the auto industry equals the value of its additional output, that is, $165 million.

Studying the impact of increased demand from the input-output table may provide the planners with other valuable information. It can help them in assessing the impact of demand increases on changes in employment, investment demand, imports, balance of payments, and national income that go beyond the immediate, direct impact. Instead of employing the tedious step-by-step procedure, planners can use input-output analysis and take advantage of high-speed computers to compute a set of simultaneous equations that express the specific production processes or technologies of each industry, taking into consideration the interrelationship of all the major industrial sectors of the economy.

5. **The Validity of Input-Output Tables.** Input-output tables are based on the following questionable assumption:

   a. The input coefficients are fixed, implying that there are no substitutions between inputs.
   b. Input functions are linear, that is, output increases by the same multiple as inputs.
   c. Production is subject to constant return to scale, that is, doubling of all inputs leads to doubling of all outputs.
   d. The marginal input coefficient is equal to the average, connoting no internal economies or diseconomies of scale.
   e. The absence of externalities, so that the total effect of implementing several activities is equal to the sum of their separate impacts.
   f. The absence of joint products, that is, each good is produced by only one industry, and every industry produces only one good.
   g. The absence of any technical change, ruling out the likelihood of, say, modern, improved agricultural techniques, decreasing the industrial and commercial inputs needed per unit of output.

Despite these limitation casting doubt on the validity of the input-output analysis, the errors may not be significant, especially in plans that cover a period of 5 years or less. For instance, given the relatively constant levels of factor prices and technology in the short run, there may not be much substitutability between inputs in the short run. Some of these problems can be alleviated if input coefficients can be calculated frequently on a regular basis by a set of simultaneous equations that (a) express the specific production processes or technologies of each industry; and (b) take into consideration the interrelationship of all the major industrial sectors of the economy. Unfortunately, some developing nations have been very slow in compiling data that are needed for the construction of the input-output tables. For many of these nations, baseline expenditure surveys in both rural and urban areas, industrial structures, transport, construction, and small-scale industry are out of date. Some developing nations' estimates are 15 to 20 years old, while others yet depend on the early benchmark estimations of the 1960s or early 1970s.[3] If a developing nation is serious about economic development one of its major priorities must be the establishment of a census and a statistical department to collect periodic economic data.

Project Appraisal and Cost-Benefit Analysis. While most planners in developing nations utilize a version of the Harrod-Domar growth model and some employ input-output tables, most of the daily operational decisions regarding the allocations of the public investment funds are based on a microeconomic method of analysis referred to as **project appraisal**. Nevertheless, one should not ignore the operational ties among the three major planning methods. Macro models provide the planner with the overall strategy. Input-output analysis assures an internally coherent array of sectoral targets. Finally, project appraisal is devised to provide for the efficient planning of individual projects within each sector. The extent to which these three major planning methods inteact will significantly affect the success of the planning process.

The technique of project appraisal is based on the theory and practice of **cost-benefit analysis**. This method rests on the simple idea that the value of a project requiring public funds must be determined by measuring the advantages (benefits) and disadvantages (costs) to the society as a whole. The need for social cost-benefit analysis stems from the existence of externalities that lead to the divergence of social costs/benefits from the private costs/benefits, as we explained before. It is based on the contention that the assumption of profit maximization that guides the private sector investment decision, leading to the equality of MPC and MPB, may not be appropriate for the public investment decisions, that is, it may not lead to the equality of SMC and SMB.

The cost-benefit analysis centers on the assessment of **social profit**, that is, the difference between social costs and social benefits, during a given period. The calculation of this variable involves the following three steps:

1. **Establishing Goals**. The usefulness of a project depends on its contribution to the national and economic goals of the developing nations. In fact all plans are devised to maximize social welfare in one way or another. Thus, it is imperative that the main measure of the social welfare be defined and quantified as precisely as possible. The following measures have been used in project analysis:
    a. **The Project's Impact on Future Consumption Levels.** Because it is hard to assign numerical values to some social goals such as political stability, life quality, self-reliance, and national cohesion, economic planners usually measure the value of a project on the basis of its contribution to the net flow of goods and services in the nation, that is, by its impact on the future consumption levels.
    b. **The Project's Impact on Income Distribution**. In this method, the planner tries to define how a particular project will benefit different income classes, especially low income classes. If the object is to increase the consumption level of low-income classes, then the planner may construct a poverty-weighted index, discussed in Chapter 2. Thus, the social welfare of a project must be calculated as a weighted sum of the distribution of its benefits to various income classes, where higher weights are assigned to the low-income classes.
    c. **The Project's Impact on the Environment**. In this approach the planners try to assess the impact of the project on the environment. This is the newest approach which has been used by the World Bank in project analysis since the beginning of 1991.
2. **Computing Shadow Prices**. The gist of the cost-benefit analysis is the calculation or estimation of prices to be employed in assessing the true values of benefits and costs associated with an investment project. However, as we already know, market prices do not reflect the social benefits and costs of an investment project due to market failure. To rectify the problem, market prices must be adjusted to account for differences between social cost-benefit and private cost-benefit calculations. Planners employ **shadow (accounting) prices** to adjust distortions in the price of capital, labor, and foreign exchange. The following examples demonstrate how this adjustment is commonly implemented:
    a. Suppose that the cost of capital in the world market is 12%, and a government of a developing nation artificially sets the cost of capital at the low rate of 6% to encourage investment. In this case, although a business can borrow money at the subsidized rate from the government, the shadow interest rate should be set at 12% to reflect the opportunity cost of capital in the world market.
    b. Assume that the unskilled worker in India earns 10 rupees an hour in the industrial sector, and only 5 rupees an hour in the agricultural sector. In this case, the shadow price is set at 5 rupees to reflect the true opportunity cost of unskilled labor to the society.
    c. Suppose, in order to control foreign trade, the Indian government set the exchange rate at 20 rupees = $1.00, when the market exchange rate is 40 rupees = $1.00. Thus, an IBM computer purchased by an Indian firm from the United States for only 40,000 rupees ($2,000) should have a shadow price of 80,000 rupees to reflect the true opportunity cost

CH. 12/DEVELOPMENT PLANNING: THEORY AND PRACTICE

of the computer to the society.

Given the existence of forces leading to sizeable distortions in prices of developing nations, it is generally agreed that a project's expected receipts and payments often do not reflects its social worth. Thus, social-cost benefit analysis is perceived to be an integral part of an efficient method of project selection in developing nations.

3. **Selecting Projects.** In selecting different investment projects, a planner needs to calculate the **net present value** (**NPV**) of time streams of project benefits and costs, using the following formula:

$$NPV = \sum_{T=0}^{T} \frac{B_t}{(1+r)^t} \qquad (12\text{-}2)$$

or

$$NPV = B_0 - C_0 + \frac{B_1 - C_1}{(1+r)} + \frac{B_1 - C_1}{(1+r)^2} + \cdots \frac{B_t - C_t}{(1+r)^T} \qquad (12\text{-}3)$$

where, B is social benefits, C is social costs, r is the **social discount rate** (the interest rate defined by the planners), t is time, and T is the life of the investment project.

For example, assume that an investment project leads to a net income stream of $1,000,000 for only 10 years. In other words, $B_t - C_t = \$1,000,000$, and t = 1,...10. The total net income stream is $1,000,000 × 10 = $10,000,000. Suppose, however, that the discount rate is 10 percent. This discounts the $1,000,000 annual net return to $$909,090 in the first year, $3,790,786 in the fifth year, and $6,144,567 in the tenth year. Thus, the discounted total income stream over the 10-year period turns out to be $6,144,567, instead of the total net income stream of $10,000,000. In other words, $6,144,565, represents the net present value of annuity of an $1,000,000 a year for 10 years, given that the discount rate is 10 percent. As formula 10-3 indicates, the NPV is significantly dependent on the social discount rate. A higher (lower) social discount rate leads to a lower (higher) NPV. It should be noted that social discount rates may be different from the market rate of interest which is used by the private sector to calculate the profitability of private investment. The extent by which the social interest rates differ from market rates depends on subjective evaluations of net benefits by planners. The higher the future benefits and costs are valued by the planners, the lower will be the social rate of discount. Having understood the concept of net present value, and chosen the proper social discount rate, the planner can then use the NPV rule to choose among alternative projects. According to this rule, a project should be accepted if its NPV is positive and rejected if its NPV is negative. However, as we explained earlier, NPV calculations are significantly affected by the choice of social discount rates. An alternative approach is to calculate the discount rate that sets NPV of a project equal to zero. This discount rate, referred to as the **internal rate of return**, can be used by the planner as the criterion for project selection. The planner should compare this rate with either the market rate of interest or a predetermined social discount rate, and select investment projects whose internal rate of returns are greater than the market rate or the predetermined social discount rate. Given that most developing nations suffer from capital shortages, the selection of investment projects usually includes a ranking of all investment projects that satisfy the NPV rule, that is, their NPVs are positive. Accordingly, the investment projects are ranked by descending order of their NPV/K ratios, and the project with the highest NPV/K ratio is chosen first, then the next highest, and so on down the line until the entire available capital investment has been used up. To illustrate the method by which investment projects are ranked, assume that the social discount rate is 10 percent and we have to make a choice between the following two investment projects:

PART III/DOMESTIC RESOURCE POLICIES & DEVELOPMENT STRATEGIES   246

on down the line until the entire available capital investment has been used up. To illustrate the method by which investment projects are ranked, assume that the social discount rate is 10 percent and we have to make a choice between the following two investment projects:

   a. An air conditioning factory with the initial capital requirement (K) of $3000,000, resulting in a net stream of $250,000 per year for a 5-year period, and $400,000 per year for an additional 15-year period.
   b. A refrigerator factory with the K cost of $3,000,000, resulting in a net stream of income of $350,00 a year for a 20-year period.

This hypothetical example is portrayed in Table 12.2. It shows how the two hypothetical investment projects are ranked by their NPVs. Although the total amount of *undiscounted* net income for the air conditioning factory ($7,250,0000) is higher than the same total for the refrigerator factory ($7,000,000), the planner should invest in the refrigerator, because it provides a higher NPV/K ratio (2,979,748/3,000,000 = 99.32) than the same ratio for the air conditioning factory (2,834,809/3,000,000 = 94.49). This example also shows the significance of higher net incomes in the first few years, before the discount factor is very high.

Defining the Duration of the Plan

The planner needs to specify the period of time during which the stated objective will be met. The plans' duration may be classified into the following three categories:

1. **Short-term plans**. These plans aim at reaching their objective in the immediate future, that is, the next calendar or budget year. They implement government policy according to a detailed budget. The size and composition of short-term plans are determined primarily by budgetary consideration, progress made in feasibility studies, and projects launched in the previous years.
2. **Medium-term plans.** These plans focus on improving economic conditions on a relatively distant future, typically 5 years. A medium-term plan can take the form of a **rolling plan**, that is, a plan revised at the end of each year. For example, given a 5-year plan for 2000-2005, at the end of 2,000 the planner would revise the plan, devising a new plan for 2001 to 2006. In this manner, the plan is renewed at the end of each year, however, the number of years stays the same as the plan rolls forward over time. In practice, the implementation of rolling plans have proven to be difficult for many developing nations. A more practical approach to updating a medium-term plan, is by implementing part of it through the short-term plan.
3. **Long-term (perspective) plans**. These plans covers a long period of time, that is, 15 years, 20 years, or longer. Long-term plans should serve as the framework for medium- and short-term plans.

THE FAILURE OF PLANNING IN DEVELOPING NATIONS

A review of the record of planning in developing nations over more than four decades reveals that, in general, such efforts have led to discouraging outcomes. The existence of empirical studies in this area reveals that there has been less success than failure. Additionally, the majority of the nations that engaged in planning have failed to achieve even modest output and income goals in their plans, except in the short-run. What is even worse is that the condition is deteriorating instead of ameliorating as nations keep on planning. [4]

Table 12.2

Present Value of Hypothetical 20-Year Net Income Streams from Two Alternative $3 Million Investment Projects in Year 0 Discounted at 10 percent a year

	Air Conditioning Factory ($3 million initial capital)			Refrigerator Factory ($3 million initial capital)	
Year	Net Income ($B_t - C_t$)	Net Income (discounted to year 0)	Year	Net Income ($B_t - C_t$)	Net Income (discounted to year 0)
1	250,000	227,272	1	350,000	318,182
2	250,000	206,611	2	350,000	289,256
3	250,000	187,829	3	350,000	262,960
4	250,000	170,753	4	350,000	239,055
5	250,000	155,230	5	350,000	217,322
6	400,000	225,790	6	350,000	197,566
7	400,000	205,263	7	350,000	179,605
8	400,000	186,603	8	350,000	163,278
9	400,000	169,639	9	350,000	148,434
10	400,000	152,217	10	350,000	134,940
11	400,000	140,198	11	350,000	122,673
12	400,000	127,452	12	350,000	111,521
13	400,000	115,866	13	350,000	101,383
14	400,000	105,333	14	350,000	92,166
15	400,000	95,7572	15	350,000	83,787
16	400,000	87,052	16	350,000	76,170
17	400,000	79,138	17	350,000	69,246
18	400,000	71,944	18	350,000	62,951
19	400,000	65,404	19	350,000	57,228
20	400,000	59,457	20	350,000	52,025
Total	7,250,000	2,834,809		7,000,000	2,979,748

The failure of planning in developing nations can be explained in the context of two interrelated elements, one dealing with limitations of theory in practice, and the other with inadequacy of planning process.

Limitations of Theory in Practice

As we explained earlier, the major economic argument for development planning is based on the notion of market failure. To rectify this problem through development planning, the government is entrusted with the task of reconciling the divergence between social costs and benefits. However, experience shows that, in practice, governments often worsen rather than reconcile such divergences. This point has been elegantly described by Killick, who writes:

> It is doubtful whether plans have generated more useful signals for the future than would otherwise have been forthcoming; governments have rarely, in practice reconciled private and social valuations except in a piecemeal manner, because they have seldom become operational documents, plans have probably had only limited impact in mobilizing resources and in coordinating economic policies.[5]

The four major cases where private and social valuations seem to diverge, and where the impacts of governmental policies have frequently led to enhance rather than reduce these divergences are:

1. **Import Substitution Policies**. As we will explain in Chapter 13, import substitution policies are policies that aim at discouraging importation of manufactured goods by encouraging their domestic production. This is achieved through protectionist means such as quotas, subsidized interest rates, overvalued exchange rates, special tax concessions to foreign investors, higher effective tariff rates designed to lower the cost of capital- and intermediate-goods imports, and the whole host of bureaucratic industrial licensing procedures. Unfortunately, such policies have failed to meet the planners' expectations in terms of leading to the low-cost efficient production processes to be enjoyed by the domestic producers. This is especially true in Latin American countries that pursue import-substitution polices. For example, in Colombia, Peru, and Chile the costs of vehicles runs two to three times higher than the costs of similar vehicles in the international market. As we explain later in Chapter 13 policies of indiscriminate import-substitution have proven to be self-defeating. Such policies which give rise to inefficient and costly production, would result in losses for both consumers and producers, thereby reducing the world's welfare.
2. **Urban Development Biased Policies**. Government policies in many developing nations are biased in favor of urban development. This is evident by the existence of considerable income differentials and disparities in economic opportunities between rural sectors and urban sectors in developing nations. Such policies have resulted in increasing urban unemployment and agriculture stagnation, leading to an excessive migration of rural workers to urban areas in search of jobs. The outcome of this process has been a net social loss to the society in terms of lost agricultural production and the higher social costs of accommodating rural migrants in cities.
3. **Industrialization and Employment Conflict**. As we explained in Chapter 7, the dual objective of rapid industrial growth and higher employment in developing nations has usually led to achieving the first objective at the expense of the second objective. However, if government policies were more tuned to adjusting factor-price movements to the real resource scarcities of developing nations, there would be no need for such a conflict to exist. In practice, however, factor-price movements have significantly deviated from their tacit social valuations. This is partly due to the fact that public policies in many developing nations have aimed at increasing the level of wages above worker's shadow price or scarcity value by various schemes such as minimum wage legislation, and

tying wages to educational attainment. Similarly, the private cost of capital has been kept way below its scarcity or social cost, by schemes such as tax allowances, low effective rate of protection, overvalued exchange rates, and quotas. The outcome of such policies has been the adaptation of the more capital-using production techniques than would be needed if public policy aimed at adjusting prices. In summary, private valuations of costs and benefits usually justify the employment of the relatively more capital-using technologies when real social valuations would dictate the adoption of the relatively more labor-using technologies.

4. **Overvaluation of Returns to Education**. As we explained in Chapter 7 the policies of many developing nations have aimed at subsidization of private costs of education, especially at the higher levels. As a result, private cost-benefit valuations have shown higher returns than are warranted by the social cost-benefit valuations. This has led to the misallocation of resources away from of alternative investment opportunities, such as the creation of productive opportunities.

Inadequacy of the Planning Process

As our foregoing discussion implies, in theory many developing nations' policies are designed to reduce income inequality, eliminate poverty, and increase employment. In practice, however, such policies seems to be worsening rather than improving these problems. Such an outcome is partially explained by the inadequacy of the planning process which stems from the following problems:

1. **Data Insufficiency and Unreliability**. In many developing nations the statistical data that are needed for planning purposes are either nonexistent, or weak and unreliable.
2. **Inadequate Supply of Planning Experts**. In many developing nations the supply of economists, statisticians, and other planning experts are inadequate. This problem coupled with the data insufficiency and unreliability in most developing nations makes the planning effort a frustrating experience.
3. **Institutional Inadequacy**. A number of variables contribute to the institutional inadequacy of the planning process in most developing nations. These variables include:
    a. The failure of political leaders, planners, and administrators to engage in a continuous communication regarding objectives and strategies.
    b. The detachment of the day-to-day decision making mechanism of government from the planning agency.
    c. The international transfer of organizational and institutional planning conventions that may be inappropriate to the local conditions existing in the developing nations
    d. The existence of unqualified and incompetent civil servants who are in charge of bureaucratic organizations marked by resistance to innovations and change, corruption, lack of commitment to national goals, and personal and interdepartmental rivalry.
4. **Absence of Political Determination**. Many developing nations' leaders and high level administrators lack the political determination to carry out a development plan. The existing evidence shows that in nations with development plans, the absence of appropriate governmental support for the plans is the major reason for their implementation's failure.

Markets Over Planning

Given the failure of planning in developing nations, many politicians and economists have advocated the enhanced use of the market mechanism as opposed to planning in developing nations. Such a position has been nurtured by the following elements:

GLOBAL INSIGHTS CASE 12.3

THE STAGES OF ECONOMIC DEVELOPMENT AND PLANNING IN CHINA

The Chinese economy has gone through the following stages in the course of its development from 1949 to the present:

1. **Stage one,** from the latter part of 1949 to 1953, was a period of coalition building during which the Communists devised the basis for a national government.
2. **Stage two** which lasted from 1943 to 1957, was a period in which the First Five-Year plan was implemented. This plan was developed with the help of Russian advisors who followed the Russian planning pattern. During this period the state played a significant role in the operation of the plan. The plan, aimed at high industrial growth and capital formation, was directed to industry and transportation. More specifically, it called for the rise in the gross value of the output of producer goods by 128 percent over the 1952 level. It targeted the production of 4 million tons of steel by 1957. It planned to increase cement production by 110 percent over the 1952 level. Finally, it planned for an increase in the gross value of the agricultural production of 23 percent in five years.
3. **Stage three**, referred to as the **Great Leap Forward,** lasted from 1958 to 1960. During this period, China departed from Russian style planning and instituted a new approach that was geared to industrial development. The philosophy behind the Great Leap Forward was to utilize domestic Chinese, labor and material, to push the economy ahead at an accelerated rate.
4. **Stage four,** which lasted from 1961 to 1965, followed the collapse of the Great Leap Forward and involved the return of development planning marked by the adoption of more rational economic policies toward agriculture and industry. This plan placed priority on the development of heavy industry.
5. **Stage five**, lasting from 1966 to 1969, was the period in which the *Proletarian Cultural Revolution* took place. It was an attempt by Mao Tse-Tung, the Chinese leader, to shape Chinese society in accordance with his model. Accordingly, it evoked ideological idiom over scientific know-how.
6. **Stage Six** is the current stage that started in 1970. This stage can be marked by a resumption of more efficient political and economic policies. In 1978, a movement toward agriculture started that led to the modification of the traditional communes by the "production responsibility system," comprising contracts between the communes and a group of farmers. The contracts determine the land to be cultivated and identify the type and quantity of products to be forwarded to the state.

These contracts provide access to land for 15 years, during which time the land can either be sold or inherited. Additionally, any excess product above what is specified in the contract can be sold in the newly revived free market. This reform has contributed to the record-breaking performance of Chinese agriculture during the 1980s.

Continued

> *Global Insights Case 12.3, Continued*
>
> The industrial reform in China started at a slower pace than its agriculture reform. Initially, the system adhered to strict Soviet-style comprehensive planning. Beginning in 1994, China introduced some new reforms to narrow the scope of the plan, permitting competition between the new private sector and the state. Accordingly, prices were to be freed, and firms were allowed to retain a portion of their profit for bonuses and investment, instead of remitting all the profits to the state. As a result of these reforms, some of small firms are now leased out, like farms. Wages in many firms now differ in accordance to the earning differentials between the firms, and workers commonly have contracts.
>
> A return toward central planning started in 1988. A major factor that contributed to the movement was a high inflation rate which reached the level of 20% in 1998. In 1990 there was a sudden slow down in reforms that checked the movement toward market pricing. Consequently, managers and local officials began to loose power to the national government, and a single price started to become more common for many goods. Such policies contributed to growth stagnation and unemployment.
>
> Chinese development plans are similar to the former Soviet's development plan and can be classified into two major categories, on the basis of the stated goals: (1) the physical output plan, which sets production, distribution, and investment goals; and (2) financial plans, which are derivatives of physical plans. Plans can also be classified into three groups, depending on the period of time that they cover: (1) long-range plans which usually concentrate on a specific aspect of the economy and may cover a 30-year period; (2) medium-range plans which commonly cover a five-year period during which the stated goals and targets have to be met; and (3) annual or operating plans that set production and distribution targets to be met by Chinese enterprises and other units during the year. Annual plans can be subdivided into quarterly or monthly periods.
>
> Today, the Chinese monetary and fiscal system exerts strong control over the economy. Because much of the financial resources of the nation are collected and distributed through the national budget, it plays a significant role in the Chinese economy. Tax and non-tax revenues are channeled through the budget to support capital investment in state firms. Monetary control is implemented through the People's Bank of China. All firms are compelled to have an account with the Bank, which can match all purchases and sales against authorized payments and receipts. The Bank is also oversees the expenditures of all state firms, and is in charge of allocating financial resources according to the Credit and Cash plans.
>
> Source: Martin C. Schnitzer and James W. Nordyke, *Comparative Economic Systems*, 2nd ed. (Pelham Manor, N.Y.: South-Western Publishing Co., 1977), Chapters 18 & 19); Dwight H. Perkins, "Reforming china's Economic System," *Journal of Economic Literature* 26, no.2 (June 1988): 601-645; D. Gale Johnson, "Economic Reforms in the People's Republic of China, " *Economic Development and Cultural Change* 36, no. 3, supplement (April 1988); the special in *The Economist*, August 1, 1987.

1. The increasing disappointment with government interventions, especially in the area of central planning.
2. The success of the Newly Industrialized Countries (NICs), especially South Korea and Taiwan who depended significantly on the private enterprise, in the later phases of their development.

However, the effectiveness of the market mechanism depends on the existence of special institutional, legal, social and cultural preconditions that are usually nonexistent in developing nations. Thus, the degree by which a developing country should depend on the market mechanism, as opposed to central planning, depends on the special conditions that exist in that nation. Nevertheless, one thing is clear, that is, developing nations are marked by the existence of market imperfection, lack of effective competition, and substantial externalities. Given these conditions, in general, these nations will not be able to depend on the market mechanism by the degree that developed nations did when they were at their early stages of development.

It would seem that low-income nations in their early stages of development need to continue to depend

252   PART III/DOMESTIC RESOURCE POLICIES & DEVELOPMENT STRATEGIES

more on planning because the cultural and institutional prerequisites for a market economy are inadequate and they confront major structural changes in the future. Middle-income nations could gradually become more market-oriented, nevertheless they would need to remain mixed economies with a large degree of government interaction. Nations in later stages of their development, such as the NICs of East Asia and Latin American, already have circumstances that permit more dependence on competitive prices. But, even these nations need to be mindful of the dangers of depending entirely on the market mechanism for the allocation and distribution of their resources in achieving the economic and social objectives of their development plan in the long run.

In closing this chapter it must be emphasized that economic decisions in developing nations are ultimately made by political leaders rather than economists. These leaders, operating within a political framework, may be more interested in satisfying the groups who keep them in power rather than launching major social and economic reforms. However, many experts predict that this situation will change and in the future we will witness a development crisis that may be impossible to rectify, without broad social and economic and improvements. Alarmed by such predictions, evidence shows that during the past few decades, governments in developing nations have assumed an increasing role for the management and direction of their economies. Such a trend is expected to continue in most developing nations. One could hope that the developing nations' policy makers have learned from their past mistakes, setting the stage for their success in the future.

SUMMARY

1. **Development planning** may be defined as the intentional government action to orchestrate economic decision process over the long run and to direct, affect, or even control a nation's the major economic variables in order to achieve a contemplated set of economic goals.
2. An **economic plan** is composed of a set of quantitative economic objectives to be attained during a given period of time. Economic plans can be divided into the following two categories: (1) **comprehensive plans** which aim at covering all aspects of national economy; and (2) **partial plans** which only deal with a part of national economy, such as agriculture, industry, foreign sector, and so forth.
3. A **planning process** can be described as an activity that is implemented by the government and composed of the following steps: (1) choosing social objectives; (2) setting various targets; (3) organizing a framework for implementation, coordination and monitoring of a development plan; and (4) defining the duration of the plan.
4. The arguments of the opponents of development planning are based on the concept of market efficiency. They argue that the market efficiently allocates scarce resources among alternative uses, leading to the following outcomes: (1) firms produce those goods that maximize their profits; (2) consumers obtain commodities for which they are willing to pay; (3) the market determines available capital and labor; (4) the market distributes income between resources and thus, individuals; and (4) resources are hired out to maximized income.
5. The plea for development planning by its proponents is based on the following two major arguments: market failures and undesirable market outcomes.
6. The failure of the market system stems from the following factors: (1) the existence of externalities; (2) lack of information; (3) monopoly distortions; government intervention; and (4) low savings rate.
7. Planning may be necessary, because the market mechanism could produce outcomes that policy makers may find unacceptable. This position is of course normative, calling for a value judgement. The following two situations illustrates the point: (1) maldistribution of income; and (2) interests of future generations.

CH. 12/DEVELOPMENT PLANNING: THEORY AND PRACTICE

QUESTIONS

1. Why do you think that there was considerable support for development planning following the World War? Why did the economists started to question the wisdom of economic planning beginning the 1970s.
2. Define the concept of economic planning and answer the following questions:
    a. What are the two categories of economics plans?
    b. What is meant by a planning process?
    c. What steps should a government take when engaging in a planning process?
3. Discuss the major arguments for and against economic planning.
4. Define the three planning models discussed in the text and elaborate on their major weaknesses and strengths from the standpoint of planning in Third World nations.
5. Elaborate on the failure of the economic planning in the Third World nations by answering the following questions:
    a. What are the major reasons for the failure of economic planning in the Third World nations?
    b. Given your answer to part a, which reason do you think is the most important? Explain.
6. Given the failure of economic planning, should Third Word nations discard this approach and rely exclusively on the market mechanism to achieve economic development? Do you agree with this statement? Discuss.
7. Elaborate on the concept of market failure by answering the following questions:
    a. What is meant by market failure?
    b. What factors give rise to market failure?
    c. What is the difference between market failure and government failure?
8. Fill in the required data, including the input coefficients for the following input-output table given for a hypothetical country and answer the following questions:
    a. Determine the impact of a 20 percent rise in foreign demand for the secondary sector's output on the numbers given in the table.
    b. Does an increased demand for the secondary sector's output affect other sectors of the economy? Discuss.

Input-Output Table for an Economy with Three Sectors
(millions of dollars; hypothetical data for a given period)

Output (sellers) / Input (buyers)	Primary Sector*	Secondary Sector**	Tertiary Sector***	Inter-sectoral Sales Total	All Other Sales	Total Output
Primary Sector	$200 ( )	$400 ( )	$100 ( )		$300	
Secondary Sector	$600 ( )	$800 ( )	$400 ( )		$200	
Tertiary Sector	$100 ( )	$300 (0.20)	$200 ( )	$750	$200	
Other Resources	$1,350 (0.56)	$300 (0.05)	$200 (0.46)	$2,550		
Total Input					$700	

* **Primary sector** consists of agriculture, forestry, and fishing.
** **Secondary sector** consists of manufacturing.
*** **Tertiary sector** consists of commerce, finance, transport, and services.

NOTES

1. W. Arthur Lewis, *Development Planning: The Essentials of Economic Policy* (London: Allen and Unwin, 1966), pp.16-17.
2. Ibid., 35-36.
3. Alan Heston, "National Accounts: A Brief Review of Some Problems in Using National Accounts Data in Level of Output Comparisons and Growth Studies," *Journal of Development Economics* 44 (June 1994): 44-45.
4. Albert Waterson, *Development Planning: Lessons of Experience* (Baltimore: Johns Hopkins University Press, 1965).
5. Tony Killick, "The Possibilities of development planning," *Oxford Economic Papers* 41 (July 1976): 163-164.

SUGGESTED READINGS

Blitzer, Charles R., Paul B. Clark, and Lance Taylor. eds. *Economy-Wide Models and Development Planning*. London: Oxford Univeristy Press, 1975.

Coase, R. H. "The Nature of the Firms." *Economica* N.S. 4 (1937): 386-405. Reprinted in George J. Stigler and Kenneth E. Boulding. Eds. *Readings in Price Theory*. Chicago: Irwin, 1952, pp. 331-51.

Devarajan, Shantayanan, Lyn Squire, and Stehaput Suthiwart-Narueput. "Beyond the Rate of Return: Reorienting Project Appraisal." *World Bank Research Observer* 12 (February 1977): 35-46.

Ghosh, Pradip K. ed. *Development Policy and Planning: A Third World Perspective*. Westport,Conn.: Greenwood Press, 1984.

Harberger, Arnold C. *"Reflections on Social Project Evaluation."* In *Pioneers in Development: Second Series*, edited by Gerald M. Meier. New York: Oxford University Press, 1987.

Heston, Alan. "National Accounts: A Brief Review of Some Problems in Using National Data in Level of Output comparisons and Growth Studies." *Journal of Development Economics* 44 (June 1994): 44-45.

Hollis, Chenery B. ed. *Studies in Development Planning*. Cambridge, Mass.: Harvard University Press, 1971.

Killick, Tony. *A Reaction Too Far: Economic Theory and the Role of the State in Developing Countries*. London: Overseas Development Institute, 1989.

Klitgaard. *Adjusting to Reality: Beyond "State Versus Market" in Economic Development.* San Francisco: ICS Press, 1991.

Lal, Deepak. *The Poverty of Development Economics.* London: Institute of Economic Affairs, 1983.

Little, Ian and James Mirrlees. *Project Appraisals and Planning for Developing Countries.* New York: Basic Books, 1974.

Lewis, Arthur W. *Development Planning: The Essentials of Economic Policy.* London: Allen and Unwin, 1966.

Miernyk, William H. *The Elements of Input-Output Analysis.* New York: Random House, 1965.

Nove, Alec. *The Economics of Feasible Socialism.* London: Allen and Unwin, 1983.

Pappas, Ivy. "Techniques of Project Appraisal." in Norman Gemmell. ed. *Surveys in Development Economics.* Oxford: Blackwell, 1987, chap. 9.

Pugh, Cedric. "The World Bank's Millennial Theory of the State: Further Attempts to Reconcile the Political and the Economic." *The Third World Planning Review* 19 (September 1997): iii-Xiv.

Rosen, Sherwin. "Transactions Costs and Internal Labor Markets." in Oliver E. Williamson and Sidney G. Winter. Eds. *The Nature of the Firms: Orgins, Evolution, and Development.* New York: Oxford University Press 1991.

Sagesti, Francisco R. "National Development Planning in Turblent Times: New Approaches and Criteria for Institutional Design." *World Development* 16 (April 1988): 431-448.

Schrenk, Martin. "The Self-Managed Firm in Yugoslavia." in Gene Tidrick and Chen Jiyuan, eds. *China's Industrial Reform.* New York: Osford Uiversity Press, 1987.

Stewart, Frances. "The Fragile Foundations of the Neoclassical Approach to Development." *Journal of Development Studies* 21 (January 1985): 282-92.

Streeten, Paul P. *Strategies for Human Development.* Copenhagen: Handelshojskolens Forlag, 1994, pt. 2.

Stigler, Joseph. "The Role of Government in Economic Development." *Annual World Bank Conference on Development Economics, 1996.* Washington, D.C.: World Bank, 1977, pp. 11-26.

_____, Ha-Joon Chang and Robert Towthorn. eds. *The Role of the State in Economic Change.* New York: Oxford University Press, 1995.

Tinbergen, Jan. *Development Planning.* London: Weidenfeld & Nicolson, 1967.

Todaro, Michael P. *Development Planning: Models and Methods.* Nairobi: Oxford University Press, 1971.

Waterson, Albert. *Development: Lessons of Experience.* Baltimore: Johns Hopkins University Press, 1965.

Williamson, Oliver E. "Hierarchical Control and Optimum Firm Size." *Journal of Political Economy* 75 (April 1967): 123-39.

PART IV

INTERNATIONAL ECONOMICS OF DEVELOPING NATIONS

CHAPTER 13

TRADE THEORY, TRADE POLICIES, AND DEVELOPMENT EXPERIENCE

International trade theories have been developed to explain various issues that are encountered in trade among nations. Some of the most important questions raised in international trade are as follows:

1. Why do nations trade?
2. What are the gains from trade?
3. How are relative prices of goods determined in international trade?
4. What factors determine the direction of trade (who exports what)?
5. What are the welfare effects of restricting trade?

This chapter examines these questions. First, we review the historical development of modern theories. The writings of the mercantilists and classical economists, including Adam Smith and David Ricardo, have been crucial in shaping the foundation of modern trade theories. Second, we present the theoretical principles and policies that are employed in analyzing the impact of international trade among nations.

HISTORICAL DEVELOPMENT OF MODERN TRADE THEORIES

The purpose of this section is to review the historical development of trade theories, and elaborate on major theories that have laid the foundation for the modern theories of international trade. First we discuss the theory of mercantilism. Second, we elaborate on the theory of absolute advantage. Third, we present the theory of comparative advantage. Finally, we explain the Heckscher-Ohlin theory which provides the foundations of modern international theory.

Theory of Mercantilism

The systematic study of international trade started in the era of mercantilism that prevailed in Europe between the sixteenth and eighteenth centuries. This period marked the beginning of the development of modern states. The basic idea of **mercantilism** was that wealth is a necessary condition for national power. National power is in turn enhanced by the increase in specie, that is, gold and silver coins. Thus, for a country without gold and silver mines, the only means of acquiring gold and silver is by encouraging exports and discouraging imports.

The problem with mercantilist ideas was that they confused the concept of wealth with precious metal. Because they assumed that wealth was limited, they concluded that one nation's gain from trade was achieved only by another nation's loss.

David Hume, the eighteenth-century British economist, essayist, historian, and philosopher, criticized mercantilism and showed that there is a self-correcting mechanism (called the price-specie-flow mechanism) that makes mercantilist policies self-defeating. He explained that as a nation increases its exports and accumulates more gold and silver coins, the money supply in the economy increases. An increase in the money supply creates an inflationary effect and increases domestic prices. The increase in domestic prices makes domestic goods more expensive for other countries to buy, resulting in a decrease in exports. On the other hand, an increase in domestic prices makes foreign-produced goods relatively cheaper than domestic ones, causing imports to increase.[1] When exports fall and imports rise, the country's money supply (precious metals) declines.

Although mercantilism continued to be criticized by later economists, such as Adam Smith and David Ricardo, some of its teachings are still practiced today, though to a lesser degree. For example, in an attempt to take away some of the United States' world economic power and leadership, General Charles De Gaulle adopted policies to increase French exports and discourage imports, particularly from the United States. Additionally, he demanded that the United States settle its payments deficit with France in gold. De Gaulle's mercantilist policy is still followed by his successors, although in a less extreme fashion.[2] Today, socialists have created a France in which key industries and banks are nationalized. As a result, about one third of France's productive capacity and 70 percent of its high-tech industries are under the government control. Today, government intervention in France has reached the same level practiced in the seventeenth century, prompting some authors to call the present government's policy "high-tech mercantilism."[3]

Theory of Absolute Advantage

The theory of **absolute advantage** was developed by Adam Smith. Smith, a leading advocate of free trade, recognized the significance of specialization and division of labor. His theory of absolute advantage states that two countries can benefit from trade if, due to natural or acquired endowments, they can provide each other with a product made more cheaply than they can be produced at home. This means that the total resource cost to produce a good in one country is absolutely less than the resource cost to produce the same good in another country. Thus, according to this theory, each country should specialize in the production of goods in which it is most efficient, that is, the goods it can make most cheaply.

Absolute advantage might be the result of natural endowment or acquired endowment. Natural endowment includes factors that are related to climate, soil, and mineral resources. For example, some nations, such as Saudi Arabia and Iran, have petroleum, but most do not. Bananas can be grown relatively cheaply in Central America because of the tropical climate. The soil and climate conditions are conducive to the production of wine and lumber in France and Sweden, respectively. Acquired endowments include special skills and technology, such as those used by the United States to produce AWACS planes and those used by Japan to produce electronic robots. Thus, according to the theory of absolute advantage, the U.S.

CH. 13/TRADE THEORY, TRADE POLICIES & DEVELOPMENT EXPERIENCE

should export AWACS to Saudi Arabia, and Saudi Arabia should export petroleum to the United States. France should export wine to Sweden and Sweden should export lumber to France. Japan should export electronic robots to Iran, and Iran should export petroleum to Japan.

The concept of absolute advantage can be explained numerically by a simple example. Let us assume that: 1) the United States and France are both able to produce two goods, cotton and wine; 2) there are no transportation costs between these countries; 3) competitive conditions prevail; 4) labor is the only factor of production and thus the only cost of production; 5) labor is freely mobile within countries but not between countries; and 6) there is no government intervention. Table 13.1 shows the production resulting from one day (eight hours) of labor.

Table 13.1

PRODUCTION FROM ONE DAY OF LABOR AT FULL EMPLOYMENT

Country	Cotton Output (Bales/Day)	Wine Output (Gallons/Day)
United States	10	5
France	5	10

According to Table 13.1, France has an absolute advantage in the production of wine because one day of labor produces 10 gallons of wine in France compared to 5 gallons of wine in the United States. The United States has an absolute advantage in the production of cotton because one day of labor produces 10 bales of cotton in the United States compared to 5 bales in France. Thus, it is sensible for the United States to specialize in the production of cotton, export the cotton to France, and import French wine. The reverse is true for France.

We may now introduce the concept of opportunity cost to show the extent by which each country benefits from trade. **Opportunity cost** is the value of the benefit foregone when choosing one alternative rather than another. This simply means what a nation would have to give up of one good in choosing to produce another good. For example, the opportunity cost of 1 gallon of wine in the United States is 2 bales of cotton, because 1 day of labor can produce either 5 gallons of wine or 10 bales of cotton.

In our example, both countries can gain from trade, if they specialize and exchange wine for cotton at a relative price ratio of 1:1, that is, by trading 1 gallon of wine for 1 bale of cotton. As a result, the United States can employ all of its resources to produce cotton, and France can use all of its resources to produce wine. The United States can import 1 gallon of wine for 1 bale of cotton, as opposed to sacrificing the production of 2 bales of cotton to make 1 gallon of wine at home, thereby saving 1 bale of cotton. In the same manner, France can save 1 gallon of wine in trade with the United States.

In summary, the theory of absolute advantage suggests that:

1. The higher the level of a country's specialization, according to its absolute advantage, the more potential gain from trade.
2. Both trading parties gain from trade. These points are in contrast to mercantilist thought, which implies one country's gain from trade is achieved by another country's loss.

Theory of Comparative Advantage

The theory of absolute advantage showed the effects of trade when each trading partner had an absolute advantage in the production of only one commodity. A more complicated situation emerges when a country has an absolute advantage in producing both goods; that is, it can make both goods at a lower cost than the other country. David Ricardo first demonstrated this case in his theory of **comparative advantage.** He showed that both trading nations can benefit from trade even when one of the nations has an absolute advantage in the production of both commodities. In terms of our previous example with two countries (the United States and France) and two goods (cotton and wine), Ricardo's theory can be explained using Table 13.2.

Table 13.2

PRODUCTION FROM ONE DAY OF LABOR AT FULL EMPLOYMENT

	Cotton Output (Bales/Day)	Wine Output (Gallons/Day)	Opportunity Costs Bales of Cotton/Gallons of Wine	Opportunity Costs Gallons of Wine/Bales of Cotton
United States	180	90	1W = 2C	1C = 0.5W
France	40	80	1W = 0.5C	1C = 2W

As the table indicates, the United States has an absolute advantage in the production of both commodities. One day of labor produces 180 bales of cotton or 90 gallons of wine in the United States as compared to 40 bales of cotton or 80 gallons of wine in France. This might lead one to think that trade is not advantageous for the United States. Yet trade is profitable to both countries because the relative cost of production in both countries is different. The opportunity costs column reveals how cotton (C) and wine (W) are exchanged in each country before trade takes place. According to these numbers, 2 bales of cotton can be exchanged for 1 gallon of wine in the United States. In other words, 1 bale of cotton commands 0.5 gallons of wine in the United States. In France, on the other hand, 1 bale of cotton is exchanged for 2 gallons of wine. This shows that cotton is relatively cheaper in the United States, whereas wine is relatively cheaper in France. If the United States exports 1 bale of cotton to France, it can receive 2 gallons of wine, as opposed to 0.5 gallons at home. If France exports 1 gallon of wine to the United States, it can receive 2 bales of cotton, as opposed to 0.5 bales at home. Therefore, the United States should export cotton to France, and France should export wine to the United States.

However, as France exports wine to the United States, the supply of wine in the United States increases and the price falls. Similarly, in France, cotton imports from the United States increase the supply, decreasing its price. This process continues until the price ratios in the United States and France become equal to each other. In other words, trade equalizes the relative prices in both countries. At this new price, it pays for both countries to specialize in the production of the commodity in which they have a comparative advantage—the United States in cotton and France in wine. In this way, both countries export the surplus of domestic production over domestic demand and import the excess of domestic demand over domestic production.

Thus, according to the theory of comparative advantage, if one country can produce two goods more efficiently than another country and can produce one of these goods more efficiently than the other, it should specialize in and export that commodity in which it is comparatively more efficient, that is, the commodity in which it has the greatest absolute advantage. The less efficient nation should specialize in and export the commodity in which it is comparatively less inefficient, that is, the commodity in which its absolute disadvantage is least.

HECKSCHER-OHLIN THEORY

Ricardo's theory of comparative advantage assumes that domestic differences in natural or acquired endowment give rise to differential factor productivities that provide the basis for trade among nations. This implies that the primary determinant of the basis for trade is factor productivity.*

Eli Heckscher and Bertil Ohlin, two Swedish economists, argued that international differentials in supply conditions explain the direction of international trade. They explained that supply includes not only factor productivities but factor endowments as well.** Their ideas gave rise to the development of a theory that considers factor endowment as the primary cause of international trade.

According to this theory the price differentials among nations are related to two factors: (1) differences in relative endowments of the factors of production that exist among countries, and (2) differences in the intensities of factor usage in the production of different commodities. Given these circumstances the Heckscher-Ohlin (H-O) theory states that each country should export those commodities that use its abundant factor more intensively, importing goods that use its scarce factor more intensively.*** This means, for example, countries that have an abundance of labor, such as India or Hong Kong, should export commodities such as cloth, which require a labor-intensive technology. On the other hand, a capital-abundant country like the United States should export commodities such as airplanes and electronic computers, which require capital-intensive technology.****

---

*The term "factor productivity" refers to the productivity of the factors of production. For example, labor productivity is measured as output per day in Table 13.1.

**The term "factor productivity" refers to the productivity of the factors of production. For example, labor productivity is measured as output per day in Table 13.1

***The term "factor" here refers to the factors of production, for example, capital and labor. A factor of production could be abundant (cheap) or it could be scarce (expensive).

****Like all economic theories, the H-O theory is based on a number of simplifying assumptions. The theory assumes the following:

1. There are two countries using two factors of production, capital and labor, to produce two goods.
2. Identical production functions exist in both countries.
3. Production functions in both countries display constant return to scale.
4. One of the commodities is capital intensive at all input prices; the other is labor intensive.
5. Perfect competition in both commodities and factor markets, as well as full employment of resources exists in both nations.
6. Both nations have identical tastes.
7. There are no transportation or similar costs and no barriers to free international trade.
8. Perfect factor mobility exists within each nation but not between nations.
9. Neither country has complete specialization in production.

For more details regarding the implications of these assumptions, see Asheghian, P., *International Economics*, 3rd. ed. Cincinnati, Ohio: Dame/Thompson Learning, 2003, pp. 70-71.

GLOBAL INSIGHTS CASE 13.1

RELATIVE RESOURCE ELATIVE RESOURCE ENDOWMENTS AND TRADE PATTERNS OF LEADING DEVELOPED NATIONS

The relative abundance of factors of production in a nation determines its role as an importer or exporter in the global market. Table A shows six leading advanced nations' resource endowment as percentages of the world's total resource in 1980. The United States, for example, has 33.6 percent of physical capital, 50.7 percent of research and development scientists, 29.3 percent of arable land, 27.7 percent of skilled labor, 19.1 percent semiskilled labor, and 0.19 percent of unskilled labor. These amount to 28.6 percent of all resources combined. As shown, the United States has a greater relative share of world resources of physical capital, research and development scientists, and arable land than any other country. Given this data, according to the Heckscher-Ohlin (H-O) theory, the United States should export capital- and technology-intensive products, and agricultural products.

Table A
RELATIVE ENDOWMENTS OF LEADING DEVELOPED NATIONS*
(AS A PERCENTAGE OF WORLD TOTAL)

Country	Physical Capital	R & D Scientists	Arable Land	Skilled Labor	Semi-Skilled Labor	Unskilled Labor	All Resources (1982 GDP)
United States	33.6	50.7	29.3	27.7	19.1	0.19	28.6
Britain	4.5	8.5	1.0	5.1	4.9	0.09	5.1
Canada	3.9	1.8	6.1	2.9	2.1	0.03	2.6
France	7.5	6.0	2.6	6.0	3.9	0.06	6.0
Japan	15.5	23.0	0.8	8.7	11.5	0.25	11.2
West Germany	7.7	10.0	1.1	6.9	5.5	0.08	7.2

Source: John Mutti and Peter Morici, *Changing Patterns of U.S. Industrial Activity and Comparative Advantage* (Washington, D.C.:National Planning Association, 1983), p. 8. and World bank, *World Development Report 1984* (Washington, D.C., 1984), pp. 222-23.

Table B shows export/import ratios for the same nations. An export/import ratio greater than one indicates that the nation is a net exporter of a specific product. On the other hand, an export/import ratio smaller than one means that the nation is a net importer of the product. As these data indicate, the United States is a net exporter of technology-intensive products and services, a pattern that reflects U.S. technological expertise and past accumulation of physical

Continued

> *Global Insights Case 13.1, Continued*
>
> capital. Although the data are from 1979, circumstances are not very different today for the United States. These results are in accord with the Heckscher-Ohlin theory.
>
> **Table B**
> **EXPORT/IMPORT RATIOS OF LEADING DEVELOPED NATIONS**
>
> | | Product | | | | |
> |---|---|---|---|---|---|
> | Country | Technology-intensive | Labor-intensive | Services | Standardized | Primary |
> | United States | 1.52 | 0.38 | 1.50 | 0.39 | 0.55 |
> | Britain | 1.39 | 0.71 | 1.28 | 0.76 | 0.81 |
> | Canada | 0.77 | 0.20 | 0.49 | 1.38 | 2.21 |
> | France | 1.38 | 0.86 | 1.22 | 1.03 | 0.52 |
> | Japan | 5.67 | 1.04 | 0.72 | 1.09 | 0.44 |
> | West Germany | 2.40 | 0.59 | 0.82 | 0.84 | 0.29 |
>
> *Source:* John Mutti and Peter Morici, *Changing Patterns of U.S. Industrial Activity and Comparative Advantage* (Washington, D.C.: National Planning Association, 1983), p. 32; and P. Morici, *Meeting the Competitive Challenge: Canada and the United States* (Washington, D.C.: Canadian-American committee, 1988), p. 49.

LEONTIEF PARADOX

In 1953, Professor Wassily Leontief provided the first major attempt to empirically examine the Heckscher-Ohlin theory. Using the U.S. trade data for 1947, he analyzed the capital to labor ratio for some 00 export industries and import-competing industries. He found that the capital to labor ratio for the U.S. export industries was lower than that of its import-competing industries. In other words, his results suggested that the United States exported goods that were relatively labor intensive and imported commodities that were relatively capital intensive. Given that the United States was considered to be a capital-abundant and a labor-scarce country at the time of the study, Leontief's results seemed to contradict the H-O theory, which predicted that a capital-abundant country would export relatively capital-intensive goods. To further examine the H-O theory, Leontief did another study, using 1951 data, and again he found that U.S. exports were relatively less capital intensive than U.S. imports. To explain the paradox, Leontief argued that the United States is two to three times more efficient than other countries. If the labor supply in the United States were adjusted to account for this efficiency, the United States could actually be considered a labor-abundant nation. Leontief's paradoxical conclusion gave rise to similar studies for other countries. For example, a case study of Japan, by Tatemoto and Ichimura in 1959, suggested that Japanese exports were capital intensive and its imports were relatively labor intensive. Because Japan was believed to be a labor-abundant country at the time of the study, the paradox was repeated. However a more careful analysis of the patterns of Japanese exports revealed that Japanese exports to developing countries tended to be relatively capital intensive, whereas its exports to advanced countries-the United States and Western countries-tended to be labor intensive. This explanation seems to conform to the H-O theory, because Japan is a relatively labor-abundant country as compared to the United States, and it is relatively capital-abundant in comparison to its developing countries trading partners.

TRADE THEORY AND ECONOMIC DEVELOPMENT

According to conventional trade theory, if each country specializes in the production of the commodity in which it is most efficient, not only does each nation gain from trade but world output also increases. The majority of Western economists support this theory and consider international trade an "**engine of growth**." To defend their position, they present historical evidence showing that in the nineteenth century, export-led growth in Great Britain and several other now-industrial nations propelled their economies into rapid growth and development. In other words, the majority of Western economists maintain that international trade served as an engine of growth for these nations during that period. This implies that today's developing nations could also benefit from international trade as the now-advanced countries did when they went through their development processes.

There are, however, some economists who do not share this view and present theories stating that international trade has hampered rather than promoted the development process. This has occurred through deterioration in terms of trade and vast oscillation in the export incomes of developing countries. Three theories that have attracted much attention are the dependency theory, the theory of immiserizing growth, and the Prebisch theory. Having elaborated on the dependency theory in Chapter 5, in this section, first, we explain the other two theories and then elaborate on ways by which international trade can contribute to the process of economic development.

Theory of Immiserizing Growth

As we discussed earlier in this chapter, according to the theory of comparative advantage, each country should specialize in and export the goods in which it is comparatively more efficient than its trading partners. Because the comparative advantage of most of the developing nations lies in the production of primary products, they should, according to the theory, specialize in and export these products. Around the mid-1950s, however, economists presented cases showing that the pursuit of comparative advantage dictates actually makes developing countries worse off; the pursuit "immiserizes" them. The possibility of *immiserizing growth*, which was emphasized by Jagdish N. Bhagwati, was later studied by Harry Johnson and Carlos Diaz Alejandro. Through their work, the concept of **immiserizing growth** came to be known as an expansion of the factor supply or productivity that makes a nation worse off. The possibility of immiserizing growth occurs when an increase in the supply of a tradable good tends to decrease its price in the world market. If the price decrease is large enough, it might have an adverse effect on the exporting country, thereby worsening its welfare.

Take the case of Brazil, which is the world's largest coffee-bean exporter. Assume that a technological advance in coffee-bean production is introduced to this country. This would encourage an individual coffee-bean grower to take advantage of the situation and increase production and sales. Because all farmers might behave in this fashion, their collective action may result in a considerable increase in output. Given that Brazil has a large share of the world's coffee-bean market, and given an inelastic demand for coffee beans, the expansion of Brazil's coffee-bean supply results in a lower world price for coffee beans. If this price decline is large enough to outweigh the increase in the quantity supplied, Brazil's revenue from coffee-bean exports will decrease. In this way, Brazil's own technological improvements and resulting increases in supply worsen its terms of trade (the amount of goods exported per unit imported). When this happens additional

CH. 13/TRADE THEORY, TRADE POLICIES & DEVELOPMENT EXPERIENCE

international trade will actually worsen Brazil's economic welfare rather than improve it.

Several conditions are necessary for immiserizing growth to occur:

1. The world's demand for the country's exports must be inelastic, such that an expansion in the quantity of exports results in a large decline in price.
2. The country's economic growth must be biased toward the export sector.
3. The country's economy must be dependent on international trade for national welfare to the extent that a decline in the terms of trade could outweigh the possible gains from increasing product supply.

Although immiserizing growth might have taken place for a developing country, like Brazil with its coffee-bean expansion, before the 1930s, it does not seem very prevalent in the real world although it is a possibility.* If it does occur, it brings unpleasant results.** Because immiserizing growth takes place only in the presence of an inelastic demand, it is possible for a country to exploit this inelasticity by imposing optimum tariffs and taxes on exports. The success of such a strategy depends on the market power exercised by the country in question; and the market power, in turn, is limited by the existence of potential new entrants into the world market.

Graphical Illustration of Immiserizing Growth.

Given our previous example of Brazil, Figure 13.1 portrays a case of immiserizing growth. The figure illustrates Brazil's production possibilities frontiers (PPFs) for coffee beans (export product) and steel (import product), both measured in terms of tons per year. Initially, before growth takes place, Brazil is producing at point P_0 on PPF_0 and consuming at point C_0 on its community indifference curve (I_0). It exports A_0P_0 tons of coffee for A_0C_0 tons of steel at the terms of trade ratio denoted by TOT_0.

Now assume that due to technological improvement, Brazil's ability to grow coffee beans increases much faster than its ability to produce steel. This causes Brazil's production possibilities frontier to shift right to PPF_1. As the figure shows, the growth is "biased" toward Brazil's export product (coffee beans), indicating more favorable technological improvement in coffee-bean production than in steel production. Given that Brazil has a large share of the world market for coffee beans and the world demand for coffee beans is price inelastic, Brazil's expanded coffee-bean supply causes the world price for coffee beans to decline substantially. Thus, Brazil's terms of trade decline to TOT. At this new price ratio, Brazil produces at point P_1 on PPF_1 and consumes at point C_1 on curve I_1. At the new terms of trade (TOT.), Brazil exports A_1P_1 tons of coffee for A_1C_1 tons of steel. Because the consumption point moves from pregrowth position C_0 on curve t Io postgrowth point C_1 on curve I_1, Brazilian welfare decreases. In other words, Brazil's own advancement in supply ability makes it worse off, plunging it to a lower indifference curve.

---

*Most developing nations are not large enough for export volume to significantly affect their terms of trade. As a result, immiserizing growth is not very prevalent in these nations.

**Both income elasticity of demand and price elasticity of demand for primary products are low.

Figure 13.1

A CASE OF IMMISERIZING GROWTH

Initially, before growth takes place, Brazil produces at point P_0 on its production possibilities curve PPF_0 and consumes at point C_0 on its community indifference curve I_0. It exports AP_0 tons of coffee for $A0Co$ tons of steel at the terms of trade ratio denoted by TOT_0. Assume that due to technological improvement, Brazil's ability to grow coffee beans increases much faster than its ability to produce steel. This causes Brazil's production possibilities frontier to shift right to PPF_1 and its term of trade to decline to TOT_1. At this new price ratio, Brazil produces at point P_1 on PPF_1 and consumes at point C_1 on. At this new terms of trade, Brazil exports A_1P_1 tons of coffee for A_1C_1 tons of steel. Because the consumption point moves from pregrowth position C_0 on community indifference curve I_0 to postgrowth point C_1 on the lower indifference curve I_1, Brazilian welfare decreases.

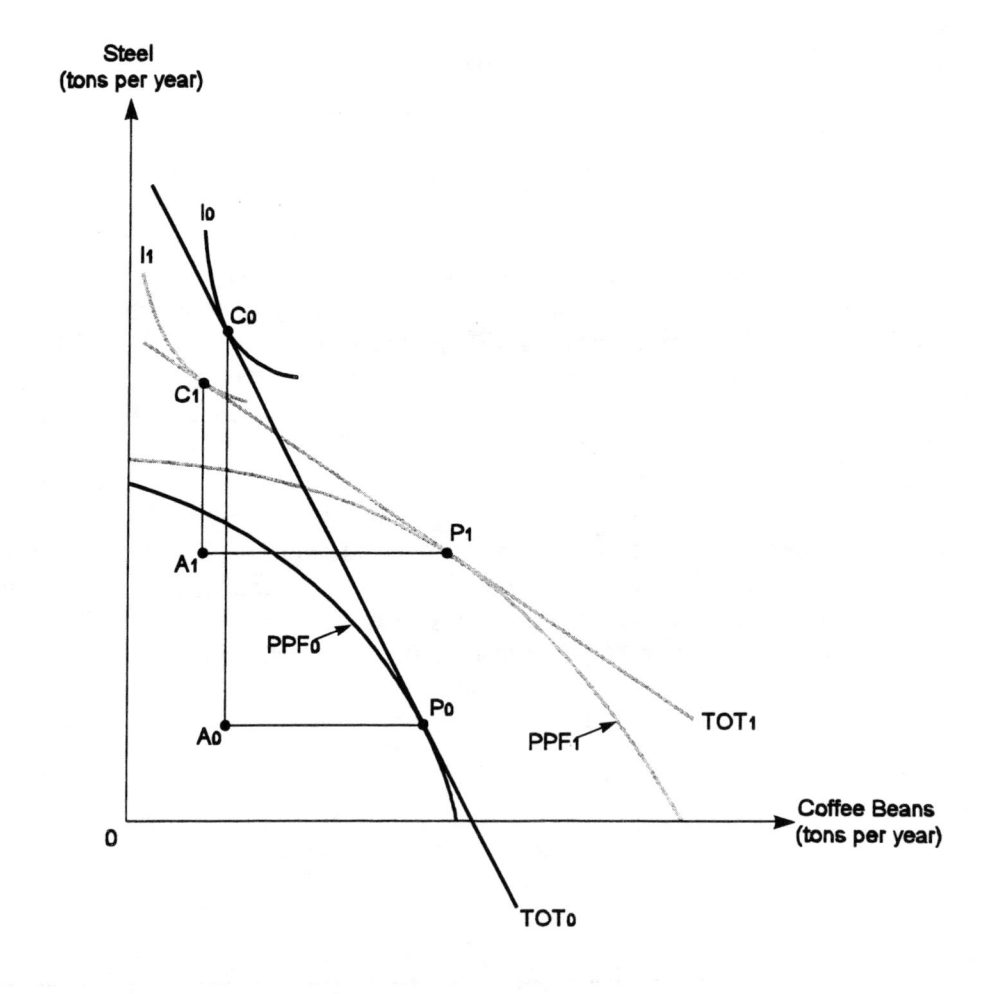

Prebisch Theory

The possibility of immiserizing growth existing in developing countries gave rise to a new argument that questioned the wisdom of pursuing policies based on the theory of comparative advantage. In the early 1950s, Raul Prebisch, an Argentinean economist, and others argued that developing countries, primarily exporters of agricultural products and raw materials, faced an inelastic demand in their export markets and were not gaining (nor would they gain) from trade with advanced countries.* Because the prices of these products relative to manufactured goods had been declining and were unstable, Prebisch and others postulated a persistent, long-run tendency for developing countries' terms of trade to deteriorate. They also hypothesized that a developing country's initial export to an advanced country would bring a greater gain to the advanced country, alleging that the advanced country was in a more advantageous position.

Given these arguments, their policy recommendation to the developing countries was as follows:

1. Developing countries should decrease the resources used for the production and export of their primary product sectors.
2. They should expand the resources used in their modern and industrial sectors.
3. They should restrict the import of the industrial goods into their countries, replacing these imports with goods produced domestically.
4. They should demand a decrease in the trade barriers imposed against their industrial products by advanced countries.

The Prebisch theory created a great deal of controversy, especially regarding the validity of the facts presented to support it. The theory was based on data related to the long-run movements of the British terms of trade from the late 1800s to the end of the 1930s. Questions have been raised concerning the adequacy of such data. To be sure, the British terms of trade did improve, whereas the terms of trade of its trading partners declined during the period. However, it is argued that the British export and import structure was unique, and, as such, it does not lend itself to generalization about the deterioration of the terms of trade of today's developing countries. Additionally, such data do not allow for product quality changes. The evidence shows that the quality of primary products usually stays fairly constant, whereas the quality of manufactured products keeps improving as time goes by. For example, the quality of Brazilian coffee beans is almost the same as it was years ago, whereas a 1995 IBM computer is much more sophisticated than a 1970 model. Thus, if quality changes are taken into consideration, one could argue that developing countries' terms of trade may not have deteriorated over time. In other words, the reason that developing nations exported more primary products per unit of manufactured goods over time could be related to the rising relative value of the manufactured goods compared to the value of primary products over the same time. In our example, the quality of the Brazilian coffee beans has stayed fairly constant. Because in a competitive market a relatively higher-quality commodity commands a relatively higher price, more Brazilian coffee beans must be exported per unit of IBM computers imported into Brazil.

To date, the evidence indicates that periods of worsening terms of trade have alternated with periods of improving terms of trade. Thus, it is believed that policymakers should not discourage investment in primary products on the grounds that these sectors inevitably face unfavorable price trends; this may not happen. Research has also shown that, contrary to the Prebisch theory, in some cases, the gain from the initial opening of trade accrued mainly to primary-product exporters in developing countries as opposed to their trading partners in advanced countries. For example, when Thailand embarked on international trade in the 1850s, the price of rice, Thailand's newly growing export, increased significantly relative to the price of cloth and other imports. Most of the benefits accrued to Thai farmers. The opening of trade had a comparable impact in Japan during the 1850s and 1860s. During these periods, Japan exported massive amounts of tea and silk in exchange for imports of manufactured goods and rice. The evidence suggests that the gains from trade were mainly accrued to Japanese producers of tea and silk.

With all its controversies, the Prebisch theory has had an enormous impact on the economic policies of developing countries, especially those in Latin America. Many of these countries, such as Colombia, Peru, and Chile, have vigorously followed the policies of import substitution, replacing imports with domestically produced goods. Such policies, implemented by the imposition of taxes and tariffs on imported manufactured goods, have resulted in high production costs for domestically manufactured goods. For example, according to a 1970 study, in Colombia, Peru, and Chile, the production costs for motor vehicles runs about two to three times higher than the production costs for similar vehicles in the international market.[4] As we explained in Chapter 6, policies of indiscriminate import substitution have proven to be self-defeating. Such policies, which give rise to inefficient and costly production, result in losses for both consumers and producers, thereby reducing the world's welfare.

EXPORT INSTABILITY

The Prebisch theory postulated a persistent, long-run tendency for developing countries' terms of trade to deteriorate. Independent of this long-run phenomenon, developing countries may also experience short-run oscillations in their export prices and revenues. This can significantly hinder their economic development process. Export instability occurs because export earnings tend to fluctuate annually to a greater extent for developing countries than for advanced countries.

In this section, we elaborate on the factors that give rise to export instability. We then review empirical studies that have tried to assess the extent of these short-run oscillations and their real effects on the economic development process. Finally, we elaborate on policies employed by developing countries to stabilize their export prices or revenues.

Factors Giving Rise to Export Instability

The factors leading to export instability can be classified as price variability and a high degree of commodity concentration. In examining these two factors, we should keep in mind that developing countries are relatively more involved in the export of raw materials and primary products than of manufactured goods.

Price Variability. Price variability refers to dramatic fluctuations developing countries experience in the prices of their primary products. These fluctuations occur because demand for and supply of primary products produced by developing countries are both price inelastic and unstable. This situation is illustrated in Figure 13.2. D and S represent demand and supply curves, respectively, for a hypothetical developing country's primary-product exports. The equilibrium price is P. If D increases (shifts to the right) to D' or S decreases (shifts to the left) to S', the equilibrium price increases to P'. If both D and S shift simultaneously to D' and S', the equilibrium price rises even more, to P''. If the reverse case takes place, that is, D' and S' fall back to D and S, the equilibrium price declines significantly to P. Thus, given inelastic and unstable (shifting) demand and supply for developing countries' primary exports, one can expect wide oscillations in the prices these countries receive for their exports.

The inelasticity of demand for developing countries' primary-product exports is attributed to the fact that individual households in advanced countries allocate only a small proportion of their budgets to primary products, such as sugar, tobacco, tea, coffee, and bananas. In other words, each of these products is such a relatively small part of the consumer's total expenditures that changes in their prices lead to less-than-proportional changes in quantities demanded, resulting in a price inelastic demand.

The inelasticity of supply of developing countries' primary-exports is attributed to the internal rigidities that exist in most of these countries regarding resource usage. As a result, changes in export prices lead to less-than-proportional changes in quantities supplied, resulting in a price inelastic supply.

CH. 13/TRADE THEORY, TRADE POLICIES & DEVELOPMENT EXPERIENCE

Figure 13.2

A CASE OF PRICE VARIABILITY FOR A DEVELOPING COUNTRY'S PRIMARY PRODUCT EXPORTS

D and S represent demand and supply curves for a hypothetical developing country's primary product exports. The equilibrium price is P. If D increases (shifts to the right) to D', the equilibrium price increases to P'. If both D and S shift simultaneously to D' and S', the equilibrium price rises even more to P". If the reverse takes place, that is D' and S' fall back to D and S, the equilibrium price declines significantly to P. Thus, given inelastic and unstable (that is, shifting) demand and supply for developing countries' exports, we can expect wide oscillations in the prices these countries receive for their exports.

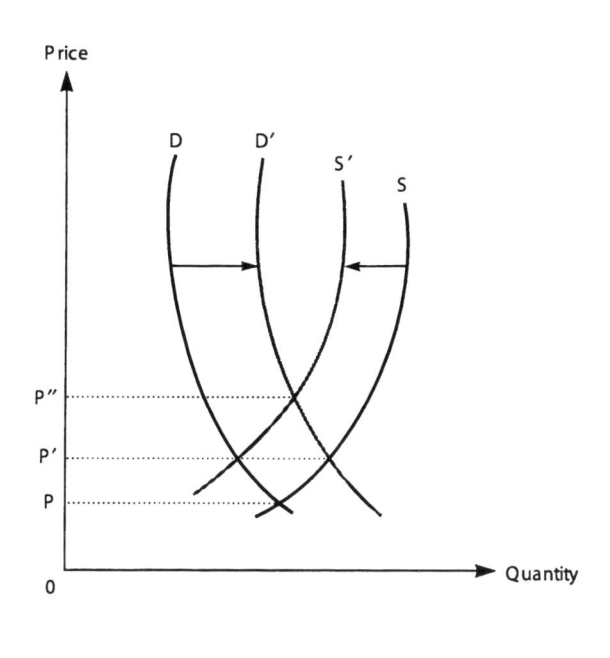

High Degree of Commodity Concentration. One of the attributes of many developing countries is that their exports are concentrated in a small number of primary products. As Table 13.3 shows, in some developing countries, one or two commodities may contribute to the bulk of export earnings. This deficiency in diversification suggests that acute changes in the price of one or two commodities could lead to sharp changes in total export revenues. If the commodities exported were more diversified or less concentrated, a price increase in some commodities could be balanced by a price decrease in other commodities, leading to higher stability in total export revenue.

Table 13.3

PERCENTAGE OF MAJOR PRIMARY EXPORTS TO TOTAL EXPORTS FOR SOME DEVELOPING COUNTRIES[1]

Country	Major Exports	Percentage of Total Export Earnings
Bolivia	Tin	4.21*
	Zinc	5.57*
Colombia	Coffee beans	6.23*
Ghana	Cocoa beans	34.61***
Indonesia	Oil	8.73***
Kuwait	Oil	93.00*
Oman	Oil	37.83***
Saudi Arabia	Oil	91.46**
Sri Lanka	Tea	14.31*
Venezuela	Oil	83.54*

* 2001 data
** 2000 data
*** 1998 data

Source: International Monetary Fund, *International Financial Statistics* (Washington, DC: IMF, August 2002)). Percentages were calculated by the author and are rounded to the nearest digit. For each country, the latest available yearly data were used.

Empirical Studies of Export Instability in Developing Countries

One of the earliest investigations of export instability in developing countries was carried out by Alasdai MacBean. Using 1946-1958 data, he examined export instability for a sample of 45 developing countries and 18 advanced nations. His analysis suggested that export instability, measured by an index, was only slightly greater for the developing countries than for the advanced countries.* He thus concluded that the significance of short-term export instability to developing countries had been overstated. In most cases, oscillations in income did not seem to be closely related at all to oscillations in export proceeds. Many nations with great export instability had relatively stable incomes, whereas many with high export stability experienced serious income instability.

MacBean's analysis also demonstrated that the greater oscillation in developing countries' export proceeds did not induce notable fluctuation in their macroeconomic variables of national income, savings, and investment. This, according to MacBean, may have been related to two factors. One is the relatively low absolute level of export instability; the other is the fact that the very low foreign-trade multipliers shielded the developing countries' economies from oscillations in their export proceeds.

MacBean rejected the commonly accepted explanations of export instability, such as specialization in primary products, commodity concentration, and geographic concentration. He explained that specialization, not simply in primary commodities, but in a specific commodity like natural rubber that is distinctively subject to instability, accounts for the oscillations in the export earnings.

MacBean's findings regarding the relative insignificance of export instability and its possible causes led him to make some policy rules. If export fluctuations did not inflict serious damage on most of the developing countries, he argued, the possible benefits of export stabilization may be negligible. Thus, according to MacBean, the costly international commodity agreements developing countries requested to stabilize their export proceeds were not defensible. The same resources could be employed more efficiently for genuine developmental objectives rather than for stabilizing export revenues that were stable at the outset.[5]

Further studies on the subject of export instability produced controversial results. Benton Massell, using 1950-1966 data and a sample of 36 developing countries and 19 advanced countries, showed that developing countries tended to experience higher export instability due to their higher product concentration. This instability, however, was mitigated by their dependence on food exports which tended to be more stable.[6]

Using 1950-1972 data and a sample of 123 developing countries and 26 advanced countries, Lancieri showed that developing countries were much more subject to fluctuations of export revenues than were advanced nations. His study supported the view that export instability is a significant obstacle to development.[7]

Love reexamined the effects of commodity concentration on instability in export earnings. Using time series data for 24 developing countries, he found a positive relationship between concentration and instability.[8] His findings, however, were rejected by Massell, who questioned whether Love employed a valid measure of export instability and whether his analysis supported his conclusions.[9]

In summary, empirical studies support the view that export instability is, in general, somewhat greater for developing countries than for advanced countries. However, the impact of export instability on economic development and its association with commodity concentration remain controversial. Nevertheless, the developing countries have continued to seek international commodity agreements in order to stabilize and enhance their export revenues.

Policies to Stabilize Export Prices or Revenues

The stabilization of a developing country's export prices or revenues can be achieved by either purely domestic strategies, such as establishing domestic marketing boards, or international strategies, such as engaging in international commodity agreements.

Domestic Marketing Boards. A domestic marketing board (DMB) is an agency that is set up by a developing country's government. The objective of this agency is to maintain price stability for the country's individual producers. To achieve this goal, the agency buys goods from individual domestic producers at a guaranteed price and then sells them on the global market at fluctuating world prices. In determining its guaranteed price, the board sets domestic prices below world prices in good years. This allows the board to accumulate funds needed in bad years to pay domestic producers prices that are higher than international prices. Examples of DMBs include the cocoa marketing boards of Ghana, the rice marketing board in Burma, and the Rice Export Corporation in Pakistan.

In practice, only a few of these agencies have met with some degree of success due to the corruption of agency officials and the difficulty in correctly forecasting domestic prices.

International Commodity Agreements. International commodity agreements (ICAs) refer to agreements between producing and consuming countries to stabilize and increase the prices and revenues of exports. The main types of ICAs are international buffer stock agreements, international export quota agreements, and multilateral agreements.

International Buffer Stock Agreements. This type of international agreement involves the establishment of an international agency by producing nations (often joined by consuming nations) to limit commodity price swings. To achieve this objective, the agency is provided with finances and supplies of a commodity to regulate its world price. If the supplies are abundant and the world price of the commodity falls below an agreed minimum price, the agency purchases the commodity, causing its price to rise to the desired level. On the other hand, if supplies are tight and the world price of the commodity rises above an agreed maximum price, the agency sells the commodity, causing its price to fall to the desired level.

The best-known example of an international buffer stock agreement is the *International Tin Agreement.* This agreement, reached in 1956, was successfully in force for a number of years before its eventual collapse in 1987. Other examples of international buffer stock agreements are the *International Cocoa Agreement* and the *International Natural Rubber Agreement.* Like the International Tin Agreement, these agreements are no longer operational.

Using the example of cocoa beans, Figures 13.3 and 13.4 illustrate how the agency regulates price. Assume that the cocoa-bean agreement calls for a minimum price of $2.50 per pound and a maximum price of $3.50 per pound. Starting at equilibrium point E in Figure 13.3, suppose the demand for cocoa rises from D to D`, causing the equilibrium price to rise from $3.00 per pound to $3.75 per pound. To bring the price down to the maximum level of $3.50 per pound, the agency has to sell 10,000 tons of cocoa beans (line AE", the excess demand at $3.50 per pound), causing the supply curve to shift to S`. This leads to the new equilibrium point E", where the price is brought down to the maximum level of $3.50 per pound.

Conversely, starting at equilibrium point E in Figure 13.4, assume the supply of cocoa beans increases from S to S`, causing the price to fall from $3.00 per pound to $2.25 per pound. To raise the price to the minimum level of $2.50 per pound, the agency must purchase 10,000 pounds of cocoa beans (line AE", the excess supply at the price of $2.50 per pound), causing the demand curve to shift to D`. This leads to the new equilibrium point E", where the price is brought up to the minimum level of $2.50 per pound.

A buffer stock agreement is subject to the following disadvantages:

1. The extended maintenance of the minimum price level may deplete the funds needed to buy excess supplies at the lowest price. This may lead to a downward revision of the minimum price.
2. The extended maintenance of the maximum price level may deplete the agency's stockpile, destroying this price-stabilization strategy's effectiveness. This may lead to the upward revision of the maximum price.
3. Some goods can be stocked only at a very high cost.

International Export Quota Agreements. This type of agreement is aimed at regulating the quantity of an exported good in order to stabilize its price. In such an agreement, producing nations select a target price for the commodity and estimate the world demand for the coming year. Given the estimated demand, they ascertain the quantity of supply that generates the target price. They then divide up this quantity among the supplying nations and rule that no nation should export more than its assigned quota. If the estimated demand is accurate and if the participating nations honor their quotas, the target price is established for the coming year. If the price deviates from the target price, the quota is adjusted to reestablish the target price. This is illustrated in Figures 13.5 and 13.6, in which we assume that the agreement calls for the stabilization of the price of coffee at $1.00 per pound. S and D portray the estimated supply and demand, respectively, that yield this targeted price at equilibrium point E, where 40 million pounds of coffee are sold. Using Figure 13.5, assume that due to world recession the market demand for coffee decreases from D to D', causing the price to fall to $0.75 (point E`). To re-establish the target price, the supplying nations' quotas must be tightened. This causes the supply curve to shift from S to S`, yielding the target price of $1.00 at equilibrium point E".

Figure 13.3

BUFFER STOCK AGREEMENT: PRICE SETTING IN\E THE CASE OF A RISE IN DEMAND

Starting at equilibrium point E, suppose the demand for cocoa rises from D to D`, causing the equilibrium price to rise from $3.00 per pound to $3.75 per pound. To bring the price down to maximum level of $3.50 per pound, the agency has to sell 10,000 tons of cocoa beans (line AE`; the excess demand at the price of $3.50 per pound), causing the supply curve to shift to S`. This leads to the new equilibrium point E`, where the price is brought down to the maximum level of $3.50 per pound.

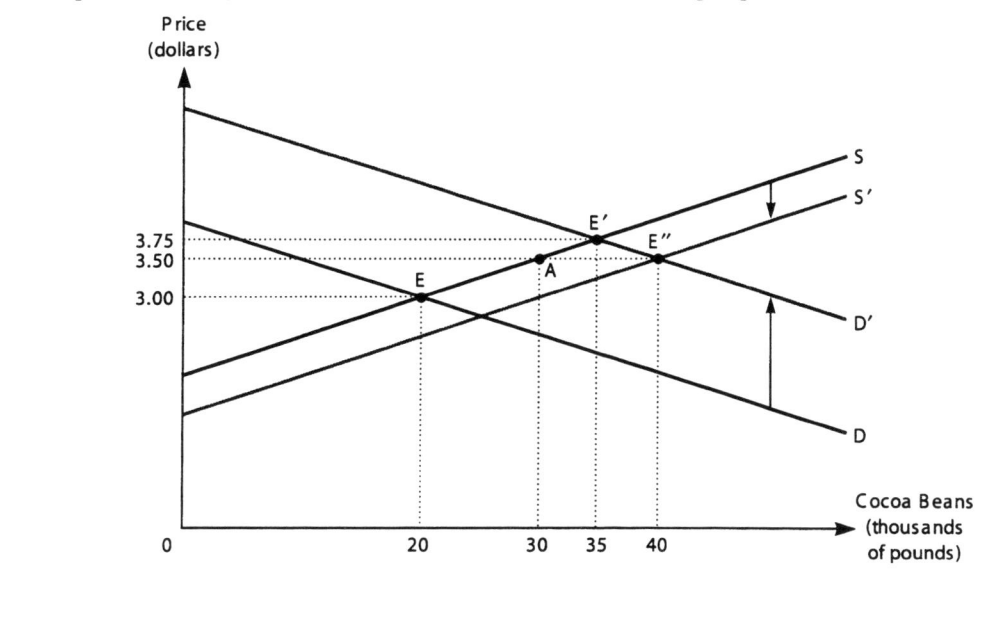

Conversely, starting from equilibrium point E in Figure 13.6, assume that demand shifts to the right, causing the equilibrium price to increase to $1.25. To re-establish the target price, the supplying nations' quotas must be relaxed. This causes the supply curve to shift from S to S', yielding the target price of $1.00 at equilibrium point E".

An example of an international export quota agreement is the *International Sugar Agreement*. This agreement, reached in 1954, has been generally ineffective in stabilizing and increasing sugar prices due to advanced countries' capability to enhance the production of their own beet sugar. Another example is the *International Coffee Agreement,* which was negotiated in 1962. Although this agreement succeeded in stabilizing coffee prices at a higher level, it was suspended in 1989. This led to a glut of coffee in the international market, causing its price to drop sharply. In 1993, the major producers were negotiating to reach a new International Coffee Agreement.

Figure 13.4

BUFFER STOCK AGREEMENT: PRICE SETTING IN THE CASE OF A RISE IN SUPPLY

Starting at equilibrium point E, assume the supply of cocoa beans increases from S to S`, causing the price to fall from $3.00 per pound to $2.25 per pound. To raise the price to the minimum level of $2.50 per pound, the agency has to purchase 10,000 pounds of cocoa beans (line AE", the excess supply at the price of $2.50 per pound), causing the demand to shift to D`. This leads to the new equilibrium point E", where the price is brought up to the minimum level of $2.50 per pound.

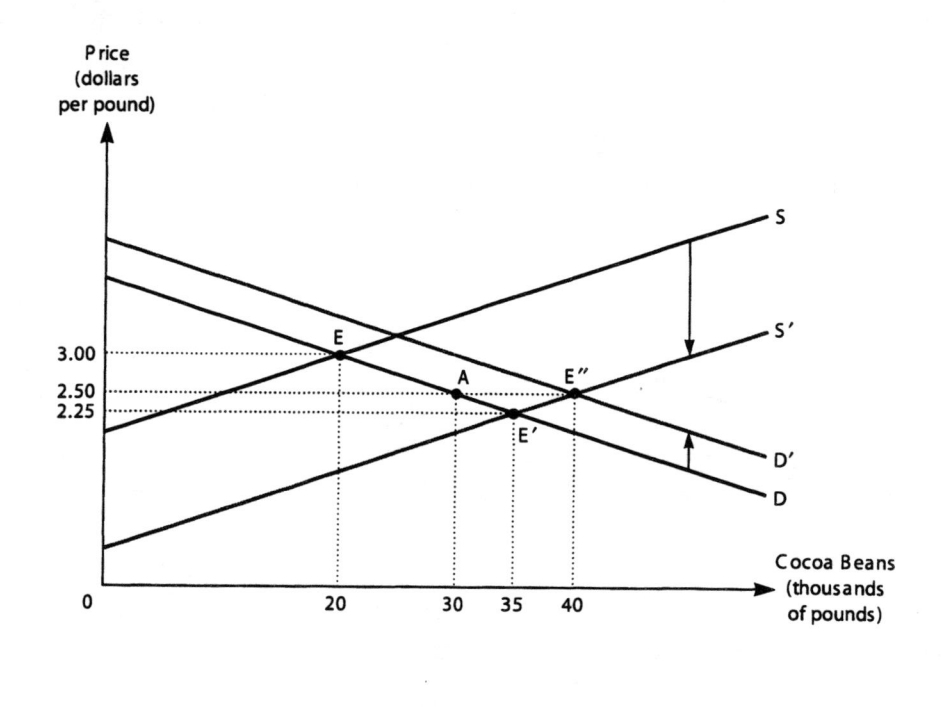

Multilateral Agreements.

A multilateral agreement is a long-term contract that determines a *minimum* price at which importing countries guarantee to buy a specified quantity of a good and a *maximum* price at which exporting countries guarantee to sell a specified quantity of a good. Thus, multilateral agreements are designed to set an upper limit (ceiling) and a lower limit (floor) on the prices of traded goods. Examples of multilateral agreements are the *International Sugar Agreement* and the *International Wheat Agreement*.

In comparison with buffer stock and export quota agreements, multilateral agreements lead to less distortion in the market mechanism and the allocation of scarce resources. This is because they usually do not impose output constraints on the commodity in question. As a result, they do not restrain the development of more efficient producers. However, given the relative ease of entry into and withdrawal from these contracts by participating nations, they tend to provide only limited market stability.

Figure 13.5

INTERNATIONAL EXPORT QUOTA AGREEMENT: PRICE STABILIZATION IN THE CASE OF A FALL IN DEMAND

Assume that the agreement calls for the stabilization of the price of coffee at $1.00 per pound. S and D portray the estimated supply and demand that yield this targeted price at equilibrium point E, where 40 million pounds of coffee are sold. Now suppose that due to world recession the market demand for coffee decreases from D to D′, causing the price to fall to $0.75 (see point E′). To reestabish the target price, the quotas of the supplying nations will be tightened. This causes the supply curve to shift from S to S′, yielding the target price of $1.00 at equilibrium point E″.

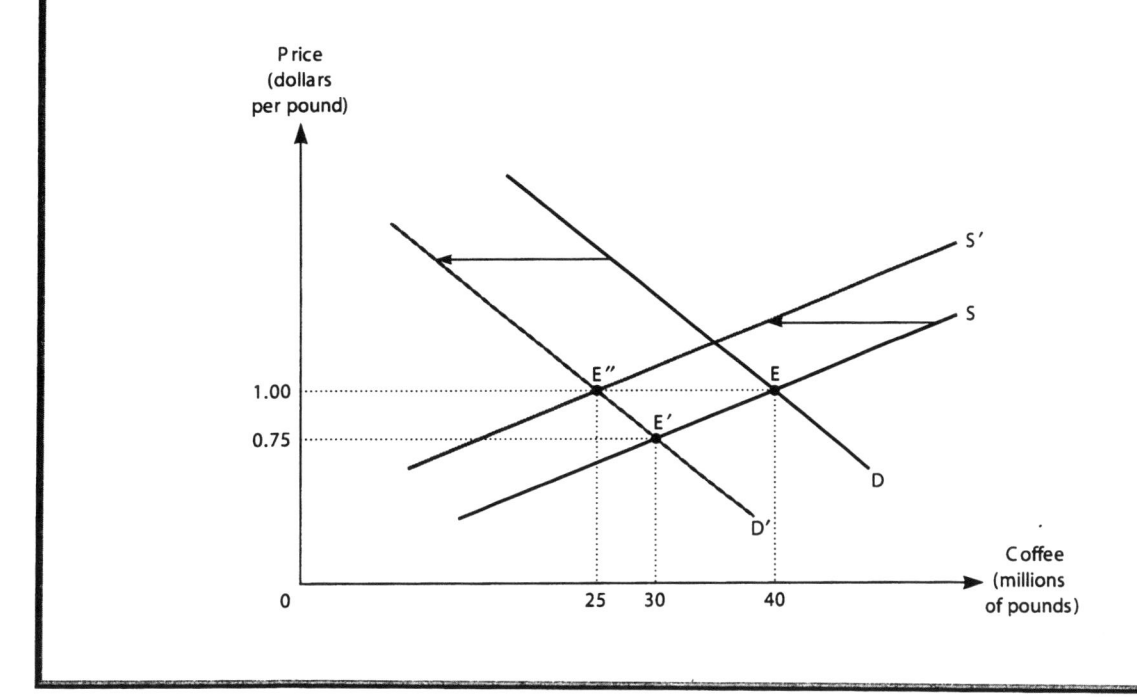

TRADE LIBERALIZATION IN DEVELOPING NATIONS

As we explained earlier, following the Prebisch theory, many developing nations, especially those in Latin American countries, pursued policies of import substitution. The 1950s and 1960s can be viewed as a period during which import-substitution industrialization was a popular trade strategy that was approved by many economists and pursued in many developing nations. Many of these nations initiated their import-substitution policies by protecting final stages of industry, such as food processing and automobile assembly. In some larger developing nations, domestic products almost entirely displaced imported consumer goods.

Although the import-substitution strategy succeeded in encouraging the growth of manufacturing, it did not promote economic development. The evidence shows that many developing nations that have followed import-substitution strategies have not shown signs of catching up with advanced nations. In some developing nations, the pursuit of import-substitution policies has led only to a marginal increase in per capita income. A case in point is India which, following the implementation of a series of economic plans between the early 1950s and the early 1970s, found itself with a per capita income that was only a few

Figure 13.6

INTERNATIONAL EXPORT QUOTA AGREEMENT: PRICE STABILIZATION IN THE CASE OF A RISE IN DEMAND

This diagram is identical to Figure 13.5; however, starting from equilibrium point E, let us assume the demand shifts to the right (as opposed to the left in Figure 13.5). This causes the equilibrium price to increase to $1.25. To reestabilsh the target price, the quotas of the supplying nations will be relaxed. This causes the supply curve to shift to the right from S to S`, yielding the target price of $1.00 at equilibrium point E".

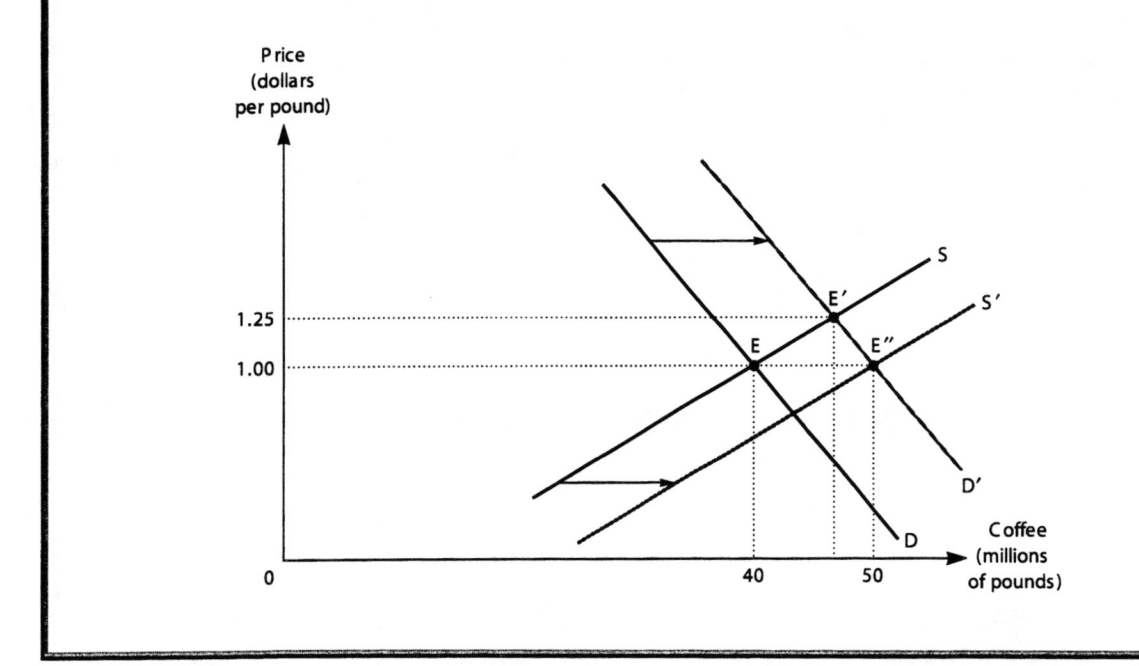

percent higher than before. In other developing nations, such as Mexico, the pursuit of import-substitution policies resulted in economic growth; however, it did not lead to narrowing the income gap between these nations and advanced countries.

A number of empirical studies measured the welfare costs of developing countries' trade barriers that were imposed to promote industrialization in the 1960s and early 1970s. These studies showed that the trade barriers inflicted notable costs on Argentina, Chile, Colombia, Egypt, Ghana, India, Israel, Mexico, Pakistan, the Philippines, South Korea, Taiwan, and Turkey. The only exception was Malaysia, where the import barriers led to a small benefit due to favorable terms of trade.[10]

Given the shortcomings of import substitution in promoting economic development, such a strategy has come under increasingly harsh criticism by economists in recent years. As a result, since the 1960s, there has been a steady movement toward trade liberalization in some developing countries that previously followed import-substitution policies. In the 1960s, several trade liberalizations were carried out in Latin American countries, notably in Brazil and Chile from 1964 and in Colombia from 1967. By decreasing bias against manufactured exports, they improved export performance. Besides Latin American countries, a small group of initially poor countries pursued trade liberalization policies by combining rapid growth of output and living standards with industrialization directed primarily toward export markets instead of domestic markets. These countries, as we explain later in this chapter, have experienced impressive economic performance and have gained the status of NICs.

The most important trade liberalizations in the 1970s took place in Argentina, Chile, and Uruguay. These nations attempted to stabilize and liberalize their economies in the face of recession, inflation, declining terms of trade, and unstable capital flow which helped to induce the international debt crisis of the 1980s. Examples of other countries that have followed trade liberalization policies include Cameroon, Costa Rica, Cote d'Ivorie, Guatemala, Indonesia, Malaysia, Thailand, Tunisia, and Turkey.[11]

The road to trade liberalization, which started gradually in the 1960s and continues today, has not always been smooth. Import-substitution policies are still practiced in many developing nations that have rightly complained about the existence of import barriers against their exports of both manufactured and agricultural products to advanced nations. In fact, trade barriers against the manufactured products of developing countries have been higher than the tariffs on manufactured goods between advanced nations. Additionally, import barriers on manufactured goods from developing countries have risen since the 1960s.

Despite an increase in their manufactured goods, most developing nations' exports are still composed of raw materials and agricultural products. Yet advanced nations have kept and even increased their restrictions on imports and their subsidies to production and exports of agricultural products.[12]

Given the existence of trade barriers against the exports of developing countries, many nations that felt neglected by previous General Agreement on Tariff and Trade (GATT) rounds looked forward to the Uruguay Round of negotiation for dismantling trade barriers against them. The United States persuaded many of these nations to join the Uruguay Round of negotiation in 1986 with promises of significant concessions. Unfortunately, following the successful negotiation of this round on December 15, 1993, many developing nations felt they did not get all they hoped for. To be sure, trade barriers will fall as a result of the round, but not as much or as quickly as the developing nations had expected. In the area of agriculture, for example, developing nations expected that major industrial nations would entirely dismantle subsidies for their products, rapidly decrease tariffs, and open markets by reducing quotas. But the developing countries learned that they had to accept much less in all three areas. Nevertheless, despite their disappointment with the Uruguay Round, some developing nations, such as Chile and Brazil, believe that the agreement will lead to an overall net benefit for their economies due to relatively freer international trade.[13]

DEMANDS FOR A NEW INTERNATIONAL ECONOMIC ORDER

Skeptical about the possible advantages of the existing international trading system, developing countries have collectively demanded that advanced nations institute policies to improve the international trading system. Such a demand for a new international economic order (NIEO) led to the assembly of the United Nations Conference on Trade and Development (UNCTAD) in Geneva in 1964. Following this event, UNCTAD became a permanent organization of the United Nations that convenes every four years to discuss issues regarding trade between advanced and developing nations.*

Developing countries' demands for an NIEO, include a number of objectives, which are discussed subsequently.

---

*Other meetings of UNCTAD were held in New Delhi, 1968; in Santiago, 1972; in Nairobi, 1976; in Manila, 1979; in Belgrade, 1983; in Geneva, 1987; and in Cartegena, 1992.

1. **Dismantling of trade barriers on agricultural products in advanced countries.** Historically, the internal political power of agricultural interests in advanced nations has opposed the removal of trade barriers on agricultural products in those countries. However, as we explained in the previous section, some progress was made during the Uruguay Round of negotiations, resulting in a lowering of trade barriers against developing countries. However, as noted earlier, developing nations are not totally satisfied with the outcome of the Uruguay Round and feel that they were shortchanged by GATT.
2. **Creation of international commodity agreements to stabilize prices of primary products.** Over the years this objective has continued to be the centerpiece of developing nations' demand for an NIEO. Unfortunately, however, not much progress has been made in meeting this goal. Over time, international commodity agreements have resulted in uncontrollable goods inventory or have led to the use of export controls, contributing to existing inefficiencies.
3. **Enhancing advanced nations' aid to developing nations.** To fulfill this objective, developing nations have demanded that advanced nations increase their financial aid to 0.7 percent of their GNP, as advocated by the United Nations (U.N). To date, little progress has been made in meeting this objective. The worldwide recession of the late 1980s and early 1990s has made it difficult for advanced nations to enhance their aid to developing nations. Table 13.3 shows the Official Development Assistance (ODA) granted to developing nations by advanced nations for years 1999-2001. As this table indicates, most advanced nations have not donated 0.7 percent of their GNP to provide financial assistance to developing nations, as recommended by the United Nations.
4. Renegotiating developing countries' international debt and decreasing their interest payments. Some steps, which we explain in the next chapter, were taken to meet this objective . Although some progress was made in defusing the international debt crisis, the debt dilemma continues in the early 2000s.
5. **Increasing the transfer of technology from multinational corporations to developing nations.** As we explain in Chapter 17, although the positive role of multinational corporations (MNCs) has been met with skepticism from both advanced and developing countries, the role of MNCs has created more heated debate and has stirred more controversy in developing countries. So far, not much progress has been made in meeting the developing nations' demands for developing appropriate technologies, increasing the flow of technology from advanced nations, and adopting a code of conduct for MNCs to eradicate abuses.
6. **Permitting developing countries to have a greater role in the international decision-making process.** The participation of developing countries in international organizations, such as the International Monetary Fund, the World Bank, and the UN, has enhanced their role in the international decision-making process. Nevertheless, in spite of the fact that developing countries surpass advanced nations in sheer numbers, they are far from governing these critical organizations.

Table 13.3

OFFICIAL DEVELOPMENT ASSISTANCE (ODA) GRANTED TO DEVELOPING NATIONS BY ADVANCED NATIONS, 1999-2001

	ODA in Millions of U.S. Dollars			ODA as Percentage of GNP Donor Nations		
Country	1999	2000	2001	19999	20000	2001
Denmark	1,733	1,664	1,599	1.01	1.06	1.01
Norway	1,370	1,264	1,346	0.91	0.8	0.83
Netherlands	3,134	3,075	3,155	0.79	0.82	0.82
Luxembourg	119	116	142	0.66	0.7	0.80
Sweden	1,630	1,813	1,576	0.7	0.81	0.76
Belgium	760	812	866	0.3	0.36	0.37
Switzerland	969	888	908	0.35	0.34	0.34
France	5,637	4,221	4,293	0.39	0.33	0.34
Ireland	245	239	285	0.31	0.3	0.33
Finland	416	371	389	0.33	0.31	0.33
United Kingdom	3,401	4,458	4,659	0.23	0.31	0.32
Spain	1,363	1,321	1,748	0.23	0.24	0.30
Germany	5,515	5,034	4,879	0.26	0.27	0.27
Portugal	276	261	267	0.26	0.26	0.25
New Zealand	134	116	111	0.27	0.26	0.25
Austria	527	461	457	0.26	0.25	0.25
Australia	982	995	852	0.26	0.27	0.25
Japan	15,323	13,062	9,678	0.35	0.27	0.23
Canada	1,699	1,722	1,572	0.28	0.25	0.23
Greece	194	216	194	0.15	0.19	0.19
Italy	1,806	1,368	1,493	0.15	0.13	0.14
United States	9,145	9,581	10,884	0.10	0.10	0.11

Source: "The US and Foreign Aid," Assistancehttp://www.globalissues.org/TradeRelated/Debt/USAid.asp?so=p2001#oda.

GLOBAL INSIGHTS CASE 13.2

U.S. POLICY ON TRADE WITH DEVELOPING COUNTRIES

Much of the surge in the growth of U.S. exports in recent years is due to demand from developing countries. During the 1990s U.S. exports to advanced nations have grown at the rate of 5 percent per year in real terms. In the mean time, U.S. exports to developing nations have grown at about twice that rate. Among developing nations, the growth of U.S. exports to Latin America have been especially impressive, increasing from 0.9 percent of U.S. GDP in 1990 to 1.4 percent in the first three quarters of 1996. In the same period, exports to other developing and transition economies rose from 1.6 percent to 2.2 percent of GDP.

The United States' strategy has aimed at encouraging the involvement and integration of developing nations into the global trading system. To achieve this goal, a number of policies have been adopted that not only benefit U.S. consumers, but also provide special encouragement for developing nations to increase and diversify their exports.

One of the main U.S. programs for promoting trade with developing nations is the Generalized System of Preferences (GSP), instituted in 1976. Under this program, about 4,600 products from 148 developing nations and territories are eligible for duty-free entry into the United States. In 1995 the United States imported $18.3 billion in duty-free goods under the program, accounting for 16 percent of total U.S. imports from the GSP recipients. More than two-thirds of all GSP imports in 1995 originated in six developing nations, including Brazil, India, Indonesia, Malaysia, the Phillipines, and Thailand.

Under this program, as nations reach certain developmental stages they are graduated from the program, to allow lower income countries to take better advantage of available preferences. For example, Malaysia graduated in January 1, 1997.

The Caribbean Basin Economic Recovery Act, implemented in 1984, provides preferential access to the U.S. market for 24 Caribbean nations and territories. In 1991 the United States activated a similar program for four South American nations. This program is the cornerstone of U.S. strategy to lead these nations to curtail their production and exports of cocaine. These two programs help support growth and development in some of the globe's less developed nations, which in turn have become better consumers of U.S. goods.

Source: U.S. Government Printing Office, *Economic Report of the President* (Washington DC: U.S. Government Printing Office, 1997), 252-254

We may close this section by stating that although developing nations have succeeded in articulating their demands for an NIEO, they still have a long way to go before completely satisfying such demands. The worldwide recession of the late 1980s and early 1990s, which has forced many industrial nations to worry abut their own domestic economic problems, has put the NIEO on a back burner so to speak. Although some modest progress was made in the Uruguay Round in dismantling some of the trade barriers against developing nations, it is unlikely that any further progress will be made in meeting the overall demands for an NIEO in the near future.

In concluding this chapter, we must emphasize that the road to economic development is not smooth and

CH. 13/TRADE THEORY, TRADE POLICIES & DEVELOPMENT EXPERIENCE

is imbued with uncertainty. A successful journey requires immense financial resources, technical expertise, and managerial know-how that are lacking in most developing countries. As a result, advanced countries have a crucial role in assisting developing countries to achieve their economic development goals. However, as NICs have demonstrated, the major effort should come from the developing countries themselves.

SUMMARY

1. The basic idea of mercantilism is that wealth is a necessary condition for national power. National power is in turn enhanced by the increase in specie. Thus, a country lacking gold and silver mines can only acquire gold and silver by encouraging its exports and discouraging its imports.
2. The theory of absolute advantage states that each country should specialize in the production of the goods in which it is more efficient, that is, the goods it can produce at the least cost.
3. According to the theory of comparative advantage, if one country can produce two goods more efficiently than another country and can produce one of these goods more efficiently than the other, it should specialize in and export that commodity in which it is comparatively more efficient, that is, the commodity in which it has the greatest absolute advantage. The less efficient nation should specialize in and export the commodity in which it has the least disadvantage.
4. Opportunity cost is the value of the benefit foregone when choosing one alternative over another.
5. According to the H-0 theory, each country should export those commodities that use its abundant factor most intensively and import goods that use its scarce factor most intensively.
6. Leontief's Paradox provided the first major test of the H-O theory. His study suggested that the United States exports goods that are relatively labor intensive and imports commodities that are capital intensive.
7. Immiserizing growth is an expansion of the factor supply or productivity that makes a nation worse off when it exports the goods it specializes in producing.
8. According to the Prebisch theory, because world prices for primary products have been declining and unstable, developing countries' terms of trade have deteriorated over time. Thus, developing countries should restrict the import of industrial goods into their countries, replacing these imports with goods produced domestically.
9. The factors leading to export instability can be classified as price variability and a high degree of commodity concentration.
10. Price variability occurs because demand for and supply of primary products produced by developing countries are both price inelastic and unstable.
11. Empirical studies support the view that export instability is, in general, somewhat greater for developing countries than for advanced countries. However, the impact of export instability on economic development and its association with commodity concentration remains controversial.
12. The stabilization of a developing country's export prices or revenues can be achieved by either purely domestic strategies, such as domestic marketing boards (DMBs), or international strategies, such as international commodity agreements.
13. A DMB is an agency that is set up by a developing country's government. The objective of this agency is to maintain price stability for the country's individual producers.
14. International commodity agreements (ICAs) refer to agreements between producing and consuming countries to stabilize and increase the prices and revenues of their exports.
15. The main types of ICAs are international buffer stock agreements, international export quota agreements, and multilateral agreements.
16. Developing countries' demands for a new international economic order (NIEO) include a number of objectives.

284 PART IV/INTERNATIONAL ECONOMICS OF DEVELOPING NATIONS

17. Newly industrialized countries (NICs) are at a relatively advanced stage of economic development. Each of these countries has a substantial and active industrial sector that is integrated into its international trade, finance, and investment systems.

QUESTIONS

1. Why do the majority of Western economists consider international trade an "engine of growth?" Is this assertion true for today's developing countries? Explain.
2. Why do some economists consider conventional international trade theory inappropriate for developing countries? Explain.
3. What is "immiserizing growth?" What conditions are necessary for immiserizing growth to occur? Explain.
4. Explain the Prebisch theory. What is the basis of this theory? What are its policy implications? Give examples of countries that are somehow following the Prebisch recommendations.
5. What is "export instability?" What factors give rise to export instability?
6. What conclusions can be drawn from many empirical studies on the subject of export instability? Explain.
7. Commodity price stabilization has been a main goal of many developing countries. What are the major methods used to achieve this objective?
8. What are international commodity agreements? Give some examples of ICAs, and explain why many of them have failed over time.
9. Developing countries' demands for an NIEO include a number of objectives. Discuss these objectives.
10. Using demand and supply analysis, show that when the supply of a good rises, its equilibrium price declines by a smaller amount, the more price elastic the demand curve for that good.
11. Graphically analyze and verbally explain how a buffer stock agreement can result in either the depletion of commodity stock or an unmanageable stock for the buffer authority.
12. Employing ordinary supply and demand curves, show that suppliers' revenue is subject to less fluctuation from a shift in the demand curve than from a shift in the supply curve.
13. Discuss the pros and cons of the argument that international trade can hamper economic development.
14. Import-substitution industrialization is more effective for a large developing country than for a small one. Do you agree with this statement? Discuss.
15. Compare the theories of comparative advantage and absolute advantage.
16. Briefly discuss the mercantilists' ideas with regard to international trade. How do these ideas differ from Adam Smith's view? Give an example of the application of the theory of mercantilism as it exists today. What are some fallacies of this theory?

PR0PBLEMS

1. Using demand and supply analysis, show that when the supply of a good rises, its equilibrium price declines by a smaller amount, the more price elastic the demand curve for that good.
2. Graphically analyze and verbally explain how a buffer stock agreement can result in either the depletion of commodity stock or an unmanageable stock for the buffer authority.
3. Employing ordinary supply and demand curves, show that suppliers' revenue is subject to less fluctuation from a shift in the demand curve than from a shift in the supply curve.
4. Discuss the pros and cons of the argument that international trade can hamper economic development.
5. Import-substitution industrialization is more effective for a large developing country than for a small one

Do you agree with this statement? Discuss.

6. Assume that a two-country trading world consists of France and Costa Rica. The following table explains the amount of output produced by each country:

	Labor Input (days)	Wine Output (gallons)	Beef Output (pounds)
France	2	140	70
Costa Rica	2	20	60

a. Which country, if any, has an absolute advantage in production? A comparative advantage?
b. In what commodity does each country specialize if the two countries specialize and exchange wine for cloth at a relative price ratio of 1:1, that is, by trading 1 gallon of wine for 1 yard of cloth.
c. What are gains from trade?

NOTES

1. David Hume, "Of Money," *Essays* (London: Green and Co., 1912), vol. 1, 319; see also, Eugene Rostow, *The Economic Writings of David Hume* (Edinburgh: Nelson, 1955).
2. Alan M. Rugman, Donald J. Lecraw, and Laurence D. Booth, *International Business: Firm and Environment* (New York: McGraw-Hill Book Company, 1985), 26-27.
3. Donald A. Ball and H. Wendell McCulloch, Jr., *International Business: Introduction and Essentials,* 2nd ed. (Plano, TX: Business Publications, Inc., 1985), 61.
4. Bernard Munk, "The Colombian Automobile Industry: The Welfare Consequences of Import Substitution," *Economic and Business Bulletin* (Fall 1970): 6-22.
5. A. I. MacBean, *Export Instability and Economic Structure.* (Cambridge, MA: Harvard University Press, 1966).
6. Benton F. Massell, "Export Instability and Economic Structure," *American Economic Review* 40 (September 1970): 618-630.
7. E. Lanceri, "Export Instability and Economic Development," *Banca del Lavoro Quarterly Review* (June 1978): 135-152.
8. J. Love, "Commodity Concentration and Export Earnings Instability: A Shift from Cross-Section to Time Series Analysis," *Journal of Development Economics* 24 (1986): 239-248.
9. Benson F. Massell, "Concentration and Instability Revisited," *Journal of Development Economics,* 33 (1990): 145-147.
10. Bela Balassa, *The Structure of Protection in Developing Countries,* (Baltimore: John Hopkins Press, 1971); Jagdish N. Bhagwati and Anne Krueger, *Foreign Trade Regimes and Economic Development,* multiple volumes (New York: Colombia University Press for the National Bureau of Economic Research, 1973-76).
11. The World Bank, *World Development Report 1987* (New York: Oxford University Press, 1987), ch. 5.
12. For a discussion on reasons for the pursuit of protectionist agricultural policies by advanced nations, see The World Bank, *World Development Report 1986* (New York: Oxford University Press, 1986), ch. 6.
13. "Developing Nations Feel Shortchanged by GATT," *The Wall Street Journal,* 15 December 1993, A6.

SUGGESTED READINGS

Balassa, B. *Comparative Advantage, Trade Policy and Economic Development*. New York: New York University Press, 1989.
Bhagwati, J. N. "Immiserizing Growth." *Readings in International Economics*. Homewood, IL: Irwin, 1967.
———. *Foreign Trade Regimes and Economic Development: Anatomy and Consequences of Exchange Control Regimes*. Cambridge, MA: Ballinger, 1978.
———. *The New International Economic Order: The North-South Debate*. Cambridge, MA: MIT Press, 1977.
Cline, W. R., ed. *Policy Alternatives for a New International Economic Order*. New York: Praeger, 1979.
Finlayson, J. A. *Managing International Markets: Developing Countries and the Commodity Trade Regime*. New York: Columbia University Press, 1988.
Frank, A. G. *Capitalism and Underdevelopment in Latin America: Historical Studies of Chile and Brasil*. New York: Monthly Review Press, 1967.
———. *Latin America: Underdevelopment or Revolution?* New York: Monthly Review Press, 1978.
Greenway D., ed. *Economic Development in International Trade*. London: MacMillian, 1987.
Gwin, C. *Integration of Developing Countries into the World Trading System*. Cambridge, MA: Ballinger, 1989.
Hecksher, E. "The Effects of Foreign Trade on Distribution of Income." *Economics Tidskrift* 21 (1919): 497-512.
Johnson, H. G. *Economic Policies Toward Less Developed Countries*. New York: Praeger, 1967.
Krueger, A. D. *Trade and Employment in Developing Countries*. Chicago: University of Chicago Press, 1983.
Lewis, J. P., ed. *Development Strategies: A New Synthesis*. Washington DC: Overseas Development Council, 1985.
Little, I., et al. *Industries and Trade in Some Developing Countries*. London: Oxford University Press, 1970.
MacBean, A. I. *Export Instability and Economic Development*. Cambridge, MA: Harvard University Press, 1966.
Martin, M., et al. *Studies of Development and Change in the Modern World*. New York: Oxford University Press, 1988.
Meier, G. *The International Economics of Development*. New York: Harper & Row, 1968, ch. 3.
Nurkse, R. "Patterns of Trade and Development in International Trade." In *Problems of Capital Formation in Underdeveloped Countries and Patterns of Trade and Development*, edited by R. Nurkse. New York: Oxford University Press, 1970.
Prebisch, R. *Toward a New Trade Policy for Development*. New York: United Nations, 1964.
Purcell, R. B., ed. *The Newly Industrializing Countries in the Third World*. Boulder, CO: Lynne Rienner, 1989. Skully, M. T. *Financing East Asia's Success*. New York: St. Martin's Press, 1988.
Taylor, L. *Varieties of Stabilization Experience*. New York: Oxford University Press, 1988.
Turner, L. and N. McMullen. *The Newly Industrializing Countries: Trade and Adjustment*. London: George Allen & Unwin, 1982.

CHAPTER 14

THE INTERNATIONAL DEBT CRISIS

One of the major problems that has plagued developing countries in recent years is a precarious debt dilemma. During the past decade, developing countries have accumulated a total international debt amounting to $1.3 trillion. Although the seeds of the debt crisis were planted during the energy crisis of the early 1970s, it did not became apparent to the world until August 12, 1982. On that date, Mexico declared that it could no longer observe its formerly scheduled payments on its foreign debt. Subsequently, many other developing countries, especially those in Latin America, announced similar problems.

The debt crisis has had far-reaching implications for both developing countries and advanced nations. From the developing countries' standpoint, it has seriously hampered their economic development process because money that could have been used to finance development projects had to be set aside for servicing external debts. From the advanced countries' standpoint, the debt crisis has threatened the stability of the international banking system. Given this situation, many solutions have been suggested to mitigate the potential threats of the debt crisis.

Although no widespread default has erupted yet, the debt problem is by no means over. In this chapter, we first elaborate on the magnitude of the debt crisis and discuss its origin. Then, we explain the debt crisis in Mexico and other developing countries. Next, we define sovereign default and examine the impact of the debt crisis on the International Monetary Fund (IMF) and the United States. Finally, we review resolutions to the debt crisis and discuss the challenge ahead.

MAGNITUDE OF THE DEBT CRISIS

Tables 14.1 and 14.2 portray the extent of the developing countries' debt burden. Table 14.1 indicates the rate of growth of the developing countries' debt from 1994 through 2003. As this table shows, the total combined debt of developing countries is expected to exceed $2.2 trillion in 2003. This figure is more than 22 times larger than the $100 billion total of these same countries debt in 1973. Measuring debt as a percentage of exports of goods and services, the developing countries' debt is projected to fall from its 1994 level (199.3 percent) to 134.4 percent in 2003. Thus, as the table illustrates, although the debt keeps on rising in absolute terms, the debt to export ratios have been declining in recent years.

According to Table 14.1, the debt is concentrated in two regions, Asia and the Western Hemisphere (Latin America). One striking difference between these two regions is how their external debt has been financed. In general, Latin American countries have been much more dependent on bank financing than

Table 14.1

TOTAL EXTERNAL DEBT OF DEVELOPING COUNTRIES (IN BILLIONS OF U.S. $)*

	1994	1995	1996	1997	1998	1999	2000	2001	2002	2003
Total Debt	1,727.2 (199.3)	1,873.3 (181.0)	1,944.8 (167.5)	2,036.8 (161.4)	2,195.3 (187.3)	2,239.8 (177.9)	2,208.1 (142.5)	2,190.4 (144.5)	2,232.0 (143.7)	2,263.7 (134.4)
Debt by Region:										
Africa	286.8 (280.9)	303.0 (252.5)	300.1 (225.0)	290.8 (213.6)	289.8 (240.2)	289.9 (226.3)	277.6 (179.5)	276.1 (185.3)	268.4 (184.7)	265.2 (174.8)
Asia	518.8 (140.0)	579.1 (121.8)	615.4 (121.8)	669.3 (118.4)	696.9 (129.1)	702.2 (121.5)	674.9 (96.4)	675.8 (96.8)	688.7 (93.7)	716.8 (89.2)
Middle East & Turkey	356.5 (191.2)	371.9 (153.7)	383.0 (153.7)	404.6 (155.0)	452.0 (205.3)	468.9 (186.6)	486.7 (144.0)	486.1 (144.0)	502.4 (168.8)	510.1 (169.6)
Western Hemisphere	565.1 (272.3)	619.2 (251.5)	646.3 (236.7)	672.1 (224.6)	756.7 (259.3)	778.8 (258.2)	768.9 (215.0)	752.4 (215.1)	772.5 (205.7)	744.5 (182.2)

*FIGURES IN PARENTHESES INDICATE DEBT AS A PERCENTAGE OF EXPORTS OF GOODS AND SERVICES.
Source: International Monetary Fund, *World Economic Outlook* (Washington, DC:IMF, April 2002) 211-212, table 38.

Table 14.2

**DEBT-SERVICE RATIOS OF DEVELOPING COUNTRIES
(AS A PERCENTAGE OF EXPORTS OF GOODS AND SERVICES)**

	1994	1995	1996	1997	1998	1999	2000	2001	2002*	2003*
Total	8.9	8.9	8.3	7.7	8.8	8.6	7.4	7.4	7.3	6.8
Africa	10.0	9.7	9.2	8.6	8.8	8.3	6.9	7.0	9.5	6.7
Sub-Sahara	8.4	7.9	7.9	7.6	7.7	7.6	6.4	6.8	10.2	6.7
Developing Asia	6.4	6.2	6.0	5.1	6.0	5.8	5.0	4.6	4.4	4.4
Excluding China & India	6.1	6.3	6.3	6.7	7.5	6.5	6.1	5.7	5.7	5.5
Middle East & Turkey	5.1	4.9	4.0	4.0	.8	4.2	3.6	4.0	4.5	5.0
Western Hemisphere	16.2	16.9	16.0	15.4	17.2	17.8	6.0	6.1	14.2	12.8

*Estimated data.
Source: International Monetary Fund, *World Economic Outlook* (Washington, DC: IMF, April 2002) 217, table A42.

Asian countries, which owe the bulk of their debts to official agencies and governments. Additionally, most private loans given to Latin American nations are made by a few major U.S. banks.

Table 14.2 shows the **debt–service ratios,** that is, payments of interest on total debt plus amortization as a percentage of total exports The debt–service ratio is an indicator of indebted countries' burden. As this table indicates, there are noticeable differences among regions with regard to the debt burden. More specifically, Latin America's burden is much larger than Asia's, and has not declined nearly as fast as Asia's. Asia's debt burden is expected to decrease by 31.25 percent (from 6.4 percent in 1994 to 4.4 percent in 2003). However, Latin America's debt burden is projected to decline by 20.98 percent (from 16.2 percent in 1994 to 12.8 in 2003).

Although the total amount of debt in Africa is the second smallest among the regions (see Table 14.1), as Table 14.2 shows, Africa's debt–service ratio is the second largest among the regions. In other words, like Latin American nations, African nations have also been suffering from a severe debt problem. However, unlike Latin American countries, which have been dependent on bank financing, the bulk of African nations' debt is owed to official agencies and governments.

The magnitude of the debt problem can also be observed by a closer look at the "Group of 15" (or G-15) heavily indebted countries, including Argentina, Bolivia, Brazil, Chile, Colombia, Cote d'Ivoire, Ecuador, Mexico, Morocco, Nigeria, Peru, the Philippines, Uruguay, Venezuela, and the former Yugoslavia. For these nations, the average ratio of external public debt to gross domestic product (GDP) increased by about 15 percentage points during the 1980s. Moreover, for the largest debtors-Argentina, Brazil, Mexico, and Venezuela-this ratio rose more than 9 percent during the same period.[1] Given the magnitude and the nature of debt in Latin American countries, it is no surprise that these countries have attracted so much attention in recent years. Yet, the debt crisis is obviously not limited to Latin America, but embraces most of the third-world nations.

ORIGIN OF DEVELOPING COUNTRIES' DEBT CRISIS

In hindsight, researchers have suggested a number of factors as having a significant role in the developing countries' debt crisis. These factors include advanced countries' tighter monetary policies, the second oil shock of the late 1970s, poor public-sector investment in developing countries, the worldwide recession (1980-1982), capital flight from developing countries, the appreciation of the dollar, and excess loanable funds in advanced countries. Attempting to assign appropriate weights to each of these factors is highly subjective and debatable. The relative significance of each factor differs depending on the nation under consideration. As a result, it is very hard to make generalizations. In this section, we elaborate on each of these factors, keeping in mind that each played a crucial role in fueling the debt crisis.

Tight Monetary Policies of Advanced Countries

To combat inflation in the late 1970s, the Federal Reserve Bank of the United States (the Fed) initiated a tight monetary policy in 1979. This led to a rise in the U.S. prime rate, which eventually peaked at 20.5 percent in 1981. It also caused the London Interbank Offer Rate (LIBOR) to increase sharply, from 9.5 percent in 1978 to 16.6 percent in 1981 (see Table 14.3).[*]

In the late 1970s, a large percentage of the developing countries' debt, especially that of Latin American countries, was based on adjustable interest rates that were tied to LIBOR. Thus, the sharp rise in LIBOR not only made new borrowing more expensive for developing countries, but also caused the interest payments on old loans to rise sharply. As a result, the debt--service ratio of the developing countries' rose significantly (see Table 14.2).

---

[*] LIBOR is the rate of interest used between banks when they provide Eurocurrency loans to each other.

Table 14.3

CHANGES IN SIX-MONTH DOLLAR LIBOR

	1978	1979	1980	1981	1982	1983	1984	1985
Percent	9.5	12.1	14.6	16.6	13.3	9.9	11.2	8.7

Source: The World Bank, *World Development Report 1986* (Washington, DC: Oxford University Press, 1986), 32.

The Second Oil Shock

One of the factors that might have contributed to the debt crisis at the start of the 1980s is the second oil shock of 1979-1980. The first oil shock occurred in 1973 and 1974, and resulted in the transfer of billions of dollars (or "petrodollars") from oil-importing nations to oil-exporting nations. This led to huge balance of payments (BOP) surpluses in the Organization of Petroleum Exporting Countries (OPEC). For example, in 1974 alone, the OPEC nations, taken as a whole, had a current account surplus of about $60 billion. Surely, given the limited capacity of OPEC nations, they could not absorb the tremendous influx of funds into goods and services; hence, they had to search for alternative ways to spend the massive funds.

As oil-exporting nations examined options for spending their surpluses, other countries searched for means to finance their deficits. More specifically, developing countries were hard stricken by the oil price hike and desperately needed new sources of capital. This situation eventually led to the recycling of petrodollars, as illustrated in Figure 14.1 The OPEC nations exported oil to advanced countries (arrow 1) in exchange for dollars (arrow 2). These dollars were deposited in the Eurocurrency market (arrow 3) and then were loaned to developing countries (arrow 4). In turn, the developing nations used the loans(arrow 5) for net imports of goods and services from advanced countries (arrow 6).

The recycling of petrodollars provided developing nations with easy access to badly needed funds. As a result, they continued to increase their borrowing in order to finance their additional import expenditures. The second oil shock only exacerbated this situation and ignited the debt crisis in 1982.

Some writers concede that oil shocks serve to explain the timing of the crisis for oil-importing developing countries, such as Argentina, Brazil, and Poland. However, the same oil shocks could have made it simpler for oil exporters, like Mexico, Nigeria, and Venezuela, to reimburse their debtors in the early 1980s. Instead, these exporters were in the same predicament as the oil importers. As a result, according to these writers, it is doubtful that the oil shocks played a significant role in touching off the debt dilemma in 1982.[2]

Poor Public Sector Investment in Developing Countries

Evidence indicates that the borrowed petrodollars were not invested wisely. First, a large percentage of loans went toward consumption and extravagance on the part of corrupt officials. Second, the funds were poorly invested in inefficient public enterprises. For example, the Las Truchas Steel complex in western Mexico, built with the help of loans from suppliers and from the World Bank, sustains production costs that are

Figure 14.1

PETRODOLLAR RECYCLING

The OPEC nations exported oil to advanced countries (arrow 1) in exchange for dollars (arrow 2). These dollars were deposited in the Eurocurrency market (arrow 3) and then were loaned out to developing countries (arrow 4). In turn, the developing nations used the loan proceeds to pay for (arrow 5) the net imports of goods and services from advanced nations (arrow 6).

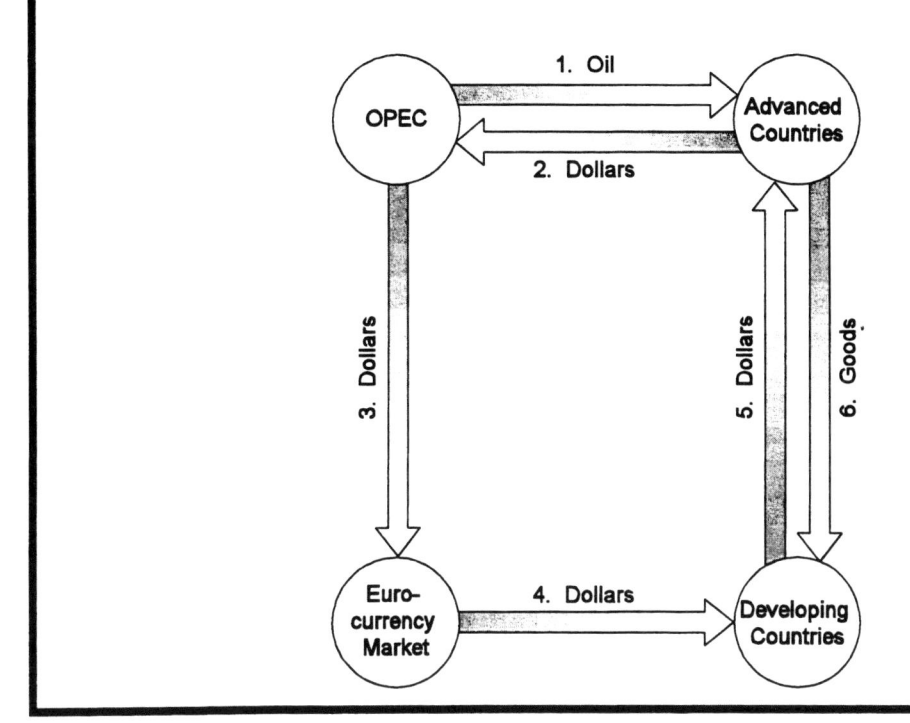

reportedly twice as large as those of the South Korean steel mills.[3] Finally, many of these investments were made with the expectation that domestic growth would continue at the same expansionary rate as in the 1970s. Consequently, some of the borrowed money was used for investment in energy production sources, especially hydroelectricity. The fact that the expected growth did not materialize made these investments, for the most part, fruitless.

The World Wide Recession

Fueled by the 1973-1974 quadrupling of oil prices, a short, sharp recession hit the world economy from 1974 through 1975. Table 14.4 illustrates the changes in key world economic indicators from 1973 through 1982. Besides the oil price hike, other factors that contributed to this recession included the 1972-1974 food crisis, the realignment of currencies following the collapse of the Bretton Woods system, and advanced countries' anti-inflationary policies. After three years of recovery, the world was hit by yet another oil shock. The oil prices doubled from 1979 through 1980, setting the stage for the 1980-1982 recession. Although this recession was milder than the previous one, it lasted longer due to the contractionary monetary policies employed by advanced countries to combat inflation. As a result, unemployment, which had remained at about 5 percent after the first recession, rose to more than 8 percent in advanced countries while real GDP growth became negative (see Table 14-4). The world recessions decreased the income of developing countries for two reasons: (a) The recession made their exports grow slowly or decline; and (b) the lower demand for developing countries' exports caused export prices to decline which, given a relatively inelastic demand for these exports, led to declining export revenues. With declining export revenues, developing countries were forced to increase their borrowing in order to meet their import requirements.

Table 14.4

KEY ECONOMIC INDICATORS, 1973-1982 (BY PERCENTAGE)

Indicators	1973	1974	1975	1976	1977	1978	1979	1980	1981	1982[a]
World Trade Growth (volume)[b]	12.5	4.0	-4.0	11.5	4.5	5.0	6.5	1.5	0.0	-2.0
Advanced Countries										
GDP growth	6.6	0.6	-7.0	5.1	3.6	3.9	3.2	1.3	1.0	-0.2
Unemployment	3.4	3.7	5.5	5.5	5.4	5.1	5.0	5.6	6.5	8.0
Inflation rate	7.7	11.6	10.2	7.3	7.4	7.3	7.3	8.8	8.6	7.5
Developing Countries										
Oil Importers										
GDP growth	6.5	5.3	4.0	5.3	5.6	6.6	4.2	5.5	2.2	2.0
Debt-service ratio[c]	12.6	11.4	13.3	12.6	12.6	15.7	14.7	13.9	16.6	21.5
Oil exporters[d]										
GDP growth	9.1	7.2	3.7	8.2	2.4	2.4	1.2	-1.3	1.2	1.9
Debt-service ratio	12.2	6.7	7.8	8.4	14.9	14.9	15.5	13.0	15.7	19.1

[a]Estimated data.
[b]IMF data for 1973 to 1981; GATT data for 1982.
[c]Service of medium- and long-term debt as a percentage of exports of goods and services.
[d]Excludes China.
Source: The World Bank, *World Development Report 1983* (Washington, DC: Oxford University Press, 1983) 1.

Capital Flight from Developing Countries

Capital flight refers to the transfer of funds from one nation to another by firms or individuals. It happens when the expected returns from keeping funds abroad are higher or more secure than from keeping them at home. During the early 1980s, a large-scale capital flight occurred in many developing countries, contributing to their debt crisis. Unfortunately, it is extremely difficult to estimate the amount of capital flight because it often goes unreported. Nevertheless, as Table 14.5 indicates, capital flight from developing countries has been relatively large and has clearly fueled the debt crisis in these countries. From 1976 through 1985, the ratio of capital flight to debt growth ranged from 13 percent for Brazil to 115 percent for Venezuela. Given such estimates, some economists think it is useless to lend money to developing countries. They maintain that flight deepens foreign exchange shortages. This may force the developing country to devalue its national currency. As a result, it would be more expensive to import the equipment and machinery needed for the economic development process.[4] Although reversing capital flight will not eradicate the debt, it can diminish

Table 14.5

ESTIMATED NET CAPITAL FLIGHT FROM\E DEVELOPING COUNTRIES, 1976-1985

Country	Capital Flight (billion of U.S. $)	Changes in External Debt (billion of U.S. $)	Flight as Percentage of Debt Growth
Argentina	26	42	62
Bolivia	1	3	33
Brazil	10	80	13
Ecuador	2	7	29
India	10	22	45
Indonesia	5	27	19
Korea	12	40	30
Malaysia	12	19	63
Mexico	53	75	71
Nigeria	10	18	56
Philippines	9	23	39
South Africa	17	16	106
Uruguay	1	4	25
Venezuela	30	26	115

Source: Morgan Guaranty Trust Company of New York, *World Financial Markets,* March 1986, 13, table 10.

it and help to strengthen commercial bankers' basis for avoiding enhanced exposure to debtor nations.[5]

Capital flight is caused by several factors. Chief among these are the following:

1. **Currency overvaluation.** As we already know, a nation's overvalued domestic currency may lead to a rise in imports and a decline in exports, deteriorating the BOP. This raises the possibility of devaluation of the currency to resolve the BOP problem. Such a possibility encourages financial investors to transfer their capital abroad in order to decrease the risk and to profit from devaluation when it transpires.
2. **Interest-rate ceilings.** To encourage the development process, many developing countries impose ceilings on interest rates. Such a repressive financial policy encourages financial investors to move their funds out of the country in order to gain from higher interest rates abroad.

3. **High and variable inflation.** This leads to uncertainty and discourages investment activities. It also causes real interest rates to decline. The higher uncertainty and lower real interest rates at home encourage financial investors to transfer their money out of the country.
4. **Taxation.** If the tax rate on either investment income or wealth is lower on assets held abroad than those held at home, investors are encouraged to transfer their funds abroad.

Other factors that contribute to capital flight are slow growth, default on government obligations, limitations on currency conversion, poor investment climate, and political instability at home.

Appreciation of the Dollar

During the 1980s, the U.S. budget deficit, induced by tight monetary policies, caused U.S. interest rates to rise. The higher U.S. interest rates compared to those of other industrial nations, encouraged the movement of short-term funds from those countries to the United States. The increase in the inflow of short-term funds to the U.S. caused the U.S. dollar to appreciate.

The higher interest rates, along with appreciation of the dollar, intensified the debt problems of developing countries in two ways. First, the rising interest rates caused developing countries' interest payments on debt to escalate. Second, because the developing countries' debt was denominated in U.S. dollars, the appreciation of the dollar caused the real value of the debt to rise.

Excess Loanable Funds in Advanced Countries

Although the oil shocks of the early 1970s (1973-1974) and the late 1970s (1979-1980) resulted in a large increase in the oil-import expenditures of many developing countries, it also provided OPEC members with ample money to spend. Most of this money was invested in predominantly Western banks, providing them with excess loanable funds. This was accompanied by deregulation of U.S. financial institutions, enhancing banks' power in managing their operations. Given the excess cash and deregulation, banks found themselves anxious to expand their loans. As a result, they invested, often recklessly, in developing countries. Loans were often made without sound economic analysis or adequate assessment of risk factors. In many instances, the developing countries' expanding debt problem was practically overlooked as their governments were lured into accepting more debt than the countries could handle.

THE MEXICAN DEBT CRISIS

As we already mentioned, the debt crisis, rooted in the 1970s, became apparent to the world in August 12, 1982. On that date, Mexico, which had been regarded as one of the most credible developing countries, declared that it could no longer service its debt. Mexico's debt, amounting to more than $80 billion at the time, made it the world's second-largest developing country debtor after Brazil. During the "Mexican Weekend," Mexico had to come up with $3 billion to meet a servicing payment due on Monday, August 16. Unable to service its debt, Mexico requested and was granted the following: (a) a rescheduling of the debt's principal; (b) a moratorium on payments of principal to commercial banks; and (c) a loan from various international sources (foreign governments, central banks, and the IMF).

The timely intervention of the IMF proved to be crucial in preventing an immediate crisis. In return for the new loans, Mexico agreed to follow a stringent austerity program, demanding a cut in its massive public-sector deficits and improvement in its balance of trade.

GLOBAL INSIGHTS CASE 14.1

DEBTS OF TRANSITIONAL ECONOMIES

Like developing countries, Eastern Europe and the former Soviet Union have suffered from debt burden. These former nonmarket economies borrowed substantially from the West before the outbreak of the debt crisis in 1982. As a result, like developing countries, they encountered debt problems in the 1980s. As the table shows, the former Soviet Union, Poland, and the former Yugoslavia were among the major debtors in the Eastern block countries. With the exception of Poland and Romania, these nations have been rated as above-average risks by the West in recent years.

The most dramatic drop ever recorded in a nation's credit rating was that of the former Soviet Union. In 1989, the international banking community placed the credit-worthiness of the former Soviet Union below that of developing countries Greece, Portugal, and Saudi Arabia. After the demise of the Soviet Union, the governments of the Russian Federation, Ukraine, and most of the other newly independent states announced their intent to pay the debts owed by the Soviet Union. Although this announcement reassured creditors initially, there was considerable difficulty in establishing a mechanism for distributing the debt burden among the independent states.

Today, world leaders realize that the smooth transition of the Eastern European countries and the former Soviet Union to market economies cannot be achieved without assistance from the West. Given this fact, in addition to humanitarian assistance, financial assistance is granted on the basis of adjustment and development plans approved by the World Bank and the IMF. Membership in these international organizations is perceived as part of the process leading to a market economy. As a result, all transitional economies have either become members or are in the process of joining these organizations.

Today, the World Bank and the IMF have become significant sources of funds for Eastern block countries. For example, in 1991, Bulgaria, Czechoslovakia, Hungary, Poland, and Romania received a combined loan of $3.6 billion and $2 billion from the IMF and the World Bank. In April 1992, the Group of Seven (Canada, France, Germany, Italy, Japan, Great Britain, and the United States) provided a multilateral financial assistance package for the Russian Federation, which included the following:

- Approximately $18 billion in financial assistance to help the Russian Federation reform its economy.
- Six billion dollars to help stabilize the ruble exchange rate.
- Early membership in the IMF.

In April 1993, Russian and Western governments agreed to reschedule $15 billion of the nation's $20 billion debt to its creditors. It remains to be seen how long the West will continue tp provide financial assistance to the transitional economies.

Continued

> **Global Insights Case 14.1, Continued**
>
> **EXTERNAL DEBTS OF THE SOVIET UNION AND EASTERN EUROPE, 1987**
>
> | | Debt* | Debt/Exports** |
> |---|---|---|
> | Bulgaria | 7.6 | 205 |
> | Czechoslovakia | 5.1 | 59 |
> | East Germy | 19.9 | 98 |
> | Hungary | 17.3 | 31 |
> | Poland | 38.9 | 427 |
> | Romania | 2.7 | 19 |
> | Yugoslavia | 22.5 | 113 |
> | Soviet Union | 40.0 | 48 |
>
> *Convertible currency debt in billions of U.S. dollars.
> **Ratio of external debt to exports to the market economies.
>
> Sources: Rudiger Dornbush, *Stabilization, Debt, and Reform* (Englewood Cliffs, NJ: Prentice Hall, 1993); United Nations, *World Economic Survey 1992* (New York: United Nations, 1992).

The Mexican debt crisis resulted in part, from the discovery of an estimated 72 billion barrels of oil reserves in 1977. This made Mexico a major oil exporter, generating additional revenue for its government to spend. By the mid-1980s, about 60 percent of Mexico's export revenue was attributed to oil. This sudden influx of income encouraged rapid public investment. Funds were used to finance subsidies, social programs, and public works. In fact, government spending increased more rapidly than oil revenue. To supplement the oil revenue, some spending was financed through **seigniorage,** that is, the benefit from printing money. Other spending was financed by borrowing abroad. Aided by the fiscal stimulus, Mexico managed to attain a high rate of economic growth. In the meantime, oil prices continued to rise, providing the country with additional revenues. Given the high rate of economic growth and the rising oil revenue, foreign commercial banks, especially U.S. banks, rushed to lend money to Mexico. By 1982, about 92 percent of Mexico's loans originated from commercial banks and the rest from official lenders. As Mexico continued its borrowing from private banks, the terms of borrowing became more unfavorable. *Floating interest rates,* which rose with the growth in market rates, were increasingly employed by the commercial banks lending money to Mexico. As a result, the percentage of Mexico's loans that was based on floating rates increased from about 47 percent in the mid-1970s to 82 percent in 1982. The rapid increase in government spending, supported by oil revenues and borrowed money, led to inflation (too much money chasing too few goods), which reached the rate of 30 percent in 1981. The worldwide recession in 1981, accompanied by rising interest rates and falling oil prices, put additional strain on the Mexican economy. The increasing interest rates raised Mexico's cost of borrowing. Falling oil prices decreased export revenues from $20 billion in 1981 to $6 billion in 1986. As a result, Mexico experienced a BOP deficit. To resolve the deficit, the Mexican authorities devalued the peso in 1982. However, they failed to reduce the government budget deficit or employ other policies that would control the deficit and thus diminish the nation's demand for additional foreign loans. Consequently, devaluation resulted in further domestic inflation without much gain to domestic employment or the BOP.

Given events described, commercial banks started to question Mexico's creditworthiness. In the summer of 1982, the country learned that its conventional foreign credit lines were drying up. By 1986, it became evident that Mexico could not meet its loan obligations. As a result, Mexican authorities entered negotiations with various commercial banks, the IMF, the World Bank, the Inter-American Development Bank, and the U.S. government. Together, they agreed on a new loan package. According to the agreement, commercial banks and multilateral institutions would increase their loans to Mexico for a two-year period. Furthermore, the United States committed a $1.5 billion contingency fund to assist Mexico for the oil revenue lost to declining prices. Accordingly, the United States pledged to make funds available to Mexico any time oil prices decreased to between $5 and $9 a barrel for 90 days or more during the first nine months of the agreement. After nine months, Mexico would have to bear the burden of falling oil prices. Additionally, if oil prices rose above $14 per barrel, Mexico would have to pay back some of its loans. The agreement proposed a number of measures to foster economic growth in Mexico. These included trade liberalization, export promotion, reduction of government subsidies and price controls, increased reliance on the private sector, and policies to enhance domestic investment.

The Mexican agreement set the stage for a new approach to dealing with the international debt crisis. Formerly, the IMF and other creditors had demanded that debtor nations employ austerity measures, which essentially required these nations to reduce their public-sector expenditures and improve their merchandise trade balances. However, starting with this agreement, creditors became more flexible and realized that austerity measures alone might be self-defeating in the long run.

DEBT CRISIS IN OTHER DEVELOPING COUNTRIES

As Mexico began to struggle with the debt crisis and search for a solution, other developing countries in Latin America found themselves in the same predicament. Notable among them were Argentina (with a total debt of about $40 billion in 1982) and Brazil (with a total debt of about $88 billion in 1982). Together, the debts of Argentina, Brazil, and Mexico ranked highest among developing countries, accounting for about one third of the total debt. Unfortunately, the debt crisis was not limited to Latin American countries but encompassed other developing countries in Africa, Asia, Europe, the Western Hemisphere, and the Middle East. As Table 14.6 indicates, at the outbreak of the debt crisis in 1982, the total debt of developing countries reached the level of $747 billion and continued to grow thereafter. In contrast to Latin American nations that owed most of their debts to commercial banks, African nations owed their debts to official agencies and governments. This provided an opportunity for the resolution of the African debt problem through the Paris Club. The **Paris Club** refers to an informal group of creditor governments who meet in the French Treasury to assure that all creditor governments grant comparable concessions. The Paris Club granted debt relief to the poorest and most heavily indebted nations, such as those in sub-Saharan Africa. However, given that most of the Latin American nations' debt was owed to commercial banks, a framework for rescheduling these debts did not yet exist. Numerous banks around the globe had invested heavily in Latin America, including major U.S. banks, such as Bank of America and Citicorp. A rampant Latin American default would have jeopardized the survival of these large banks and some of the smaller banks, threatening international financial stability. The stage was set for the international financial community to seek a solution to the debt crisis in order to prevent a potential international financial disaster.

SOVEREIGN DEFAULT

Because developing countries are sovereign, that is, independent of all other nations, they cannot be forced to pay their debts. A nation's decision to default on its external debt is known as **sovereign default.** Most of the debt of developing countries is *sovereign debt,* composed of loans that are either borrowed or guaranteed by these nations' governments. Given this fact, some economists have suggested that debtor

Table 14.6

SUMMARY OF DEVELOPING COUNTRIES' EXTERNAL DEBTS BY REGIONS

(IN BILLIONS OF U.S. DOLLARS)

	1977	1978	1979	1980	1981	1982	1983	1984	1985	1986
Africa	60.9	72.2	84.0	94.1	102.8	117.2	123.3	126.8	130.0	131.5
Asia	83.4	93.8	110.2	134.3	155.0	179.8	197.1	210.9	230.9	250.1
Europe	38.2	47.3	55.3	67.0	71.5	72.7	75.3	79.1	81.4	82.2
Nonoil Middle East	25.8	30.7	36.3	41.9	46.8	52.0	56.0	59.7	65.8	69.1
Western Hemisphere	124.1	154.4	185.2	227.8	284.3	352.3	338.9	351.1	357.1	363.6
Total	332.4	398.4	471.0	565.0	660.4	747.0	790.6	827.6	865.2	896.5

Source: International Monetary Fund, *World Economic Outlook* (Washington, DC: IMF, April 1985, 262, table 45.

nations should default on their external obligations. On the surface, this action seems to be very tempting for the debtor developing countries, and its immediate impact is to relieve the country of its external obligations. However, the potential costs associated with sovereign default have made developing countries reluctant to embark on such an action. The three main costs related to sovereign default are as follows:

1. **Confiscation of assets.** An easy option open to a creditor government is to impound the debtor nations' assets that are within its jurisdiction. However, given the small size of a developing country's assets held abroad, relative to its total external debt, confiscation of assets does not seem to be a significant obstacle to sovereign default. It may, however, serve as a minor deterrent to a country that may be contemplating the default. For example, in 1986, the government of Peru repatriated almost $700 million worth of gold and silver from abroad, fearing that these assets might be confiscated by creditor governments.
2. **Exclusion from new borrowing.** A defaulted nation may be excluded from the international capital market. Such an exclusion does not even have to be orchestrated by creditor nations. If a nation defaults, prospective lenders will view that country as a bad risk, and they will be unwilling to extend new loans to that country. Even if the country succeeds in securing an external loan, it is possible that the loan's proceeds would be impounded by the country's creditors. Given the inadequacy of domestic savings in developing countries, most of these nations count on external borrowing to finance badly needed domestic investment projects. Thus, excluding these countries from the international capital market may prove to be very damaging to their process of economic development.
3. **Trade restrictions and reductions in gains from trade.** A creditor nation may ban all trade with the defaulting nation or impose trade restrictions. In practice, such a ban or restriction may be not be very effective because a country may default on loans to banks in some countries but not in

CH. 14/THE INTERNATIONAL DEBT CRISIS

others. As a result, it could maintain its ability to engage in international trade. The most significant cost of default, resulting from reductions in gains from trade, is related to the first two costs discussed. As noted earlier, creditor nations may confiscate the assets of the debtor nations. They may also exclude the debtor nations from new borrowing. The combined effect of these actions would be a significant reduction in the volume of and gains from trade for the debtor nation.

THE INTERNATIONAL MONETARY FUND\E AND THE DEBT CRISIS

As we explained in Chapter 12, the IMF was set up to achieve two main goals: (a) to make sure that countries follow the agreed-on set of rules for engaging in international business, and (b) to help countries with temporary BOP problems. These objectives put the IMF in the position of a watch dog or a manager of international finance. From its inception in 1947 until the early 1970s, the IMF appeared as a powerful institution that dominated the international monetary system. This power stemmed from its ability to finance BOP deficits of member countries. However, with the breakdown of the Bretton Woods system and adoption of the managed floating exchange rate system by IMF members in 1973, the fund lost most of its power over the international monetary system. The first oil shock that hit the world in 1973 led to the influx of petrodollars from the oil-exporting nations to commercial banks. This event led to excess liquidity in such banks, enabling them to offer loans on much easier terms than the high-conditionality credit offered by the IMF. Commercial banks rushed to lend their excess reserves in order to boost their profits. A study of 13 major U.S. banks reports that from 1970 through 1976, earnings on domestic transactions increased by $40 million, while foreign earnings hit the level of $700 million. The study also finds that in 1975, 52 percent of total earnings were derived from international transactions. Such enormous profits encouraged commercial banks to become the major source of financing in developing countries, increasing their exposure in these countries.[6] As a result, the IMF became an insignificant source of BOP financing.

Aware of the situation, the IMF tried to make some adjustment to reestablish its dominance in the international monetary system. This included creation of the Extended Fund Facility (EFF) in 1974, and the Supplementary Financing Facility (SFF) in 1979.[7] However, only a few developing countries took advantage of these facilities during the 1970s.

The international debt crisis renewed the IMF's power in managing international finance. Lending and conditionality by the IMF became more noticeable. The IMF's **conditionality,** a quid pro quo for borrowing, requires a close economic surveillance of a nation as a prerequisite for borrowing from the Fund (the IMF). This often requires borrowing developing countries to engage in budget-deficit reduction through tax revenue enhancements and decreased social spending, trade liberalization, currency devaluation, abolishment of price controls, restrictions on public-sector employment and wage rates, and restraints on credit creation. These steps are often referred to as *austerity policies*. The IMF monitors the debt targets, the exchange rate, and domestic credit for compliance.

The IMF responded to the debt crisis by increasing its own resources and enhancing its lending to developing countries. It used its power to lead debtors and creditors in the "required direction." From August 1982 through December 1984, the IMF lent $22 billion to 70 countries to support their economic adjustment programs. Beginning in 1984, almost every prominent debtor had either secured or was in the process of negotiating a stabilization package with the IMF.[8]

By the late 1980s, the IMF's image as the manager of international finance was clearly tarnished by the failure of the stabilization programs. Such failure was either due to the refusal of officials to implement austerity policies at the level demanded by the IMF or simply to the fact that the program did not work. during the 1980s, many countries that had implemented IMF stabilization programs experienced contraction in their economies, inflation, and insignificant improvement in their current accounts. By 1987, it was evident that the assets of commercial banks were lost in Latin America, and the IMF's major management strategy of influencing and coercing commercial lending had met with scant success. This is evident from the following statement made by the seven largest Latin American nations in their Declaration of Uruguay, October 27-29, 1988:

> The conditionality of adjustment programs, sector lending, and restructuring agreements often entail measures that are inadequate and contradictory, making the economic policies more difficult in an extremely harsh economic climate.[9]

The IMF's failure in managing the debt crisis may have been related to its lack of power in implementing its strategies. The debt crisis of the 1980s strengthened its managerial position but did not provide the IMF with the necessary power. As a result, the Fund continued to rely mainly on short-term strategies of reacting to unpredictable events instead of taking initiative on long-run issues.[10]

THE UNITED STATES AND THE DEBT CRISIS

The debt crisis has had significant implications for the United States. The decrease in the growth of Latin American economies and their suppressed demand for imports means fewer exports for the United States, leading to a decline in the U.S. gross national product (GNP). Using 1985 data, a study of U.S. exports to Argentina, Brazil, Mexico, Venezuela, and the Philippines revealed that debt-related austerity programs lowered U.S. net exports in 40 out of 61 industries studied. As a result, U.S. net trade was $13.7 billion lower than what it could have been in the absence of such programs. Additionally, the study reports that overall U.S. production fell by $21.9 billion, or 0.5 percent of the 1985 GNP.[11]

The decline in developing countries' ability to pay their debts meant trouble for creditor banks in general and the United States in particular. A default by one of the larger debtors or a group of the smaller debtors could create substantial liquidity problems in the world financial system. Given the magnitude of investment by U.S. giants in Latin America in 1983 (see Table 14.7), the United States considered the responsibility of deterring default, even by a single nation, crucial. A default by even one country, such as Mexico, could have generated a chain reaction of bank failures affecting many nations. The United States and other nations did not want a replay of the rampant banking disaster that started the Great Depression.

These considerations led the United States to get seriously involved with the debt crisis, searching for viable solutions. In the next section, we study the resolutions to the debt crisis and elaborate on the plans that were suggested by the United States to deal with this dilemma.

SOLUTIONS TO THE DEBT CRISIS

During the 1970s and early 1980s, creditors took a case-by-case approach in dealing with the debt crisis. By the mid-1980s, it was evident that this approach had not greatly relieved the problem. As a result, several solutions were proposed. Although some of these solutions have proven unworthy, others have helped to alleviate the problem, though not to the degree necessary. In this section, we concentrate on some of the widely discussed proposals.

Debt-Equity Swap

Debt-equity swaps are methods used to transform some of the existing debt to equity. A foreign buyer, usually a multinational corporation (MNC), purchases a country's debt at a discount and sells it back to the debtor country in return for its domestic currency. The buyer is then required to use this currency to purchase

Table 14.7

TOP U.S. BANK LOANS TO MAJOR LATIN AMERICAN DEBTOR NATIONS, DECEMBER 1983 (IN MILLIONS OF U.S. DOLLARS)

Bank	Argentina	Brazil	Mexico	Venezuela	Total
Citicorp	1,090	4,700	2,900	1,500	10,190
Bank of America	300	2,484	2,748	1,614	7,139
Manufacturers Hanover	1,321	2,130	1,915	1,084	6,441
Chase Manhattan	775	2,560	1,553	1,226	6,114
J.P. Morgan	741	1,785	1,174	464	4,164
Chemical	370	1,276	1,414	776	3,836
Bankers Trust	230	743	1,286	436	2,695

Source: Brian Kettell and George Magunus, *The International Debt Game* (Cambridge: Ballinger Publishing Company, 1986), x.

shares of stock in a domestic enterprise or to make a direct investment in the country. As a result, the developing country's external debts and interest obligations decrease. Additionally, the creditor disposes a bond whose repayment is questionable, but instead carries shares of stock in an existing enterprise in the the country. As a result, the developing country's external debts and interest obligations decrease. Additionally, the creditor disposes a bond whose repayment is questionable, but instead carries shares of stock in an existing enterprise in the developing country.

Examples of MNCs that have engaged in debt-equity swaps include Fiat, Dow Chemical Company, and Nissan Corporation. Fiat purchased Brazilian debt at a discount and exchanged it for the cruzado (the Brazilian currency). It then used the proceeds to augment its plant in Brazil. Dow Chemical Company and Nissan Corporation engaged in similar arrangements with Chile and Mexico, respectively.

The United States supported the debt-equity swaps and proposed that the World Bank promote this arrangement. This encouraged countries such as Argentina, Brazil, Mexico, Chile, and the Philippines, to participate in debt-equity swaps.

The Baker Plan

During the early 1980s, the United States insisted that debtor developing countries pay the full interest owed to U.S. banks. By 1985, however, it was evident that the austerity policies of the previous few years had not greatly reduced the debt problem. Latin American nations found themselves deeper in debt, and U.S. policymakers realized the restraints the debt crisis inflicted upon the growth of these nations and thus their demand for U.S. exports. In the fall of 1985, the U.S. Secretary of Treasury, James Baker, presented a plan to deal with the continuing dilemma. The plan called for a number of measures to alleviate the problems of the highly indebted developing countries. These measures included:

1. Additional funding by commercial banks.
2. Provision of credit by the IMF and the Inter-American Development Bank.
3. World Bank structural assistance.
4. Subsidies from trade surplus nations, such as Japan.
5. Promotion of a world economic environment that supports continued and enlarged market access for everyone and supplements debtors' sustained growth.

In summary, the Baker Plan emphasized growth over austerity in developing countries, based on funds generated by trade surplus nations, the IMF, the World Bank, the Inter-American Development Bank, and commercial banks. The plan called for $20 billion in loans from commercial banks, and $9 billion in additional loans from multilateral agencies over and above the money that was normally lent to the 15 most

GLOBAL INSIGHTS CASE 14.2

TRADE LIBERALIZATION AND THE DEBT CRISIS

Many debt-stricken developing nations have reacted to their dilemma by trying new policies that strive to stimulate long-term economic growth and reduce fiscal debts. Many of these nations have adopted policies that aim at promotion of free markets and elimination of government restrictions of domestic and international trade. For example, soon after his inauguration in July 1989, Carlos Menem, the president of Argentina, introduced new policies to achieve the following three objectives:

1. Increase market orientation.
2. Encourage freer international trade.
3. Privatize state-owned enterprises.

These policies were a reversal of Argentina's strategies for inward-oriented development and concentrated intervention in the market mechanism that had existed for more than a decade. Other countries that have embarked on market-oriented reforms include Mexico, Venezuela, and Poland. Market-oriented reforms have been identified with the restoration of sustained growth in Chile, Mauririus (after 1984), and Mexico (after 1988). However, the new reforms have not yet eliminated economic and political instability in these nations. Efforts to execute the reforms have elicited great resistance and have not yielded fast improvement.

It seems that the worst is over for the debt-stricken countries. In many of these nations, debt-exports and debt-GNP ratios have substantially decreased. Data show that a large percentage of debt owned by affected nations in 1982 has already been paid. For example, it is estimated that from 1983 to 1989, Argentina paid 40 percent of its debt; Brazil, 38 percent; Mexico, 62 percent; Nigeria, 30 percent; and Venezuela, 75 percent.

Sources: D. Cohen, "The Debt Crisis: A Postmortem," in O. J. Blanchard and S. Fischer, eds, *NBER Macroeconomics Annual 1992* (Cambridge, MA: The MIT Press, 1992), 70--71; L. B. Krause and K. Kihwan, eds., *Liberalization in the Process of Economic Development* (Berkely, CA: University of California Press, 1991); World Bank, *World Development Report 1991* (New York: Oxford University Press, 1991).

GLOBAL INSIGHTS CASE 14.3

TIED-AID AGREEMENTS

Tied-aid is officially supported concessional financing linked to procurement in the donor country. It distorts trade when used to win contracts for capital goods exports rather than to provide true aid. Tied-aid can misallocate resources from more efficient to less efficient producers whose government offer such financing.

When used for exports promotion, tied-aid can also distort aid flows by directing scarce resources away from high-priority development projects to projects of interest to industries in donor countries. Traditionally, tied-aid has directed donor support toward, for example, large electric power generation and telecommunication projects and away from social sector projects. This skewing of resources allocation in developing countries increases the capital intensity of development and burdens the recipient country with high maintenance expenditures in the future.

In response to complaints from exporters that they often faced tied-aid competition for capital goods projects, the United States negotiated rules in the OECD to govern tied-aid programs. The rules, dubbed the Helsinki Package, became effective in February 1992. They apply to nonconcessional financing and stipulate that higher income developing countries (those with per capita above $3,035) are ineligible for all tied-aid. The least developed countries remain eligible for all types of financing because of their desperate shortage of capital. For countries in between, such as China, Indonesia, and India, tied-aid is prohibited for projects that can generate cash flows sufficient to repay debt on commercial terms.

It is hoped that the Helsinki rules will reduce dislocations and maximize the total resources—aid and commercial financing—available to promote economic development. Last year the OECD issued guidelines for the use of tied-aid, to draw the line between projects that should receive tied-aid. Since 1992, under the Helsinki Package, annual tied-aid has declined from $10 billion to about $4 billion. The tied-aid that remains has been shifted away from major capital projects capable of supporting financing on commercial terms to legitimate aid projects such as water and sewage, and health and other social services.

Source: U.S. Government Printing Office, *Economic Report of the President* (Washington DC: U.S. Government Printing Office, 1997), 275, Box 7-5, p. 275. Reprinted.

indebted nations. Unfortunately, however, the large commercial banks were very reluctant to go along with the plan. In fact, these banks actually withdrew $2 billion instead of lending the additional $20 billion called for. As the debt problem persisted into 1988, it was evident that the Baker Plan was inadequate to resolve the crisis. This resulted in a major alteration of the plan and gave birth to the Brady Plan.

The Brady Plan

The Brady Plan was an extension of the Baker Plan. It took shape in March 1989 and enhanced the Baker Plan by augmenting debt reduction and multilaterally financed loan guarantees. The plan was unclear about how its suggestions were to be implemented. However, one thing was clear: The market-based debt reduction (the decrease in nations' external debts through "voluntary" market transactions) had to be promoted by official agencies. The plan targeted a 20-percent, or $70 billion, reduction in the $350 billion that developing countries owed to commercial banks in advanced countries. The World Bank, the IMF, and Japan committed a combined total of $29.5 billion from 1989 through 1992. Although these strategies succeeded in alleviating the debt crisis to some degree by the early 1990s, the dilemma still lingers on.

PHASES OF THE DEBT CRISIS

In the last section, we elaborated on the most widely discussed proposals for resolving the debt crisis. Equipped with this knowledge, we now look at the debt crisis from an historical perspective. The debt crisis has gone through several phases since 1982. In the first phase, commercial banks put together short-term emergency packages that extended the maturity of some loans that were due over the next two years or over five to seven years. Additionally, they committed new money to cover any immediate needs, such as the 1982-1983 restructuring of Argentina, Brazil, and Mexico. Bank lending under these situations is known as *concerted lending,* a tactful terminology for lending that was, in many circumstances, involuntary. Under this arrangement, banks had to contribute new money in proportion to their loan exposure at the beginning of the crisis.

The second phase was a period aimed at buying time. Concerted lending, conceived as an emergency measure, was designed to give nations time to achieve reforms and banks time to raise reserves and capital. It was agreed that the IMF would oversee a nation's economic accomplishment and provide the resultant information to commercial banks. During this phase, in 1984, Mexico agreed with its creditor banks on the first multiyear restructuring agreement. The Mexican restructuring also highlighted the first use of debt-equity swaps.

The third phase began with the announcement of the Baker Plan in October 1985. As we mentioned earlier, this plan emphasized growth-oriented reforms for debtor countries in return for new loans from banks. Until then, the debt-relief strategy was dominated by the IMF. Beginning with this phase, however, the World Bank joined the IMF in combating the debt crisis. Also, with this phase, Mexico and Chile started to emphasize structural adjustment in the areas of privatization and trade.

The fourth phase started with the introduction of the Brady Plan in March 1989. As we explained earlier, the Brady plan built on the Baker Plan by enhancing debt reduction and multilaterally financed loan guarantees. The plan was employed to restructure the commercial bank debts of Costa Rica, Nigeria, Venezuela, the Philippines, and Uruguay. Additionally, the plan provided the basis for debt agreements with Argentina and Brazil.

THE CHALLENGE AHEAD

The debt crisis hit the world in 1982 and attracted a great deal of attention during the 1980s. Some observers suggested that the crisis would be over almost exactly 10 years after it began. As the 1980s wore on, it became apparent that these observers were overly optimistic. Debtors continued to experience problems in fully servicing their debts, and banks increasingly treated their loans to debt-stricken nations as "value impaired." In much of Africa and some segments of Latin America today, access to world capital markets is either nonexistent or remains impaired. The former communist nations of Eastern Europe and the new Commonwealth of Independent States (CIS) are in need of resource transfers from abroad as they attempt to establish market economies in the face of heavy foreign debt burdens.

Nevertheless, to date, there has been a significant amount of progress. In October 1992, Brazil agreed to restructure the $44 billion it owed to foreign banks[12] In April 1992, Argentina reached an accord with its

CH. 14/THE INTERNATIONAL DEBT CRISIS

framework for "debt and debt-service reduction."*For its part, the U.S. government has continued to follow several multilateral and bilateral initiatives to decrease debt burden of the poorest developing nations. In mid-December 1994, the Paris Club of creditor countries, including the United States, agreed on more favorable debt reduction terms, referred to as the "Naples Terms." The Naples Terms aimed at lowering the debts of heavily indebted poor nations by up to 67 percent. During the 1996 fiscal year, the United States negotiated debt-reduction agreements with seven nations under the Naples Terms. In February 1996, the United States Congress commissioned a pilot debt buyback and swap initiative for lower income Latin American and Caribbean nations that are active in economic reforms, particularly investment reforms. Countries must also meet certain political principles, including democratic governments, and a good record in the areas of human rights, narcotics, and terrorism. Such progress has convinced some observers that the debt crisis is over. To others, however, the assertion that the situation has improved is questionable. Nonetheless, it is clear there are still nations, such as Peru and Ecuador, that have yet to put the problem behind them. Additionally, the debt crisis has caused policymakers in developing countries to shift economic discussion away from income distribution and poverty, which are the crucial problems that exist in many of these countries. If the debt crisis were under control, there would be enormous pressure on policymakers in both developing and advanced countries to address these problems. This is a challenge that policymakers will have to deal with in the future.[13] A new challenge to officials in advanced countries is the growing debt burden in Russia. A solution to this problem is a prerequisite to Russia's smooth transition from communism to a free market.[14]

Today's international debt strategy reflects a realization that many of the heavily indebted developing countries cannot resolve their debt problems by themselves, and some of the debt must be written off as uncollectible. Given this fact, creditors have been increasingly willing to write off these debts as uncollectible subject to implementation of the required structural changes for adjustment by the debtor developing countries.[15]

Although the employment of the new strategy has not resulted in a significant decrease in the debt itself, progress toward resolving the problem seems well on its way. Some heavily indebted nations, chiefly in Latin America, that had been closed out of financial markets are again considered creditworthy. However, the conditions in smaller nations look less optimistic.

The vast increase in the inflow of funds to heavily indebted developing countries in 1991 underlined the major gain of the "debt-regularization process"-new lending, foreign portfolio investment, the return of capital flight, and new investment advancement. What seems to be needed in the years ahead is for the inflow of funds to continue. This, in turn, depends on the following factors: the growth of the world economy, leading to higher export earnings for developing countries; continued progress in adjustment reforms with greater social equality in developing countries; political tranquility; and an open market that is free from protectionist measures against developing countries. The likely outcome is a long, painful period in which indebted developing countries endure more economic hardships than they would prefer.

---

*The first part was signed in January 1990

SUMMARY

1. During the past decade, developing countries have accumulated a total international debt amounting to $1.3 trillion. The total combined debt of developing countries is expected to exceed $1.4 trillion in 1994.
2. Although the seeds of the debt crisis were planted during the energy crisis of the early 1970s, it did not become apparent to the world until August 12, 1982, when Mexico declared it could no longer service its debt.
3. In general, Latin American countries have been much more dependent on bank financing than Asian countries. Additionally, most private loans given to Latin American nations are made by a few major U.S. banks.
4. Researchers have suggested a number of factors as having a significant role in the developing countries' debt crisis. These factors include advanced countries' tighter monetary policies, the second oil shock of the late 1970s, poor public-sector investment in developing countries, the worldwide recession (1980–1982), capital flight from developing countries, the appreciation of the dollar, and excess loanable funds in advanced countries.
5. Capital flight refers to the transfer of funds from one nation to another by firms or individuals. It happens when the expected returns from keeping funds abroad are higher or more secure than from keeping them at home.
6. Capital flight is caused by several factors. Chief among these factors are currency overvaluation, interest-rate ceilings, high and variable inflation, and high domestic tax rates.
7. Starting with the Mexican agreement, creditors became more flexible and realized that austerity measures alone might be self-defeating in the long run.
8. Together, the debts of Argentina, Brazil, and Mexico ranked highest among developing countries, accounting for about one third of the total debt in 1982. 9. Unfortunately, the debt crisis was not limited to Latin American countries, but encompassed other developing nations in Africa, Asia, Europe, the Western Hemisphere, and the Middle East.
9. A nation's decision to default on its external debt is known as sovereign default.
10. The three main costs related to sovereign default are (a) confiscation of assets; (b) exclusion from new borrowing; and (c) trade restrictions and reductions in gains from trade.
11. The international debt crisis renewed the IMF's power in managing international finance.
12. The decline in developing countries' ability to pay their debts meant trouble for creditor banks in general and the United States in particular.
13. Debt-equity swaps are methods used to transform some of the existing debt to equity.
14. The Baker Plan emphasized growth over austerity in developing countries, based on funds generated by trade surplus nations, the IMF, the World Bank, the Inter-American Development Bank, and commercial banks.
15. The Brady Plan enhanced the Baker Plan by augmenting debt reduction and multilaterally financed loan guarantees.

REVIEW QUESTIONS

1. What factors caused the debt crisis of developing countries to occur in the 1980s? Explain.
2. Why did the debt crisis of the 1980s jeopardize the stability of the world's financial system? Explain.
3. What have been the implications of the debt crisis for both advanced and developing countries? Explain.
4. What factors give rise to capital flight? Explain.
5. What is "sovereign default?" What factors are associated with sovereign default? Explain.

CH. 14/THE INTERNATIONAL DEBT CRISIS

6. What is the major difference between the nature of the debt crisis in Latin America and Asia?
7. What factors caused the Mexican debt crisis to occur? Explain.
8. What has been the major impact of the debt crisis on the IMF? Explain.
9. What implications has the debt crisis had for the United States? Explain.
10. What is the difference between the Baker Plan and the Brady Plan? Explain.
11. What phases has the debt crisis gone through? Explain.

PROBLEMS

1. Why do you think a debtor nation prefers to borrow from a commercial bank rather than from the IMF? Explain.
2. Given the Japanese position as the United States' largest foreign creditor, the U.S. government should default on its foreign debt to Japan in order to resolve its debt problem. Do you agree with this statement? Discuss.
3. In choosing a lender, should developing countries take into consideration the currency in which the loan is denominated? Discuss.
4. The debt problem is caused by developing countries themselves. Thus, it is their responsibility to resolve the debt problem on their own, rather than involving advanced countries. Do you agree with this statement? Discuss.
5. Capital flight is one of the major factors responsible for the debt burden in some developing countries. Because capital flight creates a large debt for a government but generates a countervailing foreign asset for citizens who carry funds abroad, the overall net debt of the nation as a whole does not change. Thus, nations whose external debts are mainly due to capital flight should encounter no debt problem. Do you agree with this statement? Explain.
6. Developing countries' debt was frequently undertaken by state-owned companies. Some of these nations have embarked on privatization by selling state-owned companies to the private sector. Do you think the amount of borrowing by these nations would have been higher or lower if they had moved on privatization earlier? Discuss.
7. What is the possible impact of lifting trade barriers on a nations's ability to borrow in the international financial market? Explain.

NOTES

1. Pablo Guidotti and Manmohan S. Kumar, "Managing Domestic Public Debt," *Finance and Development* (September 1992): 9-12.
2. Peter H. Lindert, *International Economics,* 9th ed. (Homewood, IL: Irwin, 1991), 555..
3. Pedro P. Kucznski, *Latin American Debt* (Maryland: Johns Hopkins University Press, 1988), 64.
4. John T. Cuddington, *Capital Flight: Estimates, Issues, and Explanations.* Princeton Studies in International Finance, no. 58 (Princeton, NJ: Princeton University, 1986).
5. Donald R. Lessard and John Williamson, eds., *Capital Flight and Third-World Debt* (Washington, DC: Institute for International Economics, 1987); John Williamson and Donald R. Lessard, *Capital Flight: The Problem and Policy Responses* (Washington, DC: Institute for International Economics, 1987).
6. L. R. Bernal, "Resolving the Global Debt Crisis," *Economica Internazionale* 40 (May-August 1987): 155-171.
7. Jonathan D. Aronson, *Money and Power* (London: Sage Publications, 1977), 178.
8. "Muddling Through," *The Economist,* (6 February 1988), 80.
9. "Latin American Declaration Deplores Adverse Impact of Debt, Projectionism," *IMF Survey* (November 14, 1988), 354-355.
10. Parviz Asheghian, "International Banking Management and the Debt Crisis," *International Academy of Management and Marketing, 1991 Proceedings,* 716-735.

11. Gerald Berg, "The Effects of External Debts of Mexico, Brazil, Argentina, Venezuela, and the Philippines on the United States," *Applied Economics* 20 (1988): 939-956.
12. "Brazilian Accord Puts End to Debt Crisis in Region, But Not to Economic Troubles," *The Wall Street Journal,* 10 July 1992, A12.
13. Ibid; U.S. Government Printing Office, *Economic Report of the President* (Washington DC: U.S. Government Printing Office, 1998), 275.
14. "Debt Burden Is Very Perilous, Russian Warns," *The Wall Street Journal,* 14 July 1993, A9.
15. United Nations, *World Economic Survey 1992* (New York: United Nations), 157-164.

SUGGESTED READINGS

Bergsten, Fred, and William Cline. Bank Lending to Developing Countries: The Policy Alternatives. Washington DC: Institute for International Economic, November 1987.

Bouchet, M. H. *The Political Economy of International Debt.* Westport, CT: Greenwood Press, 1987.

Clark, John, and Eliot Kalter. "Recent Innovation in Debt Restructuring." Finance and Development (September 1992): 6-8.

Cline, William. "International Debt: Progress and Strategy." *Finance and Development* (June 1987): 9-11.

_____. "International Debt: From Crisis to Recovery." *American Economic Review, Papers and Proceedings* 75, no. 2 (May 1985): 185-190.

_____. *Mobilizing Bank Lending to Debtor Countries.* Washington, DC: Institute for International Economics, 1987.

Corden, W. Max. "Debt Relief and Adjustment Incentives." *International Monetary Fund Staff Papers* 35, no. 4 (December 1988): 628-643.

Darity, W. L., and B. Horn. *The Loan Pushers: The Role of Commercial Banks in the International Debt Crisis.* Cambridge, MA: Ballinger, 1988.

Dornbusch, Rudiger. "Latin American Debt Problem: Anatomy and Solutions." In *Debt and Democracy in Latin America,* edited by Barbara Stallings and Robert Kaufman. Boulder, CO: Westview Press, 1989.

Dornbusch, Rudiger, and Stanley Fischer. "The World Debt Problem: Origins and Prospects." *Journal of Development Planning* (1984): 57-81.

Fisher, Stanley, and Ishrat Husain. "Managing the Debt Crisis." *Challenge: The Magazine of Economic Affairs* 28, no. 2 (June 1990): 24-27.

Felix, David. "How to Resolve Latin America's Debt Crisis." *Challenge: The Magazine of Economic Affairs* 28, no. 5 (November/December 1985): 44-51.

Foxely, Alejandro. "Latin American Development After the Debt Crisis." *Journal of Economic Development* 27 (1987): 201-225.

Kenen, Peter. "Organizing Debt Relief: The Need for a New Institution." *Journal of Economic Perspectives* (Winter 1990): 7-18.

Lancaster, Carol, and John Williamson, eds. *African Debt and Financing.* Washington, DC: Institute for International Economics, 1986.

Nowzad, Bahman. "Lessons of the Debt Decade." *Finance and Development* 27, no. 1 (March 1990): 9-13.

Orlando, Frank, and Simon Tietel. "Latin America's External Debt Problem: Debt Servicing Strategies Comparable With Long-Term Economic Growth." *Economic Development and Cultural Change* (April 1986): 641-671.

Rhode, William R. "Third-World Debt: The Disaster that Didn't Happen." *The Economist* (12 September 1992): 21-23.

Sachs, Jeffrey D. "The Debt Crisis at a Turning Point." *Challenge* (May-June 1988): 17-26.

_____.Sachs, Jeffrey D., ed. *Developing Country Debt and the World Economy.* Chicago: University of Chicago Press, 1989.

Trebat, Thomas. "Latin American Debt in the Eighties: A Case Study of Brazil." In *Foreign Debt and Latin American Development,* edited by Antonio Jorge, et al. New York: Pergamon Press, 1983.

Ukpolo, Victor, "Foreign Debt and Economic Development: The Case of Sub-Sahran African Economies." *Journal of Third World Studies* 9, no. 1 (1992): 199-214.

Williamson, John, *Voluntary Approaches to Debt Relief.* Washington DC: September 1988, revised June 1989.

PART V

FOREIGN DIRECT INVESTMENT, MULTINATIONAL CORPORATIONS, AND FOREIGN AID

CHAPTER 15

FOREIGN DIRECT INVESTMENT AND MULTINATIONAL CORPORATIONS

In Chapter 13 we devoted our attention to international trade, that is, the export and import of goods and services. However, trade in goods and services is only part of international business. International business can be defined as those business transactions among individuals, firms, or other entities (both private and public) that occur across national boundaries. These activities include the movement of goods (the importing and exporting of commodities); the transaction of services, such as management, accounting, marketing, finance, and legal services; the investment of capital in tangible assets, such as manufacturing, agriculture, mining, petroleum production, transportation, and communications media; and transactions in intangible assets, such as trademarks, patents, and the licensing of manufacturing technology.

A multinational corporation (MNC) is the principal player in international business. To engage in international business, MNCs rely heavily on foreign direct investment (FDI), that is, the acquisition of a controlling interest in a company or facility. Although their history goes back a long way, the mid-nineteenth century can be marked as an important period in the development of MNCs. During this period, a number of companies began expanding their operations by establishing branch offices in foreign countries. Alfred Nobel, the Swedish entrepreneur, started his first foreign plant in Hamburg, Germany, in 1866. The Singer Company established a plant in Glasgow, Scotland, in 1867. Fredrick Bayer founded dye factories in Russia in 1876, in France in 1882, and in Belgium in 1908. The proliferation of MNCs and their emergence as a pivotal global economic force had to await the significant postwar advancement in transportation and communications and enormous liberalization of international trade and payments that began to gather momentum in the late 1950s. During the 1960s, U.S. direct investment in foreign countries grew rapidly-mainly in Canada and Europe-accounting for roughly 70 percent of the net FDI in the world during the post-World War II period through the 1960s. However, following this period, the share of U.S. net FDI relative to the total amount of FDI by advanced countries in the world gradually declined, reaching the approximate levels of 63 percent in 1970, 54 percent in 1975, 44.5 percent in 1980, and 39 percent in 1991.*[1]

Starting with the 1970s, the picture of international business began to change. Advances in communications media, speedier worldwide travel made possible by jet-age technology, and lower costs of

---

*As we explain later in this chapter, foreign direct investment involves an investment in the equity securities of a foreign firm that is large enough to exert effective control over the firm.

production in developing countries resulted in the expansion of international business. During this period, the former West Germany, Great Britain, other European countries, Canada, and Japan started catching up with the United States. Japan's rapid growth in the automobile and steel industries, for example, placed that country's corporations on the list of the 50 largest corporations in the world.

The international business activities of developing countries have increased in recent years as well. Many companies from developing countries (such as Argentina, Brazil, Hong Kong, India, South Korea, and Taiwan) have engaged in FDI, mainly in manufacturing in other developing countries. Because of their "scaled-down," relatively more labor-intensive technology and their lower managerial and overhead costs, these companies have been able to produce relatively low-cost products. These products have successfully competed in the world market, mainly on the basis of their low prices.

All of these events have contributed to the weakening position of the United States as the world leader in international business. Later in this chapter we use data to provide further explanations regarding the United States' position in the world of international business. [2]

Today, the yearly sales of such MNCs as General Motors, Exxon, and Ford Motor Company, surpass the total national income of all but a handful of nations. It is estimated that the sales between foreign subsidiaries of the same company may account for roughly 25 percent of global trade. Such estimates emphasize that the competitiveness of business in this age is beyond the grasp of any purely domestic company. In such a competitive environment, the life cycles of different products are getting shorter, and it is costlier and harder to develop new products. This makes the jobs of today's corporate managers more challenging. To turn these challenges into opportunities, today's managers need to develop products and bring them to global markets much faster than ever before.

The purpose of this chapter is to provide an understanding of the nature and scope of MNCs. First, we define the concept of MNC and present the world's major MNCs. Next, we differentiate between FDI and portfolio investment, providing some statistics for FDI. We also elaborate on MNCs' channels of entry into international business. Finally, we discuss technology transfer by MNCs.

DEFINITION OF MULTINATIONAL CORPORATION

There is no consensus among scholars regarding the definition of MNC. Differences in definitions stem from the different types of MNCs, each type following a specific purpose. Consequently, each definition is based on a given criterion that is considered indicative of the purpose and type of MNC. Three major criteria have been used: (a) a structural criterion, (b) a performance criterion, and (c) a behavioral criterion.

Using the **structural criterion,** an MNC can be defined by two approaches. In the first approach, multinationality is defined by the number of countries in which a firm is operating. This means that a firm has its base in one country, such as the United States, and operates in a number of other countries. In the second approach, ownership characteristics are used as the basis for definition. Since the term "multi" means "many," the multinational firm refers to a firm that is owned or operated by individuals from many nations. Thus, an MNC can be defined either by the nationality of its owners or by the nationality of its top management.

If the first definition is adopted, an MNC is a firm that makes its stocks available to all the countries in which it is operating. If the second definition is adopted, a firm could be considered an MNC if its top management is composed of people from various countries. It is assumed that such individuals would have a worldwide outlook and would be less prone to follow the interest of any specific nation.

Using the **performance criterion,** the MNC can be defined on the basis of the absolute amount or the relative share (percentage) of assets, number of employees, sales, or earnings in a foreign country. According to the absolute measure, a firm is considered an MNC if it has allocated a "certain amount" of its resources to its foreign operations. By the relative measure, a firm is considered an MNC if it allocates a "significant

CH. 15/FOREIGN DIRECT INVESTMENT & MNCs

portion," that is, a very large percentage, of its resources to foreign operations. This measure implies that the magnitude of the firm's foreign operations is so significant that it depends on other countries for its growth and financial stability.

Using the **behavioral criterion,** a firm can be classified as multinational if its top management "thinks internationally." In this definition, it is assumed that because the MNC is concerned with more than one country, its top management sees the entire world as the domain of their operation. Thus, the international manager is considered a person who searches for investment opportunities in the world market rather than being confined to the domestic market.[3]

In this book, we define a multinational corporation as a group of corporations that is operating in different countries but is controlled by its headquarters in a given country. We refer to the country that houses the headquarters of an MNC as the home country and to other countries as host countries. We maintain that the ownership of MNCs can be public, private, or mixed.

THE WORLD'S MAJOR MULTINATIONAL CORPORATIONS

Table 15.1 shows the 10 largest corporations, ranked on the basis of their total sales in 2001. Table 15.2 indicates, for each country, the number of firms, total sales, and the percentage sale of the world's ten largest corporations among the major investing countries in 2001. In 2001, The United States, with 6 firms, had the largest number of firms among the top 10 MNCs in the world, accounting for about 64.17 percent of the total sales of these corporations. Other advanced nations on the list were Britain, Germany, Netherlands, and Japan.

FOREIGN DIRECT INVESTMENT AND PORTFOLIO INVESTMENT

One must differentiate between the terms portfolio investment and foreign direct investment. The main criterion for differentiating between the two is control. **Portfolio investment** is merely a financial investment that does not give the owner the power to exert control over the assets of the firm in question. This can involve investment in debt securities (bonds) or a small amount of investment in equity securities (stocks of a firm). **Foreign direct investment** is an investment that results in control of a firm by the investor. This can involve an investment in a firm's equity securities large enough for the investor to exert effective control over the firm.

The amount of equity securities needed to classify an investment as either portfolio or FDI is a subject that is open to debate. In practice, the amount is arbitrarily set by different countries, depending on their perception of effective control. The U.S. Department of Commerce, for example, considers FDI as any investment by an individual or a firm in a foreign company that represents more than 10 percent of the outstanding stock of that company. The percentage chosen by other nations varies and is usually higher than 10 percent.

It should be noted that FDI does not necessarily involve the movement of capital from a host to a home country. In fact, FDI can be financed in a number of other ways. As a foreign investor, one could finance an investment by (a) selling technology to affiliates in a foreign country and investing the proceeds in that country, (b) raising the needed capital locally, (c) reinvesting the firm's foreign earnings in that country, or (d) using the management service fees that are earned in a foreign country. Thus, the important characteristic of FDI is not how the investment is financed but the control that it confers. As we already mentioned, it is the word "control" that differentiates FDI and portfolio investment. Portfolio investment does not involve control and is undertaken solely as a means of obtaining capital gain, rather than engaging in entrepreneurial activities.

Table 15.1

THE WORLD TEN LARGEST CORPORATIONS RANKED BY SALES

Rank	Company	Headquarters	Revenues for the year ended December 31, 2001 (millions of U.S. $)]	Profits (million of U.S.$)
1	Wal Mart Stores	U.S.	219,812.0	6,671.0
2	Exxon Mobil	U.S.	191,581.0	15,320.0
3	General Motors	U.S.	177,260.0	601.0
4	BP	Britain	174,218.0	8,01.0
5	Ford Motors	U.S.	162,412.0	-5,453.0
6	Enron	U.S.	138,718.0	N/A
7	Daimler Chrysler	Germany	136,897.3	-592.8
8	Royal Dutch/Shell Group	Britain/Netherlands	135,211.0	10,852.0
9	General Electric	U.S.	125,913.0	13,684.0
10	Toyota Motor	Japan	120,814.4	4,925.1

Source: "Global 500," *Fortune*, July 22, 2002, http://www.fortune.com/lists/F500/index.html

Table 15.2

NUMBER OF FIRMS, TOTAL SALES, AND THE PERCENTAGE SHARE OF THE WORLD'S FIFTY LARGEST CORPORATIONS AMONG THE MAJOR INVESTING COUNTRIES, 1995

Rank	Country	Number of Firms	Total Sales (Millions of U.S. $	Percentage Share
1	The United States	6	1,015,696.00	64.17
2	England	1	174,218.0	11.01
3	Germany	1	136,897.3	8.65
4	Britain/Netherlands	1	135,211.0	8.54
5	Japan	1	120,814.4	7.63

Source: Calculated by the author from "Global 500", *Fortune*, July 22, 2002,

International trade is dominated by the world's advanced industrial nations, so FDI also is led by these countries. Table 15-3 shows the outflows and inflows of foreign direct investment by major industrial countries. As this table indicates, As this table indicates, according to 2000 data, Great Britain is the major investor and the United States is the major recipient of foreign direct investment in the world. The Great Britain position as the major investor of FDI abroad is followed by France, the United States, Netherlands, Germany, Canada, Japan, and Italy. A comparison of data for 1995 and 2000 reveals that France has experienced the highest rate of growth of FDI abroad (971.302%) than any other major industrialized nations

CH. 15/FOREIGN DIRECT INVESTMENT & MNCs

in the world. This position is followed by Great Britain (483.603%), Netherlands (270.488%), Canada (261.175%), Italy (71.99%), The United States (54.323%), Japan (40.071%), and Germany.

The growing amount of U.S. FDI abroad, can be attributed, among other factors, to the economic recovery of the United States in the early 1990s, and the growth of the market economies in the world. Such growth has been aided by the collapse of the former Soviet Union, Eastern European countries' economic reforms, and the unification of Germany.

Table 15.3
DISTRIBUTION OF MAJOR INDUSTRIAL COUNTRIES' FOREIGN DIRECT INVESTMENT AT HOME AND ABROAD
(Millions of dollars)

Country	1995 Investment Abroad	1995 Investment Home	2000 Investment Abroad	2000 Investment Home	Percentage Change Abroad	Percentage Change Home
Canada	11.490	9.319	41.499	62.216	261.175	567.625
France	15.820	23.730	169.480	43.170	971.302	81.922
Germany	39.100	11.990	52.050	189.180	33.120	1477.815
Great Britain	44.460	20.320	259.470	129.840	483.603	538.976
Italy	7.024	4.8420	12.075	13.175	71.911	172.098
Japan	22.510	0.400	31.530	8.230	40.071	1957.500
Netherlands	20.192	12.228	74.809	54.138	270.488	342.738
United States	98.780	57.800	152.440	287.680	54.323	397.716

Source: International Monetary Fund. *Direction of Trade Statistics* (Washington, DC: International Monetary Fund, February 2001).

The growing amount of FDI in the United States can be attributed, among other factors, to the relative market size in the United States, the declining labor costs relative to other rich nations, the relative abundance of raw materials, and the restrictions on the importation of certain products to the United States. These factors, which encourage a firm to invest in another country, will be more fully discussed in later chapters.

Table 15-4 provide us with more detail on the activities of the United States with regard to FDI. As the column entitled "Abroad " shows , Great Britain is the major recipient of U.S. FDI abroad, accounting for 18.75 percent of the total. The next largest recipient is Canada, which accounts for 10.16 percent. It is interesting to note that the total combined shares of Canada, Australia, Japan, and Europe of the U.S. FDI abroad is 69.59 percent. This mean that the U.S. FDI is predominantly directed toward advanced nations as is U.S. trade. The column entitled "Home" shows the FDI activities of other countries in the United States. According to the data presented in this column, Great Britain is the major investor in the United States, accounting for 18.55 percent of the total. A comparison of the total combined investment of Canada, Australia, Japan, and Europe (94.39%) in the United States, and the total combined investment of the rest of the countries, shows that advanced countries have by far greater amount of investment in the United States than do developing countries, which account for only 5.61 percent of the total.

Table 15.4

PERCENTAGE DISTRIBUTION OF U.S. FOREIGN DIRECT INVESTMENT ABROAD AND AT HOME, YEAR END 2000

Countries	Abroad	Home
All Countries	100.00	100.00
Canada	10.16	8.14
Europe	52.12	71.90
France	3.14	9.61
Germany	4.31	9.92
Netherlands	9.28	12.31
Switzerland	4.41	6.60
Great Britain	18.75	18.55
Other European Countries	12.32	14.91
Latin America and Other Western Hemisphere	19.23	3.45
Africa	1.27	0.17
Middle East	0.95	0.68
Asia and Pacific	16.04	15.66
Australia	2.84	1.17
Japan	4.47	13.18
Other Asian and Pacific Nations	8.73	1.31
International	0.23	0.00

Source: All the percentages were calculated by the author from the data provided by the Bureau of Economic Analysis, "International Accounts Data." www.bea.doc.gov/.

CHANNELS OF ENTRY INTO INTERNATIONAL BUSINESS[*]

Multinational corporations conduct their overseas operations in a variety of ways. An MNC with a full global orientation usually makes use of many channels of entry to get involved in international business. The choice of different channels of entry depends on the corporation's specific product and service lines, the foreign environment in question, and the firm's operating characteristics.

The possible channels of entry from which an MNC may choose include exporting, licensing, franchising, MNC-owned foreign enterprises, joint ventures, wholly owned subsidiaries, management contracts, and turnkey operations. In the following section, we elaborate on these channels of entry.

---

[*]This section is a condensed version of "Foreign Market Entry," that was written by professor Bahman Ebrahimi of the University of North Texas for inclusion in Parviz Asheghian and Bahman Ebrahim, *International Business*, (New York: Harper Collins, 1990), Chapter 12, 316-331.

CH. 15/FOREIGN DIRECT INVESTMENT & MNCs

Exporting

Exporting is the most traditional mode of entry into international markets. Exporting and trading have been the subject of different theories of international trade, as we discussed in previous chapters.

Exporting is still the most important entry strategy for many companies. The majority of international marketing is carried out by firms that sell domestically produced goods in foreign markets. Exporting is favored by small and large companies as an initial entry strategy or as the most effective means of continuously serving foreign markets.

There are a number of motives behind exporting domestic production. Among these motives are the following:

1. The desire to use excess production capacity at home. For example, small-scale steel mills in the United States export excess supply to overseas markets. This is because they do not want to sell off excess inventory at depressed prices in home markets since doing so might depress the domestic market even further.
2. The desire to overcome problems of domestic market saturation.
3. The desire to explore new avenues for growth.
4. The desire to gain from the effects of economies of scale, thereby realizing competitive cost advantages both domestically and internationally.

Many firms lack the resources to acquire factories in foreign countries, or they fear the problems and risks associated with production abroad. As a result, these companies find some way to serve foreign markets with the products they produce in their domestic factories. Exporting takes advantage of operating leverage from domestic operations because fixed costs may already have been covered by domestic operations. Exporting also helps a firm become experienced in foreign markets. Such experience may help further expansion through other channels of entry.

Licensing

Although a firm may decide to manufacture its product abroad, this does not mean that it has to carry out the production activities itself. Foreign production can be performed by a firm in a host country through a licensing agreement. In other words, **licensing** is the process of entering a foreign market by selling technology to an independent foreign firm. This is in contrast to FDI which takes place by the "internalization" of technology, that is, using the technology in company-owned affiliates. Through licensing, a firm provides a combination of technology, brand-name use, the right to use certain patents or copyrights, and management services to another firm that produces the product in a foreign country. The supplier is called the **licensor.** The firm receiving the know-how and the right to manufacture in the host country is called the **licensee.**

By engaging in licensing, a firm avoids investing in production facilities, as well as the difficulties of producing and marketing in a foreign environment. Therefore, the licensor is only minimally involved internationally. In return for its minimal involvement, the licensor receives a modest return, perhaps 2 percent to 5 percent of sales, from the licensee. For example, Disney receives a 5-percent royalty on its licensed amusement park in Japan. Usually, the licensing agreement stipulates each party's responsibilities, the markets to be served, the rights granted, the control specifications, and the provisions for royalty payments.

Licensing has been an easy route for producers in developing countries as well as some advanced nations, such as Japan, to establish themselves as new global competitors by accessing technology from foreign MNCs. For example, after World War II, the Japanese government restricted domestic industries to local

GLOBAL INSIGHTS CASE 15.1

PIZZA HUT GOES TO BRAZIL

Brazil is a land of enormous opportunity and is one of the fastest growing developing countries in the world. Yet, the country continues to face significant economic and social upheavals. The state plays a central role in the economy, and privatization has been difficult. The huge gap between poor and rich has grown in recent years, and there are problems with affordable housing, clean water, and adequate sewage systems. However, trade restrictions have plummeted, and Brazil is luring a large amount of foreign investment.

Pizzza Hut, a company with more than 10, 000 restaurants worldwide, entered the Brazilian market in 1988 through franchisee operations. At that time, the country was suffering from high inflation and economic instability. Initially, Pizza Hut did not have a well thought-out strategy for Brazil. In 1991, the company opened up an office in Brazil with the purpose of establishing a plan for its Brazilian operations. Pizza Hut decided to follow the strategy of corporate franchises as opposed to a unit-by-unit franchise that had been adopted by other U.S. companies such as Kentucky Fried Chicken. In a Unit-by-unit franchise, an individual restaurant is franchised to a certain franchisee, but in corporate-franchise, the corporate franchisee is provided with a whole territory. The strategy of using strong corporate franchises was based on Pizza Hut's desire to have franchisees with strong financial backing and experience in operation in an inflationary economy.

In 1995, Fernando Henrique Carsoso was elected as the president of Brazil. Pizza Hut learned that it had to adopt to a new Brazilian economic condition, characterized by price stabilization and a significant drop in the exchange rate between the U.S. dollar and the Brazilian Real. This situation led to a significant decline in Pizza Hut's sales volume. To deal with this problem, the company instructed its franchisees to reduce their prices by 25 percent in order to meet its competition. In January 1992, McDonald's, the leading fast-food franchise in Brazil, raised its prices by 40 percent in order to keep up with inflation, but later decreased them by 40 percent and publicized the drop as a vote of confidence in Brazil. The strategy was very successful and contributed to McDonald's market growth. Many Pizza Hut units, on the other hand, decreased prices in the last week of October 1995. However, this strategy proved to be a failure. The news media portrayed the move as a desperate attempt by Pizza Hut compete with the McDonald's.

As 1996 was coming to an end, Pizza Hut was continuing to grapple with its problems, and in 1997 PepsiCo (Pizza Hut's parent company) declared that it was planning to sell its restaurant division. It remains to be seen if Pizza Hut would continue its expansion in Brazil under new ownership, and if it will be successful.

Source: J.R. Whitaker Penteado, "Fast Food Franchises Fight for Brazilian Aficionados," *Business week* June 7, 1993, pp. 20-24; "Pizza-Hut Cooks in Brazil," *Advertising Age*, April 4, 1994, p.45; Jeanne Whalten, "PepsiCo Restaurants Cook With Enrico," *Advertising Age*, June 5, 1995, p.4.

participants. As a result, exporting and the licensing of technology to Japanese firms became the only two alternatives for foreign producers to enter the Japanese market. Japanese companies thereby gained access to otherwise unavailable and valuable technologies that helped the country's industrialization after World War II.

In summary, licensing is an "arm's length" pattern of international involvement that plays an important role in international business. The choice of licensing versus FDI is influenced by a country's environmental factors, industry conditions, and company preferences. Usually, licensing decreases in relative importance as a host country's per capita gross national product (GNP) and industrialization rises. In countries with restrictions on FDI, such as post--World War II Japan, licensing becomes more important. On the other hand, in the presence of incentives for FDI, licensing is pursued less and less. Licensing also requires the presence of certain indigenous technical capabilities in the host country. Licensing is used more often when a firm's technology is not research intensive and when it can be codified, patented, and transferred.[4]

Franchising

Franchising is a form of licensing, and it is the fastest-growing segment of international licensing. Franchises involve giving permission to a foreign firm to produce a product and to use its name, trademark, or copyright. In producing the product, the **franchisee** (the receiver of the rights) is usually required to use a specific set of procedures and methods and to follow a set of quality guidelines. In return, the **franchiser** (the supplier of the rights) receives a franchise right fee and
royalties. The franchisee, which is the local (host country) partner, provides the capital and knowledge of the local environment. The local partner also operates the business using operational and marketing strategies provided by the franchiser.

In addition to the right to use its name, the franchiser generally sells the franchisee some array of products and services. For example, one can make a franchise contract with Hilton Hotels to buy its supplies, receive its training for staff, and connect with its reservation system. Hilton maintains the right to control the quality of services provided by the franchisee. This right is maintained so the franchisee cannot tarnish the company's image. In return for using the Hilton name and receiving its services, the franchisee pays the company a fee based on the volume of sales.

The technology that is transferred includes a well-known name, an established reputation, a management system, some marketing skills, and certain supplies. Today, franchise operations in retailing and the restaurant business are popping up all over the world. You can see familiar McDonald's and Kentucky Fried Chicken restaurants next to Hilton hotels in countries such as Japan, Britain, Canada, Malaysia, and Mexico.

MNC-Owned Foreign Enterprise

If an MNC chooses to have its production and marketing facilities in a certain country, it creates an entity under the local law of the host country. The production facilities may be in the form of assembly plants or complete manufacturing plants.

An assembly plant requires less capital investment, and it is less expensive and less complicated to operate. As a result, it may be preferable to a complete manufacturing plant. Not only does an assembly plant provide for control of operations by the MNC, but it also benefits the home country by keeping some jobs and the value-added at home.[*] Because most of the vital elements of the MNC's technologies stay out of the host nations, assembly plants are less likely to be nationalized by a host government. This type of foreign involvement may be preferred for satisfying a host government's requirements that a foreign firm be established under its local laws, or it may be used as a strategy to improve goodwill or prevent hostile actions by host nations.

---

[*]*Value-added* is the increase in the value of a product contributed by each producer or distributor as the product progresses through the stages of production and distribution. Value-added may also be defined as the value of the product (sales price) minus the cost of its inputs purchased from other firms.

GLOBAL INSIGHTS CASE 15.2

DISNEYLAND OVERSEAS

In 1983, Tokyo Disneyland opened its doors to the public. This event took five years of planning and construction since the Walt Disney Corporation signed a franchising agreement with Oriental Land Company of Japan. In its first year of operation, Tokyo Disneyland proved to be a success. In that year, more than 10 million people visited the park, spending $335 million. This was $155 million more than had been predicted, mainly because the average payment per visitor was $30, rather than the assessed $21 per visitor.

It is interesting to note that unlike firms such as Mister Donut and Lenox China that had to adapt their products to Japanese tastes, Tokyo Disneyland is identical to the two Disney parks in the United States. In fact, this was a requirement of the management of the Oriental Land Company. Based on the experience of such successful franchises as McDonald's, the company anticipated that Japanese youth would embrace American-style culture.

Although the park is a replica of those in the United States, there have been many operational adjustments. Noticeable among these are the promotional methods employed by Tokyo Disneyland. Unlike Disney in the United States that uses its own marketing division to launch advertising, Tokyo Disneyland relies on outside Japanese agencies that target the local culture. For instance, ads in Tokyo, where the park is well known, rely more on a fun image whereas ads outside Tokyo are more informational.

As a franchiser, Disney did not participate in financing Tokyo Disney operations. However, it did commit to providing design, master planning, and training services during construction, and consulting services after completion of the project. For its services during construction Disney received fees. As a franchiser, Disney continues to receive royalties from admission and from merchandise and food sales.

Responding to its successful operation in Japan, Disney decided to consider expanding into the European markets. In 1985, following careful marketing research, Disney declared that it had narrowed down its location choice to two countries, France and Spain. Finally, in 1986, Disney reached an agreement with French government to lay foundation for the establishment of Euro Disneyland. This location decision of France over Spain was based on the more central location of Paris and the large number of tourist visiting Paris every year.

On April 12, 1992, Euro Disneyland, the world largest theme park, came into existence some 20 miles east of Paris. Unfortunately, however, it did not get the same warm reception in France, which is viewed as half of the theme Park's market, as it did in Japan. Many French feared that the park was a step toward replacement of the French with American cultures, expressing their disdain with the theme park with slogans such as "not Europe's cup of tea." It seems that Disney's successful experience in Japan led the company to overlook the cultural differences between France and Japan. "Everything we imported that worked in the United States worked in Japan," said Ronald D. Pouge, managing director of Walt Disney Attractions Japan Ltd. However, the experience demonstrated that the European market presented Disney with a totally different challenge. Eventually, Disney learned that, unlike the Japanese are fond of American pop culture, Europeans tend to want a more local content in their parks. To head off criticism, Disney explained in the French press that it was of French descent, with an original name of D'Isigny rather than Disney. However, such a strategy did not seem to assuage the negative views of the French toward Disney. As a result, in 1993, the company considered closing theme park, but made financing arrangements to remain open. With the opening of the English Channel Tunnel in May 1994, and forecasts for a European economic upturn, Euro Disneyland became more optimistic about its operation and was looking forward to a brighter future.

In 1988, attendance at the original park peaked. Nevertheless, despite a 15% gain in sales in 1988, the group's net profit decreased by 52.25% to $1.7 billion. According to a Japanese analyst, over the years Tokyo Disney has

Continued

> **Global Insights Case 15.2 continued**
>
> been able to insulate itself from Japan's dwindling economy, but a plunge in guest expenditure means that those days are coming to an end. This analyst has called on Tokyo Disney to design strategies in order to boost sales; to demonstrate that is alive and well even though U.S. parks struggle to attract visitors.
>
> Today, As the Japanese economy suffers from recession, its citizens may become hesitant to pay the $46 admission fee. This is especially true since in March of 2001 Universal Studio's Japan, a $1.4 billion movie-theme park started operating in Osaka. The potential threat of this newcomer stems from its ability to offer Western Japan's resident a closer alternative than Tokyo Disney.
>
> **Source:** "Is Disney Headed for the Euro-Trash Heap?" *Business Week,* 52 (January 24, 1994); "Alarm Bells," *The Economist* January 8 (1994): 5; David J. Jefferson, "Chip Thrills," *The Wall Street Journal*, 26 March 1993, R11; Sara Khalili, "Is This Another Japanese 'Goofy' Investment?" *North American International Business* February (1991): 74–75; John Huey, "America's Hottest Export: Pop Culture," *Fortune* December 31 (1990): 50–60; Michael Dobbs, "Mickey Mouse Storms the Bosittle," *Across the Board* 23, no. 4 (1986): 9–11; *Moody's Industrial Manual* 2 (1987): 5942; "Bonjour, Mickey," *Fortune* 113, no. 2 (1986): 8; Peter Lewis, "Disney Advances in Europe," *Maclean's* 98, no. 27 (1985): 42; Terry Trucco, "How Disneyland Beat All the Odds in Japan," *Advertising Age* 55, no. 57 (1984): 14–6; "Will Tokyo Embrace Another Mouse? Disney Second Par is Facing a Swarm of Challenges," *Business Week On-Line,* September 10, 2001.

A complete manufacturing plant, however, reduces both the cost of the transportation of parts and the cost of import duties and tariffs. It can also improve marketing by providing better adaptation of a firm's products and services to the host nation's local market conditions.

MNC-owned foreign manufacturing may be 100 percent company owned (wholly owned), or it may be a joint venture with another firm. The firm with which an MNC enters a joint venture agreement may be a local firm or a firm from another country.

Joint Venture

A *joint venture* is a corporate entity or partnership created under a host country's law between an MNC and other parties. If the joint venture parties are local, it is called a **foreign-local joint venture**. If all the parties involved are foreign to the host country, the arrangement is called a **foreigners' joint venture**. For example, General Motors (the United States) and Isuzu (Japan) have a foreigners' joint venture to produce automobiles in Egypt. In order to entice the two companies to operate in their country, Egyptian officials offered a number of incentives, including an extension of the usual five-year income tax "holiday" to eight years.[5]

Formation of a joint venture with local partners may be required by a host government. A joint venture may also be desirable to improve local goodwill and to reduce the chance of possible hostile actions from local customers, the local government, or local labor. For instance, when faced with
the threat of a protectionist move from the U.S. Congress and the "Buy American" campaign, Japanese automobile makers voluntarily limited their auto exports to the United States and sought joint venture partners among U.S. automakers. For example, Toyota entered a joint venture agreement with General Motors to produce cars in the United States.

Joint ventures are also used to phase out foreign ownership over a period of time. Instead of demanding an immediate sale of a foreign MNC's affiliate to locals, a number of developing countries require the sale of 51 percent or more of the ownership to locals over a period of 10 to 20 years. For example, such a policy is followed by India (60 percent local ownership) and Nigeria (40 or 60 percent local ownership, depending on the industry). These phasing-out policies are considered partial nationalization of the industry in question, since the intent of the developing countries is to pass ownership and control away from the foreign MNC to local investors.[6]

GLOBAL INSIGHTS CASE 15.3

U.S. COMPANIES APPETITE FOR JOINT VENTURES

In recent years the U.S. economy has witnessed a rise in the popularity of joint ventures and strategic alliances by U.S. multinational corporations. The trend toward these forms of partnership underlines the change in U.S. corporations' views of the global market. Up until the 1960s many U.S. MNCs were dominating their industries and were able to develop their own technologies by using their own engineers. As a result, they had no incentive to seek foreign partnership.

However, as the global competition increased, U.S. MNCs learned that they had to acquire new technologies fast, decrease the massive investment needed to develop a new product, and penetrate new markets. In the early 1980s, Detroit's Big Three automakers joined their once Japanese rivals to manufacture the small cars consumers were demanding, setting the trends for other U.S. MNCs to follow. In today's telecommunication industry, the trend toward joint venture by U.S. MNCs has reached an unprecedented level. Some major U.S. corporations that are in fierce competition with each other, invest heavily together abroad. For example, both Quest (former U.S. West Inc.) and Tel-Communication Inc. Run a joint venture in Great Britain to supply phone and cable service on one network. Other U.S. MNCs prefer to go alone in seeking joint venture. The following examples provide cases in point:

- 1995: Ford and Mazda joined to build a pickup truck plant in Thailand.
- 1995: Case Corporation formed a construction-equipment manufacturing with Guangxi Liugong Machinery Co. Ltd. in China.
- 1996: Ford and Mahindra & Mahindra Ltd. formed a joint venture in India to build the Fiesta model.
- 1996: Morgan Stanley Group Inc. formed a joint venture with Grupo Posadas Sa to buy or build hotels in Mexico.

It is estimated that the average strategic alliance will last for seven years. Usually, the joint venture is resolved when the stronger partner buys the weaker partner.

Source: "More and More Firms Enter Joint Ventures With Big Competitors," *The Wall Street Journal*, 1 November 1995, 1; "Ford to Build Fiesta Model in India, Investing $400 Million in Joint Venture," *The Wall Street Journal*, 4 January 1996, A7; " A Joint Venture in China Creates Access to Market," *The Wall Street Journal*, 22 September 1995, A8; "Morgan Stanley in Hotel Venture With Mexico Group," *The Wall Street Journal*, 8 January 1996, A12; "Ford and Mazda Join to Build Plant To Make Pickup Trucks in Thailand," *The Wall Street Journal*, 4 August 1995, A4.

Increased nationalistic sentiments in some developing countries have encouraged many MNCs to hide their identity by seeking joint ventures with local partners. In such cases, the local partner simultaneously publicizes local ownership and a foreign technology link. The foreign technology used in the production may be indicative of superior product quality to local customers.

Joint ventures are usually less expensive to establish than wholly-owned subsidiary. An MNC may provide technology and management, and the joint venture partner may raise the necessary capital. Joint ventures can make entry into new markets easier and quicker than wholly owned subsidiaries. Using a local partner with its knowledge of the local environment and with local business contacts may be advantageous for the MNC. The local partner may know of existing product facilities and distribution capabilities that will reduce the MNC's time and effort. The local partner also can serve as a potential cushion against mishap and help the MNC avoid mistakes. It may make the MNC's presence less visible and troublesome. Lower overall investment risks make the joint venture an appealing option to some MNCs. For example, PepsiCo has a joint venture bottling plant in Minatitlan, Mexico.

On the negative side, joint ventures mean less control and flexibility for the MNC. Control is shared at best, especially if the MNC's interest is less than 50 percent. However, minority involvement by foreign MNCs may be required by local law. The MNC and its partners may have differing objectives. An MNC's global objectives are organizing operations and getting returns on an international basis. Such objectives may be meaningless to a local partner who is interested in his/her own objectives.

Joint ventures may mean revealing exclusive technology to other firms. These firms may use the technology in the future to compete with the MNC, making such technology disclosure expensive to the MNC. Thus, many MNCs are reluctant to enter into joint venture agreements. For example, Coca-Cola decided to pull out of India rather than share its long-kept secret syrup formula with the Indian government through a required joint venture.

The methods and philosophies of the MNC and the local partner may be different enough to lead to conflicts over the way the affiliate is run. Product lines and marketing approaches may not be transferable to the host country. This may cause difficulties in teaching the partners the MNC's preferred methods. Further product choices may be limited because of such difficulties.

Another disadvantage of the joint venture is the sharing of profits with a partner. Profits are shared in proportion to ownership. An MNC that needs to show a large profit from a risky venture may find this a problem. Joint ventures tend to be unstable. One obvious reason is the conflict between partners. Another less obvious, but more frequent, reason is the MNC's shifting interests and priorities. By virtue of their global orientation, MNCs must balance product and market diversification against concentration on the local area. This may lead to shifts in priorities among production facilities, product choices, market coverages, and market concentrations. Such shifts may require pulling out of a joint venture contract.

Wholly Owned Subsidiary.

Wholly owned subsidiary may be the preferred type of foreign production ownership because it provides the MNC with a great deal of control and flexibility. Under this arrangement, coordination among multinational operations can be easier, and conflicts with joint venture partners are nonexistent. At the same time, 100 percent ownership means more investment and greater commitment by the MNC. It also increases the risk associated with greater involvement in a host nation that may have a different and potentially hostile environment.

Some international markets may be closed if the MNC insists on complete ownership of a subsidiary. For instance, IBM was forced to leave India when the firm insisted on full ownership of its facilities. Strong attachments to full ownership may need modification in order to open certain markets to MNCs. The advantages and disadvantages of the wholly owned subsidiary form of foreign involvement are the opposite of those of the joint venture, discussed in the previous section.

Management Contract

A **management contract** is an arrangement by which a company provides managerial assistance to another company in return for a fee. Such managerial help can be provided for other independent companies, joint venture partners, or an MNC's wholly owned subsidiaries in foreign nations. In providing help to a wholly owned subsidiary under a management contract, the MNC is trying to extract a larger proportion of its subsidiary's profits out of a host country. This strategy can combat limitations set on the repatriation of profits for the host nation.

Contracts to manage can also be used in nationalized operations. In addition to the normal compensation, an MNC receives fees for providing vital expertise needed in operations. Such contracts may be for a specific time period or on an ongoing basis. Management contracts can also be used in combination with turnkey contracts. An example of a management contract is the operation of many U.S. hotel chains in foreign countries. Under a management contract arrangement, these hotel companies agree to operate, for a fee, hotels owned by foreign investors or governments. A management contract can also be used in combination with a franchise agreement. A franchisee can arrange for a third party to manage the franchised operation.

Turnkey Operation

A **turnkey operation** is an arrangement by which an MNC agrees to construct an entire facility or plant, prepare it for operation, and then turn the key of the plant over to the local owners. The essence of turnkey is the construction and equipping of the facility rather than the future use of its technology and operations, as is the case in licensing agreements. Typical turnkey projects include large-scale construction projects, such as dams, nuclear power plants, or airports. The operation of such projects is less complex than the initial construction. Operation of the project may also require expertise that an MNC lacks. In a licensing agreement, the purpose is the use of technology in operations. By contrast, a turnkey operation consists of the construction of facilities that can be turned over to another firm for operation. For example, many telecommunications firms, such as Siemens of Germany, NEC of Japan, and AT&T of the United States, construct telephone installations in foreign countries which are turned over to local operators on completion.

If an MNC has the expertise for operating such projects, and if the local firm or government chooses, a management contract can be arranged. If a management contract is agreed on with the turnkey project, the MNC provides the expertise to enable the project to be operational when construction is completed. The MNC provides training and instruction for local individuals to make the local firm self-sufficient. The MNC receives additional monies for providing management assistance and training services.

Turnkey operations fit the plans of some countries, such as the People's Republic of China, India, Iran, and Turkey. These countries can speed up their development process by contracting with foreign firms to build much-needed projects for these nations. For example, in 1980, the former Soviet Union contracted with firms from Germany, France, Britain, and Italy to build its $4 billion natural gas pipeline. Other examples of turnkey operations include the building of steel mills by the former Soviet Union in Iran and the building of fertilizer and chemical plants by the Japanese in Iraq and Iran.

SUMMARY

1. International business can be defined as those business transactions among individuals, firms, or other entities (both private and public) that occur across national boundaries.
2. There is no consensus among scholars regarding the definition of multinational corporation (MNC). Different definitions are based on different criteria that are considered indicative of the purpose and type of MNC.
3. Using the structural criterion, the MNC can be defined by the number of countries in which a firm is operating or by the nationalities of its owners and/or top management.

CH. 15/FOREIGN DIRECT INVESTMENT & MNCs

4. Using the performance criterion, an MNC can be defined on the basis of the absolute amount or the relative share (percentage) of assets, number of employees, sales, or earnings in a foreign country.
5. Using the behavioral criterion, a firm can be classified as multinational if its top management "thinks internationally."
6. In this book, an MNC is defined as a group of corporations that is operating in different countries but is controlled by its headquarters in a given country.
7. The main criterion for differentiating between portfolio investment and foreign direct investment (FDI) is the amount of control the investment allows the company to retain.
8. Foreign direct investment can be financed by (a) selling technology to affiliates in a foreign country and investing the proceeds in that country, (b) raising the needed capital locally, (c) reinvesting the firm's foreign earnings in that country, or (d) using the management service fees that are earned in a foreign country.
9. International business is dominated by the world's major industrial countries. The United States is the world's major exporter, the major investor, and the major recipient of FDI.
10. The United States' position as the world's leading foreign investor has weakened over the years, losing ground to countries such as Japan and Western Europe.
11. The possible channels of entry into international business include exporting, licensing, franchising, MNC-owned foreign enterprises, (joint ventures and wholly owned subsidiaries), management contracts, and turnkey operations.
12. An MNC can manufacture products in a foreign country by signing a licensing agreement with an independent foreign firm that obtains the right to produce and sell the product in return for a modest fee.
13. Franchising involves granting permission to a foreign firm to produce a product and to use its name, trademark, or copyright, in return for a fee and royalties (based on a contract).
14. An MNC may have part ownership (a joint venture) or complete ownership (a wholly owned subsidiary) of its foreign production and marketing operations.
15. In a management contract, a company provides managerial assistance to another company in return for a fee.
16. A turnkey operation is an arrangement by which an MNC agrees to construct an entire facility or plant, prepare it for operation, and then turn the key over to the local owners, for a fee.
17. Technology transfer is a complex, time-consuming, and costly process that is composed of many stages. This process ranges from research and development to product planning and design. It includes labor training, quality control, management practices, marketing skills, and service supports.
18. The successful transfer of technology requires close cooperation between the parties involved. In practice, however, both home and host countries have raised questions regarding the potential benefits or drawbacks of technology transfers to their nations.
19. Home countries have argued that the establishment of production facilities abroad decreases their export potential and increases their imports. This leads to the loss of jobs and a decrease in the GNP in the home country.
20. Suspicion of MNCs, fueled by the fear of technological dependency, has caused the residents of many host countries, especially laborers, to persuade their governments to enact regulations that control the activities of these corporations.
21. Technology transfers to host countries have met with more criticism in developing countries than in advanced countries. Two major criticisms that are raised by developing countries regarding technology transfers are (a) that the MNCs are monopolistic in nature, and (b) that the type of technology transferred by the MNCs is inappropriate for developing countries.
22. It is argued that the technology transmitted through MNCs is inappropriate for the conditions that exist in developing countries. To avoid this problem, an MNC must adapt its technology to developing countries' requirements.

23. It has been argued that as long as technology flows from the donor country to the recipient country in a perfectly competitive market, free from government intervention, both countries should benefit.
24. Modes of technology transfer include exporting, licensing, turnkey operations, management contracts, franchising, joint ventures, and wholly owned subsidiaries.
25. The factors that determine the mode of technology transfer chosen by an MNC are (a) the sophistication of the technology, (b) the national environments of the home and host countries, (c) the MNC's characteristics, (d) the characteristics of the domestic firms.
26. Transfer pricing refers to the pricing of goods and services that pass between either a parent company and its subsidiaries or the subsidiaries themselves.
27. Because transfer prices are set by the corporate family when they are dealing with each other, the prices may not reflect market prices. Often a market price for a particular good or service may not even exist.
28. An MNC may use transfer pricing to minimize taxes or to overcome foreign exchange controls that prohibit repatriation of funds.

QUESTIONS

1. What is the difference between international trade and international business?
2. What are the three criteria used in defining the MNC? Explain.
3. What are the different ways a foreign investor can finance an investment? Explain.
4. Differentiate between portfolio investment and FDI.
5. What are the different channels through which an MNC may enter international business? Discuss.
6. What factors determine the mode of technology transfer an MNC chooses? Explain.
7. What are the motives behind exporting domestic production? Is exporting favored by small firms or large firms? Explain.
8. What is the difference between licensing and franchising? Explain.
9. Explain the home countries' and host countries' reactions to the issue of technology. Why is technology transfer a source of conflict between host and home countries? Are both host and home countries correct in their opposing views of technology? Explain.
10. What is transfer pricing? Why might transfer prices not reflect market value? Explain.
11. How can an MNC minimize its costs through transfer pricing? What are the reactions of the governments in host and/or home countries to transfer pricing?

PROBLEMS

1. International business has a long history that dates back to ancient times. Why has so much attention been directed to this subject in recent years?
2. Explain the changing pattern of the United States' overall international business position in the last two decades. In your answer include a discussion of the growth of FDI in the European countries and Japan. What do you think the patterns of FDI will look like in the future?
3. To maintain its competitive position in the world market and protect jobs, the U.S. government should ban the transfer of U.S. technology to any other country. Do you agree with this statement? Discuss.
4. To alleviate some of the problems raised in the international transfer of technology, it is believed that a code of conduct is needed to govern such transfers. Whose rights do you think should be incorporated into such a code? What do you think the major objectives of such a code should be?
5. You are the manager of an MNC that is planning to install a new plant in India (a labor-abundant country) to manufacture prefabricated housing units. You have been advised by the production manager that the production process can range from a very labor-intensive to a very capital-intensive technology. How do you choose the correct technology? Why is your choice the correct one? Would your answer to

CH. 15/FOREIGN DIRECT INVESTMENT & MNCs

these questions change if the plant were to be built in an advanced country, such as Canada? What would happen if you were dealing with a different type of industry?

6. As the manager of an MNC that enjoys a technological edge in the domestic market, what factors would you consider in selecting your method for expansion into the international market?
7. Compare and contrast management contracts and turnkey arrangements. Can these two be combined? How? Give examples.
8. The major objective of all firms, whether domestic or international, is to make a profit. To achieve this goal, can we apply the same techniques and concepts we use for domestic firms to the MNCs? Discuss.
9. Compare the different criteria used to define international business. Refer to Table 15.1 and explain what criterion is used in identifying firms as MNCs. Why do you think such a criterion is used as opposed to others?
10. What are the advantages and disadvantages of exporting compared with foreign production?

NOTES

1. United Nations Center on Transnational Corporations, *Transnational Corporations in World Development* (London: Graham & Trotman, 1985), 207; International Monetary Fund, *Balance of Payments Statistics Yearbook* (Washington DC: IMF, 1992).
2. Franklin R. Root, "Some Trends in the World Economy and Their Implications for International Business," *Journal of International Business Studies* (Winter 1984): 19--23; William A. Dymsza, "Trends in Multinational Business and Global Environment: A Perspective," *Journal of International Business Studies* (Winter 1984): 25-46.
3. Yair Aharoni, "On the Definition of a Multinational Corporation," *The Quarterly Review of Economics and Business* 11 (Autumn 1971): 27-37.
4. J. Farok, "Choosing Between Direct and Licensing: Theoretical Considerations and Empirical Tests," *Journal of International Business Studies* 15, no. 3 (Winter 1984): 167-188.
5. *IL&T Egypt*.Business International Corporation, (October 1986): 4.
6. Robert Grosse and Duane Kujawa, *International Business: Theory and Managerial Applications* (Homewood, IL: Irwin, 1988), 612-613.

SUGGESTED READINGS

Aharoni, Yair. "On the Definition of a Multinational Corporation." *The Quarterly Review of Economics and Business* 11 (Autumn 1971): 27-37.

Asheghian, Parviz. "The Comparative Capital Intensities of Joint Venture Firms and Local Firms in Iran." *Journal of Economic Development* 7 (December 1982): 77-86.

_____. "The R&D Activities of Foreign Firms in a Less Developed Country: An Iranian Case Study." *Journal of Business and Economic Perspectives* 10 (Spring 1984): 19-28.

_____. "Technology Transfer by Foreign Firms to Iran." *Middle Eastern Studies* 21 (January 1985): 72--79.

Baranson, Jack. *Technology and the Multinationals: Corporate Strategies in a Changing World Economy*. Lexington, MA: Lexington Books, D.C. Heath, 1978.

Benvignati, Anita M. "International Technology Transfer Patterns in a Traditional Industry." *Journal of International Business Studies* 16 (Winter 1983): 6375.

Casson, M., ed. *Multinational Corporations*. Aldershot, England: Edward Elgar Publishing Ltd., 1990.

_____., et al. *Multinationals and World Trade*. Winchester, MA: Allen and Unwin, 1986.

Caves, Richard E. *Multinational Enterprise and Economic Analysis*. Cambridge: Cambridge University Press, 1982.

Daniels, John P., and Fernando Robles. "The Choice of Technology and Export Commitment: The Peruvian Textile Industry." *Journal of International Business Studies* 13 (Spring/Summer 1982): 67-87.

Davidson, W. H. "Key Characteristics in the Choice of International Technology Transfer Mode." *Journal of International Business Studies* 16 (Summer 1985): 5-1.

Dunning, John H. *International Production and the Multinational Enterprise*. London: Allen & Unwin, 1981, ch. 12.

_____. *International Production and the Multinational Enterprise*. London: Allen & Unwin, 1981, ch. 1.

_____. "Technology, United States Investment and European Economic Growth." In *The International Corporation: A Symposium,* edited by Charles P. Kindleberger. Cambridge, MA: Massachusetts Institute of Technology Press, 1970.

Eckaus, Richard. "The Factor Proportions Problems in Underdeveloped Areas." *American Economic Review* 45 (1955): 539-565.

Fishwick, Frances. *Multinational Companies and Economic Concentration in Europe.* New York: Praeger, 1982.

Freeman, Orille L. *The Multinational Company: Instrument for World Growth.* New York: Praeger, 1981.

Hart, Thomas, Michael E. Porter, and Eileen Rudden. "How Global Companies Win Out." *Harvard Business Review* 60 (September-October 1982): 98-08.

Kindleberger, C. P., and D. B. Audretsch, eds. *The Multinational Corporations in the 1980s.* Cambridge, MA: MIT Press, 1983.

Kujawa, Duane. "Technology Strategy and Industrial Relations: Case Studies of Japanese Multinationals in the United States." *Journal of International Business Studies* 16 (Winter 1983): 9-22.

Magee, Stephen P. "Multinational Corporations, the Industry Technology Cycle and Development." *Journal of World Trade Law* 11 (1977): 297321.

Mansfield, Edwin. *The Economics of Technological Change.* New York: Norton, 1968.

Mason, Hal H. "The Multinational Firm and the Cost of Technology to Developing Countries." *California Management Review* 15 (Summer 1973): 5-13.

_____. "Some Aspects of Technology Transfer: A Case Study Comparing U.S. Subsidiaries and Local Counterparts in the Philippines." *The Philippine Economic Journal* 9 (September 1970): 83-108.

Morley, Samuel A., and Gordon Smith. "Limited Search and the Technology Choices of Multinational Firms in Brazil." *Quarterly Journal of Economics* 91 (1977): 263-287.

Pavitt, Keith. "The Multinational Enterprise and the Transfer of Technology." In *The Multinational Enterprise,* edited by John H. Dunning. London: Allen & Unwin, 1971.

Peck, Morton J. "Technology." In *Asia's New Giant: How the Japanese Economy Works,* edited by Hugh Patrick and Henry Rosovsky. Washington, DC: Brookings Institution, 1978, ch. 8.

Pickett, James D., J. C. Forsyth, and N. S. McBain. "The Choice of Technology, Economic Efficiency and Employment in Developing Countries." *World Development* 2 (1974): 47-54.

Pitelis, Christos N., and Roger Sugden, eds. *The Nature of Transnational Firms.* New York: Routledge, 1991.

Steward, Frances. *Technology and Underdevelopment.* Boulder, CO: Westview Press, 1977.

_____. "Choice of Technique in Developing Countries." *Journal of Development Studies* 9 (October 1972): 99-122.

Teece, David J. *The Multinational Corporation and the Resource Cost of International Technology Transfer.* Cambridge, MA: Ballinger, 1976.

United Nations Commission on Transnational Corporations. *Transnational Corporations in World Development: A Re-examination.* New York: United Nations, 1978.

Vernon, Raymond. *Sovereignty at Bay: The Multinational Spread of United States Enterprises.* New York: Basic Books, 1971.

_____. *The Technology Factor in International Trade.* New York: National Bureau of Economic Research, 1970.

Vernon, Raymond, and Louis T. Wells, Jr. *Manager in the International Economy,* 5th ed. Englewood Cliffs, NJ: Prentice-Hall, 1986, ch. 2.

Wilkins, Mira. *The Emergence of Multinational Enterprise: American Business Abroad from the Colonial Era to 1914.* Cambridge, MA: Harvard University Press, 1971.

_____. *The Maturing of Multinational Enterprise: American Business Abroad from 1914 to 1970.* Cambridge, MA: Harvard University Press, 1971.

CHAPTER 16

TECHNOLOGY TRANSFER BY MULTINATIONAL CORPORATIONS TO DEVELOPING NATIONS

Theoretically, foreign direct investment (FDI) in the developing countries is perceived not only as a source of capital inflow but also as a vehicle for acquiring modern technology and the necessary managerial know-how that these countries require for their development. Following World War II, when a shortage of capital existed, FDI was emphasized as a significant source for providing the needed capital for developing countries. As shortage of capital was slowly resolved, however, and as many development efforts that were based solely on capital failed, the technology transfer role of FDI became the center of attention.

The purpose of this chapter is to provide us with a broad understanding of the issues that are raised when technology is transferred through MNCs to developing nations. First we describe the variables that affect the choice of technology by an MNC. Second, we discuss the issue of technology transfer and appropriate technology. Third, we explain the modes by which technologies are transferred. Finally, we elaborate on the strategies that are used in choosing among these modes of technology transfer.

CHOICE OF TECHNOLOGY

As our preceding discussion indicated, different technological alternatives can be used for the production of a given type of product. The question to ask, then, is what alternative should be chosen? To answer this question, one must take into consideration the variables that affect the choice of technology. Chief among these variables are the costs of capital and labor, the availability of technological alternatives, the size and growth of the market, and the obsolescence of the existing technology.

The Cost of Capital and Labor

What determines a firm's choice to use a relatively capital-intensive technology or to use a relatively labor-intensive technology? Obviously, a firm attempts to achieve the lowest possible production cost when producing a given product. As a result, the choice of technology will depend on the relative cost of labor as compared with the cost of capital. Thus, given two alternative methods of production, if labor is relatively more expensive than capital, assuming everything else is the same, the firm would use a more capital-intensive technology. On the other hand, if capital is relatively more expensive than labor, the firm would use a labor-intensive technology. This means a firm that operates in an advanced country like the United States, which has an abundance of capital, should use a relatively capital-intensive technology. However, a firm that is located in an LDC, like India, should use a relatively labor-intensive technology.

The research and development (R&D) efforts of the United States in recent decades are indicative of the choice of technology on the basis of the relative cost of capital and labor. Given the relative scarcity of labor in the United States, these R&D efforts have resulted in the development of technologies that are largely labor saving, that is, capital intensive. However, today, when the relative scarcity of natural resources is expected to increase, as we will explain in Chapter 21, there are signs that some of the U.S. industries are shifting away from labor-savings to natural resource-saving technologies, that is, those technologies that reduce the amount of natural resources needed in the production of different goods.

The Availability of Technological Alternatives

The choice of technology by a firm is affected by the commercial feasibility of the technology and the availability of technological alternatives to the firm. These, in turn, depend on the industry in which a firm is operating. In some industries, numerous technological alternatives exist from which a firm can choose its desired production technique. For example, in the textile industry the production process is broken down into a number of different operations, each allowing trade-offs between capital and labor. In other industries, however, there may be only a very few alternatives from which a firm can choose. For example, in the petroleum industry, the refinery of raw materials is achieved by the distillation process, using heat to separate different products. In this process, there is little room for intervention. Consequently, the substitution of capital for labor is not feasible in the basic distillation process.

The Size and the Growth of the Market

Because the objective of a firm is the production of a product that can be sold for a profit, the market size and its growth are among the most significant factors that should be taken into consideration in choosing a technology. Given that the demand for the products of an MNC is generated by both the domestic and the foreign markets, the size and the potential growth of these markets are important factors that should guide the MNC in choosing the technology that produces products in the quantity and of the quality that are warranted by these markets. Thus, it is necessary for us as managers of MNCs to have some knowledge of the market size and the share of the market that could be captured by our company. If the market is too small, and we choose a relatively large size plant, then our plant has to operate under its capacity. This unused plant capacity, leading to a higher production cost and higher prices, erodes our competitiveness in the marketplace. On the other hand, if our market is too large, and we choose a relatively small-size plant, we would not be able to satisfy the market demand and would lose some of our customers to our rivals. Thus, it is important to gather as much information about the market as is possible. Such information should include data on the total sales in the market, the rate of market growth, the price of substitutes and complimentary goods, the labor training costs, the labor relations problems, the government regulations, and information on major competing firms with regard to their market share, product quality, customer satisfaction, and distribution channels. Such information not only guides us to choose the optimum plant size but also allows us to define the right price for the product-a price that covers our full cost and yields the desired rate of return on the invested capital.

The Obsolescence of the Existing Technology

Because in any industry the introduction of a new invention might result in the obsolescence of the

GLOBAL INSIGHTS CASE 16.1

GILLETTE'S BLUNDER

When the Gillette Company developed a superior stainless steel razor blade, it feared that such a superior product might mean fewer replacements and sales. Thus, the company decided not to market it. Instead, Gillette sold the technology to Wilkinson, a British garden tool manufacturer. Because Gillette thought that Wilkinson would use the technology only in the production of garden tools, it did not restrict its use in the razor blade market. However, when Wilkinson Sword Blades were introduced they sold quickly, and Gillette realized the magnitude of its mistake. Only superior marketing skills and experience enabled Gillette to eventually recover.

Source: David A. Ricks, *Big Business Blunders: Mistakes in Multinational Marketing* (Homewood, Ill.: Dow Jones-Irwin, 1983), p.21.

existing technology, it is important for us as managers of MNCs to predict the possibility of such an occurrence before undertaking an investment project. This prediction is helpful in guiding us to select those technologies that would generate sufficient revenues to justify their initial costs before they become obsolete. Take the case of the textile industry, which has gone through numerous innovations regarding each specific production operation. A recent study lists 40 different innovations in textile machinery, and it shows the number and the nature of the innovations for each improvement is rising over time, we might assume that it would continue to rise. The shortcoming of this approach is that the variables that have caused a trend in the past might change in the future. As a result, the forecasting might turn out to be completely wrong. specific production operation. According to this study, there have been six different innovations regarding fiber preparation. For example, one of the innovations, called the automatic hopper feeder, was introduced in West Germany in 1959 and was later used by Automatic Material Handling, Inc., in 1973, leading to the obsolescence of the existing technology.[1] To ensure that the expected revenue justifies the initial cost of the product, any firm investing in the textile industry prior to 1959 should have tried to predict the possibility that the existing process would become obsolete at a certain time. But what about those firms who have already invested in an old technology when a new technology is introduced? Should a firm that uses the nonautomatic hopper feeder convert to the automatic one? To answer this question one needs to undertake a cost-benefit analysis, taking into consideration the initial cost of the equipment, the cost of labor, the cost of capital, the cost of discarding the old equipment, and the expected additional revenue that would be generated by the new technology as compared with the old technology. If revenues are greater than the costs, then the firm should use the new technology, otherwise it should continue to use the old technology.

The question of obsolescence in the selection of technology has become even more significant and pressing in today's world since the computer has tremendously changed the speed at which new innovations are introduced.

TECHNOLOGY TRANSFER AND APPROPRIATE TECHNOLOGY

As we already know, one of the potential benefits of MNCs to host countries, especially developing countries, is their ability to generate and transfer technology to these countries. Aware of the importance of technology in the process of economic development, many developing countries have considered it to be an important consideration in deciding to favor foreign direct investment. For example, a government official in prerevolutionary Iran stated that:

> Since our development plan reserves a high place for the private sector, the role of foreign private investment in this sector is very important. For it should also bring with it administrative and managerial skills, innovations and entrepreneurship to our private sector, creating a true and genuine partnership, but also laying the foundation for self-sustained and sound expansion.[2]

Having realized the importance of FDI as a vehicle for technology transfer, an important issue that is raised is the question of appropriate technology.

Appropriate Technology

It has become evident that much of the success of investment projects in developing nations depends on the selection of **appropriate technology**, that is, a technology that better fits the economic and social environment of the country in question. What may be appropriate technology for the capital-abundant United States, however, may be totally inappropriate for a labor-abundant country like India. Thus, it is necessary for an MNC to adapt its technology to the national environment of the country in which it operates. However, the existing empirical studies cast doubt on the willingness and ability of MNCs to engage in such a process. The existing empirical evidence shows that, in general, MNCs in developing countries have used capital-intensive technologies that are inappropriate for labor-abundant developing countries. This tendency can be attributed to the following factors:

1. **Engineering mentality.** Engineers who design a plant for an MNC are usually trained according to an advanced country's curricula. Thus, an engineer's interest is in **technical efficiency**, that is, to produce the maximum amount of output from a given amount of input. Given such an orientation, machines are often considered more efficient than humans, a capital-intensive technology is chosen.[7]
2. **Fixed factor proportions.** In some industries, such as chemicals, petroleum refining, and steel, capital--labor ratios are not alterable to a significant degree. Thus, capital and labor should be combined in a relatively fixed proportion. As a result, there may be no substitute for a highly capital-intensive technology.
3. **Scarcity of skilled workers.** In many developing countries, the technical, administrative, and managerial resources needed to implement labor-intensive technology are scarce. As a result, it may be cheaper for an MNC to use a capital-intensive technology, conserving expensive personnel.
4. **High cost of adaptation.** Corporations may find that modifying their capital-intensive technology is more expensive than employing it without modification.
5. **Factor market distortions.** The policies of some developing countries may make capital cheaper than its equilibrium price, that is, the price determined by market forces of demand and supply. The cheaper capital, in turn, may encourage the use of capital-intensive technology. Policies that lead to factor market distortions include minimum wage legislation, capital subsidization, and artificially low foreign exchange prices. The minimum wage legislation, resulting from organized labor pressure, artificially raises the level of wages in a developing country and discourages the use of a

labor-intensive technology. On the other hand, capital subsidies and low foreign exchange prices, designed to promote industrialization, encourage the use of a capital-intensive technology.

The ineffectiveness of MNCs in transferring the appropriate technology to developing nations has fueled resentment toward these corporate giants and has added to the list of their criticisms, as we will discuss in the next section.

GLOBAL INSIGHT CASE 16.2

THE GLOBAL DIFFUSION OF TECHNOLOGY

Throughout the 1990s, the beneficial effect of technology on productivity and growth appear to have been enjoyed most strongly in the United States. Although growth has rebounded in Europe and the emerging market economies of East Asia, these events so far appear to be cyclical rather than structural in nature. That is, recovery in these countries seems to be bringing them back up to their economic potential, but not yet accelerating the expansion of the potential. The situation in the United States has been otherwise. From 1995 to 2000, according to OECD estimates, potential output in the United States grew at an annual rate of 3.5 percent, compared with only 2.2 percent for the countries that have adopted the Euro, and only 1.4 percent for Japan. Growth in total factor productivity—the efficiency with which capital and labor are used in combination—also lags in most European and other industrial countries as compared to that of the United States. There is little sign in other industrial nations of the acceleration that the United States has experienced over the past several years.

The lagging pace of investment in information technology in much of Europe compared with the United States may be one reason for the divergence in trend growth. This lag is evident even after taking into account differences in the measurement of purchases of high-technology products. The United States also leads other industrial countries on several measures of the usage of information technology, including numbers of telephone lines, Internet hosts, and secure servers used in e-commerce. Yet the United States is not ahead in every aspect of technology. For example, wireless technology has taken off in Europe and the Far East far more than the United States.

There are some signs that the use of the new technologies, the pervasiveness of which has so benefitted the United States, is beginning to approach critical mass in other advanced economies, including Germany, the Netherlands, the Nordic countries, and the United Kingdom. For example, Germany now boasts a technology-oriented stock market, the Neuer Market, similar to the Nasdaq, and is reported to have the largest European contingent of Internet enterprises, larger even than in the United Kingdom. Firms in Scandinavia are innovators in important areas of technology, notably wireless communication. Perhaps not coincidentally, the Nordic countries (excluding Denmark) benefitted more from higher total factor growth in the latter of half of the 1990s than did European countries. Meanwhile other developed countries that have lagged in productivity growth are attempting to catch up. Japan, for example, has recently taken steps to deregulate its telecommunications industry and provide incentives for firms to upgrade their information technology equipment and employee skills. Burgeoning information technology sectors have also begun to appear in some developing counties. One notable example is the development of Indian software programming industry. However, additional policy steps are needed to ensure that these countries fully enjoy the benefits of the new technologies.

Sources: U.S. Government Printing Office, *Economic Report of the President* (Washington D.C.: U.S. Government Printing Office, 2001), 162-166, Reprinted.

CONFLICTS SURROUNDING TECHNOLOGY TRANSFER BY MNCs

Technology transfer is a complex, time-consuming, and costly process that is composed of many stages. This process ranges from research and development to product planning and design. It includes labor training, quality control, management practices, marketing skills, and service supports. The successful implementation of such a process demands continuous communication and requires close cooperation between the parties involved. Unfortunately, however, both home and host countries have raised questions regarding the potential benefits of technology transfers to the developing countries. This has led to controversy and conflict between home and host countries, further complicating the management of MNCs.

Home Countries' Reactions to Technology Transfer

Home countries have often reacted against the export of technology on the ground that it is harmful to their economic base. They argue that the establishment of production facilities by MNCs' subsidiaries abroad decreases their export potential. Additionally, they claim, because some of the MNCs' imports come from their subsidiaries abroad, the volume of imports to the home country increases. Given the decrease in exports and increase in imports for the home countries, it is argued that the availability of jobs in the home country will be diminished. It is also argued that by providing technological know-how to foreign nations, a country might lose its international competitiveness in the world. This in turn leads to the loss of GNP, causing the rate of economic growth of the home country to diminish.

The above arguments have caused some groups, especially labor unions, to oppose the expansion of MNCs to foreign countries. In the United States this has been especially a sensitive issue in recent years. Many U.S. MNCs have chosen to set up plants in countries such as Mexico, Singapore, and Taiwan in order to take advantage of the cheaper labor costs in these countries. These plants are used to assemble U.S.-made components into products that are then exported back to the United States. For example, in 1982 some U.S. automobile manufacturers set up assembly plants in Mexican border towns to make cars using the U.S. parts and inexpensive Mexican labor.[3] As another example, Zenith Radio Corporation closed its television plant in Sioux City, Iowa, in 1979, and set up plants in Mexico and Taiwan.[4] Such incidents have caused a bitter confrontation between MNCs and labor unions, whose members have been asked to accept wage cuts in order to keep jobs at home. The U.S. labor unions have blamed MNCs not only for exporting jobs abroad, but also for exploiting foreigners by paying them low wages.

Host Countries' Reactions to Technology Transfer

The subject of technology transfer by MNCs has been a more touchy and sensitive issue in the host countries than it has been in the home countries. Suspicion of MNCs, fueled by the fear of technological dependency, has caused the residents of many host countries, especially laborers, to persuade their governments to enact regulations that control the activities of these corporations. For example, in the hope of upgrading the skill level of jobs in Canada, the Canadian government has encouraged MNCs to locate their entire operation of one line of their product in Canada. As another example, Japan has feared that MNCs, through their superior technology, might dominate their local firms. As a result, Japan has restricted the flow of technology through MNCs by "taking the foreign investment package apart," that is, by buying capital, management, and technology separately, rather than acquiring them together through the MNC.

Although the positive role of MNCs in technology transfer has been met with skepticism from both advanced countries and developing countries, the role of the MNCs has created more heated debates and has stirred more controversy in the developing countries as compared with the advanced countries. This has led some economists to question the possible advantages of technology transfers by MNCs to developing countries. Two types of criticisms can be differentiated concerning MNC transfer of technology.

The first criticism is related to the monopolistic nature of MNCs. It is argued that an MNC that is transferring technology to a developing country can dictate conditions that are favorable to its own interest. This is due to the MNC's monopolistic power over the technical and managerial know-how, the capital, and the foreign exchange (currency) that is transferred to the developing country through its investment. Consequently, it is argued, the real cost to developing countries of obtaining foreign private technical knowledge may well be higher than it first appears. For example, a study of U.S. subsidiaries abroad finds that these subsidiaries are established mostly in industries that are oligopolistic in nature, and that their purpose is to protect a market that previously was served by exports.[5]

The second criticism is related to the type of technology that is transferred. It is argued that the technology that is transmitted through the multinational corporation is not "appropriate" for conditions that exist in developing countries. In comparison with advanced countries, developing countries are mostly located in the tropical and subtropical zones and, therefore, have a climate different from the advanced countries. Their factors of production are locally available in quite different proportions. Educated managers, skilled workers, technicians, and professionals are relatively scarce. Given these conditions, if a technology that is designed for an advanced country is transferred to a developing country, it will have a distorting effect on the developing countries' economy as a whole. To avoid this problem, it is necessary for the MNC to adapt its technology to the conditions that exist in the developing countries. However, it must be realized that technology is not transferred in a vacuum. The successful transfer of technology and its adaptation to the national environment of a developing country not only depends on the willingness and the ability of the MNCs, but also on the absorptive capacity of the recipient host country and its relationship with the MNC. The lack of technical and managerial skills needed to operate a successful manufacturing process, the existence of small and stagnant markets, and the restrictive government policies in developing countries are among factors that have provided serious obstacles to the process of technology transfer and adaptation. Consequently, although MNCs have been the means of some technology transfer in a few cases, they have not, in general, performed this task up to their potential.[6] For example, a study of U.S. MNCs in developing countries found that these corporations adapted their technologies, in some degree, to meet the factor proportion problem, that is, the relative abundance of labor to capital of the developing country in question. It was also found that American firms had more of a tendency to get by without some of the most automatic devices as compared with the local firms. This was related to the American reliance on their own technical know-how and training abilities.[7] As another example, in a study of Latin America it was learned that the Latin American companies usually took the same approach as the foreign firms in selecting a production technique. Often Latin American companies utilized the capital-intensive techniques that were developed in advanced countries. The use of the capital-intensive techniques, according to the study, was mostly related to the lack of skilled labor in Latin America. The study also emphasizes that the MNCs had not tried to design labor-intensive techniques that could solve, partially, the unemployment problem of Latin America.[8] As a third example, in a study of Brazil it was found that MNCs were reluctant to fully adapt their technology to the conditions prevailing in Brazil. According to the study, the failure of the MNCs to adapt their technology to Brazil was related to their unwillingness to do an adequate search in Brazil's ""permissive environment," that is, an environment that allowed MNCs to operate profitably without fully adapting their technologies to the national environment of Brazil.[9]

Reconciling Host and Home Countries' Reactions

The question to ask at this point is whether or not the host countries and the home countries are both correct in their negative views of technology transfer. Theoretically speaking, as our discussion of trade theories in Chapter 2 indicated, free trade would lead to a maximization of the world's economic welfare. Thus, we could argue that as long as technology is flowing from the donor to the recipient country in a perfectly competitive market, free from government intervention, both countries would benefit. However, because in actual market settings both government intervention and market imperfections exist, disturbing the free flow of technology, there is reason to believe that both the recipient host and donor home countries might not benefit from the process of technology transfer. Thus, what seems to be needed is the absence of government intervention, allowing the free forces of market demand and supply to direct the flow of technology transfer, as is dictated by the precepts of the comparative advantage theory of trade. Unfortunately, however, what seems to be theoretically right is not implemented in a practical way. This is due to noneconomic variables, such as xenophobia, nationalistic ideology, and labor union demands, that enter the decision-making process, each playing a significant role in the process of technology transfer.

MODES OF TECHNOLOGY TRANSFER

The transfer of technology through international business depends on the patterns of international involvement, which are fully described in Chapter 15. These patterns provide us with the modes of technology transfer. These modes of transfer include the export of goods and services, licensing, turnkey operations, management contracts, franchises, joint ventures, and wholly owned subsidiaries. Among these modes, the wholly owned subsidiaries are potentially the best means of technology transfer to developing countries. This is because they provide not only the technology needed for successful operation, but also the knowledge and the skills that are required for the actual production to take place.

TECHNOLOGY TRANSFER STRATEGIES

Given that the international transfer of technology can take different modes, the question to ask at this point is what mode should be chosen by the MNC? The answer depends on the relative cost and the feasibility of technology transfer. These, in turn, are determined by four interrelated factors: (1) the sophistication of the technology, (2) the national environments of the home and host countries, (3) the characteristics of the MNC, and (4) the characteristics of the domestic firms.

The Sophistication of the Technology

If a product is relatively new or it involves a highly sophisticated technology, an MNC is more apt to establish a wholly owned subsidiary rather than choose other modes of technology transfer. This is because the MNC has full ownership and, therefore, full control over its subsidiary. This enables the corporation to better protect and internalize those technologies that have been obtained through its own substantial research and development expenditures.

The Environments of the Home and Host Countries

The existing laws and the competitive environment in both the home and the host countries have a bearing on the technology transfer mode that is chosen by the MNC. Many MNCs move their production facilities abroad in order to protect a market that is in danger of being lost either due to the takeover of the market by competitors or because the tax structure of the host or home country makes such a move profitable.

The choice of technology transfer modes by MNCs is especially limited in the developing countries. These countries that usually lack the technical and managerial know-how, yet they often insist on national ownership and staffing. Consequently, most developing countries, such as Kuwait and United Arab Emirates, do not even allow the establishment of wholly owned subsidiaries in their countries. These countries usually set percentage ceilings on the foreign equity that can be invested in each firm of an industry. They also may limit foreign direct investment in joint ventures.

The Characteristics of the MNC

The financial capability of an MNC and its top executive strategy with regard to long-run profit maximization are important elements that affect the choice of the technology transfer modes. If the top executives view technology as an essential ingredient of the MNCs marketing-manufacturing package, and if they believe that such a strategy would lead to long-run profit maximization, then a wholly owned subsidiary is preferred over other modes of technology transfer. The top executive view with regard to long-run profit maximization can be formulated in terms of the cost-benefit analysis.

Different investment projects are expected to generate different costs and revenues, leading to different profits. At one extreme, the exporting mode could be chosen. This alternative is relatively costless because it does not require investment in equipment and machinery in a foreign country. On the other extreme, the wholly owned subsidiary could be chosen, involving the commitment of financial and managerial resources for a long period of time. Which alternative should be chosen? This depends on the expected profit from these projects and the attitudes of the top executives with regard to risk. If the top executives are risk takers, they would choose the mode that is expected to have the higher risk and the higher profit. On the other hand, if they are risk averters, they would select the mode that is expected to involve lower risk and lower profit.

The Characteristics of Domestic Firms

The size, the degree of competitiveness, and the ability of the domestic firms to absorb the imported technology are among the factors that affect the choice of the technology transfer mode by the MNC. For example, when an MNC plans to invest in a developing country, foreign direct investment might be the preferable mode of technology transfer, due to problems in exporting technology to such countries. However, in advanced countries, where domestic firms are capable of imitating an imported technology, licensing arrangements might be preferable to foreign direct investment. Additionally, licensing might be suitable for relatively small corporations that do not have the necessary capital, management, or experience to get involved in foreign direct investment.

PRICING OF TECHNOLOGY TRANSFER

Because the market for technology is highly imperfect and the pricing information is not readily available, the pricing decisions for technology transfer represent a complex issue. This complexity is further amplified by the existence of different compensation packages from which an MNC can choose. These packages range from simple royalties and licensing fees to more comprehensive agreements that include additional payments to the licensor for technical assistance and other services rendered. Other payments to the licensor might be made based on profits, on goods supplied by the licensor, on dividends from an equity share granted by the licensee, and on tax savings resulting from the agreement.

Given the complexity of the pricing of international technology transfer, and the lack of a standard model for negotiation, the success of the MNC's manager in dealing with a nonaffiliated foreign buyer of technology depends on his or her negotiating skills and bargaining power.

Transfer Pricing

The issue of the pricing of technology transfer is further complicated by what is known as transfer pricing. Transfer pricing refers to the pricing of goods and services that pass between either a parent company and its subsidiaries or between the subsidiaries themselves. Because transfer prices are set by the corporate family when dealing with each other, they may not reflect the market prices. Often a market price for a particular good or service may not even exist. As a result, an MNC may use transfer pricing to minimize taxes or to overcome foreign exchange controls that prohibit the repatriation of funds.

Because tax rates are different between nations, a parent company exporting goods and services to a subsidiary in a high-tax nation (as compared with the taxes charged in the home country) could set a high transfer price. This has the effect of decreasing the profits of the foreign subsidiary and leading to lower taxes in the host country. In the same manner, if the subsidiary is located in a low-tax nation, an MNC could minimize taxes by charging a low transfer price. However, if import tariffs are present, the MNC will consider both taxes and tariffs in formulating the transfer pricing policy. This is because a high transfer price means a high value for the goods and services sold. Similarly, a low transfer price means a low value for the goods and services sold. Because import tariffs are imposed on the declared value of imports, this leads to a higher or lower tariff cost as the case may be. Thus, an MNC should measure the tax benefit of a higher or lower transfer price against the resulting higher or lower tariff cost. A high transfer price will be charged if the savings on the host country's taxes are greater than the additional tariff costs. A low transfer price will be used if the savings on tariffs are greater than the additional taxes.

Foreign exchange controls prevent repatriation of funds by MNCs. To circumvent such controls, an MNC can charge high transfer prices to its subsidiaries, thus repatriating profits from those host countries that impose foreign exchange controls.

Other circumstances in which an MNC may use transfer pricing to minimize its costs occur when taxes are imposed on dividends or when a host country's currency is rapidly depreciating. Because dividend taxes, in essence, tax the MNC's profit two times, the MNC can transfer funds using a high transfer price instead of repatriating dividends. If a host country's currency is rapidly depreciating, that is, its value is falling as compared with other currencies, the MNC can protect itself by adopting a high-transfer pricing policy. This allows the MNC to exchange the depreciating currency to stronger currencies, thus minimizing the exchange losses that may result from the weaker currency.

To modify the impact of transfer pricing practices by MNCs, many host country governments have tried to intervene in the negotiations on agreements for technology payments. In the United States, the government is given the right to reallocate gross income, deductions, credits, or allowances between the parent company and the subsidiaries if arbitrary pricing or allocation of expenses may have taken place to avoid taxes. If the taxpaying company is not happy with the government reallocation procedure, it has to prove that the reallocation was not warranted and a refund is in order. An example of the tax implication of transfer pricing is seen in the case of Eli Lilly & Company in the 1950s. In this case, the IRS ended up collecting $4 million from the company. Although the company appealed the decision, it did not win the case. The tax court maintained that the company's pricing policy had resulted in ""tax avoidance and does not clearly reflect the income of the related organizations."[10]

TECHNOLOGICAL FORECASTING

New technologies are introduced every day, and the forecasting of technological change is an integral part of a firm's decision-making process. Such forecasting not only prepares a firm to deal with the question of obsolescence, but it also allows the firm to predict the number of workers and the kinds of workers that are needed for the production activities. This prepares the firm to plan for the recruitment and training of people with the needed skills, thereby enabling it to better compete in the marketplace.

There are three different approaches to technological forecasting: seeking expert opinions, extrapolating from statistical trends, and forecasting with the aid of models.

The first and the easiest approach is to simply bring scientific experts together and ask their opinion about the future with regard to a given technology. Unfortunately, however, such predictions, even by highly respected scientists, may result in large errors. For example, Ernest Rutherford, the Nobel Prize-winning nuclear scientist, predicted that the use of nuclear energy on a large scale was not probable. However, as we

> **GLOBAL INSIGHTS CASE 16.3**
>
> **MATSUSHITA'S FORECAST OF THE GROWTH OF ELECTRONICS AND RELATED TECHNOLOGIES**
>
> Matsushita Electric Industrial Company is the largest of Japan's electronics manufacturers. In 1983 Matsushita implemented a three-year corporate strategy. The major thrust of this strategy was a "metamorphosis from a manufacturer of home-appliance products to a manufacturer of consumer and industrial electronics." The reason for this shift in strategy was the slow rate of growth in the home-appliance industry. If Matsushita had continued as a manufacturer of home-appliance products after 1986, they might have had less than 5 percent average sales growth per year.
>
> Matsushita's strategic shift to consumer and industrial electronics is based on their belief that electronics and related technologies will be key to their survival and growth. The Japanese Association for Electronics Industries Development forecasted the average annual growth rate for the whole industry at 12.6 percent for the 1980s. Matsushita responded to the forecast by establishing a semiconductor laboratory in the summer of 1985. This exemplifies Matsushita's strong strategic planning capabilities.
>
> *Source*: Gen-Ichi Nakamura, "Strategic Management in Major Japanese High-Tech Companies," *Long Range Planning*, vol 19, no. 6 (December 1986), pp. 82-91.

know today, he was proven to be wrong.

The second approach is based on the extrapolation of statistical trends. This means plotting the historical data regarding the rate of improvement of a given product or process and examining the trend as it develops over time. For example, if the trend is positive, that is, if the rate of improvement is rising over time, we might assume that it would continue to rise. The shortcoming of this approach is that the variables that have caused a trend in the past might change in the future. As a result, the forecasting might turn out to be completely wrong.

The third approach is based on the use of forecasting models.* This is a scientific approach that tries to relate different aspects of technological change to a set of quantifiable variables. With improvements in statistical techniques and advances in computer applications in recent years, the reliability of this approach has significantly increased over the years.[11]

---

*A model is a means for explaining the relationship between different variables. Models can be presented in three different forms: tables, graphs, and equations. An example of a simple model is the demand-supply model. This model could be presented in tables, showing the quantity demanded, the quantity supplied, and the prices of a given good. It could also be presented graphically as a demand curve and a supply curve, or mathematically as a demand equation and a supply equation.

SUMMARY

1. The variables that affect the choice of technology are the cost of capital and of labor, the availability of technological alternatives, the size and the potential growth of the market, and the obsolescence of the existing technology.
2. Technology transfer is a complex, time-consuming, and costly process that is composed of many stages. This process ranges from research and development to product planning and design. It includes labor training, quality control, management practices, marketing skills, and service support.
3. The successful transfer of technology requires close cooperation between the parties involved. In practice, however, both home countries and host countries have raised questions regarding the potential benefits or drawbacks of technology transfers to their nations.
4. Home countries have argued that the establishment of production facilities abroad decreases their export potential and increases their imports. These lead to the loss of jobs and a decrease in the GNP in the home country.
5. Suspicion of MNCs, fueled by the fear of technological dependency, has caused the residents of many host countries, especially laborers, to persuade their governments to enact regulations that control the activities of these corporations.
6. Technology transfers to the developing countries have met with more criticism in the developing countries than in the advanced countries. Two major criticisms that are raised by developing countries regarding technology transfers are (a) that the MNCs are monopolistic in nature and (b) that the type of technology that is transferred by the MNCs is inappropriate for developing countries.
7. It is argued that the technology that is transmitted through an MNC is not ""appropriate" to the conditions that exist in developing countries. To avoid this problem, it is necessary for an MNC to adapt its technology to the requirements of the developing countries.
8. It has been argued that as long as a technology is flowing from the donor country to the recipient country in a perfectly competitive market, free from government intervention, then both countries would benefit.
9. Modes of technology transfer include exporting, licensing, setting up turnkey operations, establishing management contracts, franchising, setting up joint ventures, and creating wholly owned subsidiaries.
10. The factors that determine the mode of technology transfer that is chosen by an MNC are (a) the sophistication of the technology, (b) the national environment of the home and the host countries, (c) the characteristics of the domestic firms in both countries and (d) the characteristics of the MNC.
11. Given the complexity of international technology transfer and the lack of a standard model for negotiation, the success of the MNC's manager in dealing with a nonaffiliated foreign buyer of technology depends on his or her negotiating skills and bargaining powers.
12. Transfer pricing refers to the pricing of goods and services that pass between a parent company and its subsidiaries or between the subsidiaries themselves.
13. Because transfer prices are set by the corporate family when they are dealing with each other, the prices may not reflect the true market prices. Often a market price may not even exist for a particular good or service.
14. An MNC may use transfer pricing to minimize taxes or to overcome foreign exchange controls that prohibit repatriation of funds.
15. The three different approaches that are used in technological forecasting are (a) seeking expert opinion, (b) extrapolating trends from statistical data, and (c) using forecasting models.

CH. 16/TECHNOLOGY TRANSFER BY MNCs TO DEVELOPING NATIONS

QUESTIONS

1. Explain the home countries' and the host countries' reactions to the issue of technology. Why is technology transfer a source of conflict between host and home countries? Are both host countries and home countries correct in their opposing views of technology? Explain.
2. How can an MNC minimize its costs by means of transfer pricing? What are the reactions of the governments of host countries to transfer pricing?
3. What factors determine the mode of technology transfer an MNC chooses? Explain.

PROBLEMS

1. To maintain its competitive position in the world market and protect jobs, the U.S. government should ban the transfer of U.S. technology to any other country. Do you agree with the above statement? Discuss.
2. To alleviate some of the problems that are raised in the international transfer of technology, it is believed that a code of conduct is needed that should govern such transfers. Whose rights do you think should be incorporated into such a code? What do you think the major objectives of such a code should be?
3. You are the manager of an MNC that is planning to install a new plant in India (a labor-abundant country) to manufacture prefabricated housing units. You have been advised by the production manager that the production process can range from a very labor-intensive to a very capital-intensive technology. How do you choose the correct technology. Why is your choice the correct one? Would your answer to these questions change if the plant were to be built in an advanced country, say, for example, Canada? What would happen if you were dealing with a different type of industry?
4. As the manager of an MNC that enjoys a technological edge in the domestic market, what factors would you consider in selecting your strategy for expansion into the international market?

NOTES

1. Anita M. Benvignati, "International Technology Transfer Patterns in a Traditional Industry," *Journal of International Business Studies* (Winter 1983): pp. 63-75.
2. Mehdi Samii, "The Role of Foreign Private Investment in Iran's Economic Development," *Bank Markazi Iran, Bulletin* (January/February 1971), p. 531.
3. "American Auto Makers Using More Mexico Assembly Lines," The New York Times, 25 July 1982, p. 1.
4. "Sioux City Still Suffers After Its Top Employer Moves Business Abroad," *The Wall Street Journal, 5 April 1979*, p. 1
5. Raymond Vernon, *The Multinational Spread of the U.S. Enterprise* (New York: Basic Books, 1971).
6. R. S. Eckaus, "Technological Change in the Less Developed Countries" in Stephen Spiegelglas and Charles J. Welsch, eds., Economic Development: Challenge and Promise (Englewood Cliffs, N.J.: Prentice-Hall, 1970), also see, chap. 2, pp. 18-23 for a summary of other empirical studies in the area of technology transfer.
7. Roy B. Helfgott, "Multinational Corporations and Manpower Utilization in Developing Nations," *Journal of Developing Areas* 7 (January 1973): 225-246.
8. Doug Hellinger and Steve Hellinger, "The Job Crisis in Latin America: A Role for Multinational Corporations in Introducing More Labor-Intensive Technologies," *World Development* 3 (June 1975): 399-410.
9. Samuel A. Morely and Gordon W. Smith,""Limited Search and Technology Choices of Multinational Firms in Brazil," *Quarterly Journal of Economics* 31 (May 1977): 263-287
10. *U.S. Tax Cases*, Vol. 67-1, 1967 (Chicago: Commerce Clearing House, Inc., 1967).
11. Edwin Mansfield, *The Economics of Technological Change* (New York: Norton, 1968).

SUGGESTED READINGS

Asheghian, Parviz. "Technology Transfer by Foreign Firms to Iran." Middle Eastern Studies 21 (January 1985): 72-79.

_____. "The R&D Activities of Foreign Firms in a Less Developed Country: An Iranian Case Study." *Journal of Business and Economic Perspectives* 10 (Spring 1984): 19-28.

_____. "The Comparative Capital Intensities of Joint Venture Firms and Local Firms in Iran." *Journal of Economic Development* 7 (December 1982): 77-86.

Baranson, Jack. Technology and the Multinationals: Corporate Strategies in a Changing World Economy. Lexington, Mass.: Lexington Books, D.C. Heath, 1978.

Benvignati, Anita M. "International Technology Transfer Patterns in a Traditional Industry." *Journal of International Business Studies* 16 (Winter 1983): 63-75.

Daniels, John P., and Fernando Robles. "The Choice of Technology and Export Commitment: The Peruvian Textile Industry." *Journal of International Business Studies* 13 (Spring/Summer 1982): 67-87.

Davidson, W. H. "Key Characteristics in the Choice of International Technology Transfer Mode." *Journal of International Business Studies* 16 (Summer 1985): 5-21.

Donaldson, Loraine. *Economic Development*: Policy and Analysis. New York: West, 1984. Chap. 5.

Dunning, John H. *International Production and the Multinational Enterprise*. London: Allen & Unwin, 1981. Chap. 12.

_____. "Technology, United States Investment and European Economic Growth." In Charles P. Kindleberger, The International Corporation: A Symposium. Cambridge, Mass.: Massachusetts Institute of Technology Press, 1970.

Eckaus, Richard. "The Factor Proportions Problems in Underdeveloped Areas." *American Economic Review* 45(1955): 539-565.

Kujawa, Dune. "Technology Strategy and Industrial Relations: Case Studies of Japanese Multinationals in the United States." *Journal of International Business Studies* 16 (Winter 1983): 9-22.

Magee, Stephen P. "Multinational Corporations, the Industry Technology Cycle and Development." *Journal of World Trade Law* 11 (1977): 297-321.

Mansfield, Edwin. *The Economics of Technological Change*. New York: Norton, 1968.

Mason, Hal H. "The Multinational Firm and the Cost of Technology to Developing Countries." *California Management Review* 15 (Summer 1973): 5-13.

_____. "Some Aspects of Technology Transfer: A Case Study Comparing U.S. Subsidiaries and Local Counterparts in the Philippines." *The Philippine Economic Journal* 9 (September 1970): 83-108.

Morley, Samuel A., and Gordon Smith. "Limited Search and the Technology Choices of Multinational Firms in Brazil." *Quarterly Journal of Economics* 91 (1977): 263-287.

Pavitt, Keith. "The Multinational Enterprise and the Transfer of Technology." In John H. Dunning, ed., *The Multinational Enterprise*. London: Allen & Unwin, 1971.

Peck, Morton J. "Technology." In Hugh Patrick and Henry Rosovsky, eds., Asia's New Giant: *How the Japanese Economy Works*. Washington, D.C.: Brookings Institution, 1978, Chap. 8.

Pickett, James D., J. C. Forsyth, and N. S. McBain. "The Choice of Technology, Economic Efficiency and Employment in Developing Countries." *World Development* 2 (1974): 47-54.

Steward, Frances. "Choice of Technique in Developing Countries." *Journal of Development Studies* 9 (October 1972): 99-122.

_____. Technology and Underdevelopment. Boulder, Colo.: Westview Press, 1977.

Teece, David J. *The Multinational Corporation and the Resource Cost of International Technology Transfer*. Cambridge, Mass.: Ballinger, 1976.

Vernon, Raymond. *The Technology Factor in International Trade*. New York: National Bureau of Economic Research, 1970.

CHAPTER 17

CONFLICTS BETWEEN HOME AND HOST COUNTRIES

The growth of MNCs in recent years has given rise to heated debates regarding the usefulness of these corporations for both host countries and home countries. Nations differ in their attitudes toward the presence of foreign corporations, and they display different degrees of tension about this situation. In general MNCs have met with more resistance in developing countries than in developed (advanced) countries.

Some writers in developed (advanced) countries have considered MNCs as the chief instrument in abolishing poverty in developing countries. Other writers in developing countries, however, have referred to MNCs as the main device of the developed nations for achieving "economic imperialism." These writings have fueled tensions and have contributed to the imposition of governmental restrictions on activities of MNCs.

Although objection to the presence of MNCs has an economic tone, political or nationalistic considerations have played a significant role in shaping conflicting views toward MNCs. Xenophobia and the fear of economic dependence have lured some politicians to suggest the economic confinement of foreign interests and the reserving of certain sectors exclusively for exploitation by local entrepreneurs.[1]

The purpose of this chapter is to provide us with a general understanding of the major opposing views on the activities of MNCs in host countries. First, we list the major criticisms of MNCs. Second, we study the sources of conflict. Third, we elaborate on host countries' reactions to MNCs. Finally, we raise the question as to who is right— MNCs or the countries in which the MNCs do business.

MAJOR CRITICISMS OF MNCS

The subject of MNCs is imbued with a variety of complaints that are raised by host countries against these corporations. The criticisms of MNCs with regard to technology transfer and social issues were discussed in Chapters 10. Some other major criticisms that are aimed at MNCs are the following:

1. MNCs raise their needed capital locally, contributing to the rise in interest rates in those countries.

2. The majority (sometimes even 100 percent) of the stocks of a subsidiary of an MNC is owned by the parent company. Consequently, the host country's residents do not have much control over the operations of these corporations within their borders.
3. MNCs reserve the key managerial and technical positions for expatriates. As a result, they do not contribute to the "learning-by-doing" process in the host countries.
4. MNCs do not provide training for their host countries' workers.
5. MNCs do not adapt their technology to the conditions that exist in host countries.
6. MNCs concentrate their research and development activities in their home countries. As a result, they restrict the transfer of modern technology and know-how to the host countries.
7. MNCs give rise to the demand for luxury goods in host countries at the expense of essential consumer goods.
8. MNCs start their foreign operations by the purchase of existing firms, rather than by developing a new productive facility from scratch in the host country.
9. MNCs do not contribute to the exports of their host countries.
10. MNCs worsen the income distribution of their host countries.
11. MNCs do not observe the objectives of the national plans for development in host countries.
12. MNCs earn excessively high profits and fees, due to their monopoly power in host countries.
13. MNCs dominate major industrial sectors.
14. MNCs are not accountable to their host nations, but only respond to their home country's government.
15. MNCs contribute to inflation by stimulating demand for scarce resources.
16. MNCs recruit the best personnel and the best managers from the host country at the expense of local entrepreneurs.
17. MNCs form alliances with corrupt developing countries elites.
18. MNCs interfere with the political conditions of host countries in the developing countries.
19. MNCs disregard the impact of their actions on consumer safety and environmental conditions.
20. MNCs disregard the cultural and social impact of their actions on the host country.

To understand the elements that give rise to these criticisms, one should look at the sources of conflicts.

SOURCES OF CONFLICTS

Conflicts arise from a clash of goals between constituencies. A firm must satisfy different groups of people, each group with its own specific goals. Employees, customers, stockholders, and the governments of home and host countries have different objectives that may not be compatible. Employees strive for a higher compensation package and better working conditions. Customers expect high quality goods at a lower price. Stockholders would like higher rates of return on their investment. Governments, in both host and home countries, may want higher exports or strive for the achievement of certain social goals.

Thus, the incompatibility of objectives of the parties involved in international business may set the stage for confrontation among them.

MNCs' Objectives

The main objective of an MNC is to maximize its global profit. The pursuit of this goal leads the MNC (1) to choose the type of operation that best suits its objective; (2) to improve efficiency by allocating its resources within the corporate family; and (3) to retain as much of its profit as possible.

Because MNCs operate in different host countries, each with its own governmental jurisdiction, they are not accountable to these nations concerning most aspects of their operations. Each nation controls only that part of the MNC's activities that fall within its borders. This gives MNCs more power vis-a-vis local firms, when dealing with the host country's demands. MNCs can counter the pressure of any given host country by simply threatening to curtail their activities or to shut down their operations in that country. This unique characteristic of MNCs goes against a host country's goal of achieving certain economic and social objectives. For example, a host government might be interested in export promotion; however, the MNC may find exporting unprofitable and hence does not cooperate with the host government in achieving this goal. This situation may lead to a conflict of interests and can raise tensions between the MNC and the host country's government.

Home Countries' Objectives

Conflicts between MNCs and home countries can arise both from economic goals and noneconomic goals.

Economic Goals. Economically speaking, there is often not much conflict between the goals of MNCs and the objectives of home countries. In its striving for profit maximization, an MNC generates earnings for (1) its stockholders in terms of dividends and capital appreciation; (2) its employees in the form of wages and salaries; and (3) its home government through the payment of corporate profit taxes. Because increases in the earnings of their residents is an economic objective that host countries try to achieve, there seems to be no conflict of interest between these countries and MNCs on that score.

Because most managers and owners of an MNC are residents of the MNC's home country, they have a tendency to identify their interests with those of their home country. As a result, they may try to fuse the corporate interest with the home country's interest. For example, an MNC may try to buy most of its resources at home, as long as it is compatible with its profit maximization objectives.

However, in spite of this tendency, an MNC cannot ignore world economic conditions when allocating its resources. Thus, if labor costs are high at home, or if the home country's economy is not strong, the MNC may close its factories at home and invest its capital abroad, helping increase employment in a foreign country rather than at home. Such an action leads to higher unemployment at home and may cause depression in areas where the MNC's factories have been closed. For example, when General Electric (GE) moved its plant from Ashland, Massachusetts, to Singapore, it caused the loss of 1,100 jobs in Ashland. As another example, 4,000 jobs were lost at home when RCA closed its Memphis, Tennessee, facilities and moved to Taiwan.[2]

Such incidents lead to tension between the unemployed workers and the MNCs. This might cause the home country government to step in and restrict the activities of MNCs abroad. For example, U.S. labor's opposition to MNCs contributed to the passage of the Trade and Investment
Act of 1972, known as the "Burke-Hartke Bill" after its original cosponsors. This bill introduced certain measures that have restricted both U.S. imports and foreign direct investment by U.S.
corporations. According to the bill, the President of the United States has the right to forbid any person within U.S. jurisdiction from making transfers of capital to or within any foreign nation, if in the President's judgment the transfer would lead to a net increase in unemployment in the United States.

Noneconomic Goals. Conflicts between MNCs and governments can also stem from noneconomic goals that are set by the home or host country's government. Chief among these goals is national defense. A home country government might impose restrictions on: (1) the exportation of certain products, such as computer hardware and electronic devices, that might be strategically significant to hostile nations; (2) the licensing and the technology that are needed to produce such goods; and (3) the investment in facilities in host countries needed to produce these goods. While these restrictions might be necessary from the home

GLOBAL INSIGHTS CASE 17.1

THE EXXON VALDEZ DISASTER

On March 24, 1989, Exxon Valdez, a 987-foot supertanker loaded with 1,264,164 barrels of crude oil hit ground on Bligh Reef in Prince William Sound, Alaska. The oil that leaked from the tanker eventually moved along the Alaskan Coastline contaminating portions of the shoreline of Prince William Sound, the Kenai Peninsula, lower Cook Inlet, the Kodiak Archipelago and the Alaska Peninsula. The lands that were considered affected included a National Forest, four National Wildlife Refuges, three National Parks, five State Parks, four State Critical Habitat Areas and a State Gaming Sanctuary. The oil had ultimately reached shorelines almost 600 miles southwest from the original spill site at Bligh Reef.

Following the accident, efforts focused on containing and cleaning up the spill, and fighting to revive oil covered wildlife. The clean-up work was centered on containing the spill area and on the rescuing of wildlife who had come in contact with the oil. Under the direction of the U.S. Coast Guard and with the advice from federal and state agencies and local communities, Exxon was put in charge of cleaning up operation.

On October 9, 1991, the U.S. District Court entered into a plea agreement that brought criminal charges against Exxon and a civil settlement for recovery of natural resource damages resulting from the spill. Exxon received a fine of $150 million; the largest fine ever imposed for an environmental crime. The courts gave $125 million in recognition of Exxon's cooperation in cleaning up the spill and paying private claims. Upon receipt of the settlements, The Exxon Valdez Oil Spill Trustee Council was formed to direct restoration. Additionally, Exxon agreed to pay $50 million to the United States and the State of Alaska for restitution. Finally, Exxon agreed to pay $900 million over a 10 year period to reimburse the federal and state governments for clean-up costs, damage assessment, litigation and continuing restoration.

Unfortunately, despite the massive clean-up efforts that had taken place, a 1989 shoreline assessment concluded that a large amount of oil still was lingering on the shorelines. In 1990, another shoreline assessment was completed in a joint effort by Exxon and the state and federal governments. This study concluded that some levels of oil still persisted on the shorelines and there was still much work to be done.

During 1991-1994, limited clean-up efforts occurred. In 1992, Exxon and the state and federal governments concluded that seven miles of the 21.4 miles of shoreline surveyed still showed some surface oil residue. However, this study was subject to two limitations that led to underestimation of the actual number of shorelines that were still polluted. One limitation was that the assessment included no surveying of shorelines that were set aside for monitoring natural recovery. Another limitation of the study was the fact that no sites were studied on Kodiak Island or the Alaska Peninsulas during this 1992 assessment.

During 1994, restoration workers manually treated the shoreline to speed up the degradation of surface oil William Sound.

The spill has put an enormous hardship on many species including mammals, birds, fish and intertidal plants and animals such as mussels, chitons, and fucus. A recent study conducted in 1996, estimated that the total number of species and resources that were threatened or lost due to the spill was 28. There has been only one species, the bald eagle, which has been officially declared as recovered by the Trustee Council. The good news is that more species seem to be on their way to recovery. The massive injuries also took its toll on Alaska's inhabitants. This occurred because the archeological sites were looted, subsistence harvests declined, commercial fishing shut down for a season, recreational land use became limited, and in many cases, the myth of unspoiled water and lands has been tainted forever.

At the end of 1995, the total assets of Exxon were $91.3 billion, with an output of 3.4 million barrels of crude oil per year, the company seemed to have recovered from the *Exxon Valdez* oil spill disaster. The company has taken responsibility for its action regarding the spill and made huge efforts to take corrective measures. Today, the company is more aware of the issue of the corporate social responsibility and tries to promote this issue within its worldwide Organizational Structure. Perhaps this attitude, following the spill, saved Exxon from failure.

Sources: George Laycock, "The Disaster that Won't Go Away," *Audubon*, September 1990, pp.106-112; "Oil Spill Leaves Crude Mark on Alaska, "*National Parks*", March/April 1991, pp. 13-14; Nina Munk, "We're Praying Hearty," *Forbes*, 24 October 1994, pp. 84-90; Sharon Bagley, "One Deal that Was Too Good for Exxon," *Newsweek*, 6 May 1991, p.54; Art Davidson, *In the Wake of the Exxon Valdez: The Devastating Impact of Alaska's Oil Spill* (San Francisco, California: Sierra Club Books, 1980); John Cable, *Out of the Channel: The Exxon Valdez Oil Spill in Prince William Sound* (New York: Harper Collins, 1991); Bruce M. Owen, et. al. *The Economics of a Disaster: The Exxon Valdez Oil Spill* (Westport, Conn.: Quorum Books, 1995).

country's national security standpoint, they may prove to be detrimental to the profit maximization process of the MNC.

Another noneconomic goal that might lead to conflict between an MNC and a home or host country's government is the government's objective of environmental protection. A host government may desire an environment which is free from water pollution, air pollution, and toxic wastes. Yet MNCs might not take these issues seriously because of the high cost of alleviating these problems. This may cause the host government to step in and force the MNCs to take responsibility for cleaning up the environment.

Host Countries' Objectives

The subject of MNCs is a more touchy issue in host countries than it is in home countries. While home countries perceive MNCs as an integral part of their economic systems, host countries may view them as foreign agents whose benefits are not worth their costs. Such a negative attitude toward MNCs is especially strong in developing countries. The notion that these large MNCs somehow undermine the independence of developing countries raises nationalistic fever in these countries and invites emotional reaction against MNCs. Nevertheless, the host countries' responses vary, depending on (1) the relative dominance of MNCs in their economy, (2) their perceived degree of dependence on the MNCs, and (3) the extent to which MNCs' activities are subsidized by the host government.

The sources of conflict between MNCs and host countries can be traced not only to the economic goals of the host countries, but to their noneconomic goals as well. A new area of conflict between host countries and MNCs is the so-called transborder data flow (TDF) problem. Given the increasing importance of this issue, with its economic and noneconomic implications, a separate discussion of this topic is included in this section.

Economic Goals. The economic objectives of a host country in allowing MNCs to operate in their country can be stated as three separate goals: (1) the economic growth goal, (2) the distributive and allocative goal, and (3) the balance of payments goal.

The Economic Growth Goal. The increase in the rate of economic growth is the primary reason for a country to open its doors to MNCs. It is hoped that foreign investment will augment national resources, contributing to the growth of GNP. It is also hoped that MNCs will transfer their technology and provide training for the local workers. This is critical to a country's economic growth, because it allows the nation to become technologically independent in the long run, achieving its economic growth goals without foreign help. However, because MNCs have obtained their superior knowledge and technology through their investment in research and development, they do not have any incentive to transfer completely their technology and know-how to the host countries. Such a transfer would cause these corporations to lose their competitive edge over local firms. The unwillingness of MNCs to transfer their technology to host countries leads to a technological dependence of these nations on MNCs, setting the stage for future conflicts.

The Distributive and Allocative Goal. The second economic goal of host countries is related to: (1) the distribution of profits earned by the MNCs and (2) control over the allocation of resources by these corporations.

The objective of host countries is to maximize the benefits that accrue to them from the MNCs' activities in their countries. To achieve this goal, they believe that they should have control over the allocation of resources flowing across their borders. This belief is based on the contention that the profits of MNCs in host countries arise from the employment of local resources and from access to domestic markets. MNCs, however, challenge this view. They maintain that their profits in host countries stem from the efficient utilization and allocation of their firm-specific advantages. Because MNCs have property rights over these advantages, they argue, the profits generated by their operations should accrue to them alone. Additionally, they should have the right to control their own scarce resources.

The controversy over the control of resources and distribution of profit is a major issue that has not yet been resolved, and it continues to intensify the tension between MNCs and their host countries.

The Balance of Payments Goal. The third economic goal of a host country in allowing MNCs to operate within its borders is to improve its balance of payments. Because foreign exchange is a scarce resource, especially in developing countries, many countries look to MNCs as a source of financing their foreign currency needs.

The impact of an MNC on the balance of payments of a host country changes with the passage of time. Initially, an MNC may bring in capital to a host country and contributes to the balance of payments position. This is because payment for this capital is usually made in a foreign currency, strengthening the country's holding of international reserve assets. However, if a well-developed capital market exists in the host country, an MNC might raise the demand for capital in the local market, causing the home country's interest rates to rise. If this happens, then the MNC's initial investment is not helpful to the balance of payments. For this reason, most countries, especially the developing countries, insist that MNCs pay for the initial cost of their new investment with foreign currencies that have been raised outside their national borders.

After the initial investment is made and the plant becomes operational, there is a second impact on the balance of payments. If the plant produces goods that can effectively compete with commodities that are imported from foreign countries, there would be a decrease in payments for imports. This results in a decline in the outflow of foreign currencies, causing improvement in the balance of payments. Additionally, if the plant produces goods that can be exported, there would be an increase in the inflow of foreign exchange, leading to further improvement in the balance of payments.

There is also a third impact on the balance of payments that results from the initial investment by an MNC in a host country. If the investment is profitable, then the foreign owners may wish to repatriate their capital in the form of royalties, licensing fees, and eventually dividends. This results in an outflow of foreign currencies from the host country worsening the balance of payments. Aware of this negative outcome on their balance of payments, many countries have passed ceilings on the amount of profits, licensing fees, and royalties that can be repatriated by the MNCs. Unfortunately, however, this has caused some MNCs to engage in deceptive policies, such as transfer pricing, to circumvent restrictions imposed by their host governments on the repatriation of their capital. Other MNCs have preferred to plow their earnings into future investment and further growth. This, in turn, has caused additional complaints by the host countries, who relate the size of MNCs in their countries to the degree of foreign domination that is imposed upon them.

A major way in which MNCs can contribute to the balance of payments position of their host countries is through the export of goods and services. However, many MNCs feel that the conditions which exist in developing countries are not conducive to exports from those countries. This is because production in many of these countries is supported by protectionist policies such as import tariffs. As a result, the products that are produced by these nations are relatively expensive and hence incapable of competing with the cheaper and better quality goods abroad.

Noneconomic Goals. The main noneconomic goal of a host country in dealing with MNCs is to maintain its independence. Another noneconomic goal is the maintenance of a social, political, and cultural atmosphere that is free from friction.

GLOBAL INSIGHTS CASE 17.2

HISTORICAL EVIDENCE AGAINST MULTINATIONAL CORPORATIONS

There is historical evidence that the actions undertaken by some MNCs in the past have led to undesirable, often disastrous, outcomes for the societies in which these MNCs have operated. The following examples are cases in point:

1. Some MNCs have formed alliances with corrupt Third World elites. This has led many observers to believe that MNCs, whether they know it or not, are siding with elites and promoting inequalities in these societies.[1]
2. MNCs' excessive interference in the political conditions of host countries in the Third World is a sore issue that has been documented on many occasions. The well publicized alleged role of ITT in the 1973 coup d'etat against Salvador Allende's regime in Chile is a prime example. Another example is Gulf Oil's political involvement in Angola.[2]
3. The increase in African infant mortality that resulted from the introduction of Western-style baby formula into that continent by Nestle and a number of other MNCs is seen as an example of their irresponsibility.[3]
4. The excessive use of transfer pricing, tax havens, and the manipulation of currency fluctuations by some MNCs exemplify the abuse of both home and host country laws. Examples of these abuses include the Hoffman-LaRoche use of transfer pricing and Lonrho's use of tax havens.[4]
5. The MNCs are also seen as disregarding the impact of their actions on consumer safety and environmental conditions. This is especially true when host government regulations to protect the consumer or the environment are absent. These activities can take different forms, such as the dumping of industrial wastes and pollutants, the use of harmful pesticides, and the sale of unsafe products. A well publicized example is the leakage of a deadly gas at Union Carbide's chemical plant in Bhopal, India, in 1984. The accident caused the death of approximately 2,500 people, exposed 200,000 people to the gas, and made about 50,000 people sick. It killed thousands of animals and destroyed vegetation.[5] Another example is the case of a U.S. children's carcinogenic fire retardant that has been banned in the United States, but the company continues to sell the banned product in other countries.[6]
6. There have been unfair labor practices by some MNCs in some host countries. For example, Kodak, Nestle, and IBM have been associated with abuses in trade union recognition.[7]
7. Reports of illegal payments, bribery, and other corrupt practices by MNCs have been frequently written about in the press. Aircraft manufacturers and oil companies have been implicated in these illegal dealings. For example, Lockheed has been accused of trying to influence the Japanese government's military purchases through multimillion dollar "commissions." Overall, the company has been accused of giving $25 million in bribes to government officials in different countries in order to win orders for its new aircraft. Similarly, Exxon was accused of making payoffs of $28 million in the form of political contributions. United Brands was accused of attempting to alter a tax law in Honduras by making a $1.25 million payoff in political contributions to influential individuals. And there have been bribery convictions against Imperial Chemical Industries of the United Kingdom and Marubeni Trading Company of Japan.[8]

Continued

> *Global Insights Case 17.2, continued*
>
> The above examples illustrate why MNCs, despite the use of the most sophisticated public relations services in the world, have gained such dubious reputations.
>
> **NOTES**
>
> 1. L. M. Turner, "There's No Love Lost between Multinational Companies and the Third World, "*Business and Society Review*", vol.11, no.2 (autumn 1974), pp. 75-78.
> 2. Michael Z. Brook, and H. Lee Remmers, International Management and Business Policy (Boston: Houghton Mifflin, 1978), p. 311.
> 3. Ibid., p.310.
> 4. Ibid., p.311.
> 5. *The New York Times*, 6 December 1984, p.1.
> 6. James Brady, "An Export Trade in Death," Advertising Age, vol. 49, patt 2, 15 May 1978, p. 99.
> 7. Brook and Remmers, *International Management*, p. 311.
> 8. Annat Negandhi, *International Management* (Boston: Allyn and Bacon, 1987) p. 55.

Many developing countries view MNCs with suspicion, and they fear that their interaction with these corporate giants will lead to a loss of control over their political, cultural, and economic lives. They feel that in dealing with MNCs they will become subservient, providing raw materials and cheap labor to these corporations, but never playing a crucial role in a production process that is based on advanced technology controlled by the MNCs. These nations feel that the intention of MNCs in investing in their countries is to serve the local market exclusively. They charge that MNCs reserve the exporting functions only for their parent companies or for some of their advanced subsidiaries. Such a view is a is a very gloomy picture of the role of MNCs in developing countries. This view, in turn, causes some of these countries to eventually pursue policies that are aimed at curtailment of MNCs' activities within their borders.

Even in an advanced country, such as the United States, MNCs cannot escape resistance. For example, in 1987 when a Japanese company gave in to pressure from the U.S. government and abandoned its bid to take over a semiconductor company, an American politician stated that "We have won one for America's national security."[3] Worried about the ever-increasing size of foreign investment in the United States, another politician was wondering if Americans would lose "... control over our economic destiny."[4] Yet such views are not shared by many economists, who believe the inflow of foreign direct investment (FDI) to the United States will provide the country with know-how and capital. The restriction of FDI is detrimental, it is argued, to a nation that has assumed a new role as the world's largest debtor, requiring roughly $150 billion a year from overseas to finance its growth.[5]

Pessimistic attitudes toward MNCs stem, to a large extent, from (1) the experience of developing countries with colonialism and (2) the income distribution effect of MNCs' investment.

Colonialism. In the past, colonialism in many developing countries crippled their efforts to industrialize. Colonies were forced by the mother countries, who made the resource allocation decisions, to specialize in the production of primary and intermediate goods. As a result, colonies did not develop an industrial base conducive to their economic independence. Today, some of the developing countries see a close resemblance between the former mother countries of colonialism and present-day MNCs. They believe that if the resource allocation decisions are made at the MNC's headquarters, the subsidiaries in the developing countries will end up producing goods that will not make any significant contribution toward the economic development of the host countries.

The Income Distribution Effect of MNCs The activities of an MNC may disturb the income distribution in a host country, leading to social and political unrest. Investment by an MNC may cause the emergence of new entrepreneurs, whose fortunes may increase at the expense of those in power. The reverse may also be true, that is, an MNC may further intensify the strength of the group already in power. It is also possible that an MNC may pay higher wages than the wages paid by local firms. Any of these scenarios would cause one group to gain wealth and power at the expense of another group, at least in the short run. This may cause those who benefit from the operations of an MNC to lobby their government in support of such corporations. Those who lose from the activities of the MNCs, however, may demand that their government restrict the activities of these corporations. The power of those who lose from the activities of MNCs may be enhanced by support from those who feel a sense of subservience, weakness, and inferiority in dealing with these corporate giants. These feelings may stem from a suspicion that they may not be able to invent, produce, or market a product on their own without the help of MNCs. Whatever the reasons, this situation leads to social and political unrest and sets the stage for governmental intervention that leads to more restrictive policies toward MNCs.

Transborder Data Flow Transborder data flow (TDF) refers to the flow of electronically transmitted information across national boundaries. The immense growth in the computer and telecommunication industries since the 1970s has tremendously facilitated the storing and transmission of massive amounts of information across national boundaries. This has enabled MNCs to collect information in different host countries and transmit it to their home country for use in their worldwide operations. For example, an MNC with its headquarters in New York can build a computerized marketing data file in Europe and transfer this information electronically to its headquarters in New York.

Information collected by MNCs in host countries covers a wide range of subjects. This information includes data on production, distribution, research and development, finance, marketing, personnel, and payroll. Europe is the end point for the transmission of information by many MNCs. Information is transmitted from Europe for storing and processing in the United States, and the results are then transmitted back to Europe for many MNCs.

Given the large volume of information collected by MNCs and the significance of this information in shaping today's global markets, host countries, both developed countries and developing countries, have come to realize the impact of TDF on their countries' economic and noneconomic goals.

Economically speaking, information is an economic resource, and as such it is a marketable, transferable, and exportable commodity. The ability of one country to store and process information may give that country technological advantage over other countries. A case in point is the United States, which has derived immense benefits not only by processing and storing data in U.S.-based computer systems but also by exporting sophisticated computer equipment.

From a noneconomic standpoint, host countries are worried that the collection and storing of certain types of data may give the home countries a political advantage and may jeopardize their national sovereignty. Indeed, it has been argued that in times of war or national emergencies, host countries might not be able to gain access to vital information stored in hostile home countries.

Given the economic and noneconomic implications of TDF, European countries have decided to deal with the problem through a new form of privacy protection legislation. In addition, due to the diversity of laws in different countries and the importance of this issue globally, the Organization of Economic Cooperation and Development (OECD) devised guidelines on TDF in 1980. These voluntary guidelines were adopted by Canada in 1984. The purpose of these guidelines is to encourage the cooperation of member nations with regard to the exchange of information. Adherence to these guidelines means that the OECD member countries will consider the OECD guidelines equivalent to their own privacy laws. This may result in the relaxation or removal of barriers to the free flow of information between OECD members and the United States.

The legislation regarding TDF can be considered as a form of nontariff trade barriers. The effects of these trade barriers can be viewed from two perspectives: international and domestic. Internationally, the decrease in the flow of information increases the uncertainty felt by potential importers and exporters. As a result, the volume of international trade in goods and services decreases. Service sector industries that are heavily dependent on TDF, such as the airlines, banking, financial services, and tourism, are especially affected by barriers against TDF. Domestically, as the flow of information into a country diminishes, the prices charged by the data-processing industries rise. Also, as the cost-cutting technological information of foreign origin is denied to the domestic producers their production costs rise. Thus, the legislation of TDF, like tariff barriers, may result in losses for business on both the national and international levels. We must stress that the abuse of TDF is a serious problem that would be best resolved by international cooperation rather than by protectionist barriers that retard the free flow of international trade.

HOST COUNTRIES' REACTION TO MNCS

Given the conflicting goals of MNCs vis-a-vis the goals of host countries, the reactions of different nations to these corporations vary considerably. The factors that determine the intensity of these reactions are (1) the perceived degree of foreign domination and control and (2) the extent to which the activities of the MNCs are subsidized by the government of the host countries.

Suspicions concerning the presence of some foreigners have led some countries to go so far as to confiscate foreign enterprises in their country. For example, after the downfall of the Shah of Iran in 1979, the new Islamic Republic government of that country confiscated all American companies. Some other countries, however, have been indecisive about the presence of MNCs and have gone from one extreme to another. For example, the French government has shifted its policies regarding FDI three times within a five-year period.

Some countries have developed different policy measures that have the intention of lessening the effects of FDI on their economic systems without banning FDI altogether. It is hoped that such policies would provide them with the benefits of FDI — technology, managerial know-how, labor training, the needed capital, and access to foreign markets — without forcing them to yield completely to foreign ownership and control.

Some of the major policies employed by host countries in dealing with MNCs are: requiring joint venture arrangements; controlling entries and takeovers; excluding foreigners from specific activities; controlling the local content and local employment; export requirements; controlling the local capital market; debt equity requirements; taking the foreign investment package apart; requiring disinvestment; and controlling remittances, rates, and fees.

Joint Venture Arrangements

As we explained in Chapter 18, a joint venture arrangement calls for the partnership of an MNC with either the private entrepreneurs or the government of a host country. There are two advantages of engaging in a joint venture arrangement (rather than having a wholly owned subsidiary) for an MNC. First, by making a host country's residents part owners of the operation, it minimizes the control measures that are used by that country's government against the foreign operation. Second, by placing indigenous partners on the board of directors, it better equips an MNC to deal with the cultural elements that exist in a host country. For example, American Telephone and Telegraph (AT & T), the world's largest communication company, began to expand into the European market. After spending millions of dollars to figure out a strategy for Europe, the company decided to try local partnership. This decision was based on the realization that the European market was crowded, the governments were hostile, and the trade barriers were formidable. In 1983, AT & T began to form joint ventures with different European companies with the intention of gaining local expertise, political power in Europe's protected market, and faster growth. Accordingly, joint ventures were arranged with Phillips for producing communication gear, Olivetti for producing computers, and Cia. Telefonica Nacionale de Espara for producing microchips. There are signs that AT & T's strategy has paid off, and the company plans to form more partnerships with other European countries.[6]

The advantages of joint venture arrangements for host countries' residents are: (1) their ability, as partial owners, to decide about the operations of the firm and (2) their ability to share in the profits that result from the activities of the firm in their country.

Unfortunately, however, joint venture arrangements, like any other kind of partnership, are not without problems. First, a joint venture is composed of partners with different cultural backgrounds and different objectives. This can lead to disagreements between the partners regarding different aspects of the firm's day-to-day operations. For example, foreign partners are more likely to opt for plowing back their earnings into the company, whereas local partners might prefer higher dividends. The time may also come when the corporation needs to build up its capital, but the local partners are unwilling to contribute their share. As another example, a host government might desire a more equitable income distribution. However, an MNC might have entered into partnership with the wealthy class of the host country. If such a partnership is successful, then the high profit earned by the joint venture would further increase power and wealth of the wealthy class, thereby worsening the income distribution in the country as a whole.

Given the nature of problems associated with joint ventures, some MNCs have gone so far as to shut down their existing operations rather than engage in such arrangements. For example, in response to India's demand that IBM and Coca-Cola sell 60 percent of the equity of their Indian subsidiaries to domestic interests, both companies pulled out of that country.[7]

Today, joint venture arrangements are still popular in some countries, such as Japan and South Korea. Such arrangements have enabled these host countries to have access to the advanced technology of the West, without yielding complete ownership and control to foreign interests. Unfortunately, however, cultural gaps between partners have diminished the potential benefits of joint venture arrangements. For example, in a move to acquire aerospace technology, a group of Japanese companies negotiated a joint venture with Boeing, the American aerospace company. From the beginning of negotiations there were signs of disagreements between the two sides. For instance, the Japanese complained that "... Boeing assigns to the project too many young executives who don't understand Japanese business practice."[8] Americans complained about "... the Japanese negotiator's lack of technical knowledge."[9]

Joint venture arrangements are not only popular in market economies, but they are also encouraged in nonmarket economies, such the People's Republic of China. However, due to difficulties that have afflicted Western joint venture projects in the former Soviet Union, in Eastern Europe, before its recent economic reform, and in China, Western entrepreneurs have remained reluctant to expand their investment into nonmarket economies.[10]

Following the economic reforms of the Eastern European countries and the collapse of the Soviet Union, the activities of MNCs in these nations have increased. As a result, countries such as Hunagry and Russia have become popular sites for joint ventures.[11]

Controlling Entries and Takeovers

In most developing counties and in some developed countries, the entry of foreign firms into their country is controlled. Such firms are required to obtain approval for a new investment venture or for the takeover of an existing firm. In Canada, for example, the Foreign Investment Review Agency (FIRA) is in charge of screening foreign direct investment. In India, a Foreign Investment Board is given the responsibility of reviewing foreign direct investment.

Although different countries have different requirements for approving foreign direct investment, most nations demand a detailed description of the applicant's operations and financial position. Additionally, they require the potential investor to explain the way in which the investment project would contribute to national objectives. The approval process puts the reviewing board of the country in the driver's seat, so to speak, enabling the board to approve only those projects that are potentially beneficial to the country.

There is a tendency by many countries to prohibit the purchase of existing plants, requiring that a foreign investment project start from scratch. This tendency arises from the argument against monopoly. It is felt that the takeover of an existing firm by an MNC keeps the number of firms in an industry constant and does not contribute the market competition. Thus, for example, if an industry is composed of 10 firms, a takeover of an existing firm by an MNC leaves the total number at 10. A new entry, however, raises the number to 11, increasing the degree of competitiveness in the industry.

Although the above argument is theoretically strong, practically speaking it loses its appeal when an industry is already competitive and when the government feels, for no good reason, that a new investment is somehow preferable to a takeover of an existing one. Suppose an ailing domestic firm is operating in a relatively competitive situation and its operators are not capable of running it efficiently. In this situation, the plant and equipment are worth more to the foreign entrepreneurs who wish to invest in that country than the domestic entrepreneurs who are sustaining losses. Thus, both parties would gain from the takeover by the foreign entrepreneurs. In this situation, a policy of forcing the foreign entrepreneurs to start from scratch and causing the domestic entrepreneurs to scrap their plants seems to be unproductive.

Today, countries that are open to foreign investment gladly hand over the control of their troubled companies in the hope of acquiring as much foreign investment and technology as they can. For example, in pursuing its new policy of openness to foreign investment in 1986, Spain allowed four takeovers of domestic firms by foreign firms: SEAT group was taken over by Volkswagen AG of West Germany, a locally known maker of natural cosmetics was taken over by Gillette, a local meat packer was taken over by Unilever, and a canner was taken over by Pillsbury.[12]

Excluding Foreigners from Specific Activities

A host country may reserve certain business fields for domestic entrepreneurs only, prohibiting foreign involvement in those areas. The business activities that are usually prohibited to foreigners by host countries are banking, insurance, public utilities, communications and the media, and the exploitation of certain natural resources.

Banking, insurance, and other financial institutions in general are prohibited as investments for foreigners because of the fear by some host countries, such as Canada and Mexico, that these institutions have the potential for providing foreigners with influence and control over their economic system. Such control, it is argued, may be in conflict with the economic policies of the host country.*[13]

Public utilities are prohibited as investments for foreigners by many host governments because such businesses are considered to be an inseparable part of national development.

The operation of communications and the media—radio, television, and newspapers—is usually restricted by host governments to the local entrepreneurs or to the host country government itself. It is argued that they represent a vital national interest that should not be entrusted to foreign hands.

Involvement of foreigners in the exploitation of certain natural resources in many host countries, such as Brazil, Finland, Mexico, and Morocco, is very limited, because these resources are considered a gift of nature that should be exploited only for public use, rather than for private gain. Many other developing countries have limited foreign involvement and investment in their mineral deposits, oil reserves, and forestry

---

* All of these prohibitions do not apply for to trade between the United States, Mexico, and Canada. As explained in Chapter 9, trade between Mexico, Canada, and the United States is covered under the provisions of NAFTA agreements.

resources to purchases of concessions by foreigners. Such concessions have provided foreign firms with the exclusive rights to explore a given resource, but only for a limited time period. In return for these rights the host governments have received royalties on the extracted resource and income taxes on the net profits of the foreign firms.

Controlling the Local Content and Local Employment

To ensure that the operations of foreign firms are conducive to the industrialization process and that they increase the employment in host countries, many developing countries have demanded foreign firms continually increase the amount of locally produced goods that are used as content of their final products. Additionally, they have required that a certain percentage of the foreign firm's total employees be citizens of the host country. The local contents policies have been widely used by Latin American countries where MNCs are engaged in automobile manufacturing. Mexico has gone so far as to require foreign firms to employ a labor force that is 90 percent Mexican.

Nations that impose local content requirements in a new industry hope to improve their economy not only through that industry, but also via that industry's linkages with the suppliers of component parts and materials. Unfortunately, however, the local content requirement may prove costly. This happens if the local market is not large enough to allow economies of scale in the production of the related component parts and materials.

Export Requirements

Foreign exchange is scarce in many countries, especially developing countries. It provides these countries with the needed funds for the importation of items that they need in the process of their industrialization. Exports are the surest way of acquiring the necessary foreign exchange, and foreign investments projects are often evaluated on the basis of their potential contribution to the country's exports.

Many nations have learned that the overall strategies of MNCs may not permit or inspire their new subsidiaries to compete against the old subsidiaries in securing markets for their exports. This has led host countries to be skeptical of the MNCs' role in enhancing their exports. As a result, some countries have considered the ability of a subsidiary to freely export a prerequisite for its approval as a foreign investment.

Unfortunately, however, many developing countries' markets are protected with high tariffs and quotas. If a foreign firm's subsidiary is forced to operate in a protected industry, its high production cost will erode its competitiveness in the world market. Thus, the ability of the subsidiary to freely export should be weighed against the government's desire to engage in protectionist policies.

Controlling the Local Capital Market

Because most developing countries lack the needed capital and technology for their own development process, they look upon MNCs as a major source of financing. However, the foreign exchange authorities of these countries often fear that an MNC might raise all or some of its capital in the host country, further draining capital out of the country. To ensure against this possibility, many developing countries exclude foreigners from their local capital market, requiring that all capital funds be raised outside their national boundaries. The impact of this requirement is to increase the inflow of foreign exchange into the host country, improving its balance of payments at the time of investment.

The policy of forcing foreign investors to bring in their own money, without furnishing any local capital, must be exercised with caution. Such a policy may discourage some prospective investors who might potentially be a significant source of technology transfer to the developing country.

Debt Equity Requirements

Some countries provide guidelines on debt equity ratios. The purpose of such guidelines is to ensure that the investing firm has sufficient financial resources to minimize the possibility of bankruptcy. For example, a regulation by the People's Republic of China requires that: (1) for joint ventures with an investment of $3 million or less, there can be no debt; (2) for investments of $3 million to $10 million, the amount of debt cannot be greater that the equity investment; (3) for investments of $10 million to $30 million, the amount of debt cannot be greater than two times the equity; and (4) for investments greater than $30 million, the debt cannot exceed triple the equity investment. The problem with this requirement is that it might discourage some potential small investors from entering the marketplace. In the case of China, it is predicted that many people who had hoped to set up electronics assembly plants in China may now be forced out of business in China.[14]

Taking the Foreign Investment Package Apart

One way for host countries to resist foreign investment, yet enjoy foreign capital and foreign technology, is by "taking the foreign investment package apart." This means buying the needed technology, management, and capital separately, rather than acquiring them in one package in the form of an MNC's investment.

Although this is a sound strategy, and it has been successfully implemented in Japan, its application in other countries is questionable. This is because many countries, especially developing countries, do not have the necessary skill of imitating foreign technology and of adapting it to their national requirements as Japanese did. Additionally, many corporations are reluctant to break their package apart and leave control of their technology in foreign hands. As a result, for most developing countries the opportunity to pursue such a strategy is relatively limited. Nevertheless, it pays off for a host country to explore the possibility of purchasing only those parts of an investment package that are needed. For example, South Korea has attempted to follow Japan's lead by importing technology from Europe and the United States. To explain such a strategy, the South Korean head of technology transfer stated that "We're very weak in designing technology. We're very weak in process technology, so we import what we can't create."[15]

Although South Korea's strategy with regard to technology transfer has been relatively successful, it has met with some problems. For example, South Korea has been unable to transfer robot technology from Japanese robot makers. The Japanese have refused to provide South Korea with the software that controls robot operation, stating that South Koreans are not ready for such technology.[16]

A more recent example involved the People's Republic of China and Chrysler Corporation. According to a contract, the Chrysler Corporation had agreed to the transfer of engine equipment to China's First Automotive Works. However, it remains to be seen if Chrysler can overcome the market pitfalls that other Western investors have experienced in China.[17]

Requiring Disinvestment

According to this policy, the host government requires the potential foreign investor to disinvest over a period of time. This is achieved by transferring the corporation's ownership to the host country at a specified time for a predetermined price.

The problem with this strategy is the determination of a price that both parties can agree upon, given the uncertainty associated with the future course of events. Even if an agreement is reached, it may still lead to a distortion of incentives by the foreign firms and the host country. Assume that an MNC invests in a host country and agrees to surrender its ownership to that country at a predetermined price of $1 billion at the end of a 10-year period. Under the agreement, the MNC has the incentive to devise strategies to ensure that it will not have more than $1 billion worth of assets in its investment at the end of the 10-year period. However, at the same time, the host country tries to ensure that the value of the corporation's asset does not fall below $1 billion. Thus the stage is set for a conflict between the MNC and the host country. As a result, the company might follow strategies in the next 10 years that may not be helpful to its future, when its ownership is reverted to the host country.

Controlling Remittances, Rates, and Fees

Some of the policies that can be used by host countries to improve their balance of payments, to fulfill their national domestic policies, or to prevent MNCs from reaping excess profits involve the restriction of remittances, the imposition of ceiling rates on royalties, and the imposition of limits on fees paid for technology. However, the problem with these policies is that an MNC may be in a position to circumvent these restrictions through extra charges for training, research and development, machinery, advice, use of overhead facilities, corporate overhead, interest, and other services. An MNC also has the power to circumvent the system by altering its transfer prices for raw materials, component parts, and final products. All these actions have the effect of increasing the flow of funds from the host country to the corporation's headquarters in the home country, thus dampening the effort of the host country's government to diminish the foreign exchange outflow.

Other Policies

Other policies used by host countries in securing some of the benefits of MNC investment are requiring foreign firms to engage in labor training, requiring that certain key managerial positions be held by nationals, prohibiting foreign firms from engaging in technologically stagnant industries, and demanding that foreign firms engage in research and development in the host country.

The host countries hope that these measures will contribute to the internalization of the firm's technological and managerial know-how within the nation, thereby improving the country's balance of payments. Empirical studies suggest that host countries have been at least partially successful in implementing such measures. These studies show that MNCs usually engage in the training of the local labor. Studies also show that MNCs' training budgets might be greater than the training budgets of domestic firms.[18] However, the research and development activities carried out by MNCs in developing countries seem to be of an elementary nature, and these efforts usually do not lead to the adaptation of technology by these corporations. Additionally, there seems to be no significant difference between the amount of research rendered by foreign firms as compared with domestic firms.[19]

WHO IS RIGHT?

Our prior discussion suggests that all the activities of MNCs do not have the same impact on either host countries or home countries. Additionally, it is difficult to measure these effects and to reach a general conclusion that can be applied to all countries and all MNCs. In fact, much of the literature in the area of FDI is composed of studies that deal with the isolated problems of individual countries. As a result, any generalization about the conclusions reached by these studies is questionable. One thing is clear: many host countries believe that there are gains to be made from the operations of MNCs within their borders, and they continue to receive these corporations with open arms. This is especially true for countries with market economies. For example, Brazil offers a number of incentives to attract foreign investment. These include tax rebates for MNCs that reinvest corporate earnings into the economy, convertibility of earnings into the dollar, fiscal incentives, and the free repatriation of corporate earnings up to 12 percent of the invested

GLOBAL INSIGHTS CASE 17.3

U.S. TOBACCO EXPORTS: A HEALTH-TRADE CONTROVERSY

Since January 11, 1964, when the *Surgeon General's Report* documented the health problems associated with smoking, U.S. cigarette and other tobacco products consumption has been steadily declining. Such a decline is not only related to the public awareness of the adverse health effect of smoking, but other factors as well, such as government restriction on where smoking is permitted, and higher local and federal taxes. This has resulted in higher cigarettes prices, affecting the decline of the sale of tobacco related products in the U.S.

Considering the diminishing sales in its domestic market, the U.S. tobacco industry has been actively promoting cigarette export in the international market. As a result, U.S. export of tobacco has continued to experience a rapid growth overseas, leading to more than $2 billion trade surplus in cigarettes. Such a surplus could be attributed to the opening of new overseas markets in Asia to American tobacco products. The opening of these markets was achieved with the help of United States Trade Representative (USTR).

Under the banner of free trade, the USTR engages in negotiations that are aimed at the removal of unfair trade practices against U.S. goods. Japan, South Korea, Taiwan, and Thailand are examples of countries that have negotiated with USTR regarding their high import tariffs, discriminatory taxes and unfair marketing and distribution practices. For example, in 1985 USTR was successful in getting Japan to agree to remove cigarette tariffs, as well other discriminatory barriers directed against import cigarettes.

Besides USTR efforts to ensure fair treatment for U.S. cigarettes abroad, the U.S. government funds three specific programs that are designed to promote tobacco exports: the Department of Agriculture's Cooperator Market Development Program, the Targeted Export Assistance Program, and the Export Credit Guarantee Programs.

Paradoxically, the government continues to vigorously support the sales of tobacco companies abroad, even though it appears to be a powerful supporter of the global antismoking movement. This is evident by the activities of the Department of Health and Human Services. This organization acts as a collaborating headquarters for the United Nations World Health Organizations and maintains close relationships with other health organization around the globe in disseminating information regarding the adverse effects of smoking. It is obvious that the U.S. trade policy of promoting tobacco exports is clearly in conflict with its stated health policy of reducing the use of tobacco products.

Sources: United States General Accounting Office, "Trade and Health Issues: Dichotomy Between U.S. Tobacco Export Policy and Antismoking Initiatives," May 1990; "Tobacco Industry: Stubbed Out," *The Economist*, August 20, 1994, 26.

capital. But even in the case of nonmarket economies, the most unlikely countries, such as the People's Republic of China and Nicaragua, are not reluctant to seek foreign investment. China has gone so far in receiving FDI that it even offers incentives to MNCs to engage in the exploration of one of its most precious resources, oil.[20] In 1986, the former Marxist government of Nicaragua was hosting about 60 MNCs, which contributed about 13 percent to its GNP.[21]

Much of the conflict between MNCs and nation-states seems to be political. The sheer size of MNCs is indicative of their power. For example, data show that the sales of General Motors and Exxon are greater

CH. 17/CONFLICTS BETWEEN HOST AND HOME COUNTRIES

than the GNPs of Switzerland and Saudi Arabia.[22] As a result, these corporations can negotiate business contracts that may have a greater impact on the negotiating countries than many treaties would have.

There is considerable concern that MNCs can be used as a means by which home countries could impose their political wills on host countries. For example, the U.S. government has forbidden the affiliates of U.S. MNCs from selling to certain communist nations. This goes against the laws of France and Canada, which require that the sales be made. Enforcement of this law could thus be considered an intrusion by the United States into the sovereignty of France and Canada. A more IBM and GM, under pressure at home, have reluctantly pulled out of this country because of its past racial policies.[23] Some observers doubt that such a political move is significant in changing the South African racial policies. So far, the move has resulted in economic hardship on many South Africans, recent example is the case of South Africa. The foreign affiliates of some of the U.S. MNCs, such as who have had to face the loss of jobs and fringe benefits that were associated with the operations of these companies.[24]

As the above example indicates, the curtailment of MNCs' operations does not seem to resolve political problems. A useful means for reaching agreements might be a forum for discussing controversial issues that have given rise to conflicting views between parties involved in international business.

SUMMARY

1. MNCs have been criticized by host countries for many reasons.
2. An MNC must satisfy different groups. These groups include employees, customers, stockholders, and the governments of the home and host countries. Because the objectives of these different groups are not necessarily compatible with each other, conflicts among these groups involved in international business are bound to arise.
3. The pursuit of the profit maximization goal leads an MNC (a) to choose that mode of operation that best suits its objective, (b) to improve efficiency by allocating its resources within the corporate family, and (c) to retain as much of its profit as possible.
4. Economically speaking, there are few conflicts between the goals of MNCs and the objectives of home countries. Conflicts do arise, however, if an MNC closes its factory at home and invests money abroad, leading to higher unemployment at home.
5. The conflicts between the MNC and its home country can also stem from noneconomic goals that are set by the government in the home country. Conflicts may arise over exports and over the licensing and production of certain products in certain host countries. Conflicts may also arise over environmental issues.
6. The objectives of a host country in allowing MNCs to operate within its borders can be divided into economic goals and noneconomic goals.
7. The economic goals of a host country in receiving MNC investment are: (a) to achieve economic growth, (b) to achieve better distribution and allocation of resources, and (c) to improve the balance of payments of the host nation.
8. The main noneconomic goal of a host country is independence. Other noneconomic goals are the maintenance of a social, political, and cultural atmosphere that is free from friction.
9. TDF refers to the flow of electronically transmitted information across national boundaries. TDF is an economic resource and, as such, is a marketable, transferable, and exportable commodity. The legislation regarding TDF may be considered as a form of nontariff trade barrier. The effect of this trade barrier may be viewed from two perspectives: international and domestic.
10. The factors that determine the intensity of reactions of a host country to an MNC are (a) the perceived degree of foreign domination and control and (b) the extent to which the activities of MNCs are subsidized by the government of the host country.

11. Some of the major policies that can be adopted by host countries to enjoy FDI without yielding to complete foreign ownership and control are requiring joint venture arrangements, controlling entries and takeovers, excluding foreigners from specific activities, controlling the local content and local employment, export requirements, controlling the local capital market, debt equity requirements, taking the foreign investment package apart, requiring disinvestment, and controlling remittances, rates and fees.
12. A joint venture arrangement calls for a partnership of an MNC with either private entrepreneurs or the government of a host country.
13. Controlling market entries and takeovers of foreign firms is achieved by requiring these firms to have approval for a new investment venture or for the takeover of an existing firm. In most countries the purchase of an existing firm is not allowed.
14. Excluding foreigners from certain business activities is usually achieved by prohibiting their engagement in banking, insurance, public utilities, communications and the media, and in the exploitation of certain natural resources.
15. To control the local content of products and local employment, host countries can require foreign firms to continually increase the amount of the locally produced content of their products. Additionally, they can require that a certain percentage of the foreign firm's employees be citizens of the host country.
16. According to the policy of export requirement, the approval of a potential investment project by an MNC is contingent upon its contribution to the host country's exports.
17. The policy of controlling the local capital market calls for the exclusion of foreigners from the host country's local capital market.
18. The control of debt equity by a host government provides guidelines on the debt equity ratio of the potential investment project by the MNC in the host country.
19. "Taking the foreign investment package apart" means that a host country buys the needed technology, management, and capital in separate business deals, rather than acquiring all these ingredients in one package in the form of an MNC investment.
20. A policy of disinvestment calls upon the investing MNC to disinvest over a period of time. This is achieved by transferring the corporation's ownership to the host country at a specified time for a predetermined price.
21. The policies of controlling remittances, rates, and fees are used by host countries to improve their balance of payments position, to fulfill national domestic policies, and to prevent MNCs from reaping excess profits.
22. Other policies used by host countries in securing some of the benefits of MNCs investment are requiring foreign firms to engage in labor training, requiring certain key positions to be held by nationals of the host countries, prohibiting foreign firms from engaging in technologically stagnant industries, and demanding that foreign firms engage in research and development in the host countries.

QUESTIONS

1. In order to dampen the effect of foreign ownership and control, some host developing countries have forced MNCs to share their ownership with the host country nationals. Such policies have reduced the amount of capital inflow that MNCs can transfer to the host countries. Given the scarcity of capital in developing countries, why do you think that they continue to press for joint foreign-local ownership?
2. Some countries prohibit the purchase of an existing firm by an MNC, requiring a foreign investment project to start from scratch. What theoretical justification is given for such a prohibition? Explain. Does this theoretical justification hold true in practice? Explain.
3. Given the conflicts between MNCs and home and host countries, who do you think is correct-MNCs,

CH. 17/CONFLICTS BETWEEN HOST AND HOME COUNTRIES

home countries, or host countries? Explain. What is one possible way of alleviating the conflicts? Explain.

4. Suppose you are responsible for attracting foreign direct investment to your country. Which incentives do you use to attract FDI to your country, and why? How do you deal with the possible resistance to FDI in your country? Under what conditions do you prevent foreign firms from acquiring domestic firms in your country?

5. Choose a developed country and a developing country and undertake a research project to determine the following:
   a. The restrictions that are imposed by the developing country and the developed country governments on foreign ownership.
   b. The incentives offered to attract FDI by the developing country and the developed country.
   c. Compare your chosen developing country and developed country. Which one seems to be pro-foreign investment, and why?

6. Some host countries have objected to the presence of MNCs inside their borders on the grounds that MNCs impinge upon their national independence. What factors have contributed to the existence of such an attitude? Explain.

7. Given the presence of hostility on the part of some developing countries toward the United States, do you think that the U.S. government should take any action against developing countries that expropriate the investments of the U.S. MNCs? Discuss.

PROBLEMS

1. International business has a long history that dates back to ancient times. Why has so much attention been directed to this subject in recent years?

2. Explain the changing pattern of the United States' overall international business position in the last two decades. In your answer include a discussion of the growth of FDI in the European countries and Japan. What do you think the patterns of FDI will look like in the future?

3. To maintain its competitive position in the world market and protect jobs, the U.S. government should ban the transfer of U.S. technology to any other country.
   Do you agree with this statement? Discuss.

4. To alleviate some of the problems raised in the international transfer of technology, it is believed that a code of conduct is needed to govern such transfers. Whose rights do you think should be incorporated into such a code? What do you think the major objectives of such a code should be?

5. You are the manager of an MNC that is planning to install a new plant in India (a labor-abundant country) to manufacture prefabricated housing units. You have been advised by the production manager that the production process can range from a very labor-intensive to a very capital-intensive technology. How do you choose the correct technology? Why is your choice the correct one? Would your answer to these questions change if the plant were to be built in an advanced country, such as Canada? What would happen if you were dealing with a different type of industry?

6. As the manager of an MNC that enjoys a technological edge in the domestic market, what factors would you consider in selecting your method for expansion into the international market?

7. Compare and contrast management contracts and turnkey arrangements. Can these two be combined? How? Give examples.

NOTES

1. Thomas W. Allen, "Industrial Development Strategies and Foreign Investment Policies of Southern Asia and South Pacific Developing Countries," in R. Hal Mason, ed., *International Business in the Pacific Basin* (Lexington, Mass.: Lexington Books, D.C. Heath, 1978), pp. 51-92.
2. California Newsreel, *Controlling Interest: The World of Multinational Corporation* (San Francisco: California Newsreel, 1978), video tape.
3. "U.S. Efforts to Deter Foreign Investor Vie with Need for Capital," *The Wall Street Journal* 5 August 1987, p.1.
4. Ibid.
5. Ibid., pp. 1, 13.
6. "AT & T Finding Success in Europe Elusive, So It Tries Local Partners New Strategies, *The Wall Street Journal*, 19 December 1985, p. 33.
7. "IBM Shuts Down Operations in India," *The New York Times*, 2 June 1978, p. D5; "India Demands "Know-How' and 60% Share of Coca-Cola Operation," *The New York Times*, 9 August 1977, p. 45.
8. "Venture with Boeing Is Likely to Give Japan Big Boost in Aerospace," *The Wall Street Journal*, 14 January 1986, p. 22.
9. Ibid.
10. "Capitalists Wary of Moscow's Hard Sell to Invest in Joint-Venture Enterprises," *The Wall Street Journal*, 6 April 1987, p. 25; Joint Ventures in China Get Clobbered By Beijing's Draconian Credit Squeeze," *The Wall Street Journal*, 29 March 1989, p. A 10.
11. "Progress in Work: Joint Ventures Raise Hungry's Hope for Future," *The Wall Street Journal* 5 April 1990, p. A 14. "Space Race Becomes a Joint Venture," *The Wall Street Journal*, 11 November, 1992, p. A 10; "The Pioneers A Small Joint Venture is Leading the Way in Getting Russian Oil,' *The Wall Street Journal*, 29 , January 92, p. 1.
12. "Spain's New Openness to Foreign Investment Is a Boon to Consumers," *The Wall Street Journal*, 29 July 1987, p.1.
13. "Foreign Ownership and Structure of Canadian Industry," *Report of the Task Force on the Structure of Canadian* (Oawa: Queen's Printer, 1968), p. 389.
14. "China Sets Equity Requirement for Its Partners in Joint Ventures," *The Wall Street Journal*, 19 December 1985, p. 33.
15. "Weak in Technology, South Korea Seeks Help from Overseas," *The Wall Street Journal*, 7 January 1986, p. 1.
16. Ibid., pp. 1, 14.
17. "Chrysler Corp. to Enter Chinese Market with Major Sale of Engine Equipment," *The Wall Street Journal*, 21 July 1987, p. 12.
18. Parviz Asheghian, "Joint Venture Firms and Labour Training in Iran," *Management Research News*, no. 3 (1983):16-19.
19. Parviz Asheghian, "The R & D Activities of Foreign Firms in a Less Developed Country: An Iranian Case Study," *Journal of Business and Economic Perspectives* (Spring 1984):19-28.
20. "China to Give Foreign Companies Better Terms in Oil Exploration," *The Wall Street Journal*, 3 December 1985, p. 34.
21. "Multinational Corporations Continue to Be Crucial to Nicaraguan Economy," *The Wall Street Journal*, 14 November 1986, p. 34.
22. John Heim, "The Top 100 Economies," *Across the Board* (May 1980), pp. 8-11. This study uses data for 1978.
23. "GM, IBM, and Others Departing South Africa Are Faulted for Plans to Continue Sales There," *The Wall Street Journal*, 24 October 1986.
24. "South Africans Face Pain in Life Without U.S. Firms," *The Wall Street Journal*, 24 October 1986, p. 24; "U.S. Exodus Touches Many South Africans," *The Wall Street Journal*, 6 November 1986, p. 36.

SUGGESTED READINGS

Agmon, Tamir, and Seev Hirsch. "Multinational Corporations and the Developing Economies: Potential Gains in a World of Imperfect Market and Uncertainty." *Oxford Bulletin of Economics and Statistics*, 41 (November 1979):333-344.

Asheghian, Parviz. "Comparative Efficiencies of Foreign Firms and Local Firms in Iran. *Journal of International Business Studies*, 13 (Winter 1982):113-120.

_____."Joint Venture Firms and Labour Training in Iran." Management Research 3 (1983):16-19.

_____, and William G. Foote. "X-Inefficiencies and Interfirm Comparison of U.S. and Canadian Manufacturing Firms in Canada." *Quarterly Journal of Business and Economics*, 24 (Autumn 1985): 3-12; the abstract is printed in the *Journal of Economic Literature*, 24 (June 1986), p. 1085.

_____, and William G. Foote. "The Productivities of U.S. Multinationals in the Industrial Sector of the Canadian Economy." *Eastern Economic Journal*, 11 (April/June 1983):123-133.

_____, and William G. Foote. "Capital Efficiency, Capital Intensity and Debt-Equity: A Comparison of U.S.-Owned and Canadian-Owned Firms in Canada." *Midwestern Journal of Business and Economics*, 2 (Fall 1986):39-48.Banai Moshe and William D. Reisal. "Enterprise Manager's Loyalty to the MNC: Myth or Reality? An Exploratory Study." *Journal of International Business Study*, (Second Quarter 1993): 233-248.

Behrman, Jack N. *National Interests and the Multinational Enterprise: Tensions Among the NorthAtlantic Countries*. Englewood Cliffs, N.J.: Prentice-Hall, 1970.

_____, and Robert E. Grosse. *International Business and Governments*. Columbia, S.C.: University of South Carolina Press, 1990.

Bergstan, C. F., and T. Moran. *American Multinationals and American Interests*. Washington, D.C.:Brookings Institution, 1978.

Brash, D. T. *American Investment in Austrian Industry*.Cambridge, Mass.: Ballinger, 1976.

Buss, Martin D. J. "Legislative Threat to Transborder Data Flow." *Harvard Business Review*, 62 (May/June 1984):111-118.

Cassers-Gomes Benjamin. "Firm Ownership Preferences and Host Government Restrictions: AnIntegrated Approach." *Journal of International Business Studies*, (First Quarter 1990) 1-22..

Casson, Mark. *Alternatives to the Multinational Enterprise*. London: Macmillan, 1979.

Dunning, John H. *American Investment in British Manufacturing Industry*. London: Allen & Unwin, 1958.

_____. "Multinational Enterprises and Nation States." In A. Kapoor and Philip D. Grulb, eds. *The Multinational Enterprise in Transition*. Princeton, N.J.: Darwin Press, 1972, Chap. 28.

Forsyth, David J. C. U.S. *Investment in Scotland*. New York: Praeger, 1972.

Globerman, Stephen. "Technological Diffusion in the Canadian Tool and Die Industry." *Review of Economic Statistics*, 57 (November 1975):428-434.

_____. "Foreign Direct Investment and Spillover Efficiency Benefits in Canadian Manufacturing Industries." *Canadian Journal of Economics*, 12 (February 1979): 42-56.

Johnson, Harry G. "The Efficiency and Welfare Implications of the International Corporation." In Charles P. Kindleberger, ed. *The International Corporation*. Cambridge, Mass.: Massachusetts Institute of Technology Press, 1970.

Kindleberger, Charles P. *American Business Abroad*. New Haven, Conn.: Yale University Press, 1969.

Garg, Arun Kumar. *Multinational Corporations in India: Export Promises*. Mearut, India: Friends Publications, 1992.

Gedicks, Al. *The New Resource Wars: Native and Environmental Struggles Against Multinational Corporations*. Boston: South End Press, 1993.

Lafalce, John J. "TDF Barriers to Service Trade." *International Data Report*, 8, no. 4 (1985): 190-193.

Lall, Sanjaya. "Performance of Transnational Corporations in Less Developed Countries." *Journal of International Business Studies*, (Spring 1983): 13-33.

Langlois, Catherine C. and Bodo B. Schlegelmilch. "Do Corporate Codes of Ethics Reflect National Character? Evidence from Europe and the United States." *Journal of International Business Studies*, (Fourth Quarter 1990): 519-539.

Mansfield, Edwin, J. Teece, and S. Wagner. "Overseas Research and Development by U.S.-Based Firms." *Review of Economics and Statistics*, 46 (May 1979):187-196.

Organization for Economic Cooperation and Development. *Trade, Investment, and Technology in the 1990s*. Paris:

OECD, 1991.

Rearden, John J. *America and Multinational Corporation: the History of a Troubled Partnership.* Westport, Conn.: Praeger, 1992.

Rugman, Alan M. *Multinationals in Canada: Theory, Performance and Economic Impact.* Boston: Martinus Nijhoff, 1980.

Safarian, A. E. *The Performance of Foreign Owned Firms in Canada.* Washington, D.C.: Canadian-American Committee, National Planning Association, 1969.

_____. *Storm over the Multinationals.* Cambridge, Mass.: Harvard University Press, 1977.

Sethi, S. Prakash. *Multinational Corporations and the Impact of Public Advocacy on Corporate Strategy: Nestle and Infant Formula Controversy.* Boston: Kluwer Academic, 1994.

Streeten, Paul. "Costs and Benefits of Multinational Enterprises in Less Developed Countries." In John H. Dunning, ed. *The Multinational Enterprise.* London: Allen & Unwin, 1971, Chap. 9.

Twomey, Michael J. *Multinational Corporations and the North American Free Trade Agreement.* Westport, Conn.: 1993.

Tsanacas, Demetri. "The Transborder Data Flow in the New World Information Order: Privacy or Control." *Review of Social Economy,* 43 (December 1985): 357-370.

United Nations. *Transnational Corporations in World Development: Trends and Prospects.* New York: United Nations, 1988. Overview and Part 1.

Vaistos, Constantine V. "Income Distribution and Welfare Considerations. In John H. Dunning, ed. *Economic Analysis and the Multinational Enterprise.* New York: Praeger, 1974, Chap. 12.

Vernon, Raymond. *Sovereignty at Bay: The Multinational Spread of U.S. Enterprise.* New York: Basic Books, 1971

CHAPTER 18

FOREIGN AID

Besides foreign direct investment, portfolio investment, and exports, another major source of foreign exchange earnings for developing nations is foreign aid. The purpose of this chapter is to provide us with a broad understanding of the issues that are involved in foreign aid. First, we study the history of foreign aid. Second, we elaborate on the two major types of foreign aid. Third, we discuss measurement problems in calculating development assistance. Fourth, we present the foreign aid incentives of the donor nations. Fifth, we explain the foreign aid incentives of the receiving nations. Sixth, we talk about controversies surrounding foreign aid. Finally, we look at the future and conclude the chapter.

THE HISTORY OF FOREIGN AID

The history of foreign aid shows that the objectives and the patterns of foreign aid have gone through a continuous transformation since the end of World War II. Post-war foreign aid was primarily aimed at nations that were devastated by the war. The Marshall Plan, a program of dollar grants from the United States to European countries, was initiated in 1948. This plan channeled aid to Western Europe on a large scale. The objective of the plan was to advance economic recovery while maintaining social stability and democracy. During the Marshall Plan years of 1949-52, the United States granted $18.6 billion in foreign aid. This amounted to 1.5 percent of the U.S. GNP in those years which is by far larger than the percentage of the U.S. GNP that is granted by the United States as foreign aid to other nations today.

To help developing nations acquire technical know-how, in 1949 President Truman introduced his "Point Four" program. This program was first described as the fourth point in the 1949 inaugural address of President Truman, who stated:

> Fourth, we must embark on a bold new program for making the benefit of our scientific advances and industrial process available for improvement and growth of underdeveloped areas...I believe that we should make available to peace-loving people the benefits of our store of technical knowledge in order to help them realize their aspirations for a better life...We invite other countries to pool their technical resources in this...world-wide efforts for the achievement of peace, plenty, and freedom.[1]

At that time much was expected from a simple transfer of technological know-how from advanced nations to developing countries. Such an attitude was especially echoed in the following statement that was made by then U.S. Secretary of State, Webb:

It is important to us and to the rest of the world that people in these areas realize that, through perseverance, hard work, and a little assistance, they can develop the means of taking care of their material needs and at the same time can preserve and strengthen their individual freedoms.[2]

Given the attitude of advanced nations during the early 1960s, the United States and other developed nations provided relatively little foreign aid to developing nations. What was offered generally came in the form of technical assistance. At the time, the prevailing view was that the income gap between rich and poor countries would close over time, without much special effort on the part of advanced nations. Additionally, many of today's developed nations were still way behind the United States. As a result, the concern was not focused exclusively on the developing nations.

In his Inaugural Address, President Kennedy emphasized the moral commitment to assist less fortunate people, by making the following statement:

To those peoples in the Huts and villages of half the globe struggling to break the bonds of mass misery, we pledge our best efforts to help them to help themselves, for whatever period is required—not because the Communists may be doing it, not because we seek their votes, but because it is right. If a free society cannot help the many who are poor, it cannot save the few who are rich.[3]

Following this statement, in the early 1960s, under Kennedy's administration, the resources devoted by the United States to help developing nations rose significantly. Accordingly, U.S. foreign economic assistance, measured in 1996 dollars, rose from $13 billion in 1958 to $22 billion in 1962.

Throughout the 1960s the United States remained the major contributor of official development assistance. Not only did this country provide direct assistance to developing nations, but it also coordinated bilateral assistance from other nations by engaging in the following activities:

1. In 1961, the Development Assistant Committee (DAC) was established as the primary mechanism for coordinating aid among the Organization for Economic Cooperation and Development (OECD).
2. The United States led the way in providing development assistance and non concessional development finance through the multilateral development banks.
3. The IDA was organized in 1960 to provide concessional financing to the poorest countries.
4. The first two regional development banks, the Asian Development Bank and the Inter-American Development Bank, began operation in the 1960s, with the United States as a founding member of both.

By the early 1960s, as U.S. involvement in foreign aid intensified, the intellectual focus of development assistance changed. With the passage of time the bilateral and multilateral technical assistance failed to produce the expected results in developing nations. However, the large-scale capital assistance under the Marshall plan led to significant increases in productivity in Europe. As a result, the emphasis shifted for a while from technical assistance to industrialization and massive transfer of capital. It was assumed that a shortage of investment resources was behind this lack of growth. Long term growth models that were developed in the 1950s postulated a direct relationship between a nation's investment level and growth of its GDP. These models provided theoretical justification for assuming that a nation's rapid growth hinges upon its ability to generate sufficient resources to fund high investment requirements. The role of aid was to ameliorate bottlenecks to growth, by closing the gap between the desired level of investment and the saving and private foreign capital available to finance. The notion that resource transfer was an important determinant of growth was in accord with the U.S. successful experience with the Marshall plan.

In the 1970s, the focus of assistance shifted once again and concentrated on the direct reduction of poverty. Although fast economic growth was expected to eradicate poverty over the long term, it was believed that poverty could in fact get worse in the beginning stages of development. As a result, in the allocation of foreign aid, the projects directly designed to meet basic needs of the poorest populations in developing countries were given the first priority. These projects were mainly focused on measures aimed at population control, health, education, and rural development.

In the early 1970s, the growth rates of developing countries began to diverge widely. During that time the Asian and Latin American nations were generally growing steadily and many African nations were beginning to stagnate. The bottlenecks that were inhibiting development not only included investment but also encompassed the following factors:

1. How investment was used.
2. The environment in which the investment was made.

During this period the domain of development broadened to encompass the necessity to develop agriculture, exports, and human resources, as well as industry and infrastructure.

In the 1980s, it became clear that there is no simple causal relationship between the quantity of assistance, rate of economic growth, and changes in poverty. As a result, the policy focus changed once again, underlying the impact of a nation's domestic economic and social policies on development and growth. Given this new focus, the quantity of aid, which had been the centerpiece of the earliest models, came to be viewed as just one of many elements affecting development. The effectiveness of aid in enhancing a nation's growth was considered to depend on the existence of sound domestic policies in that nation. The concerns about poverty also focused on the policy environment. Growth did not necessarily cause poverty to worsen; in fact, the East Asian experience showed that growth was the most effective antidote to poverty and that egalitarian policies could facilitate growth.

This idea led to an increased emphasis on conditionality. Accordingly, it was decided that aid would only be granted if a nation agreed to a specific set of reforms, which usually included the following:

1. Fiscal discipline.
2. Open capital and trade flows.
3. Deregulation and reform of public enterprises.
4. The establishment of efficient banking systems.
5. Legal reforms.
6. The liberalization of prices, exchanges rates and interest rates.

In implementing this new strategy, The IMF and the World Bank led the way in negotiating the structural adjustment programs that include these reforms. Such reforms were instituted as a condition for providing funds to developing nations, many of which had been devastated by the debt crises that began in 1982. Several empirical studies during this period reported that these types of reforms were a necessary, although not a sufficient, condition for economic growth.

During the 1970s and 1980s, as other developing nations enhanced their assistance to developing nations, the United States' supremacy as the world's major provider of foreign aid diminished. The diminishing significance of the United States as the major aid donor in the world can be inferred from its shrinking contribution to the total aid in the world during the last five decades. The statistics show that during the 1950s and most of the 1960s the United States accounted for over half of all official development assistance provided by the market democracies. Following this era, other advanced nations' share of the world debt continued to increase, reaching the levels of 55 percent in 1970, 72 percent in 1980, and 88 percent in 1995.

Today, most of advanced nations have decreased their bilateral assistance, and the resources of multilateral institutions and regional development banks are coming under increased pressure. Following the end of Cold War, the increasing demand for assistance by the transition economies has stretched development resources ever thinner. With the disappearance of a need to fight communism in developing nations, the political support of development assistance has continued to erode in recent years. The statistics show that official development assistance from the 21 DAC members has diminished by about 6 percent in real terms since 1991 to $59 billion, or only 0.27 percent of their aggregate GNP in 1995. As a result, nations without the social, economic, and political bases for development, in Africa and other developing nations, are likely to be left behind as other developing nations enjoy rapid economic growth.

THE MAJOR TYPES OF FOREIGN AID

Foreign aid can be divided into the two categories of public aid and private aid, depending on whether the source of financing is the public sector or the private sector.

Public Aid

Official assistance provided by the public sector of the donor nation in the form of loans or grants is given either directly from one government to another government (*bilateral assistance*) or indirectly through vehicle of an international agency (*multilateral assistance*). Among the main sources of multilateral assistance are:

1. The World Bank, established by a United Nations charter in 1944.
2. The Agency for International Development (AID). This is an American organization that was established in 1961, as the main U.S. foreign aid unit.
3. The Organization for Economic Cooperation and Development (OECD), established in 1961. Although members of this organization are European nations, it also includes the major industrial countries of Australia, Canada, Japan, New Zealand, and the United States. The major objectives of OECD are: (1) to assist its member countries in pursuing policies that promote economic and social welfare and (2) to coordinate and encourage members' assistance to the developing nations.

Private Aid

Unofficial aid is provided by the private organizations of the donor nations. They are referred to as **private voluntary organizations (PVOs)** in the United Sates, **nongovernmental organizations (NGOs)** in Europe, and **voluntary agencies (Volags)** in Asia. They are composed of private foundations and charities, research organizations, religious groups, and federations of nurses, doctors, economists, engineers, and agricultural scientists. These organizations include the Red Cross and Red Crescent, Interaction, World Vision, Misereor (Germany), Mani Tese (Italy), Maisons Gamiliales Rurales (France), The Gga Khan Foundation, and many others. During the 1970-1990 period, funding sponsored by nongovernmental organizations grew from about $1 billion to over $5 billion. Today, it is estimated that nongovernmental organizations affect the lives of some 250 million people in developing nations. Although the highest per capita contribution came from Sweden, Switzerland, Norway, and Germany, approximately 50 percent of this total originated in the United States. The advantages of private aid as opposed to public aid stem from its following characteristics:

1. Because private aid is largely motivated by humanitarian considerations, it is less concerned by political constraints. As a result, most nongovernmental institutions are able to work much more effectively with the indigenous people that they are attempting to help than massive public aid

programs could.
2. The direct involvement of nongovernmental institutions with indigenous people and organizations enables them to circumvent the distrust and skepticism that their help is less sincere, likely to be short lived, or has an ulterior motive.

Given the above two classifications of foreign aid, it should be noted that only public aid is commonly reported in the official statistics. As a result, the official reports on foreign aid usually underestimate the true amount of aid received by a developing nation during a given time period. But even if we set this problem aside, we should note that foreign aid suffers from both a conceptual and measurement problem. For example, preferential tariffs granted by an advanced nation to a developing nation allow the recipient to sell its industrial products in the advanced nation's market at higher prices than otherwise would be feasible. Such implicit aid should be counted as part of foreign aid, however, this is not usually the case.

Economists define foreign aid as any capital flow to developing nations that satisfies the following two characteristics:

1. Its goal must be noncommercial from the standpoint of the donor.
2. It must be categorized by **concessional terms**, that is, the interest rate and the repayment period for borrowed capital should be softer (less rigid) than commercial terms.

But even the above definition may be inadequate, because it implies that military aid, which is usually noncommercial and concessional, should be included in the calculation of foreign aid. However, military aid is often excluded from such a measurement. As a result, in practice, foreign aid comprises all official grants and concessional loans, either in kind or in currency, that are directed at transferring resources from advanced to developing countries in order to aid developing nations to achieve their development or income distribution goals. Although this definition is widely accepted and used, its precision is open to question. This is because it is often difficult to distinguish between developmental grants and loans from those motivated by security or commercial interests.

MEASUREMENT PROBLEMS IN CALCULATING DEVELOPMENT ASSISTANCE

Not only there are conceptual problems associated with the definition of foreign aid, there are also measurement problems in the assessment of actual development assistance flows. More specifically, the measurement of foreign aid suffers from the following general problems:

1. **Underestimating Loans Tied to the Source or to the Project.** Loans can be tied either by source or by project. If a loan is tied to the source, then grants or loans have to be used to buy goods and services from the donor nation. If a loan is tied to the project, then the loan amount must be spent on a specific project, such as steel manufacturing, or power generating plant. In both of these cases, the actual value of the aid to the recipient declines. This happens because the specified source could be a high-priced supplier or the specified project may not be very advantageous to the loan recipient.
2. **Miscalculating Loans Tied to the Importation of Capital-Using Equipment.** If the loan is tied to the importation of capital-using equipment, it may lead to an increase in unemployment in the recipient nation. This happens because the importation of the capital-using equipment displaces worker who otherwise could be employed. The rise in unemployment imposes an additional real cost to the importing nation.

GLOBAL INSIGHTS CASE 18.1

PATTERNS OF U.S. AID TODAY

In 1996, Congress authorized $6.7 billion for foreign assistance spending. That amounts to 0.1 percent of GDP, or a per capita expenditure of $27. Contrary to conventional wisdom, evidence indicates that American public attitudes are sufficiently supportive of foreign assistance to justify a modest increase.

Over 1993-95, 30 percent of U.S. non-military bilateral aid was allocated to Egypt and Israel. Other allocations went to Ethiopia, Haiti, India, Peru, Russia, South Africa, Turkey, and the Ukraine. The share of U.S. aid going to the sub-Saharan African countries has grown in recent years, while the share to Latin America and East and South Asia has diminished. A special initiative to assist the transition to democracy in South Africa allocated over $600 million, to be disbursed over 1995-97. During the 1990s the United States and other donors also developed assistance programs for transition economies. U.S. aid has supported a wide range of projects, including privatization programs in the Czech Republic and Russia; legal reform in Kazakstan, the Kyrgyz Republic, and Russia; public health programs in Russia and the Ukraine; and humanitarian assistance in Bosnia and Herzegovina. A large portion of U.S. aid goes to social infrastructure such as health and education; less than 6 percent of U.S. bilateral development assistance is spent on economic infrastructure—in sharp contrast with Japan, which expends almost one quarter of its aid on the promotion of transport and communications alone. An increasing amount of aid from the United States and other countries is absorbed by crises and humanitarian relief.

In addition to providing bilateral aid, the Administration strongly supports the international financial institutions which provide multilateral aid. In its 1998 budget request, the Administration has asked that funding for multilateral development banks to be restored to fiscal 1990 levels of more than $1.4 billion.

As already noted, in addition to their regular nonconcessional lending the international financial institutions provide concessional financing for the poorest countries that lack access to alternative financing. Funds for these "soft" loans come from contributions by the wealthier countries and income earned from past projects. The World Bank's IDA remains the single most important source of such funding, having approved an annual average of $6 billion in concessional lending over the past 5 years. It is therefore vitally important that the United States deliver in full on its outstanding commitments to the IDA. The IMF's Enhanced Structural Adjustment Facilities (ESAF), established in 1987 to provide concessional financing to low-income countries experiencing balance of payments problems, has been enlarged to $15 billion—roughly double its original size. Thus far, over 40 countries have borrowed from the ESAF; in return for these funds they agree to undertake 3-year structural adjustment programs. Recently the United States, together with the World Bank and the IMF, spearheaded a new initiative to reduce debt burdens for highly indebted low-income countries.

Source: U.S. Government Printing Office, *Economic Report of the President* (Washington DC: U.S. Government Printing Office, 1997), pp. 264-266, Reprinted.

3. **Nominal Versus Foreign Assistance**. Aid flows are usually assessed in terms of nominal value. Given the inflation rate, this causes the nominal value of loans to keep rising over time. However, when loans are deflated for increase in prices, the real value of aid from most donor nations declines substantially over time. For instance, during the 1960-1990 period, the nominal total value of U.S. foreign aid given to other nations raised by 130%, while its real value decreased by about 30%. Thus, when assessing the

value of a loan received by a developing nation, it is important to differentiate between nominal and real value.

THE FOREIGN AID INCENTIVES OF DONOR NATIONS

The major motivating factors that cause an advanced nation to given aid to a developing nation can be classified into two major categories: political incentives, and economic incentives.

Political Incentives

These incentives constitute the most important elements that have given rise to the supply of foreign aid by advanced nations to the developing nations. This is especially true for the United States which has been quite frank in admitting this fact. Following the "Truman Doctrine," after World War II, The United States provided aid to Greece and Turkey in order to neutralize the threats of internal subversion by groups hostile to Americans. U.S. aid to war-torn Europe, cumulating in the Marshal plan, which was basically provided as means of controlling the international dissemination of communism. The "Point Four" program of technical assistance to developing nations, initiated by president Truman, stemmed from political concerns.

During the 1951-1953 period, the U.S. aid program was guided by the so called "Mutual Security Agency" implying that the security consideration was the main motivating factor in providing aid to other nations. In the 1960s, the United States' concern with security in granting of aid was clearly stated in the following sentence, appeared in a pamphlet that was prepared for public distribution by the Agency for International Development (AID):

> The major objective of the U.S. foreign assistance program is to assist other countries that seek to maintain their independence and develop into self-supporting nations. The resulting community of free nations, cooperating on matters of mutual concern, offers the best-long-run prospect for security and peace for the United States.[4]

The history shows that the flow of funds has varied on the basis of the United States' assessment of political conditions as opposed to the real needs of potential recipient nations. This can be detected from the U.S. continuous changes in emphasis in different parts of the world, depending on the political condition. The following list summarizes the shifting pattern of the U.S. aid program over time:

1. During the 1950s and 1960s, the emphasis shifted from South Asia to Southeast Asia to Latin America to the Middle East and back to Southeast Asia.
2. In the late 1970s, attention was directed toward Africa and the Persian Gulf.
3. In the 1980s, the Caribbean and Central America became the center of attention.
4. In the 1990s, the Russian Federation, Bosnia, Ukraine, Asia (especially China), and the Middle East dominated the U.S. attention.

Other major donor countries such as England, France, and Japan have portrayed aid patterns similar to the United States. In other words, these nations have used foreign aid as political means to support those developing countries that they perceive to be "friendly," that is, those nations whose regimes prove to be in their national security interests. It is interesting to note that even socialist aid, which was mainly generated by the former Soviet Union, was inspired by political and strategic considerations.

With the demise of the Soviet Union and the end of the Cold War, one may assume that these political impetuses will eventually dissipate. However, there are signs that may not be the case. During the early

2000s, the granting of aid was still contingent on the recipient nation's willingness to advance free markets, open its economy, and restructure itself according to the donor's democratic and free market ideology.

GLOBAL INSIGHTS CASE 18.2

FOREIGN AID AND U.S. PUBLIC OPINION

Most Americans think the U.S. Government spends far too much on foreign aid, to the neglect of domestic needs. Yet a number of surveys and polls have found that this widespread attitude toward aid is based on false premises. In one survey the median respondent guessed that the United States provides 40 percent of all aid to developing countries; the true figure, according to OECD, is 12 percent. Likewise, most of those surveyed believe that the United States spends a larger percentage of its GDP on aid than other industrial countries, whereas in fact we spend the smallest. Those surveyed estimate that 18 percent of the Federal budget goes to foreign aid; the true figure is well below 1 percent. The median respondent (before being told the actual level of aid) would raise the amount of aid provided to 20 percent of all international aid and 5 percent of the Federal budget. Focus group and polls have found that Americans, in general, retain some sense of moral obligation to help those in need.

Source: U.S. Government Printing Office, *Economic Report of the President* (Washington DC: U.S. Government Printing Office, 1997), 265, Box 7-3, Reprinted.

Economic Incentives

Economically speaking, a donor nation's incentive for giving aid to a developing nation stems from its desire to generate interest revenue and to expand its own export. This is evident from the increasing tendency of donor nations in providing loans instead of outright grants, and tying aid to the exports of donor nations. Today, interest bearing loans constitute over 80 % of all loans, as compared to less than 40% in the earlier period. This has put tremendous pressure on the debt-stricken developing nations who have been facing substantial debt repayment burden.

Such a pressure is further intensified by a 40% increase in these nations' import costs in recent years. The increased import costs have stemmed from the mechanism provided by tied aid, limiting the receiving country's freedom in searching for low-cost and suitable capital and intermediate goods.

The following quotation form a former British minister of overseas development portrays the economic goal of a donor nation with regard to granting aid to a developing nation:

> About two-thirds of our aid is spent on goods and services from Britain...Trade follows aid. We equip a factory overseas and later on we get orders for spare parts and replacements...[Aid] in our long-term interest.[5]

CH. 18/FOREIGN AID

THE FOREIGN AID INCENTIVES OF THE RECEIVING NATIONS

The elements that motivate developing nations to accept aid from advanced nations could be divided into two categories: the major impetuses, and the minor impetuses.

Major impetuses are composed of economic factors that are believed by the developing nations to facilitate their economic development process. Such belief stems from the economic training of development economists who were taught in all university development courses that foreign aid, in currency or kind, is an essential element of economic development because it achieves the following:

1. Alleviates foreign exchange constraints in the developing nations, enabling them to direct their excess productive resources, especially labor, into productive investment, contributing to economic growth.
2. Assists and expedites the process of economic development by leading to additional domestic savings that result from the higher growth rates that it is assumed to generate. It is hoped that eventually the need for aid disappears as domestic resources become adequate to allow for a self-maintaining development process.
3. It provides the developing nation with managerial and technical assistance that they need in their economic development process.

Although there is no disagreement between developing nations and advanced nations regarding the role of aid in the process of economic development, conflict arises over the amount and conditions. Developing nations prefer to receive more aid in terms of outright grants or long-term low-cost loans with minimum contingent requirements. As a result, they do not want to tie their loan to the donor's exports. They also would like to have greater freedom in deciding what policies to use to satisfy long-run economic goals. Unfortunately, however, the evidence shows that the majority of loans that have come in this fashion have proved to be wasteful. The funds provided by such loans have either been wasted in elaborate but unproductive projects (e.g., showcase mosques, oversized airports, and monuments to the ruling family) or have been robbed by dishonest government administrators and their associates.

Minor impetuses can be divided into the political impetus and the moral impetus. Political impetus stems from the desire of both the donor and the receiving nation as a ploy to support the current government in containing opposition and keeping itself in power. Examples include South Vietnam in the 1960s, Iran in the 1970s, and Cental America in the 1980s, whose acceptance of foreign aid was based on political impetus. The problem associated with this kind of loan is that its acceptance undermines the political sovereignty of the recipient nation, by implicitly allowing the donor nation to interfere in its internal affairs.

Moral impetus may either stem from humanitarian obligations of the advanced nation to the developing nation, or it may be based on the belief that the rich nations should compensate the poor nations for past exploitation.

Today, the prevailing views of many proponents of foreign aid in both advanced and developing nations assert that rich countries have a duty to support the economic and social development of the developing nations. Additionally, they believe that such support should not undermine the autonomy of the developing nations in the allocation and utilization of the aid funds.

GLOBAL INSIGHTS CASE 18.3

GAUGING PUBLIC SUPPORT FOR U.S. GOVERNMENT AID

Public perceptions of foreign aid reflect U.S. values and principles. In public opinion polls Americans have always ranked domestic affairs higher than international ones. Even before the September 11 terrorist attacks, the U.S. public named as its top five priorities reducing the threat of international terrorism, stopping international drug trafficking, halting the spread of AIDS around the world, protecting the global environment, and getting Saddam Hussein out of Iraq.

Until the mid-1990s, 65-75 percent of Americans believed that the country was spending too much on foreign aid. But in 2000 several surveys found that only 40-47 percent of Americans still held that view. A study in the early 1990s, after the end of the Cold War, found that Americans were becoming more interested in aid for humanitarian than for security purposes. Whether that has remained true since the September 11 attacks is unknown. But in general, Americans have never strongly supported economic aid to other countries. For example, three surveys conducted by the Chicago Council on Foreign Relations since the end of the Cold War have found that the U.S. public is divided on whether to give economic aid to other countries. In the most recent survey, in line with the previous two, only 13 percent of Americans favored increasing federal spending on foreign economic aid-while 48 percent favored reducing it.

Americans strongly endorse supporting the United Nations, ending world hunger, and alleviating human pain and suffering worldwide. Yet they historically have had doubts about the effectiveness of foreign aid, including concerns about corrupt foreign governments. These misgivings may be related to general distrust of the federal government and international organizations, which consistently rank near the bottom in U.S. surveys on confidence in institutions. Much as they advocate self-reliance in welfare programs, Americans want foreign aid that shows results in countries with honest and compassionate governments.

Source: USAID, *Foreign Aid in the National Interest,* http://www.usaid.gov/fani/ch06/objectives.htm , Chapter 6, Box 6.1, p. 2, Reprinted

CONTROVERSIES SURROUNDING FOREIGN AID

Like foreign direct investment and multinational corporations, foreign aid constitutes is a very controversial issue between advanced and developing nations. We will study controversies surrounding MNCs in Chapter 14. The purpose of this section is to elaborate on the views of proponents and opponents of foreign aid.

Proponents of foreign aid argue that the aid has in fact promoted economic growth in developing nations by supplementing their savings, providing them with the needed foreign exchange and technical assistance.[6]

Opponents of foreign aid have presented the following arguments:

1. **Tied Aid.** One major problems with aid is that bilateral aid is often tied aid, requiring the recipient to spend the funds received on commodities produced in the donor nation. The problem with this approach, it is argued, is that the donor may not be the cheapest producer of those commodities.
2. **Mixed Credits.** Closely analogous to tying aid is the practice of awarding of "mixed credits," that is, a credit for the purchase of the advanced country's exports at below market rate of discount and thus

encompassing a subsidy. Opponents argue that this type of credit has led to fierce competition in promotion of advanced-nation exports and has led to a clear bias toward capital intensity and import intensity. Given that competition for sales is the greatest and the possibilities for gain most lucrative in the relatively rich developing nations, mixed credits have shifted the aid from the poorer and more needy to the richer developing nations.

3. **Aid Politicization**. Aid has been used as a political ploy by advanced nations to impose their own will on developing nations. For example, France significantly decreased its aid to the Republic of Guinea when it learned that the Republic would not assent to French policy.

4. **Aid Widens the Income Distribution Gap**. Aid focuses on stimulating the growth of the modern sector, and thus, widens the income distribution between the rich and the poor in the developing nations.

5. **Aid Helps Corrupt Officials and Breeds a Welfare Mentality**. In practice, foreign aid has proved to be a failure, because it has been largely appropriated by corrupt officials and has bred a welfare mentality on the part of recipient countries. Over the last two decades, domestic issues such as government deficits, the balance of payments problem, and unemployment have gained precedence over global politics in advanced nations. Additionally, the taxpayers in advanced nations have become increasingly aware of the fact that the funds allocated to foreign aid usually end up benefitting a small elite group in developing nations who are usually richer than themselves. As a result, they have become increasingly disillusioned with the issue of aid, wanting their officials to concentrate on domestic economic problems, instead of funneling their tax dollars to developing nations.

LOOKING INTO THE FUTURE

Given the disenchantments of both donors and recipients of foreign aid, what are the prospects for the future? It can be argued that unhappiness with the issue of foreign on both sides may breed an atmosphere that is more conducive to a new arrangement which fuses the interests and motivations of donors and recipients. There are signs that movement in such a direction has already begun. This is evident by the growing proportion of development assistance funds that continue to be channeled through agencies such as the World Bank, whose political motives incentives are more narrowly explicated in comparison to those of individual donor nations. It is also evident from the growing number of private organizations who have become active in providing foreign aid to the Third World.

Today, many observers believe that enhancing the opportunities for profitable trade with advanced nations is much more crucial to the growth of developing nations than increasing official assistance. The successful conclusion of the Uruguay Round of negotiations, and the United States decision to channel half of its future funds through PVOs indicates that movement toward such real-development oriented trade and aid policies is gathering momentum. Will this movement continue? Will officials in advanced countries realize the virtue of transferring some of their aid funds to private voluntary organization to capitalize on the latter's growing image? Only time will tell.

SUMMARY

1. The history of foreign aid shows that the objectives and the patterns of foreign aid have gone through a continuous transformation since the end of World War II.
2. Post-war foreign aid was primarily aimed at nations that were devastated by the war.
3. The Marshall Plan, a program of dollar grants from the United States to European countries was initiated in 1948. This plan channeled aid to Western Europe on a large scale. The objective of the plan was to advance economic recovery while maintaining social stability and democracy.

4. To help developing nations acquire technical know-how, in 1949 President Truman introduced his "Point Four" program. This program was first described as the fourth point in the 1949 inaugural address of President Truman.
5. By the early 1960s, as U.S. involvement in foreign aid intensified, the intellectual focus of development assistance changed. With the passage of time the bilateral and multilateral technical assistance failed to produce the expected results in developing nations As a result, the emphasis shifted for a while from technical assistance to industrialization and massive transfer of capital.
6. In the 1970s the focus of assistance shifted once again and concentrated on the direct reduction of poverty. Although fast economic growth was expected to eradicate poverty over the long term, it was believed that poverty could in fact get worse in the beginning stages of development. As a result, in the allocation of foreign aid the projects directly designed to meet basic needs of the poorest populations in developing countries were given the first priority.
7. In the 1980s, it became clear that there is no simple causal relationship between the quantity of assistance, rate of economic growth, and changes in poverty. As a result, the policy focus changed once again, underlying the impact of a nation's domestic economic and social policies on development and growth. The effectiveness of aid in enhancing a nations' growth was considered to depend on the existence of sound domestic policies in developing nations.
8. During the 1970s and 1980s, as other developing nations enhanced their assistance to developing nations, the United States' supremacy as the world's major provider of foreign aid diminished.
9. Today, most advanced nations have decreased their bilateral assistance, and the resources of multilateral institutions and regional development banks are coming under increased pressure.
10. Foreign aid can be divided into the two categories of public aid and private aid, depending on whether the source of financing is the public sector or the private sector.
11. Public aid refers to the official assistance provided by the public sector of the donor in the form of loans or grants either directly from one government to another government (*bilateral assistance*) or indirectly through the vehicle of an international agency (*multilateral assistance*). Among the main sources of multilateral assistance are: (a) The World Bank, (b) The Agency for International Development (AID), and (c) The Organization for Economic Development and Cooperation (OECD).
12. Private aid refers to the unofficial aid that is provided by the private organizations of the donor nations. They are referred to as **private voluntary organizations (PVOs)** in the United Sates, **nongovernmental organizations (NGOs)** in Europe, and **voluntary agencies (Volags)** in Asia.
13. The advantages of private aid as opposed to public aid stems from its following characteristics: (a) because private aid is largely motivated by humanitarian considerations, it is less concerned by political constraints; and (b) the direct involvement of nongovernmental institutions with indigenous people and organizations enables them to circumvent the distrust and skepticism that their help is less sincere, likely to be short lived, or has an ulterior motive.
14. Only public aid is commonly reported in the official statistics. As a result, the official reports of foreign aid usually underestimate the true amount of aid received by a developing nation during a given time period.
15. The measurement of foreign aid suffers from the following general problems: (a) underestimating loans tied to the source or to the project, (b) miscalculating loans tied to the importation of capital-using equipment, and (c) nominal versus foreign assistance.
16. The major motivating factors that cause an advanced nation to given aid to a developing nation can be classified into two major categories: political incentives and economic incentives.
17. Political incentives constitute the most important elements that have given rise to the supply of foreign aid by advanced nations to the developing nations.
18. History shows that the flow of funds has varied on the basis of the United States' assessment of political

CH. 18/FOREIGN AID

conditions as opposed to the real needs of potential recipient nations.

19. During the early 2000s, the granting of aid was still contingent on the recipient nation's willingness to advance free markets, open its economy, and restructure itself according to the donor's democratic and free market ideology.
20. Economically speaking, a donor nation's incentive for giving aid to a developing nation stems from its desire to generate interest revenue, and to expand its own export.
21. The elements that motivate developing nations to accept aid from an advanced nations could be divided into two categories: the major impetuses and the minor impetuses. Major impetuses are composed of economic factors that are believed by the developing nations to facilitate their economic development process. Minor impetuses can be divided into the political impetus and moral impetus. Political impetus stems from the desire of both the donor and the receiving nation as a ploy to support the current government in containing opposition and keeping itself in power. Moral impetus may either stem from humanitarian obligations of the advanced nation to the developing nation, or it may be based on the belief that the rich nations should compensate the poor nations for past exploitation.
22. Proponents of foreign aid, consisting of economists traditionalists, argue that the aid has in fact promoted economic growth in developing nations by supplementing their savings, providing them with the needed foreign exchange and technical assistance.
23. Opponents of foreign aid have presented the following arguments: (a) tied aid, and (b) mixed credits.
24. Today, many observers believe that enhancing the opportunities for profitable trade with advanced nations is much more crucial to the growth of developing nations than increasing official assistance.

QUESTIONS

1. Elaborate on the changing patterns and objectives of foreign aid from the end of World War II to present.
2. Elaborate on the Marshall Plan and the Point Four program by answering the following questions:
    a. When did these plans come into existence?
    b. What are the main objectives of these plans?
    c. How do these plans differ from each other?
3. Elaborate on the impact of foreign aid on developing nations by answering the following questions:
    a. How significant is foreign aid to developing nations as compared to other sources of foreign exchange income?
    b. What are different forms of official development assistance?
    c. Compare bilateral and multilateral foreign aid. Explain which one is more desirable and why.
4. What are measurement problems in calculating development assistance? Explain.
5. What are the major motivating factors that cause an advanced nation to give aid to a developing nation? Explain.
6. What are the elements that motivate a developing nation to accept aid from an advanced nation? Explain.
7. Elaborate on tied aid by answering the following questions:
    a. What is meant by tied aid?
    b. What is one of the major problems associated with tied aid?
    c. How does tied aid differ from mixed credits?
8. Distinguish between public aid and private aid and answer the following questions:
    a. Which one of these two types of aid is more desirable from the viewpoint of a developing nation that is receiving such a loan?
    b. Why do official reports on foreign aid commonly underestimate the true amount of aid received by a developing nation?

9. Given the disenchantments of both donors and recipients of foreign aid, elaborate on the prospects for the future by answering the following questions:
   a. Under what conditions do you think that a developing nation should accept foreign aid in the future?
   b. Given your answer to Part (a), assuming that such conditions stated could not be met, do you think that the developing nation should accept whatever it can receive? Explain.

NOTES

1. Paul Samuelson, *Economics*, 3rd ed. (New York: McGraw-Hill, 1973), p. 709
2. Charles Wolf, Jr., *Foreign Aid: Theory and Practice in Southern Asia* (Princeton, 1960), p. 59.
3. Benjamin Higgins, *Economic Development: Problems, Principles, and Policies*, Revised ed. (New York: W.W. Norton, 1968), p.576.
4. U.S. Agency for International Development, *Principles of Foreign Economic Assistance*, Rev. ed. (Washington, D.C., September 1965), p.1.
5. Earl Grinstead, *Overseas Development* (November 1968); p.9.
6. See, for example, Hollis B. Chenry and Nicholas G. Carter, "Foreign Assistance: Objectives and Consequences," *American Economic Review* 63 (1973): 459-468.

SUGGESTED READINGS

Abott, George C. "Two Concepts of Foreign Aid." *World Development* 1 (September 1973).
Baur, Peter T. "Foreign Aid: What is at Stake?" *Public Interest*. Summer 1982.
_____. "Foreign Aid: Rewarding Impoverishment?" *Swiss Review of World Affairs*. October 1985.
_____, and B. Jamey. "The Political Economy of Foreign Aid." *Lloyds Bank Review*. October 1981.
Bhagwati, Jagsih, N. and Richard S. Eckaus, eds. *Foreign Aid*. Harmondswoth, England: Penguin, 1970.
Cassen, Robert et al. *Does Aid Work?* New York: Oxford University Press, 1980.
_____. "The Contribution of Foreign Aid to Development and the Role of the Private Sector." *Development* 1 (1992): 7-15.
Chenery, Hollis B. and Alan M. Strout. "Foreign Assistance and Economic Development." American Economic Review 56 (September 1966): 679-733.
Commision, Brandt. *North South: A Program for Survival*. Cambridge, Mass.: MIT Press, 1980.
Hunter, Shireen. *OPEC and the Third World: The Politics of Aid*. Bloomington, Ind., 1984.
Iqbal, Zubair. "Arab Concessional Assistance, 1975-81." *Finance and Development*. 20, no. 2 (1983): 31-33.
Krueger, Ann O. "Aid in the Development Process." *World Bank Research Observer* 1 (January 1986): 57-78.
Leipziger, Danny P. "The Concessionality of Foreign Assistance." *Finance and Development* 21, no.1 (1984): 44-46.
Maizels, Alfred and Machiko Nissanke. "Motivations for Aid to Developing Countries. *World Development*. 12, no. 9 (September 1984): 879-900.
Mosely, Paul. *Overseas Aid: The Challenge and the Opportunity*. Oxford, 1987.
_____, Paul, Jane Harrington, and John Toye. *Aid and Power: The World Bank and Policy-Based Lending*. London: Routledge, 1991.
Myrdal, Cunnar. *The Challenge of World Poverty*. New York: Pantheon, 1970, Chaps. 10 and 11.
Riddel, Roger C. *Foreign Aid Reconsidered*. Baltimore: Johns Hopkins University Press,1987.
Rix, Alan. *Japan's Foreign Aid Challenge: Policy Reform and Aid Leadership*. London: Routledge, 1993.
Ruttan, Vernon W. "Why Foreign Economic Assistance." *Economic Development and Cultural Change* 37 (January 1989): 411-424.
Shihata, Ibraihim, F. I. And Naiem A. Sherbiny. "A Review of OPEC Aid Efforts. *Finance and Development*. 23, no. 1 (1986): 17-20.

PART VI

CRITICAL ISSUES FOR THE NEW MILLENNIUM

CHAPTER 19

TRANSITION ECONOMICS

The global economy has changed drastically in recent years, presenting the world with new economic opportunities and intensifying international competition for goods and services. Movement toward market-oriented economic systems and free international trade has exemplified itself in expanded and new free-trade agreements and the collapse of communist power, continuing to change the picture of the world economy.

This chapter has three main purposes. First, to elaborate on the political events that gave rise to economies in transition. To this end, we discuss the Eastern European economic reforms, study the unification of Germany, and elaborate on the demise of the Soviet Union. Second, to discuss transition and economics, a new subject that has attracted the attention of economists in recent years. Third, to elaborate on experience with economic reform and the need for a new theory.

POLITICAL EVENTS GIVING RISE TO ECONOMIES IN TRANSITION

The economic reforms in Eastern European countries, the fall of the Berlin Wall and the reunification of Germany, and the demise of the Soviet Union brought an end to the Cold War. These events, which occurred in such a remarkably short time frame, surprised everyone in the world and opened a new chapter in the global economy. The purpose of this section is to explain these events and elaborate on their global economic impact.

Eastern European Countries Economic Reforms

Following World War II, the Eastern European countries (Bulgaria, Czechoslovakia, the former East Germany, Hungary, Poland, Romania, and Yugoslavia) adopted the command economy that was initiated and practiced by the former Soviet Union. The collapse of Communist power in 1989 brought an end to Soviet domination in this part of the world and laid the foundation for the transformation of Eastern European economies into market-oriented economic systems. For the global economy, as a whole, this transformation is good news, providing the free world with new markets for exports, new sources of raw materials for imports, and new investment opportunities. The economic forces that contributed to the collapse of Soviet power in Eastern Europe are related to inefficiencies that stem from a command economy. With no competition and the absence of a profit-maximization objective, firms in Eastern Europe had little or no incentive to produce efficiently, cut costs, develop new markets, improve quality, or innovate. As a result, by the late 1980s, the income growth of these countries had fallen significantly behind that of advanced market-oriented economies and newly industrial countries (NICs). Countries such as Poland and Hungary found themselves facing huge external debts, the proceeds of which had been used, for the most part, to finance unproductive investments. In their economic planning, they stressed a growth process that demanded significant increases in factor input rather than a surge in productivity. Such a growth process was not feasible, however, due to a decrease in the growth of labor input. This resulted from the virtual halt of labor migration from the agricultural sector to the industrial sector.

The integration of the Eastern European countries into the global market has created new channels for exports and has offered rich commercial opportunities for Western companies. Many manufacturing firms are now being attracted to the emerging Eastern European nations as a low-cost, conceivably high-technology zone on their borders.[1] Most of the impact on world trade volumes will result from the closing standard-of-living gap between Eastern and Western Europe. The overall trade impact of economic reform is expected to be small, accounting for an approximate 2- to 3-percent expansion of global trade. Countries directly affected by such integration are the middle-income countries.* These countries are expected to see some of their exports displaced from the European Union (EU) markets.** Additionally, middle-income countries are not expected to be able to compensate for the lost market by enhancing their exports to Eastern European countries.[2]

Working within the IMF and the World Bank, the United States has been very active in facilitating the transition of the Eastern Europan countries into market economic systems. In the late 1990s there were signs that the economic conditions were improving in Eastern European countries. For example, Poland's economy was booming, inflation was less than 20%. Foreign investors like Citibank referred to Poland as "Eastern Europe's tiger economy." It was even predicted by some observers that "Poland would become the regional headquarters of many companies."[3]

Unification of Germany

One significant event that took place in November 1989 was the fall of the Berlin Wall, which paved the way for German unification. On July 2, 1990, economic union of the two Germanies was achieved. East Germany agreed to scrap its currency and adopt the West German mark. It also adopted West German economic rules and laws, joining the market-oriented economic system.[4] This unification created a Germany with a population of approximately 80 million people and a land mass half the size of Texas.[5]

German unification has economic implications for both Germany and the rest of the world. In the short run, it is expected that eastern Germany will experience hard economic times. West Germany's absorption of the poor and decaying East German economy was estimated to cost $1 trillion in the next decade, a cost financed by West Germany. It was also estimated that it would take about five years for the former East Germany's economic structure to meet the level of its western counterpart. During this period, Germany was expected to experience significant social and economic problems in its eastern section. It was estimated that 70 percent of 8,000 enterprises in the East would face bankruptcy, and 75 to 100 billion West German marks would be spent annually on unemployment relief, social security, wage increases, and reconstruction in the East.

---

*Middle-income countries include some of the Mediterranean countries, the East Asian NICs, and the more industrialized Latin American countries.

**Previously referred to as the European Community (EC), the European Economic Community (ECC), and the European Common Market (ECM). The EU provides an example of a customs union that developed into a common market and eventually evolved into an economic union. The EU was formed in 1958 by Belgium, France, Italy, Luxembourg, West Germany, and the Netherlands. In 1973, Denmark, Ireland, and Great Britain joined; Greece joined in 1981; and Portugal and Spain joined in 1986.

In the long run, Germany's benefits from unification are expected to widen as western investment in eastern industries continues to expand. German economic power, measured by GNP, might increase by one tenth after unification. Given the huge size of a united German market and the inability of German companies to satisfy market demand, the EU and the rest of the world are offered the incredible opportunity of exporting more goods to this vast market.

Before unification, West Germany—one of the six original founders of the EU—provided the biggest share of the EU budget (about 27 percent) and accounted for more than half of the EU's total trade. With the unification of its eastern and western sections, Germany naturally has an even greater impact on the EU. In the short run, Germany's effort to finance the development of its eastern part drains potential funds available for the EU's less developed member states. Additionally, following unification, eastern Germany started to receive $4.8 billion annually in subsidies from the EU budget. Eighty percent of this amount is contributed by western Germany. This will eventually lead to a decrease in Germany's contribution to the EU.

German unification has also made the implementation of the EU's agricultural policy difficult because the abundant agricultural products from eastern Germany have added to the existing surplus of the EU agricultural product market.

In 1991, Germany was expected to remain an economic giant, experiencing healthy economic growth (2.5 percent to 3 percent for the early 1990s) despite growing political problems at home and abroad following unification. From the global standpoint, given the need for rebuilding eastern Germany, the demand for imports was expected to increase well in excess of 10 percent a year.[6] This would benefit Germany's major trading partners: the United States, Japan, Great Britain, the Netherlands, Belgium, Australia, and especially France, which were already doing the most business with West Germany. Other countries benefitting directly from German unity include Italy, Spain, Switzerland, and Korea. However, against this optimistic forecast for Germany, 1992 was marked as the year of German "recession and helplessness."[7] In 1993, Germany experienced a number of problems, such as an escalation in "far-right" disorder, a destabilizing inflow of immigrants, and growing cynicism about Germany's construction plans for eastern Germany.

Another aspect of German unification with global implications is the country's decision to unify its currency. In order to exchange East German currency for West German money on a one-for-one basis, West Germany committed itself to giving large amounts of subsidies to East German citizens and businesses. A concurrent decision was to not raise taxes to pay for these subsidies. To prevent a surge in inflation from the influx of subsidies into Germany's economy, the country decided to support higher interest rates. As we explained earlier in this chapter, this contributed to the currency turmoil in Europe, threatening to kill the Maastricht Treaty that was to be voted on by the French on September 20, 1992. Fortunately for the EU, French voters ratified the treaty by a narrow margin, paving the way for the intensified efforts of EU members to implement that treaty. However, Germany's support of high interest rates ignited yet another crisis in the currency market in the summer of 1993, bringing the European Exchange Rate mechanism (ERM) to the brink of collapse[*]. Once again, under pressure from European allies, Germany's central bank cut its two key lending rates, precipitating a series of interest cuts throughout Europe. Other European central banks followed Germany's lead in cutting interest rates, and the ERM was revived.[8]

The impact of the German reunification on the world economy has been compared to that of the OPEC price increase in 1973 and the "Reaganomics" of the 1980s. These events shocked the world's economy for years to come, significantly affecting international trade and investment flows.

---

[*]A joint floating exchange rate system that was designed by the six original members of the EU in March 1972. Under this system, member nations' currencies were tied closely to each other, but they were allowed to fluctuate against a given currency (the U.S. dollar), rising or falling as a group.

In the mid-1990s, five years following the unification, German taxpayers had spent $575 billion on the former East Germany for development of an infrastructure of 14,000 state-owned companies and the overhauling the late phone system. This has resulted in soaring economic growth, reaching the level of 8.5% in 1994.

The present economic conditions in Germany, is well described by the CIA which states:

Germany possesses the world's third most technologically powerful economy after the US and Japan, but structural market rigidities - including the substantial non-wage costs of hiring new workers - have made unemployment a long-term, not just a cyclical, problem. Germany's aging population, combined with high unemployment, has pushed social security outlays to a level exceeding contributions from workers. The modernization and integration of the eastern German economy remains a costly long-term problem, with annual transfers from western Germany amounting to roughly $70 billion. Growth picked up to 3% in 2000, largely due to recovering global demand; newly passed business and income tax cuts are expected to keep growth strong in 2001. Corporate restructuring and growing capital markets are transforming the German economy to meet the challenges of European economic integration and globalization in general.[9]

It remains to be seen how soon the former East Germany can stand on its own, and whether or not growth in the former East Germany can be sustained.[10]

Demise of the Soviet Union

In the late 1950s, Nikita Khrushchev claimed that Soviet economic output would overtake and surpass that of the United States. He told the United States, "We will bury you." Such statements set the stage for a bitter cold war between the two superpowers. The United States and the Soviet Union fought a political battle that most observers believed would end in a final nuclear war. However, economic and political problems within the Soviet Union created an inefficient, bureaucratic system. This led to shortages of agricultural and industrial products, forcing the nation to continue to expand its imports from Western Europe and, ironically, from the United States, the country Khrushchev was supposed to bury.

The political and economic problems in the former Soviet Union set the stage for the emergence of one of the century's pivotal leaders, Mikhail S. Gorbachev, who came to power in 1985. His reforms, referred to as "perestroika" (restructuring) and "glasnost" (openness), transformed the political and economic structure of the Soviet Union and helped to end the Cold War. However, he became the victim of the very reforms that he initiated. Gorbachev's reforms opened Soviet society to the world and ended the Communist party's seven-decade monopoly on power. He allowed the fall of the Communist regimes in Eastern Europe, introduced multiple-party and multiple-candidate elections, and strengthened the elected legislature. He stopped religious oppression, freed political prisoners, and gave Soviet citizens the freedom to travel and emigrate. In talks with the United States, Gorbachev agreed to drastic reductions in nuclear and conventional arms, thereby strengthening the world's prospect for peace. However, despite his accomplishments in reshaping his country's political and economic systems, he made some mistakes. Many observers believe Gorbachev moved too slowly on economic reforms. As a result, shortages of food, fuel, housing, and consumer goods worsened. In planning and implementing his reforms, Gorbachev did not consult sufficiently with republics, nor did he give them enough autonomy. Finally, he chose his aides unwisely, ending up with colleagues who eventually turned against him. These mistakes not only cost Gorbachev his presidency, but they paved the way for the demise of the Soviet Union and the birth of the new Commonwealth of Independent States (CIS).

Western leaders welcomed the formation of the CIS; U.S. President George Bush referred to the demise of the Soviet Union as "a defining moment in history." He said that U.S. security would be enhanced by offering aid to the region, and added that "If this democratic revolution is defeated, it would plunge us

GLOBAL INSIGHTS CASE 19.1

BILATERAL INVESTMENT TREATIES

For much of the last decade the United States has been actively pursuing the negotiation of bilateral investment treaties with emerging-market countries around the world. The U.S. government places priority on negotiating such treaties with countries undergoing economic reform where it believes the United States can have a significant impact on the adoption of liberal policies on the treatment of FDI. The structure of these treaties has also laid the policy groundwork for broader multicountry initiatives in the OECD (the MAI) and eventually the WTO. The structure of our bilateral investment treaties provides U.S. inventors with the following six basic guarantees:

- Treatment that is as favorable as that received by their competitors—this implies the better of national or most-favored nation treatment.
- Clear limits on the expropriation of investments, and fair compensation when expropriation does occur.
- The right to transfer all funds related to an investment into and out of the country without delay, at the market rate of exchange.
- Limits on the ability of the host government to impose inefficient and trade-distorting performance requirement.
- The right to submit an investment dispute with the host government to international arbitration.
- The right of U.S. investors to engage the top managerial personnel of their choice, regardless of nationality.

In cases where national treatment is the binding standard, the treaty ensures that U.S. inventors are treated in a manner equivalent to domestic inventors; where it is most-favored nation treatment, U.S. inventors are assured treatment no worse than investors from any third country receive. As the table indicates, to date, the United States has successfully negotiated bilateral investment treaties with some countries and is actively engaged in pursuing a multilateral version of the treaty under the auspices of the OECD.

Countries with which the United States

Country and date		Country and date		Country and date		Country and date	
Albania	pending	Croatia	pending	Jordan	pending	Romania	1994
Argentina	1994	Czech Republic	1992	Kazakhstan	1994	Russia	Pending
Armenia	1996	Ecuador	1997	Kyrgyzstan	1994	Senegal	1990
Azerbaijan	pending	Egypt	1992	Latvia	1996	Slovakia	1992
Bangladesh	1989	Estonia	1997	Moldova	1994	Sri Lanka	1993
Belarus	pending	Georgia	1997	Mongolia	1997	Trinidad and Tobago	1996
Bulgaria	1994	Grenada	1989	Morocco	1991	Tunisia	1993
Cameroon	1989	Haiti	pending	Nicaragua	pending	Turkey	1990
Congo (Brazzaville)	1994	Honduras	pending	Panama	1991	Ukraine	1996
Congo (Kinshasa)	1989	Jamaica	1997	Poland	1994	Uzbekistan	Pending

Note: Years are those when the treaty entered into force.
*The MAI stands for Multilateral Agreement on Investment.

Source: U.S. Government Printing Office, *Economic Report of the President* (Washington DC: U.S. Government Printing Office, 1998), 259, Box 7-6. Reprinted.

into a world more dangerous in some respects than the dark years of the Cold War."[11]

The CIS has many obstacles to overcome before becoming a modern market-oriented society. Russia, comprising 51.3 percent of the former Soviet Union's population and 75 percent of the land mass, has especially attracted the attention of the Western world and is being closely watched by Western leaders. Boris Yeltsin, the former Russian leader, faced tremendous economic and political problems that threatened his own survival. Such problems came to a head in the fall of 1993 when hard-line lawmakers took a stand against Yeltsin by encamping inside the Parliament. This standoff ended in violence and led to the dissolution of the Parliament and approval of the final draft of a new Russian constitution (written by Yeltsin) that would augment presidential powers and legally grant citizens the right to own property.[12] Russian voters' approval of the draft on December 12, 1993, gave Yeltsin a significant political victory.[13] Yeltsin was successful in keeping many of the government's free-market programs on course, but the economic challenges facing him were overwhelming. Yeltsin dealt with an economic system marked by a significant drop in production. It was expected that some sectors of the economy would experience as much as a 50 percent decline in their output levels. Yeltsin had to deal with a variety of other problems as well, including inflationary pressures caused by shortages and unemployment that resulted from dismantling the communist system.[14] Added to the economic problems were the political problems of keeping the CIS together and preventing the disintegration of the awesome military structure that were left by the Soviet government.[15] Following a number of health problems, finally Yeltsin stepped down on January 1, 2000. He was replaced by one of his closest allies. It remains to be seen how the new leader of Russia manages numerous problems that are facing his country.

From the outset of independence, it was clear that it would be extremely difficult for the CIS to be transformed to market-oriented systems without economic aid from the West. Realizing this, Western leaders have been quick to pour economic aid to the region, contingent upon market-oriented economic reforms. On April 2, 1992, President Bush and Allied leaders pledged to funnel a combined $24 billion of additional aid to Russia.[16] The aid was given to help Yeltsin implement market-oriented economic reform. The U.S. and European officials made it clear that "any backpedaling on economic reform could jeopardize billions of dollars in planned Western aid."[17] In July 1992, the leaders of the G-7 nations (Great Britain, Canada, France, Germany, Italy, Japan, and the United States) promised to provide debt relief to Russia. They also pledged to extend export credit to Russia, lift their trade barriers, and provide the Russians with more technical assistance.[18]

Following Bill Clinton's presidential victory over George Bush, Russia continued to receive billions of dollars in grants, credits, and special funds to sustain its demolished economy. However, the outflow of funds was just as massive as the inflow. An estimated $10 to $15 billion flew out of Russia in 1992—an amount totaling about 15 percent of Russia's gross domestic product (GDP) for the year. Capital flight is a manifestation of the malfunctioning economy and is expected to reverse itself once the Russian economy stabilizes.[19]

With focus on international trade, at their September 1994 summit in Washington, both presidents of the United States and Russia signed a Partnership for Economic Cooperation that serves as a framework for reducing barriers to expanded economic cooperation. A number of U.S. agencies, including the Overseas Private Investment Corporation, the Export-Import Bank, the Trade and Development Agency, and the Department of Commerce, have programs that are aimed at facilitating trade and investment in Russia. Since 1992, the U.S. Agency for International Development (USAID) has offered about $2 billion in assistance to help Russia develop democratic and market institutions.[20]

The present economic condition of Russia is well described by the CIA which states:

> A decade after the implosion of the Soviet Union in 1991, Russia is still struggling to establish a modern market economy and achieve strong economic growth. In contrast to its trading partners in Central Europe - which were able to overcome the initial production declines that accompanied the launch of market reforms

within three to five years - Russia saw its economy contract for five years, as the executive and legislature dithered over the implementation of many of the basic foundations of a market economy. Russia achieved a slight recovery in 1997, but the government's stubborn budget deficits and the country's poor business climate made it vulnerable when the global financial crisis swept through in 1998. The crisis culminated in the August depreciation of the ruble, a debt default by the government, and a sharp deterioration in living standards for most of the population. The economy rebounded in 1999 and 2000, buoyed by the competitive boost from the weak ruble and a surging trade surplus fueled by rising world oil prices. This recovery, along with a renewed government effort in 2000 to advance lagging structural reforms, have raised business and investor confidence over Russia's prospects in its second decade of transition. Yet serious problems persist. Russia remains heavily dependent on exports of commodities, particularly oil, natural gas, metals, and timber, which account for over 80% of exports, leaving the country vulnerable to swings in world prices. Russia's agricultural sector remains beset by uncertainty over land ownership rights, which has discouraged needed investment and restructuring. Another threat is negative demographic trends, fueled by low birth rates and a deteriorating health situation - including an alarming rise in AIDS cases - that have contributed to a nearly 2% drop in the population since 1992. Russia's industrial base is increasingly dilapidated and must be replaced or modernized if the country is to achieve sustainable economic growth. Other problems include widespread corruption, capital flight, and brain drain.[21]

Given the preset economic conditions of Russia, it seems that it has a rough road ahead in its transition process. This calls on economic assistance on the free world to prevent this country from reverting to its past communist ideology.

TRANSITION AND ECONOMICS

The fall of Berlin Wall in the 1989 led a large group of economists to examine the process of transformation from socialism to capitalism in the former socialists economies. This gave rise to a new field of study in economics, called *transition economics*, or *transformation economics*.[22]

Today, the transformation of the economic institutions of the nations concerned has led to a significant change in economic conditions of the population, affecting the lives of more than 1.5 billion people.[23] This process has presented humanity with one of the most important events of the twentieth century, along with the Great Depression and the transition of capitalism to socialism. However, in spite of the triumph of capitalism over socialism, capitalism has not been introduced everywhere, and we still face the challenge of fostering prosperity and growth by well-tuned institutions in the poorest nations. What is alarming is that the achievement of such an objective is by no means guaranteed for nations that have embarked on the transition process. Transition in the former Soviet Union, for instance, has met with enormous problems which has been marked by unprecedented political crises and economic failure. Fall of the ruble, high inflation, growing decline in output, proliferation of organized crime, lack of fiscal revenues, generalized asset diversion, and capital flights have severely hampered the transition process. The prevalence of these conditions in transition economies like Russia present substantial risks that could direct that nation to continued economic stagnation and underdevelopment. Thus, devising transition policies that lead to successful capitalist development in the former socialist nations is an important task that not only provides the free world with economic benefits, but it also contributes to global peace and security.

In the initial stages of transition, the policy prescription focused on macroeconomic reforms and put strong emphasis on the following three major strategies:

1. Price liberalization.
2. Privatization of state-owned enterprises in order to evoke profit-maximizing behavior.
3. Tight monetary policies and balanced budget to stabilize the economy.

Although structural reform was also considered as part of the transition process, unfortunately, however, it did not attract the attention that it deserved.[24] In this section, first we study the principles of economic transition. Equipped with this knowledge, in the next section we reflect on the experience with economic reform and elaborate on the need for a new theory.

PRINCIPLES OF ECONOMIC TRANSITION

At the outset it must be emphasized that there is no agreed upon theory of transition among economists. Additionally, there is no universal policy prescription that can be applied to the problems arising from the process of transition in each nation. This stems from the fact that each nation that embarks on transition starts with different initial conditions. Nations differ in terms of natural resource endowments, the initial level of per capita income, the degree of industrialization, the extent of state ownership, the dependence on COMECON trade, the proximity to existing or potential partners, and the intensity of effort that they are willing to devote to transition process.* Given the lack of agreed upon theory of transition among economists, however, the majority of them agree on a number of principles needed for a successful transition from a command economy to a market economy. These principles can be studied in the context of two major reforms: macroeconomic reforms and structural reforms. We devote the rest of this section to examining these reforms. However it should kept in mind that to date, no modern economy has yet accomplished successful reforms that encompass simultaneous implementation of all of these principles. It should also be emphasized that contrary to the false expectations by some nations that the transformation can occur quickly, the economic transition is a long process that might take decades for completion. Given the sheer magnitude of the tasks involved in the process of transition, policy makers must be patient and avoid the implementation of policies that might be desirable in the short-run, but prove to be detrimental in the long-run.

Macroeconomic Reforms

Macroeconomic reforms hinge on three significant principles: price liberalization, launching sound fiscal and monetary policies, and opening the economy to global market forces. These are often described as macroeconomic reforms because they apply to the entire economy. They are central to creating the conditions for economic stability. However, it must be emphasized that implementation of these macroeconomic principles is not adequate to produce a healthy market economy. Indeed, without structural reform to infuse a competitive private sector into the economy, macroeconomic reforms will not succeed in restoring sustained growth. In other words, macroeconomic reforms can only produce rapid output growth when the basic structure of a market economy is in place.

Price Liberalization. In command economies prices are controlled by the government on the basis of either domestic costs or international prices. As such, they do not reflect the opportunity costs of resources involved in their production. In market economies, however, production and investment decisions are

---

*In January 1949, the then Soviet Union and communist bloc countries in Eastern Europe formed the **Council of Mutual Economic Assistance (CMEA or COMECON)**. Besides the Soviet Union, the original members of the council included Bulgaria, Czechoslovakia, Hungary, Poland, and Rumania. Late in 1949, Albania and East Germany joined the council. In 1962, Mongolia and Cuba joined, and Albania withdrew. The purpose of forming the council was to divert trade away from Western market economies and achieve a higher level of self-sufficiency among CMEA members. Although CMEA was successful in certain areas, trade among its members continued to be mostly bilateral, and their craving for Western technology induced them to pursue trade with Western market economies.

decentralized and are determined by the market forces of demand and supply. The interaction of demand and supply leads to price flexibility that guides the allocation and distribution of resources throughout the economic system.

In transitional economies, concerns about sharp price rises, especially for basic commodities such as bread, have led some economists to propose postponing price reform, at least until after steps have been taken to deal with the monetary "overhang". But, the dilemma with this approach is that unless the old system is promptly replaced with an incentive system based on correct prices to assure efficient production, output will diminish as the command system is torn down. Given this problem, an early and comprehensive price decontrol is what is needed in the case of economies in transition.

Price liberalization encompasses not only commodity prices, but the prices of labor and wages, as well. In a well tuned market economy, wages, just like prices, fluctuate freely in response to the market forces of demand and supply. This causes each worker to be rewarded according to his/her contribution to the production process. As a result, price flexibility allows the market mechanism to guide the workers to switch to professions and regions where they are most productive. However, a prerequisite for this process is for firms to operate under market incentives. Otherwise, they have little reason to set wages appropriately or to control their costs. Thus, to escape a wage-price spiral during the transition period, it may be desirable to impose temporary and limited restrictions on wage increases in state firms. But, after firms face market constraints, all wage limitations should be dismantled to permit wages to adjust to their proper amounts.

Price liberalization also involves interest rates. This will require the liberalization of financial markets to enable savers to receive an appropriate return and investors to offer correct incentives in making investment decisions. As an initial step in this direction, the policy makers should ensure that the real interest rate is positive, at least in the initial stages of transition. Experience demonstrates that government intervention in financial markets often leads to negative real interest rates, contributing to capital flight and poor investment.

Launching Appropriate Fiscal and Monetary Policies.

A major ingredient of a successful economic transition is the creation of sound monetary and fiscal policies that ensure economic stability. This is necessary especially because it infuses a sense of certainty into the economic system, enabling producers and consumers to have a firm basis for planning. It also promotes long-term investment and economic restructuring in an economic environment that is marked by highly uncertain conditions caused by high and volatile inflation.

A sound **fiscal policy** requires tight controls on government spending and credit policies, and it encompasses the following ingredients:

1. The government should restrict the subsidies it gives to consumers and to loss-generating state firms.
2. State firms must face the so-called "hard budget constraints", that is, the government should not cover the losses they may incur.
3. Establishment of a tax system that generates revenue. This eases the pressure on government to print money in order to finance necessary government spending. Such a tax system should limit distortions to prices and economic incentives. This calls for the design of a broad tax base that allows marginal tax rates to be reduced. Tax revenues that are generated from only a few sources, such as tariffs, can be highly distortionary. This is true in the case of most Latin American nations. One exception is Colombia, which has one of the most advanced income tax systems in the third world.

Having a sound fiscal discipline in place, the government should strive for the implementation of a **monetary policy** that is aimed at precluding undue money creation and rendering a steady supply of credit to the economy. This calls upon the following initiatives:

1. **Achieving Price Stability**. This requires launching effective mechanisms for controlling

GLOBAL INSIGHTS CASE 19.2

THE 1948 WEST GERMAN ERHARD REFORMS

At the end of World War II, the German economy lay in ruins. Industrial output in 1948 was one-third its 1936 level because of a massive disruption in production and trade patterns, even though capacity had been increased by capital formation in the intervening years. Economic disruption was aggravated by wartime money creation, pricing controls, and uncertainty about economic policy. Each day vast crowds traveled to the countryside to barter food from farmers; an extensive black market development; and cigarettes replaced in currency in many transactions.

The extensive reform package of June 1948 created a new currency, the deutsche mark. Most currency and bank accounts were converted at a rate of 100 to 6.5, but debts were converted at a rate of 10 to 1. In addition, price controls were lifted on most goods, a restrictive monetary policy was adopted, tax rates were lowered, and incentives were provided for investment. Much of the credit for the reform went to German economic advisors, foremost among them Ludwing Erhard.

These reforms almost immediately established sound and stable macroeconomic conditions. Consumer prices increased 20 percent between June and December of 1948, but inflation then subsided to an average annual rate of just over 1 percent between 1949 and 1959. Goods that had been hoarded or sold only in the black market became generally available. Real industrial production increased 40 percent in the second half of 1948 and grew an average of 11 percent annually between 1949 and 1959. Real GNP and productivity also grew rapidly. But the reform was not painless: unemployment rose from 3 percent in the first half of 1948 to more than 10 percent in the first half of 1950.

Macroeconomic reform could not have produced such impressive results if West Germany after the war had not had key structural elements in place. It had the legal framework necessary for a market economy, many intact businesses, and highly skilled workers and managers. Restrictive fiscal policies in place since 1946 helped set the stage for the reforms to succeed. In addition, the Marshall plan and private aid from abroad were critical during the initial reconstruction phase. By the early 1950s, however, foreign aid had diminished; robust economic growth worldwide and the Korean war stimulated demand for German exports and fueled economic growth.

Source: U.S. Government Printing Office, *Economic Report of the President* (Washington D.C.: U.S. Government Printing Office, 1991), Box 6-2, p. 201, Reprinted.

---

the growth of money and credit. The first step in achieving this goal is the reform of central banking. It is imperative for the central bank to have a high degree of independence from the central government. This would allow the bank to withstand the political forces to finance government spending with money creation, enabling the bank to pursue the goal of price stability. The central bank's independence is especially crucial during the transition period, which is marked by uncertainty and inflation pressures and may need a strong anti-inflation position, with severe limits on money growth. Controlling the growth of money and credit also calls up a sound banking system. Such a system should allow the central bank to play an important role in monitoring the banking system and in serving as the lender of last resort. This enables central bank to oversee the operation of the banking system, ensuring that firms are subject to a hard budget constraint. Given the importance of controlling the growth of money and credit, sufficient supervisory capabilities also must be developed early, rather than late into the transition process. The Case of Chile illustrates this point, where the collapse of its financial system in the late 1970s was linked to inadequate supervision of external borrowing and domestic lending by its banks.

2. **Reducing Monetary Overhangs.** In nations that have curbed inflation and allocated goods through rationing, the stock of domestic monetary assets outstanding is usually unsustainably large. Where such a so-called, "monetary overhang" exists, sound economic stabilization policy requires that it be diminished. Otherwise, decontrolling prices could lead to an inflationary surge in demand. The government could decrease the monetary overhang by the following methods:

   a. **Selling Real Assets.** The government could sell real assets such as housing. Although the privatization of real assets should be considered as a high priority item, however, as we explain later in this chapter, it may be difficult to sell these assets quickly.

   b. **Selling Financial Assets.** The sale of financial assets such as government bonds, at market interest rates helps to facilitate the establishment of a bond market. This, in turn, provides the monetary authorities with an instrument to control the money supply. Bonds must be serviced, and so using bond issues to resolve the monetary overhang could worsen the fiscal deficit. During the transition, bond issues may need to pay high real interest rates, which would lead to higher interest payments on national debt. That in turn, could cause lenders to be concerned about the government's ability to service its debt. If a government chooses to sell bonds to deal with the monetary overhang, it is critical to adopt monetary and fiscal policies that are both credible and strong. Since buyers must be guaranteed that government bonds will be serviced in full, governments should consider using whatever assets they have to support these bonds. Nations could use their available resources-such as copper, gold, or future oil revenues-to back bonds wholly or in part. Such bonds should be tradeable, and legal mechanisms would be developed to assure the public that the assets would be available to service the debt.

3. **Currency reform.** This approach presents an alternative to reducing the monetary overhang. Currency reform calls on the central government to replace the existing monetary assets with new assets that usually have a lesser value. A confiscatory currency reform acts as a tax on holders of currency and other financial assets and they are useful only as a component of an overall economic reform policy. As a result, repeated currency reforms should be avoided because they can disrupt economic activity, diminish the government's credibility, shake the public's confidence in the monetary assets, and fuel capital flight.

Opening the Economy to International Market Forces

Given the globalization of the world economy, a significant ingredient of economic reform for transitional economies is the opening of their economies to international market forces. This can be achieved by establishing currency convertibility, and trade liberalization.

Currency Convertibility. Although currency convertibility has more than one definition, in the context of transition economics it refers to the ability of a nation to trade its currency, either at home or abroad. Domestically, this means that the nation's currency should be a credible medium of exchange and convertible within its borders. In the former Soviet Union, certain cities and republics restricted the purchase of rubles by nonresidents and imposed trade barriers against each other. Additionally, certain deposit accounts were not convertible to currency.

Internationally, currency convertibility requires the currency of a nation to be tradeable in the foreign exchange market at the going market rate. To be sure, this does not necessarily imply free trade. Many nations with convertible currencies have hindered the free flow of goods and services to their boundaries by imposing tariffs and other impediments to trade. Thus, currency convertibility should be conceived as a first step among many steps that could lead to the elimination of trade barriers, promoting free international trade.

From a global perspective, currency convertibility, along with other measures to liberalize trade, constitute a crucial initial reform. It enhances the range of commodities that consumers can purchase. It allows producers to import the needed inputs and capital goods from abroad. The increasing amount and variety of the needed inputs, in turn, may enhance domestic production. Additionally, currency convertibility, along with free trade, stimulates competition in the following two distinct ways:

1. It exposes firms to the discipline of the international market. This is especially significant in smaller nations in which firms in some industries are relatively large in comparison to the size of the domestic market. In the absence of foreign competition, state firms in these nations may not face enough domestic competition at the initial stages of a reform effort. This may allow them to survive by increasing their prices at the expense of consumers, rather than attempting to enhance their efficiencies.
2. It allows new domestic enterprises to overcome domestic barriers to competition. This happens because, in order to be competitive, domestic firms are forced to cut costs and increase efficiency.

Currency convertibility is subject to the following two potential problems that could occur during the transition process:

1. Enterprises that are likely to survive in the long run might face serious financial problems during transition from controlled to world prices.
2. During the early phases of transition, the balance of payments could deteriorate.* This is due to the fact that it takes time for the supply side of the economy to respond to the new market incentives and the increase in demand stemming from a rise in exports.

These problems could be alleviated by converting existing trade barriers to temporary tariffs. This method, sometimes referred to as the "tariffication" approach, has the following merits:

1. It replaces a potentially complicated range of trade barriers with a single gap between domestic and world prices.
2. It makes the degree of protection more transparent.
3. It clears the way for eventual tariff reduction.

It should be noted that is not necessary for a nation to undertake full convertibility. In fact, many economists suggest that it is desirable to focus on convertibility of trade and other current account transactions, before embarking on international capital flow convertibility.**They argue that the existence of market distortion and a lack of confidence might foster capital flight in the initial stages of transition.

---

*The **balance of payments** (BOP) can be defined as an accounting statement that summarizes all transactions between the residents of one nation and the residents of all other nations during a given period of time. In other words, the BOP indicates the amount of foreign currency that was pumped into and out of a nation's economic system during a given period.

The **current account includes those transactions that do not result in any future obligations. In general, current account items are caused by (a) purchasing from and selling to foreigners and (b) unilateral transfers—-remittances and grants given to or received from foreigners free of charge. Capital account items result when (a) a country invests in foreign nations or when foreign nations invest in that country; (b) a nation provides loans to foreigners or receives loans from foreigners and (c) a nation deposits money in foreign banks or foreigners deposit money in the country's local banks.

However, they concede that it is not wise to delay the capital account convertibility too long. This is due to the fact that convertibility of capital account transaction is significant in furnishing venture and working capital to private enterprise during the process of transition. Additionally, it helps the transfer of technology and know how to the nation that is going through transition.

One of the issues that arises in currency convertibility is the choice of the exchange rate system. Accordingly, a nation's authorities must choose between fixing the exchange rate or allowing it to move freely in response to the market forces of supply and demand. They may adopt a fixed exchange rate system as part of a complete stabilization program. Assuming that such a system is backed up by a credible noninflationary monetary policy, it may help diminish inflation expectations, easing the transition to price stability. However, the choice of an appropriate level for the fixed rate is not a simple one. If the value of foreign currency in terms of domestic currency is set too low, foreign-made goods would become cheaper to purchase, as compared to domestic goods. This gives rise to a higher demand for imports. The higher demand for imports, in turn, reduces the initial inflation pressure. On the other hand, if the value of foreign currency in terms of domestic currency is set too high, foreign goods become more expensive in comparison to domestic goods. This causes exports to rise, enhancing the competitiveness of domestic firms in world markets and reducing the likelihood of large trade deficits.

If a freely fluctuating exchange rate system is chosen, the value of exchange rate is determined by the forces of demand and supply. This introduces uncertainty into the system and might discourage business activities.

STRUCTURAL REFORMS

The success of economic reforms requires a framework that is conducive to the implementation of the individual policies discussed above. This calls on structural reforms that establish private property and property rights, and promote competition.

Establishing Private Property and Property Rights

As we already know from our discussion of Marxism in Chapter 4, socialism and communism are based on social ownership of property. Accordingly, private property is not only a tool by which capitalists can exploit the working class to obtain an unearned share of the social product, it is also the foundation for dividing society into two classes: proletariat and the bourgeoisie. Thus, a major step in dismantling socialism and communism is to establish private property rights and erect a legal system to protect these rights. Using the process of privatization, productive assets must come under the control of the private sector. Failure to achieve these objectives would leave producers with no incentive to react to prices and to assume risks. As a result, the reform efforts will not succeed in generating the growing supplies of commodities that consumers would like to purchase.

Privatization of state enterprises is a complicated task in the process of economic transition that must be implemented with urgency. The task is more complicated to a large extent than the privatization efforts that have been implemented in developed market economies over the years. This complexity stems from the following factors:

a. Inadequacy of financial markets to provide the needed credit for the process of privatization.
b. Political concerns that may rise from the sale of domestic equity to foreigners.
c. The prevalent supposition that those who benefitted under the old regime are among those who can afford to make large equity investments, unjustifiably benefitting from the privatization process.
d. The inaccuracy of the books of large enterprises in not reflecting the economic realities. This might make it easier for insiders to buy these enterprises at very low prices and enjoy sizeable profits.

GLOBAL INSIGHTS CASE 19.3

IMPORTS OF FOREIGN TECHNOLOGY ON JAPAN'S ECONOMIC TRANSITION

One historically important example in which the import of foreign technology was the centerpiece of a reform effort followed the MeUi restoration in Japan in 1868. Spurred by a desire to emulate the economic success of the West, Japan within a remarkably short period of time overhauled its central government, changed what was being taught in its schools, and shifted the energies of its people toward commerce. The linchpins of the Japanese transition were the concentration on importing foreign technology and technical assistance, the development of a transportation infrastructure conducive to commerce and trade, and the privatization of government production facilities. Entire factories were imported, along with technical advisers who operated the machinery until Japanese workers and managers were capable of doing it on their own.

Source: U.S. Government Printing Office, *Economic Report of the President* (Washington, D.C., U.S. Government Printing Office, 1991), 206.

The Order of Privatization. One question that arises in the process of privatization is the order in which it should take place. The following is a list of possible methods that can be adopted:

1. Firms with positive net worth should be privatized first. Firms that are sustaining losses, have high debt burdens, or are anticipated to require notable internal restructuring before they become viable, should to be privatized later after the restructuring takes hold. This approach was tried in Poland.
2. By contrast to the first method, this second method focuses on privatizing of loss-sustaining industries first, supposedly because this method would diminish the subsidies that must be paid by the government. This method was employed in Yugoslavia.
3. Selling firms to workers or to the highest bidder.
4. Distributing vouchers to the general public. This allows citizens to buy portions of enterprises, either directly or by investing in holding enterprises that assume management function. This approach has been considered by Czechoslovakia.
5. Using a combination of methods in a single privatization.

Creation of a Private Housing Market. A significant component of privatization should be generation of a private housing market. Experience shows that in most nations that embark on transition the lack of adequate housing and the inadequacy of existing housing provide real impediments to the free movement of workers, preventing them from moving to areas where jobs are. Thus, the establishment of private housing is an important first step toward both ameliorating labor mobility and elevating living conditions. The authorities should ensure that property is transferable so that existing and new housing can be allocated in an efficient manner.

Privatization Experience. In the transition economies, the evidence shows that Central and Eastern Europe and the Baltic States have been relatively successful in achieving favorable results from privatization. The evidence also indicates fewer promising results in the case of a number of countries, including Armenia, Georgia, Kazakhstan, the Kyrgyz Republic, Moldova, Mongolia, Russia, and Ukraine. In these nations the privatization experience produced the following results:

> # GLOBAL INSIGHTS CASE 19.4
>
> # PROPERTY RIGHTS AND PRIVATE PROPERTY IN THE FORMER SOVIET UNION, EASTERN EUROPEAN NATIONS AND LATIN AMERICAN COUNTRIES
>
> Private property and property rights were most notably absent in the command economies of Eastern Europe and the former Soviet Union, where economic activity was based on the idea that almost all property belonged to the state. Although small-scale entrepreneurial activity was tolerated in some Eastern European countries during the late 1980s, most control over the allocation of resources remained in the hands of the government. The public debate about private property in the former Soviet Union had also been a political debate about commitment to change following 70 years of indoctrination about the evils of profit and capitalist enterprise. During Lenin's New Economic Policy of the 1920s, reforms encouraged private producers, especially farmers, to expand production. Many farmers successfully raised output and prospered, only to have that very success considered criminal during the Stalinist purges and collectivization drives of the late 1920s and 1930s. As a result, the most successful farmers and entrepreneurs were punished by expropriation of their property, exile to labor camps, and, in many cases, execution.
>
> In Latin America, the institution of property rights has long been established but has not always been well respected. Government nationalization of industries, sometimes through expropriation, is one aspect of a legacy of not respecting property rights. More recently, inefficient and slow legal systems have discouraged private entrepreneurship.
>
> Source: Source: U.S. Government Printing Office, *Economic Report of the President* (Washington, D.C., U.S. Government Printing Office, 1991), 207-208.

- Some privatized firms performed worse than state-owned enterprises.
- Private ownership did not necessarily lead to restructuring, that is, it did not make the necessary changes to an enterprise to make it viable in competitive market.
- In some nations, there were few differences in performance between privately-owned enterprises and state-owned enterprises.

The inadequate results of privatization do not imply that it should be abandoned as a vital element of transition. Rather, it connotes that privatization relies for its success on the support of capitalism. This is clearly stated by a report of the International Monetary Fund, which states:

> "... privatization is the generally preferred course of action, but its short-term economic effectiveness and social acceptability depend on the institutional underpinnings of capitalism.[...] the heart of the matter is whether and how privatization can be achieved where governments are unwilling or incapable.[...] The reasonable short-term course of action is probably to push ahead with case-by-case and tender privatization and reprivatization...in cooperation with international assistance community, in hope of producing some success stories to emulate."[25]

Advancing Domestic Competition

As we already know, competition is the essence of capitalism. It is the driving force in market economies that leads to the efficient allocation and distribution of scarce resources. Advancing domestic competition is one of the major steps that must be taken in the process of transition. This objective can be achieved through the implementation of the following strategies:

1. Breaking existing state-owned enterprises into smaller firms.
2. Fostering the adoption of new technologies by the above smaller firms.
3. Promoting sound accounting and financial procedures in order to ensure that firms are operating on a reliable financial basis.
4. Encouraging the sale of the assets of state firms to the private sector.
5. Removing barriers to creation of new firms. Given their small sizes, these firms are often at a disadvantage in competing with the state enterprises for inputs and credit.
6. Establishing policies that protect competition. This can be achieved by enacting basic antitrust laws that aim at the following two main objectives:
    a. Precluding cartel behavior by firms that are producing the same commodities
    b. Preventing mergers that create monopoly.
7. Developing basic banking and credit function as quickly as possible. This requires the establishment of a competitive banking system that provides access to credit for new and restructured banks.
8. Developing sound financial markets. This allows risks to be shifted to those who are most willing to assume them. It also enables firms to diversify and hedge and to mobilize private savings.
9. Overhauling the role of government. This calls on authorities to rebuild the government in a framework that is conducive to the operation of a market economy. It encompasses activities that include the creation of a sensible tax, collection of meaningful economic data, and creation and enforcement of environmental regulation.
10. Developing a social safety Net. The restructuring of the economic system leads to the failure of inefficient firms that are not viable under private management. This would result in unemployment of workers that were hired by these firms. Although dislocations of inefficient firms are a prerequisite for establishing a more efficient economic system, the calamities that befall workers and their families can and should be buffered. This calls for creation of unemployment compensation, and unemployment insurance.
11. Facilitating the establishment of a sound educational system. This is an important step in transition because it allow authorities to produce a work force that is able to build and operate a contemporary market economy.

We close this section by emphasizing that it is important for the policymakers and populace to comprehend the economic rationale for market-based reforms, so that they can be supportive of the government efforts to embark on the transition process. There is no doubt that the failure of government to win support for its reform programs will lead to the failure of the economic transition process.[26]

Experience with Economic Reform and the Need for a New Theory

The experience has shown that classic policy prescription for economic reform has been subject to many flaws. More specifically, liberalization did not generate as positive a response as expected. Rather, it led to a sharp drop in output. Stabilization efforts were markedly unsuccessful in different nations. Mass privatization has usually led to enormous asset dislodging and expropriating by managers. Finally, organized crime has thrived more rapidly than markets in some transition nations. Given the disappointing outcomes of transition experiments, economists have shifted their focus in thinking about economics and have begun to emphasize the institutional perspective in grappling with the process of transition. Accordingly, they have emphasized the significance of various institutions underpinning a successful transition to a capitalist economy. This has led to a shift from market and price theory to contracting and the legal, social, and political environment of contracting. It has also forced economists to think about institutions in a dynamic, as opposed to a static system. They have come to realize that the word "transition" itself might be misleading, by giving the impression that transition is "simply" a short-run policy problem that might take a few years at most.

In reality, however, we can not be certain about the process of transition and its outcome. In other words, there is no guarantee that nations engaged in the process of transition will be successful in achieving prosperous capitalist economies. We may draw a parallel here with economic development. As we already know, development policies were devised decades ago with the goal of assisting developing nations to catch up with the advanced nations. Although some nations, like NICs have been successful in achieving their development goals, other nations, especially in Africa, have experienced even further impoverishment.

The transition hinges upon a given set of institutions as the point of departure. Setting up specific goals for the destination point by adopting advanced nations model does not guarantee that we reach that point, as was the case with economic development of third world nations. To be sure, the institutions of other nations can not be imitated or copied. Such an attempt may lead to unintentional outcomes.

Although there is still no consensus among economists regarding the path to a successful transition from socialism to capitalism, there are a few principles that have attracted more attention in recent years. These principles, have stemmed from more than a decade of experience with economic transition. According to Michel Camdessus, managing director of the International Monetary Fund (IMF), who elaborated on some of these principles, "They are principles that can act as lodestars for all countries at all stages of the transition."[27] These principles include the following:

1. **Promoting the highest standard of governance.** This requires erecting a framework that calls for government, firms, financial institutions, and individuals to deal with each other in a transparent way. More specifically, it includes the following policies:
    a. Placing a greater emphasis on the rule of law and respect for property. This objective should be achieved not only thorough legislation but also through an independent judiciary and court system that is capable of enforcing property rights and contracts.
    b. Implementing comprehensive administrative and fiscal reforms to advance government's efficiency and to foster the cognition of citizens' obligation toward the government.
2. **Creating government institutions "adequate" for a market economy.** This calls for fostering political and institutional stability, protecting private property from encroachment, and shielding taxpayers from government's lobbyist groups who act on self-interest:
    a. A simple, efficient, equitable tax system.
    b. A regulated and well managed financial system that is open to competition, on both domestic and global levels.
    c. Expenditure policies that minimize unproductive spending.
    d. Monetary polices that progressively depend on contemporary, market-based means.
    e. Transparency in implementing all of the above policies.
3. **Ameliorating allocative efficiency** by rectifying socialism's distortions via the launching of flexible relative prices and the generation of a competitive market environment that is open to the global economy.
4. **Stabilizing the economy** to allow the market system to function correctly.
5. **Furnishing better incentives and corporate governance organizations** to allow enterprises to react to market signals. This requires large scale privatization and encouragement of the entry of new private firms and the generation of an entrepreneurial class.
6. **Emphasizing poverty reduction.** This objective should be considered as a key goal in the process of transition and it encompasses the following features:
    a. A cost-effective program that aims at poverty reduction, and human development.
    b. A well aimed social safety net.

GLOBAL INSIGHTS CASE 19.5

THE ECONOMIC HARDSHIP IN SUB-SAHARAN AFRICA

Following a period of economic stagnation, many African nations embarked on a series of structural reforms and adjustments policies in order to restore economic growth in the mid-1980s. Now after almost two decades into adjustment, the economic climate in Sub-Saharan Africa still remains uncertain, and the region finds itself with the following problems:

1. Civil disarray.
2. Macroeconomic instability.
3. Slow economic growth.
4. Slow progress in privatization.
5. Inward orientation and burdensome regulations.
6. Poor infrastructure.
7. High wage and production costs.
9. Rapid increase in population.
10. Loss of export revenues.
11. Destruction of the fragile ecosystem.
12. The inability of many of these nations to feed their growing populations.

Some numbers help to illustrate the economic crisis in sub-Saharan Africa. Annual GNP growth (excluding South Africa) averaged 2.3% percent during 1983-1989 and 1.4% during 1990-1997, as compared with 3.8% and 5.1% for all other third world nations.

The elements that gave rise to the sub-Saharan African predicament can be divided into the following two major categories:

1. Factors beyond the region's control, including drought, foreign capital withdrawals, depressed goods prices, and diminishing foreign aid.
2. Poor government policies, including inefficient state-owned firms, failure to promote export growth, neglect of the agricultural sector, and failure to control the growth of population

Fortunately, after a long period of poor performance, the economic conditions in sub-Saharan Africa began to show signs of improvement. The following facts illustrate this point:

1. After reaching the level of 47% in 1994, annual inflation subsided to 10% in 1998.
2. The overall fiscal deficit declined from about 9% of GDP in 1992 to less than 5% in 1998.

The improved economic performance of sub-Saharan African countries in recent years can be contributed to improved policies in these nations. During the 1990s many of these nations began to implement the following structural reforms:

Continued

CH. 19/TRANSITION ECONOMICS

Case 19.5 continued

1. Abolishing price controls.
2. Dismantling inefficient public sector monopolies and privatizing state enterprises.
3. Eliminating nontariff trade barriers.
4. Lowering import duties.
5. Freeing the exchange rates.
6. Eliminating direct control on bank credit.
7. Establishing market-determined interest rates.

Given the recent economic improvement in the region, the future growth will depend on the degree by which each individual African nation is capable of achieving the following objectives:

1. To increase investment, especially private investment.
2. To maintain a stable economic environment.
3. To develop and maintain a transparent and stable legal and regulatory environment that minimizes the risks that discourage both domestic and foreign investment.
4. To bring an end to armed conflict that wipes out human and physical capital and deviates resources from investment in infrastructure and human capital.

Sources: Ernesto Hernandez-Cata, "Sub-Saharan Africa: Economic Policy and Outlook for Growth," Finance and Development 36, No.2 (March 1999):10-12; Eshrat, Husain, "Results of Adjustment in Africa: Selected Cases," *Finance and Development,* 31, No. 2 (June 1994): 6-9.; Amar Bhattacharya, Peter J. Montiel, and Sunil Sharma, "How Can Sub-Saharan Africa Attract More Private Capital Inflows?" Finance and Development, 34, No.2, (June 1997): 3-6.

---

    c. A tax system that assures a fair distribution of the tax burden without impeding incentives to work.
    d. Fostering labor market policies that supports high levels of productive employment.
    e. Undertaking pension reforms to reconcile the objective of ensuring a decent standard for the elderly with the goal of the long-term viability of public finances.[28]

It should be noted that these objectives are not implemented in a vacuum. The following constraints must be considered before undertaking a transition process:

1. **Uncertainty associated with the outcome of the transition process.** Because transition from socialism to capitalism is a process that is directed by people who are facing a number of unknowns, a transition model should incorporate uncertainty, experimentation and the learning process that must occur during the transition process.
2. **The complementarities and interactions between reforms.** There are complementarities between individual reforms which must be considered in the formulation of the transition process. For example, there are complementarities between price liberalization and privatization. In the absence of privatization, free prices alone do not lead to optimal allocation of resources since firms do not enjoy incentives for profit maximization.
3. **Political framework.** Even if the transition process leads to enhancement of aggregate welfare, it still gives rise to winners and losers in the economic system. This underlines the significance of not separating economic and political reforms. Economic reforms may adversely affect the economic well-being of politicians and interest groups who might not be supportive of the process of transition.

Thus, it is necessary for the architects of transition to keep the political implications of their economic prescription in mind and not treat political and economic reforms as separate issues.[29]

Because no preestablished theory of transition existed before the fall of the Berlin Wall, the subject is still in its elementary phases of development. Today, transition is history in the making, and can be considered as a branch of economic development with specific characteristics, as compared to the developing nations studied in this textbook. These include over industrialization, a relatively high level of human capital and economic development, generalized ownership and state power, and low initial income inequality. Such characteristics call for more research on the subject to pave the way for the establishment of more theories that are supported by the majority of economists.

We conclude this chapter by noting that movement toward a market-oriented economy and free international trade is reaching a new and unprecedented height. Recent world events, such as those explained here, have opened up a new chapter in the world of free trade, changing the nature of East-West trade relations. However, the transition from a command economy to a market-oriented economy is not painless. Experience has shown that the dismantling of subsidies and price controls, and the suspension of regulations regarding employment and worker dismissals may initially lead to higher unemployment and inflation. It may also worsen income inequality before economic growth and higher productivity induce an improvement in standards of living. Higher inflation, leading to a rise in the prices of domestically produced goods, may cause exports to fall and imports to rise, generating foreign exchange shortages. These factors, along with political considerations, may force some countries to move away from further openness. Given these problems, some observers have argued that a rapid transition toward a market economy is preferable to a slow one because the faster the economic reforms take place, the lower the probability of their being blocked by those who benefitted from the previous system. Additionally, it is argued that public support for reform may best be achieved when tangible benefits of the reforms are felt more quickly. One thing is clear: Eastern European countries cannot achieve a successful transformation to market-oriented economic systems without help, especially financial assistance from the West. Such a transformation requires political leadership and demands global cooperation between the leaders of the advanced market-oriented economies. Aware of this fact, the United States and its allies have cooperated in easing restrictions on the sale of high-technology goods to Eastern European countries that are adopting democratic reforms.[30]

SUMMARY

1. The collapse of Communist power in 1989 brought an end to Soviet domination in Eastern European countries and laid the foundation for the transformation of these nations' economies into market-oriented economic systems.
2. The economic forces that contributed to the collapse of Soviet power in Eastern Europe are related to inefficiencies that stem from a command economy.
3. The overall trade impact of the economic reforms in Eastern Europe is expected to be small, accounting for an approximate 2- to 3-percent expansion of global trade.
4. On July 2, 1990, the economic union of the two Germanies was achieved. East Germany agreed to scrap its currency and adopt the West German mark. It also adopted West German economic rules and laws, joining the market-oriented economic system.
5. In the short run, it was expected that eastern Germany would experience hard economic times.
6. In the long run, Germany's benefits from unification are expected to widen as Western investment in Eastern industries continues to expand.
7. The impact of Germany's reunification on the world economy has been compared to that of the OPEC price increase in 1973 and the "Reaganomics" of the 1980s, which shocked the world's economy for years to come, significantly affecting international trade and investment flows.
8. The demise of the Soviet Union led to the creation of the new Commonwealth of Independent States (CIS). The CIS has many obstacles to overcome before becoming a modern market-oriented society.

9. The fall of the Berlin Wall in 1989 led a large group of economists to examine the process of transformation from socialism to capitalism in the former socialist economies. This gave rise to a new field of study in economics, called *transition economics*, or *transformation economics*.
10. In the initial stages of transition, the policy prescription focused on macroeconomics reforms and put strong emphasis on three major strategies: (1) Price liberalization; (2)Privatization of state-owned enterprises in order to evoke profit-maximizing behavior; and (3)Tight monetary policies and balanced budget to stabilize the economy.
11. Macroeconomic reforms hinges on three significant principles: Price liberalization, launching sound fiscal and monetary policies, and opening the economy to global market forces
12. Price liberalization encompasses not only commodity prices, but wages, interest rates.
13. A sound **fiscal policy** requires tight controls on government spending and credit policies, and includes three features: (1) The government should restrict the subsidies it gives to consumers and to loss-generating state firms; (2) State firms must face the so-called "hard budget constraints", that is, the government should not cover the losses they may incur; and (3) establishing a tax system that generates revenue.
14. Having a sound fiscal discipline in place, the government should strive for the implementation of a **monetary policy** that is aimed at precluding undue money creation and rendering a steady supply of credit to the economy. This includes three features: (1) achieving price stability; (2)reducing monetary overhangs; and (3)currency reform.
15. Given the globalization of the world economy a significant ingredient of economic reform for transitional economies is the opening of their economy to international market forces. This can be achieved by establishing currency convertibility, and trade liberalization.
16. Although currency convertibility has more than one definition, in the context of transition economics, it refers to the ability of a nation to trade its currency, either at home or abroad. Domestically, this means that the nations's currency should be a credible medium of exchange and convertible within its borders. Internationally, currency convertibility requires the currency of a nation to be tradeable in the foreign exchange rate at the going market rate.
17. The success of economic reforms require a framework that is conducive to the implementation of the individual policies discussed above. This calls for structural reforms that establish private property and property rights, and promote competition.
18. Experience has shown that classic policy prescription for economic reform has been subject to many flaws.
19. Although there is still no consensus among economists regarding the path to a successful transition from socialism to capitalism, there are a few principles that have attracted more attention in recent years. These are: (1) promoting the highest standard of governance; (2) creating government institutions "adequate" for a market economy; (3) ameliorating allocative efficiency by rectifying socialism's distortions via the launching of flexible relative prices and the generation of a competitive market environment that is open to the global economy; (4) stabilizing the economy to allow the market system to function correctly; (5) furnishing better incentives and corporate governance organizations to allow enterprises to react to market signals; and (6) emphasizing poverty reduction.
20. It should be noted that these objectives are not implemented in a vacuum. The following constraints must be considered before undertaking a transition process: (1) uncertainty associated with the outcome of the transition process; (2) the complementarities and interactions between reforms; and (3) political framework.

QUESTIONS

1. Elaborate on the economic forces that contributed to the demise of Soviet power in Eastern Europe, and discuss the overall trade impact of Eastern European economic reforms.
2. Discuss the economic implications of German unification, in both the short run and the long run.
3. Who are the major beneficiaries of German unification? Explain.

4. Following unification, why did Germany support a high interest rate policy? Elaborate on the impact of this policy on the EU and the global economy.
5. Theoretically, what do economic development and transition economics have in common? Explain.
6. What were the major components of policy prescription for economies in transition? What was the major shortcoming of these policies? Explain.
7. Elaborate on the features of monetary polices and fiscal policies by answering the following questions:
    a. What is the major purpose of undertaking these polices?
    b. What tools are used in implementation of each of these polices?
    c. Why is the implementation of both these polices necessary for a successful transition from a command economy to a market economy?
8. How can a transitory nation achieve the objective of opening its economy to the global market? Explain.
9. What major policies of transition have attracted more attention in recent years? What constraints should be considered in implementation of these policies.? Explain.

NOTES

1. "Exporting Labor: Western Europe Finds That It's Pricing Itself Out of the Job Market," *The Wall Street Journal*, 9 December 1993, 1, A8.
2. Susan M. Collins and Dani Rodrik, *Eastern and the Soviet Union in the World Economy* (Washington, DC: Institute for International Economics, May 1991).
3. "Booming Economy in Poland Brings Jobs, Wealth and Apathy," *The Wall Street Journal*, November 1996, p.1.
4. "German Merger to Affect Economies around World," *Los Angeles Times*, 22 July 1990, B2.
5. "A Transatlantic Partnership: Germany and the United States," *Forbes*, 23 July 1990, A1.
6. "Unified Germany Likely to Remain an Economic Giant," *Los Angeles Times*, 5 May 1991, D1.
7. "Germany Faces a Year Worsening Ills: Recession Is Accented by Violence, Refugee Influx," *The Wall Street Journal*, 4 January 1993, A6.
8. Ibid.
9. CIA, "Germany," *The World Factbook 2001*, http://www.odci.gov/cia/publications/factbook/.
10. "East-West Divide Lives on in Germany: Leipzing Show Progress, but no Economic Miracle," *The Wall Street Journal*, 3 August 1995, p. A8.
11. "Bush, Allies Pledge $24 Billion to Russia," *The Wall Street Journal*, 2 April 1992, A2
12. "Yeltsin's Foes Holed up in Parliament Given a Way Out: Job, Cash to Defeat," *The Wall Street Journal*, 1 October 1993, A6; "Yeltsin Clears the Final Draft of Constitution," *The Wall Street Journal*, 9 November 1993, A19.
13. "Yeltsin's Constitution Appears to Gain Thin Victory in Russia," *The Wall Street Journal*, 13 December 1993, A10.
14. "Russia's Crisis Over Reforms Seems to Ease," *The Wall Street Journal*, 15 April 1992, A15.
15. "Armed Forces of Former Soviet Union Are Fast Falling Apart, Analysts Say," *The Wall Street Union*, 13 April 1992, 18.
16. "Bush, Allies Pledge $24 Billion to Russia," *The Wall Street Journal*, 2 April 1992, A2.
17. "Russian Cabinet Offers to Quit to Save Reforms," *The Wall Street Journal*, 14 April 92, A14.
18. "G-7 Nations Offer Yeltsin Relief on Debt," *The Wall Street Journal*, 9 July 1992, A2.
19. "Russia Should Turn to Latin America for Advice as Capital Flight Worsens," *The Wall Street Journal*, 15 November 1993, A9.
20. "U.S. Government Printing Office, *Economic Report of the President* (Washington, D.C.: United States Government Printing Office, 1997), 258.
21. CIA, "Russia," *The World Factbook 2001*, http://www.odci.gov/cia/publications/factbook/.
22. Gerard Ronald, *Transition and Economics* (Cambridge, Mass: The MIT Press, 2001), p. XVII.
23. *Ibid.*
24. *Ibid.*, p. XVIII.

25. John Nellie, "Time to Rethink Privatization in Transition Economies, *Finance and Development* 36, No.2 (June 1999), http://www.imf.org/external/pubs/ft/fandd/1999/06/index.htm.
26. A major source of the topic of "Principles of Economic Transition," that was covered in this textbook is Chapter 6: Economies in Transition," *Economic Report of the President,*" (Washington, D.C.: U.S. Government Printing Office, 1999): 193-232.
27. International Monetary Funds, "Achievements and Prospects after Ten Years of Transition: Remarks by Michel Camdessus, Managing Director of International Monetary Fund at the Warsaw School of economics, Warsaw, Poland, December 10, 1999, p. 8, http://www.imf.org/external/np/speeches/1999/121099.HTM.
28. Gerard Ronald, Ibid., p.11; International monetary Fund, "Achievements and Prospect after Ten Years of Transition".
29. Ibid. pp. 12-13.
30. "U.S., Allies to Ease More Curbs on High-Tech Sales to East Europe," *The Wall Street Journal,* 20 February 1990, A20.

SUGGESTED READINGS

Aghion, P., and Blanchard. "On Privatization Methods in Eastern Europe and Their Implication." *Economics of Transition*, 6 (1, 1998):87-99.
Alexeev, M. "Privatization and the Distribution of Wealth in Russia." *Economics of Transition*, 7 (1999): 449-465.
Anderson, R., and C. Kegels. *Transition Banking: The Financial Development of General and Eastern Europe.* Oxford, UK: Oxford University Press, 1997.
Aslund, A. *How Russia Became a Market Economy.* Washington, D.C.: Brookings Institution, 1995.
BardhamP., and Roemer, J. *Market Socialism.* Oxford, UK: Oxford University Press, 1992.
Black, Cyril E., et al. *Common Sense in U.S.—Soviet Trade.* Washington, DC: American Committee on East-West Accord, 1979.
Boycko, M., A. Shleifer, and R. Vishny. *Privatizing Russia.* Cambridge, MA: MIT Press, 1995.
Brus, W., and K. Laski. *From Marx to the Market.* Oxford, UK: Oxford University Press, 1989.
Byrd, M.A. *The Market Mechanism* in China. New York: M.E. Sharp, 1991.
Collins, Susan M. *Eastern Europe and the Soviet Union in the World Economy.* Washington DC: Institute for International Economics, May 1991.
Dewartripont, M. And J. Tirole. *The Prudential Regulation of Banks.* Cambridge, MA: MIT Press, 1994.
Dixit, A. *Investment Under Uncertainty. Princeton University Press, 1996.*
Fingleton, J., E. Fox, D. Neven, and P. Seabright. Competition Policy and the Transformation of Central Europe. London: Center for economic Policy Research, 1998.
Frydman, R., and A. Rpaczynski. *Privatization in Eastern Europe: Is the State Withering Away?* London: Central European University Press, 1994.
Gros, D., and A. Steinherr. *Winds of Change: Economic Transition in Central and Eastern Europe.* London: Longman, 1995.
Havrylyshyn, Oleh, and John Williamson. *From Soviet Disunion to Eastern Economic Community.* Washington DC: Institute for International Economics, October 1991.
Kaiser, Karl. "Germany's Unification." *Foreign Affairs* 70, no. 1 (1990): 179-225.
Kenneth, David and Mark Liberman, *The Road to Capitalism: Economic Transformation in Eastern Europe and the Former Soviet Union* (New York: Dryden Press, 1992).
Klaus, Valclav, "A Perspective on Economic Transformation in Eastern Europe and the Former Soviet Union," *Proceeding of the World Annual Conference on Development Economics* (Washington, D.C.: World Bank, 1991): 13-18.
Kornai, J. *The Road to Free Economy.* New York: Norton, 1990.
_____. *The Socialist System: The Political Economy of Communism.* Oxford, UK: Oxford University Press, 1995.
Marrel, Peter "How Far Has the Transition Progressed?" *Journal of Economic Perspective* 10 (Spring 1996): 25-44.
Layard, R. And J. Parker. *The Coming Russian Boom: A Guide to New Markets and Politics.* New York: Simon and Schuster, Free Press, 1996.
Manne, H.G. *Insider Trading and the Stock Market.* New York: Free Press, 1966.

McKinnon, R. *The Order of Economic Liberalization.* Baltimore: John Hopkins University Press, 1991.

Milanovic, B. *Income, Inequality, and Poverty During the Transition from Planned to Market Economy.* World Bank Regional and Sectoral Studies, Washington, D.C., 1998.

North, D. *Institutions, Institutional Changes and Economic Performance.* Cambridge, UK: Cambridge University Press, 1990.

Sachs, J. *Poland's Jump to the Market Economy.* Lionel Robbins Lectures. Cambridge, MA, and London: MIT Press, 1993.

Shleifer, A., and D. Treisman. Without a Map: *Political Tactics and Economic Reform in Russia.* Cambridge, MA: MIT Press, 2000.

Sinn, H. W., and G. Sinn. *Jumpstart.* Cambridge, MA: MIT Press, 1993.

Staniszkis, J.*Dynamics of the Breakthrough in Eastern Europe.* Berkeley, CA: Berkeley University Press, 1991.

Williamson, O. *The Economic Institutions of Capitalism.* New York: Free Press, 1985.

Van Ham, Peter. "Soviet Economic Reform and East-West Relations." *Problems of Communism* 40 (Jan-April 1991): 144-149.

Williamson, John. *The Economic Opening of Eastern Europe.* Washington, DC: Institute for International Economics, May 1991.

CHAPTER 20

GLOBALIZATION, LOCALIZATION, AND THE ENVIRONMENT

Today, the spread of industrialization and industrial innovation has led the world economy into a new era in which nations are becoming more and more interdependent. In pursuing economic development in the new millennium, policy makers have found themselves faced with an environment that has been transformed socially, politically, and economically. Three issues that will dominate the world in the new millennium are globalization, localization and the environment.

In covering different issues related to economic development in the proceeding chapters, this textbook has tried to maintain a global perspective. Given such an orientation, we end this textbook, first, by providing a more in depth coverage of the concept of globalization. Second, we elaborate on the other contemporary issues, localization and environment, that are highly related to globalization.

GLOBALIZATION

Globalization can be defined as the growing integration of national economies into expanding international markets. The term "globalization" was first introduced in the 1980s. However, as we already know from our discussion of Chapter 1, globalization is not a new phenomenon. Forty centuries ago, Greek, Mesopotamian, and Phoenician merchants engaged in global business through the exportation and importation of goods and services.[1]

Given the experience of the Great Depression in the United States, the 1930s cast doubt on the wisdom of globalization. Nations began to follow inward polices by drawing back into their shells, realizing that international markets could lead to poverty and unemployment.

Following World War II, the efforts of Western states to build and strengthen international ties laid the foundation for today's globalization. This has brought nations closer together, fusing individual national markets. The dismantling of protectionist barriers has stimulated free movement of capital and paved the way for multinational corporations to establish their subsidiaries around the globe. The rise of the internet and recent advances in telecommunications have further fueled the process of globalization.

As we already know, the standard international economic theory has been supportive of globalization of the markets, asserting that it would lead to the most efficient way of allocating the world's scarce resources. Trade theories have also shown that if countries specialize according to their comparative advantage, not only do they benefit as participants of trade, but also world output is maximized. However, as the street protests against World Trade Organization conference in Seattle (November 2001) showed there is an increasing opposition to the forces of globalization. Such an opposition is based on the following points, raised by the opponents of globalization:

- The West's gain has come at the expense of developing nations. The already meager share of the global income of the poorest people in the world has dropped from 2.3% to 1.4% in the last decade.
- In advanced nations, the freedoms granted by globalization are leading to growing insecurity in the workplace. This is especially true in the case of blue collar workers, who have witnessed the exodus of MNCs overseas to low-wage countries.
- The spread of satellite TV, international media networks and increased personal travel is threatening national cultures. For example, Hollywood movies constitute about 70% of all films shown in France's cinemas.
- Large multinational corporations (MNCs) are becoming more influential and powerful, as compared to democratically-elected governments. As a result, MNCs put shareholder interests above those of communities and even their own customers.
- Corporations are disregarding the environment in the quest for huge profits and marketplace domination.
- Corporate power is limiting individual freedom.
- The global economies of scale enjoyed by MNCs will put small business out of work.[2]

Having gained an understanding of the globalization issues, we devote the next section to a comprehension of globalization and dependency to show the changing position of developing nations in the global market place.

Globalization and Dependency

For developing nations, dependence on rich nations is nothing new. What is new is that the developed nations have come to the realization that in an era of growing scarcity of natural and mineral resources, and escalating global trade, they too are becoming more dependent on the developing countries. Rich nations dependence on developing nations arises from the following major two factors:

1. The existence of energy and raw materials in developing nations that are needed by advanced nations.
2. The existence of a vast market in developing nations, providing a significant outlet for the exports of advanced nations.

Some numbers help illustrate the growing dependance of advanced nations on developing nations. For example, in the case of the United States, developing nations supply eighty percent of its fuel imports, more than fifty percent of its imports of consumer goods, and a quarter of its imports of capital goods. Additionally, developing nations account for more than forty percent of the total exports of the United States. As another example, developing nations account for about 50% of the goods exported by Japan abroad.

Today, developing nations are expected to absorb about seventy percent of the growth in global imports over the next quarter of century. Some theoreticians even foresee that Third World nations may become "the engine for growth" for advanced nations, early in the twenty-first century. Other scientists predict a gloomier picture for advanced nations, by maintaining that the movement of manufacturing production to low-wage developing nations, may trigger enormous layoffs and stagnant wages for workers in Third Word countries.[3]

Given the growing significance of developing nations, as the source of scarce resources and exports outlets for developed nations, it is essential for advanced nations to assist third world nations in achieving economic growth in a changing global environment.

LOCALIZATION

Although globalization is bringing the world's nations together, it is also tilting the balance of power within them, giving rise to the desire for self-determination and relegation of power, that is, localization. The speedy flow of information across national boundaries, made possible by electronic network systems, has resulted in a new international economic order that is highly integrated. In this new economic order, all markets are highly interconnected and the amount of private capital flowing in financial markets overshadows the resources of many nations. In such an environment, the demand for self-determination has taken the following forms:

- The replacement of authoritarian political or single party units by multiparty politics.
- Greater autonomy of subnational political units.
- Involvement of community groups and nongovernmental organizations (NGOs) in governance.

In the new millennium, although some businesses continue to integrate to enhance their power on the global market, many nations are moving in the reverse direction, fragmenting, questioning existing authorities, and searching for procedures to orchestrate their efforts.

Globalization and localization might appear to be countervailing forces, but they usually originate from the same source and reinforce each other. In fact, in the same manner that advances in information and communications technologies have been important in spreading global economic forces, they have also been instrumental in allowing local groups to short-circuit central authorities in looking for information, visibility, even financing. Reinforcing each other, these global and local forces have revolutionized traditional forms of centralized governance, significantly affecting development thought.[4]

GLOBALIZATION, LOCALIZATION, AND ECONOMIC DEVELOPMENT

Following World War II, economic development was born and came to existence in a period when autonomous states were run by authoritarian decision makers in the developing nations. But globalization has contributed to the erosion of that autonomy. Markets, for example, have the potential of disciplining states, punishing their mistakes and calling their bluff. These circumstances have resulted in new ways of thinking about how to manage the world's economies and how to create new institutions to achieve this goal. These institutions will be required at the following three levels:

1. **Supranational government**. These institutions, needed for shaping and channeling the forces of globalization have already been established and include World Trade Organization (WTO), The Basle Accords, and the Montreal Protocol. These institutions affect trade, banking systems, and the depletion of ozone worldwide, respectively.
2. **National level**. At this level many nations are learning about the policies that work well and policies that are not conducive to economic stability and hence should be avoided. Given the increasing exposure of developing nations to globalization, they are discovering that a stable macroeconomic environment, a liberalized domestic business service sector, and a legal framework that induces transparency and protects investors' interests is appropriate.
3. **Subnational level**. At this level, localization has induced governments to grant political, fiscal and administrative power to local government. However, attempts at sustaining workable intergovernmental relations have not kept pace with the speed of decentralization.[5]

THE ENVIRONMENT

Given the globalization of the world economy and the growing dependence of advanced nations on developing nations, a significant issue that has attracted the attention of academicians and policy makers around the world is the question of environment. Having entered the new millennium, we have come to realize that environmental issues are a matter of both national and global concerns. Many of them generate spillovers that inflict sizeable costs not only on those near the source of the problem but on the entire society and on future generations. Environmental problems encompass many issues, including desertification, persistent organic pollutants, the fate of Antarctica, and the environmental health of the high seas and the seabed. Among these issues, some of the problems that have attracted growing attention are ozone depletion, acid rain, global climate change, deforestation, desertification, and threat to biodiversity. The purpose of this chapter is to examine these issues and elaborate on their implications for developing nations, within a global context.

Since an understanding of climate change hinges upon a comprehension of acid rain and ozone depletion, we begin by examining these issues first before elaborating on climate change.

Acid Rain

Rain is naturally slightly acidic. This acidity arises from its interaction with CO_2 in the atmosphere that causes the formation of a dilute carbonic acid. However, human activities that lead to the generation of sulphur dioxide (SO_2) and nitrogen oxides (NO_X) significantly contribute to the rain acidity.[6]

"Acid rain" is a general term that is used to describe the various ways that acids fall out of the atmosphere. A more accurate term is "acid deposition", which is composed of the following two types:

1. **Wet deposition.** This includes acidic rain, fog, and snow. When this type of acid flows over and seeps through the ground, it impacts a number of animals and plants on the earth. The potency of this type of acid rain depends on a number of factors, including how acidic the water is, the chemistry and buffering capacity of the soils involved, the types of fish, trees, and other living things that rely on the water for survival.
2. **Dry deposition.** This includes acidic gases and particles. Approximately fifty percent of the acidity in the atmosphere falls back to earth through dry deposition. These acidic particles and gases are blown away by the wind onto buildings, cars, homes, and trees. Rainstorms can wash dry deposited gases and particles from trees and other surfaces. When that occurs, the runoff water adds those acids to the acid rain, making the combination more acidic than the falling rain alone. The compounds that generate both wet and dry acid deposition are blown by prevailing winds across state and national boundaries, and occasionally over hundreds of miles.

Causes of Acid Rain

As we explained earlier, the primary causes of acid rain are sulfur dioxide (SO_2) and nitrogen oxides (NOx). In the United States, about 65% of all SO_2 and 25% of all NOx stem from electric power generation that depends on burning fossil fuels like coal.

Interaction of these gases in the atmosphere with water, oxygen, and other chemicals form various acidic compounds which leads to the generation of acid rain. Sunlight enhances the strength of most of these reactions. The outcome is a mild solution of sulfuric acid and nitric acid, forming the acid rain.

GLOBAL INSIGHTS CASE 20.1

U.S. ACID RAIN PROGRAM

In 1990, Congress established the Acid Rain Program under the Clean Air Act. The principal goal of the program is to achieve reductions of 10 million tons of sulfur dioxide (SO2) and 2 million tons of nitrogen oxides (NOx), the primary components of acid rain. These pollutants, in their various forms, lead to the acidification of lakes and streams rendering some of them incapable of supporting aquatic life. In addition, they impair visibility in our national parks, create respiratory and other health problems in people, weaken forests, and degrade monuments and buildings.

Source: U.S. Environmental Protection Agency, "Acid Rain Program Progress Report,"http://www.epa.gov/airmarkets/progress/arpreport/index.html, Reprinted.

The Effects of Acid Rain

Acid deposition leads to the following adverse effects on our planet:

1. It damage forests and soils.
2. It harms fish and other living things, materials, and human health.
3. It causes "visibility reduction", that is, it reduces how far and how clearly we can see through the air.
4. It causes acidification of lakes and streams and contributes to damage of trees at high elevations (for example, red spruce trees above 2,000 feet) and many sensitive forest soils.
5. It enhances the decay of building materials and paints, including scars to buildings, statues, and sculptures.
6. It harms public health.[7]

How to Reduce Acid Rain

Some of the steps that can be taken to reduce, or even eliminate, the acid deposition problem, include cleaning up smokestacks and exhaust pipes, using alternative energy sources, and restoring a damaged environment.

Cleaning Up Smokestacks and Exhaust Pipes. Nearly all of the electricity that we use today is generated from burning fossil fuels like coal, natural gas, and oil. The burning of these fuels releases sulfur dioxide (SO_2) and nitrogen oxides (No_x) into the atmosphere, causing acid rain. Sulfur is an impure component of coal. When coal is burned it reacts with air, forming SO_2. NO_x, however, is generated when any type of fossil fuel is burned. Catalytic converters can be used to reduce NO_X emissions from automobiles. To reduce SO_2, the following actions can be taken:

- Use coal containing less sulfur.

- Wash the coal, and employ instruments called scrubbers to chemically remove the SO_2 from gases leaving the smokestack.
- Establish power plants that employ technologies that do not require fuel.
- Change power plant's fuels. For instance burning natural gas generates much less SO_2 than burning coal.

Some alternatives will also have the added benefits of diminishing other pollutants like mercury and carbon dioxide. Comprehending these "co-benefits" has become significant in pursuing cost-effective air pollution reduction strategies. Finally, power plants can use technologies that do not burn fossil fuels. Although such devices have been required for more than two decades in the United States, they have not been tried in most of the developing nations.

Using Alternative Energy Sources. Besides fossil fuels, other sources of electricity include: nuclear power, hydropower, wind energy, geothermal energy, and solar energy. Although, nuclear and hydropower have been used in the United States, and other advanced nations, wind, solar, and geothermal energy have not yet been employed on a large scale in any nation. Acid rain can also be reduced by using alternative energies to power automobiles, including natural gas powered vehicles, battery-powered cars, fuel cells, and combinations of alternative and gasoline powered vehicles. It should be kept in mind that all sources of energy have environmental costs as well as benefits. This necessitates the implementation of costs-benefits analyses before any of these alternatives is chosen by a nation.

Restoring A Damaged Environment. Acid rain affects an ecosystem by altering the chemistry of the soil and the chemistry of the streams. This narrows, or may even deplete, the place where certain plants and animals can live. Since there are many changes that occur as a result of the acid rain it takes a long time for ecosystems to recover from the inflicted damage, even after emissions are reduced and the rain becomes normal again.

Although some minor improvements can occur in a short period of time, major improvements do not come for a very long time. For example, visibility might improve within days, and the streams chemistry can improve within months, however, it might take years or even centuries for the chronically acidified lakes, streams, forests, and soils to show improvement.

The recovery of lakes and streams can be hastened by adding limestone or lime (a naturally-occurring basic compound) to eliminate the acidity. This process, referred to as **liming**, has been employed particularly in Norway and Sweden. However, it has not been used very often in the United States. Liming is subject to the following problems:

a. High cost, associated with the need to be used repeatedly in order to prevent the water from returning to its acidic condition.
b. It is considered as a short-term solution in only specific areas rather than a vehicle for reducing or preventing pollution.
c. It does not rectify the broader problems stemming from changes in soil chemistry and forest health in the watershed.
d. It does not resolve visibility reduction, material damage, and risk to human health.

Aside from the above problems, liming does permit fish to remain in a lake, enabling them to survive in place until emissions reductions decrease the amount of acid deposition in the their environment.[8]

OZONE DEPLETION

The atmosphere is made up of nitrogen (78%), oxygen (21%), water vapor and a small amounts of some other gases.[9] Between 15 and 39 km above the earth's surface, the action of ultraviolet (UV) light on oxygen generates and extinguishes ozone. In the ozone layer there are only a very few molecules of ozone per million molecules of air. But, this is sufficient to shield UV, which would otherwise cause skin cancers, cataracts and inflict damage on plant and animal life. Although about 75% of ozone is broken down by nitric oxide, adequate ozone remains to harness UV penetration. However, chemicals such as chlorofluorocarbons (CFCs) and other halocarbons that are manufactured on earth destroy some of the remaining ozone molecules. These chemicals are commonly utilized as solvents, aerosol propellants, refrigerants and in foam production. When these are dumped into the atmosphere they move up to the stratosphere where they are broken up by UV light.[10]

The Ozone Agreements

The issue of ozone depletion attracted global attention in the early and mid-1980s. This has resulted in the signing of the following agreements:

1. **Vienna Convention.** This convention which occurred in 1985, presents the first major attempt by the international community that is aimed at the protection of the ozone layer. Although this convention led to the generation of a framework for future cooperation, it did not encompass a protocol restraining the use of CFCs.
2. **The Montreal Protocol.** This agreement was reached in 1987, and emerged as a major cooperative endeavor to control ozone depletion. The participants in this agreement acknowledged that the risk of ozone depletion, resulting from CFCs and other chemicals including chlorine and bromine, is costly. They realized that there was technological and institutional ability to explore cost-effective, environmentally-friendly substitutes. They also agreed that the solution to the problems calls on the participation of all parties, each having a significant role to play in combating ozone depletion. These considerations led the participants to agree to reduce ozone depletion via decreasing output of chlorine and bromine that are known to lead to ozone depletion. These agreements were aided by the London amendment (1990) and the Copenhagen amendment (1992) whereby the participants agreed to phase out CFCs altogether by 1995 (DOE, 1994). Following the world community's efforts in combating ozone depletion, the global annual production of CFCs fell significantly (from 1 metric tons in 1985 to 0.36 metric tons in 1995). Today, global production of CFCs has declined substantially, and the problem of ozone depletion is basically behind us. Full compliance with the Copenhagen amendment is expected to be accomplished by the middle of the next century.[11]

CLIMATE CHANGE

Once, all climate changes occurred naturally. During the Industrial Revolution, we began altering our climate and environment through changing agricultural and industrial practices. Before the Industrial Revolution, human activity released very few gases into the atmosphere, but now through population growth, fossil fuel burning, and deforestation, we are affecting the mixture of gases in the atmosphere. As a result, the rate of climate change is accelerating as the amount of carbon dioxide, methane, and other so called "green house gases" that are dumped into atmosphere every day keep rising.

The 20th century can be marked as the warmest century in the past 600 years. Fourteen of the warmest years since the 1860s occurred in the 1980s and 1990s. Temperatures in 1998 were higher than the mean temperatures for the 118 years on record, even after taking the effect of El Nino into account.[12]

To understand the speed of the global climate over time, it is necessary to have an understanding of the greenhouse gases, as discussed in the next section.

GLOBAL INSIGHTS CASE 20.2

GOOD AND BAD OZONE

How Can Ozone Be Both Good and Bad?

Ozone occurs in two layers of the atmosphere. The layer surrounding the earth's surface is the troposphere. Here, ground-level or "bad" ozone is an air pollutant that damages human health, vegetation, and many common materials. It is a key ingredient of urban smog. The troposphere extends to a level about 10 miles up, where it meets the second layer, the stratosphere. The stratospheric or "good" ozone layer extends upward from about 10 to 30 miles and protects life on earth from the sun's harmful ultraviolet rays (UV-b).

What is Happening to the "Good" Ozone Layer?

Ozone occurs naturally in the stratosphere and is produced and destroyed at a constant rate. But this "good" ozone is gradually being destroyed by manmade chemicals called chlorofluorocarbons (CFCs), halons, and other ozone depleting substances (used in coolants, foaming agents, fire extinguishers, and solvents). These ozone depleting substances degrade slowly and can remain intact for many years as they move through the troposphere until they reach the stratosphere. There they are broken down by the intensity of the sun's ultraviolet rays and release chlorine and bromine molecules, which destroy "good" ozone. One chlorine or bromine molecule can destroy 100,000 ozone molecules, causing ozone to disappear much faster than nature can replace it.

It can take years for ozone depleting chemicals to reach the stratosphere, and even though we have reduced or eliminated the use of many CFCs, their impact from years past is just starting to affect the ozone layer. Substances released into the air today will contribute to ozone destruction well into the future.

Satellite observations indicate a world-wide thinning of the protective ozone layer. The most noticeable losses occur over the North and South Poles because ozone depletion accelerates in extremely cold weather conditions.

Source: United States Environmental Protection Agency, "Ozone: Good Up High, Bad Nearby," http:/www.epa.gov/oar/oaqps/gooduphigh.

Greenhouse Gases

Greenhouse gases are gases that shield the reflected thermal radiation from the sun in the Earth's atmosphere.[13]

Although some greenhouse gases occur naturally in the atmosphere, some gases stem from human actions. Naturally occurring greenhouse gases encompass water vapor, carbon dioxide, methane, nitrous oxide, and ozone.

The following is the list of human activities that add to the levels of most of these naturally occurring gases:

- Burning of solid waste, fossil fuels (oil, natural gas, and coal), and wood and wood products, leading to carbon dioxide emission.
- The production and transport of coal, natural gas, and oil, leading to methane emission.

GLOBAL INSIGHTS CASE 20.3

THE IMPACT OF OZONE ON HUMAN HEALTH AND ENVIRONMENT

How Does the Depletion of "Good" Ozone Affect Human Health and the Environment?

As the stratospheric ozone layer is depleted, higher UV-b levels reach the earth's surface. Increased UV-b can lead to more cases of skin cancer, cataracts, and impaired immune systems. Damage to UV-b sensitive crops, such as soybeans, reduces yield. High altitude ozone depletion is suspected to cause decreases in phytoplankton, a plant that grows in the ocean. Phytoplankton is an important link in the marine food chain and, therefore, food populations could decline. Because plants "breathe in" carbon dioxide and "breathe out" oxygen, carbon dioxide levels in the air could also increase. Increased UV-b radiation can be instrumental in forming more ground-level or "bad" ozone.

How Does "Bad" Ozone Affect Human Health and the Environment?

Repeated exposure to ozone pollution may cause permanent damage to the lungs. Even when ozone is present in low levels, inhaling it triggers a variety of health problems including chest pains, coughing, nausea, throat irritation, and congestion. It also can worsen bronchitis, heart disease, emphysema, and asthma, and reduce lung capacity. Healthy people also experience difficulty in breathing when exposed to ozone pollution. Because ozone pollution usually forms in hot weather, anyone who spends time outdoors in the summer may be affected, particularly children, the elderly, outdoor workers and people exercising. Millions of Americans live in areas where the national ozone health standards are exceeded. Ground-level ozone damages plant life and is responsible for 500 million dollars in reduced crop production in the United States each year. It interferes with the ability of plants to produce and store food, making them more susceptible to disease, insects, other pollutants, and harsh weather. "Bad" ozone damages the foliage of trees and other plants, ruining the landscape of cities, national parks and forests, and recreation areas.

Source: United States Environmental Protection Agency, "Ozone: Good Up High, Bad Nearby," http:/www.epa.gov/oar/oaqps/ gooduphigh.

- The decomposition of organic wastes in municipal solid waste landfills, and the raising of livestock, leading to methane emissions.
- Agricultural and industrial activities that lead to nitrous oxide emission.
- Combustion of solid waste and fossil fuels, leading to nitrous oxide emission.
- Industrial processes that lead to the generation of perfluorocarbons (PFCs), and sulfur hexafluoride (SF$_6$), which are generated in a variety of industrial activities.

These greenhouse gases vary in terms of their ability to absorb heat in the atmosphere. The most heat-absorbent gases are HFCs and PFCs. Methane absorbs more than 21 times the heat per molecule than carbon dioxide, and nitrous oxide traps 270 times more heat per molecule than carbon dioxide. Usually, greenhouse gas emissions are estimated in terms of units of millions of metric tons of carbon equivalents (MMTCE), which weight each gas by its Global Warming Potential. (GWP) value.[14]

> # GLOBAL INSIGHTS CASE 20.4
>
> # THE ANTARCTIC OZONE HOLE
>
> The ozone hole is a well-defined, large-scale destruction of the ozone layer over Antarctica that occurs each Antarctic spring. The word "hole" is a misnomer; the hole is really a significant thinning, or reduction in ozone concentrations, which results in the destruction of up to 70% of the ozone normally found over Antarctica.
>
> The science of the ozone hole is quite complex, but our understanding of the many factors that combine to create it has improved greatly since the first investigations in the 1980s. Unlike global ozone depletion, the ozone hole occurs only over Antarctica. Using several instruments on satellites, planes, and balloons, scientists have produced detailed graphs of the size of the ozone hole.
>
> Source: U.S. Environmental Protection Agency, "Ozone Depletion," http://www.epa.gov/docs/ozone/science/hole/.

Global Warming

Our weather and climate are affected by the sun which heats the earth's surface. The earth, in turn, radiates energy back into the space. However, some of the outgoing energy is trapped by atmospheric greenhouse gases like water vapor, carbon dioxide, and other gases. These gases, functioning like the glass panels of a greenhouse, retain the heat in our planet.

In the absence of "greenhouse effect," the planet's temperatures would be much lower than they are now. As a result, life as it is known, would not exist. Today, because of greenhouse gases, the earth's temperature, averaging 60°F is very favorable. But if the atmospheric concentration of greenhouse gases rises we may face problems.

The existing data show that beginning with the industrial revolution, atmospheric concentrations of carbon dioxide have risen nearly 30%, methane concentrations have more than doubled, and nitrous oxide concentrations have increased by about 15%. These increases have caused the heat-trapping capability of the earth's atmosphere to rise.[15]

Factors Giving Rise to Greenhouse Gases

One of the elements that affect the Earth's temperature is sulfate aerosols. This common air pollutant, cools the atmosphere by reflecting light back into space. However, these substances have short lives and their use varies from region to region.

Scientists generally believe that the primary cause for the enhanced combustion concentration of carbon dioxide is the burning of fossil fuels and other human activities. To be sure, plant respiration and the decomposition of organic matter emits more than 10 times the CO_2 in comparison to human activities.

GLOBAL INSIGHTS CASE 20.5

CHANGING CLIMATE

Global mean surface temperatures have increased 0.5-1.0°F since the late 19th century. The 20th century's 10 warmest years all occurred in the last 15 years of the century. Of these, 1998 was the warmest year on record. The snow cover in the Northern Hemisphere and floating ice in the Arctic Ocean have decreased. Globally, sea level has risen 4-8 inches over the past century. Worldwide precipitation over land has increased by about one percent. The frequency of extreme rainfall events has increased throughout much of the United States.

Increasing concentrations of greenhouse gases are likely to accelerate the rate of climate change. Scientists expect that the average global surface temperature could rise 1-4.5°F (0.6-2.5°C) in the next fifty years, and 2.2-10°F (1.4-5.8°C) in the next century, with significant regional variation. Evaporation will increase as the climate warms, which will increase average global precipitation. Soil moisture is likely to decline in many regions, and intense rainstorms are likely to become more frequent. Sea level is likely to rise two feet along most of the U.S. coast.

Calculations of climate change for specific areas are much less reliable than global ones, and it is unclear whether regional climate will become more variable.

Source: U.S. Environmental Protection Agency, "Global Warming: Climate," http://www.epa.gov/globalwarming/climate/index.html.

However, such emissions have generally been in balance during the centuries preceding the industrial revolution.

With the advent of the industrial revolution the growing emission of carbon dioxide, resulting from industrial activities, began to change the picture of the atmosphere. Fossil fuels burned to operate automobiles, heat homes and businesses, and power factories significantly raised the release of carbon dioxide into the atmosphere. Today, fossil fuels account for 98% of U.S. carbon dioxide emissions, 24% of methane emissions, and 18% of nitrous oxide emissions. Enhanced agriculture, deforestation, landfills, industrial production, and mining also contribute a significant share of emissions. In 1997, the United States emitted about one-fifth of total global greenhouse gases.[16]

The Impact of Climate Changes on the Environment

Climate changes are likely to increase sea levels, endangering island economies and low-lying nations such as the Maldives and Bangladesh. Climate changes also threaten agricultural production in developing nations. The overall effect of doubling carbon dioxide in the atmosphere would be to decrease the GDP of developing nations by 2-9 percent, as compared to 1.0-1.5 percent decrease in GDP of advanced nations. Within the developing nations, the cost of inaction is likely to be inflicted upon the poorest populous, who have meager resources to react to climate changes.[17] Although these facts are now widely accepted by the international community, there still remain a number of issues that are not well comprehended. Chief among these issues are the following:

1. How intensive variations in weather will be in a warming world.

2. How the impact of climate fluctuations on agriculture and living conditions will be distributed globally.
3. How fast climate changes occur.
4. How people who will be displaced by elevating sea levels, in nations such as Bangladesh, will be served.

Such issues make accurate measurement of the economic effects of climate changes very problematic. Nevertheless, the impact is expected to be tremendous and will primarily affect developing nations. The alleviation of this problem requires a sharp reduction of global emissions, and calls on the international community to reach an agreed upon solution. Unfortunately, an international agreement to restrain climate changes faces the following obstacles:

1. The uncertainty associated with the magnitude of possible gains and the range of adaptation.
2. The difficulty of monitoring compliance with emission rules and plausible sanctions.
3. Distributional considerations.
4. Resistence to costs associated with reaching the objectives of restraining climate changes.

Today, the industrial nations account for 60 percent of all energy related carbon-dioxide. Of this amount, the United States alone is responsible for 25 percent of all carbon-dioxide released into the atmosphere. Given this fact, developing nations have argued that because gases are the outcomes of industrialization in advanced nations, those nations should accept the major responsibility in rectifying the problem. Additionally, third world nations have faced enormous difficulty in erecting regulatory capacity to harness the release of gases and other pollutants. Nevertheless, some progress has been made on the international level in coping with climate change. To this end, two international agreements have been reached. The first international agreement was ratified in Rio in 1992, and the second international agreement was signed in Tokyo in 1997.[18]

Rio Convention

In this first agreement, advanced nations voluntarily committed themselves to decrease the level of their emissions in 2000 to the level in 1990. In this convention, the emissions levels for each country was defined on the basis of their past history. This implies that the nations that polluted more in the past were permitted to pollute more in the future. From the developing nations' perspectives, this did not seem to be equitable. They felt that there was no justification in allowing advanced nations to emit higher levels of omissions per capita simply on the basis of their past behavior.[19]

Tokyo Convention

At this second convention, more ambitious goals were established and more binding commitments were set. An important step was set forward in trying to ensure efficiency in reducing emissions, through the Clean Development Mechanism (CDM). This mechanism would permit advanced nations to assist developing nations to lower their emissions. In the mean time it would allow advanced nations to earn "credit" for these lower emission. However, the equity issue raised in the previous convention in Rio was not effectively addressed. This contributed to the reluctance of developing nations to enter into binding commitments. As a result, the United States and several other industrial nations have been reluctant to take binding commitments upon themselves. They realized that without sufficient global enforcement, nations with stronger legal frameworks would end up sustaining inequitable burdens once treaties were endorsed.[20]

BIODIVERSITY

The issue of biodiversity has been imbued with heated debates in the academic community. It has also been subject to misunderstanding among the general public, decision makers, and even the scientific community. Since its first appearance in the proceedings of the National Forum on Biodiversity in September, 1986, numerous writers have elaborated on this subject. The purpose of this section is to provide us with an understanding of the concept of diversity and its significance to our planet.

Definition of Biodiversity

Biological diversity, or biodiversity, is a term that refers to the variations of life on our planet. In other words, it encompasses all species, organism and population. A more thorough definition is presented by botanist Peter H. Raven, who writes:

> At the simplest level, biodiversity is the sum total of all the plants, animals, fungi and microorganisms in the world, or in a particular area; all of their individual variation; and all of the interactions between them. It is the set of living organisms that make up the fabric of the planet Earth and allow it to function as it does, by capturing energy from the sun and using it to drive all of life's processes; by forming communities of organisms that have, through the several billion years of life's history on Earth, altered the nature of the atmosphere, the soil and the water of our planet; and by making possible the sustainability of our planet through their life activities now. [21]

We still do not know how many species have existed on our planet, but so far about 1.4 million species have been named. It has also been estimated that there are about 9 million more species that have not been identified yet. We do know, however, that some numbers of species are declining at a fast rate.[22]

Levels of Biodiversity

Biodiversity can be divided into the following three categories:

1. **Ecosystem diversity.** This category refers to all the various habitats, biological communities and ecological processes, as well as variations within individual ecosystems.
2. **Genetic diversity.** This category relates to all the various genes embodied in all individual plants, animals, fungi, and microorganism. It happens both within species and between species.
3. **Species diversity.** This category pertains to all the variations within and between populations of species, as well as between species.[23]

The Significance of Protecting Diversity

An important issue that has attracted increasing attention in recent years is the preservation of diversity. Today, it is an established fact that the diversity of life enriches the quality of our lives in a variety of ways and is crucial for our physical and psychological well being. Although reasons for protecting biological diversity are complex, they can be classified into the following four major categories:

1. **Loss of diversity leads to the weakening of the entire natural system.** This happens because every species performs a significant function in maintaining a healthy ecosystem. The loss of diversity interferes with the system and goes against its natural checks and balances. As a result, the system becomes more susceptible to natural and artificial disturbances. This enhances the possibility of a system-wide collapse. For example, in parts of the Midwestern United States, during the dust

bowl years of the 1930s, soil was kept intact only by the remnant areas of natural prairies. Simplified ecosystems are almost always expensive to maintain. For example, when synthetic chemicals are relied upon to control pests, the target species are not the only ones affected. But their natural predators are almost always killed or driven away, exacerbating the pest problem. In the meantime, people are unintentionally breeding pesticide resistant pests.

To deal with this problem, a process has begun where people become perpetual guardians of the affected area, which requires the expenditure of financial resources and human ingenuity to keep the system going.

2. **Every species is a potential source of food supply.** Our sources of food supply are composed of a variety of species that are hunted, fished, gathered, as well as those that are cultivated for agriculture, forestry, and husbandry. Today, only about 20 species provide 90% of the world's food. Out of these 20, only three species provide us with wheat, maize and rice, accounting for more than 50 % of the world food supply. New varieties are always needed to compete with pests and diseases that afflict farming. Wild strains of wheat are critical genetic reservoirs for these new varieties. In 1970, for example, the U.S. corn crop was threatened by a new race of corn leaf blight that had reduced corn yields by 50% in many states. The gene that creates resistance to the blight was discovered in a wild strain of corn found only in Mexico.

3. **Every species is a potential source of human medicine.** Every species has the potential of being the source of both traditional medicine and those synthesized from biological resources and processes. For example, organic alkaloids, a type of chemical compound, are found in an estimated 20% of plant species. Still only 2% of plant species have been tested for these compounds. According to a report published in 1980, the market value of prescription drugs from higher plants was more than $3 billion.

4. **Human Psychological Needs.** As human species, we evolved in a diverse natural environment surrounded by forests, grasslands and water. As such, we are part of nature and we need to preserve it to enjoy a holistic , and organic experience. Today, our urban environment is imbued with pollution, noise, and traffic congestion, just to name a few. Extended living in such an environment has contributed to emotional and psychological problems that have inflicted our lives. Natural diversity lifts the human spirit, providing a cure for ills resulting from prolonged urban exposure.

The above reasons have focused on the benefits of the natural world from the human standpoint. It is argued, however, that all things have intrinsic value just because they exist. In this context, a fifth reason for protecting diversity is related to the notion that species and natural systems are intrinsically valuable and for that reason they must be protected.

DEFORESTATION

One of the major global problems that has afflicted our planet is deforestation. Deforestation has a severe negative impact on the climate, biodiversity, and atmosphere, and endangers physical and cultural survival of the indigenous peoples. According the available data, deforestation has contributed to the extinction of tribal people in this century as compared to previous centuries. Just in Brazil, For example, we lost 87 tribes between 1900 and 1950.[24]

Deforestation encompasses the cutting down, burning, and damaging of forests. It is estimated that if deforestation continues at its current rate, the globe's rain forests will disappear within 100 years. This would have a devastating impact on global climate, eliminating most of plants and species on the earth.[25]

The impact of deforestation on global climate stems from the fact that the forest plays a significant function in the water cycle, recycling rain into the clouds as it receives rainfall. If land is cleared, flooding

> # GLOBAL INSIGHTS CASE 20.6
>
> # BIODIVERSITY AND THE GREAT LAKES BASIN'S HUMAN POPULATION
>
> Historically, the lack of attention to biological diversity, and the ecological processes it supports, has resulted in economic hardships for segments of the basin's human population. The first Europeans that settled in the basin came in pursuit of fur-bearing animals, exhausted the populations and were forced to move on to areas more rich in pelts. In the early 1800s, the virgin forests of the basin appeared to be without limit. They were harvested to support the building boom in the basin, often with a view to farming the cleared land. Frequently, poorer soils could not support agriculture after the forests were cleared, the farms failed, and the forests have yet to be fully regenerated. The Great Lakes commercial fishery reached its peak in the late 1800s. An entire industry, and the families it supported, suffered because of the introduction of exotic species, the overharvest of the lakes and pollution. Today, only pockets remain of the once large commercial fishery.
>
> United States Environmental Protection Agency, "The Conservation of Biological Diversity in Great Lakes Ecosystem: Issues and Opportunities,"http://www.epa.gov/glnpo/ecopage/issues.html#Overview, Reprinted.

and drought would become serious problems.

Causes of Deforestation

The elements giving rise to deforestation can be divided into the following three categories:

1. **Agricultural activities**. This is the most common type of deforestation. Given the dependence of poor nations on agricultural, farming is a basic way of life . Driven by the basic human need for food, a peasant farmer usually chops down trees in order to graze cattle or raise crops for self-subsistence. Mechanized , or contemporary, agriculture takes place on a much larger scale. This results in deforestation of several square miles at a time. To satisfy the global demand for beef, large cattle pastures often replace rain forests, contributing to deforestation.
2. **Commercial logging**. This is another common form of deforestation that is undertaken by the logging industry in order to make profit. It occurs by cutting trees for sale as timber or pulp. Logging can take the following two forms:
    a. **Selective logging**. In this type of logging only the economically valuable species are cut.
    b. **Clearcutting**. In this type of logging all the trees are cut. This method uses
heavy machinery, such as bulldozers, road graders, and log skidders, to remove cut trees and build roads, which is just as damaging to a forest overall as the chainsaws are to the individual trees.
3. **Other causes**. Other causes of deforestation include the desire to construct towns or dams which flood large areas. However, these cases constitute only a very small part of the whole problem of

deforestation.[26]

The Rate of Deforestation

The determination of the actual rate of deforestation is a difficult task. The deforestation rate is determined by analyzing satellite imagery of forested areas that have been cleared.[27] According to estimates by the Food and Agriculture Organization (FAO) during the 1980s, 53,000 square miles of tropical forests (rain forest and other) were destroyed each year. Out of this amount, 21,000 square miles were deforested annually in South America; most of this occurred in the Amazon Basin. Assuming that these estimates are accurate, we can say that an area of tropical forest large enough to cover North Carolina is deforested each year.[28]

The Impact of Deforestation on Climate

Deforestation affects climate in the two following ways:

1. **Enhancing the amount of carbon dioxide and other trace gases in the atmosphere.** The plants and soil of tropical forests hold 460-575 billion metric tons of carbon globally. Each acre of tropical forest stores about 180 metric tons of carbon. If a forest is cut and burned to set up cropland and pastures, the carbon that was stored in the tree trunks (wood is about 50% carbon) mixes with oxygen and is released into the atmosphere as CO_2.[29]

2. **Affecting evaporation process.** Tropical deforestation impacts the local climate of a region by decreasing the evaporative cooling that is generated from both soil and plant life. When trees and plants are chopped dwon, the moist canopy of the tropical rain forest quickly decreases. According to recent studies, about half of the precipitation that falls in a tropical rain forest stems from of its moist, green canopy. Evaporation and evapotranspiration processes cause a large amount of water to be returned to the local atmosphere. This, in turn, boosts the formation of clouds and precipitation. If the level of evaporation is diminished, more of the Sun's energy would be able to warm the surface, causing the temperature to rise.[30]

Deforestation and Biodiversity

The rain forest is the natural habitat for many plants and animals that can only be found in small areas of the forests. Deforestation destroys their habitat and may lead to their extinction. The evidence shows that every day species are vanishing from the tropical rain forests as they are cleared. Although the exact rate of extinction is not known, estimates show that up to 137 species disappear globally each day.[31]

As we know from our earlier discussion of biodiversity, the loss of species will have dire consequences for the planet, and hence our own well being. We may be losing species that might have great potential in preventing deadly diseases such as AIDS and cancer, Alzheimer, just to name a few. What is even more disturbing is that other organisms are losing species that are crucial for their survival. The loss of such species ensures the extinction of these organisms.

The Impact of Deforestation on the Ecosystem

The impact of deforestation on the ecosystem depends on various cutting techniques and uses of land, each having a different impact on the earth and surviving organisms that constitute a forest. and its regeneration.

GLOBAL INSIGHTS CASE 20.7

TROPICAL DEFORESTATION AND HABITAT DEGRADATION IN THE BRAZILIAN AMAZON BASIN

The Brazilian Amazon is the largest continuous region of tropical forest in the world, containing nearly 31 percent of the world total. Tropical deforestation is a major component of the carbon cycle and has profound implications for biological diversity. Deforestation increases atmospheric carbon dioxide (CO_2) and other trace gases, possibly affecting climate. Conversion of forests to cropland and pasture results in a net flux of carbon to the atmosphere because the concentration of carbon in forests is higher than that in the agricultural areas that replace them. Furthermore, while occupying less than 7 percent of the terrestrial surface, tropical forests provide homes to half or more of all plant and animal species. The primary adverse effect of tropical deforestation is massive extinction of species including, for the first time, large numbers of vascular plant species.

Deforestation affects biological diversity in three ways: (1) destruction of habitat, (2) isolation of fragments of formerly contiguous habitat, defined as areas of less than 100 square kilometers surrounded by deforestation, and (3) edge effects within a boundary zone between forest and deforested areas, defined as 1 kilometer into the forest from adjacent areas of deforestation. In the boundary zone there are greater exposure to winds; dramatic micrometeorological differences over short distances; easier access for livestock, other nonforest animals, and hunters; and a range of other biological and physical effects. The result is a net loss of plant and animal species in the edge areas. Spatial analysis of the geometry of deforestation is critical to the estimation of forest isolation and the edge effect. If 100 km2 of tropical deforestation occurs as a 10 km by 10 km square and we assume that the edge effect is 1 km, the total area affected is approximately 144 km2. In contrast, if the 100 km2 of deforestation is distributed as 10 strips, each 10 km by 1 km, the affected area is approximately 350 km2.

An analysis of change over a 10-year period of the entire Brazilian Amazon area was performed using Landsat data. For 1988, 210 black and white photographic images from the 1.55-to-1.75 micrometer channel of the Landsat Thematic Mapper, with a ground resolution of about 30 meters, were obtained. The deforested areas were digitized with visual deforestation interpretation and standard vector geographic information system (GIS) techniques. Image 4-07a is a Landsat Thematic Mapper color composite image of southern Rondonia state, Brazil, and illustrates this type of analysis. Taken on June 5, 1988, this image shows areas of tropical forest, deforestation, regrowth, and isolated forest. The area labeled as "isolated forest" is about 3 km by 15 km in size.

To determine the extent of deforestation in 1978, maps produced from single (visible) channel Landsat Multispectral Scanner (MSS) data were digitized. The ground resolution of the MSS channel was about 80 meters.

The numerical results of the analysis shows that deforestation increased between 1978 and 1988 (78,000 to 230,000 km2) as did the total affected habitat (208,000 to 588,000 km2). About 5.6 percent (230,324/4,092,831) of closed canopy forest had been cleared as of 1988 and about 14.4 percent (587,604/4,092,831) of the forested.

Continued

> *Global Insights Case 20.7 continued*
>
> Amazon was affected by deforestation-caused habitat destruction, habitat isolation, and edge effects. The preponderance of affected habitat results from proximity to areas of deforestation (approximately 341,000 km2 for a 1-km edge-effect) and not from isolation of forest (approximately 16,000 km2) or deforestation per se (approximately 230,000 km2). While the rate of deforestation averaged approximately 15,000 km2/year [(230,324 - 78,268)/10] in the Brazilian Amazon from 1978 to 1988, the rate of habitat fragmentation and degradation was approximately 38,000 km2/year [(587,604 - 208,229)/10]. Implications for biological diversity are not encouraging and provide added impetus for the minimization of tropical deforestation in the future.
>
> MTPE's future plans include continuing analyses using data from such instruments as the Enhanced Thematic Mapper (ETM), scheduled for flight on Landsat-7, and the Advanced Spaceborne Thermal Emission and Reflection Radiometer (ASTER), provided by Japan and scheduled for flight on an EOS satellite.
>
> Source: NASA's Earth Observing System, http://eocpso.gsfc.nasa.gov/eos_edu.pack/p.24.html, Reprinted.

We may distinguish between the following techniques of farming:

1. **Burning the tree trunks.** In a tropical rain forest, almost all the nutrients that are conducive to life are embodied in the plants and trees, not in the ground as is the case in a northern, or temperate forest. After the plants and trees are chopped off to sow the land, farmers ordinarily burn the tree trunks to free the nutrients essential for a fertile soil. However, the rains wash away most of the nutrients, leaving the soil much less fertile. Consequently, in as little as 3 years, the ground is no longer be capable of supporting crops. When the land becomes less fertile, farmers abandon the nutrient-deficient soil and move to other areas to clear and plant. Thus, the area that was previously under cultivation is left to grow back to a rain forest. But after the land is abandoned it might take up to half a century for the forest to replenish itself.
2. **Shade agriculture.** In this method of farming, trees are left alone to provide shade for shade-thriving crops like coffee or chocolate. Because in this type of farming much of the forest is left untouched, the forests replenish themselves and can grow back as fast as in two decades.
3. **Intensive agricultural systems.** In this type of farming large quantities of chemicals like pesticides and fertilizers are used. The application of these chemicals causes a lot of the living organisms in the area to die. These dead organisms, in turn, seep into the soil and wash into the surrounding areas. For example, the application of intensive agricultural systems to grow bananas harms the ecosystem in the following two ways:
    a. The use of chemicals on the plants and in the soil to kill pest animals also leads to the destruction of other animals as well, and weakens ecosystem's health.
    b. The use of irrigation ditches and underground pipes for water transport, changes the water balance of the land.

Given the above problems associated with intensive agricultural systems, it can take many centuries for a forest to replenish itself.[32]

Looking Into The Future of Deforestation

Deforestation has presented humanity with a global problem that is market by global climate changes and the extinction of thousands of species every year. Given the global nature of the problem, its solution requires worldwide attention and calls on international cooperation. Fortunately, such a movement has already started and the desire to mitigate deforestation has fueled cooperation among nations in finding ways to halt the loss

GLOBAL INSIGHTS CASE 20.8

THE LEVEL OF INCOME AND DEFORESTATION IN TROPICAL COUNTRIES

Most tropical nations are very poor by U.S. standards, and farming is the basic way of life for a large part of population. In Brazil, for example, the average annual earnings per person is U.S. $5400, compared to $26,980 per person in the United States (World Bank, 1998). In Bolivia, which holds part of the Amazon rain forest, the average earnings per person is $800. Farmers in these countries do not have the money to buy necessities and must raise crops for food and to sell. Deforestation by a peasant farmer is often done to raise crops for self-subsistence, and is driven by basic human need for food. Poor farmers chop down a small area (typically a few acres) and burn the tree trunks-a process called Slash and Burn Agriculture. Intensive, or modern agriculture, occurs on a much larger scale, sometimes deforesting several square miles at a time. Large scale cattle pastures often replace rain forest to grow beef for the world market, Thus, contributing to the deforestation process.

There are other reasons for deforestation, such as to construct towns or dams which followed large areas. Yet, these latter cases constitute only a very small part of deforestation.

Source: NASA, Earth Observatory, "Tropical Deforestation: Why Deforestation Happens," http://eathobservatory.nasa.gov/LibraryDeforestation//deforestation / 2.html., Reprinted

GLOBAL INSIGHTS CASE 20.9

SELECTIVE LOGGING IN INDONESIA

A study in Indonesia found that when only 3% of the trees were cut, a logging operation damaged 49% of the trees in the forest. Yet, even with that much damage, the rain forest will grow back relatively quickly if left alone after selective logging, because there are still many trees to provide seeds and protect young trees from too much sun.

Source: NASA, Earth Observatory, "Tropical Deforestation: After Deforestation," http://earthobservatory.nasa.gov/gov/Library/Deforstation/deforestation_4.ht..

GLOBAL INSIGHTS CASE 20.10

REGIONAL VARIATIONS IN THE RATE OF DEFORESTATION

The rate of deforestation varies from region to region. Recent research results showed that in the Brazilian Amazon, the rate of deforestation was around 6200 square miles per year from 1978-1986, but fell to 4800 square miles per year from 1986-1993. By 1988, 6% of the Brazilian Amazon had been cut down (90,000 square miles, an area the size of New England). However, due to the isolation of fragments and the increase in forest/clearing boundaries, a total of 16.5% of the forest (230,000 square miles, an area nearly the size of Texas) was affected by deforestation. Scientists are currently analyzing rates of deforestation for the current decade, as well as studying how deforestation changes from year to year.

The much smaller region of Southeast Asia (Cambodia, Indonesia, Laos, Malaysia, Myanmar, Thailand, and Vietnam) lost nearly as much forest per year as the Brazilian Amazon from the mid-1970s to the mid-1980s, with 4800 square miles per year converted to agriculture or cut for timber.

Source: NASA, Earth Observatory: "Tropical Deforestation: The Rate of Deforestation" http://eathobservatory.nasa.gov/Library/Deforestation/deforestation_2.htm., Reprinted.

GLOBAL INSIGHTS CASE 20.11

NASA MISSIONS TO STUDY DEFORESTATION

NASA's Earth Science Enterprise future plans to study the effects of deforestation include continuing analyses using data from such instruments as the Enhanced Thematic Mapper Plus (ETM+), scheduled for flight on Landsat-7, and the Advanced Spaceborne Thermal Emission and Reflection Radiometer (ASTER) and the Moderate Resolution Imaging Spectroradiometer (MODIS), scheduled for flight on the EOS AM-1 satellite. The observational capabilities and scientific studies planned as part of the Earth Science Enterprise, including the Earth Observing System, will help to assess the impacts of deforestation on the global climate system. An overarching objective of the Earth Science Enterprise is to improve our understanding of the causes and effects of climatic and environmental change so that we may become more effective and efficient managers of our natural resources, as well as mitigate potential impacts from natural disasters.

Source: Reprinted from NASA's Earth Observatory, http://earthobservatory.nasa.gov/Library/Deforestaton/deforestation_4.html.

of rain forests.

From a global standpoint, deforestation is a complicated issue that is caused by a number of factors, requiring a complex solution. Thus, simple solutions that do not take the nature of global and rain forest ecology into account, do not have much chance of success. In the context of economic development, the problem of deforestation is rooted in economic crises of nations holding rain forests. It also stems from the living conditions of the poor inhabitants who depend on deforestation related particles as a major source of income. Thus, the solution to this worldwide problem not only depends on educating people on the issue of deforestation, but it also demands improvements of living conditions of poor people who depend on deforestation to make a living. [33]

DESERTIFICATION

Desertification refers to the degradation of dry land. It happens when productive land in arid, semi-arid, or sub-humid-dryland is degraded either by human endeavors or by prolonged drought. Desertification may strengthen a general climatic tendency toward greater aridity, or it may instigate a change in local climate.[34] Desertification does not take place in a predictable manner. It occurs erratically, leading to formation of patches on deserts borders. Poor land management could lead to quick degradation of areas far from desert to barren soil, rock, or sand. Thus, there is no direct relationship between the presence of a nearby desert and desertification.[35]

Causes of Desertification

The major elements that give rise to desertification can be divided into the following two major categories:
1. **Prolonged drought.** Variability in the rate and severity of drought has significant effect on dryland degradation and desertification. The following two major factors contribute to prolonged drought:
    a. **Declining rain fall.** The Sahel region of Northen Africa provides us with an example of this cause of deforestation. In this region, the rain levels have fallen 20-40% in recent decades and the land has been significantly ruined. Declining rainfall may also lead to changes in vegetation with, for instance, shrubs giving way to grass cover.
    b. **Long periods of high winds**. Prolonged periods of high winds may lead to the removal of fertile top-soil causing it to erode. This is true in tropical sub-humid regions, where fields that lack vegetation are susceptible to erosion by undue runoff at the onset of a rainy season.
2. **Human endeavors.** Human activity is the major source of desertification. This is due to the extreme vulnerability of dryland ecosystems to inappropriate land use and over-utilization. This is especially true during the times of environmental strain such as drought, high wind, or seasonal dryness. Over-utilization may arise from the following two factors:
    a. The existence of land shortages, poverty, and other forces beyond a farmers controls might force them to use unsustainable lands.
    b. Over-cultivation of the few available areas of fertile land by farmer's in order to enhance the production of export crops.[36]

The Impact of Desertification on the Environment.

Desertification is a complex process. It encompasses many causes, and it proceeds at varying rates in various climates. It leads to the loss of biological productivity and complexity in croplands, pastures and woodlands. It also contributes to both regional and global climate change. This is due to the following two factors:

1. Diminished soil quality, resulting from deforestation, may affect local climate by increasing temperature and decreasing moisture level. These impacts may go beyond the desertified area, leading to regional changes in climate and atmospheric circulation. This, in turn, may intensify dryland degradation process.
2. Desertification and efforts to eliminate it may affect the climate by changing the emission and absorption of greenhouse gases. Diminishing soil quality and vegetation may lead to the release of carbon. Re-vegetation can lead to the absorption of more carbon from the air. Animals raised on desert scrub may produce more methane which can be absorbed from the atmosphere by dry soils. Efforts to reclaim the land by using fertilizers may lead to the emission of nitrous oxide.[37] The problem of climate change, stemming from deforestation, is amplified by the fact they reinforce each other. In other words, not only does deforestation lead to global climate change, but the global climate change, in turn, leads to deforestation. This fact is recognized by the UN Framework Convention on Climate Change, which states:

> "arid and semi-arid areas or areas liable to floods, drought and desertification" are "particularly vulnerable to the adverse effects of climate change..."(Article 4).[38]

Today, desertification is a wide spread environmental problem that afflicts more than one hundred nations. Unfortunately, when an area experiences desertification it does not attract public attention until after the process is well underway. Usually, little or no data are available to show the rate of degradation or previous conditions of the ecosystem. Scientists are still learning about the desertification process and they have not reached any consensus regarding the issue of deforestation.

GLOBAL INSIGHTS CASE 20.12

THE UNITED NATIONS CONFERENCE ON DESERTIFICATION (UNCOD)

The year 2002 marks the twenty-fifth anniversary of the United Nations Conference on Desertification (UNCOD) held in Nairobi, Kenya, and the tenth anniversary of the United Nations Conference on Environment and Development (UNCED), better known as the Earth Summit, in Rio de Janeiro, Brazil. The first conference raised the world's awareness to the causes and effects of desertification. The second provided a programme of action for sustainable development worldwide (Agenda 21). The United Nations Convention to Combat Desertification, which was born out of these two conferences, emphasizes the importance of participation at the community level in planning, decision-making and implementation of actions needed to combat desertification and mitigate the effects of drought. It is essential that communities develop the capacity to make informed decisions about their development strategies.

Source: United Nations, "Combating Disertifcation," http://des2002.az.blm.gov/preface.htm., Reprinted

Global Monitoring of Desertification

The launching of satellites into orbit has opened a new window of opportunity for scientists to study the desertification process. Over the last twenty five years satellites have started to furnish us with the global monitoring needed for a better understanding of the desertifiation process. They have provided us with Landsat images of the same region that are taken every several years, during the same seasons.* This has enabled scientists to study the possibility of changes in the susceptibility of land to desertification. Research, using Landsat data shows the effect of people and animals on our planet. But, a more thorough comprehension of the process and problems of desertification calls on employment of other kinds of remote-sensing devices, such as land-monitoring networks, and global data bases of field observations.[39]

GLOBAL INSIGHTS CASE 20.13

HISTORY OF DESERTIFICATION

Desertification became well known in the 1930's, when parts of the Great Plains in the United States turned into the "Dust Bowl" as a result of drought and poor practices in farming, although the term itself was not used until almost 1950. During the dust bowl period, millions of people were forced to abandon their farms and livelihoods. Greatly improved methods of agriculture and land and water management in the Great Plains have prevented that disaster from recurring, but desertification presently affects millions of people on almost every continent. Increased population and livestock pressure on marginal lands has accelerated desertification. In some areas, nomads moving to less arid areas disrupt the local ecosystem and increase the rate of erosion of the land. Nomads are trying to escape the desert, but because of their land-use practices, they are bringing the desert with them. It is a misconception that droughts cause desertification. Droughts are common in arid and semiarid lands. Well-managed lands can recover from drought when the rains return. Continued land abuse during droughts, however, increases land degradation. By 1973, the drought that began in 1968 in the Sahel of West Africa and the land-use practices there had caused the deaths of more than 100,000 people and 12 million cattle, as well as the disruption of social organizations from villages to the national level. While desertification has received tremendous publicity by the political and news media, there are still many things that we don't know about the degradation of productive lands and the expansion of deserts. In 1988 Ridley Nelson pointed out in an important scientific paper that the desertification problem and processes are not clearly defined. There is no consensus among researchers as to the specific causes, extent, or degree of desertification. Contrary to many popular reports, desertification is actually a subtle and complex process of deterioration that may often be reversible.

Source: USGS, "Deforestaton," http://pubs.usgs.gov/gip/deserts/deforestification/

---

*Landsat is a U.S. satellite used to acquire remotely sensed images of the Earth's land surface and surrounding coastal regions.

Local Treatments of Desertification.

Land can be protected and reclaimed by individuals and governments at the local levels by taking the following actions:

1. **Covering the dunes with large boulders or petroleum in sand dunes areas.** This action will disrupt the wind close to the face of the dunes and stop the sand from moving. Sand fences are employed throughout the Middle East and the United States, in the same way snow fences are used in the north.
2. **Planting tree fences or grass belt to protect oases and farmlands in windy regions belts.** Sand that penetrates through the grass belts can be caught in strips of trees. To further protect the land against the wind, small plots of trees may also be scattered inside oases. In northeastern China, a "Green Wall," which will eventually stretch more than 5,700 kilometers in length, much longer than the famous Great Wall, is being planted to protect "sandy lands"—deserts, believed to have been generated by human endeavors.
3. **The more efficient use of existing water resources and control of salinization.** New methods are being developed to utilize surface–water resources such as rain water harvesting or irrigating with seasonal runoff from adjacent highlands. New methods also being developed to detect and tap groundwater resources and to find more effective methods of irrigating arid and semiarid lands.

Studies on the reclamation of deserts are also concentrating on the following issues:

- Appropriate crop rotation to protect the fragile soil.
- Understanding how sand-fixing plants can be adapted to local environments
- How grazing lands and water resources can be developed effectively without being overused.

To stop and reverse the degradation of arid and semiarid lands, we need to comprehend how and why the rates of climate change, population growth, and food production negatively impact these environments. This hinges upon more scientific research and the wise use of the available earth-science information.[40]

RELATIONSHIP BETWEEN ECONOMIC DEVELOPMENT AND THE ENVIRONMENT

Being equipped with a knowledge of environmental issues, we devote this section to more in depth understanding of the linkage between economic development and the environment. As our discussion of the environmental issues throughout this chapter has indicated, there is a two-way relationship between economic development and the environment. This is the case due to the following two reasons:

1. Development attempts to improve the welfare of developing nations also include amelioration of environmental quality that is exemplified by safe and abundant water, and healthy air to breath. If the gains from increasing the level of incomes in the developing nations are canceled out by increased expenditures on health and quality of life, stemming from pollution, then such outcomes could not be called development.
2. Environmental damage can weaken productivity. The potential of earning income for the future can be endangered by soil that is degraded, and aquifers that are depleted for the purpose of raising income today.

Although the environmental problems such as carbon dioxide emission, ozone depletion, and acid rain are global problems, calling for international cooperation by both developing and developed nations, the most immediate environmental problems facing developing nations are somewhat different. These nations are still struggling with the problems of unsafe water, inadequate sanitation, oil depletion, indoor smoke from cooking fires, and outdoor smoke from coal mining. It is incumbent upon developed nations not only to solve the universal environmental problems, impacting both developing and developed nations, but also to assist developing nations in resolving their immediate environmental issues. Since all the environmental problems feed upon each other, the benefits of such assistance for the advanced nations themselves is clear. However, developing nations have a crucial role to play in cooperating with advanced nations in order to resolve environmental problems. To this end, developing and developed nations should keep the following points in mind:

1. Developing countries should have access to less polluting technologies, and capitalize on the experience of developed nations in dealing with environmental problems.
2. Some of the gains in resolving environmental problems in developing nations, such as tropical forests and biodiversity, also benefit developed nations.
3. Some of the potential problems of global warming and ozone depletion facing developing nations, stem from a high level of consumption in advanced nations. As a result, these nations must take on the burden of finding and implementing solutions for these problems.
4. The strong relationship between environmental goals and poverty reduction provides a compelling case for enhanced support for programs aimed at reducing poverty and population growth.
5. The maintenance of a sustained economic growth in developing nations hinges upon advanced nations attempt at:

   - Improving access to trade and capital market.
   - Fostering policies that enhance savings and decrease global interest rates.
   - Promoting policies that advance an economic growth that is conducive to the environmental quality and is helpful to the economic conditions of developing nations.

To be sure, policy reforms and institutional changes are essential in generating accelerated economic development and bettering environmental management.

We close this chapter by stating that we have entered an era that is unprecedented in its potential for change. The increasing realization of the significance of environmental issues, the economic reforms of transitional economies, and movements toward democratization and participation in the development process, are all steps in the right direction. It remains to be seen how and when we succeed in resolving the environmental problems that are rooted in our quest for industrialization and profit.[41]

SUMMARY

1. Trade theories have also shown that if countries specialize according to their comparative advantage, not only do they benefit as participants of trade, but also world output is maximized. However, there is an increasing opposition to the forces of globalization.
2. Rich nations' dependence on developing nations arises from the following major two factors: (a) the existence of energy and raw materials in developing nations that are needed by advanced nations; and (b) the existence of a vast market in developing nations, providing a significant outlet for the exports of advanced nations.
3. Localization, that is, the demand for self-determination has taken the following forms: (a) the replacement of authoritarian political or single party unit by multiparty politics; (b) greater autonomy of subnational

political units; and (c)involvement of community groups and nongovernmental organizations (NGOs)in governance.
4. New ways of thinking about how to manage the world's economies and how to create new institutions that help to achieve this goal, calls on establishment of three institutions at three levels:(a) supranational government, (b) national level; and (c) subnational level.
5. "Acid rain" is a general term that is used to describe various ways that acids fall out of the atmosphere. A more accurate term is "acid deposition", which is composed of the following two types: (a) wet deposition; and (b) dry deposition.
6. The primary causes of acid rain are sulfur dioxide (SO_2) and nitrogen oxides (NOx).
7. Some of the steps that can be taken to reduce, or even eliminate, the acid deposition problem, include cleaning up smokestacks and exhaust pipes, using alternative energy sources, and restoring a damaged environment.
8. The recovery of lakes and streams can be hastened by adding limestone or lime (a naturally-occurring basic compound) to eliminate the acidity. This process, referred to as **liming**, has been employed particularly in Norway and Sweden. Liming is subject to a number of problems, as discussed in the textbook.
9. In the ozone layer there are only a very few molecules of ozone per million molecules of air. But, this is sufficient to shield UV, which would otherwise cause skin cancers, cataracts and inflict damage on plant and animal life.
10 The issue of ozone depletion attracted global attention in the early and mid-1980s. This has resulted in the signing of the following agreements: (1) Vienna Convention; and (2)he Montreal Protocol.
11. Before the Industrial Revolution, human activity released very few gases into the atmosphere, but now through population growth, fossil fuel burning, and deforestation, we are affecting the mixture of gases in the atmosphere. As a result, climate changes are accelerating as the amount of carbon dioxide, methane, and other green house gases that are dumped into the atmosphere every day keep on rising.
12. Greenhouse gases are gases that shield the reflected thermal radiation from the sun in the earth's atmosphere.
13. In the absence of the "greenhouse effect," the planet's temperatures would be much lower than they are now. As a result, life as it is known, would not exist. Today, because of greenhouse gases, the earth's temperature, averaging 60°F is very favorable. But if the atmospheric concentration of greenhouse gases rises we may face problems.
14. Scientists generally believe that the primary cause for the enhanced combustion concentration of carbon dioxide is the burning of fossil fuels and other human activities.
15. Climate changes are likely to increase sea levels, endangering island economies and low-lying nations such as the Maldives and Bangladesh. Climate changes also threaten agricultural production in developing nations.
16. Some progress has been made on the international level in coping with climate change. To this end, two international agreements have been reached. The first international agreement was ratified in Rio in 1992, and the second international agreement was signed in Tokyo in 1997.
17. Biological diversity, or biodiversity, is a term that refers to the variations of life on our planet. In other words, it encompasses all species, organisms and populations.
18. Biodiversity can be divided into the following three categories: (1) ecosystem diversity; (2) genetic diversity; and (3) species diversity.
19. Although reasons for protecting biological diversity are complex, they can be classified into the following four major categories: (1) loss of diversity leads to the weakening of the entire natural systems; (2) every species is a potential source of food supply; (3) every species is a potential source of human medicine; and (4) human's psychological needs from prolonged urban exposure.

CH. 20/GLOBALIZATION, LOCALIZATION, AND THE ENVIRONMENT

20. Deforestation encompasses the cutting down, burning, and damaging of forests. Deforestation has a severe negative impact on the climate, biodiversity, the atmosphere, and endangers the physical and cultural survival of the indigenous peoples.
21. The elements giving rise to deforestation can be divided into the three categories: (1) agricultural activities; (2) commercial logging; and (3) other causes.
22. The deforestation rate is determined by analyzing satellite imagery of forested areas that have been cleared.
23. Deforestation affects climate in the following two ways: (1) enhancing the amount of carbon dioxide and other trace gases in the atmosphere; and (2) affecting the evaporation process.
24. The rain forest is the natural habitat for many plants and animals that can only be found in small areas of the forests. The deforestation destroys their habitat and it may lead to their extinction.
25. We many distinguish between the following techniques of farming: (1)burning the tree trunks; (2) shade agriculture; and (3) intensive agricultural systems.
26. Desertification refers to the degradation of dry land. It happens when productive land in arid, semi-arid, or sub-humid dry land is degraded either by human endeavors or by prolonged drought.
27. The major elements that give rise to desertification can be divided into the following two major categories: (1) prolonged drought; and (2) human endeavors.
28. Desertification is a complex process. It encompasses many causes, and it proceeds at varying rates in various climates. It leads to the loss of biological productivity and complexity in croplands, pastures and woodlands. It also contributes to both regional and global climate change. This is due to the following two factors: (1) diminished soil quality, resulting from deforestation; and (2) desertification and efforts to eliminate it may affect the climate by changing the emission and absorption of greenhouse gases.
29. The launching of satellites into orbit has opened a new window of opportunity for scientists to study the desertification process.
30. Land can be protected and reclaimed by individuals and governments at the local levels by taking the following actions: (1) covering the dunes with large boulders or petroleum in sand dunes areas; (2) planting tree fences or grass belts to protect oases and farmlands in windy regions; and (3) the more efficient use of existing water resources and control of salinization.
31. Studies on the reclamation of deserts also is concentrating on the following issues: (1) appropriate crop rotation to protect the fragile soil; (2) understanding how sand-fixing plants can be adapted to local environments; and (3) how grazing lands and water resources can be developed effectively without being overused.
32. There is a two-way relationship between economic development and the environment. This is the case due to the following two reasons: (1) development attempts on improving the welfare of developing nations also include amelioration of environmental; and (2) environmental damage can weaken productivity. The potential of earning income for the future can be endangered by soil that is degraded, and aquifers that are depleted for the purpose of raising income today.
33. Developing and developed nations should keep the following points in mind: (1) developing countries should have access to less-polluting technologies, and capitalize on the experience of developed nations in dealing with environmental problems; (2) some of the gains of resolving environmental problems in developing nations also benefits developed nations; (3) some of the potential problems of global warming and ozone depletion facing developing nations stem from a high level of consumption in advanced nations; (4) the strong relationship between environmental goals and poverty reduction provides a compelling case for enhanced support for programs aimed at reducing poverty and population growth; (5) and the maintenance of a sustained economic growth in developing nations hinges upon developed nations' economic policies.

QUESTIONS

1. Elaborate on globalization by answering the following questions:
   a. What is meant by globalization.
   b. Is globalization a new phenomenon? Explain.
   c. Why has globalization met with so much resistance in recent years? Explain.
2. According to the standard microeconomic theory, given a budget constraint, the objective of a firm is to maximize its profit. In a perfectly competitive market, the pursuit of this object should lead to the most efficient allocation of scarce resources. Do you agree with that objective? Discuss.
3. Elaborate on localization by answering the following questions:
   a. What is meant by localization?
   b. What factors have given rise to localization?
4. Discuss the relationship between localization, globalization and development.
5. Elaborate on the concept of acid rain by answering the following questions:
   a. What is meant by acid rain?
   b. What are the different types of acid rain?
   c. What causes acid rain?
   d. What is the impact of acid rain on the environment?
   e. How can we reduce acid rain?
6. Discuss ozone depletion by answering the following questions:
   a. What is meant by ozone depletion?
   b. What factors cause Ozone depletion?
   c. When did the ozone problem attract worldwide attention?
   d. What has been done to rectify the problems of ozone depletion?
7. Elaborate on global warming by answering the following questions:
   a. What is meant by global warming?
   b. What causes global warming?
   c. What can be done about global warming?
   d. What is the impact of global warming on the environment?
8. Explain the concept of greenhouse gases by answering the following questions:
   a. What are greenhouse gases?
   b. What causes greenhouse gases?
9. Elaborate on biodiversity by answering the following questions:
   a. What is meant by biodiversity?
   b. What are the different types of biodiversity?
   c. What is the significance of protecting biodiversity?
10. Discuss deforestation. What is meant by deforestation? What are the causes of deforestation?
11. What are the impacts of deforestation on the ecosystem and biodiversity? Explain.
12. What is meant by desertification? What are causes of desertification?
13. What is the impact of desertification on the environment? What are local remedies in dealing with the problems of desertifiation?

NOTES

1. Parviz Asheghian, and Bahman Ebrahimi, *International Business: Economics, Environments, and Strategies*. (New York: Harper Collins, 1990), p. 7.
2. BBC News, E-Cylopedia, "Globalization: What on Earth is it About?" http://news.bbc.co.uk/1/hi/special_report/1999/02/99/e-cyclopedia/711906.stm.
3. Adrian Wood, *North-South Trade, Employment, and Inequality* (New York: Oxford University Press, 1995); Richard b. Freeman, "Are Your Wages Set in Beijing?" *Journal of Economic Perspective* 9(Summer 1995): 15-32; and Pam Woodall, "The Global Economy: War of Words" *Economist*, October 1, 1994, pp. 14-19.
4. The World Bank, *The World Development Report 1999/2000* (New York: Oxford University Press, 2000), Chapter 1, pp. 31-32.
5. *Ibid.*
6. D. Adams, P. Freund, P. Riemer and A. Smith, *Technical Response to Climate Change, IEA Greenhouse Gas R&D Program*, July 1996, p.2., hpp://WWW.ieagreen.org.uk/tec2.htm.
7. U.S. Environmental Protection Agency, Clean Air Markets-Environmental Issues: Acid Rain, http://www.epa.gov/airmarkets/acidrain/.
8. U.S. Environmental Protection Agency, Clean Air Markets-Environmental Issues: What Society Can Do About Acid deposition, http://www.epa.gov/airmarkets/acidrain/society/index.htm..
9. Hohghton J., *Global Warming, and Complete Briefing*. Lion Publishing, 1994., p. 192.
10. D. Adams, P. Rreund, P Rimer and A. Smith, Technical Responses to Climate Change, IEA Greenhouse Gas R & D Programme, July 1996, page 1. Also available on line athttp://www.ieagreen.org.uk/tec8.htm.
11. Technical Response to Climate Change, "The Atmosphere and Environmental Issues" http://www.iegreen.org.uk/tec2.htm.
12. "Human Influence on Climate Are Becoming Clearer," *New York Times*, June 29, 1999.
13. Futurepast, Inc., *A Greenhouse Gas Primer: What are Greenhouses And Should be Concerned*, p.1, http://www.futurepast.com/ghg_intro.htm?source=overture.
14. U.S. Environmental Protection Agency, "Global Warning: Emissions", http://www.epa.gov/globalwarming/emissions/index.htm.
15. U.S. Environmental Protection Agency, "Our Changing Atmosphere," http://www.epa.gov/globalwarming/climate/index.htm.
16. U.S. Environmental Protection Agency, "Global Warning: Climate", http://www.epa.gov/globalwarming/climate/index.htm.
17. The World Bank, *The World Development Report 1999/2000* (New York: Oxford University Press, 2000), Chapter 4, p. 97.
18. The World Bank, *The World Development Report 1999/2000* (New York: Oxford University Press, 2000), Chapter 1, pp. 41-42.
19. The World Bank, Ibid, p. 42. "Rio Convention", *http://www.earthsummit2002.org/es/issues/Conventions/rio_conventions.htm*.
20. The World Bank, Ibid; http://www.health.fgov.be/WHI3/krant/krantarch2001/kranttekstnov1/011129 m 10un.htm.
21. Raven, Peter H., *Defining Biodiversity*, Nature Conservancy 44 (1):11-15, The Nature Conservancy, Arlington, Virginia, 1994.
22. Wilson, Alexander, *The Culture of Nature*, Blackwell Publishers, Cambridge Massachusetts, 1992; Hoose, Phillip M., *Building an Ark-Tools for the Preservation of Natural Diversity through Land Protection*, Island Press, Covelo, California, 1981.
23. Ecological Society of America, "Biodiversity," http//www.esa.org/education/factsheets/biodiversity.htm.
24. "Deforestation: Causes and Solutions," p.1, http//davison.k12.mi.us/academic/golal/defores.htm
25. NASA, Earth Observatory, "Tropical Deforestation," p.1, http://earthobservatory,nasa.gov/ Library/ Deforestation/.
26. *Ibid.*

27. United States Environmental Protection Agency, "The Conservation of Biological Diversity in Great Lakes Ecosystem: Issues and Opportunityies,"http://www.epa.gov/glnpo/ecopage/issues.html#Overview; Ecological Society of America, "Biodiveristy,"http://www.esa.org./education/factsheets/biodiversity.htm.
28. NASA, Earth Observatory, "Tropical Deforestation: Rate of Deforestation" http://earthobservatory,nasa.gov/Library/Dforestation/deforestation_2.html.
29. NASA, Earth Observatory, "Tropical Deforestation: Deforestation and the Global Carbon Cycle" http://earthobservatory,nasa. gov/Library/Dforestation/deforestation_3.html.
30. NASA, Earth Observatory, "Tropical Deforestation: Deforestation and the Hydrologic Carbon Cycle" http://earthobservatory, nasa.gov/Library/Dforestation/deforestation_3.html.
31. NASA, Earth Observatory, "Tropical Deforestation: Deforestation and Biodiversity" http://earthobservatory, nasa. gov/Library/Dforestation/deforestation_3.html.
32. NASA, Earth Observatory, "Tropical Deforestation: After Deforestation" http://earthobservatory,nasa. gov/Library/Dforestation/deforestation_4.html.
33. NASA, Earth Observatory, "Tropical Deforestation: The Future" http://earthobservatory ,nasa. gov/ Library/Dforestation/deforestation_4.html.
34. IUCC, "Desertification and Climate Change," http://www.unep.ch/iucc/fs103.htm.
35. USGS, "Desertification," http://pubs.usgs.gov/gip/deserts/deforestation/.
36. IUCC, "Desertification and Climate Change," http://www.unep.ch/iucc/fs103.htm.
37. *Ibid.*
38. *Ibid.*
39. USGS, "Desertification: Global Monitoring," http://pubs.usgs.gov/gip/deserts/deforestation/.
40. USGS, "Desertification: Local Remedies," http://pubs.usgs.gov/gip/deserts/deforestation/
41. The World Bank, *The World Development Report 1992* (New York: Oxford University Press, 1992), p. 1-2.

SUGGESTED READINGS

Andersen Terry, and Donald R. *Free Market Environmentalism.* Boulder, Colo.: Westview Press, 1991.
Arnold, Ron, and Alan Gottlieb. *Trashing the Economy: How Runaway Environmentalism is Wrecking America.* Bellevue, Washington: Free Enterprise Press, 1991.
Berle, Gustav. *The Green Entrepreneur.* New York: McGraw-Hill, 1991.
Brown, Lester r.. et al. *Saving the Planet: How to Shape an Environmentally Sustainable Global Economy.* New York: Norton, 1991.
Bruntland, G.H., et al. *Our Common Future: World Commission on Environment and Development.* New York: Oxford University Press, 1987.
Caldwell, Lynton K. *Between Two Worlds: Science, the Environmental Movement, and Policy Choice.* New York: Cambridge University Press, 1990.
_____. *International Environmental Policy.* 2nd ed. Durham, North Carolina: Duke University Press, 1990.
Campbell, Monica E., and William M. Glenn. *Profit from Pollution Prevention.* Willowdale, Ontario: Firefly Books, 1982.
Constanza, Robert, ed. *Ecological Economics: The Science and Management of Sustainability.* New York: Columbia University Press, 1992.
Cook, R. U., and Warren, Andrew, 1973, *Geomorphology in Deserts.* Berkeley, California: University of California Press, 1973.
Daly, Herman E., and Kenneth W. Towsend, eds. *Valuing the Earth: Economics, Ecology, Ethics.* Cambridge, Mass: MIT press, 1993.
Davis, John. *Green Business: Managing for Sustainable Development.* New York: Basil Blackwell, 1991.
During, Alan . *Poverty and the Environment: Reversing the Downward Spiral.* Washington, D.C.: Worldwatch Institute, 1989.
Eigeland, Tor, et.al. *The desert realm:.*Washington.:National Geographic Society, 1982.
Ericksen, G. E."The Chilean nitrate deposits." *American Scientist* 71 (1983):366-374.
Elkins, Paul, and Jakop von Uexhull. *Grass Movements for Global Change.* New York: Routledge, 1992.

George, Susan. *The Road from Rio*. East Haven, Conn.: Inbook, 1993.
Gerster, Georg., 1960, *Sahara-desert of destiny*. New York: Coward-McCann, 1983.
Greeley, Ronald, and Iversen, J. D., 1985, *Wind as a geological process on Earth, Mars, Venus and Titan*. New York: Cambridge University Press, 1985.
Hare, F. K., 1983. "Climate on the desert fringe" in Gardner, Ritz, and Scoging, Helen, eds., *Mega-geomorphology*: Oxford: Clarendon Press, 1983.
Mikesell, Raymond F., and Lawrence F. Williams. *International Banks and the Environment*. San Francisco: Sierra Club books, 1992.
Miller, Jr. Tyler, G. *Environmental Science*: Working With the Earth, 5th. ed. Belmont, California: Wadsworth Publishing Co., 1995.
Office of Technology Assessment,. *Trade and Environment: conflicts and opportunities*. Washington, D.C.: Office of Technology Assessment, 1992.
Paepke, C. Owen. *Environmentalism and the Future of Progressive Politics. New York: Random House, 1993.*
Renner, Michael. *The Economics and Environmental Dimensions*. Washington, D.C.: Worldwatch Institute, 1989.
Roddick, Anita. *Body and Soul: Profit With Principles*. New Crown, 1991.
Sachs, Wolfgang, ed. *Global Ecology: A New Arena of Political Conflict*. Atlantic Highlands, N.J.: Zed Books, 1990.
Schmidheiny, Stephan. *Changing Course: A Global Business Perspective on Development and the Environment*. Cambridge, Mass: MIT Press, 1992.
Schmucher, E.F. *Small is Beautiful: Economics As if the Earth Mattered*. New York: Harper & Row, 1973.
Shiva, Vadana. *Staying Alive: Women, Ecology, and Development*. London: Zed, 1989.
World Bank, *World Development Report 1999/2000*. New York: Oxford University Press, 2000. Chapters 1 and 4.
_____. *World Development Report 1992*. New York: Oxford University Press, 2000.
World Resource Institute. *A New Generation of Environmental Leadership: Action for the Environment and the Economy*. Washington, D.C.: World Resources Institute, 1993.

GLOSSARY

A

Absolute poverty
Below the income level that secures the bare essentials of food, clothing, and shelter. This income level, referred to as the absolute poverty line, is a global measure of poverty. In other words, it is an international poverty line that does not recognize any national boundary.

Absolute advantage
A theory developed by Adam Smith that states that two countries could benefit from trade if, due to natural or acquired endowment they could provide each other with a product cheaper than they could produce it at home.

Accelerator principal
A proposition that a favorable impact of population growth, is that it leads to higher output and hence to an increase in net investment.

Acid deposition
See acid rain.

Acid rain
A general terminology that is used to describe the various ways that acids fall out of the atmosphere. A more accurate term is "acid deposition", which is composed of wet deposition and dry deposition.

Age-specific fertility rate
The number of babies born to a certain population at a specific point in time.

Age-specific death rate
The number of deaths in a given population during a specific period of time.

Agricultural extension programs
Programs that are designed to familiarize farmers with the results of agricultural research.

Appropriate technology
A technology that better fits the economic and social environment of the country in question. What may be appropriate technology for the capital-abundant United States, however, may be totally inappropriate for a labor-abundant country like India.

Autonomous technological progress
Technological progress that results from scientific curiosity. The inventor makes discoveries for the sheer pleasure of it.

B

Baker Plan
A plan presented in 1985 by James Baker, the U.S. Secretary of the Treasury, to deal with the debt crisis of developing nations. The plan emphasized growth over austerity in developing countries, based on funds generated by trade surplus nations, the International Monetary Fund, the World Bank, the Inter-American Development Bank, and the commercial banks.

Balance of payments (BOP)
An accounting statement that summarizes all transactions between the residents of one nation and the residents of all other nations during a given period of time. In other words, the BOP indicates the amount of foreign currency that was pumped into and out of a nation's economic system during a given period.

Balanced growth
A theory that calls for simultaneous application of capital to a wide range of various industries in order to achieve economic growth.

Basic-needs approach
A measure of economic development that focuses not only on *how much* is being produced, but also *what* is being produced, in *what ways*, for *whom*, and *with what impact*.

Behavioral criterion
A criterion used to define MNC. According to this criterion, a firm can be classified as multinational if its top management "thinks internationally." In this definition, it is assumed that because the MNC is concerned with more than one country, its top management sees the entire world as the domain of their operation. Thus, the international manager is considered a person who searches for investment opportunities in the world market rather than being confined to the domestic market

Big-push thesis
A theory stating that massive activity is fundamental to defeat the sluggishness that is deep-seated in the stagnant economy of a developing nation.

Bilateral assistance
Official assistance provided by the public sector of the donor in the form of loans or grants directly from one government to another government.

Biodiversity

The same as biological diversity and species diversity, that is, the variations of life on our planet. In other words, biodiversity encompasses all species, organism and population.

GLOSSARY

Biological approach
An approach to agriculture that calls on increasing yield through the utilization of improved plant varieties such as hybrid corn or the new varieties of rice developed at the International Rice Research Institute in the Philippines. Due to the significant effect on yields of some of these new varieties, the phenomenon is frequently referred to as the green revolution.

BOP
See balance of payments

Bourgeoisie
The capitalist and middle classes

Brady Plan
A plan proposed by Nicholas Brady, former U.S. Secretary of the Treasury, to deal with the developing countries' debt crisis. The Brady Plan enhanced the Baker Plan by augmenting the debt reduction and multilaterally financed loan guarantees.

Brain drain
The emigration of highly skilled workers from developing countries to advanced countries.

Burke-Hartke bill
A Trade and Investment Act that was passed in 1972. This bill introduced certain measures that have restricted both U.S. imports and foreign direct investment by U.S. corporations.

C

Capital spending
Expenditures on the purchases of machinery and equipment.

Capital flight
The transfer of funds from one nation to another by firms or individuals. It happens when the expected returns from keeping funds abroad are higher or more secure than from keeping them at home.

Capital saving (labor using) technological progress
A technological progress that leads to a lower capital/labor ratio, assuming that factor prices stay constant.

CIS
Commonwealth of Independent States.

Classical theory of economic stagnation
Theory which holds that continuous growth of the population would lead to economic stagnation. At this so-called stationary state there would exist low income for masses and the population growth would be checked by poverty.

Clean development mechanism (CDM)
A mechanism that permits advanced nations to assist developing nations to lower their emissions, and allowing advanced nations to earn "credit" for these lower emissions.

Clearcutting
In this type of logging all the trees are cut. This method uses heavy machinery, such as bulldozers, road graders, and log skidders, to remove cut trees and build roads, which is just as damaging to a forest overall as the chainsaws are to the individual trees.

Communism
The final and perfect goal of historical development in Marxist ideology, characterized by the following features:
- A classless society in which all people live by earning and no one lives by owning. The wage system is entirely eliminated and all people live according to the following motto: "From each according to his ability to each according to his needs."
- The state has been dismantled and transferred to the museum of antiques "along with the bronze ax and the spinning wheel."

Comparative advantage
A theory first presented by David Ricardo that two nations can benefit from trade even when one of the nations has an absolute advantage in the production of all commodities.

Comprehensive Plan
An economic plan that is aimed at covering all aspects of the national economy.

Concessional terms
A borrowing requirement that calls on the interest rate and the repayment period for borrowed capital to be softer (less rigid) than commercial terms.

Conditionality
A quid pro quo for borrowing, requires a close economic surveillance of a nation as a prerequisite for borrowing from the Fund (the IMF).

Counterpressure
A proposition that population pressure generates counterpressure

Crude birth rate
The number of births per thousand of population.

Crude death rate
The number of deaths per thousand of the population. It portrays changes in the birth rate, the changes in age structure, and changes in the age-specific death rate.

Currency substitution
The use of foreign currency (e.g., U.S. dollars) as a medium of exchange instead of or along with the domestic currency.

D

DAC
See Development Assistant Committee.

Debt-service ratio
Payments of interest on total debt plus amortization as a percentage of total exports.

Debt-equity swaps
Methods used to transform some of the existing debt to equity. A foreign buyer, usually a multinational corporation (MNC), purchases a country's debt at a discount and sells it back to the debtor country in return for its domestic currency. The buyer is then required to use this currency to purchase shares of stock in a domestic enterprise or to make a direct investment in the country. As a result, the developing country's external debts and interest obligations decrease.

Debt-service ratio
Payments of interest on total debt plus amortization as a percentage of total exports.

Decentralization
The process of reorganizing the SOFs to allow for more flexibility, and provide better incentives for managers in order to enhance efficiency. It also calls for providing capital at its market price to prevent wasteful use of capital-intensive technology.

Deforestation
The cutting down, burning, and damaging of forests.

Demographic transition
A process by which a population pattern eventually shifts from a stage characterized by high birth rates and high death rates to a stage in which both birth and death rates are low and almost equal. This process is composed of the following four distinct stages:

- Stage 1: High Fertility and Mortality.
- Stage 2: Decreasing Mortality.
- Stage 3: Declining Fertility.
- Stage 4: Stationary Population.

Dependency burden
An index which measures the proportion of the total population aged 0 to 14, and 65 years and older, which are considered unproductive years and thus not included in the labor force.

Demography
The formal study of population and the elements that affect its rate of change.

Dependency theory
A theory developed by an influential group of writers sympathetic to Karl Marx. This theory attributes the sluggishness of economic growth and development in developing nations to their dependent

relationships with advanced countries.

Dependency burden
People between ages 15 and 64, representing economically nonproductive members of the society that must be supported by others.

Desertification
The degradation of dry land. It happens when productive land in arid, semi-arid, or sub-humid-dryland is degraded either by human endeavors or by prolonged drought.

Development Assistant Committee (DAC)
An organization that was established in 1961as the primary mechanism for coordinating aid among the Organization for Economic Cooperation and Development (OECD).

Development planning
The intentional government action to orchestrate the economic decision process over the long run and to direct, affect, or even control a nation's major economic variables in order to achieve a contemplated set of economic goals. Development planning is implemented by the means of an economic plan.

Dialectic materialism
A concept developed by Karl Marx on the basis of Hegelian dialectic. Dialectic materialism is a logical method of historical analysis which suggests that every economic system develops to a stage of maximum efficiency and then breeds internal opposing forces that eventually leads to its own demise. At this stage, the foundations of an opposing system have already been shaped and it eventually replaces the old system. This metamorphosis continues pulling the society from one historical stage to another as each old system yields to the new one.

Direct taxes
Taxes that are composed of primary property, wealth, income, and inheritance taxes. Indirect taxes include items such as import, export, sales, purchase, and turnover, and value-added taxes.

Discouraged workers
Those who, unable to find a job, have dropped out of the labor force.

Disguised unemployment
A condition in which the available functions are distributed among workers in such a manner that all appear to be fully employed, but in fact much of their time is wasted in unproductive endeavors.

Diversified (mixed) agriculture
One of the stages of agricultural development. In this stage part of the agricultural output is used for self-consumption and the other part for sale to the commercial sector.

Dry deposition.
One of the two types of acid deposition. This includes acidic gases and particles. Approximately fifty percent of the acidity in the atmosphere falls back to earth through dry deposition.

E

Economic plan
A plan composed of a set of quantitative economic objectives to be attained during a given period of time.

Economic growth
The rate of increase in a nation's full employment real output or income over time.

Ecosystem diversity
All the various habitats, biological communities and ecological processes, as well as variations within individual ecosystems.

Equal-weights index
One of the weighted indexes for GNP growth. This index is calculated by giving equal weight to a one percent increase in income of any member of the society. Thus, weights in equation (1) are set in proportion to the number of people in each income class, and would be equal to 4% for the upper income class ($W_1 = 0.40$), and 4% for the middle- income class ($W_2 = 0.40$), and 20% for the lowest income class. This approach causes a one-percent increase in income in the lowest income class to have the same weight in the overall performance as a one-percent rise in income of the other two incomes, in spite of the fact that the absolute increment is by far smaller.

Elasticity of substitution
A measure determining the relative responsiveness of the K/L ratio to a change in relative factor prices (i/w), where i is the interest rate and w is the wage rate.

External diseconomy
Conditions that lead to increases in a firm's long run average cost or scale of production as a result of factors that are totally outside of the firm as a producing entity.; It exists when marginal social cost is greater than marginal social benefit.

External economy
Conditions that lead to declines in a firm's long run average cost or scale of production as a result of factors that are totally outside of the firm as a producing entity.; It exists when marginal social cost is less than marginal social benefit.

Extrapolation of statistical trends
A forecasting technique that requires plotting the historical data regarding the rate of improvement of a given product or process and examining the trend as it develops over time.

F

FAO
Food and Agriculture Organization.

Fed
See below.

Federal Reserve Bank of the United States
The central bank of the United States.

Fertility
The inclination of a population to have children.

Financial repression
The rationing of loanable funds in order to deal with shortages.

First oil shock
Oil price increases in 1973–1974.

First world
The capitalist nations, where capital and land are owned by people.

Fiscal policy
The deliberate taxation and spending decisions by the government to attain efficiency and growth. Efficiency is obtained by stabilizing the economy at full employment, hence mitigating the swings of business cycles. Growth is achieved by extending tax incentives to work, save and invest.

Fisher ideal index
A price index used to compare a nation's GNP over time.

Foreign direct investment
An investment that results in control of a firm by the investor. This can involve an investment in a firm's equity securities large enough for the investor to exert effective control over the firm.

Foreigner's joint venture
A joint venture that is composed of parties that are all foreign to the host country.

Foreign-local joint venture
A joint venture that is composed of parties that are local to the host country.

Four Dragons (Gang of Four)
A terminology that has been facetiously used to describe a group of four newly industrialized countries (Hong Kong, South Korea, Singapore, and Taiwan) who have performed very well the past three decades.

Fourth-world nations
A designation used to refer to the least-developed nations in order to identify them as the "poorest of the poor".

Franchisee
The receiver of the rights to produce a product or use a name, trademark, or copyrights.

Franchiser
The supplier of the rights to produce a product or use a name, trademark, or copyrights.

Franchising
A form of licensing that involves giving permission to a firm to produce a product and to use its name, trademark, or copyright.

Functional (factor) share distribution of income
A rather crude measure of income inequality that deals with the distribution of income to factors of production. More specifically, this measure compares the percentage of total income that the labor receives as a whole, with the percentages of total income distributed in the form of rent, interest, and profit to land, capital, and entrepreneur, respectively.

G

G-7 nations
Group of seven advanced nations including Great Britain, Canada, France, Germany, Italy, Japan, and the United States.

GDI
See Gender Development Index.

Gender development index (GDI)
A measure of economic development that was designed by the United Nations in 1995 in order to reflect gender equality in developing nations.

Genetic diversity
All the various genes embodied in all individual plants, animals, fungi, and microorganism. It happens both within species and between species.

Glasnost
Openness, literally; Russian term for specific economic policy.

Globalization
The growing integration of national economies into expanding international markets.

Green revolution
See biological approach.

Greenhouse gases
Gases that shield the reflected thermal radiation from the sun in the Earth's atmosphere.

Guided capitalism
A modernization strategy that was employed by Japan under the Meiji emperor, 1868-1912. This strategy depended on state initiative for larger investments in infrastructure. Government established about half

of the investment in non agricultural ventures and helped private industries through a number of schemes such as low taxes on businesses, subsidies, tax rebates, loans, and a low-wage labor policy.

H

Hagen's stages of economic industrialization

A stage theory developed by Evert Hagen, stating that the process of economic industrialization can be divided into six stages:

1. The emergence of self-contained factory processes.
2. The development of initial interrelationships.
3. The expansion of light engineering.
4. The improving control of quality and tolerances.
5. The elaboration of the industrial complex.
6. The stage of industrial complexity.

Harris-Todaro model

A two-sector model that assumes migrants respond to urban-rural differences in expected as opposed to actual earnings.

Harrod-Domar growth model

An economic growth model that shows the elements that give rise to economic growth. Application of of the Harrod-Domar model to the stages-of-economic-growth theories tells us that to accelerate economic growth all we have to do is raise the percentage of national income that is saved.

Headcount index

An index used to measure poverty. It is calculated as the ratio of number of poor people to population. The magnitude of this index is much lower in advanced nations as compared to the developing nations.

Heckscher-Ohlin (H-O) theory

A theory holding that each country should export those commodities that use its abundant factor more intensively, importing goods that use its scarce factor more intensively.

Hegelian dialectic

The cornerstone of Hegelian philosophy; a method of logic or reasoning which maintains that any concept, called a *thesis*, can have meaning only when it is compared to its opposite concept, called an *anthesis*; the interplay of the two then generates a new concept of comprehension referred to as *synthesis*. For example, the concept of "high" (thesis) induces the opposite concept of "low" (antithesis), and the two interact to shape the new concept of "height" (synthesis).

Hidden unemployment

A situation in which individuals are engaged in nonemployment endeavors, such as education and household chores, as a "second choice."

Human Poverty Index (HPI)

An index that is based on the assumption that human poverty should be measured in terms of the

following three major deprivations :
- Survival. This variable reflects the vulnerability to death at relatively early age. It is measured by the percentage of people who are expected to die before reaching the age of 40.
- Knowledge. This variable is measured by the percentage of adults that are illiterate.
- Overall Economic Provision. This variable is measured by the percentage of people with access to health services and safe water plus the percentage of children younger than five years of age who are malnourished.

Gini coefficient of inequality
A yardstick of income inequality, named after Corrodo Gini. It may be defined as the numerical value of the area between the Lorenz curve and the line of perfect equality divided by th numerical value of the entire area beneath the line of perfect equality. In other words, it is the ratio of the inequality area to the whole triangular area under the line of perfect equality, That is:

$$\text{Gini coefficient of inequality} = \frac{\text{inequality area}}{\text{triangular area}}$$

Human development index (HDI)
A measure of economic development that was developed in 1990, with the support of the United Nations. This index was designed to incorporate quality of life components with national products, adjusted for purchasing power.

HDI
See Human Development Index.

I

ICAs
See International Commodity Agreements

ICP
See International Commission Project

IDA
International Development Association

Immiserizing growth
An expansion of the factor supply or productivity that makes a nation worse off.

Income shares method
One of the two most common methods used by economists to measure income In this method, the first step is to divide the population into successive quintiles (fifth) or deciles (tenth) in accordance to ascending income levels. The next step is to determine what percentage of the total national income is received by each income group.

Indirect taxes
Taxes, paid indirectly by individuals and corporations through the purchase of goods; these taxes are

composed of import, export, and excise duties.

Induced technological progress
Technological progress that results from the desire for profit, in the private sector. It may also be caused by aspiration for social progress in the public sector.

Infant death rate
The number of deaths per thousand of births during the first year of life.

Infant mortality rate
The number of children who die before their first birthday out of every 1000 live births.

Innovation
The practical application of an invention to production for a market.

Input-output (interindustry) tables

An approach to development that is composed of a set of simultaneous equations that express the specific production processes or technologies of each industry, taking into consideration the interrelationship of all the major industrial sectors of the economy. All industries are considered both as employers of inputs and producers of output.

Instrumental variables
Policy devices that are used to achieve economic objectives. These devices include monetary, fiscal, subsidy, tariff, quota, labor training, exchange rate, technology transfer, foreign investment, foreign aid, education, wage, price control, capital rationing, business incentives, and interest rate policies.

Intensive agricultural systems
In this type of farming large quantities of chemicals like pesticides and fertilizers are used. The application of these chemicals causes a lot of the living organisms in the area to die. These dead organisms, in turn, seep into the soil and wash into the surrounding areas.

Interindustry tables
See input-output tables.

International Development Association (IDA)
An organization that was established in 1960 to provide concessional financing to the poorest countries.

International Commission Project (ICP)
A new measurement system that was designed by the International Commission Project (ICP) of the United Nations Statistical Office and the University of Pennsylvania. This measurement is based on determination of the purchasing power of income. This new approach changes a nation's GDP from domestic currency into international dollars ($1) by calculating P (the price level of GDP) as the ratio of the purchasing power parity (PPP) exchange rate to actual (or market) exchange rate.

International export quota agreements
Agreements that are aimed at regulating the quantity of an exported good in order to stabilize its price. In such an agreement, producing nations select a target price for the commodity and estimate the world demand for the coming year. Given the estimated demand, they ascertain the quantity of supply that generates the target price. They then divide this quantity among the supplying nations and rule that no nation should export more than its assigned quota. If the estimated demand is accurate and if the participating nations honor their quotas, the target price is established for the coming year. If the price deviates from the target price, the quota is adjusted to reestablish the target price.

International commodity agreements (ICAs)
International commodity agreements (ICAs) refer to agreements between producing and consuming countries to stabilize and increase the prices and revenues of exports. The main types of ICAs are international buffer stock agreements, international export quota agreements, and multilateral agreements.

International buffer stock agreements
International agreements involving the establishment of an international agency by producing nations (often joined by consuming nations) to limit commodity price swings. To achieve this objective, the agency is provided with finances and supplies of a commodity to regulate its world price. If the supplies are abundant and the world price of the commodity falls below an agreed minimum price, the agency purchases the commodity, causing its price to rise to the desired level. On the other hand, if supplies are tight and the world price of the commodity rises above an agreed maximum price, the agency sells the commodity, causing its price to fall to the desired level.

Inverted-U hypothesis
A hypothesis proposed by Simon Kuznet to explain the secular behavior of income inequality. According to Kuznet, there is a wide oscillation in the income inequality gap characterizing the secular income framework: expanding in the initial stages of economic growth, when the transition from the traditional sector to the modern sector is fast, stabilizing for a while, and then narrowing in the final stages. This is, in fact where the theory got its name.

Invisible unemployment
A situation in which workers' capabilities are used inadequately.

Isoquant
A curve that shows various combinations of two factor inputs, such as capital (K) and labor (L) that yield the same level of total output, say 100 units.

J

Joint venture
A corporate entity or partnership created under a host country's law between an MNC and other parties.

L

Labor using (capital saving) technological progress
A technological progress that leads to a higher capital/labor ratio, assuming that factor prices stay constant.

Labor productivity
Output per worker.

Laspeyres price index
A price index used to compare a nation's GNP over time.

Paashe price index
A price index used to compare a nation's GNP over time.

Leontief Paradox
An empirical study suggesting that the United States export goods that are relatively labor intensive and import goods that are capital intensive. This is contrary to the Heckscher-Ohlin theory which predicts that, as a capital-abundant nation, the United States should export capital-intensive commodities.

Lewis model
An economic model developed by Sir W. Arthur Lewis, an economist, in the mid-1950s, to explain how economic growth takes place in labor-abundant third world nations. Lewis recommends the following simple strategies for launching economic development: (a) the total agricultural surplus should be increased; (b) the economy should accumulate as much capital as possible; and (c) there should be as much investment and labor-using innovation in the industrial sector as possible.

LIBOR
See London Interbank Offer Rate.

Licensee
The firm receiving the know-how and the right to manufacture in a host country.

Licensing
An agreement through which production is performed by a firm in a host country.

licensor
The supplier of technology, a brand name, the right to patents or copyrights, or management services to another firm which produces the product in a foreign country.

Life expectancy
The average number of remaining years that people of a given age group can expect to live, given that the age-specific death rate stays constant.

Localization
Developing nations' desire for self-determination and relegation of power.

Current account
A balance of payments account. It includes those transactions that do not result in any future obligations. In general, current account items are caused by (a) purchasing from and selling to foreigners and (b) unilateral transfers—remittances and grants given to or received from foreigners free of charge. Capital account items result when (a) a country invests in foreign nations or when foreign nations invest in that country; (b) a nation provides loans to foreigners or receives loans from foreigners and (c) a nation deposits money in foreign banks or foreigners deposit money in the country's local banks.

London Interbank Offer Rate (LIBOR)
The rate of interest used between banks when they provide Eurocurrency loans to each other.

Long-term (perspective) plans
Plans that cover a long period of time, that is, 15 years, 20 years, or longer.

Lorenz curve
A curve was devised in 1905 by Conrad Lorenz, an American statistician. The Lorenz curve is the most widely used diagram that shows the relationship between population groups and their respective income shares.

Lower (extreme) poverty line
The absolute level of income, defined by international standards. It is based on standards set in India and amounts to $275 per capita income.

M

Maastricht Treaty
A treaty providing the blueprint for monetary union and closer cooperation among European Union members.

Malthusian theory of population
Unchecked population growth would increase at a geometric ratio, while food supply would increase at an arithmetic ratio. Thus, unchecked population growth would have increased 512 times after 225 years, but the food supply would have increased only 10 times during this same period. There are positive checks and preventive checks to population growth.

Management contract
An arrangement by which a company provides managerial assistance to another company in return for a fee. Such managerial help can be provided for other independent companies, joint venture partners, or an MNC's wholly owned subsidiaries in foreign nations.

Marshall plan
A program of dollar grants from the United States to European countries that was initiated in 1948. This plan channeled aid to Western Europe on a large scale. The objective of the plan was to advance economic recovery while maintaining social stability and democracy.

Mechanical approach
An approach to agriculture that calls on the utilization of tractors, combines, and other types of machinery primarily as a substitute for labor.

Medium-term plans
Plans that focus on improving economic conditions on a relatively distant future, typically 5 years. A medium-term plan can take the form of a rolling plan, that is, a plan revised at the end of each year.

Mixed credits
A credit for the purchase of the advanced country exports at below market rate of discount and thus encompassing a subsidy.

Modern sector
An economic sector in which technology is characterized by a very low elasticity of substitution that is close to zero. In this sector, one skilled worker is combined with one machine, as an inseparable team. For example, modern petrochemical, chemical, and metallurgical process are very inflexible in their requirement of inputs of all kinds.

Modern Agriculture
The final stage of agricultural development in which substantial productive capacity and high output per worker allows a very small number of farmers to feed entire nations.

Monetary policy
The intentional implementation of the Federal Reserve's authority to stimulate expansions or contractions in the money supply in order to attain price stability, to help mitigate the swings of business cycles, and to bring countries' output and employment to the preferred level.

Montreal protocol
An agreement that was reached in 1987, and emerged as a major cooperative endeavor to control ozone depletion.

Mortality rate
The rate of death of a specific population.

Multilateral agreement
A long-term contract that determines a *minimum* price at which importing countries guarantee to buy a specified quantity of a good and a *maximum* price at which exporting countries guarantee to sell a specified quantity of a good. Thus, multilateral agreements are designed to set an upper limit (ceiling) and a lower limit (floor) on the prices of traded goods. Examples of multilateral agreements are the *International Sugar Agreement* and the *International Wheat Agreement*.

Multilateral assistance
Official assistance provided by the public sector of the donor in the form of loans or grants indirectly through vehicle of an international agency.

N

Naples Terms
Favorable debt reduction terms that were agreed upon by the Paris Club of creditor countries, including the United States, in mid-December 1994. The Naples Terms aimed at lowering the debts of heavily indebted poor nations by up to 67 percent.

Net reproduction rate
The number of daughters a newborn female will deliver throughout her life, given constant age-related and fertility and mortality rates.

Neutral technological progress
A technological progress by which the same level of output can be obtained with less inputs, combined at the same proportion

Newly industrialized countries (NICs)
These countries include Argentina, Brazil, Greece, Hong Kong, South Korea, Mexico, Portugal, Singapore, Spain, and Taiwan. These countries are at a relatively advanced stage of economic development. Each of these countries has a substantial and active industrial sector that is integrated into its international trade, finance, and investment systems.

O

OECD
The Organization for Economic Cooperation and Development

Open unemployment
A condition in which people who are willing and able to work cannot find jobs.

Opportunity cost

The value of the benefit foregone when choosing one alternative rather than another. This simply means what a nation would have to give up of one good in choosing to produce another good.

P

Paris Club
An informal group of creditor governments who meet in the French Treasury to assure that all creditor governments grant comparable concessions.

Partial Plan
An economic plan that only deals with a part of the national economy, such as agriculture, industry, the foreign sector, and so forth.

Perestroika
Restructuring literally; Russian term for specific economic policy.

Performance criterion
A criterion used to define MNC. According to this criterion, the MNC can be defined on the basis of the absolute amount or the relative share (percentage) of assets, number of employees, sales, or earnings in a foreign country.

Physical quality of life index (PQLI)
A composite index that combines indicators of infant mortality, life expectancy, and basic literacy to measure the performance of a nation in terms of the most basic needs of the populace.

Planning process
An activity that is implemented by the government and involves choosing social objectives, and setting various targets.

Population density
The number of people per unit area of land (e.g., per square kilometer).

Portfolio investment
A financial investment that does not give the owner the power to exert control over the assets of the firm in question. This can involve investment in debt securities (bonds) or a small amount of investment in equity securities (stocks of a firm).

Poverty gap
A yardstick of poverty that measures the total amount of money needed to bring the income of every poor person up to the poverty line, thereby eradicating poverty.

Poverty-weighted index
One of the weighted indexes for GNP growth. This index is calculated by giving a higher weight to a one-percent increase in income of the lowest income class than for the upper income. In this manner more emphasis is placed on the welfare of the lower-income classes.

POVs
See Private Voluntary Organizations.

PPF
See Production Possibilities Frontier

Prebisch theory
A theory stating that because world prices for primary products have been declining and unstable, the terms of trade for developing countries have deteriorated over time. Thus, developing countries should restrict their imports of industrial goods, replacing these imports with domestically produced goods.

Price variability
Price variability refers to dramatic fluctuations developing countries experience in the prices of their primary products.

Private voluntary organizations (PVOs)
An unofficial aid provided by the private organizations in the United States.

Privatization
The process of transferring the ownership and control of SOFs from the government to the private sector. This approach is rooted in the neoclassical theory that privatization leads to a higher productivity.

Production possibilities frontier (PPF)
A curve that shows all possible combinations of two products that a country can produce with available technology and full employment of all resources.

Progressive taxes
Taxes that are based on a positive relationship between the level of income and the percentage of taxes paid by an individual. In other words, people at the higher level of income are supposed to pay a larger proportion of their income in taxes.

Purchasing parity power (PPP)
The number of units of a nation's currency needed to buy the identical quantity of goods and services in the domestic market as $1 would purchase in the United.

PPP
See Purchasing Power Parity.

R

Rate of natural increase of population
The difference between the crude death rate and crude birth rate.

Recurrent spending
For most nations this item includes the following:
- Expenditures on nondurable goods, and services, consisting of those for maintenance, public sector employees, and all expenditures on military equipment.
- Interest payments of the government.
- Subsidies and other transfers to individuals.
- Transfers to substantial governments.

Rio convention
The first convention regarding the impact of climate changes on the environment. In this convention, advanced nations voluntarily committed themselves to decrease the level of their carbon dioxide emission in 2000 to the level in 1990.

Rolling plan
A medium plan revised at the end of each year.

Rostow's stages of economic growth
A stage theory developed by W.W. Rostow, stating that the process of economic growth can be divided into five stages: (a) the traditional stage, (b) the preconditions for takeoff, (c) the takeoff, (d) the drive to maturity, and (e) the age of mass consumption.

S

Second oil shock
Oil price increases in of 1979—1980.

Second world
The socialist or the centrally directed nations, where the government owns the means of production.

Seigniorage
The gains accruing to a country from printing its currency or when its currency is employed as an international currency and reserve.

Selective logging
In this type of logging only the economically valuable species are cut.

Shade agriculture
In this method of farming, trees are left alone to provide shade for shade-thriving crops like coffee or chocolate.

Sharecropping
An arrangement by which a peasant farmer utilizes the landlord's farmland in return for a percentage of food output, such as 50% of the wheat or rice that is grown.

Short-term plans
Plans that aim at reaching their objective in the immediate future, that is, the next calendar or budget year. They implement government policy according to a detailed budget.

Size (personal) distribution of income
The most commonly used measure of income inequality employed by economists; it is usually used as a direct indicator of welfare. Theoretically, income distribution is largely determined by the ownership structure of the productive factors of production and the function that each factor performs in the production process, and as such, it is an important measure of welfare. The size distribution of income focuses on individuals, households, and the total incomes they receive. The manner by which the income is earned is immaterial.

Social discount rate
The interest rate defined by the planners.

Social profit
The difference between social costs and social benefits, during a given period.

Socialism
A transitory stage between capitalism and communism. That is characterized by the following two major features:"Dictatorship of Proletariats." This is a stage in which the bourgeoisie has been stripped from power and is controlled by the proletariats. Capitalists' properties are under the control of the workers

who also run the state. As Marx put it, this is a stage in which "expropriators have been expropriated." Payment according to work accomplished. The wages received by workers depends on their contribution to the production process. It is a stage in which means of production are owned by the state, and the state in turn is controlled by the proletariats, and the output is allocated according to the following motto:

"From each according to his ability to each according to his labor"

SOFs
See state owned firms.

Sovereign default
A nation's decision to default on its external debt.

Species diversity
The same as biological diversity, or biodiversity, that is, the variations of life on our planet. In other words, species diversity encompasses all species, organisms and population.

Stages of agricultural development
The evolution of agricultural production can be divided into three stages of subsistence agriculture, diversified agriculture, and modern agriculture.

State-owned firms (SOFs)
Public enterprises that are owned and managed by government.

Stationary population
A population in which age and sex-specific mortality rates have stayed at replacement stage, that is, one.

Structural criterion
A criterion used to define MNC. According to this criterion an MNC can be defined by two approaches. In the first approach, multinationality is defined by the number of countries in which a firm is operating. This means that a firm has its base in one country, such as the United States, and operates in a number of other countries. In the second approach, ownership characteristics are used as the basis for definition. Since the term "multi" means "many," the multinational firm refers to a firm that is owned or operated by individuals from many nations. Thus, an MNC can be defined either by the nationality of its owners or by the nationality of its top management.

Subnational governments
Government organizations, including provinces, departments, counties, and municipalities.

Subsistence agriculture
One of the stages of agricultural development, characterized by the existence of subsistence farming, that is marked by the most primitive agricultural production method and low productivity. At this stage, although some agricultural products may be sold or traded in local markets, most output is produced for family consumption. Few staple food crops, such as wheat, barely, rice and corn are the major sources of food intake.

T

Target variables
The specific quantitative goals that economic planners wish to achieve. Examples include achieving annual GDP growth rate of 8 percent, reducing poverty by 2 percentage points of population, and reducing the balance of payments deficit to $100 million.

TDF
See Transborder Data Flow.

Technical efficiency
A production efficiency that results in either producing more output with the same inputs, or producing the same quantity of output with fewer inputs. Changes in technical efficiency stem from invention and innovation.

Technological dualism
An economy which is composed of a traditional sector and a modern sector, each with its own type of technology.

Technology
The method or technique for converting inputs to outputs in accomplishing a specific task. In the above definition, the terms "method" or "technique" are used to mean not only the knowledge, but also the skills and the means for accomplishing a task.

Theory
An abstraction of reality and is based on certain simplifying assumptions

Theory of Mercantilism
Theory stating that wealth is a necessary condition for national power. National power is in turn enhanced by the increase in specie, that is, gold and silver coins. Thus, for a country without gold and silver mines, the only means of acquiring gold and silver is by encouraging exports and discouraging imports.

Theory of socialist and communist revolution
A theory developed by Karl Marx, stating that capitalism will eventually die and the class struggle is resolved when the bourgeoisie is ousted by the proletariat. At this stage, capitalism will be replaced by socialism, which Marx considered a *transitionary stage* preceding communism.

Theory of value and wages.
A theory developed by Karl Marx, stating that the value of each commodity is determined by the amount of labor embodied in its production.

Theory of surplus value and capital accumulation
A theory developed by Karl Marx. According to this theory, in production of a commodity, the capitalist hires a worker and sets the length of the working day. Although the value of a commodity that is produced

is defined by the amount of time embodied in its production, the capitalist pays only a constant subsistence wage to the worker. Because the worker does not stop producing when the value of the commodity that is created is equal to the subsistence wage, the value of the commodity that is produced is greater than the subsistence wage that the worker receives. This difference, referred to as the surplus value, is the driving force of capitalist system.

Third world nations
A designation developed in the early post-World War II decades. By refraining from affiliating themselves with either the United States or the former Soviet Union, these 127 Asian, African, and Latin American members of the UNCTAD formed a third political unit in the United Nations. Today, the "third world" designation does not imply nonalignment, as it did originally.

Tied Aid
A type of aid that requires the recipient to spend the funds received on commodities produced in the donor nation.

Tokyo convention
The second convention regarding the impact of climate changes on the environment. At this convention, more ambitious goals were established and more binding commitments were set. An important step was set forward in trying to ensure efficiency in reducing emissions, through the Clean Development Mechanism (CDM).

Total population increase of a population
The natural increase plus net migration.

Total fertility rate
The total of the age-specific fertility rate for a specific group over time, that is, over the total childbearing years.

Traditional sector
An economic sector in which technology is characterized by factor proportion flexibility, that is, high elasticity of substitution. In this sector, which is predominantly agricultural, workers and their implements could be combined in broadly flexible proportion.

Transborder data flow (TDF)
The flow of electronically transmitted information across national boundaries.

Transfer pricing
The pricing of goods and services that pass between either a parent company and its subsidiaries or between the subsidiaries themselves.

Turnkey operation
An arrangement by which an MNC agrees to construct an entire facility or plant, prepare it for operation, and then turn the key of the plant over to the local owners.

U

UN
United Nations.

Unbalanced growth
As theory developed by Albert O. Hirschman, who contends that *deliberate unbalancing* of the economy, according to a pre-formulated strategy, is the best approach for accomplishing economic growth.

UNCTAD
The United Nations Conference on Trade and Development.

Underemployment
A situation in which individuals work less than they would like to work.

Unemployment
Situation which exists whenever individuals who are actively seeking and presently available for work among a given age range can not find work.

Upper poverty line
An income level of $370 per capita. This figure is derived from studies of a number of nations with low average income—Bangladesh, the Arab Republic of Egypt, India, Indonesia, Kenya, Morocco, and Tanzania.

USAID
U.S. Agency for International Development.

V

Value-added tax.
Devised by French economists, the value-added tax is a tax imposed on the value that is added at each stage of production of a given good. It is calculated as the difference between the sales of the firm and its purchases from other firms.

Vienna convention
This convention which occurred in 1985, presents the first major attempt by the international community that is aimed at the protection of the ozone layer. Although this convention led to the generation of a framework for future cooperation, it did not encompass a protocol restraining the use of CFCs.

Vicious circle of poverty
A well known theory which is based on the notion that a lack of capital is the major impediment to growth and economic development. In other words, this theory relates economic stagnation to very low levels of per capita output.

GLOSSARY

Visible underemployment
A condition in which workers are compelled to work short hours as an alternative to being out of a job.

Volags
See Voluntary Agencies.

Voluntary agencies (Volags)
An unofficial provided by the private organizations in Asia.

W

Wet deposition
One of the two types of acid deposition. It includes acidic rain, fog, and snow. When this type of acid flows over and seeps through the ground, it impacts a number of animals and plants on the earth. The potency of this type of acid rain depends on a number of factors, including how acidic the water is, the chemistry and buffering capacity of the soils involved, the types of fish, trees, and other living things that rely on the water for survival.

INDEX

A

Absolute advantage, 87, 259-263, 283-285
Accelerator Principal, 127
Acid Rain, 408, 428
ACQUIRED IMMUNODEFICIENCY SYNDROME, 44
Adam Smith, 24, 259, 260
Advanced nations, 272, 273, 277, 279-282, 287, 291, 406
Afghanistan, 64
Africa, 3, 9, 14, 102, 157, 160, 169, 223,288, 289, 293, 297, 298, 304, 306, 397
African-American, 44
age-specific death rate, 117
Agency for International Development (AID), 371
Agenda 21, 426
Aggregate Growth Models, 238
Agricultural Extension Programs, 166
Alasdai MacBean, 272
Albania, 388
Albert Hirschman, 127
Alfred Nobel, 311
allocative efficiency, 397
allocative goal, 347
American Telephone and Telegraph (AT & T), 352
Angola, 349
ANTARCTIC OZONE HOLE, 414
Appropriate Technology, 332
Argentina, 33, 204, 224, 278, 279,289, 290, 293, 297, 300-302, 304, 306, 312
arithmetic progression, 116
Arizona, 152
Asia, 3, 102, 14, 157, 158, 160, 162, 169, 287, 368, 371
ASIAN "MIRACLE", 333
Asian Development Bank, 77, 366
ASIAN GROWTH MODEL, 214
Asset Redistribution, 108
asthma, 413
AT&T, 325
Australia, 145, 281, 368
austerity policies, 299
Automatic Material Handling, Inc, 331
Autonomous technological progress, 179

B

bad ozone, 412
backward linkages, 72
Baker Plan, 301-304, 306, 307
Balance of payments (BOP), 290, 392

balance of payments goal, 347, 348, 392
Balanced Growth, 70
Bangladesh, 203, 64, 415
Basic Needs, 24
behavioral criterion, 313
Belgium, 27, 31 64, 281, 311, 383
Benton Massell, 222, 273
Bertil Ohlin, 263
Bhopal, India, 349
BIG-PUSH THESIS, 69
BILATERAL INVESTMENT TREATIES, 385
Bill Clinton, 37
biodiversity, 408, 417, 420, 429
Biological approach, 165
Birth Control Programs, 130
Boeing, 223, 224, , 272, 353, 289, 293, 423
Boris Yeltsin, 386
bourgeoisie, 31
Bosnia, 151, 371
Brady Plan, 303, 304, 306, 307
brain drain, 150, 202
Brazil, 3, 26, 41, 121, 204 304, 318, 266-269, 279, 282,289, 290, 292-294, 297, 300-302, 304-306, 312, 313, 354
Brazilian Amazon, 421
Bretton Woods system, 291, 299
Britain, 264-266, 295, 319, 325
bronchitis, 413
Budapest, 128
budget deficit, 213, 294, 296
BUFFER STOCK AGREEMENT, 276
Bulgaria, 295, 296, 388

C

California, 146, 152, 302
Cambodia, 43, 44, 424
Cameroon, 279
Canada, 3, 14, 24, 40, 64, 126, 145, 177, 264, 265, 281,295, 311, 312, 314, 319, 334, 353, 359 , 368
Capital account, 392
capital flight, 289, 292-294, 305-307
CAPITAL FORMATION , 205, 279
Capital Saving (Labor Using) Technological Progress, 185
Capital Spending, 219, 227
carbon dioxide, 413, 428
Caribbean, 44, 89, 282, 305, 371
Carlos Diaz Alejandro, 266
Causes of Deforestation, 419
Central America, 3, 260, 371
Central Asia, 43
CHANGING CLIMATE, 415
CHANNELS OF ENTRY INTO INTERNATIONAL BUSINESS, 316

463

Characteristics of Domestic Firms, 337
Characteristics of the MNC, 337
Charles De Gaulle, 260
Chile, 40, 121, 204, 224, 270, 278, 279, 289, 301, 302, 304, 349
China, 14, 36, 38, 39, 44, 104, 121, 129, 158, 168, 170, 206, 250, 251, 288, 292, 303, 353
chlorofluorocarbons (CFCs), 411, 412
CHOICE OF TECHNOLOGY, 329
Chrysler Corporation, 356
CIA, 384, 386
Cia. Telefonica Nacionale de Espara, 353
Citibank, 382
Citicorp, 297, 301
classical economists, 259
Clearcutting, 419
CLIMATE CHANGE, 412, 415
CO_2, 408, 414, 420
Coca-Cola, 324, 353
Cold War, 37, 222, 368, 371, 384
Colombia, 40, 163, 223, 270, 272, 278, 279, , 289
Colonialism, 350
COMECON, 388
Commercial banks, 212, 213, 294, 296, 297, 299, 300, 302-306
Commercial logging, 419
Commonwealth of Independent States (CIS), 37, 304, 384
communism, 14
Communist revolution, 36
Comprehensive Plans, 233
concerted lending, 304
concessional financing, 303
concessional terms, 369
Congo (Dem. Rep.), 130
contractionary monetary policies, 292
Copenhagen amendment, 411
Corporate Income Taxes, 218
Corrodo Gini, 96
Costa Rica, 3, 40, 121, 279, 285, 304
cost-benefit analysis, 243
Cote d'Ivorie, 279, 289
Council of Mutual Economic Assistance (CMEA or COMECON), 388
Counterpressure, 127
Criticisms of the Big-Push Thesis, 70
crowding, 104
crude birth rate, 117
crude death rate, 118
Cub, 121, 171
Currency Convertibility, 391, 392
Currency devaluation, , 88, 104, 239, 299
Currency overvaluation, 293, 306
Currency reform, 391
currency substitution, 212
Current account, 290, 392
Czechoslovakia, 295, 296, 388

D

David Hume, 260
David Ricardo, 259, 260
Debt crisis, 223, 279, 280, 287, 289, 290, 292, 294-297, 299-302, 304-307
Debt Equity Requirements, 356
Debt-equity swaps, 300, 301, 304, 306

DEBTS OF TRANSITIONAL ECONOMIES, 295
Debt-service ratio, 292
debt-service ratio, 222, 288
Decentralization, 227
Definition of Biodiversity, 417
DEFINITION OF MULTINATIONAL CORPORATION, 312
Deforestation, 408, 415, 421, 422
Demographic Factors, 90
Demographic Transition, 118
Demography, 117
demonstration effect, 189
Dependency, 266, 406
dependency burden, 45, 121
desertification, 408, 425
deutsche mark, 390
developing countries, 3
Development Assistant Committee (DAC), 366
Development planning, 233
Direct taxes, 215
Direct Transfer Payments and Public Expenditures, 108
discouraged workers, 45
diseconomies of scale, 243
disguised unemployment, 123, 140, 163
dismal science, 115
Disney, 317
Diversified (Mixed) Agriculture, 161, 163
Domestic Marketing Boards, 273, 283
Dominican Republic, 121
Dow Chemical Company, 301
Droughts, 427
Dry deposition, 408
Dust Bowl, 427

E

EARHARD, 390
Earnings, 201, 270-273, 299, 305
Earth Summit, 426
East Asia, 89, 191, 214
East Asian crisis, 78
East Germany, 228, 388
Eastern Europe, 37, 44, 295, 296, 304
Eastern European countries, 381, 382, 395
Eastern European nations, 14
Economic development, 11, 266, 270, 273, 277-279, 282-284, 287, 292, 298, 302, 303, 305
Economic growth, 11, 267, 278, 296, 297, 302, 305
Economic plan, 233
Economies of Scale, 128
Ecosystem, 417, 420
Ecuador, 40, 289, 293, 305
Education, 24, 25, 108, 201, 203
Educational Budgets, 202
Effects of Acid Rain, 409
Efficiency, 211, 265
Egypt, 13, 26, 126, 278, 322, 370
Elasticity of Substitution, 186
Eli Heckscher, 263
Eli Lilly & Company, 338
emphysema, 413
energy crisis of the early 1970s, 287, 306
Energy Sources, 410
England, 31, 178
Enhanced Structural Adjustment Facilities (ESAF), 370

enusu , 206
Environment, 260, 302, 408, 410, 415, 425
equal-weights index, 21
ERM, 383
Essay on Principles of Population, 115
Ethiopi, 64, 130, 370
Ethnic Minorities, 104
EU commission, 150
EU markets, 382
Eurocurrency market, 290, 291
Europe, 35, 43, 103, 295-298, 304, 306, 260, 311, 351
European Union (EU), 150
Evaporation process, 420
Excluding Foreigners from Specific Activities, 354
export of goods and services, 336
Export Requirements, 355
Export-Import Bank, 386
exporting, 317
exports, 365
extended family, 48
Extended Fund Facility (EFF), 299
External Dependence, 42
external diseconomy, 236
External economies, 69
external economy, 236
Externalities, 48, 234, 236, 243, 251
Exxon, 312

F

FACTOR INTENSITY AND TECHNOLOGICAL PROGRESS, 182
Factor market distortions, 332
factor- price-distortions, 107
Family-Farms, 159
FAO, 171
Federal Reserve Bank of the United States (the Fed), 289
Fel'dman investment strategy, 38
Fernando Henrique Carsoso, 318
fertility rate, 117
Fiat, 301
Fidel Castro, 126
Financial Assets, 391
financial liberalization, 215
financial repression, 213
Finland, 281, 354
first world, 14
Fiscal policy, 211, 389
Fisher, 16, 17, 305
Fixed factor proportions, 332
Floating interest rates, 296
Florida., 146
Food and Agriculture Organization (FAO) , 420
Food, 24, 273, 277, 291
Ford Motor Company, 312
foreign direct investment (FDI), 63, 311, 313 , 329, 365
Foreign Investment Review Agency (FIRA), 353
foreigners' joint venture, 322
foreign-local joint venture, 322
Foreign private investment, 205
forward linkages, 72
Four Dragons, 34
France, 24, 31, 150, 260-262, 264, 265, 281, 285, 295, 314, 325, 386
franchisee, 319

franchiser, 319, 336
franchising, 317 , 319
Frederick Harbison, 2
Fredrick Bayer, 311
French Treasury, 297
functional or factor share distribution of income, 93
Future of Deforestation, 422

G

G-7 nations, 37, 386
Gang of Four, 34
Gender Development Index (GDI), 26
GENDER DISCRIMINATION, 203
gender inequality, 26
General Agreement on Tariff and Trade (GATT), 279
General Motors, 312, 322
General Theory of Employment, Interest and Money, 142
Genetic diversity, 417
Geneva, 279
geometric progression, 115
Germany, 2, 31, 145, 150, 295, 264, 265, 281, 311, 314, 325, 386
Gga Khan Foundation, 368
Ghana, 163, 206, 272, 273, 278
Gillette, 354
Gini Coefficient, 96
Glasgow, 311
glasnost, 37, 384
global climate change, 425
Global Monitoring of Desertification , 426
Global Warming, 6, 415
globalization, 3, 405, 407
GM, 359
good ozone, 412
Gorbachev, 37
government consumption, 220
Government Expenditures, 219
Government Intervention, 236, 260, 261
Great Britain, 31, 145, 266, 295, 312, 314, 383, 386
Great Depression, 140, 300, 387, 405
Great Leap Forward, 250
Great Plains in the United States, 427
Greece, 33, 281, 295, 371
Greek, 405
green revolution, 165, 171
greenhouse effect, 414
Greenhouse Gases, 412
Group of 15, 289
Guatemala, 40,, 64, 279
guest workers, 150
Gulf Oil's, 349
Gustav Ranis, 72

H

Hagen's stages of economic industrialization, 66
Haiti, 151, 370
halocarbons, 411
halons,, 412
Hamburg, 311
Harris-Todaro Model, 139
Harrod-Domar model, 79, 238

Harry Johnson, 266
headcount index, 89
Health, 24, 303
heart disease, 413
HECKSCHER-OHLIN THEORY, 263, 264, 265
Helsinki Package, 303
Herzegovina, 370
hexafluoride (SF6), 413
Hidden Unemployment, 138
High and variable inflation, 294, 306
High Degree of Commodity Concentration, 270, 271, 283
high-income economies, 14
Hirschman, 71
Hispanic men and women, 44
HISTORY OF DESERTIFICATION, 427
HIV, 44
Hoffman-LaRoche, 349
Holland, 32
Home Countries' Objectives, 345
Honduras, 64
Hong Kong, 3, 33, 35, 36, 78, 127, 263, 312
Host Countries' Objectives, 347
HOST COUNTRIES' REACTION TO MNCs, 352
Housing, 24
hui, 206
Human Development Index, 24
Human Poverty Index (HPI), 102
Hungary, 295, 296, 353, 382, 388

I

IBM, 269, 353, 359
Ichimura, 265
IDA, 370
IMF, 272, 287, 288, 294, 295, 297-300, 302, 304, 306, 307, 382
IMF's conditionality, 299
Immigration Reform and Control Act (IRCA), 151
immiserizing growth, 266-269, 279, 283, 284
impediments to monetary policies, 211
Imperial Chemical Industries, 349
Import Substitution, 12, 248, 277-279, 284
Inadequacy of Financial Institutions in Developing Nations, 212
Income gap, 278
Income Share Method, 94
Income Distribution Effects of MNCs, 351
India, 13, 40, 44, 88, 103, 104, 129, 163, 239, 263, 277, 278, 282, 288, 293, 303, 312, 325, 330, 353, 370
indirect taxes, 108, 219
indivisibilities, 69
Indonesia, 13, , 40 223, 272, 279, 282, 293, 303, 423, 424
Induced technological progress, 179
Industrial Revolution, 178
industrial innovation, 405
industrial production, 415
industrialization, 12, 157, 277-279, 284, 405
Infant Mortality, 19, 23, 41, 117
Inflation, 206, 279, 289, 292, 294, 296, 299, 306
Innovation, 305
Input-Output Tables, 240
instrumental variables, 238
Intensive agricultural systems, 422
Interaction, 368
Inter-American Development Bank, 297, 302, 306, 366
Interest Payments, 222, 280, 289, 294

Intergovernmental Transfers, 224
interlocking factor markets, 161
Internal Educational Policies, 202
internal rate of return, 245
International Buffer Stock Agreements, 273, 274, 283
International business, 260, 299, 311
International Cocoa Agreement, 274
International Commission Project (ICO), 18
International Commodity Agreements, 273, 280, 283, 284
International Conference on Population and Development (ICPD), 125
INTERNATIONAL EXPORT QUOTA AGREEMENT, 277, 278
International Export Quota Agreements, 273, 274, 277, 283
International Labor Organization (ILO), 104
international media networks, 406
International migration, 145
International Monetary Fund (IMF), 205, 287, 280, 397
International Natural Rubber Agreement, 274
International Sugar Agreement, 275, 276
International Tin Agreement, 274
International Wheat Agreement, 276
internet, 405
Invention, 178
inverted-U hypothesis, 104
Invisible Unemployment, 138
Iran, 104, 260, 261, 325, 352
IRS, 338
isoquant, 182
Israel, 126, 278, 370
Isuzu, 322
Italy, 281, 295, 314, 383, 386
ITT, 349

J

Jagdish N. Bhagwati, 266, 278
Jamaica, 40
James Baker, 301
Japan, 3, 14, 27, 31 , 35, 36, 40, 77, 140, 171, 177, 178, 192, 214, 260, 261, 264-266, 269, 281, 295, 302, 304, 307, 312, 314, 318, 319, 322, 325, 349, 334, 358, 368,383, 386, 394, 406
Jawaharlal Nehru, 239
John Fei, 72
Joint Venture, 317, 322, 336, 352, 356
Jordan, 203

K

Karens, 104
Kentucky Fried Chicken, 319
Kenya, 13, 40, 41, 121, 103, 163, 171, 426
Keynes, 142
Keynesian economics, 211
Keynesian theory, 142
Kodak, 78, 214, 224, , 278, , 293, 349, 383
Kosygin, 235
Kuwait, 41, 272

L

Labor productivity, 46, 263
Labor Saving (Capital Using) Technological Progress , 186
Lancieri, 273
Land Reform, 108, 171

landfills, 415
Laos, 43, 424
Laspeyres price index, 16
Latifundio, 159
Latin America, 14, 44, 39, 89, 102 157, 159, 160, 169 , 204, 228, 270, 279, 282, 287, 289, 297, 300, 304, 305, 307, 371
LATIN AMERICAN COUNTRIES, 395
Latin American, 277-279, 287-289, 291, 297, 300, 301, 305, 306
LEONTIEF PARADOX, 265
less developed countries (LDCs), 3
Levels of Biodiversity, 417
Lewis theory of labor transfer, 138
LEWIS THEORY OF DEVELOPMENT, 72
Lewis's model, 158
Libya, 40
lincensee, 317
Licensing , 317, 336
licensor, 317
Life expectancy at birth, 117
Life Expectancy, 19
liming, 410
Lim's study, 222
line of perfect equality., 96
Literacy, 19
loanable funds, 215, 289, 294, 306
Local Treatments of Desertification, 427
LOCALIZATION, 407
London Interbank Offer Rate (LIBOR), 289
Long-term (perspective) plans, 246
Los Angeles County, 152
Love , 273
Low Savings Rate, 236
lower (extreme) poverty line, 89
lower-middle-income, 14
low-income countries, 14
low-income, 14
Ludwing Earhard, 390

M

M atsushita, 339
Maastricht Treaty, 383
Mackenzie, 411
Mahalanobis model, 38
Mahatma Gandhi, 181
Malaysia, 36, 40, 121, 224, 278, 279, 282, 293, 319, 424
Maldistribution of Income, 237
Maldives, 415
Malthusian theory of population, 115
Management Contract , 317, 325
Mani Tese, 368
Mao Tse-Tung, 250
management contracts, 336
marginal private benefit (MPB), 234
marginal social cost (MSC), 234
Market economy, 295, 397
Market Failures, 234
Marketing and Storage Facilities, 167
Marshall Plan, 365, 366
Marubeni Trading Company, 349
Maternal mortality rate , 118
Mauririus, 302
McDonald, 318, 319
Mechanical Approach, 165

Medium-Sized (Multi Family) Farms, 159
mercantilists, 259
Mesopotamian, 405
MeUi restoration, 394
Mexic
MEXICAN DEBT CRISIS, 294, 296, 307
MEXICAN ECONOMIC REFORMS, 216
Mexico, 33, 40, 121, 163, 171, 304, 228, 278 , 296,287, 289, 290, 293, 294, 296, 297, 300-302, 304, 306, 319, 324, 334, 354
Michel Camdessus, 397
Middle East, 39, 121, 288, 297, 298, 306, 371
middle-income countries, 14
Mikhail S. Gorbachev, 235, 384
Minatitlan, 324
Minifundios, 159
mining , 415
Misereor, 368
Mixed Credits, 374
MNC-Owned Foreign Enterprise, 317, 319
MNCs' Objectives, 344
MNCs, 182, 218, 329
Modern agriculture, 161, 164
Modern Sector, 72, 188
MODES OF TECHNOLOGY TRANSFER, 336
Moldova, 40
mordida (bite), 220
monetarist theory, 211
Monetary Overhangs, 391
Monetary policy, 211, 289, 389
Mongolia, 14
Monopoly Distortions, 236
Montreal Protocol, 407, 411
Morocco, 13, 289, 354
Mortality (death) rate, 117
Multilateral agreements, 273, 276, 283
multinational corporation (MNC), 280, 300, 311
Myanmar, 104, 424

N

NAFTA, 354
Nairobi, 279, 426
Naples Terms, 305
NEC , 325
negative interest rates, 213
Nepal, 203
Nestle, 349
net present value (NPV), 245
net reproduction rate, 117
Netherlands, 31, 281, 314, 383
Neutral Technological Progress, 183
New England, 424
New international economic order (NIEO), 279, 283
new millennium, 405, 407
New York, 146, 260, 278, 279, 293, 296, 302, 305
New Zealand, 14, 281
newly industrial countries (NICs), 14, 33, 382
Nicaragua, 358
NICs , 252, 279, 282, 283, 284, 397
Nigeria, 126, 130, 163, 240, 289, 290, 293,302, 304, 322
Nikita Khrushchev, 37,38, 384
nitrogen, 410
Nissan Corporation, 301
nitrogen oxides (NOX), 408, 409, 426

nnovation, 178
Noncash Income, 89
nonconcessional financing, 303
Nondurable Goods and Services, 220
nongovernmental organizations (NGOs), 407
nontariff trade barriers, 399
North America, 4, 35, 44, 103, 140
North American Free Trade Agreement (NAFTA), 151
Norway, 24, 281, 368, 410
Nurkse, 189, 279

O

OECD, 303, 385
Official Development Assistance (ODA), 280
on-the- Job Training, 200
OPEC (Organization for Petroleum Exporting Countries), 14, 290
Open Unemployment, 45, 138
Opportunity cost, 261, 283
Organization of Economic Cooperation and Development (OECD), 14, 178, 191, 351, 366, 368
Organization of Petroleum Exporting Countries (OPEC), 290
Overvaluation of Returns to Education, 249
oxygen, 410
Ozone Agreements, 411
OZONE DEPLETION, 410, 428

P

Paashe price index, 17
Pacific Rim, 43
Pakistan, 64, 126, 163, 203
Paris Club, 297, 305
Partial Plans, 233
People's Republic of China, 356, 358
Pepsico, 324
perfluorocarbons (PFCs), 413
performance criterion, 312
perestroika, 37, 235, 384
Personal Income Taxes, 217
Peru, 171, 270, 289, 298, 305
PHASES OF THE DEBT CRISIS, 304
Philippines, 26, 64, 163, 278, 289, 293, 300, 301, 304
Phoenician, 405
physical quality of life index (PQLI), 19
Phytoplankton, 413
PIZZA HUT, 318, 346
planning process, 233
Point Four, 365, 371
Poland, 290, 295, 296, 302, 382, 388
POLIOMYELITIS, 43
population density, 45
POPULATION PROJECTIONS, 131
Porfirio Diaz rule, 64
Portfolio investment, 305, 313, 365
Portugal, 33, 150, 281, 295
positive checks, 116
poverty gap, 89
poverty-weighted index, 21
Prebisch Theory, 266, 269, 270, 277, 283, 284
President George Bush, 37, 384
President Kennedy, 366
President Truman, 365
Pretax or Aftertax Income, 90

preventive checks, 116
Price Liberalization, 388
Price stability, 273, 283, 389
Price Variability, 270, 271, 283
Pricing and Exchange Rate Policies, 168
PRICING OF TECHNOLOGY TRANSFER, 337
Primary sector, 254
Private Aid, 368
PRIVATE PROPERTY, 395
Privatization, 227, 304, 307
Progressive income taxes, 108
production possibilities frontier (PPF), 182
project apprisal, 243
Proletarian Cultural Revolution, 250
Prolonged drought, 425
PROPERTY RIGHTS, 395
Property Taxes, 218
Public Goods and Services, 90
purchasing parity power (PPP, 87
Quotas, 204, 274, 275, 277-279

R

Rangar Nurkse, 71
rate of deforestation, 420, 424
rate of natural increase of population, 118
rationing, 213
Raul Prebisch, 269
Reagan administration, 178
Reaganomics, 383
Real Assets, 391
Recurrent Spending, 219
Red Crescent, 368
Red Cross, 368
redistribution from growth, 108
regressive taxes, 108
Reichel, 24
Requiring Disinvestment, 356
research and development (R & D), 330
Research and Technological Improvements, 164
Rio Convention, 416
Rio de Janerio, Brazil, 426
rolling plan, 246
Romania, 295, 296
Rosenstein-Rodan, 69
ROSTOW'S STAGES OF ECONOMIC GROWTH, 64
Rumania, 388
Rural Industrialization, 168
Rural Poverty, 102
Russia, 31, 178, 305, 311, 370
Russian Federation, 295, 371
Rwand, 151

S

Sabah, 224
Sahel of West Africa, 427
Sahel region of Northen Africa, 425
Salvador Allende's, 349
Singer Companh, 311
Samurai bonds, 77
Sanitation, 24
Sarawak, 224

satellite TV, 406
Saudi Arabia, 126, 260, 261, 272, 295
savings, 206, 272, 298
Scale of Production, 188
Scotland, 311
Second Oil Shock, 289, 290, 306
second world, 14
Secondary sector, 254
seigniorage, 296
Selective logging, 419
SELECTIVE LOGGING, 423
Shade agriculture, 422
shadow (accounting) prices, 244
Sharecropping, 161
Short-term plans, 246
Siemens, 325
Sierra Leone, 27, 40
Simon Kuznets, 2, 140
Singapore, 3, 33, 36, 78, 137, 129
Sioux City, Iowa, 334
size or the personal distribution of income, 94
skin cancer, 413
social benefits, 236
social discount rate, 245
Social Relations of Production, 190
Social Safety Net, 396
Socioeconomic Development, 130
Sophistication of the Technology, 336
SOURCES OF CONFLICTS, 344
Sources of Taxation, 217
South Africa, 40, 121, 293, 359, 370
South America, 178
South Asia, 89
South Korea, 3, 33, 36, 40, 61, 121, 171, 203, 278, 312, 356, 358
Southeast Asia, 371, 424
sovereign debt, 297
sovereign default, 287, 297, 298, 306
Soviet Union, 14, 37, 235, 295, 296, 353, 381, 395
soybeans, 413
Spain, 33, 150, 281, 383
Species diversity, 417
Speed of Change, 190
Sri Lanka, 104, 121, 272
stabilization program, 393
Stalinist Development Model, 36
Standard of living, 25
Star Wars weapons, 181
state-owned firms (SOFs), 225
stationary population, 118
STRATEGIES OF AGRICULTURAL AND RURAL DEVELOPMENT, 164
structural criterion, 312
STRUCTURAL REFORMS, 393
subnational governments, 224
subnational political units, 407
Sub-Saharan Africa, 39, 89, 158, 121, 160, 168, 297, 398
Subsidies, 204, 223, 279, 296, 297, 302
Subsistence agriculture, 161, 162
sulphur dioxide (SO2), 408
surplus labor, 72
Sweden, 40, 126, 260, 261, 281, 410
Syria, 203

T

Taiwan, 3, 33, 36, 40, 61, 121, 171, 278, 334, 358
Tamils, 104
Tanzania, 13, 40
target variables, 238
tariffication, 392
Tatemoto, 265
Taxation, 215, 294
Taxation Potential, 217
technical efficiency, 178, 332
technological dualism, 188
TECHNOLOGICAL FORECASTING, 338
Technology, 178, 260, 263-265, 280
technology transfer, 334
Terrorism, 305
Tertiary sector, 233, 254
Thailand, 64, 36, 44, 121, 163, 269, 279, 282, 358, 424
Theory of Absolute Advantage, 260
Theory of Comparative Advantage, 262
Theory of Immiserizing Growth, 266
Third Word countries, 3, 14406
Tibetans, 104
Tied Aid, 374
TIED-AID AGREEMENTS, 303, 374
Tokyo Convention, 416
total population increase, 118
Toyota, 322
Trade and Development Agency, 386
traditional economics, 7
Traditional Sector, 72, 188
Transborder Data Flow, 347, 351
Transfer Pricing, 218, 337
transformation economics, 387
transition economics, 387, 261, 263
Truman Doctrine, 371
Tunisia, 279
Turkey, 150, 278, 279, 288, 325, 370, 371
Turnkey Operation, 317, 336, 325

U

U.S. ACID RAIN PROGRAM, 409
U.S. Agency for International Development (USAID), 39, 386
U.S. Department of Commerce, 313
U.S. Immigration and Naturalization Service, 152
U.S. TOBACCO EXPORTS, 358
U.S., 204, 260, 264, 265, 281, 282, 288, 289, 293, 294, 296-301, 305-307
Ukraine, 295, 370, 371
ultraviolet (UV), 411, 412
UN, 14, 280
Unbalanced Growth, 71
underdeveloped countries, 3
Underemployment, 45, 138
underground economy, 150
Unification of Germany, 382
United Kingdom, 281, 349
United Nations, 24, 279, 280, 296, 305
United Nations (U.N), 280
UNITED NATIONS CONFERENCE ON DESERTIFICATION

(UNCOD) ,14, 426
United Nations Conference on Trade and Development (UNCTAD), 279
United Nations Food and Agriculture Organization (FAO), 158
United Nations World Health Organizations , 358
United States, 3, 14, 24, 27, 31, 126, 138, 145, 150, 151,177,222, 260-266, 279, 281-283, 287, 289, 294, 295, 297, 300, 301, 303, 305-307, 312, 314, 322, 325, 330, 354, 356, 366-368, 382-384, 386, 405, 406, 410, 415
United States Trade Representative (USTR), 358
upper poverty line, 89
upper-middle-income, 14
Urban, 248
Uruguay Round, 279, 280, 282

V

Validity of Input-Output Tables, 243
value-added tax, 217
Venezuela, 272, 289, 290, 292, 293, 300-302, 304
Vicious Circle of Poverty, 67, 206
Vienna Convention, 411
Vietnam , 14, 43, 44, 126, 424,
Visible Underemployment, 138

W

Wassily Leontief, 265
Water Supply, 24
water vapor, 410
Webb, 365
WEIGHTED INDICES FOR GNP GROWTH , 20
West Germany, 264, 265, 312
Western Europe, 44, 138, 140, 365, 382
Western European countries, 14
Western Hemisphere, 223, 287, 288, 297, 306
Wet deposition, 408
Wholly Owned Subsidiary, 317, 324, 336
World Bank, 14, 48, 205, 264, 279, 280, 290, 292, 295, 297, 301, 302, 304, 306, 367, 368, 382, 423
World Trade Organization (WTO), 385, 405, 407
World War II, 2, 160, 192, 233, 318, 365, 371, 381, 390, 405, 407
World Wide Recession, 291

Y

Yeltsin, 37, 386
Yugoslavia, 289, 295, 296

Z

Zaire, 224
Zenith Radio Corporation, 334